Legal Aspects of Business

Text and Cases

(With Leading Decided Cases of Supreme Court and High Courts)

Dr. K. RAMACHANDRA
M.Com., MBA, LL.B., DPM & IR, Ph.D.
Former High Court Advocate,
Presently Professor and HOD of Commerce & Management,
Maharani's Arts, Commerce & Management College for Women.
NAAC Accredited 'A' Grade College,
BANGALORE -560 001.
E-mail: drkrc@rediffmail.com

Dr. B. CHANDRASHEKARA
M.Com., MBA, MTM, M.Phil., Ph.D.
Professor,
P.G. Department of Commerce & Management,
Government R.C. College of Commerce & Management,
Palace Road, BANGALORE – 560 001.
E-mail: drbcs2007@rediffmail.com

Prof. CHANDRAKANT KANAKATTE
M.Com., LL.M., PGDHR
Advocate
and
Visiting Faculty to B' School
BANGALORE – 560 020.
E-mail: chandu934@gmail.com

Himalaya Publishing House
ISO 9001 : 2015 CERTIFIED

First Edition : 2010
Edition : 2012
Second Revised Edition : 2016
Edition : 2017
Reprint : 2018
Reprint : 2023
Reprint : 2024

Published by : Mrs. Meena Pandey
for **Himalaya Publishing House Pvt. Ltd.,**
"Ramdoot", Dr. Bhalerao Marg, Girgaon, Mumbai - 400 004.
Phone: 022-23860170, 23863863; **Fax:** 022-23877178
E-mail: himpub@bharatmail.co.in; **Website:** www.himpub.com

Branch Offices :

New Delhi : "Pooja Apartments", 4-B, Murari Lal Street, Ansari Road, Darya Ganj, New Delhi - 110 002. Phone: 011-23270392, 23278631; Fax: 011-23256286

Nagpur : Kundanlal Chandak Industrial Estate, Ghat Road, Nagpur - 440 018. Phone: 0712-2721215, 2721216

Bengaluru : Plot No. 91-33, 2nd Main Road, Seshadripuram, Behind Nataraja Theatre, Bengaluru - 560 020. Phone: 080-41138821; Mobile: 09379847017, 09379847005

Hyderabad : No. 3-4-184, Lingampally, Besides Raghavendra Swamy Matham, Kachiguda, Hyderabad - 500 027. Phone: 040-27560041, 27550139

Chennai : No. 34/44, Motilal Street, T. Nagar, Chennai - 600 017. Mobile: 09380460419

Pune : "Laksha" Apartment, First Floor, No. 527, Mehunpura, Shaniwarpeth (Near Prabhat Theatre), Pune - 411 030. Phone: 020-24496323, 24496333; Mobile: 09370579333

Cuttack : Plot No. 5F-755/4, Sector-9, CDA Markat Nagar, Cuttack - 753 014, Odisha. Mobile: 09338746007

Kolkata : 3, S.M. Bose Road, Near Gate No. 5, Agarpara Railway Station, North 24 Parganas, West Bengal - 700 109. Mobile: 09674536325

DTP by : **ASHA**

Printed at : Geetanjali Press (P) Pvt. Ltd., Nagpur. On behalf of HPH.

This Book is
Dedicated
to
Our Beloved Parents
and
Teachers

Preface to the Second Revised Edition

Orderly conduct of human behaviour is the touchstone of Law. Morality ensures self-control, whereas law regulates social control. If every individual in the society practice morality, then there is no need for law. It cannot be possible because the universe consists of equal number of saints and sinners and that way, it is balanced. Law provides the rules of the game for the individuals in the civilised society. The journey of life of a mortal from womb to tomb is comprehensively governed, guided, and directed by law of the land.

Business Law is a part of general law, wherein the orderly conduct of business affairs is ensured by it. Our country is gifted with creative and innovative entrepreneurs like Ratan Tata, Brijmohanlal Munjal of Hero Honda, Narayana Murthy of Infosys, Azim Premji of Wipro, Shivnadar of HCL, Kiran Mazumdar Shaw of Biocon Limited, Karshanbhai Patel of Nirma Industries, Mukesh and Anil Ambani of Reliance Group and host of others. These established stars and best brains of India possess entrepreneurial skills and business acumen, but certainly they are not familiar with business laws, for sure. They have to avail the services of legal luminaries at all point of time, because business and law are inseparable.

To develop a textbook that would stand out in an extremely competitive and discerning market, it was important to produce a high quality book that would be comprehensive and flexible. It was felt that a text book entitled ***Legal Aspects of Business – Text and Cases,*** shall to be delivered to the beginners and vigorous readers of Business Law of national and international importance.

People in business, whether they own, manage, or simply work for someone else, must be familiar with the law. Everyday people in business do things that may result in serious legal consequences for their employers or themselves. When a person plans on entering into an agreement with another person, he or she needs to know the formalities necessary to create an enforceable agreement. Business people are called upon to sign a wide variety of forms and need to understand the nature and consequences of the documents they are signing.

An employer who hires workers needs to be aware of the law governing employment relationships. People contemplating entering into a business relationship with someone else need to be aware of the types of business entities used in the Indian context. Of course, business people do not need to be lawyers in order to engage in business. However, the client who understands the law can avoid many legal problems. Sometimes business people end up in court because they have entered into a transaction without first consulting with a lawyer. Knowing when to call a lawyer is very important.

One of the functions of this text is to introduce the student to various topics in law important to business people, to familiarise the student with common problems, and teach the student when to consult with a lawyer before taking any action. Of course, no one is a walking encyclopedia of the law. For this reason, it will probably be useful for you to keep this text after you have completed your management course. When a problem arises, you can refer to the text to refresh your memory of the legal terminology.

The entire text book is presented in twelve modules ranging from Introduction to Business Law, to IPR, Cyber Law, RTI, Contract Act, Companies Act, Human rights, Competition Laws and Environmental Laws. Each module is pregnant with rich contents, meticulously arranged case laws of Supreme Court, High Courts and International Conventions. As a ready reckoner, the present book caters to the needs of business people, teachers, students, professionals and lay persons. For easy understanding of legal concepts and jargons, paragraph summary is provided at appropriate places. The meticulous arrangement of the contents serves the purpose of the book. We invite constructive suggestions from the reading community for further improvement of the book.

We have harped upon the above topics and believe this new book is more comprehensive, more flexible and more interesting. The content of this text book is based on extensive experience, research, successful teaching and a careful analysis of the strengths and weaknesses of competing textbooks. Every module in the book starts with learning objectives followed by meticulous arrangement of sub-chapters and concludes with a detailed summary, objective, analytical, and essay type questions. It is a comprehensive book with leading decided cases chapter-wise for management students, professionals, academicians, entrepreneurs, business persons and the researchers.

We thank profoundly our spiritual gurus - **Bhagawan Sri Sai Ram and Sri Sri Dr. Shivakumara Swamiji of Siddaganga Mutt**, Tumkur, **Sri Sri Dr.Balagangadharanatha Swamiji of Sri Adichunchanagiri Mutt**, Karnataka, for their grace and benevolence in bringing out this text book.

We also thank **Sri Niraj Pandey, Sri Vijay Pandey** and the staff of **Himalaya Publishing House** Pvt. Ltd., Mumbai. We also thank **Sri Madhu** and family for excellent DTP work, and Sri Rajashekar for wonderful cover design.

Dr. K. Ramachandra
Dr. B. Chandrashekara
Prof. Chandrakanth Kanakatte

Brief Contents

Detailed Contents

INTRODUCTION TO BUSINESS LAW

Module Objectives

After reading this chapter, you should be able to

- Explain the Nature of law
- Discuss the Overview of Business Laws in India
- List the Sources of Law
- Know the Constitution of India with special reference to Economic Principles

1.1 INTRODUCTION

People in business, whether they own, manage, or simply work for someone else, must be familiar with the law. Everyday people in business do things that may result in serious legal consequences for their employers or themselves. When a person plans on entering into an agreement with another person, he or she needs to know the formalities necessary to create an enforceable agreement. Business people are called upon to sign a wide variety of forms and need to understand the nature and consequences of the documents they are signing.

An employer who hires workers needs to be aware of the law governing employment relationships. People contemplating entering into a business relationship with someone else need to be aware of the types of business entities used in the Indian context.

Of course, business people do not need to be lawyers in order to engage in business. However, the client who understands the law can avoid many legal problems. Sometimes business people end up in court because they have entered into a transaction without first consulting with a lawyer. Knowing when to call a lawyer is very important.

One of the functions of this text is to introduce the student to various topics in law important to business people, to familiarise the student with common problems, and teach the student when to consult with a lawyer before taking any action. Of course, no one is a walking encyclopedia of the law. For this reason, it will probably be useful for you to keep this text after you have completed your management course. When a problem arises, you can refer to the text to refresh your memory of the legal terminology.

1.2 THE NATURE OF LAW

Law is the entire body of principles that govern conduct and can be enforced in the courts.

People often say, "You cant do that. It's against the law!" Exactly what do they mean when they use the word law? Many definitions of law have been suggested. We define law as the entire body of principles that govern conduct and can be enforced in the courts.

Everyone in society is subject to a variety of rules. Not all of these rules are laws. For example, many religions set rules of behaviour. Violating these rules, however, does not mean that a person has violated the law. If a group of men gets together one afternoon to play a game of baseball, certain rules govern the conduct of the game. These rules are not laws. If four people sit down at a card table to play bridge, an elaborate set of rules governs the players. These rules are not laws. If a boy and girl go out on a date and their parents tell them to be in by midnight, the parents are enforcing rules but not laws. In all of these cases, the rules are not laws and cannot be enforced in Court.

If a person does violate a law, in the event of a court finds him or her in violation of the law, the court generally imposes some form of penalty, called a sanction. Typically sanctions require a person to do or not to do something; to pay money to someone else; or impose a prison sentence on someone. For example, if a man agrees to purchase a guitar and takes possession of it, he may be used for whatever amount of money he agreed to pay for the guitar. A court, if it finds that the person agreed to pay Rs. 3000 for the guitar, may order the person to pay the seller Rs. 3000. If a married couple splits up, and the wife has custody of the children, a judge can order the husband to pay her for child support. If a thief robs a convenience store, a judge may sentence the thief to prison.

1.3 OVERVIEW OF BUSINESS LAWS IN INDIA

What Business Law Regulates?

Business law, or commercial law as it is sometimes called, is the body of rules that regulate and control the everyday activities of exchange. It is concerned with procurement of raw materials, manufacturing and producing, the sale of merchandise and commodities, brokerage, agency, shipping, bailment insurance, commercial paper, and all sorts of arrangements for financing or banking business deals.

Business law, also called merchantile law, is that branch of legal system, which regulates business activities. The same meaning is revealed in the two definitions given below:

Business law is that portion of the legal system which guarantees an orderly conduct of business affairs and the settlement of legitimate disputes in a just manner.

Business law establishes a set of rules and prescribes conduct that enables us to avoid misunderstanding and injury in our business relationships.

Business law is that portion of the legal system which guarantees an orderly conduct of business affairs and the settlement of legitimate disputes in a just manner.

1.4 SCOPE OF BUSINESS LAW

The scope of business law is indeed vast. It usually deals with topics of licences, large business houses, monopolies, issue of securities, contracts, property, agency, negotiable instruments, foreign exchange and its management, partnerships, companies, insurance, sales, bailment, guarantees, labour, suretyship, bankruptcy, consumer interest, business crimes, raising loans from financial institutions, obtaining electricity, iron and steel, customs clearance, allotment of materials, import of capital goods, pollution control and the like. These and the other aspects are covered by legislations enacted by Central, State or local bodies.

1.5 SOURCES OF LAW

The important sources of Indian law are:

- **Constitution**
- **Legislation/Statute**
- **Custom**
- **Case law/Common law**
- **Natural law**
- **English law**
- **Ordinances**
- **Administrative law**
- **Dharma**
- **Law Merchant and**
- **Equity**

The brief explnations of the above are:

Constitution

Constitution is the fundamental law of a nation.

A Constitution is the fundamental law of a nation. It was written with specific goals in mind. They wrote the Constitution so that the three branches of government — the legislative, the executive, and the judicial — had checks over one another to prevent an abuse of power by one branch of government. The Constitution also created a system of checks and balances between the powers of the states and the central government.

Sometimes constitutional law is classified as an additional category of public law. It is sometime defined as the fundamental law which sets out the powers and limitations of government as prescribed in the constitution. Whether you have the right to have your own lawyer when under prosecution for a serious crime is a constitutional law problem. Constitution is one of the sources of law. All the Central and State laws should be within the confines of Indian Constitution Law.

Legislation/Statute

A Statute is a law passed by a legislative body. A statute is defined as "the will of the legislature." A statute is thus a written "will" of the legislature expressed according to the form necessary to constitute it as a law of the state. The statutes are subject to assent by the President in case of central laws and by the governors in respect of state laws.

Legislation is the common source of law. Both Parliament and state assemblies have enacted a number of legislations that cover various aspects of business.

Legislation is the common source of law. Both Parliament and state assemblies have enacted a number of legislations that cover various aspects of business. For example: Indian Income Tax Act, 1961, Information Technology Act, 2000, Competition Act, 2002 and so on.

Custom

A custom, when accepted by courts and incorporated in judicial interpretations, becomes a law.

A substantial part of business law is customary, not withstanding advances made in science and technology. This is true both in developed and developing countries. A custom, when accepted by courts and incorporated in judicial interpretations, becomes a law. Many of the business customs or usages have already been adopted and legalised. The Indian Contract Act provides that nothing their contained, "shall affect any usage or custom of trade." Similarly, the Negotiable Instruments Act provides that nothing therein contained, "shall affect any local usage relating to instruments in an oriental language."

Case Law/Common Law

Case law is a judgement of a superior court including a point of law or principle and which necessitates its adoption and adherence in a subsequent case involving the same point.

A distinguishing feature of Anglo-American law is its reliance upon previously decided cases as a primary source of law. Reliance or judicial decisions is known as Case law or Common law. The term, Common law, originated in England and referred to a body of law that was common throughout England.

Case law, popularly called "Precedent" by lawyers is a judgement of a superior court including a point of law or principle and which necessitates its adoption and adherence in a subsequent case involving the same point. Case law is useful in as much as it helps courts to render uniformity with regard to the interpretation of statutes or formulation of principles.

In spite of prevalence of multiple laws, we still find vacuum on any given matter. Such gaps are filled by case laws. The Contract Act, for example, is not clear whether an agreement with a minor is voidable at his option or altogether void. It was the judgement by the Judicial Committee of the privy council in *Moharibibi vs. Dharmodas Ghose* (1903) that an agreement with a minor was declared absolutely void. This decision has become precedent for subsequently pronouncing all agreements with minors as void. In fact, the Indian Contract Act has not been amended till now ever since it came into effect on the first day of September, 1872. Not that the Act has been foolproof in all respects. But case laws were ably filling the gaps in the Act.

Natural Law

Natural law or natural justice is another source of law. The natural justice that no man can be punished twice for the same crime is a guiding principle for any legisaltion. Similarly, natural justice demands that no individual can be dubbed guilty unless the charges are proved against him.

The natural justice that no man can be punished twice for the same crime is a guiding principle for any legisaltion. Similarly, natural justice demands that no individual can be dubbed guilty unless the charges are proved against him.

A historic case to be quoted in this context is the *National Textile Unions vs. Ramakrishna* (1983). The dispute raised before the Supreme Court involved the point whether or not the workers of a company have *locus standi* to be heard in proceedings relating to the winding up of the company. The court found no provision to the effect in the Companies Act though it runs into more than 650 sections. The court actually created the rights for the workers by falling upon the principle of natural law and natural justice.

English Law

Our business laws are largely based on English Acts applicable in England. Our Sale of Goods Act, for instance, has been taken directly from the English Sale of Goods Act. Similarly, our Companies Act corresponds with the English Companies Act. Again in any discussion on the Indian Contract Act, reference is invariably made to the English Law.

Ordinances

Laws are also passed by local authorities like Municipality, Zilla Panchayats, Mahanagar palika, State governments and Central government. These laws are like the statutes passed by the above authorities and governments. Although ordinances apply in only relatively small geographical areas, business people must be aware of the ordinances that apply where they operate. Bangalore Mahanagar palika (BBMP) has passed an ordinance stating that goods that enter Bangalore city are subject to entry tax called "octroi." Business people entering into Bangalore city with the goods shall have to comply with this ordinance. However, business people outside the Bangalore city need not comply with. Similarly, the Government of Karnataka in order to regulate admissions of students into professional courses of medicine, dental and engineering had promulgamated an ordinance in this regard. This is applicable only within the territory of Karnataka.

Laws are also passed by local authorities like Municipality, Zilla Panchayats, Mahanagar palika, State governments and Central government.

Administrative Law

Administrative law adjust differences arising from disputes between administrative officials of governmental agencies and the general public.

Administrative law is one of the major divisions or branches of public law. Administrative law adjust differences arising from disputes between administrative officials of governmental agencies and the general public. Whether the post office has authority to limit the size of parcel post packages is an example of administrative law.

Dharma

Dharma was the main source of law during ancient periods and we have no doubt in asserting that it continues to be main spirit behind every law even today.

What is unfortunately ignored is the fact that Dharma was the main source of law during ancient periods and we have no doubt in asserting that it continues to be main spirit behind every law even today. To prove the role of Dharma in judiciary we quote A.H. Basham, "Though we know very little about the legal system of the Rigveda period", wrote he, "it is clear that the idea of a divine cosmic order already existed. Rta, the regulatory of the universal process, was perhaps the forerunner of the alter concept of Dharma."

As well as Dharma there are, according to the textbooks, other bases of law; contract, customs and royal ordinance. The earlier religious law books paid little attention to these, but their importance increased with line. It was recognised that, owing to the decadence of the age, Dharma was not now known in its fullness, and purity and therefore supplementary sources of law were needed. Generally Dharma was thought to override all other bases of law, but the Arthasastra and one other lawbook maintain that the royal ordinance overrides the other, a doctrine which we must ascribe to the totalitarianism of the Mauryas, which few later jurist have supported.

"The king's duty of protection was chiefly the protection of Dharma, and as protector of Dharma he was Dharma incarnate. From Ashoka onwards kings sometimes assumed the title of Dharmaraja, which was also one of the names of Yama, the god of death and departed. Both Yama and King maintained the sacred law by punishing evil-doers and rewarding the righteous."

Dharma is guiding principle of justice even today.

Dharma continues to be the guiding principle of justice even today. For example, a debtor who owed Rs. 100 and who executed a bond by which he was required to put forth manual labour until the amount was repaid and in case of default would be required to pay exhorbitant interest would be freed from such an obligation. In other words, the agreement would be declared void (*Ram Sarup V. Bansi Mandir*, 1915). It is Dharma which makes such agreements void.

Merchant Leagues and the "Law Merchant"

After considerable isolation, medieval merchants in logical commercial centers and coastal towns gradually began to reopen some of the old Roman trade routes. The governments of Europe were unable to furnish much help, however, since they remained weak, small, and isolated. Intent on combining private merchants organised into trading firms and eventually into leagues of trading cities. Since they could obtain little protection from local governments, these merchant organisations hired their own guards and protective agents. Continuing to grow and cooperate in these ventures, leagues of traders functioned in areas that today make up parts of Germany, Italy, Spain, France, Belgium, Holland and England.

As the merchant leagues became common, the local courts were often found inadequate to settle disputes among league members. The local governmental courts had no understanding of diverse business and trade customs and problems, especially those relating to trade between nations. Furthermore, there was no uniformity in court decisions or in the way laws were applied from country to country. In addition, foreign traders frequently had no standing in local courts.

Setting up their own courts, the large league's judges travelled to the busier ports, major trade centers, and large country fairs. In each place the league's judges settled mercantile and shipping disputes and gradually built up a recognized code of business law.

Members of these international trade leagues realized that they needed speedy, inexpensive, and non-technical ways of settling business disputes among members. The leagues already had regulations and rules that were understood among individual merchants, but local courts would not enforce rules when a member ignored them. The trade leagues, therefore, set up their own courts and code of international law for business transactions. This system included definite rules for honouring contracts, purchase and sales agreements, and enforcing shipping requirements in all commercial countries in Europe. An individual trader who ignored the league rules and resorted to the local governmental courts soon learned that it was almost impossible to do business on a large scale. Setting up their own courts, the large league's judges travelled to the busier ports, major trade centers, and large country fairs. In each place the league's judges settled mercantile and shipping disputes and gradually built up a recognized code of business law. Thus, the law merchant legal system did not originate in any one country exclusively, but came to be used and accepted throughout the Western commercial world.

For several hundred years, these merchants courts continued to operate on their own — no connection whatever with the existing governmental court system. This separation from the regular court systems continued in France, Belgium, and Latin American colonies of Spain until comparatively recent times.

In England, however, by the end of the seventeenth century, law merchant courts had ceased to exist. Their rules and decisions were gradually absorbed into the English common law and came to be recognized in English court decisions. In short, then, the principles of the law merchant became English commercial law eventually serving as the basis for all business law in the United States and India. This body of rules and principles, drawn from the practical ideas of these medieval merchants, is still the source of most of our current business laws. This includes, our law in the areas of contracts, agency, sales, bailments, torts, partnership, shipping, insurance, corporations, and marine law, loans from financial institutions, obtaining electricity, iron and steel, customs clearance, allotment of materials, import of capital goods, pollution control and the like.

Equity

Many years ago, the courts in the U.K. and U.S.A. were divided into courts of law and courts of equity. Today, in the U.K., U.S.A., Indian and other courts hear both law and equity matters.

Whenever monetary relief is not an adequate remedy, the courts grant some form of equitable relief that is called equity.

Generally, people who went to law courts wanted monetary damages. People who desired some remedy other than money went to the equity courts. Today whenever monetary relief is not an adequate remedy, the courts grant some form of equitable relief. For example, a person enters into a contract to purchase a particular painting and paid the amount thereon, subsequently, if the seller refuses to deliver the paintings to the buyer, the buyer may file suit. In this situation, the court requires the defendant (seller) to honour the contract and deliver the painting. The order is an example of an equitable remedy. In India, we have the Specific Performance Act, 1963, which ensures equitable remedy.

1.6 CLASSIFICATION OF LAW

Substantive and Procedural Law

Substantive law regulates rights and duties.

Substantive Law includes the laws that create, define, and regulate rights and obligations. Substantive law regulates rights and duties. If a student agrees to rent an apartment during the school year, the legal rights and obligations of the student to the apartment are determined by the law that governs the relationships between the owner of the apartment and the student. *For example:* IPL

Procedural Law specifies the methods of enforcing rights and obligations created by substantive law.

Procedural Law specifies the methods of enforcing rights and obligations created by substantive law. If the student in the example above feels the apartment owner has somehow violated the students rights, she may file suit in court. The laws that determine in which court the case should be filed. How the trial is conducted and how a court judgement is enforced are all part of procedural law. For the most part, this text deals with substantive law, although some procedural law is discussed. *For example:* Civil Procedure Code, 1908, The Indian Evidence Act, 1872, The Criminal Procedure Code, 1973.

Public Law and Private Law

Public law deals with the rights and powers of the government and citizens.

Public law deals with the rights and powers of the government. An example of public law is criminal law. Suppose that the owner of an apartment and a student get into an argument and the student hits the owner with a baseball bat. By engaging in such behaviour, the student probably has violated the criminal laws of the state she is living in.

Private law is administrated between private citizens.

Private law is administrated between private citizens. If the student fails to pay her rent, the landlord may file suit to collect it. The case will be governed by Private law, because the government is not involved. Figure 1.1 shows classification of laws.

Civil Law

Civil law deals with violations against an injured party and recovery for the injury the plaintiff has sustained as a result of the defendant's conduct.

Civil law deals with violations against an injured party. In a civil case, a private party, the plaintiff, files suit against the defendant to recover for the injury the plaintiff has sustained as a result of the defendant's conduct. To win the suit, the plaintiff must establish his or her case by a preponderance of the evidence. That is, the court must find that more evidence favours the plaintiff's position in the case than supports the defendant's position. The purpose of a civil law suit is to compensate the injured person.

Suppose that Mr. Harish purchased a new motorcycle from a dealer for Rs. 42,500. The dealer delivered the motorcycle to Mr. Harish, who agreed to pay the dealer Rs. 7,500 per month. After Mr. Harish got the motorcycle, he refused to make payments. In this situation, the dealer could file a civil suit against Mr. Harish either for Rs. 42,500 or to force Harish to return the cycle to the dealer. The dealer would be the plaintiff, and Harish would be the defendant. The dealer would have to convince the court that Harish agreed to purchase the cycle for Rs. 42,500. If the court agreed and Harish had no defense, the court would order Harish to pay the Rs. 42,500 or to return the cycle to the dealer.

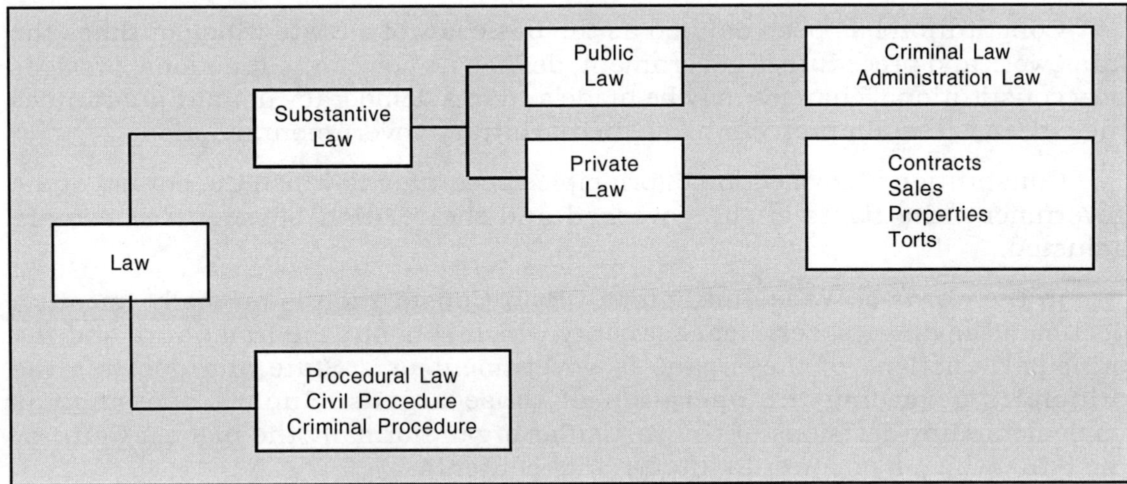

Fig. 1.1 Classification of Law

Civil case — a case brought by a private individual trying to enforce a private right

Plaintiff — is a person who brings a lawsuit

Defendant — a person being sued

Criminal law establishes the duties people owe to society. If a person violates any of these duties, he or she has committed a wrong against society. Criminal cases are brought by the government (local, state or central) against the accused. The police, the prosecutor files the case on behalf of the government. To win the suit, the prosecutor must establish, beyond a reasonable doubt, that the defendant committed the crime which the prosecutor asserts he or she committed. In a criminal case, but not in a civil case, a judge/magistrate may impose fine and imprisonment term against an accused/criminal as punishment for violating the law.

Criminal law establishes the duties people owe to society. If a person violates any of these duties, he or she has committed a wrong against society.

In some cases, if a person is found guilty of murder, he or she may be executed (capital punishment). It should be noted that juveniles, defined by law as people under the age of 16, are tried in a separate court called juvenile court, for violations of criminal law. Table 1.3 distinguishes civil law from criminal law.

Table 1.3 Comparison of Civil and Criminal Law

	Civil Law	*Criminal Law*
Who files suit	Private individual (Plaintiff) sues	Government Prosecutes
Burden of Proof	Preponderance of the evidence	Beyond a reasonable doubt
Principal Action	Monetory damages Equitable remedies	Death Imprisonment Fines

1.7 THE CONSTITUTION OF INDIA

Nature of Constitution and Constitutional Law

Constitution has been defined as the basic law of a State which outlines the framework and procedure of government, defines its power and functions, provides how constitutional changes may be made and in a democracy usually guarantees the citizens certain protections against arbitrary governmental action.

Constitution is a collection of principles according to which the powers of the government, the rights of the governed and the relation between the two are adjusted.

By a Constitution is normally meant a document having a special legal sanctity which sets out the framework and the principal functions of the organs of government or a State and declares the principles governing the operation of those organs.

In the words of Wade and Philips, "By a Constitution is normally meant a document having a special legal sanctity which sets out the framework and the principal functions of the organs of government or a State and declares the principles governing the operation of those organs. Such a document is implemented by decisions of the particular organ normally the highest Court or the State which has power to interpret its contents."

In short, Constitution is the collection of principles or body of fundamental rules (written or unwritten) which usually provides for the establishment, Constitution and organisation of the organs of government, their power and functions, manner in which the said power and functions are to be exercised, their inter-relationships, the relation between these organs of the government and the people of the country.

"A constitution does not necessarily or usually contain the detailed rules upon which depend the working of the institutions of government. Legal processes, rules for elections, the mode of implementing services provided by the State, so far as these are matters for enactment, are to be found, not in the Constitution, but in ordinary statutes made by the legislature within the limits set by the Constitution itself. Such statute can be altered by the same method as that which they were originally enacted whereas changes in the constitution call for a more elaborate process."

Constitutional law has been defined as the rules which regulate the structure of the principal organs of government and their relationship to each other and determine their principal functions. These rules consist both of legal rules in the strict sense and of usages, commonly called conventions, which without being enacted are accepted as binding by all who are concerned in government. The constitutional law, in short, is the basic law of a State which usually provides for the Constitution and structure of the organs of government, their powers and functions, their inter-relations and their relations with the people.

The Constitutional law may be in the form of a written document or unwritten conventions. In U.K. there is no Constitution in the form of a written document or code, however, there is a body of law which forms the Constitution partly statutory, partly common law and partly conventional.

1.8 MAJOR KINDS OF CONSTITUTIONS

The major classification of constitutions across the globe are shown in figure 1.3.

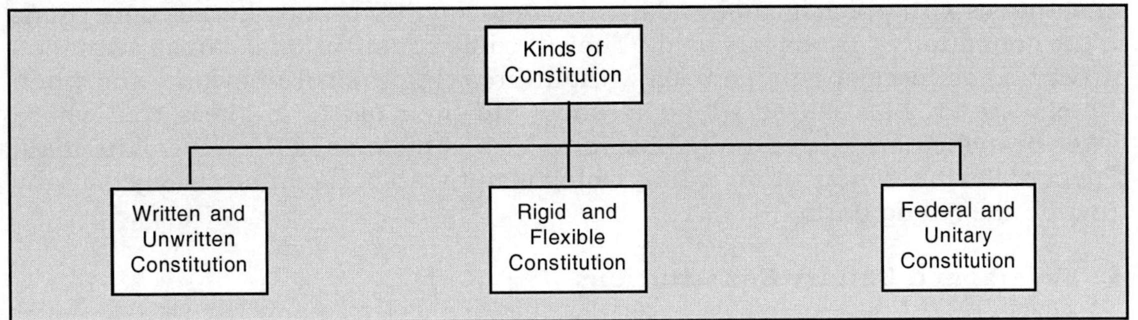

Fig. 1.3 Kinds of Constitution

1. Written and Unwritten Constitutions

Constitutions may be classified as (a) written constitution and (b) unwritten constitution. The Constitutions of most of the countries are written. The best example of an unwritten Constitution is that of the U.K. Actually, all the constitutions are a mixture of written and unwritten elements. The written constitution contain some unwritten elements in the form of customs and conventions and unwritten Constitutions contain written elements in the form of statutes, judicial decisions, etc. Even the Constitution of U.K. which is regarded as the best example of unwritten constitution contains many written elements in the form of statutes, judicial decisions and charters. All Constitutions are in fact a mixture of written law and unwritten custom. K.C. Wheare has rightly observed, "We cannot agree that there is any country, least of all the United Kingdom, which has a system of government embodied solely in written rules or solely in unwritten rules. Consequently, the classification of constitution into written and unwritten has lost its significance."

The best example of an unwritten Constitution is that of the U.K.

2. Rigid and Flexible Constitutions

A Constitution is called rigid if, for the amendment or revision of its provisions, a special procedure, is required to be followed and a constitution is called flexible if its provisions can be amended or revised by the ordinary legislative process. Thus, the distinction between rigid and flexible constitution is based on the existence or non-existence of a special amending procedure. In the case of a flexible constitution, its provisions may be amended or modified by ordinary legislative process, but in the case of a rigid constitution, a special procedure is required to be followed for the amendment or revision of its provisions. The constitution of U.K. may be mentioned as an example of flexible constitution. The provisions of the Constitution of U.K. may be amended or revised by an Act of Parliament. The Constitution of U.S.A. may be mentioned as an example of rigid constitution.

A Constitution is called rigid if, for the amendment or revision of its provisions, a special procedure is required to be followed and a constitution is called flexible if its provisions can be amended or revised by the ordinary legislative process.

The rigid constitution possesses the quality of stability. Its provisions cannot be changed easily at the desire of the ruling party. The Constitution is regarded as a body of superior laws and commands much respect. Under such constitution the rights of the people are more secure. However, the main defect of the rigid constitution is that it cannot be changed in accordance with needs. It places obstacles in the required social changes. The merit of the flexible constitution is that it can be changed according to the need of the society. Friedrich has rightly observed, "The great and outstanding advantage of a flexible constitution is the

The rigid constitution possesses the quality of stability. It cannot be changed in accordance with needs.

Flexible constitution is that which is not stable. It can be changed at any time by the ruling party

smoothness with which it can be adapted to new conditions and altered conceptions in the community." Bryce has said, "They (flexible constitutions) can be stretched or bent so as to meet emergencies without breaking their framework; and when the emergency has passed they slip back into their old form like a tree whose outer branches have been pulled aside to let a vehicle pass. However, the main defect of flexible constitution is that which is not stable. It can be changed at any time by the ruling party."

3. Federal and Unitary Constitutions

Constitution which provides for a federal system of government is called a federal constitution, while a constitution which provides for a system of Unitary government is called a Unitary Constitution. Thus, Unitary Constitution establishes a unitary government while the federal constitution establishes a federal government. In the system of Unitary government the whole power of government is conferred upon a single central organ or organs from which the local government derive whatever authority or autonomy they possess. In the system of unitary government the Central Government has exclusive power to determine the pattern of relationship between central and local governments and also the manner of distribution of powers among them.

In the unitary constitution all the powers of government are given to the Centre.

In the unitary constitution all the powers of government are given to the Centre and the local governments enjoy the powers delegated to them by the Centre. Thus, in the unitary constitution the regional governments are totally subordinate to the Centre. The constitution of U.K. may be mentioned as an example of unitary constitution.

Federal constitution establishes a system of double government–Central Government (General Government) and State Governments (Regional governments).

The federal constitution establishes a federal system of government. It establishes a system of double government-Central Government (General Government) and State Governments (Regional governments). A constitution will be a federal constitution, if it possesses the following characteristics:

(1) System of double government: A federal constitution always provides for double governments — Central government (general government) and State governments (regional governments). A system of double governments is, thus, an essential feature of a federal constitution.

(2) Distribution of powers: A federal constitution provides for the distribution of the powers of State between Central government (general government) and State governments (regional governments). Under the federal constitution both the Central government and State or regional governments are supreme in the spheres allotted to them and none of them is subordinate to the other. Thus, under the federal constitution the Central or general government and State Governments (or regional governments) are coordinate and independent in their spheres and not subordinate to one another. However, in practice such arrangement is not possible. Even the American Constitution which is regarded as an ideal federal constitution has not established such system of government. The modern tendency has been to provide more powers to the Central Government. In short, if the federal principle is predominant in the constitution, it is regarded as federal constitution.

(3) Rigidity: The federal constitution provides for distribution of powers between the Central Government and the State or regional governments and such distribution of powers will be of no importance, if the constitution can be amended at the desire of the Central Government, because in such conditions the Central Government can take any power by amending the Constitution. Consequently, rigid process of amendment is an essential feature of the federal constitution. The process of amendment will be rigid if it involves the participation of both, the Central Government and State or regional governments. In the case of flexible constitution its provisions can be amended or revised by the ordinary legislative process but in the case of a rigid constitution a special procedure is required to be followed for the amendment or revision of its provisions.

(4) Written: The federal constitutions should be written. Actually, it is not necessary for a federal constitution to be written but in practice it is always found written. Its main reason is that on account of distribution of powers between the Central Government and State or regional governments an unwritten federal constitution will create much confusion, conflict and uncertainty. **Wheare** has rightly said that the written constitution is essential if federal government is to work well.

(5) Independent judiciary: The federal constitution provides for the division of powers between Central Government and State or regional governments. On account of it, there may be disputes between the Central Government and the State or regional governments. Independent judiciary is required to determine such disputes. The judiciary should not be under the control of the Central government or State (regional) government because if the judiciary will be under the control of Central Government or State governments, the government having the control over the judiciary may compel the judiciary to decide the issue or resolve the dispute in its favour. To maintain the federal nature of the Constitution, an independent judiciary is required.

Independent judiciary is required to determine disputes between Central and State government.

(6) Supremacy of Constitution: Supremacy of the constitution is an essential feature of the federal constitution. In the case of federal constitution the constitution is regarded as the supreme law of the country. The distribution of powers provided by the constitution will be of no importance, if Central government or state (or regional) governments can ignore it. **Wheare** has rightly said that supreme constitution is essential, if Government is to be federal.

Federal Constitution the constitution is regarded as the supreme law of the country.

1.9 FEATURES OF INDIAN CONSTITUTION

The main feature of the Indian constitution are discussed under the following headings:

Indian Constitution — Federal or Unitary

It is a controversial issue as to whether the Indian Constitution is a federal constitution or unitary constitution. It is better to examine the federal and unitary features of the Indian Constitution and then to make an attempt to derive a conclusion as to its exact nature. A constitution is called a federal constitution if —

(a) It establishes double governments, Central (or general) Government and State (or regional) governments;

(b) It provides for the distribution of powers of the state between Central Government and State (or regional) governments;

(c) It is rigid and written;

(d) It establishes independent judiciary;

(e) It is the supreme law of the country.

Now we may examine as to how far the Indian Constitution possesses the afore-said essential characteristics of the federal constitution.

1. System of Double Governments

A federal constitution always provides for double governments — Central or general government and State or regional governments. The Indian Constitution creates double governments — Central government and State governments.

2. Distribution of Powers

Under the federal constitution the Central and State governments are independent in their sphere and not subordinate to one another.

A federal constitution provides for the distribution of powers of the State between the Central (or general) government and State (or regional) governments. Under the federal constitution the Central and State governments are coordinate and independent in their sphere and not subordinate to one another.

The Indian Constitution also provides for the distribution of powers. The distribution of powers provided under the Constitution of India may be explained as follows:

Legislative: The subjects have been divided into three categories — Union list, State list and Concurrent list. The subjects of all India importance (e.g., Defence of India, Naval, Military and Air forces, Foreign Affairs, War and Peace, Railways, National Highways, Posts and Telegraphs, Currency, Coinage, Foreign Exchange, Reserve Bank of India, Banking, etc.) have been placed in the Union list. The subjects of local interest (public order, police, local government, public health and sanitation, hospitals and dispensaries, libraries and museum, agriculture, water supplies, irrigation, land etc.) have been placed in State list. The subjects which are of local interest but require uniform treatment all over the country (e.g., education, factories, newspaper, criminal law, criminal procedure, contracts, etc.) have been placed in the concurrent list.

The Parliament has exclusive power to make laws with respect to any of the matters or subjects enumerated in the Union list and the legislature of any state has power to make laws for such state or any part thereof with respect to any of the matters or subjects enumerated in the State list.

The Parliament (i.e., the Central Legislature) has exclusive power to make laws with respect to any of the matters or subjects enumerated in the Union list and the legislature of any state has power to make laws for such state or any part thereof with respect to any of the matters or subjects enumerated in the State list. Parliament and state legislature both have power to make laws with respect to any of the matters or subjects enumerated in the Concurrent list, but in case of conflict between a law made by the Parliament and a law made by the State legislature with respect to such matter the law made by the Parliament (i.e., the Central legislature)will prevail and the laws made by the State legislature shall, to the extent of the repugnancy, be void, unless the law made by the state legislature has received the assent of the President. The residuary power vested in the Parliament.

3. Rigid and Written Constitution

Actually it is not necessary for a federal constitution to be written but in practice it is always found written, because due to distribution of powers between the Central Government and State governments, an unwritten federal constitution will create confusion and conflict. The Indian Constitution is a written constitution.

The Federal Constitution provides for distribution of powers between the Central Government and the State Governments.

The federal constitution provides for distribution of powers between the Central Government and the State Governments. Such distribution of powers will be of no importance, if the Constitution can be amended at the desire of the Central Government because in such condition the Central Government can take any power by amending the Constitution. Thus rigid of amendment is an essential feature of the federal constitution. The process of amendment will be rigid if it involves the participation of both, the Central Government and State Governments. In a rigid constitution a special procedure is required to be followed for the amendment of its provisions, even in this respect the Indian Constitution has adopted a middle course. Some of its provisions, e.g., Articles 4, 239A, 312 etc., may be amended by Parliament by simple majority, i.e., by ordinary legislative process, while some of its provisions, i.e., the provisions relating to Fundamental Rights, Directive Principle of State Policy, Emergency provisions, etc., may be amended by Parliament by special majority (i.e., the Bill for the amendment must be passed by each House of Parliament by a majority of total membership of the House and by a majority of not less than two-thirds of the members present and voting in the House), and some of the provisions (e.g., the provisions relating to distribution of legislative powers, any of the lists in the 7th Schedule, the representation of States in Parliament, the Union Judiciary, the High Courts in the States, Articles 368 etc.) can be amended only if the bill for amendment is passed by each House of Parliament by a Majority of total membership of the House and by a majority of not less than two-thirds of the members present and voting in the House and this amendment is ratified by the legislatures of not less than one-half of the States. Then the provisions relating to federal features the ratification by not less than one-half of the State Legislature is required.

In a rigid constitution a special procedure is required to be followed for the amendment of its provisions even in this respect the Indian Constitution has adopted a middle course.

4. Independent Judiciary

The federal constitution provides for division of powers between general or Central Government and regional or State Governments. On account of it there may be disputes between the Central and the State governments. Independent judiciary is required to determine such dispute. The judiciary, thus, should not be under the control of the Central Government or the State Governments, because, if the judiciary will be under the control of Central government or State governments, the Government having the control over the judiciary may compel it to divide the dispute in its favour. The independent judiciary is, thus necessary to maintain the federal nature of the constitution. Various methods are adopted to maintain the independence of judiciary, e.g., appointment of the judges by the head of the executive or through independent commission, difficult procedure for their removal, no variation in conditions of their services to their disadvantages after their appointment, prohibition of any discussion with respect to the conduct of any judge, etc. Various provisions have been incorporated in the Indian Constitution with the object to establish an independent judiciary in India.

Various provisions have been incorporated in the Indian Constitution with the object to establish an independent judiciary in India.

5. Supremacy of Constitution

Actions of any organ of the government which is against the Constitution of India is invalid and of no force.

The Constitution of India is the Supreme law of the country. Act of any organ of the government which is against the Constitution of India is invalid and of no force. The legislature, executive or judiciary cannot violate the Constitution. Thus, the Constitution of India controls all the organs of the government. No person or governmental authority is above the Constitution and, therefore, act of any person or of any governmental authority which is contrary to the Constitution will be invalid and of no force.

Rule of Law

The rule of absolute supremacy or predominance of regular law as opposed to the influence of arbitrary power.

According to Dicey, A.V., Rule of law has three meanings:

(1) It means, in the first place, the absolute supremacy or predominance of regular law as opposed to the influence of arbitrary power and excludes the existence of arbitrariness, of prerogative or even of the wide discretionary authority on the part of the government. It implies that a man may be punished for a breach of law but he can be punished for nothing, else. No man can be punished except for a breach of Law.

Rule of law is equality before the law or the equal subjection of all classes to the ordinary law of the land administered by the ordinary law Courts.

(2) It means, again, equality before the law or the equal subjection of all classes to the ordinary law of the land administered by the ordinary law Courts. In this sense, the "rule of law" excludes the idea of any exemption of officials or other from the duty of obedience to the law which governs other citizens or from the jurisdiction of the ordinary tribunals. This implies that no man is above law.

(3) The rule of law, lastly may be used as a formula for expressing the fact that the law of the constitution is not the source but the consequence of the regular activities of individuals as defined and enforced by the courts. The constitution is the result of the ordinary law of the land. This implies that the legal rights of the people are secured not by guaranteed rights proclaimed in the constitution but by the operation of the ordinary remedies of private law available against those who lawfully interfere with his rights. Free access to Courts of justice is an efficient guarantee against the wrong doers.

Judicial Review

Judicial review, in short, is the authority of the Courts to declare void, the acts of the legislature and executive, if they are found in the violation of the provisions of the Constitution. Judicial Review is the power of the highest court of a jurisdiction to invalidate on Constitution-grounds, the acts of other government agency within that jurisdiction.

Judicial review is the authority of the Courts to declare void, the acts of the legislature and executive, if they are found in the violation of the provisions of the Constitution.

The doctrine of judicial review has been originated and developed by the American Supreme Court, although there is no express provision in the American Constitution for the judicial review. In *Marbury v/s Madison*, the Supreme Court made it clear that it had the power of Judicial Review. Chief Justice George Marshall said: "Certainly all those who have framed the written constitution contemplate them as forming the fundamental and paramount law of the nations, and consequently, the theory of every such government must be that an act of the legislature, repugnant to the constitution, is void." There is supremacy of Constitution in U.S.A. and therefore, in case of conflict between the Constitution and the Acts passed by the Legislature, the Courts follow the Constitution and declare the Acts to be unconstitutional and therefore, void. The Courts declare void the acts of the legislature and executive, if they are found in the violation of the provisions of the Constitution even in our country.

In case of conflict between the Constitution and the Acts passed by the Legislature, the Courts follow the Constitution and declare the Acts to be unconstitutional and therefore, void.

In England there is supremacy of Parliament and therefore, the Act passed or the law made by Parliament cannot be declared to be void by the Court. The function of the judiciary is to ensure that the administration or executive function conforms with the law. The Constitution of India expressly provides for judicial review. Like U.S.A. there is supremacy of the Constitution in India. Consequently, an Act passed by the legislature is required to be in conformity with the requirements of the Constitution and it is for the judiciary to decide whether or not the Act is in conformity with the Constitutional requirements and if it is found in violation of the constitutional provisions the Court has to declare it unconstitutional and, therefore, void, because the Court is bound by its oath to uphold the Constitution. The courts can declare the acts of the executive and Acts passed by the legislature void if they are found in violation of the Constitution. In the written and federal constitution the power of judicial review is of special importance. The federal constitution provides for division of powers between the Central Government and the State Government and on account of it there may be disputes between the Central Government and the State Governments. In such a condition there must be independent judiciary having power to declare the acts of any Government or any of the organs of the Government void if they are found in violation of the Constitution.

The Constitution of India expressly provides for judicial review. Like U.S.A. there is supremacy of the Constitution in India.

Let us discuss the Preamble, important terms, fundamental rights, and Directive Principle of State Policy as envisaged in our Constitution one by one.

THE CONSTITUTION OF INDIA

INTRODUCTORY

THE PREAMLBE

WE, the people of India, having solemnly resolved to constitute India into a sovereign, socialist, secular, democratic republic and to secure to all its citizens

JUSTICE, social, economic and political;

LIBERTY of thought, expression, belief, faith and worship;

EQUALITY of status and of opportunity;

and to promote among them all;

FRATERNITY, assuring the dignity of the individual and the unity and integrity of the Nation.

In our Constituent Assembly, this twenty-sixth day of November, 1949, do hereby **ADOPT, ENACT AND GIVE TO OURSELVES THIS CONSTITUTION.**

Meaning, Object and Importance of Preamble

Preamble is an introductory paragraph or part in a statute deed or other document, setting forth the grounds and intention of it.

The word "preamble" has been defined as an introductory paragraph or part in a statute, deed or other document, setting forth the grounds and intention of it. It is introduction of preliminary statement especially to a legal document setting

The preamble to an Act sets out the main objectives which the legislation is intended to achieve. It contains in a nutshell the ideals and aspirations of the Act.

forth its ground and intention. The preamble to an Act sets out the main objectives which the legislation is intended to achieve. It contains in a nutshell the ideals and aspirations of the Act. Preamble is a key to open the minds of the maker of the Act and the mischief which they intent to redress. Preamble is very useful to understand the intention of the makers of the Act and the general purpose behind the provisions of the Act. The preamble to the Constitution indicates the type of Government which the Constitution is intended to establish and rights and freedoms which the Constitution is intended to provide to the Citizens. The preamble to the Indian Constitution makes it clear that the people of India have adopted and given to themselves the Constitution and, thus, the sovereignty lies in the people. It indicates that the ultimate source for the validity of, and the sanction behind the Constitution is the will of the people. In short, reading through the preamble one can see the purpose that it serves, namely, the declaration of the sources of the Constitution, a statement of its objectives and the date of its adoption.

The preamble is very useful in the interpretation of the Constitution. In case the word used in a particular statute is capable of being both the narrower and the liberal interpretation and a doubt arises as to whether the narrower or the more liberal interpretation should be adopted, the court may look into the object and policy of the Statute as recited in the Preamble.

Preamble forms part of the Constitution and the Constitution.

The view that Preamble does not form the part of the Constitution has been rejected by the Supreme Court in the case of *Kesavanand Bharti vs. State of Kerala.* The Supreme court has held that the Preamble forms part of the Constitution and the Constitution should be read and interpreted in the light of the ground and noble vision expressed in the Preamble.

As regards the issue of the power of the Parliament to amend the Preamble, it may be concluded that the preamble is the part of Constitution and therefore it can be amended by the Parliament under Article 368 but the "basic features' in the preamble cannot be amended. The preamble has been amended by the Constitution (Forty-Second Amendment) Act, 1976.

Meaning of Expression Occurring in the Preamble

The Preamble of the Indian Constitution says — we, the people of India, having solemnly resolved to constitute India into a Sovereign, Socialist, Secular, Democratic Republic and to secure to all its citizens; justice—social, economic and political. Liberty of thought, expression, belief, faith and worship; equality of status and opportunity, and to promote among them all; fraternity assuring the dignity of the individual and the unity and integrity of the Nation.

The aforesaid provisions may be explained under the following headings:

We, the People of India: The words, "We, the People of India" indicates that the people of India are the source of authority behind the Constitution. These words indicate that the sovereignty is in the People of India. The people of India, thus, Constitute the sovereign political body who hold the ultimate power and who conduct the government of the country through their elected representatives.

Sovereign, Socialist, Secular & Democratic Republic

Sovereign: The word "sovereign" indicates that India is a sovereign nation free from any external control.

Socialist: The word "socialist" has been added by the Constitution (Forty-Second Amendment) Act, 1976 w.e.f. 3-1-1977. After the addition of the word "socialist" it has become more clear that the goal of Indian Policy is socialism. The addition of the word "socialist" in the Preamble may enable the Courts to lean more and more in favour of nationalisation and state ownership of an industry.

It indicates that the state does not recognise any religion as its own religion and, thus, treats all religions equally.

Secular: The word "secular" has been added by the Constitution (Forty Second Amendment) Act, 1976 w.e.f. 3-1-77. It indicates that the state does not recognise any religion as its own religion and, thus, treats all religions equally.

Democratic Republic: The term "Democratic Republic" indicates that the government is carried on by the people of the state through their representative and executive head of the State (i.e., the President of India) is an elected representative of the people (and not a hereditary monarch as like the king of England).

Democratic Republic indicates Government is carried on by the people of the state through their representative and executive head of the State.

Justice, Liberty, Equality, Fraternity, Unity and Integrity of Nation: these words indicate the objects to be achieved. The Preamble secures to all its citizens social, economic and political justice. The Directive Principles have been inserted for this purpose. Article 15 makes it clear that state shall not discriminate against any citizen, on ground only of religion, race, caste, sex, place of birth or any of them. It provides that no citizen shall, on ground only of religion, race, sex, place of birth or any of them, be subject to any disability restriction or condition with regard to access to shops, public restaurants, hotels and place of public entertainment or the use of wells, tanks, etc. Article 17 abolishes "untouchability." Article 38 and 39 makes provisions for socio-economic justice. Socio-economic justice implies also the forced distribution of wealth for the purpose of fair division of material resources among the members of society. Political justice has been secured by providing for universal adult franchise.

The Preamble ensures the liberty of thought, expressions, faith and worship. Article 19 (1), Article 25 and Article 26 make provisions for such liberty.

The Preamble also ensures the Equality of Status and Opportunity. Articles 14 to 18 make provisions for such Equality.

The Preamble aims to promote, among the people of India Fraternity assuming the dignity of the individual. Many provisions have been made to promote the feeling that the people of India are members of the same family. For example, the Indian Constitution provides for a single citizenship. All citizens have been given the right to move freely throughout the territory of India and to reside and settle in any part of the territory of India (Article 19 (1) and 19 (1) (e)).

All citizens have been given the right to move freely throughout the territory of India and to reside and settle in any part of the territory of India [Article 19(i) (e)]

The Preamble aims to promote the unity and integrity of the Nation. The word "integrity" has been added by the Constitution (42nd Amendment) Act 1976 w.e.f. 3.1.1977.

1.10 THE FUNDAMENTAL RIGHTS

The Constitution has eight Fundamental Rights as mentioned below:

1. Right to equality;
2. Right to six freedoms, viz.,
   (a) freedom of speech and expression;

(b) freedom to assemble peacefully and without arms;

(c) freedom to form associations or unions;

(d) freedom to move freely throughout the territory of India;

(e) freedom to reside and settle in any part of the territory of India; and

(f) freedom to practice any profession or to carry on any occupation, trade or business.

3. Right to life and [personal property];
4. Right to freedom of religion;
5. Right to cultural and educational freedom;
6. Right against exploitation;
7. Right to private property; and
8. Right to Constitutional remedies.

The right to property has been repealed with effect from June 20,1979.

1.11 CONSTITUTION OF INDIA WITH SPECIAL REFERENCE TO ECONOMIC PRINCIPLES

The right to equality, prohibits discrimination against any citizen on grounds of religion, race, caste, sex or place of birth.

Some of the Fundamental Rights have economic significance. The right to equality, for example, prohibits discrimination against any citizen on grounds of religion, race, caste, sex or place of birth. Implied in the right to equality is the concept of protective discrimination which assures protection to Scheduled Castes who have suffered discrimination for centuries. Special efforts are to be made for the development of the socially and economically backward sections of society.

Right to freedom is an important and the most valuable fundamental right guaranteed by the Constitution. As Nani Palkhivala has said, "The Constitution is a part of the great heritage of every Indian. Its founding fathers wanted to ensure that even while India remained poor in per capita income, it should be rich in individual freedom."

The right to practice any profession or to carry on any occupation, trade or business has great economic significance.

Particularly, the right to practice any profession or to carry on any occupation, trade or business has great economic significance. The Constitution guarantees to citizens the fundamental right of freedom to take up any job or carry on any trade or business. The freedom of profession is however, exceptional in three cases, viz., (a) public interest, (b) requiring technical or professional qualifications, and (c) when a State itself decides to engage in any trade or occupation, the individual freedom is restricted.

The fundamental right against exploitation prohibits the exploitation of the weaker sections of society by individuals as well as by the State. Article 23 prohibits traffic in human beings and forced labour. Article 23 reads thus: "Traffic in human beings and other similar forms of forced labour are prohibited and any contravention of this provision shall be an offence punishable in accordance with the law." Article 24 provides special protection to children. It reads thus: " No child below the age of fourteen years shall be employed to work in any factory, mine or engaged in any other hazardous employment."

Thus, the fundamental rights enshrined in the Constitution guarantee several economic rights to the citizens, at the same time, the State is empowered to impose reasonable restrictions on such economic rights in public interest. It is this power that has enabled the government to impose a series of statutory controls over business.

1.12 DIRECTIVE PRINCIPLES OF STATE POLICY

The Directive Principles of State Policy are a unique feature of our Constitution. Speaking on the Directive Principles, Dr. Ambedkar observed: "The Directive Principles are like the instruments of instructions which were issued to the Governor-General and the Governors of colonies, and those of India by the British Government under the 1935 Government of India Act. What is called "Directive Principles' is merely another name for the instruments of instructions the only difference is that they are instructions to the legislature and the executive. Whoever captures power will not be free to do what he likes with it. In the exercise of it, he will have to respect these Instruments of Instructions which are called Directive Principles. He cannot ignore them.

The Directive Principles are the directives to the various governments and government agencies and are fundamental in the governance of the country.

The Directive Principles are the directives to the various governments and government agencies and are fundamental in the governance of the country. As Pylee observed, "The Directive Principles enshrine the fundamentals for the realisation of which the State in India stands. They guide the path which will lead the people of India to achieve the noble ideals which the Preamble of the Constitution proclaims: Justice—social, economic and political, liberty, equality and fraternity."

The Directive Principles may be classified, for convenience, under four heads as shown below:

1. Provisions dealing with Welfare (Articles 38, 42, 45, 47).
2. Provisions dealing with Social Justice (Articles 39, 41, 43, 46).
3. Provisions promoting Democracy (Articles 40, 44, 45).
4. Miscellaneous Provisions (Articles 48, 49, 50, 51).

The first two categories of provisions have **economic significance**.

Article 38 (1) lays down that the State shall promote the welfare of the people by securing a social order in which justice—social, economic and political—shall inform all the institutions of national life. Justice and welfare are the twin objectives of our Constitution.

Article 38 (2) lays down that the State shall strive to minimise the inequalities in income, and eliminate inequalities in status, facilities and opportunities, not only among individuals but also among groups of people.

Article 39 emphasises that the State shall direct its policy towards securing: (a) adequate means of livelihood to all citizens; (b) a proper distribution of the material resources of the community to the common good; (c) the prevention of concentration of wealth to the common detriment; (d) equal pay for equal work for both men and women; (e) the protection of the strength and health of workers and avoiding circumstances which force citizens to enter avocation unsuited to their age or strength; and (f) the protection of childhood and youth against exploitation or moral and material abandonment.

Article 41 lays down that the State shall, within the limits of its economic capacity and development, make provision for securing the right to work, to education and to public assistance in cases of unemployment, old age, sickness and disablement.

Article 42 states that the State shall make provision for securing just and humane conditions of work and for maternity relief.

Article 43 emphasises the necessity of an adequate or living wage in all sectors of economic activity. The article enjoins that healthy conditions of work should be provided and a decent standard of living should be guaranteed. It also stresses the right to leisure for all working people. The cottage industries in rural areas should be promoted either through individual or cooperative efforts.

Article 43 (A) states that the State shall take steps to secure the participation of workers in the management of undertakings, establishments or other organisations engaged in any industry.

The State shall promote, with special care, the educational and economic interest of the weaker sections of the people, and in particular, of the Scheduled Castes, Scheduled Tribes and shall protect them from social injustice and all forms of exploitation (Article 46).

The State shall endeavour to protect and improve the environment and to safeguard the forests and wildlife of the country {Article 48(A)}.

Thus, the Directive Principles of State Policy enjoin upon the State varied responsibilities and provide vast scope for State intervention in the economy.

1.13 DISTINCTION BETWEEN FUNDAMENTAL RIGHTS AND DIRECTIVE PRINCIPLES

The Fundamental Rights are justiciable. If a fundamental right is violated, a legal remedy is provided for that. But the Directive Principles are non-justiciable and if they are violated, there is no provision for legal remedy.

There is a difference between the Fundamental Rights and the Directive Principles and it is useful to know the distinction. The Fundamental Rights are justiciable. If a fundamental right is violated, a legal remedy is provided for that. But the Directive Principles are non-justiciable and if they are violated, there is no provision for legal remedy. Article 38 says that the 'State shall strive', it does not mean that the State must fulfil these principles. If, for example, the State does not make provisions for compulsory free education for children under the age of 14 or if the judiciary is not separated from the executive, nobody can challenge it in a court of law.

However, one thing should be kept in mind that the Directive Principles have been declared as fundamental in the governance of the country. This means that these principles are not to be lightly taken and the legislature and the government must make sincere efforts to fulfil these principles. In the words of Dr. Ambedkar, "the word 'strive' was purposely used because their intention was that, however adverse the circumstances that stand in the way for a government in giving effect to these principles and however unpropitious the time may be, they should always strive for the fulfilment of the principles. Otherwise, it would be open to the government to say that the circumstances were not good and the finances were so bad that they could not implement them."

The Directive Principles are subsidiary to the Fundamental Rights and in case of conflict with Fundamental Rights, the former shall be declared unconstitutional. In the case of *State of Madras Vs. Champakan Dorairajan*, the Supreme Court observed, "The Directive Principle of State Policy which are expressly made unenforceable by a Court cannot override the provisions in Part III which... are made enforceable by appropriate writs, orders or directions under Article 32." Thus, the Directive Principle must have to conform to run subsidiary to the chapter on Fundamental Rights. The State can act in accordance with the Directive Principles if that does not amount to the infringement of the Fundamental Rights conferred by the Constitution. The legal superiority of the Fundamental Rights over the Directive Principles has been established by the decisions of the Supreme Court in India.

Another difference between the Fundamental Rights and the Directive Principles is that the former are negative in character whereas, the latter are positive. The Fundamental Rights are in the nature of injunctions requiring the State not to do certain acts and are prohibitive in character. The Directive Principles, on the other hand, are positive directions to the State to perform certain things for the good of the citizens. They urge that it is the duty of the State to implement the social and economic policy as embodied in the directives for the attainment of economic democracy and social justice. In the words of Gledhill: "Fundamental Rights are injections to prohibit the government from doing certain things; the Directive Principles are affirmative instructions to the government to do certain things."

1.14 RELATIONS BETWEEN THE UNION AND THE STATES (ARTICLE 245 AND 246)

Distribution of Legislative Powers

The Parliament may make laws for the whole or any part of the territory of India, and the Legislature of a State may make laws for the whole or any part of the State. No law made by Parliament shall be deemed to be invalid on the ground that it would have extra-territorial operation (Article 245).

The Parliament has exclusive power to make laws with respect to any of the matters enumerated in List I in the Seventh Schedule (Union List). The Parliament and the Legislature also have power to make laws with respect to any of the matters enumerated in List III in the Seventh Schedule (Concurrent list). The Legislature of any State has exclusive power to make laws for such State or any part thereof with respect to any of the matters enumerated in List II in the Seventh Schedule (State List). The Parliament has power to make laws with respect to any matter for any part of the territory of India not included in list II notwithstanding that such matter is a matter.

> The Parliament has power to make laws with respect to any matter for any part of the territory of India not included in list II notwithstanding that such matter is a matter.

Article 246 read with Schedule 7 of Indian Constitution (Business Related Matters Only)

(A) Union List — 7th Schedule (List – I)

- Currency, coinage and legal tender; foreign exchange (Item 36)
- Foreign loans (Item 37)

- Post Office Savings Bank (Item -39)
- Lotteries organised by the Government of India or the Government of a State (Item 40)
- Trade and commerce with foreign countries; import and export across customs frontiers; definition of customs frontiers (Item 41)
- Inter-State trade and commerce (Item 42)
- Incorporation, regulation and winding up of trading corporations, including banking, insurance and financial corporations, but not including co-operative societies (Item 43)
- Incorporation, regulation and winding up of corporations, whether trading or not, with objects not confined to one State, but not including universities (Item 44)
- Banking (Item 45)
- Bills of exchange, cheques, promissory notes and other like instruments (Item 46)
- Insurance (Item 47)
- Stock exchanges and futures markets (Item 48)
- Patents, inventions and designs; copyright; trade-marks and merchandise marks (Item 49)
- Establishment of standards of weight and measure (Item 50)
- Establishment of standards of quality for goods to be exported out of India or transported from one State to another (Item 51)
- Industries, the control of which by the Union is declared by Parliament by law to be expedient in the public interest (Item 52)
- Regulation and development of oilfields and mineral oil resources; petroleum and petroleum products; other liquids and substances declared by Parliament by law to be dangerously inflammable (Item 53)
- Regulation of mines and mineral development to the extent to which such regulation and development under the control of the Union is declared by Parliament by law to be expedient in the public interest (Item 54)
- Regulation of labour and safety in mines and oilfields (Item-55)
- Regulation and development of inter-State rivers and river valleys to the extent to which such regulation and development under the control of the Union is declared by Parliament by law to be expedient in the public interest (Item 56)
- Fishing and fisheries beyond territorial waters (Item-57)
- Manufacture, supply and distribution of salt by Union agencies; regulation and control of manufacture, supply and distribution of salt by other agencies (Item 58)
- Cultivation, manufacture, and sale for export, of opium (Item 59)

- Sanctioning of cinematograph films for exhibition (Item 60)
- Industrial disputes concerning Union employees (Item 61)
- Taxes on income other than agricultural income (Item 82)
- Duties of customs including export duties (Item 83)
- Duties of excise on tobacco and other goods manufactured or produced in India except —

  (*a*) alcoholic liquors for human consumption;

  (*b*) opium, Indian hemp and other narcotic drugs and narcotics, but including medicinal and toilet preparations containing alcohol or any substance included in sub-paragraph (*b*) of this entry (Item 84)
- Corporation tax (Item 85)
- Taxes on the capital value of the assets, exclusive of agricultural land, of individuals and companies; taxes on the capital of companies (Item 86)
- Estate duty in respect of property other than agricultural land (Item 87)
- Terminal taxes on goods or passengers, carried by railway, sea or air; taxes on railway fares and freights (Item 89)
- Taxes other than stamp duties on transactions in stock exchanges and futures markets (Item 90)
- Rates of stamp duty in respect of bills of exchange, cheques, promissory notes, bills of lading, letters of credit, policies of insurance, transfer of shares, debentures, proxies and receipts (Item 91)
- Taxes on the sale or purchase of newspapers and on advertisements published therein (Item 92)
- Taxes on the sale or purchase of goods other than newspapers, where such sale or purchase takes place in the course of inter-State trade or commerce (Item 92A)
- Taxes on the consignments of goods (whether the consignment is to the person making it or to any other person), where such consignment takes place in the course of inter-State trade or commerce (Item 92B)

(B) STATE LIST – 7TH SCHEDULE (LIST –II)

- Trade and commerce within the State subject to the provisions of entry 33 of List III (Item 26)
- Production, supply and distribution of goods subject to the provisions of entry 33 of List III (Item 27)
- Markets and fairs (Item 28)
- Money-lending and money-lenders; relief of agricultural indebtedness (Item 30)

- Incorporation, regulation and winding up of corporations, other than those specified in List I, and universities; unincorporated trading, literary, scientific, religious and other societies and associations; co-operative societies (Item 32).
- Betting and gambling (Item 34)
- Taxes on agricultural income (Item 46)
- Duties in respect of succession to agricultural land (Item 47)
- Estate duty in respect of agricultural land (Item 48)
- Duties of excise on the following goods manufactured or produced in the State and countervailing duties at the same or lower rates on similar goods manufactured or produced elsewhere in India:
  (a) alcoholic liquors for human consumption;
  (b) opium, Indian hemp and other narcotic drugs and narcotics, but not including medicinal and toilet preparations containing alcohol or any substance included in sub-paragraph (b) of this entry (Item 51)
- Taxes on the entry of goods into a local area for consumption, use or sale therein (Item 52)
- Taxes on the consumption or sale of electricity (Item 53)
- Taxes on the sale or purchase of goods other than newspapers, subject to the provisions of entry 92A of List I (Item 54)
- Taxes on advertisements other than advertisements published in the newspapers and advertisements broadcast by radio or television (Item 55)
- Taxes on goods and passengers carried by road or on inland waterways (Item 56)
- Taxes on vehicles, whether mechanically propelled or not, suitable for use on roads, including tramcars subject to the provisions of entry 35 of List III (Item 57)
- Taxes on animals and boats (Item 58)
- Tolls (Item 59)
- Taxes on professions, trades, callings and employments (Item 60)
- Capitation taxes (Item 61)
- Taxes on luxuries, including taxes on entertainments, amusements, betting and gambling (Item 62)
- Rates of stamp duty in respect of documents other than those specified in the provisions of List I with regard to rates of stamp duty (Item 63)

C) Concurrent List — (LIST-III)

- Contracts, including partnership, agency, contracts of carriage, and other special forms of contracts, but not including contracts relating to agricultural land (Item -7)

- Bankruptcy and insolvency (Item 9)
- Trust and Trustees (Item 10)
- Adulteration of foodstuffs and other goods (Item -18)
- Economic and social planning (Item 20)
- Commercial and industrial monopolies, combines and trusts (Item 21)
- Trade unions; industrial and labour disputes (Item 22)
- Legal, medical and other professions (Item 26)
- Trade and commerce in, and the production, supply and distribution of —
  - a) the products of any industry where the control of such industry by the Union is declared by Parliament by law to be expedient in the public interest, and imported goods of the same kind as such products;
  - b) foodstuffs, including edible oilseeds and oils;
  - c) cattle fodder, including oilcakes and other concentrates;
  - d) raw cotton, whether ginned or unginned, and cotton seed; and
  - e) raw jute (Item 33)
- Weights and measures except establishment of standards (Item -33A)
- Price control (Item -34)

The above items contained in the union, state and concurrent list have economic significance. They influence the business in one way or the other.

Questions

Section — A: Objective Type

1. What is business law?
2. Name the sources of business law.
3. What is common law?
4. What is equity?
5. What is Law Merchant?
6. What is an Ordinance?
7. What is Administrative Law?
8. What is Substantive Law?
9. What is Procedural Law?
10. What is Public Law?
11. What is Private Law?
12. What is Civil Law?
13. What is Criminal Law?
14. Name the nobel ideals as given in Indian Constitution.
15. What is secularism?
16. What is fratenity?
17. What is Federal Constitution?
18. What is Uniter Constitution?

19. What is rule of law?
20. What is judicial law?
21. What is democratic republic?
22. What is Article 14 of Indian Constitution?
23. What is Article 19 of Indian Constitution?
24. What is Article 21 of Indian Constitution?
25. What is Article 245 of Indian Constitution?
26. What is Article 246 of Indian Constitution?
27. What is schedule VII of Indian Constitution?
28. What is List -1 of Schedule VII ?
29. What is List -2 of Schedule VII ?
30. What is List -3 of Schedule VII ?
31. What is concurrent list ?
32. How many matters are included in Union List ?
33. How many matters are included in State List ?
34. How many matters are included in Concurrent List ?
35. Name any two business related matters in Union List.
36. Name any two business related matters in State List.
37. Name any two business related matters in Concurrent List.

Section — B: Analytical Type

1. Explain the scope of business law.
2. Explain common law and dharma as sources of business law.
3. Distinguish between civil law and criminal law.
4. Differentiate between federal and unitery consitution.
5. Distinguish between written and unwritten consitution.
6. Distinguish between rigid and flexible constitution.
7. Explain the features of Indian Constitution.
8. Explain the rule of law.
9. Explain the judicial review process.
10. How Articles 14, 19, 21 of Indian Constitiution are related to business.
11. Distinguish between Fundamental Rights and Directive Principles of State Policy.
12. List the business related matters of union list.
13. List the business related matters of State list.
14. List the business related matters of concurrent list.

Section — C: Essay Type

1. Define business law and thus bring out the sources and scope of business law.
2. Explain the different kinds of constitution.
3. Bring out the nobel ideals as enunciatied in the Indian Constitution.
4. Explain substantive, procedural, criminal, civil, public and private laws.
5. Explain the features of Indian Constitution in the context of Federal and Unitary System.
6. Bring out the articles of Indian Constitution which have economic significance.
7. Discuss the business related matters incorporated in Schedule –VII read with Article 246 of Indian Constitution.

INFORMATION TECHNOLOGY ACT, 2000

Module Objectives

After reading this chapter, you should be able to

- Explain the Nature of Cyber Law, advantages of Cyber Law
- Discuss the Overview of Cyber Laws in India
- List the characteristics of IT Act, 2000
- Know the concepts of E-commerce, and E-Governance with the decided cases
- Understand all about paperless society
- Know the concept of Digital Signatures and the procedure for Legal recognition of electronic records
- Comprehend cyber crimes, and their offences level including penalties

INFORMATION TECHNOLOGY ACT, 2000

(The first cyber law of India with latest amendments)

2.1 CYBERLAW IN INDIA — INTRODUCTION

When internet was developed, the founding fathers of Internet hardly had any inclination that internet could transform itself into an all pervading revolution which could be misused for criminal activities and which required regulation. Today, there are many disturbing things happening in cyberspace. Due to the anonymous nature of the Internet, it is possible to engage into a variety of criminal activities with impunity and people with intelligence, have been grossly misusing this aspect of the internet to perpetuate criminal activities in cyberspace. Hence the need for Cyber laws in India.

Cyber laws are meant to set the definite pattern, some rules and guidelines that defined certain business activities going on through internet-legal and certain illegal and hence punishable.

Cyber laws are meant to set the definite pattern, some rules and guidelines that defined certain business activities going on through internet-legal and certain illegal and hence punishable. The IT Act 2000, the cyber law of India, gives the legal framework so that information is not denied legal effect, validity or enforceability, solely on the ground that it is in the form of electronic records.

One cannot regard government as complete failure in shielding numerous e-commerce activities on the firm basis of which this industry has got to its skies, but then the law cannot be regarded as free from ambiguities.

MMS porn case in which the CEO of bazee.com(an Ebay Company) was arrested for allegedly selling the MMS clips involving school children on its website is the most apt example in this reference. Other cases where the law becomes hazy in its stand includes the case where the newspaper Mid-Day published the pictures of the Indian actress kissing her boyfriend at the Bombay nightspot and the arrest of Krishan Kumar for illegally using the internet account of Col. (Retd.) J.S. Bajwa.

Essence of the IT Act

Information Technology Act 2000 addressed the following issues:

1. Legal Recognition of Electronic Documents
2. Legal Recognition of Digital Signatures
3. Offenses and Contraventions
4. Justice Dispensation System for Cyber crimes

ITA 2008 as the new version of Information Technology Act 2000 is often referred has provided additional focus on Information Security. It has added several new sections on offences including Cyber Terrorism and Data Protection.

2.2 IMPORTANCE OF CYBERLAW

Cyber law is important because it touches almost all aspects of transactions and activities on and concerning the internet, the world wide web and cyberspace.

Initially it may seem that a cyber law is a very technical field and that it does not have any bearing to most activities in cyberspace. But the actual truth is that nothing could be further than the truth. Whether we realize it or not, every action and every reaction in Cyberspace has some legal and cyber legal perspectives.

As the nature of internet is changing and this new medium is being seen as the ultimate medium ever evolved in human history, every activity of yours in Cyberspace can and will have a cyber legal perspective. From the time you register your domain name, to the time you set up your website, to the time you promote your website, to the time when you send and receive e-mails, to the time you conduct electronic commerce transactions on the said site, at every point of time, there are various cyber law issues involved.

2.3 CHARACTERISTICS OF INFORMATION TECHNOLOGY ACT IN INDIA

The IT Act 2000 attempts to change outdated laws and provides ways to deal with cyber crimes. Let's have an overview of the law where it takes a firm stand and has got successful in the reason for which it was framed.

- **E-Transactions:** The E-commerce industry carries out its business via transactions and communications done through electronic records. It thus becomes essential that such transactions be made legal. Keeping this point in the consideration, the IT Act 2000 empowers the government departments to accept filing, creating and retention of official documents in the digital format. The Act also puts forward the proposal for setting up the legal framework essential for the authentication and origin of electronic records / communications through digital signature.
- **Legalising E-mail Message:** The Act legalizes the e-mail and gives it the status of being valid form of carrying out communication in India. This implies that e-mails can be duly produced and approved in a court of law, thus can be regarded as substantial document to carry out legal proceedings.
- **Digital Signature and Digital Relooks:** The Act also talks about digital signatures and digital records. These have been also awarded the status of being legal and valid means that can form strong basis for launching litigation in a court of law. It invites the corporate companies in the business of being Certifying Authorities for issuing secure Digital Signatures Certificates.
- **E-governance:** The Act now allows Government to issue notification on the web thus heralding e-governance.
- **Filling E-Form:** It eases the task of companies of the filing any form, application or document by laying down the guidelines to be submitted at any appropriate office, authority, body or agency owned or controlled by the government. This will help in saving costs, time and manpower for the corporates.
- **Statutory Remedy for Cyber Crimes:** The Act also provides statutory remedy to the coporates in case the crime against the accused for breaking into their computer systems or network and damaging and copying the data is proven. The remedy provided by the Act is in the form of monetary damages, not exceeding Rs. 1 crore ($200,000).

- **Cyber Appellate Tribunal:** Also the law sets up the Territorial Jurisdiction of the Adjudicating Officers for cyber crimes and the Cyber Regulations Appellate Tribunal.
- **Guidelines for Licences:** The law has also laid guidelines for providing Internet Services on a licence on a non-exclusive basis.

2.4 ADVANTAGES OF CYBER LAWS

We need Cyber Laws so that people can perform purchase transactions over the Net through credit cards without fear of misuse.

The IT Act 2000 attempts to change outdated laws and provides ways to deal with cyber crimes. We need such laws so that people can perform purchase transactions over the Net through credit cards without fear of misuse. The Act offers the much-needed legal framework so that information is not denied legal effect, validity or enforceability, solely on the ground that it is in the form of electronic records.

In view of the growth in transactions and communications carried out through electronic records, the Act seeks to empower government departments to accept filing, creating and retention of official documents in the digital format. The Act has also proposed a legal framework for the authentication and origin of electronic records / communications through digital signature.

From the perspective of e-commerce in India, the IT Act 2000 and its provisions contain many positive aspects.

- The implications of these provisions for the e-businesses would be that e-mail would now be a valid and legal form of communication in our country that can be duly produced and approved in a court of law.
- Companies shall now be able to carry out electronic commerce using the legal infrastructure provided by the Act.
- Digital signatures have been given legal validity and sanction in the Act.
- The Act throws open the doors for the entry of corporate companies in the business of being Certifying Authorities for issuing Digital Signatures Certificates.
- The Act now allows Government to issue notification on the web thus heralding e-governance.
- The Act enables the companies to file any form, application or any other document with any office, authority, body or agency owned or controlled by the appropriate Government in electronic form by means of such electronic form as may be prescribed by the appropriate Government.
- The IT Act also addresses the important issues of security, which are so critical to the success of electronic transactions. The Act has given a legal definition to the concept of secure digital signatures that would be required to have been passed through a system of a security procedure, as stipulated by the Government at a later date.
- Under the IT Act, 2000, it shall now be possible for corporates to have a statutory remedy in case if anyone breaks into their computer systems or network and causes damages or copies data. The remedy provided by the Act is in the form of monetary damages, not exceeding Rs. one crore.

2.5 SALIENT FEATURES OF THE IT ACT, 2000 (Section-wise)

Information Technology Act 2000 consisted of 94 sections segregated into 13 chapters. Four schedules form part of the Act.

The salient features of the Information Technology Act, 2000 are as follows:

- Extends to the whole of India (Section 1)
- Authentication of electronic records (Section 3)
- Legal Framework for affixing Digital signature by use of asymmetric crypto system and hash function (Section 3)
- Legal recognition of electronic records (Section 4)
- Legal recognition of digital signatures (Section 5)
- Retention of electronic record (Section 7)
- Publication of Official Gazette in electronic form (Section 8)
- Security procedure for electronic records and digital signature (Sections 14, 15, 16)
- Licensing and Regulation of Certifying authorities for issuing digital signature certificates (Sections 17-42)
- Functions of Controller (Section 18)
- Appointment of Certifying Authorities and Controller of Certifying Authorities, including recognition of foreign Certifying Authorities (Section 19)
- Controller to act as repository of all digital signature certificates (Section 20)
- Data Protection (Sections 43 & 66)
- Various types of computer crimes defined and stringent penalties provided under the Act (Section 43 and Sections 66, 67, 72)
- Appointment of Adjudicating officer for holding inquiries under the Act (Sections 46 & 47)
- Establishment of Cyber Appellate Tribunal under the Act (Sections 48-56)
- Appeal from order of Adjudicating Officer to Cyber Appellate Tribunal and not to any Civil Court (Section 57)
- Appeal from order of Cyber Appellate Tribunal to High Court (Section 62)
- Interception of information from computer to computer (Section 69)
- Protection System (Section 70)
- Act to apply for offences or contraventions committed outside India (Section 75)
- Investigation of computer crimes to be investigated by officer at the DSP (Deputy Superintendent of Police) level

- Network service providers not to be liable in certain cases (Section 79)
- Power of police officers and other officers to enter into any public place and search and arrest without warrant (Section 80)
- Offences by the Companies (Section 85)
- Constitution of Cyber Regulations Advisory Committee who will advice the Central Government and Controller (Section 88)

2.6 E-COMMERCE

Electronic commerce, consists of the buying and selling of products or services over electronic systems.

Electronic commerce, commonly known as (electronic marketing) e-commerce or eCommerce, consists of the buying and selling of products or services over electronic systems such as the internet and other computer networks. The amount of trade conducted electronically has grown extraordinarily with widespread Internet usage.

The use of commerce is conducted in this way, spurring and drawing on innovations in electronic funds transfer, supply chain management, internet marketing, online transaction processing, electronic data interchange (EDI), inventory management systems, and automated data collection systems. Modern electronic commerce typically uses the World Wide Web at least at some point in the transaction's lifecycle, although it can encompass a wider range of technologies such as e-mail as well.

A large percentage of electronic commerce is conducted entirely electronically for virtual items such as access to premium content on a website, but most electronic commerce involves the transportation of physical items in some way. Online retailers are sometimes known as e-tailers and online retail is sometimes known as e-tail. Almost all big retailers have electronic commerce presence on the World Wide Web.

Online retailers are sometimes known as e-tailers and online retail is sometimes known as e-tail.

Electronic commerce that is conducted between businesses is referred to as business-to-business or B2B. B2B can be open to all interested parties (e.g., commodity exchange) or limited to specific, pre-qualified participants (private electronic market). Electronic commerce that is conducted between businesses and consumers, on the other hand, is referred to as business-to-consumer or B2C. This is the type of electronic commerce conducted by companies such as Amazon.com.

Electronic commerce is generally considered to be the sales aspect of e-business. It also consists of the exchange of data to facilitate the financing and payment aspects of the business transactions.

Early Development of E-Commerce

The meaning of electronic commerce has changed over the last 30 years. Originally, electronic commerce meant the facilitation of commercial transactions electronically, using technology such as Electronic Data Interchange (EDI) and Electronic Funds Transfer (EFT). These were both introduced in the late 1970s, allowing businesses to send commercial documents like purchase orders or invoices electronically. The growth and acceptance of credit cards, automated teller machines (ATM) and telephone banking in the 1980s were also form of electronic commerce. Another form of e-commerce was the airline reservation system typified by the Indian Airlines and Kingfisher.

During the 1980s, online shopping was also used extensively in the UK by auto manufacturers such as Ford, Peugeot-Talbot, General Motors and Nissan. From the 1990s onwards, electronic commerce would additionally include enterprise resource planning systems (ERP), data mining and data warehousing.

An early example of many-to-many electronic commerce in physical goods was the Boston Computer Exchange, a marketplace for used computers launched in 1982. An early online information marketplace, including online consulting, was the American Information Exchange, another pre-internet online system introduced in 1991.

In 1990 Tim Berners-Lee invented the World Wide Web and transformed an academic telecommunication network into a worldwide everyman everyday communication system called internet/www. Commercial enterprise on the Internet was strictly prohibited until 1991. Although the internet became popular worldwide around 1994 when the first internet online shopping started, it took about five years to introduce security protocols and DSL allowing continual connection to the internet. By the end of 2000, many European and American business companies offered their services through the World Wide Web. Since then people began to associate a word "e-commerce" with the ability of purchasing various goods through the internet using secure protocols and electronic payment services. In India also e-commerce is slowly gaining momentum.

In 1990 Tim Berners-Lee invented the World Wide Web and transformed an academic telecommunication network into a worldwide everyman everyday communication system called internet/www.

2.7 SIGNIFICANCE OF E-COMMERCE

Faster and Easy Access

Electronic commerce or e-commerce can be said as set of well-defined commercial process related to internet for easy online business transactions. E-commerce is a novel concept used worldwide for making best use of technologies related to electronic data exchange that can be done electronically for faster and easy access.

Virtual Stores

In case of electronic transactions there is transfer of ownership rights for better usage. E-commerce stores can be termed as virtual stores showing entire range of concerned products through websites.

According to recent market surveys it has been found that the total profit earned through physical stores is lower than the overall revenue they have to bear to sustain their existence.

Direct Links to Customer

In difficult times of global economic recession more and more companies are experimenting with e-commerce for promotion of their products/services. Here they also get the opportunity to directly get linked to the customers.

Saving Time

The fast paced life of modern time has restricted people of wasting time in activities like shopping. With the advent of plastic money and internet, people are turning towards websites for purchasing many products they need. To fulfill it, the best option is definitely e-commerce websites.

Showcasing the Products and Services

Keeping in consideration the present market situation e-commerce solutions has proved to be a boon for many sinking businesses giving them ideal place to showcase their range of products/services and explore new markets spread worldwide.

Online Transactions

The procedure of buying and selling of goods online has been totally undergone transformation and changed the method of online business conduction. Now people can purchase, sell, advertise, make online payments, accept payments through plastic money, etc., with e-commerce solutions.

Exploring New Global Markets

Many small scale as well as big companies have realized the potential of ecommerce solutions and have started exploring newer global markets through it. It is one of the cheapest medium for online business conduction and its further expansion. Customers just by a click of the mouse experience enhanced technology and get virtual exposure to various types and forms of products.

Integrated Services

Internet has become integral and one of the most important parts of any country's economic set-up and infrastructure. Several e-commerce service providers are available online that provide professional customized designing services that suit their client's needs.

Business Applications

Some common applications related to electronic commerce are the following:

- E-mail
- Enterprise content management
- Instant messaging
- Newsgroups
- Online shopping and order tracking
- Online banking
- Online office suites
- Domestic and international payment systems
- Shopping cart software

- Teleconferencing
- Electronic tickets

2.8 ELECTRONIC GOVERNANCE

What is E-Governance?

E-Governance is managing, controlling and reporting of processes, using electronic systems such as computers, internet, etc. within a private as well as public organization. E-Governance forces organizations to consider all the relevant stakeholders, such as employees, financers, shareholders, government, customers, suppliers and the community at large; by using Information Technology. Governance has become a major requirement in most organizations and business communities. Do not confuse with the word 'Governance' with 'Government.' E-Governance applies to both, Government as well as private organizations.

E-Governance is managing, controlling and reporting of processes, using electronic systems such as computers, internet, etc. within a private as well as public organization.

Where any law provides that information or any other matter shall be in writing or in the typewritten or printed form, then, notwithstanding anything contained in such law, such requirement shall be deemed to have been satisfied if such information or matter is–

- rendered or made available in an electronic form; and
- accessible so as to be usable for a subsequent reference.

Where any law provides that information or any other matter shall be authenticated by affixing the signature or any document shall be signed or bear the signature of any person then, notwithstanding anything contained in such law, such requirement shall be deemed to have been satisfied, if such information or matter is authenticated by means of digital signature affixed in such manner as may be prescribed by the Central Government.

E-Governance in India

- **Delivery of Government Services:** E-governance is now also practiced by the government of India. Information technology enables the delivery of government services as it caters to a large base of people across different segments and geographical locations.
- **Saving Cost and Ensuring Transparency:** The effective use of IT services in government administration can greatly enhance existing efficiencies, drive down communication costs, and increase transparency in the functioning of various departments.
- **Access to Tangible Benefits:** E-governance also gives citizens easy access to tangible benefits such as online form filling, bill sourcing and payments, or complex applications like distance education and tele-medicine.
- **National e-Governance Plan (NeGP):** The Government of India has launched the National e-Governance Plan (NeGP) with the intent to support the growth of e-governance within the country. The Plan envisages creation of right environments to implement G2G, G2B, and G2C services.

- **Web-based Economy:** Biggest benefit of e-governance is its potential to give birth to an entire web-based economy in private as well as public organizations.

Bhoomi Project

- The Karnataka government's 'Bhoomi' project has led to the computerisation of the centuries-old system of handwritten rural land records. Through it, the revenue department has done away with the corruption-ridden system that involved bribing village accountants to procure land records; records of right, tenancy and cultivation certificates (RTCs).
- The project is expected to benefit seventy lakh villagers in 30,000 villages.

E-Seva

- In Gujarat there are websites where citizens log on and get access to the concerned government department on issues such as land, water and taxes.
- In Hyderabad, through e-Seva, citizens can view and pay bills for water, electricity and telephones, besides municipal taxes. They can also avail of birth / death registration certificates, passport applications, permits / licenses, transport department services, reservations, Internet and B2C services, among other things.

2.9 NATIONAL E-GOVERNANCE PLAN (NEGP)

All Government services accessible to the common Citizen in his or her locality, throughout his or her life through a One-stop-shop (integrated service delivery) ensuring efficiency, transparency and reliability at affordable costs to meet the basic needs of the common citizen. This is possible through NeGP. National E-Governance Action Plan approved for implementation 10 components and 25 Mission Mode Projects ambitious outlay of over Rs. 12,000 crores involving public and private investments to provide components and framework of proliferation of e-Governance in India.

This includes core policies, core projects, core infrastructure, integrated services, projects support infrastructure, human resource, development/training, technical assistance, awareness & assessment, organizational structures, R&D, Income Tax, passport, visa and immigration project, insurance, national citizen database, central excise, pensions, banking.

NeGP: Central Mission Mode Projects

Mission Mode Projects (MMP) is identified on the basis of high citizen or business interface, land records, road transport, property registration, agriculture, treasuries, municipalities.

NeGP: State Mission Mode Projects

It is identified on the basis of high citizen or business interface grampanchayats, commercial taxes policy, employment exchange, EDI (E-

Commerce), E-Biz, common service centers, Indian portal, EG Gateway, E-Courts, E-Procurement.

NeGP: Integrated Mission Mode Projects

MMPs identified on the basis of high citizen or business interface, focus on public service delivery and outcomes, radically change the way Government delivers services process re-engineering and change management are critical integrated service delivery through common services centres.

2.10 ADVANTAGES OF E-GOVERNANCE

E-Governance sees the people in government, business and citizens working together for the benefit of all. If properly implemented, the benefits of e-Governance are enormous. Some of its obvious benefits are:

(a) Integrated Information

E-Governance targets to use a government-wide electronic information infrastructure to simplify service delivery, reduce duplication, and improve the level and speed of service to clients at a lower cost. It recommends creating, managing, and prudently sharing information electronically among the various government departments and the different services offered by them. That is, information will be captured once, as close to the source as possible, then shared and re-used by all authorized users. This will avoid manual transcription and re-entering of the same information repeatedly whenever a citizen goes to a new government department for some services.

(b) Integrated Services

The integrated information approach automatically lends itself to offering integrated services. Different types of services offered by different government departments like collecting taxes, granting licences, administering regulations, paying grants and benefits, can be availed at one place. This greatly facilitates the citizens by allowing them to perceive the government as a single body to interact with instead of a number of unrelated entities, operating at different locations in different government buildings.

(c) Anywhere Services

Provision of fully interactive on-line services by e-Governance gives public access to government services with quicker responses at convenient times. This on-line accessibility of stored information from remote locations allows government officials to serve any citizen from a government office located in any part of the state or country.

(d) Anywhere, Anytime Information

Delivery of services may require interaction between government officials and citizens, but delivery of public-domain information to citizens can be done without any such interaction. Citizens can obtain information related to government processes and procedures through an on-line system without interacting with any government official. In fact, e-Governance can give the average citizen quick, interactive access to a vast array of information, through computers at home or work or through kiosks in convenient public locations, because this access to information can be available at many different locations and at all hours, there is no pressure on individuals to physically visit a Government Office.

(e) Improved Overall Productivity

E-Governance will significantly contribute to improved overall productivity of both the government officials and the citizens, as it ensures faster interaction among them by electronic mail instead of moving paper files and letters, and in streamlining the workflow of internal government administrative processes such as procurement, recruitment, evaluation, budgeting, planning. On the other hand, improved productivity of citizens results because of the facility of anytime, anywhere services and information.

(f) Better Decision Making and Planning

The integrated information base of e-Governance helps planners and decision makers to perform extensive analysis of stored data to provide answers to the queries of the administrative cadre. This facilitates taking well informed policy decisions for citizen facilitation and accessing their impact over the intended section of the population. This in turn helps them to formulate more effective strategies and policies for citizen facilitation.

(g) Better Security and Protection of Information

E-Governance uses the integrated information approach for keeping all information at one place in electronic form. Thus, keeping the information secure against theft or leakage. Proper backup mechanisms also help in protecting the valuable information from getting lost due to natural calamities such as fires, earthquakes, and floods.

E- GAZETTE

Where any law provides that any rule, regulation, order, byelaw, notification or any other matter shall be published in the Official Gazette.

Where any law provides that any rule, regulation, order, byelaw, notification or any other matter shall be published in the Official Gazette, then, such requirement shall be deemed to have been satisfied if such rule, regulation, order, byelaw, notification or any other matter is published in the Official Gazette or Electronic Gazette: Provided that where any rule, regulation, order, byelaw, notification or any other matter is published in the Official Gazette or Electronic Gazette, the date of publication shall be deemed to be the date of the Gazette which was first published in any form.

The Central Government may by rules, prescribe—

- the type of digital signature;
- the manner and format in which the digital signature shall be affixed;
- the manner or procedure which facilitates identification of the person affixing the digital signature;
- control processes and procedures to ensure adequate integrity, security and confidentiality of electronic records or payments; and
- any other matter which is necessary to give legal effect to digital signatures.

2.11 PAPERLESS SOCIETY

Meaning

The paperless society is a concept, where the use of paper as a document is replaced by the electronic document in the form of personal computers, laptops, palmtops and other electronic devices.

The paperless society is a concept, where the use of paper as a document is replaced by the electronic document in the form of personal computers, laptops, palmtops and other electronic devices.

The paperless society concept is enabled by a combination of technologies and processes mediated through the personal computer, is already facilitated by such technologies as the PDF document system. Electronics and Computer Science (Communications and Information) relating to means of communication, record keeping, and so on, especially electronic medium that does not use paper in human and economic activity of the society is called the paperless society.

Paperless society does not require paper because of the use of computers and other electronic media to record, convey, and store information. The term Paperless is used to describe business or office work which is done by computer or telephone, rather than by writing things down. It is recording or relaying information by electronic media rather than on paper. It also involves storing and communicating information in electronic form rather than on paper.

Paperless Society — An Overview

The advent of the computer age and electronic documents is second in importance only to Johann Gutenberg's invention of the printing press in the 1450s. Once computers were firmly entrenched in the world's offices in the early 1980s, it did not take long for business people to start wondering whether electronic documents could become the primary means of communication. Futurists were quick to dream about the day when books would be presented strictly online as electronic documents, available to all and at much lower prices. Others saw electronic documents putting paper companies and many printers out of business.

While the reality of the electronic document revolution has panned out differently than the futurists predicted, the computer has brought extraordinary changes to communication. For example, the broad acceptance of electronic documents in everyday and business life has prompted the development of style guides and resources for citing electronic documents as references. Another sign of the impact of electronic documents is the arrival of the electronic reading room which citizens can visit online to read about items of national interest. Likewise, physicians are more and more frequently getting away from thick patient files and instead relying on electronic charts. This move to electronic documents reduces the chances of losing vital information and also dramatically cuts down the chance of prescription errors.

The broad acceptance of electronic documents in everyday business life has prompted the development of style guides and resources for citing electronic documents as references.

Advantages of Paperless Society

Today, electronic documents are increasingly becoming the norm for handling personal business. More and more people each year do their banking and bill paying via electronic documents. It saves time, effort and postage. Plus, many contend that it is actually more secure than mailing a check from your mailbox and risking it being stolen.

Today what is classified as an electronic document has expanded to include a wide range of items such as e-mails, photographs, letters, depositions, x-rays, claims, medical records, video clips and even voice mail. Today, organizations use Document Management Systems to organize and manage these electronic documents. With the addition of each item, the move toward a paperless society again takes a step forward.

Who knows what would follow? Once the public warms to the idea of not worrying about receipts, perhaps paper currency itself can be phased out (saving not only many trees, but billions of dollars a year). Or maybe train/metro/bus/lightrail/subway tickets via cell phones.

A significant percentage of each professional's workday is spent searching, manipulating, and reviewing documents. With the increasing popularity of creating and maintaining documents on personal computers as part of sophisticated networks, it is imperative major improvements be made in tools that support the creation, review, collaboration, modification, dissemination, editing, and archiving of documents.

2.12 IMPORTANT TERMS IN INFORMATION TECHNOLOGY ACT

Access, means gaining entry into, instructing or communicating with the logical, arithmetical or memory function resources of a computer, computer system or computer network.

Addressee means a person who is intended by the originator to receive the electronic record but does not include any intermediary.

Affixing Digital Signature means adoption of any methodology or procedure by a person for the purpose of authenticating an electronic record by means of digital signature.

Asymmetric Crypto System means a system of a secure key pair consisting of a private key for creating a digital signature and a public key to verify the digital signature.

Certifying Authority means a person who has been granted a licence to issue a Digital Signature Certificate under section 24.

Computer means electronic, magnetic, optical or other high-speed data processing device or system which performs logical, arithmetic and memory functions by manipulations of electronic, magnetic or optical impulses, and includes all input, output, processing, storage, computer software or communication facilities which are connected or relates to the computer in a computer system or computer network.

Computer Network means the inter-connection of one or more computers through (i) the use of satellite, microwave, terrestrial lime or other communication media; and (ii) terminals or a complex consisting of two or more interconnected computers whether or not the interconnection is continuously maintained.

Computer Resources means computer, computer system, computer network, data, computer database or software.

Computer System means a device or collection of devices, including input and output support devices and excluding calculators which are not programmable and capable being used in conjunction with external files which contain computer programmes, electronic instructions, input data and output data that performs logic, arithmetic, data storage and retrieval, communication control and other functions.

Data means a representation of information, knowledge, facts, concepts or instruction which are being prepared or have been prepared in a formalized manner, and is intended to be processed, is being processed or has been processed in a computer system or computer network, and may be in any form (including computer printouts magnetic or optical storage media, punched cards, punched tapes) or stored internally in the memory of the computer.

Digital Signature means authentication of any electronic record by a subscriber by means of an electronic method or procedure in accordance with the provisions of section 3 of IT Act, 2000.

Digital Signature means authentication of any electronic record by a subscriber by means of an electronic method or procedure in accordance with the provisions of section 3 of IT Act, 2000.

Digital Signature Certificate means a Digital Signature Certificate issued under sub-section (4) of section 35 of IT Act, 2000.

Electronic Form means, any information generated, sent, received or stored in media, magnetic, optical, computer memory, micro film, computer generated micro fiche or similar device.

Electronic Gazette means Official Gazette published in the electronic form.

Electronic record means data, record or data generated, image or sound stored, received or sent in an electronic form or micro film or computer generated micro fiche.

Information includes data, text, images, sound, voice, codes, computer programmes, software and databases or micro film or computer generated micro fiche.

Key Pair, in an asymmetric crypto system, means a private key and its mathematically related public key., which are so related that the public key can verify a digital signature created by the private key.

Originator means a licence granted to a Certifying Authority under section 24.

Private Key means the key of a key pair used to create a digital signature.

Private Key means the key of a key pair used to create a digital signature;

Public Key means the key of a key pair used to verify a digital signature and listed in the Digital Signature Certificate.

Public Key means the key of a key pair used to verify a digital signature and listed in the Digital Signature Certificate;

Secure System means computer hardware, software and procedure that—

(a) are reasonably secure from unauthorised access and misuses;

(b) provide a reasonable level of reliability and correct operation;

(c) are reasonably suited to performing the intended functions; and

(d) adhere to generally accepted security procedures.

Verify, in relation to a digital signature, electronic record or public key, with its grammatical variations and cognate expressions, means to determine whether—

(a) the initial electronic record was affixed with the digital signature by the use of private key corresponding to the public key of the subscriber;

(b) the initial electronic record is retained intact or has been altered since such electronic record was so affixed with the digital signature.

Any reference in this Act to any enactment or any provision thereof shall, in relation to an area in which such enactment or such provision is not in force, be construed as a reference to the corresponding law or the relevant provision of the corresponding law, if any, in force in that area.

2.13 DIGITAL SIGNATURES

Digital Signature means authentication of any electronic record by a subscriber by means of an electronic method or procedure in accordance with the provisions of section 3 of IT Act, 2000.

Digital Signature means authentication of any electronic record by a subscriber by means of an electronic method or procedure in accordance with the provisions of section 3 of IT Act, 2000.

Subject to the provisions of the Information Technology Act, 2000, any subscriber may authenticate an electronic record by affixing his digital signature. The authentication of the electronic record shall be effected by the use of asymmetric crypto system and hash function which envelop and transform the initial electronic record into another electronic record.

For the purposes of this Act "hash function" means an algorithm mapping or translation of one sequence of bits into another, generally smaller, set known as "hash result" such that an electronic record yields the same hash result every time the algorithm is executed with the same electronic record as its input making it computationally infeasible—

- To derive or reconstruct the original electronic record from the hash result produced by the algorithm.
- That two electronic records can produce the same hash result using the algorithm.
- Any person by the use of a public key of the subscriber can verify the electronic record.
- The private key and the public key are unique to the subscriber and constitute a functioning key pair.

"Hash function" means an algorithm mapping or translation of one sequence of bits into another

2.14 SECURE ELECTRONIC RECORDS AND SECURE DIGITAL SIGNATURES

Where any security procedure has been applied to an electronic record at a specific point of time, then such record shall be deemed to be a secure electronic record from such point of time to the time of verification.

Secure Electronic Record

If by application of a security procedure agreed to by the parties concerned, it can be verified that a digital signature, at the time it was affixed, was—

(a) unique to the subscriber affixing it;

(b) capable of identifying such subscriber;

(c) created in a manner or using a means under the exclusive control of the subscriber and is linked to the electronic record to which it relates in such a manner that if the electronic record was altered the digital signature would be invalidated, then such digital signature shall be deemed to be a secure digital signature.

Security Procedure for Commercial Purposes

The Central Government prescribes the security procedure for commercial circumstances prevailing at the time when the procedure is used, including—

- the nature of the transaction;
- the level of sophistication of the parties with reference to their technological capacity;
- the volume of similar transactions engaged in by other parties;
- the availability of alternatives offered to but rejected by any party;
- the cost of alternative procedures; and
- the procedures in general use for similar types of transactions or communications.

2.15 LEGAL RECOGNITION OF ELECTRONIC RECORDS

Legal recognition of digital signatures and authentication of electronic records:

In the Information Technology Act, signed with reference to a person, mean affixing of his hand written signature or any mark on any document and the expression "signature" shall be construed accordingly.

In the Information Technology Act, signed with reference to a person, mean affixing of his hand written signature or any mark on any document and the expression "signature" shall be construed accordingly.

Where any law provides that documents, records or information shall be retained for any specific period, then, that requirement shall be deemed to have been satisfied if such documents, records or information are retained in the electronic form, if—

- the information contained therein remains accessible so as to be usable for a subsequent reference;
- the electronic record is retained in the format in which it was originally generated, sent or received or in a format which can be demonstrated to represent accurately the information originally generated, sent or received; Retention of electronic records, Use of electronic records and digital signatures in Government and its agencies.
- the details which will facilitate the identification of the origin, destination, date and time of despatch or receipt of such electronic record are available in the electronic record.

Nothing in this section shall apply to any law that expressly provides for the retention of documents, records or information in the form of electronic records.

2.16 CERTIFYING AUTHORITIES

Certifying Authority means a person who has been granted a licence to issue a Digital Signature Certificate under section 24.

Certifying Authority means a person who has been granted a licence to issue a Digital Signature Certificate under section 24.

2.17 REGULATION OF CERTIFYING AUTHORITIES

The Central Government may, by notification in the Official Gazette, appoint a Controller of Certifying Authorities for the purposes of this Act and may also by the same or subsequent notification appoint such number of Deputy Controllers and Assistant Controllers as it deems fit. The Controller shall discharge his functions under this Act subject to the general control and directions of the Central Government. The Deputy Controllers and Assistant Controllers shall perform the functions assigned to them by the Controller Secure digital signature (Section 17).

Duties of Certifying Authority

- Make use of hardware, software and procedures that are secure from intrusion and misuse; provide a reasonable level or reliability in its services which are reasonably suited to the performance of intended functions;
- Adhere to security procedures to ensure that the secrecy and privacy of the digital signatures are assured; and
- Observe such other standards as may be specified by regulations, (Section 30).

Every Certifying Authority shall ensure that every person employed or otherwise engaged by it complies, in the course of his employment or engagement, with the provisions of this Act, rules, regulations and orders made thereunder (Section 31).

Every Certifying Authority shall display its licence at a conspicuous place of the premises in which it carries on its business. Power to investigate contraventions (Section 32).

Every Certifying Authority whose licence is suspended or revoked shall immediately after such suspension or revocation, surrender the licence to the Controller. Where any Certifying Authority fails to surrender a licence under sub-section (1), the person in whose favour a licence is issued, shall be guilty of an offence and shall be punished with imprisonment which may extend up to six months or a fine which may extend up to ten thousand rupees or with both (Section 33).

Every Certifying Authority shall disclose in the manner specified by regulations—

— its Digital Signature Certificate which contains the public key corresponding to the private key used by

— that Certifying Authority to digitally sign another Digital Signature Certificate;

— any certification practice statement relevant thereto;

— notice of the revocation or suspension of its Certifying Authority Certificate, if any; and

— any other fact that materially and adversely affects either the reliability of a Digital Signature Certificate, which that Authority has issued, or the Authority's ability to perform its services.

Where in the opinion of the Certifying Authority any event has occurred or any situation has arisen which may materially and adversely affect the integrity of its computer system or the conditions subject to which a Digital Signature Certificate was granted, then, the Certifying Authority shall—

— use reasonable efforts to notify any person who is likely to be affected by that occurrence; or

— act in accordance with the procedure specified in its certification practice statement to deal with such event or situation.

Functions of Controller Towards Certifying Authority

The Controller may perform all or any of the following functions, namely:

- exercising supervision over the activities of the Certifying Authorities;
- certifying public keys of the Certifying Authorities;
- laying down the standards to be maintained by the Certifying Authorities;
- specifying the qualifications and experience which
- employees of the Certifying Authorities should possess;
- specifying the conditions subject to which the Certifying authorities shall conduct their business;
- specifying the contents of written, printed or visual materials and advertisements that may be distributed or used in respect of a Digital Signature Certificate and the public key;
- specifying the form and content of a Digital Signature Certificate and the key;
- specifying the form and manner in which accounts shall be maintained by the Certifying Authorities;
- specifying the terms and conditions subject to which auditors may be appointed and the remuneration to be paid to them;
- facilitating the establishment of any electronic system by a Certifying Authority either solely or jointly with other Certifying Authorities and regulation of such systems;
- specifying the manner in which the Certifying Authorities shall conduct their dealings with the subscribers;
- resolving any conflict of interests between the Certifying Authorities and the subscribers.

Controller duties towards the Certifying Authorities and Digital Signature Certificates:

- The controller shall maintain a data base containing the disclosure record of every Certifying Authority containing such particulars as may be specified by regulations, which shall be accessible to public (Section 18).
- Subject to such conditions and restrictions as may be specified by regulations, the Controller may with the previous approval of the Central

Government, and by notification in the Official Gazette, recognise any foreign Certifying Authority as a Certifying Authority for the purposes of this Act (Section 19).

- Where any Certifying Authority is recognised, the Digital Signature Certificate issued by such Certifying Authority shall be valid for the purposes of this Act.
- The Controller may, if he is satisfied that any Certifying Authority has contravened any of the conditions and restrictions subject to which it was granted recognition under sub-section (1) he may, for reasons to be recorded in writing, by notification in the Official Gazette, revoke such recognition.
- The Controller shall be the repository of all Digital Signature Certificates issued under this Act. The Controller shall—
  - — make use of hardware, software and procedures that are secure from intrusion and misuse;
  - — observe such other standards as may be prescribed by the Central Government; to ensure that the secrecy and security of the digital signatures are assured.
- The Controller shall maintain a computerised data base of all public keys in such a manner that such data base and the public keys are available to any member of the public.
- Subject to the provisions of sub-section (2), any person may make an application, to the Controller, for a licence to issue Digital Signature Certificates.
- No licence shall be issued under sub-section (1), unless the applicant fulfills such requirements with respect to qualification, expertise, manpower, financial resources and other infrastructure facilities, which are necessary to issue Recognition of foreign Certifying Authorities.

2.18 COMPUTER RESOURCES

Computer resource means computer, computer system, computer network, data, computer database or software.

Computer resource means computer, computer system, computer network, data, computer database or software.

Section 69 empowers the Central Government/State Government/ its authorized agency to intercept, monitor or decrypt any information generated, transmitted, received or stored in any computer resource if it is necessary or expedient so to do in the interest of the sovereignty or integrity of India, defence of India, security of the State, friendly relations with foreign States or public order or for preventing incitement to the commission of any cognizable offence or for investigation of any offence.

2.19 CYBER CRIMES

Cyber crime is unlawful act wherein the computer is either a tool or a target or both. Cyber crimes can involve criminal activities that are traditional in nature, such as theft, fraud, forgery, defamation and mischief, all of which are subject to the Indian Penal Code. The abuse of computers has also given birth to a gamut of new age crimes that are addressed by the Information Technology Act, 2000.

Category of Cyber Crimes

The cyber crime is committed with the help of computers. The computers are used in two ways. They are computer as a target, and computer as a weapon.

1) The Computer as a Target : Using a computer to attack other computers. For example, Hacking, Virus/Worm attacks, distributed Denial of Service (DOS) attack and the like.

2) The Computer as a Weapon: Using a computer to commit real world crimes, for example, Cyber Terrorism, Intellectual Property Rights violations, Credit card frauds, Electronic Fund Transfer frauds, Pornography and the like. The Cyber Crimes are regulated by Cyber Laws or Internet Laws.

2.20 VARIANTS OF CYBER CRIMES

From the above two types of broad classification of cyber crimes on the basis of the usage of computers as a target and as a weapon, the following variants are explained in great detail.

(1) UNAUTHORIZED ACCESS

Access means gaining entry into, instructing or communicating with the logical, arithmetical, or memory function resources of a computer, computer system or computer network.

Access means gaining entry into, instructing or communicating with the logical, arithmetical, or memory function resources of a computer, computer system or computer network.

Unauthorized access would therefore mean any kind of access without the permission of either the rightful owner or the person in charge of a computer, computer system or computer network.

(2) HACKING

Every act committed towards breaking into a computer and/or network is hacking. Hackers write or use ready-made computer programs to attack the target computer. They possess the desire to destruct and they get the kick out of such destruction. Some hackers hack for personal monetary gains, such as to stealing the credit card information, transferring money from various bank accounts to their own account followed by withdrawal of money.

Every act committed towards breaking into a computer and/or network is hacking.

Web Hijacking

By hacking web server taking control on another person's website called as web hijacking.

TYPES OF HACKERS

Black and White Hat Hackers

A black hat is a person who compromises the security of a computer system without permission from an authorized party, typically with malicious intent.

A black hat is a person who compromises the security of a computer system without permission from an authorized party, typically with malicious intent. The term white hat is used for a person who is ethically opposed to the abuse of computer systems, but is frequently no less skilled. The term cracker was coined by Richard Stallman to provide an alternative to using the existing word hacker for this meaning. The somewhat similar activity of defeating copy prevention devices in software which may or may not be legal in a country's laws is actually software cracking.

A white hat hacker, also rendered as ethical hacker, is, in the realm of information technology, a person who is ethically opposed to the abuse of computer systems. Realization that the Internet now represents human voices from around the world has made the defense of its integrity an important pastime for many. A white hat generally focuses on securing IT systems, whereas a black hat (the opposite) would like to break into them.

The term white hat is used for a person who is ethically opposed to the abuse of computer systems, but is frequently no less skilled.

The term white hat hacker is also often used to describe those who attempt to break into systems or networks in order to help the owners of the system by making them aware of security flaws, or to perform some other altruistic activity. Many such people are employed by computer security companies; these professionals are sometimes called sneakers. Groups of these people are often called tiger teams.

Difference between White and Black Hackers

The primary difference between white and black hat hackers is that a white hat hacker claims to observe ethical principles. Like black hats, white hats are often intimately familiar with the internal details of security systems, and can delve into obscure machine code when needed to find a solution to a tricky problem.

Grey Hat Hackers

A Grey Hat in the computer security community, refers to a skilled hacker who sometimes acts legally, sometimes in good will, and sometimes not.

Some use the term grey hat and fewer use brown hat to describe someone's activities that cross between black and white. A Grey Hat in the computer security community, refers to a skilled hacker who sometimes acts legally, sometimes in good will, and sometimes not. They are a hybrid between white and black hat hackers. They usually do not hack for personal gain or have malicious intentions, but may or may not occasionally commit crimes during the course of their technological exploits.

A person who breaks into a computer system and simply puts their name there while doing no damage can also be classified as a grey hat.

Cracker

A group that calls themselves hackers refers to a group that consists of skilled computer enthusiasts.

Use of the term "cracker" is mostly limited (as is "black hat") to some areas of the computer and security field and even there, it is considered controversial. Until the 1980s, all people with a high level of skills at computing were known as "hackers." A group that calls themselves hackers refers to a group that consists of skilled computer enthusiasts.

The common usage of the term cracker, refers to those who attempt to gain unauthorized access to computer systems. Over time, the distinction between those perceived to use such skills with social responsibility and those who used them maliciously or criminally, became perceived as an important divide.

The common usage of the term cracker, refers to those who attempt to gain unauthorized access to computer systems.

Many members of the first group attempt to convince people that intruders should be called crackers rather than hackers, but the common usage remains ingrained. The former became known as "hackers" or (within the computer security industry) as white hats, and the latter as "crackers" or "black hats." The general public tends to use the term "hackers" for both types, a source of some conflict when the word is perceived to be used incorrectly; for example Linux has been criticised as "written by hackers." In computer jargon the meaning of "hacker" can be much broader.

Usually, a black hat is a person who uses their knowledge of vulnerabilities and exploits for private gain, rather than revealing them either to the general public or the manufacturer for correction. Many black hats hack networks and web pages solely for financial gain. Black hats may seek to expand holes in systems; any attempts made to patch software are generally done to prevent others from also compromising a system they have already obtained secure control over. A black hat hacker may write their own zero-day exploits (private software that exploits security vulnerabilities; 0-day exploits have not been distributed to the public). In the most extreme cases, black hats may work to cause damage maliciously, and/or make threats to do so as extortion.

Zero-day exploits (private software that exploits security vulnerabilities; 0-day exploits have not been distributed to the public).

(3) TROJAN ATTACK

The program that acts like something useful but do the things that are quite damping. The programs of this kind are called as Trojans. The name Trojan Horse is popular. Trojans come in two parts, a Client part and a Server part. When the victim (unknowingly) runs the server on its machine, the attacker will then use the Client to connect to the Server and start using the trojan.

Trojan attack referst to the program that act like something useful but do the things that are quite damping.

(4) VIRUS AND WORM ATTACK

A program that has capability to infect other programs and make copies of itself and spread into other programs is called virus. Programs that multiply like viruses but spread from computer to computer are called as worms.

(5) E-MAIL AND INTERNET RELATED CRIMES

(a) Email spoofing

E-mail spoofing refers to e-mail that appears to have been originated from one source when it was actually sent from another source.

(b) Email Spamming

E-mail "spamming" refers to sending e-mail to thousands and thousands of users - similar to a chain letter.

(c) Sending malicious codes through e-mail

E-mails are used to send viruses, Trojans etc., through e-mails as an attachment or by sending a link of website which on visiting downloads malicious code.

d) Email bombing

E-mail "bombing" is characterized by abusers repeatedly sending an identical e-mail message to a particular address.

e) Sending threatening e-mails, defamatory e-mails, and committing email frauds and IRC related attacks such as verbal attacks, clone attacks, and flood attacks.

6. DENIAL OF SERVICE ATTACKS (DOS)

Flooding a computer resource with more requests than it can handle. This causes the resource to crash thereby denying access of service to authorized users.

Flooding a computer resource with more requests than it can handle. This causes the resource to crash thereby denying access of service to authorized users. The examples include:

- Attempts to "flood" a network, thereby preventing legitimate network traffic
- Attempts to disrupt connections between two machines, thereby preventing access to a service
- Attempts to prevent a particular individual from accessing a service
- Attempts to disrupt service to a specific system or person.

Distributed Denial of Service (DOS)

A distributed denial of service (DoS) attack is accomplished by using the internet to break into computers and using them to attack a network.

Hundreds or thousands of computer systems across the Internet can be turned into "zombies" and used to attack another system or website.

There are three basic types of attack

- Consumption of scarce, limited, or non-renewable resources like NW bandwith, RAM, CPU time. Even power, cool air, or water can affect.
- Destruction or Alteration of Configuration Information.
- Physical Destruction or Alteration of Network Components.

7. PORNOGRAPHY

The literal meaning of the term 'Pornography' is "describing or showing sexual acts in order to cause sexual excitement through books, films, and the like."

This would include pornographic websites; pornographic material produced using computers and use of internet to download and transmit pornographic videos, pictures, photos, writings and the like. Adult entertainment is largest industry on internet. There are more than 420 million individual pornographic webpages today.

Research shows that 50 percent of the websites containing potentially illegal contents relating to child abuse were 'Pay-Per-View'. This indicates that abusive images of children over Internet have been highly commercialized. Pornography delivered over mobile phones is now a burgeoning business, "driven by the increase in sophisticated services that deliver video clips and streaming video, in addition to text and images."

Effects of Pornography

Research has shown that pornography and its messages are involved in shaping attitudes and encouraging behaviour that can harm individual users and their families. Pornography is often viewed in secret, which creates deception within marriages that can lead to divorce in some cases. In addition, pornography promotes the allure of adultery, prostitution and unreal expectations that can result in dangerous promiscuous behaviour. Some of the common, but false messages sent by sexualized culture. Sex with anyone, under any circumstances, any way it is desired, is beneficial and does not have negative consequences. Women have one value — to meet the sexual demands of men. Marriage and children are obstacles to sexual fulfillment. Everyone is involved in promiscuous sexual activity, infidelity and premarital sex.

8. FORGERY

Counterfeit currency notes, postage and revenue stamps, mark sheets etc. can be forged using sophisticated computers, printers and scanners. Also impersonate another person is considered forgery.

9. INTELLECTUAL PROPERTY RIGHTS VIOLATIONS

These include software piracy, copyright infringement, trademarks violations, theft of computer source code, patent violations and the like.

Cyber Squatting — Domain names are also trademarks and protected by ICANN's domain dispute resolution policy and also under trademark laws. Cyber Squatters registers domain name identical to popular service provider's domain so as to attract their users and get benefit from it.

2.21 OFFENCES AND PENALTIES UNDER THE IT ACT

Whoever knowingly or intentionally conceals, destroys or alters or intentionally or knowingly causes another to conceal, destroy or alter any computer source code used for a computer, computer programme, computer system or computer network, when the computer source code is required to be kept or maintained by law for the time being in force, shall be punishable with imprisonment up to three years, or with fine which may extend up to two lakh rupees, or with both.

If any person without permission of the owner or any other person who is incharge of a computer, computer system or computer network,

- accesses or secures access to such computer, computer system or computer network;
- downloads, copies or extracts any data, computer data base or information from such computer, computer system or computer network including information or data held or stored in any removable storage medium;
- introduces or causes to be introduced any computer contaminant or computer virus into any computer, computer system or computer network;

- damages or causes to be damaged any computer, computer system or computer network, data, computer data base or any other programmes residing in such computer, computer system or computer network;
- disrupts or causes disruption of any computer, computer system or computer network;
- denies or causes the denial of access to any person authorised to access any computer, computer system or computer network by any means;
- provides any assistance to any person to facilitate access to a computer, computer system or computer network in contravention of the provisions of this Act, rules or regulations made thereunder;
- charges the services availed of by a person to the account of another person by tampering with or manipulating any computer, computer system, or computer network, Penalty for damage to computer, computer system, etc. he shall be liable to pay damages by way of compensation not exceeding one crore rupees to the person so affected (Section 43).

If any person who is required under this Act or any rules or regulations made thereunder to—

(a) furnish any document, return or report to the Controller or the Certifying Authority fails to furnish the same, he shall be liable to a penalty not exceeding one lakh and fifty thousand rupees for each such failure;

(b) file any return or furnish any information, books or other documents within the time specified therefore in the regulations fails to file return or furnish the same within the time specified therefore in the regulations, he shall be liable to a penalty not exceeding five thousand rupees for every day during which such failure continues;

(c) maintain books of account or records, fails to maintain the same, he shall be liable to a penalty not exceeding ten thousand rupees for every day during which the failure continues (Section 44).

Penalty for Failure to Furnish Information Return and the Like

Whoever contravenes any rules or regulations made under this, for the contravention of which no penalty has been separately provided, shall be liable to pay a compensation not exceeding twenty-five thousand rupees to the person affected by such contravention or a penalty not exceeding twenty-five thousand Rupees (Section 45).

Recovery of penalty. Tampering with computer source documents. Hacking with computer system.

Whoever commits hacking shall be punished with imprisonment up to three years, or with fine which may extend upto two lakh rupees, or with both (Section 66). Now it has been amended and hacking is not an offence to make it cyber friendly.

Whoever publishes or transmits or causes to be published in the electronic form, any material which is lascivious or appeals to the prurient interest or if its effect is such as to tend to deprave and corrupt persons who are likely, having regard to all relevant circumstances, to read, see or hear the matter contained or embodied in it, shall be punished on first conviction with imprisonment of either description for a term which may extend to five years and with fine which may extend to one lakh rupees and in the event of a second or subsequent conviction with imprisonment of either description for a term which may extend to ten years and also with fine which may extend to two lakh rupees (Section 67).

Any person who secures access or attempts to secure access to a protected system in contravention of the provisions of the act shall be punished with imprisonment of either description for a term which may extend to ten years and shall also be liable to fine.

Whoever makes any misrepresentation to, or suppresses any material fact from, the Controller or the Certifying Authority for obtaining any licence or Digital Signature Certificate, as the case may be, shall be punished with imprisonment for a term which may extend to two years, or with fine which may extend to one lakh rupees, or with both.

Any person who has secured access to any electronic record, book, register, correspondence, information, document or other material without the consent of the person concerned discloses such electronic record, book, register, correspondence, information, document or other material to any other person shall be punished with imprisonment for a term which may extend to two years, or with fine which may extend to one lakh rupees, or with both (Section 72).

No person shall publish a Digital Signature Certificate or otherwise make it available to any other person with the knowledge that—

(a) the Certifying Authority listed in the certificate has not issued it; or

(b) the subscriber listed in the certificate has not accepted it; or

(c) the certificate has been revoked or suspended, unless such publication is for the purpose of verifying a digital signature created prior to such suspension or revocation.

Penalty for Breach of Confidentiality and Privacy

Penalty for publishing Digital Signature Certificate false in certain particulars may extend to two years, or with fine which may extend to one lakh rupees, or with both.

Whoever knowingly creates, publishes or otherwise makes available a Digital Signature Certificate for any fraudulent or unlawful purpose shall be punished with imprisonment for a term which may extend to two years, or with fine which may extend to one lakh rupees, or with both. (Section 73).

Any computer, computer system, floppies, compact disks, tape drives or any other accessories related thereto, in respect of which any provision of this Act, rules, orders or regulations made thereunder has been or is being contravened, shall be liable to confiscation.

2.22 THE INFORMATION TECHNOLOGY (AMENDMENT) ACT, 2008

The Government of India has brought major amendments to Information Technology Act 2000 in form of the Information Technology Amendment Act, 2008.

New Provisions Added Through Amendments

- New Section to address technology neutrality from Section 3A its present "technology specific" form (i.e., Digital Signature to Electronic Signature)
- New Section to address promotion of e-Governance Section 6A & other IT application
  — Delivery of Service
  — Outsourcing
  — Public Private Partnership
- New Section to address electronic contract Section 10A
- New Section to address data protection and privacy Section 43
- Body corporate to implement best security practices Sections 43A & 72A
- Multimember Appellate Tribunal Sections 49-52
- New Section to address new forms of computer misuse
  — Impersonation Section 419A
  — Identity theft and E-commerce frauds Section 417A like publishing
  — Video voyeurism Section 502A
  — Offensive messages and Spam Section 66A
  — Pornography Section 67A
- Preservation and Retention of Data/Information Section 67C
- Revision of existing Section 69 to empower Central Section 69, Government to designate agencies and issue direction for interception and safeguards for monitoring and decryption
- Blocking of Information for public access Section 69A, monitoring of Traffic Data and Information for Section 69B

Cyber Security

- New section for designating agency for protection Section 70A of Critical Information Infrastructure
- New Section for power to CERT-In to call and Section 70B analyse information relating to breach in cyber space and cyber security
- Revision of existing Section 79 for prescribing liabilities Section 79 of service providers in certain cases and to Empower Central Government to prescribe guidelines to be observed by the service providers for providing services. It also regulates cyber cafes.

- New Section for Examiner of Digital Evidence Section 79A
- New Section for power to prescribe modes of Encryption Section 84A
- Punishment for most of offences were reduced from three years to two years

Cyber Terrorism

- For the first time, defined the concept of cyber terrorism and has made it a heinous crime.
- Cyber terrorism as an offence that has been made punishable with life imprisonment and fine.
- This move should do tremendous service to the cause of the Indian nation as also the sovereignty, integrity and security of India.
- Highly commendable move after Mumbai 26/11 attacks.

New Cyber Crimes Added

— Provide far more exhaustive coverage off cyber crimes in the law.

— Various new cyber crimes have been added

— Like the activities defined in Section 43 off the IT Act,, 2000.

— The new amendments have added identity theft and publishing as cyber crimes.

— Have also covered breach of privacy, child pornography as specific offences.

Interception

— The new amendments have strengthened

— The hands of the nation by increasing the ambit of the powers off interception of the Government,

— Interception, blocking and monitoring powers have been more detailed and elaborately stated.

IT ACT AMENDMENTS AND CORPORATES

— Huge ramifications of the new amendments on corporate India

— Law has begun to flex its muscles

— The clock is slowly churning.

Section 2 Amendments

"Communication Device" means cell phones, personal digital assistance or combination of both or any other device used to communicate, send or transmit any text, video, audio or image (Section 2(ha).

"Computer network" means the interconnection of one or more computers or computer systems or communication device through (Section 2j).

The use of satellite, microwave, terrestrial line, wire, wireless or other communication media; and (section 2(i)

Terminals or a complex consisting of two or more inter-connected computers or communication device whether or not the inter-connection is continuously maintained (section 2(ii).

Highlights of the 2008 Amendments

— Hacking no longer an offence hacking as an offence has been deleted from the law book.
— existing Section 66 of the IT Act, 2000
- the said section has been substituted by new language
- existing language of the offence of hacking does not find mention in the current manner and the friendly cyber crime legislation amendments seek to make Indian cyberlaw friendly cyber crime legislation:
- a legislation that goes extremely soft on cyber criminals, with a soft heart cyber crime friendly

— a legislation that chooses to encourage cyber criminals by lessening the quantum of punishment accorded to them in the existing laws
— cyber crimes are bailable
— distinct absence of logic and rationale in reducing of the quantum of punishments for various offences
— now cyber crimes to be investigated not by a DSP but by an inspector

A Terror SMS From Your Cell? Possible, Sending `Masked SMS' Can Attract 3-Year Jail Term

Imagine getting a lewd SMS from a number you know, going to police with a complaint and then finding out that the supposed sender is clueless about what happened.

Two such cases have been reported to Mumbai police in the past. Though they are yet to track down the sender, they have managed to unearth a bizarre truth, that of the `masked SMS'. The user has to register on a website (for as little as $10) and can send text messages to and from any mobile number on the planet without being identified.

Mumbai police have managed to track down two or three websites that are used to send masked messages and are collaborating with IT experts to get to the bottom of the matter. ``We have received two complaints in the last one month where the sender's number was camouflaged," joint commissioner of police (crime) Rakesh Maria told TOI on a Saturday.

Masked Messages

- Sender looks for **'sending masked SMS'** in search engine
- Logs on to any of these websites and registers under a false identity
- Pays a nominal fee ($10) and gets an activation code
- Enters numbers in **'to'** and **'from'** slots
- SMS sent without either party's knowledge

IT industry sources said, ``It's rare for the real miscreant to be caught in such a situation because people might register under false identities and also commit credit card fraud to pay the small registration fee," says IT expert Vijay Mukhi.

If caught, can the culprit be charged under our laws? ``Yes," says IT expert Vijay Mukhi. ``Section 66 A of the IT Act talks about sending offensive messages using any communication device, Section 66 C is the identity theft section and Section 66 D the cheating by impersonation section." A pornographic message will be charged under Section 66 E, while Section 66 F is quoted in the case of cyber terrorism.

If proved, the offence of identity theft attracts a 3-year jail term plus a cash fine of upto Rs. 1 lakh in India. While there is a misuse of computer act that is invoked in such cases in the US, the law in India is still inadequate to handle such innovative mobile spoofing. ``Based on our findings we will decide what action should be taken against these websites. If need be, we could pull them down as well," he added. The masked SMS service is easy to operate. Giving TOI a demo, the IT expert logged on and sent this reporter an SMS from his colleague's number with utmost ease. Of course, the friend had no record of the said message in his outbox. Senior Nasscom officials say these websites can be blocked but it's long process.

Can anything be done at all? "Not immediately," says Mukhi. "As of now, one just has to be careful and cross-check the credibility of a message before filing a complaint." He added that the need of the hour is to spread awareness about the problem. "Time was when wifi was misused but we've managed to tackle that. Camouflaging is a dangerous issue and must be dealt with seriously and immediately," he added.

Can Existing Laws Help?

- Section 66A of the Indian IT Act talks about sending offensive messages using any communication device. Section 66C is the identity theft section and Section 66D the cheating by impersonation section. In the two cases reported to the Mumbai police, a combination of these three sections will apply.
- A pornographic message will be charged under Section 66E, while Section 66F is quoted in the case of cyber terrorism.
- If proved, the offence of identity theft attracts a 3-year jail term plus a cash fine of upto Rs. 1 lakh in India. While there is a 'misuse of computer act' that is invoked in such cases in the US, the law in India is still inadequate to handle such innovative mobile spoofing.

Questions

Section — A Objective Type

1. What is cyber law?
2. State the essence of the IT Act, 2000.
3. State any two characteristics of IT Act, 2000.
4. What is E-Gazette?
5. What is Digital Signature?
6. What is a private key?
7. What is a public key?
8. What is cyber security?
9. What is cyber terrorism?
10. What is E-Commerce ?
11. What is E-Governance?
12. What is paperless society ?
13. What is Cyber Crime ?
14. Who is a black hat hacker ?
15. Who is a white hat hacker ?
16. Who is a grey hat hacker ?
17. Who is a Sneaker ?
18. Who is a Cracker ?

Section — B Analytical Type

1. Explain the objectives of E-Commerce
2. State the Advantages of E-Commerce
3. State the Demerits of E-Commerce
4. Briefly explain the advantages and disadvantages of E-governance
5. Explain the advantages of paperless society
6. Distinguish between White hat hacker, and black hat hacker
7. Explain the importance of cyber law.
8. Analyse the characteristics of IT Act.
9. State the advantages of Cyber Law.
10. Explain the functions of controller towards certifying authority.

Section — C Essay Type

1. Discuss in great detail the merits and demerits of E-commerce.
2. Discuss the practical applications of information technology in Karnataka, Gujarat, and Andhra Pradesh.
3. "Paperless society is a myth." Do you agree ? Comment.
4. Explain the salient features of the IT Act, 2000.
5. Discuss the offences and penalties under the IT Act, 2000.

THE COMPETITION ACT, 2002

Module Objectives

After reading this chapter, you should be able to

- Comprehend the significance, objectives and salient features of Indian Competition Act, 2002
- Know the components of Competition Act, 2002
- Distinguish between the MRTP Act, 1969 and the Competition Act, 2002
- Diagnose all about the competition commission of India (CCI)
- Appreciate the nuances of competition appellate tribunal (CAT)
- Understand the offences and penalties under the competition law
- Know the history of Competition Law and policy across the nations of the world.

COMPETITION ACT, 2002

3.1 INTRODUCTION TO COMPETITION ACT, 2002

Since attaining Independence in 1947, India, for the better part of half a century thereafter, adopted and followed policies comprising what are known as command-and-control laws, rules, regulations and executive orders. The competition law of India, namely, the Monopolies and Restrictive Trade Practices Act, 1969 (MRTP Act, for brief) was one such. It was in 1991 that widespread economic reforms were undertaken and consequently the march from command-and-control economy based more on free market principles commenced its stride. As is true of many countries, economic liberalization has taken root in India and the need for an effective competition regime has also been recognized.

In the context of new economic policy paradigm, India has chosen to enact a new competition law called the competition Act, 2002. The MRTP Act has metamorphosed into the new law, competition Act, 2002. The new law is designed to repeat the extent MRTP Act. As of now, only a few provisions of the new law have been brought into force and the process of constituting the regulatory authority, namely, the competition commission of India under the new act, is on. The remaining provisions of the new law will be brought into force in a phased manner.

For the present, the outgoing law, MRTP Act, 1969 and the new law Competition act, 2002 are concurrently in force though as mentioned above, only some provisions of the new law have been brought into force. Competition Law for India was triggered by Articles 38 and 39 of the constitution of India. These Articles are a part of the Directive Principles of State Policy.

Pegging on the Directive Principles, the first Indian Competition Law was enacted in 1969 and was christened the Monopolies and Restrictive Trade Practices Act, 1969 (MRTP Act). Articles 38 and 39 of the Constitution of India mandate, *inter alia*, that the state shall strive to promote the welfare of the people by securing and protecting as effectively, as it may, a social order in which justice, social, economic and political shall inform all the institutions of the national life, and the state shall, in particular, direct its policy towards securing—

1) That the ownership and control of material resources of the community are so distributed as best to sub-serve the common good; and
2) That the operation of the economic system does not result in the concentration of wealth and means of production to the common detriment.

In October 1999, the Government of India appointed a High Level Committee on Competition Policy and competition law to advise a modern competition law for the country in line with international developments and to suggest a legislative framework, which may entail a new law or appropriate amendments to the MRTP

Act. The committee presented its competition policy report to the Government in May 2000 (The report will be referred to hereinafter as High Level Committee (2000)]. The draft competition law was drafted and presented to the Government in November 2000. After some refinements following extensive consultations and discussions with all interested parties, the parliament passed in December 2002 the new law, namely, the Competition Act, 2002.

3.2 OBJECTIVES OF COMPETITION ACT, 2002

The Competition Act, 2002 was enacted in January 2003. Its main objectives are to :

(1) Ensure fair competition in India, by prohibiting trade practices that have an adverse effect on competition

(2) Promote and sustain competition

(3) Protect the interests of consumers; ad

(4) Ensure freedom of trade for other participants in incidental and connected markets

3.3 ESSENTIALS / FEATURES OF COMPETITION ACT, 2002

The main features of the Competition Act are :

- Prohibition of anti-competitive agreements
- Prohibition of abuse of dominant position
- Regulation of combinations
- Establishment of the competition commission of India
- Penalties for contravention and non-compliance
- Competition advocacy and
- Constitution of the competition fund.

3.4 COMPONENTS OF THE COMPETITION ACT, 2002

The rubric of the new law, Competition Act, 2002 (Act, for brief) has essentially four compartments.

- Anti-competition agreements
- Abuse of dominance
- Combinations regulation (Mergers, amalgamations, acquisitions and takeovers)
- Competition advocacy (fostering competition).

Let us discuss each of the above component in great detail.

(1) ANTI-COMPETITION AGREEMENT

Firms enter into agreements, which may have the potential of restricting competition.

Firms enter into agreements, which may have the potential of restricting competition. A scan of the competition laws in the world will show that they made a distinction between horizontal and vertical agreements between firms. The former, namely the horizontal agreements are those among competitors and the latter, namely the vertical agreements are those relating to an actual or potential relationship of purchasing or selling to each other. A particularly pernicious type of horizontal agreements is the cartel.

Vertical agreements are pernicious, if they are between firms in a position of dominance. Most competition laws view vertical agreements generally more leniently than horizontal agreements, as *prima-facie,* horizontal agreements are more likely to reduce competition than agreements between firms in a purchaser, seller relationship. An obvious example that comes to mind is an agreement between enterprises dealing in the same product or products, such horizontal agreements, which include membership of cartels, are presumed to lead to unreasonable restrictions of competition and are therefore presumed to have an appreciable adverse effect on competition. In other words, they are per se illegal. The underlying principle in such presumption of illegality is that the agreements in question have an appreciable anti-competitive effect. Barring the aforesaid for type of agreements, all the others will be subject to the rule of reason test in the Act.

(2) ABUSE OF DOMINANCE

Dominant position has been appropriately defined in the Act. In terms of the position of strength enjoyed by an enterprise, in the relevant market, in India, which enables it to (i) operate independently of competitive forces prevailing in the relevant market; or (ii) affects its competitors or consumers or the relevant market in its favour.

Dominant position is the position of strength enjoyed by an enterprise in the relevant market which enables it to operate independently of competitive forces prevailing in the market affects its competitors or consumers or the relevant market in its favour.

Section 4 of the Competition Act, no enterprise shall abuse its dominant position. Dominant position is the position of strength enjoyed by an enterprise in the relevant market which enables it to operate independently of competitive forces prevailing in the market affects its competitors or consumers or the relevant market in its favour. Dominant position that is abused when an enterprise imposes unfair or discriminatory conditions in purchase or sale of goods or services. Again, the philosophy of Competition Act is reflected in this provision, where it is clarified that a situation of monopoly *per se* is not against public policy but, rather, the use of the monopoly status such that it operates to the detriment (loss) of potential and actual competitors.

Abuse of dominance arises if an enterprise

- Imposes unfair/ discriminatory purchase or sale prices (including predatory prices)
- Limits production, markets or technical development
- Denies market access

- Concludes contracts subject to obligations having no connection with the subject of the contracts
- Uses dominance to move into or protect other markets

Relevant market =	Relevant product market	+	Relevant geographic market

At this point it is worth mentioning that the Act does not prohibit or restrict enterprises from coming into dominance. There is no control whatsoever to prevent enterprises from coming into or acquiring position of dominance. All that the Act prohibits is the abuse of that dominant position. The Act therefore, targets the abuse of dominance and not dominance *per se*. This is indeed a welcome stop, a step towards a truly global and liberal economy.

(3) THE COMPETITION ACT ON COMBINATIONS REGULATION

Combinations, a term, which contemplates acquisitions, mergers or amalgamations.

The competition law also is designed to regulate the operation and activities of combinations, a term, which contemplates acquisitions, mergers or amalgamations. Thus, the operation of the competition Act is not confined to transactions strictly within the boundaries of India but also such transactions involving entities existing and / or established overseas.

Herein again lies the key to understanding the Competition Law. The intent of legislation is not to prevent the existence of a monopoly across the board. There is a realization in policy making circles that in certain industries, the nature of their operations and economies of scale indeed indicate the creation of a monopoly in order to be able to operate and remain viable and profitable. This is insignificant contrast to the philosophy, which propelled the operation and application of the MRTP Act, the trigger for which was the existence or impending creation of monopoly situation in a sector of industry.

The competition law has made the pre-notification of combinations voluntary for the parties concerned. However, if the parties to the combination choose not to notify the competition commission of India (CCI), as it is not mandatory to notify, they run the risk of a post-combination action by the CCI, if it is discovered subsequently, that the combination has an appreciable adverse effect on competition. There is a rider that the CCI shall not initiate an inquiry into a combination after the expiry of one year from the date on which the combination has taken effect.

(4) COMPETITION ADVOCACY

In line with the high level committee's recommendation, the Competition Act extends the mandate of competition commission of India beyond merely enforcing the law (High Level Committee, 2000). Competition advocacy creates a culture of competition. There are many possible valuable roles for competition advocacy, depending on a country's legal and economic circumstances.

Competition Advocacy is nothing but Competition commission of India advising Central Government on country's economic policies and review of laws relating to competition in India.

The Regulatory Authority under the Act, namely, competition commission of India, in terms of the advocacy provisions in the Act, is enabled to participate in the formulation of the country's economic policies and to participate in the reviewing of laws related to competition at the instance of the Central Government. The Central Government can make a reference to the CCI for its opinion on the possible effect of a policy under formulation or of an existing law related to competition. The commission will therefore be assuming the role of competition advocate, acting pro-actively to bring about Government policies that lower barriers to entry, that promote deregulation and trade liberalization and that promote competition in the market place.

Perhaps one of the most crucial components of the Competition Act is contained in a single section under the chapter entitled competition advocacy.

3.5 DIFFERENCES BETWEEN MRTP ACT, 1969 AND COMPETITION ACT 2002

In view of the policy shift from curbing monopolies to promoting competition there was a need to repeal the Monopolies and Restrictive Trade Practices Act. Hence, the competition law aims at doing away with the rigidly structured MRTP Act. The Competition Law is flexible and behaviour oriented. After the Act was passed and came into the public domain, a question often asked is whether it is not still the old law in substance although not in form. A clear answer to this question is in the title of this sub-section the act is a new wine in a new bottle. The differences between the old law (namely, the MRTP Act, 1969) and the new law (the Competition Act, 2002) may perhaps be best captured in the form of Table 3.1 displayed below.

Table 3.1 MRTP Act and Competition Act — Distinguished

Sl. No.	MRTP Act, 1969	Competition Act, 2002
1	Based on the pre-reforms scenario	Based on the post-reforms scenario
2	Based on an undertaking's size as a factor	Based on an undertaking's structure as a factor
3	Competition offences are implicit or not defined	Competition offences are explicit and defined
4	Complex in arrangement and language	Simple in arrangement and language and easily comprehensible
5	14 percent offences negating the principles of natural justice	14 percent offences and all the rest subjected to rule of reason.
6	Frowns upon dominance	Frowns upon abuse of dominance
7	Registration of agreements compulsory	No requirement of registration of agreements
8	No combination regulation	Combinations (mergers and amalgamations) beyond a high threshold limit are regulated
9	MRTP Act, 1969	Competition Act, 2002
10	MRTP commission appointed by the Government	Competition commission selected by a collegiums (search committee)
11	Very little administrative and financial autonomy for the competition commission	Relatively more autonomy for the competition commission
12	No competition advocacy role for the MRTP commission	Competition commission has competition advocacy role
13	No penalties for offences	Penalties for offences
14	Reactive and rigid	Proactive and flexible
15	Unfair trade practices (UTPs) covered	Unfair Trade Practices omitted are
16	Does not vest MRTP commission to inquire into cartels of foreign origin in a direct manner	Competition law seeks to regulate cartels of Indian and Foreign origin of India

The Competition Act is therefore a new wine in a new bottle—wine gets better as it ages. The law provides for a competition fund, which shall be utilized for promotion of competition advocacy, creating awareness about competition issues and training in accordance with the rules that may be prescribed. The extent MRTP Act, 1969 has aged for more than three decades and has given birth to the new law (the Act) in line with changed and changing economic scenario in India and rest of the world and is in line with the current economic thinking comprising liberalization, privatization, and globalization.

The message is loud yet clear that a well planned exhaustive competition compliance programme can be a great benefit to all enterprises irrespective of their size, area of operation jurisdiction involved, nature of products supplied or services rendered and the same is essential for companies, its directors and the delegate key corporate executives to avoid insurmountable hardships of monetary fines, and civil imprisonment besides loss of hard-earned reputation when the competition authorities, the media and others reveal the misdeeds in public.

In the changed scenario, India required a fresh law for competition and new regulatory authority, which under this policy is the competition commission of India.

6. COMPETITION COMMISSION OF INDIA (CCI)

The Competition Act, 2002 provides for the establishment of the Competition Commission of India, which like its predecessor — the MRTP Commission is a quasi-judicial body. The CCI, *inter alia* has the power to :

1) Issue cease and desist orders
2) Grant interim relief
3) Award compensation
4) Impose fines and
5) Order the division of dominant undertakings

In its first year, the CCI engaged in competition advocacy. In the second year, it tackled cases related to anti-competitive practices other than Mergers and Acquisitions, which was dealt from the third year.

The functioning of the CCI has been affected by a writ petition filed in the Supreme Court, which challenged the appointment of a non-judicial person as its Chairman, asserting the doctrine of the separation of the powers of the executive and the Judiciary.

In response, the Government of India has suggested that the Act will be modified and the CCI will be split into two bodies: one the regulatory body to be headed by an expert, and an appellate body to be headed by a judge. The amendment bill is yet to be finalized and approved by the parliament.

India is likely to emerge as the second largest market in the world in the not so distant future. In this scenario, the CCI will be expected to play a balanced role, protecting both consumer interests and those of the Indian businesses. The CCI will also have an important task of collaborating with the various sectoral regulators and herein competition advocacy will play a vital role.

3.6 COMPOSITION OF COMMISSION (CCI)

The Commission shall consist of a Chairperson and not less than two and not more than six members to be appointed by the Central Government (Sec. 8).

The Chairperson and every other member shall be a person of ability, integrity and standing and who has special knowledge of, and professional experience of not less than fifteen years in, international trade, economics, business, commerce, law, finance, accountancy, management, industry, public affairs, which in the opinion of the Central Government, may be useful to the commission. The chairperson and other members shall be whole — time members.

Selection Committee for Chairperson and Members

The Chairperson and other members of the commission shall be appointed by the Central Government from a panel of names recommended by a selection committee consisting of —

(a) The chief justice of India or his nominee	Chairperson
(b) The Secretary in the Ministry of Company Affairs	Member
(c) The Secretary in the Ministry of Law	Member

The term of the office of chairperson or other member shall be for five years. They shall not hold office as such after they have attained the age of sixty five years. The chairperson shall have the powers of general superintendence, direction and control in respect of all administrative matters of the Commission.

Appointment of Director General and other Directors

The Central Government may, by notification, appoint a Director General for the purposes of assisting the commission in conducting inquiry into contravention of any of the provisions of this Act and for performing such other functions as are, or may be, provided by or under this Act.

The number of other additional, joint, deputy or assistant directors General of such officers or other employees in the office of Director General and the manner of appointment of such additional, joint, deputy or Assistant Director General or such officers or other employees shall be such as may be prescribed.

Appointment of Secretary, Experts, Professionals and Officers and other Employees of Commission.

The commission may appoint a secretary and such officers and other employees as it considers necessary for the efficient performance of its functions under this Act.

The salaries and allowances payable to and other terms and conditions of services of the secretary and officers and other employees of the commission and the number of such officers and other employees shall be such as may be prescribed.

The commission may engage in accordance with the procedure specified by regulations such number of experts and professionals of integrity and outstanding ability, who have special knowledge of, and experience in, economics, law, business or such other disciplines related to competition, as it deems necessary to assist the commission in the discharge of its function under this Act.

Meeting of Commission

The commission shall meet at such times and Paces, and shall observe such roles of procedure in regard to the transaction of business at its meetings as may be provided by regulations.

The Chairperson, if for any reason, is unable to attend a meeting of commission, the senior — most member present at the meeting shall preside at the meeting.

All questions which come up before any meeting of the commission shall be decided by a majority of the members present and voting, and in the event of an equality of votes, the Chairperson or in his absence the member presiding shall have a second or/ casting vote; provided that the quorum for such meeting shall be three members.

Procedure for Inquiry of Offences Under the Act

(1) On receipt of a reference from the Central Government or a State Government or a statutory authority or on its own knowledge or information received under section 19, if the commission is of the opinion that there exists a *prima-facie* case, it shall direct the Director General to cause an investigation to be made into the matter.

(2) Where on receipt of a reference from the Central Government or a State government or a statutory authority or information received under section 19, the Commission is of the opinion that there exists no prima facie case, it shall close the matter forthwith and pass such orders as it deems fit and send a copy of its order to the Central Government or the State government or the statutory authority or the parties concerned, as the case may be.

(3) The Director General shall, on receipt of direction under sub-section (1) submit a report on his findings within such period as may be specified by the commission.

(4) The commission may forward a copy of the report referred to in sub-section (3) to the parties concerned.

Provided that in case the investigation is caused to be made based on reference received from the Central Government or the State Government or the statutory authority, the commission shall forward a copy of the report referred to in sub-section (3) to the Central Government or the State Government or the statutory authority, as the case may be.

(5) If the report of the Director General referred to in sub-section (3) recommends that there is no contravention of the provisions of this Act, the commission shall invite objections or suggestions from the Central Government or the State Government or the Statutory authority or the parties concerned, as the case may be, on such report of the Director General.

(6) If, after consideration of the objections and suggestions referred to in sub-section (5), if any the commission agrees with the recommendation of the Director Genera, it shall close the matter both with and pass such orders as it deems fit and communicate its order to the Central

Government or the State Government or the Statutory authority or the parties concerned, as the case may be.

(7) If, after consideration of the objections or suggestions referred to in sub section (5), if any, the commission is of the opinion that further investigations are called for, it may direct further investigations in the matter by the Director General or cause further inquiries to be made by in the matter or itself proceed with further inquiry in the matter in accordance with the provisions of this Act.

(8) If the report of the Director General referred to in sub-section (3) recommends that there is contravention of any of the provisions of this act, and the commission is of the opinion that further inquiry is called for it shall inquire into such contravention in accordance with the provisions of this Act.

Power of Commission to Regulate its Own Procedures

1) In the discharge of its functions, the commission shall be guided by the principles of natural justice and subject to the other provisions of this Act and of any rules made by the Central Government, the commission shall have the powers to regulate its on procedure.

2) The commission shall have, for the purposes of discharging its functions under the Act, the same powers as are vested in a Civil Court under the code of Civil Procedure, 1908, while trying a suit, in respect of the following matters, namely:

- summoning and enforcing the attendance of any person and examining him on oath;
- requiring the discovery and production of documents;
- receiving evidence on affidavits;
- issuing commissions for the examination of witnesses or documents;
- subject to the provisions of sections 123 and 124 of the Indian Evidence Act, 1872 (1 of 1872), any public record or document or copy of such of record or document from any office.

(3) The commission may call upon such experts, from the field of economics, commerce, accountancy, international trade or from any other discipline as it deems necessary, to assist the commission in the conduct of any inquiry by it.

(4) The Commission may direct any person—

(a) to produce before the Director General or the Registrar or an officer authorised by it, such books, accounts or other documents in the custody or under the control of such person so directed as may be specified or described in the direction, being documents relating to any trade, the examination of which may be required for the purposes of this Act;

(b) to furnish to the Director General or the Registrar or any officer authorised by it, as respect the trade or such other information as may be in his possession in relation to the trade carried on by such person, as may be required for the purposes of this Act.

3.7 COMPETITION APPELLATE TRIBUNAL (CAT)

The Central Government through notification is proposed to establish an Appellate Tribunal to be known as Competition Appellate Tribunal. This is to hear and dispose of appeals against any direction issued or decision made or passed by the CCI. Further to adjudicate on claim for compensation that may arise from the findings of the CCI and pass orders for the recovery of compensation.

Composition of Appellate Tribunal

The Appellate Tribunal shall consist of a Chairperson and not more than two other members to be appointed by the Central Government.

Qualifications for appointment of Chairperson and member of Appellate Tribunal:

The Chairperson of the Appellate Tribunal shall be a person, who is, or has between, a judge of the Supreme Court or the Chief Justice of a High Court.

A member of the Appellate Tribunal shall be a person of ability, integrity and standing having special knowledge of, and professional experienced of not less than twenty-five years in, competition, international trade, economics, business, commerce, law, finance, accountancy, management, industry, public affairs, administration or in any other matters which in the opinion of the Central Government, may be useful to the Appellate Tribunal.

Selection Committee

The Chairperson and members of the Appellate Tribunal shall be appointed by the Central Government from a panel of names recommended by the selection committee, composition of which has been specified for CCI.

Term of Office of Chairperson and Members of Appellate Tribunal

The chairperson or a member of the Appellate Tribunal shall hold office as such for a term of five years from the date on which he enters upon his office, and shall be eligible for re-appointment.

Provided, that no chairperson or other member of the Appellate Tribunal shall hold office as such after he has attained —

(a) in the case of the Chairperson, the age of sixty-eight years

(b) in the case of any other member of the Appellate Tribunal, the age of sixty-five years.

3.8 OFFENCES AND PENALTIES UNDER THE COMPETITION ACT, 2002

Any person or company or body-corporate or firms which deals in anti-competition agreements, abuse by way of dominance, or resort to corporate crimes through mergers, amalgamations, acquisitions and hostile takeovers which are detrimental to the general public causing downfall of competition, the central government or a state government or a local authority or the associations may refer the matter to CCI. The commission, which is having the power of a civil court, after following the due process of law and the principles of natural justice shall pass appropriate orders. Let us discuss the penalties and offences under the Act.

(1) If a person fails to pay any monetary penalty imposed on him under this Act, the commission shall proceed to recover such penalty in such manner as may be specified by the regulations.

(2) In a case where the commission is of the opinion that it would be expedient to recover the penalty imposed under the Act in accordance with provisions of the Income Tax Act, 1961, it may make a reference to this effect to the concerned Income Tax Authority under the Act for recovery of the penalty as tax due under the said Act.

(3) Where a reference has been made by the commission for recovery of penalty as tax due, the person upon whom the penalty has been imposed shall be deemed to be the assessee in default under the Income Tax Act, 1961.

(4) Without prejudice to the provisions of this Act, if any person violates any directions issued or contravenes without any reasonable ground, any decision or order of the commission issued under sections 27, 28, 31, 32 and 33 or any condition or restriction subject to which any approval, sanction, direction or exemption in relation to any matter has been accorded, given, made or granted under this Act or fails to pay the penalty imposed under this act, then he shall without prejudice to any proceeding under section 39, be liable for imposition of additional penalty not exceeding Rupees 120 lakh or imprisonment for a term upto one year or both as the civil court having jurisdiction in the matter may deem fit.

The commission may cause an investigation to be made into compliance of its orders, and based on the results of the investigation or otherwise, file a complaint before the civil court having jurisdiction in the matter, which shall pass such order under this section as it may deem fit.

Provided that the civil court shall not take cognizance of any offence punishable under this section save on a complaint filed by the commission (or) any of its officers authorized by it.

(5) Where during an inquiry, the commission is satisfied that an act in contravention of the provisions of the act has been committed and continues to be committed or that such act is about to be committed, the commission may, by order, grant a temporary injunction restraining any parties from carrying on such act until the conclusion of such inquiry or until further orders, without giving notice to the opposite party, where it deems it necessary.

3.9 APPEAL TO APPELLATE TRIBUNAL [SECTION 53(B)]

(1) The central government or the state government or a local authority or enterprise or any person, aggrieved by any direction, decision or order referred to in clause (a) of Section 53A may prefer an appeal to the Appellate Tribunal.

(2) Every appeal under sub-section (1) shall be filed within a period of sixty days from the date on which a copy of the direction or decision or under madc by the commission is received by the Central Government or the State Government or a local authority or enterprise or any person referred to in that sub-section and it shall be in such form and be accompanied by such fee as may be prescribed.

Provided that the Appellate Tribunal may entertain an appeal after the expiry of the said period of sixty days if it is satisfied that there was sufficient cause for not filing it within that period.

(3) On receipt of an appeal under sub-section (1), the Appellate Tribunal may, after giving the parties to the appeal, an opportunity of being heard, pass such orders thereon as it thinks fit, confirming, modifying or setting aside the directions, decision or order appealed against.

(4) The appellate tribunal shall send a copy of every order made by it to the commission and the parties to the appeal.

(5) The appeal filed before the appellate tribunal under sub -section (7) shall be dealt with by it as expeditiously as possible and endeavour shall be made by it to dispose of the appeal within six months from the date of receipt of the appeal.

3.10 AWARDING COMPENSATION (SECTION 53(N)

(1) Without prejudice to any other provisions continued in this Act, the Central Government or a State Government or a local authority or any enterprise any person may make an application to the Appellate Tribunal to adjudicate on claim for compensation that may arise from the findings of the commission and to pass an order for the recovery of compensation from any enterprise for any loss or damage shown to have been suffered, by such person as a result of any contravention of the provisions under the Act, having been committed by enterprise.

(2) Every application made under sub-section (1) shall be accompanied by the findings of the commission, if any, and also be accompanied with such fees as may be prescribed.

(3) The Appellate Tribunal may, after an inquiry made into the allegations mentioned in the application made under sub-section (i) pass an order directing the enterprise to make payment to the applicant, of the amount determined by it as realizable from the enterprise as compensation for the loss or damage caused to the applicant as a result of any contravention of the provisions under the Act having been committed by such enterprise.

Provided that in a case no decision or order has been made or direction issued on the contravention alleged on the application by the commission, the Appellate Tribunal may obtain the recommendations of the commission before passing an order of compensation.

Contravention of Orders of Appellate Tribunal (Section 53 Q)

Without prejudice to the provisions of this Act, if any person contravenes, without any reasonable ground, any order of the Appellate Tribunal, he shall be liable to be detained in civil prison for a term which may extend to one year, unless in the meantime the civil court directs his release and he shall also be liable to a penalty not exceeding rupees ten lakhs.

3.11 HISTORY OF COMPETITION LAW & POLICY ACROSS THE WORLD

— About 90 countries have competition laws.

— Canada and United states enacted competition legislation towards the end of the 10th century (in 1889 and 1890 respectively).

COMPETITION LAW of USA
Federal Government of USA enacted Sherman Anti-Trust Act, 1890, Clayton Act, 1914, and Fair Trade Commission Act, 1914. Subsequently, Robinson-Patman Act, 1946 and the Celler-Kefauver Act, 1950 were enacted.

Focus Areas for Competition Laws

Three areas of enforcement provide the focus for most competition laws around the world—

- Agreements among enterprises
- Abuse of Dominance
- Mergers, or more generally, combinations among enterprises.
- Body of competition law of USA constitutes those statutes judicial interpretations and the priorities and interpretations of enforcement agencies—
  - — Articles 81 and 82 of 1957 Treaty of Rome Serves as Principal competition law of EC (Former constitutes "Agreements between firms" and latter "abuse of dominance")
  - — Most recent enactment is the UK Law— Competition Act, 1998 came into force w.e.f. 1st March, 2000.
- More closely in line with EC Law.
- Major difference being mergers which are compulsorily required to be notified under EC law, are not so in UK law.

INDIAN CONTEXT

- Adopted the new competition law (Competition Act, 2002) to replace MRTP Act, 1969
- At the cross-roads of implementing new competition law.
- However, the country is yet to have a stated competition policy.

Competition Policy and WTO Regime

- A Central function of WTO is to ensure equality of competitive opportunities for members of WTO in the World Trading System.

- Agreements of Uruguay Round Final Act notified at Marrakesh relate to competition policy issues in one way or another, although not explicitly.
- Number of WTO agreements allow member to take or maintain measures that affect competition within and outside their domestic markets.

CONCLUSION

The competition law is very significant in the post liberalization era. Since India is a member country of WTO, the latter insists on fair and free competition in the trade across the nations of the globe. In line with, WTO requirements, the Government. India replaced the old MRTP Act, 1969 with the new Competition Act, 2002.

The objectives of Act are to ensure fair competition in India by prohibiting trade practices that have an adverse effect on competition, promoting and protecting competition, protecting the interests of consumers and ensures fair trade.

The law has four components to deal with, they are: anti-competition agreements, abuse of dominance, combinations regulations in relation to mergers, amalgamations, strategic alliance and take-over and also having competition advocacy through a commission called competition commission of India. For redressing the grievances of orders of CCI, the government set-up Competition Appellate Tribunal. Further, this chapter discussed the history of competition law and policy across the world.

KEY WORDS

- Competition
- Competition Law
- Anti-competition agreements
- Combinations
- Competition Advocacy
- WTO
- CCI
- CAT
- Competition Policy
- Offences and Penalties
- Compensation

Questions

Section — A Objective Type

1. State any two objectives of Competition Act, 2002.
2. Mention any two salient features of Competition Act, 2002.
3. Which Act is the predecessor of Competition Act, 2002 ?
4. What is Article 38 of India Constitution ?
5. State the intent of Article 39 of Indian Constitution.
6. Name the components of Competition Act, 2002.
7. What are anti-competition agreements ?
8. State any two horizontal restraints under anti-competition agreements.
9. State any two vertical restraints under anti-competition agreement.

10. What do you mean by abuse of dominance ?
11. State when abuse of dominance arises.
12. State any two pejorative effects of amalgamation.
13. What is competition advocacy ?
14. Expand CCI and CAT.
15. State any two difference between MRTP Act, 1969 and Competition Act 2002.
16. State any two powers of CCI.
17. What should be the qualification to become the Chairperson of CCI ?
18. What should be the qualification to become the Chairperson of CAT ?
19. State the important officials under the Competition Act, 2002.
20. Mention the composition of CCI.
21. Mention the composition of CAT.
22. State the focus area of competition laws.

Section — B Analytical Type

1. Mention the objectives and salient features of the Competition Act, 2002 ?
2. Briefly explain (j) Anti-competition agreements and (ii) abuse of dominance ?
3. Analyze the mergers and the amalgamations, regulation under Competition Act, 2002?
4. Briefly explain competition advocacy as per the Competition Act, 2002 ?
5. Bring out any five differences between the MRTP Act, 1969 and the Competition Act, 2002 ?
6. State the powers of CCI.
7. Write about the meetings of the CCI.
8. Explain the procedure for enquiry of offences under the Compensation Act, 2002. Explain the power of CCI to regulate its own procedure.

Section — C Essay Type

1. Explain in great detail the various components of the Competition Act, 2002.
2. Bring out in great detail the differences between the MRTP Act, 1969 and the Competition Act, 2002.
3. Give an account of (i) CCI and (ii) CAT.
4. Discuss the offences and penalties under the Competition Act , 2002.
5. Give an account of competition law and policy across the world.
6. "Is competition laws a boon or bane in the Indian Context ? " Comment.

THE RIGHT TO INFORMATION ACT, 2005

Module Objectives

After reading this chapter, you should be able to

- Understand the nature, scope and objectives of the RTI Act, 2005
- Know the salient features of the RTI Act, 2005
- Comprehend the concepts such as information commissioner, public authority, and information officer
- Distinguish between the information that are included and exempted from disclosure
- List the characteristics of the RTI Act, 2005
- Know the procedure to get information under RTI Act
- Understand all about the Act with interesting cases and landmark judgements.

THE RIGHT TO INFORMATION ACT, 2005 (With Latest Amendments)

4.1 Right To Information Act — Background

Right To Information Act, 2005 (RTI) empowers a citizen to access the information for disclosure from the public authority and bring transparency.

Right To Information Act, 2005 (RTI) empowers a citizen to access the information for disclosure from the public authority and bring transparency. Awareness of the people about the Act has increased after the slow start. The national campaign for people's right to information was initiated by social activists, journalists, lawyers, professionals, retired civil servants and academics, in 1996 with the objectives of a national law facilitating the exercise of the fundamental Right To Information. The "Right to Information Act, 2005" was came into force from 12th October 2005.

Right to Information Act, 2005 is an Act to provide for setting out the practical regime of right to information for citizens to secure access to information under the control of public authorities, in order to promote transparency and accountability in the working of every public Authority.

Right to Information Act, 2005 is an Act to provide for setting out the practical regime of right to information for citizens to secure access to information under the control of public authorities, in order to promote transparency and accountability in the working of every public Authority. As per the Act, Information means, material in the form of documents, memos, e-mails, press release, circulars, orders, contracts, reports, data materials.

The Act covers central, state and local governments, and all bodies owned, controlled or substantially financed by the Government or any non-government organization substantially financed, directly or indirectly by the appropriate Government. The information, which affect the sovereignty and integrity of India are not to be disclosed. Information, which relates to personal information the disclosure of which has no relationship to any public activity or interest, or which, would cause unwarranted invasion of the privacy of the individual is also not supposed to be disclosed.

The objective of the Act is to hold government and their instrumentalities accountable to the governed and to contain corruption. With potential application in meeting government's obligations to provide information on request and proactively, e-governance is a viable option for public authorities to address the information needs of RTI Act.

The objective of the Act is to hold government and their instrumentalities accountable to the governed and to contain corruption.

Similar to RTI Act, 2005 of our country, it also exists in other countries. In other countries the implementation of such Act has taken more than one year (Table 4.2). However, In India the RTI Act, 2005 is implemented in just four months (Table 4.2). This fast implementation encourages to know the problems (if any) faced by the organization due to the implementation of RTI Act.

Table 4.2 Global Implementation of RTI Act

Country / Attributes	India	USA	UK	JAPAN
Title of the Act.	Right to Information Act.	Freedom of Information Act.	Freedom of Information Act	Freedom of Information Act
Date of enactment	15 June 2005	4 July 1966	30 Nov. 2000	May 1999
Date of Implementation	12 Oct. 2005	4 July 1967	January 2005	April 2001
Time in implementation	4 Month	1 Year	4 Year	2 Year
Delivery of information	30 Day	20 Day	20 Day	30 Day

All the 24 hours in a day, millions of virtual fuse wires have been snaking across India, connecting to mini-bombs under chairs and tables in government offices that have gone progressively arrogant since Independence. In these government cells are pockets of information, concealing which, bureaucrats and politicians derive and share power and pelf.

Information is the ultimate ammunition in democracies, where citizens empowered with it, they will take governance back from oppressors. Social workers in education, health care, legal aid and other basic rights and services are admired by civil society and gleefully encouraged by the government. They deliver today what governments must. In a perfect society, where transparency reigns and corruption ceases, social workers would be redundant.

This optimism is caused by the path traveled so far. Until we adopted our Constitution in 1950, there had been no scope for individual freedom at any time in India's history. Arbitrary rule has been the norm. It is our Constitution's Article 19 that guarantees us the right to freedom of speech and expression. It is on this Article that India's celebrated freedom of the press based. While most people intuitively connect and see the need for media to be free, they do not quite presume the same right for themselves. The media must know to inform. And because it is a principle of democracy that people are their own masters.

The first stirrings of people to claim the right to know began in Rajasthan in the early nineties. Aruna Roy, an ex-IAS officer brought her experience as a government insider to bear in favour of villagers wanting to know where their unpaid wages went. Partnering with Nikhil Dey and Shankar Singh, she formed the Mazdoor Kisaan Shakti Sangathan [MKSS]. From those little reported days, grew a nation wide movement demanding the right to know. In Maharashtra Anna Hazare applied the pressure.

Finally in 2002, politicians were dragged kicking, to pass a token law, the Freedom of Information Act. It was still-born, because the Act was never notified. Not that it mattered, because it was a toothless law, any way: it did not provide for any punishment for an officer who failed to provide the information sought. But the demand to know did not die down. Nine states had already yielded to public pressure and passed their own state-level laws, most weak but some [as in Delhi, Rajasthan, Maharashtra and Karnataka], quite effective.

The right to information is implicitly guaranteed by the Constitution. However, with a view to set out a practical regime for securing information, the Indian Parliament enacted the Right to Information Act, 2005 and thus gave a powerful tool to the citizens to get information from the Government as a matter of right. This law is very comprehensive and covers almost all matters of governance and has the widest possible reach, being applicable to Government at all levels — Union, State and Local as well as recipients of government grants.

4.2 OBJECTIVES OF THE RTI ACT

Evidently, the major objectives of the Act are:

1. Greater Transparency in functioning of public authorities.
2. Improvement in accountability and performance of the Government.
3. Promotion of partnership between citizens and the Government in decision making process; and
4. Reduction in corruption in the Government departments.

All these parameters are critical elements of good governance. An attempt is therefore made below to examine the extent to which the RTI has been successful in influencing the above factors in desirable direction.

Thus, basic object of the Right to Information Act is to empower the citizens, promote transparency and accountability in the working of the Government, contain corruption, and make our democracy work for the people in real sense. It goes without saying that an informed citizen is better equipped to keep necessary vigil on the instruments of governance and make the government more accountable to the governed. The Act is a big step towards making the citizens informed about the activities of the Government.

4.3 SCOPE OF THE RTI ACT

The Act covers the whole of India except Jammu and Kashmir. It is applicable to all constitutional authorities, including the executive, legislature and judiciary; any institution or body established or constituted by an act of Parliament or a state legislature. It is also defined in the Act that bodies or authorities established or constituted by order or notification of appropriate government including bodies "owned, controlled or substantially financed" by government, or non-Government organizations "substantially financed, directly or indirectly by funds" provided by the government are also covered in it.

Private bodies are not within the Act's ambit directly. However, information that can be accessed under any other law in force by a public authority can also be requested for. In a landmark decision of 30th Nov., 2006 ('*Sarbajit Roy versus DERC*') the Central Information Commission also reaffirmed that privatised public utility companies continue to be within the RTI Act, their privatisation notwithstanding. The Act also explicitly overrides the Official Secrets Act and other laws in force on 15-June-2005 to the extent of any inconsistency.

4.4 NEED FOR RIGHT TO INFORMATION

1. Translating Right into Reality: The Right to Information has already received judicial recognition as a part of the fundamental right to free speech and expression. An Act is needed to provide a statutory framework for this right. This law will lay down the procedure for translating this right into reality.

2. People Kept Informed about Current Affairs and Broad Issues: Information is indispensable for the functioning of a true democracy. People have to be kept informed about current affairs and broad issues - political, social and economic. Free exchange of ideas and free debate are essentially desirable for the Government of a free country.

3. Information and Economic Development: In this Age of Information, its value as a critical factor in socio-cultural, economic and political development is being increasingly felt. In a fast developing country like India, availability of information needs to be assured in the fastest and simplest form possible. This is important because every developmental process depends on the availability of information.

4. Right to know relations with other Basic Rights: Right to know is also closely linked with other basic rights such as freedom of speech and expression and right to education. Its independent existence as an attribute of liberty cannot be disputed. Viewed from this angle, information or knowledge becomes an important resource. An equitable access to this resource must be guaranteed.

5. Transparency: Soli Sorabjee stressing on the need of Right to Information aims at bringing transparency in administration and public life, says, "Lack of transparency was one of the main causes for all pervading corruption and Right to Information would lead to openness, accountability and integrity."

According to Mr. P.B. Sawant, "the barrier to information is the single most cause responsible for corruption in society. It facilitates clandestine deals, arbitrary decisions, manipulations and embezzlements. Transparency in dealings, with their every detail exposed to the public view, should go a long way in curtailing corruption in public life."

4.5 SALIENT FEATURES OF RIGHT TO INFORMATION ACT, 2005

Right to information (RTI) is inherent in democratic functioning and a precondition to good governance and realization of all other human rights, including education and health care that have intense and pervasive impact on all the human activities.

Specifically, the main objectives of the law on RTI are:

- To operationalise the fundamental right to information;
- To set up systems and mechanisms that facilitate people's easy access to information;
- To promote transparency and accountability in governance;
- To minimize corruption and inefficiency in public offices and to ensure people's participation in governance and decision making.

RTI is based on the key concepts:

- The right of the public to access the information and the corresponding duty of the Government to meet the request, unless specifically defined exemptions apply;
- The duty of the Government to proactively provide certain key information even in absence of a request.

The RTI Act Promises to make the right to information more progressive, participatory and meaningful, as it encourages the common citizen to enthusiastically participate in the whole process of governance.

1. More Progressive, Participatory and Meaningful Role: The Act promises to make the right to information more progressive, participatory and meaningful, as it encourages the common citizen to enthusiastically participate in the whole process of governance. The citizens are not only free to ask for information from the Government, but also have the right to get it. The scope of the Act extends to all authorities and bodies under the Constitution or any other law, and inter alia includes all authorities under the Central Government, State Governments and Local Bodies. The non-governmental organizations (NGOs) substantially funded, directly or indirectly, by the public funds also fall within the ambit of this Act.

2. *Suo motu* Information: A duty has been cast, in section 4 of the Act, on every public authority to *suo motu* provide to the public with the information as prescribed therein, so that the public has to take minimum recourse to the use of this legislation for obtaining information.

3. Procedure for Securing Information: The procedure of securing information as provided in section 6 of the Act, prescribes a procedure, which is very simple. A citizen has to merely make a request to the concerned Public Information Officer (PIO) specifying the information sought by him. The fee payable is reasonable and information is to be provided free of cost to citizens living below the poverty line.

4. Speedy Delivery of Information: To assure that the information sought is provided quickly, section 7 of the Act, makes it mandatory for the PIO to provide the information within 30 days. If the information requested concerns the life or liberty of a person, it has been made mandatory to providc it within 48 hours of the receipt of the request. The Act provides for penalties in case of failure to provide information in time, or for refusing to accept application for information, or for giving incorrect, incomplete or misleading information, or destroying information and so on. In addition, the Information Commission has also been empowered to recommend disciplinary action against the government servants.

5. Two-Tier Mechanisms for Appeal: The Act establishes a two-tier mechanism for appeal. The first appeal lies to an officer within the organization who is senior in rank to PIO. The second appeal lies in the Information Commission. The jurisdiction of the lower court is barred under section 20 of the Act. The categories of information exempted from disclosure in this Act are kept to a bare minimum. Even the exemptions are not absolute if disclosure of the information outweighs the harm to the public authorities.

6. No Exemption for Human Right Violations and Corruption: Even in the case of security and intelligence agencies and organizations, which are exempted from the provisions of this Act, if there were cases of allegation of corruption and human rights violation, such exemption would not be available. In cases of allegations of violation of human rights, information would be made available after the approval of the Information Commission. This Act, thus, paves the way for an empowered citizen, as well as an alert, efficient, responsive, transparent and accountable government.

7. State Information Commission Powers of Court: The Central/State Information Commission has a major role in enforcing the implementation of the provisions of the Act as well as for educating the parties, mainly information seekers and providers. The Commission is vested with the power of a Court. Under Section 20, the Commission may impose penalty on the concerned officials for denial of information and recommend disciplinary action against the errant officials, who do not comply with the requirements of the Act. Moreover, under Section 25(5) of the Act, the Commission may also advise the appropriate Government in the matters of maintenance and preservation of records and the norms for disclosure of information with a view to enabling the people to observe and scrutinize the decision making process. The powers vested with the Information Commissioners, who are appointed by the President of India/Governor of a state, ensure effective implementation of the Information.

The Act specifies that citizens have a right to:

- Request any information (as defined).
- Take copies of documents.
- Inspect documents, works and records.
- Take certified samples of materials of work.
- Obtain information in the form of printouts, diskettes, floppies, tapes, video cassettes 'or in any other electronic mode' or through printouts.

4.6 IMPORTANT TERMS IN THE RTI ACT

Information means any material in any form including
- Records
- Documents
- Memos
- E-mails
- Opinions
- Advices
- Press Releases
- Circulars
- Orders
- Log Books
- Contracts
- Reports
- Samples
- Models
- Data material in any electronic Form, etc.

Central Information Commission means the Central Information Commission constituted under sub-section (1) of section 12 — [Section 2(b)]

Central Public Information Officer means the Central Public Information Officer designated under sub-section (1) and includes a Central Assistant Public Information Officer designated as such under sub-section (2) of section 5 [Sec. 2(c)]

Chief Information Commissioner and Information Commissioner mean the Chief Information Commissioner and Information Commissioner appointed under subsection (Section 2(d)

Information means any material in any form, including records, documents, memos, e-mails, opinions, advices, press releases, circulars, orders, logbooks, contracts, reports, papers, samples, models, data material held in any electronic form and information relating to any private body which can be accessed by a public authority under any other law for the time being in force [Section 2(f)]

Public Authority means any authority or body or institution of self-government established or constituted—

- by or under the Constitution;
- by any other law made by Parliament;
- by any other law made by State Legislature;
- by notification issued or order made by the appropriate

Government, and includes any—

- body owned, controlled or substantially financed;
- non-Government organization substantially financed;

- directly or indirectly by funds provided by the appropriate Government; Section 2(h)

Record includes—

- any document, manuscript and file;
- any microfilm, microfiche and facsimile copy of a document;
- any reproduction of image or images embodied in such microfilm (whether enlarged or not); and
- any other material produced by a computer or any other device; [section 2(i)]

Right To Information means the right to information accessible under this Act which is held by or under the control of any public authority and includes the right to—

- inspection of work, documents, records;
- taking notes, extracts or certified copies of documents or records;
- taking certified samples of material;
- obtaining information in the form of diskettes, floppies, tapes, video cassettes or in any other electronic mode or through printouts where such information is stored in a computer or in any other device; [Section 2(j)]

State Information Commission means the State Information Commission constituted under sub-section (1) of section 15; [Section 2(k)]

State Chief Information Commissioner and State Information Commissioner mean the State Chief Information Commissioner and the State Information Commissioner appointed under sub-section (3) of section 15; [Section 2(l)]

State Public Information Officer means the State Public Information Officer designated under sub-section (1) and includes a State Assistant Public Information Officer designated as such under sub-section (2) of section 5; [Section 2(m)]

Third Party means a person other than the citizen making a request for information and includes a public authority. [Section 2(n)]

4.7 SUO MOTU (ON HIS OWN) DISCLOSURE

Every public authority should provide as much information *suo motu* to the public through various means of communications so that the public have minimum need to use the Act to obtain information. Internet being one of the most effective means of communications, the information may be posted on the website.

Public Authorities to Disclose 16 Categories of Information

Section 4(1)(b) of the Act, in particular, requires every public authority to publish following sixteen categories of information:

1. the particulars of its organisation, functions and duties;
2. the powers and duties of its officers and employees;
3. the procedure followed in the decision making process, including channels of supervision and accountability;
4. the norms set by it for the discharge of its functions;
5. the rules, regulations, instructions, manuals and records, held by it or under its control or used by its employees for discharging its functions;
6. a statement of the categories of documents that are held by it or under its control;
7. the particulars of any arrangement that exists for consultation with, or representation by, the members of the public in relation to the formulation of its policy or implementation thereof;
8. a statement of the boards, councils, committees and other bodies consisting of two or more persons constituted as its part or for the purpose of its advice, and as to whether meetings of those boards, councils, committees and other bodies are open to the public, or the minutes of such meetings are accessible for public;
9. directory of its officers and employees;
10. the monthly remuneration received by each of its officers and employees, including the system of compensation as provided in its regulations;
11. the budget allocated to each of its agency, indicating the particulars of all plans, proposed expenditures and reports on disbursements made;
12. the manner of execution of subsidy programmes, including the amounts allocated and the details of beneficiaries of such programmes;
13. particulars of recipients of concessions, permits or authorisations granted by it;
14. details in respect of the information, available to or held by it, reduced in an electronic form;
15. the particulars of facilities available to citizens for obtaining information, including the working hours of a library or reading room, if maintained for public use;
16. the names, designations and other particulars of the Public Information Officers.

Besides the categories of information enumerated above, the Government may prescribe other categories of information to be published by any public authority. It needs to be stressed that publication of the information as referred to above is not optional. It is a statutory requirement which every public authority is bound to meet.

Another important point to note is that it is not sufficient to publish the above information once. The public authority is obliged to update such information every year. It is advisable that, as far as possible, the information should be updated as and when any development takes place. Particularly, in case of publication.

Information Exempted From Disclosure

The following is exempt from disclosure [S.8)]:

1. information, disclosure of which would prejudicially affect the sovereignty and integrity of India, the security, strategic, scientific or economic" interests of the State, relation with foreign State or lead to incitement of an offence;
2. information which has been expressly forbidden to be published by any court of law or tribunal or the disclosure of which may constitute contempt of court;
3. information, the disclosure of which would cause a breach of privilege of Parliament or the State Legislature;
4. information including commercial confidence, trade secrets or intellectual property, the disclosure of which would harm the competitive position of a third party, unless the competent authority is satisfied that larger public interest warrants the disclosure of such information;
5. information available to a person in his fiduciary relationship, unless the competent authority is satisfied that the larger public interest warrants the disclosure of such information;
6. information received in confidence from foreign Government;
7. information, the disclosure of which would endanger the life or physical safety of any person or identify the source of information or assistance given in confidence for law enforcement or security purposes;
8. information which would impede the process of investigation or apprehension or prosecution of offenders;
9. cabinet papers including records of deliberations of the Council of Ministers, Secretaries and other officers;
10. information which relates to personal information the disclosure of which has no relationship to any public activity or interest, or which would cause unwarranted invasion of the privacy of the individual (but it is also provided that the information which cannot be denied to the Parliament or a State Legislature shall not be denied by this exemption);
11. Notwithstanding any of the exemptions listed above, a public authority may allow access to information, if public interest in disclosure outweighs the harm to the protected interests. (Note: This provision is qualified by the proviso to sub-section 11(1) of the Act which exempts disclosure of "trade or commercial secrets protected by law" under this clause when read along with 8(1)(d)))

4.8 POWERS AND FUNCTIONS OF CENTRAL INFORMATION COMMISSION (CIC) AND STATE INFORMATION COMMISSION (SIC)

(1) The Central Information Commission/State Information Commission has a duty to receive complaints from any person —

(a) who has been refused information that was requested;

(b) who has received no response to his/her information request within the specified time limits ;

(c) who thinks the fees charged are unreasonable ;

(d) who thinks information given is incomplete or false or misleading;

(e) any other matter relating to obtaining information under this law.

(2) Power to order inquiry if there are reasonable grounds.

(3) CIC/SIC will have powers of Civil Court such as —

(a) summoning and enforcing attendance of persons, compelling them to give oral or written evidence on oath and to produce documents or things

(b) requiring the discovery and inspection of documents;

(c) receiving evidence on affidavit ;

(d) requisitioning public records or copies from any court or office;

(e) issuing summons for examination of witnesses or documents;

(f) any other matter which may be prescribed.

(4) All records covered by this law (including those covered by exemptions) must be given to CIC/SIC during inquiry for examination.

(5) Power to secure compliance of its decisions from the Public Authority includes—

(a) providing access to information in a particular form;

(b) directing the public authority to appoint a PIO/APIO where none exists;

(c) publishing information or categories of information;

(d) making necessary changes to the practices relating to management, maintenance and destruction of records ;

(e) enhancing training provision for officials on RTI;

(f) seeking an annual report from the public authority on compliance with this law;

(g) require it to compensate for any loss or other detriment suffered by the applicant ;

(h) impose penalties under this law; or

(i) reject the application. (S.18 and S.19)

4.9 PUBLIC INFORMATION OFFICERS (PIOs)

Public Information Officers (PIOs) are officers designated by the public authorities in all administrative units or offices under it to provide information to the citizens requesting for information under the Act. Any officer, whose assistance has been sought by the Public Information Officer for the proper discharge of his or her duties, shall render all assistance and for the purpose of contraventions of the provisions of this Act, such other officer shall be treated as a Public Information Officers.

Public Information Officers (PIOs) are officers designated by the public authorities in all administrative units or offices under it to provide information to the citizens requesting for information under the Act.

Duties of a Public Information Officer

Public information officer shall deal with requests from persons seeking information and where the request cannot be made in writing, to render reasonable assistance to the person to reduce the same in writing.

1. If the information requested for is held by or its subject matter is closely connected with the function of another public authority, the PIO shall transfer, within 5 days, the request to that other public authority and inform the applicant immediately.
2. PIO may seek the assistance of any other officer for the proper discharge of his/her duties.
3. PIO, on receipt of a request, shall as expeditiously as possible, and in any case within 30 days of the receipt of the request, either provide the information on payment of such fee as may be prescribed or reject the request for any of the reasons specified in S.8 or S.9.
4. Where the information requested for concerns the life or liberty of a person, the same shall be provided within forty-eight hours of the receipt of the request.
5. If the PIO fails to give decision on the request within the period specified, he shall be deemed to have refused the request.
6. Where a request has been rejected, the PIO shall communicate to the requester —
   (i) the reasons for such rejection,
   (ii) the period within which an appeal against such rejection may be preferred, and
   (iii) the particulars of the Appellate Authority.
7. PIO shall provide information in the form in which it is sought unless it would disproportionately divert the resources of the Public Authority or would be detrimental to the safety or preservation of the record in question.
8. If allowing partial access, the PIO shall give a notice to the applicant, informing
   (a) that only part of the record requested, after severance of the record containing information which is exempt from disclosure, is being provided;

(b) the reasons for the decision, including any findings on any material question of fact, referring to the material on which those findings were based;

(c) the name and designation of the person giving the decision;

(d) the details of the fees calculated by him or her and the amount of fee which the applicant is required to deposit; and

(e) his or her rights with respect to review of the decision regarding non-disclosure of part of the information, the amount of fee charged or the form of access provided;

(f) if information sought has been supplied by third party or is treated as confidential by that third party, the PIO shall give a written notice to the third party within 5 days from the receipt of the request and take its representation into consideration;

(g) third party must be given a chance to make a representation before the PIO within 10 days from the date of receipt of such notice.

4.10 ASSISTANT PUBLIC INFORMATION OFFICERS (APIOs)

These are the officers at sub-divisional level to whom a person can give his RTI application or appeal. These officers send the application or appeal to the Public Information Officer of the public authority or the concerned appellate authority. An Assistant Public Information Officer is not responsible to supply the information.

The Assistant Public Information Officers appointed by the Department of Posts in various post offices are working as Assistant Public Information Officers for all the public authorities under the Government of India.

4.11 TRANSPARENCY

With a view to ensuring maximum disclosure of information regarding government rules, regulations and decisions, every public authority is mandated to `maintain all its records duly catalogued and indexed in a manner and the form which facilitates the right to information under the Act.'

The public authorities are therefore required to make pro-active disclosures through publication of relevant documents. Besides, the public authorities are also required to 'provide as much information *suo motu* to the public at regular intervals through various means of communication, including internet, so that the public have minimum resort to the use of this Act to obtain information.'

> The public authorities are also required to 'provide as much information *suo motu* to the public at regular intervals through various means of communication, including internet.

In compliance of the above provisions of the Act, all the levels of the Government — the Centre, States and Local Bodies, including Village level Panchayats — have put the records in public domain, through publications as well as internet in the regional languages. And, to facilitate the access to information, a citizen has the right to:

- inspection of work, documents, records;
- taking notes, extracts or certified copies of the documents or records;
- taking certified sample of material; and
- obtaining information in electronic form, if available.

Thus, all the public authorities have duly placed the information in public domain and that a citizen has the right to observe as to what is going on inside the organization. In the cases where the information sought for are not provided within the stipulated period of 30 days or the information furnished are incomplete, misleading or incorrect, a requester is free to file a complaint or appeal before the Information Commission (IC), for necessary directions to the parties as per the provisions of the Act.

The Commission has the mandate, *inter-alia*, to impose penalty and/or to recommend disciplinary action against the information providers, if held responsible for obstructing the free flow of information. Accordingly, information seekers and the NGOs have put pressure on the public authorities for promoting the culture of openness in functioning of the Government.

A large number of PIOs have already been fined for violation of the provisions of the Act, which has, in effect, created conditions for providing information to a requester. Due to perceived benefits of transparency and accountability, RTI applications have annually increased by 8 to 10 times. There is thus massive use of the right to know. Of the millions of applications for information, less than 5 percent have been denied information under various exemption categories. In effect, thus, there is greater transparency than before in the working of the public bodies.

RTI applications have annually increased by 8 to 10 times. There is thus massive use of the right to know. Of the millions of applications for information, less than 5 percent have been denied information under various exemption categories.

Checking Corrupt Practices in Government

In a large number of cases, the Commission has ordered for providing the details of the decision-making processes, which include file notings, cabinet papers, records of recruitment, selection and promotion of staff, documents pertaining to tender processes and procurement procedure, the lists of beneficiaries of the Government's subsidized schemes, such as, food grains supplied through ration shops, water and electricity, domestic gas, educational and health facilities, shelter for poor, muster rolls under employment guarantee schemes, etc. The disclosure of vital information, such as above, has thus resulted in checking corrupt practices in delivery of services and ensuring the reach of entitlements to the poor. The disclosure of information relating to use of funds allocated to rural employment guarantee scheme, MLA/MP local area funds, etc. have contributed to advocacy in favour or against the policies and/or political leaderships.

4.12 GREATER ACCOUNTABILITY

1. Accessing Information: The RTI provides people with the mechanism to access information, which they can use to hold the government to account or to seek explanation as to why decisions have been taken, by whom and with what consequences or outcomes. In addition, every public authority is required 'to provide reasons for its administrative or quasi-judicial decisions to the affected persons' u/s 4(1)(d) of the Act.

The RTI provides people with the mechanism to access information, which they can use to hold the government to account or to seek explanation as to why decisions have been taken, by whom and with what consequences or outcomes.

2. Darkness in Policy Planning is Over: Until the implementation of the RTI Act, it was not possible for an ordinary persons to seek the details of a decision making process, which was found most often, as ineffective in terms of its outcome. It was, therefore, not possible to hold a free and frank discussion on issues of common concern of people or to fix the responsibility for any action. Such an era of darkness in policy planning is over.

3. Better Understanding of How the Government Works: The information regime has, in effect, created conducive conditions for every one to have a better understanding of how the government works or how a particular decision was reached. Such a chance given to people empowers them to make appropriate choice of leadership and the policies that affect them. This has begun to happen with salutary effects on delivery of socio-economic services, particularly for the poor. For instance, being full aware that the records pertaining to the decision making process, including file notings, are required to be put in public domain, the concerned officials at all levels objectively record the reasons for the observations made by them. Attempts are also made to effectively implement the programmes as the relevant details are proactively disclosed.

4. Quality Decision-making and Delivery of Services: In effect, thus, the quality of decision making and delivery of services have duly improved. Also, due to effective implementation of the flagship programmes for alleviation of wide-spread poverty, the mis-match between the planned targets and actual realization has been minimized. Specific mention may be made about the following schemes, which have been provided necessary financial resources as well as administrative support by the Centre and the States for effective implementation of the programmes.

- National Rural Employment Guarantee Scheme (Assured jobs)
- Sarva Shiksha Abhiyan (Education for all)
- Mid-day Meal Scheme
- Drinking Water Mission
- Integrated Child Development Services
- National Rural Health Mission
- Bharat Nirman (Rural Infrastructure, mainly road, electricity, drinking water, sanitation etc.)
- Indira Awas Yojana (Shelter for poor)

All these programmes and several other similar schemes covered under the MP/MLA Local Area Development Fund aim at providing the basic human needs for maintaining a decent standard of living. These schemes, moreover, enable them to build their strengths and abilities to realize their socio-economic objectives.

Even before the enactment of the right to information, similar programmes were implemented but the achievements were always below the general expectations. Reason? Lack of legal right to know and to scrutinize the public action and to question the authority. With empowered citizens and free flow of information, there is significant quantitative and qualitative improvement in the delivery of services and realization of benefits of the programmes designed and implemented for the poor.

Interesting Revealations and Transformation

For instance, disclosure of information relating to:

- attendance of staff in schools has helped in checking teachers' absenteeism and students' drop out;
- attendance of doctors and nurses at primary health centres has led to improvement in health care facilities in rural areas;
- the details of supplies and distribution of food grains through ration shops has assured the reach of entitlements to the beneficiaries;
- the supply and demand for petroleum products, such as, domestic gas has reduced black marketing;
- muster rolls and beneficiary of employment guarantee schemes has exposed corruption and ensured effective delivery of services to the poor; and
- allotment of retail outlets (petrol pumps) and agencies for distribution of LPG gas has ensured fair play and objective decisions, as reflected from substantial reduction in litigation cases in the matter.

As a result of increased Government's accountability in delivery of services, rural to urban migration has, of late, decelerated, as widely reported in the media. This is also corroborated by the findings of a national level survey, jointly conducted by the Transparency International and the Centre for Media Studies. The survey has revealed that in the opinions of 40 per cent of respondent (all below the poverty line), corruption and malpractices in implementation of poverty alleviation programmes have declined due to RTI induced accountability of the Government and its functionaries at various levels. RTI route has generally been followed by a large number of people for resolving disputes between the parties on the issues pertaining to the decisions on administrative and commercial matters.

Disclosure of information regarding the process of decision making or the grounds for action taken has helped resolve disputes on such issues as claim of refund of taxes paid by the individuals/companies, settlement of insurance claims, payment of dues of contractors, process of sanction and recovery of loans, etc. Since a reply is to be given within thirty days, disputes have been resolved faster. A large number of grievances pertaining to service matters, mainly promotion and pension benefits have also been redressed due to openness and promptness in taking action on requests made under the RTI.

Disclosure of information regarding the process of decision making or the grounds for action taken has helped resolve disputes on such issues as claim of refund of taxes paid by the individuals/companies, settlement of insurance claims, payment of dues of contractors, process of sanction and recovery of loans, etc.

As a result, filing of appeals in the Courts has substantially declined, as reported, for instance, by the Oil Companies, which grant dealerships for distribution of petroleum products. The Courts have also advised the petitioners to obtain information under the RTI before filing the cases before the Courts. It thus shows a strong and positive impact of RTI on transparency and accountability of the Government.

4.13 PUBLIC AUTHORITY

A "public authority" is any authority or body or institution of self-government established or constituted by or under the Constitution; or by any other law made by the Parliament or a State Legislature; or by notification issued or order made by the Central Government or a State Government. The bodies owned, controlled or substantially financed by the Central Government or a State Government and non-Government organisations substantially financed by the Central Government or a State Government also fall within the definition of public authority. The financing of the body or the NGO by the Government may be direct or indirect.

Public authorities are the repository of information which the citizens have a right to have under the Right to Information Act, 2005. The Act casts important obligations on public authorities so as to facilitate the citizens of the country to access the information held under their control. The obligations of a public authority are basically the obligations of the head of the authority, who should ensure that these are met in right earnest. Reference made to public authority in this document is, in fact, a reference to the head of the public authority.

Obligations of Public Authority

It shall publish within one hundred and twenty days of the enactment:

(i) the particulars of its organization, functions and duties;

(ii) the powers and duties of its officers and employees;

(iii) the procedure followed in its decision making process, including channels of supervision and accountability;

(iv) the norms set by it for the discharge of its functions;

(v) the rules, regulations, instructions, manuals and records used by its employees for discharging its functions;

(vi) a statement of the categories of the documents held by it or under its control;

(vii) the particulars of any arrangement that exists for consultation with, or representation by the members of the public, in relation to the formulation of policy or implementation thereof;

(viii) a statement of the boards, councils, committees and other bodies consisting of two or more persons constituted by it. Additionally, information as to whether the meetings of these are open to the public, or the minutes' of such meetings are accessible to the public;

(ix) a directory of its officers and employees;

(x) the monthly remuneration received by each of its officers and employees, including the system of compensation as provided in its regulations;

(xi) the budget allocated to each of its agency, indicating the particulars of all plans, proposed expenditures and reports on disbursements made;

(xii) the manner of execution of subsidy programmes, including the amounts allocated and the details and beneficiaries of such programmes;

(xiii) particulars of recipients of concessions, permits or authorizations granted by it;

(xiv) details of the information available to, or held by it, reduced in an electronic form;

(xv) the particulars of facilities available to citizens for obtaining information, including the working hours of a library or reading room, if maintained for public use;

(xvi) the names, designations and other particulars of the Public Information Officers.[S.4(1)(b)]

4.14 CITIZENS SEEKING INFORMATION FROM PUBLIC AUTHORITY

A citizen has a right to seek such information from a public authority which is held by the public authority or which is held under its control. This right includes inspection of work, documents and records; taking notes, extracts or certified copies of documents or records; and taking certified samples of material held by the public authority or held under the control of the public authority. It is important to note that only such information can be supplied under the Act which already exists and is held by the public authority or held under the control of the public authority. The Public Information Officer is not supposed to create information; or to interpret information; or to solve the problems raised by the applicants; or to furnish replies to hypothetical questions.

A citizen has a right to seek such information from a public authority which is held by the public authority or which is held under its control. This right includes inspection of work, documents and records; taking notes, extracts or certified copies of documents or records; and taking certified samples of material held by the public authority or held under the control of the public authority.

The Act gives the citizens a right to information at par with the Members of Parliament and the Members of State Legislatures. According to the Act, the information which cannot be denied to the Parliament or a State Legislature, shall not be denied to any person.

A citizen has a right to obtain information from a public authority in the form of diskettes, floppies, tapes, video cassettes or in any other electronic mode or through print-outs provided such information is already stored in a computer or in any other device from which the information may be e-mailed or transferred to diskettes etc.

The information to the applicant should ordinarily be provided in the form in which it is sought. However, if the supply of information sought in a particular form would disproportionately divert the resources of the public authority or by cause harm to the safety or preservation of the records, supply of information in that form may be denied.

Guidelines to Stakeholders Seeking Information Under Right to Information Act, 2005

In some cases, the applicants expect the Public Information Officer to give information in some particular proforma devised by them on the plea that they have a right to get information in the form in which it is sought. It needs to be noted that the provision in the Act simply means that if the information is sought in the form of photocopy, it shall be provided in the form of photocopy, or if it is sought in the form of a floppy, it shall be provided in that form subject to the conditions given in the Act. It does not mean that the PIO shall re-shape the information. This is substantiated by the definition of the term 'right to information' as given in the Act, according to which, it includes right to obtaining information in the form of diskettes, floppies, tapes, video cassettes or in any other electronic mode or through print-outs provided such information is already stored in a computer or in any other device. Everywhere in the Act, the word 'form' has been used to represent this meaning.

Some Information Seekers request the Public Information Officers to cull out information from some document(s) and give such extracted information to them. A citizen has a right to get 'material' from a public authority which is held by or under the control of that public authority. The Act, however, does not require the Public Information Officer to deduce some conclusion from the 'material' and supply the 'conclusion' so deduced to the applicant. It means that the Public Information Officer is required to supply the 'material' in the form as held by the public authority, but not to do research on behalf of the citizen to deduce anything from the material and then supply it to him.

4.15 METHOD OF SEEKING INFORMATION

It is the PIO's obligation to provide information to citizens of India who request information under the Act.

Under the Act, all authorities covered must appoint their Public Information Officer (PIO). Any person may submit a request to the PIO for information in writing. It is the PIO's obligation to provide information to citizens of India who request information under the Act. If the request pertains to another public authority (in whole or part) it is the PIO's responsibility to transfer/forward the concerned portions of the request to a PIO of the other within 5 days. In addition, every public authority is required to designate Assistant Public Information Officers (APIOs) to receive RTI requests and appeals for forwarding to the PIOs of their public authority. The citizen making the request is not obliged to disclose any information except his name and contact particulars.

Time Limit for Replying to the Request

The Act specifies time limits for replying to the request.

1. If the request has been made to the PIO, the reply is to be given within 30 days of receipt.
2. If the request has been made to an APIO, the reply is to be given within 35 days of receipt.
3. If the PIO transfers the request to another public authority (better concerned with the information requested), the time allowed to reply is 30 days but computed from the day after it is received by the PIO of the transferee authority.
4. Information concerning corruption and Human Rights violations by scheduled Security agencies (those listed in the Second Schedule to the Act) is to be provided within 45 days but with the prior approval of the Central Information Commission.
5. However, if life or liberty of any person is involved, the PIO is expected to reply within 48 hours.

Since the information is to be paid for, the reply of the PIO is necessarily limited to either denying the request (in whole or part) and/or providing a computation of "further fees." The time between the reply of the PIO and the time taken to deposit the further fees for information is excluded from the time allowed.

If information is not provided within this period, it is treated as deemed refusal. Refusal with or without reasons may be ground for appeal or complaint. Further, information not provided in the times prescribed is to be provided free of charge.

If information is not provided within this period, it is treated as deemed refusal.

For Central Departments as of 2006, there is a fee of Rs. 10 for filing the request, Rs. 2 per page of information and Rs. 5 for each hour of inspection after the first hour. If the applicant is a Below Poverty Card holder, then no fee shall apply. Such BPL Card holders have to provide a copy of their BPL card along with their application to the Public Authority. State Governments and High Courts fix their own rules.

If the applicant is a Below Poverty Card holder, then no fee shall apply. Such BPL Card holders have to provide a copy of their BPL card along with their application to the Public Authority.

A citizen who desires to obtain any information under the Act, should make an application to the Public Information Officer of the concerned public authority in writing in English or Hindi or in the official language of the area in which the application is made. The application should be precise and specific. He should make payment of application fee at the time of submitting the application

As prescribed in the Fee Rules. The applicant can send the application by post or through electronic means or can deliver it personally in the office of the public authority. The application can also be sent through an Assistant Public Information Officer.

4.16 WHO IS ELIGIBLE TO GET INFORMATION UNDER RTI ACT

The Act gives the right to information only to the citizens of India. It does not make provision for giving information to Corporations, Associations, Companies etc. which are legal entities/persons, but not citizens. However, if an application is made by an employee or office-bearer of any Corporation, Association, Company, NGO etc. indicating his name and such employee/office bearer is a citizen of India, information may be supplied to him/her. In such cases, it would be presumed that a citizen has sought information at the address of the Corporation etc.

The Act gives the right to information only to the citizens of India.

Fee for Seeking Information

A person who desires to seek some information from a public authority is required to send, along with the application, a demand draft or a banker's cheque or an Indian Postal Order of Rs. 10/- (Rupees ten), payable to the Accounts Officer of the public authority as fee prescribed for seeking information. The payment of fee can also be made by way of cash to the Accounts Officer of the public authority or to the Assistant Public Information Officer against proper receipt.

A person who desires to seek some information from a public authority is required to send, along with the application, a demand draft or a banker's cheque or an Indian Postal Order of Rs. 10/- (Rupees ten), payable to the Accounts Officer of the public authority as fee prescribed for seeking information.

The applicant may also be required to pay further fee towards the cost of providing the information, details of which shall be intimated to the applicant by the PIO as prescribed by the Right to Information (Regulation of Fee and Cost) Rules, 2005.

Rates of fee as prescribed in the Rules of RTI

- Rupees two (Rs. 2/-) for each page (in A-4 or A-3 size paper) created or copied;
- Actual charge or cost price of a copy in larger size paper;
- Actual cost or price for samples or models;
- For information provided in diskette or floppy, rupees fifty (Rs. 50/-) per diskette or floppy; and
- For information provided in printed form, at the price fixed for such publication or rupees two per page of photocopy for extracts from the publication.

As already pointed out, a citizen has a right to inspect the records of a public authority. For inspection of records, the public authority shall charge no fee for the first hour. But a fee of rupees five (Rs. 5/-) for each subsequent hour (or fraction thereof) shall be charged.

If the applicant belongs to below poverty line (BPL) category, he is not required to pay any fee. However, he should submit a proof in support of his claim to belong to the below poverty line. The application not accompanied by the prescribed fee of Rs. 10/- or proof of the applicant's belonging to below poverty line, as the case may be, shall not be a valid application under the Act. It may be pointed out that there is no bar on the public authority to supply information in response to such applications. However, provisions of Act would not apply to such cases.

Process of Information Gathering

In order to get the information as per the RTI Act, 2005 the information seeker has to send the request for information with the requisite fee to the Public Information Officer (PIO). Then the PIO gathers the information from the concerned department. The PIO is facing difficulties in gathering the information where medium or low level of information technology is used. However, the PIO is not finding any difficulties in gathering and disseminating the information where high level of information technology is used. The process of information gathering is shown in figure 4.1.

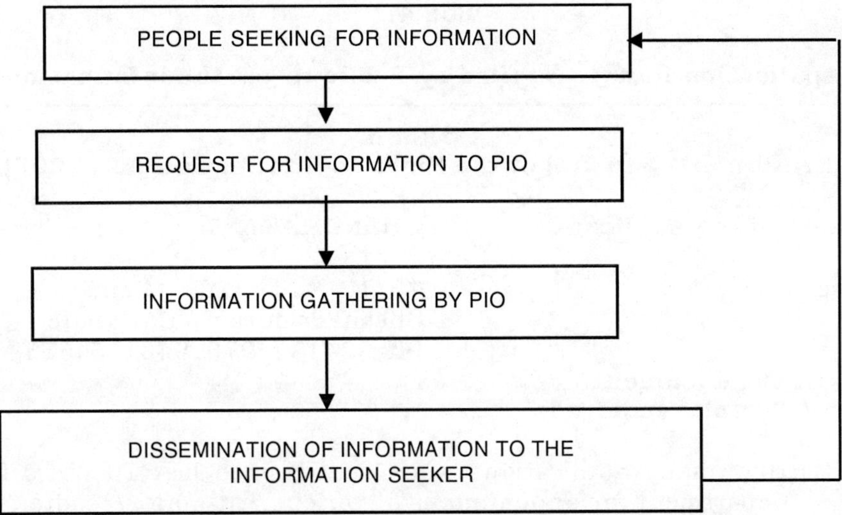

Figure 4.1 Process of Information Gathering

4.17 FORMAT OF APPLICATION

There is no prescribed format of application for seeking information. The application can be made on plain paper. The application should, however, have the name and complete postal address of the applicant. Even in cases where the information is sought electronically, the application should contain name and postal address of the applicant. The information seeker is not required to give reasons for seeking information.

The proforma of RTI application on a certain case is exhibited herein below for simple understanding (see Box 4.1).

Application to the Concerned Public Authority

The applicant should make application to the concerned public authority. It is advised that he should make all efforts to ascertain as to which is the public authority concerned with the information and should send application to the Public Information Officer of that public authority.

It is observed that some applicants seek information in respect of many subjects by way of one application. It creates problem for the Public Information Officer as well as the applicant. The applicant should, therefore, see to it that by way of one application, he seeks information in respect of one subject only.

Time Period for Supply of Information

In normal course, information to an applicant shall be supplied within 30 days from the receipt of application by the public authority. If information sought concerns the life or liberty of a person, it shall be supplied within 48 hours. In case the application is sent through the Assistant Public Information Officer or it is sent to a wrong public authority, five days shall be added to the period of thirty days or 48 hours, as the case may be.

In normal course, information to an applicant shall be supplied within 30 days from the receipt of application by the public authority. If information sought concerns the life or liberty of a person, it shall be supplied within 48 hours.

Box 4.1

Application form to be filed by Public to get the information

FORM A
(Section 6(1) and 7(1) of the Right to Information Act, 2005)

(1) Full Name of the Applicant : **CHANDRAKANT**

(2) Address : 45/1, 1st Floor, 2nd Main,
Sheshadripuram, Bangalore
Ph: 9341824976, 9481454655

(3) Details of the document / Inspection / Samples required :

(1) How many notifications were issued since last 10 years from your department for appointment of various categories/ cadre. Issue the copies of all those appointment notifications.
(2) How many disabled are appointed since last 15 years in your corporation ? Give the details of appointment and cadre with names and cadre of candidate.
(3) What are the norms for appointment of disables / physically handicapped in your corporation. What are the Acts applicable for appointment of disabled?
(4) What is the basis for not entertaining the application of the handicapped in the notification dated : 13.07.2009 vide No. ksrtco/recruitment/c1/510/09-10, Advertisement No. 1/2009 Class-2 and what is the basis for giving reservation for handicapped in the class-3 appointments such as Traffic Superintendent and other categories?
(5) How many vacancies meant for handicapped are unfilled?

(4) Year to which the above pertains : 2009

(5) Designation and address of the public information officer from whom the information is required : **The Managing Director**
KSRTC, Shanthinagar,
Bangalore

Place : Bangalore
Date : 15.10.2009

Signature of the applicant

Complaints

If any person is unable to submit a request to a Public Information Officer either by reason that such an officer has not been appointed by the concerned public authority; or the Assistant Public Information Officer has refused to accept his or her application or appeal for forwarding the same to the Public Information Officer or the appellate authority, as the case may be; or he has been refused access to any information requested by him under the RTI Act; or he has not been given a response to a request for information within the time limit specified in the Act; or he has been required to pay an amount of fee which he considers unreasonable; or he believes that he has been given incomplete, misleading or false information, he can make a complaint to the Information Commission.

4.18 APPEALS

If an applicant is not supplied information within the prescribed time of thirty days or 48 hours, as the case may be, or is not satisfied with the information furnished to him, he may prefer an appeal to the first appellate authority who is an officer senior in rank to the Public Information Officer. Such an appeal, should be filed within a period of thirty days from the date on which the limit of 30 days of supply of information is expired or from the date on which the information or decision of the Public Information Officer is received. The appellate authority of the public authority shall dispose of the appeal within a period of thirty days or in exceptional cases within 45 days of the receipt of the appeal.

If an applicant is not supplied information within the prescribed time of thirty days or 48 hours, as the case may be, or is not satisfied with the information furnished to him, he may prefer an appeal to the first appellate authority who is an officer senior in rank to the Public Information Officer.

If the first appellate authority fails to pass an order on the appeal within the prescribed period or if the appellant is not satisfied with the order of the first appellate authority, he may prefer a second appeal with the Central Information Commission within ninety days from the date on which the decision should have been made by the first appellate authority or was actually received by the appellant.

Disposal of Appeals and Complaints by the CIC

The Central Information Commission decides the appeals and complaints and conveys its decision to the appellant/complainant and first appellate authority/ Public Information Officer. The Commission may decide an appeal/ complaint after hearing the parties to the appeal/complaint or by inspection of documents produced by the appellant/complainant and Public Information Officer or such senior officer of the public authority who decided the first appeal. If the Commission chooses to hear the parties before deciding the appeal or the complaint, the Commission will inform the date of hearing to the appellant or the complainant at least seven clear days before the date of hearing. The appellant/ complainant has the discretion to be present in person or through his authorized representative at the time of hearing or not to be present.

PENALTY PROVISIONS

Every PIO will be liable for fine of Rs. 250 per day, up to a maximum of Rs. 25,000/-, for —

i. Not accepting an application;

ii. Delaying information release without reasonable cause;

iii. Malafidely denying information;

iv. Knowingly giving incomplete, incorrect, misleading information;

v. Destroying information that has been requested and

vi. Obstructing furnishing of information in any manner.

The Information Commission (IC) at the Center and the State levels will have the power to impose this penalty. The Information Commission can also recommend disciplinary action for violation of the law against an erring PIO. (S.20)

Jurisdiction of Courts

Lower Courts are barred from entertaining suits or applications against any order made under this Act (S.23). However, the writ jurisdiction of the Supreme Court and High Courts under Articles 32 and 225 of the Constitution remains unaffected.

4.19 SUCCESS STORIES UNDER THIS CAMPAIGN

This section provides RTI success stories from rural and urban areas.

SUCCESS STORY — 1

ATTENDANCE OF THE VILLAGE SCHOOL TEACHER

In a Pre-Middle School in Panchampur village, situated 70 kilometers away from the District Headquarters of Banda, a teacher was appointed for the school. However, the teacher was absent for most of the times. The workers and volunteers from the Delhi based organisations like Kabir and Parivartan, along with the local workers from the Chingari Sangathan under the 'Action Research Villages' Campaign, propagated the use of the Right to Information.

Finally, the villagers witnessed a ray of hope when they learned that they could question the Government and ask for information related to the attendance records, leave records and medical records of the absconding village school teacher. Fifteen villagers drafted an application regarding the same and filed a number of applications with the Primary Education Officer at the Banda District Head Quarters. They asked for the records of the teacher but also questioned the Primary Education Department about the Department's role and responsibilities in such situations. Immediate action was taken on the issue by the Department.

The Primary Education Officer summoned the teacher the very next day and asked for an explanation. Living up to his accountability and responsibility, the officer appointed a new school teacher for the village school. The school was opened On the next day itself and regular teaching began in the school. An enquiry was ordered against the teacher and he was asked to report to the school instantly.

The villagers were overwhelmed with the fact that their use of Right to Information could reap such instant results.

Source: PACS

SUCCESS STORY 2

CAMPAIGN REPORT TO THE DISTRICT MAGISTRATE, BANDA

Another interesting facet of the campaign was the process of filing RTI applications in Banda (UP). A group of ten volunteers and villagers went to various offices for submitting their RTI applications. None of the applications could be filed easily. Most of the offices were ill-equipped for the task. One of the major problems faced during the filing process was that the clerks, and sometimes even the officers, appeared non-conversant and at times completely ignorant about the RTI Act itself. The applications were filed after a lot of trepidation, struggle and running around the offices. These experiences were submitted in the form of a report to the District Magistrate of Banda District, which had the desired effect and considerably improved the situation in most of the offices.

Source: PACS Report

SUCCESS STORY 3

TRANSPARENCY IN PUBLIC DISTRIBUTION SYSTEM FOR BPL FAMILIES

The 'Mere Gaon Ke Sawaal' Campaign volunteers noticed that the residents of Nai Basti (Bahraich, UP) were also facing the same problems as the other economically backward villages of the region. The 'Kotedar' had been apathetic towards their requests. The use of Right to Information by the villagers, the women being in majority, was successful in curbing the corruption that had seeped in the Public Distribution System to some extent.

When the campaign volunteers saw the BPL ration cards of the villagers, they found that no entries had been made during February 2006 to December 2006. It was evident that the villagers had not received any ration in the said time period. Immediately, 51 village residents agreed to file group RTI applications on the issue and demanded information regarding the acquisition and the distribution of the ration and also asked for copies of the ration records. The applications were filed by the applicants personally after a lot of difficulty at the District Supply Office. Exactly within a fortnight, the Kotedar reached the village and narrated a long sob story, which moved few of the innocent villagers so much that they even agreed to take back their RTI applications. They very next day the Kotedar brought a mini bus to the village along with "pooris" made with one quintal flour and asked the villagers to come to the SDM's office and take back their RTI applications. But, the women of the forest village rights forum refused to do so.

This initiative by the women of the village encouraged the other villagers and they also refused to take back their RTI applications. The Kotedar trying another of his tactics, one day announced in the village that all those who requested for information can collect it from him. When few villagers reached to take the information, they were forced to make thumb imprints on a blank paper. The Dehat Sanstha volunteers immediately reported this scam to the SDM. Finally, the Kotedar was suspended.

Source: PACS Report

SUCCESS STORY 4

SCHOOL UNIFORMS DISTRIBUTED AT THE END OF THE DECEMBER SESSION

Despite several claims of the Government, school uniforms of the session — December 2006-07 — were not PricewaterhouseCoopers Final Understanding the "Key Issues and Constraints" in implementing the RTI Act distributed among the students of the Gulrahai Primary School in Allahabad. Workers from KABIR and ABSSS conducted a meeting with the villagers of Gulrahai and educated them on the RTI Act. Immediately thereafter, nine parents prepared an RTI application and questioned the administration regarding the school uniforms of the children. In the first week of January 2007, the school dresses were distributed to the children. Similarly, in the Bharthaul Village primary school of Chitrakoot district, school dresses were not distributed among the children till December. Under 'Mere Gaon Ke Sawaal' Campaign, KABIR & ABSSS conducted a meeting with the villagers of Gulrahai and educated them on the RTI Act. The very next day, parents of these children submitted an RTI application with the District Education Officer and within 15 days, school dresses were distributed and a video shoot of the court was also conducted.

Source: PACS report

SUCCESS STORY 5

EXPOSING CORRUPTION IN MEDICINE PROCUREMENT AT PUBLIC SECTOR UNIT

Applicants belonging to Anuppur, Madhya Pradesh and Koria district of Chhattisgarh filed RTI applications with the PIO of South Eastern Coal Fields Ltd. (SECL) situated at its head office in Bilaspur during the months of February — April 2006. They sought the following information:

" Names of all medicines procured by SECL for distribution through its primary health centres and its OPD clinics in the Hasdev coal mines area during the financial year 2005-06. (They cater exclusively to the employees of SECL and their families).

" Quantity of medicines procured during the same period.

" Supply price of each item.

" Copies of all purchase orders issued by SECL for these medicines.

" Name and contact details of suppliers who bagged the purchase order. All three applicants received the requested information within the 30 day deadline stipulated in the RTI Act. Armed with these documents, applicants worked for several weeks crosschecking the data along with a team of about 25 committed volunteers. Based on the research it was found out that fictitious companies were shown as suppliers of luxury items in the name of procurement of medical supplies.

Next, the volunteers cross checked the rates at which the medicines had been supplied only to find that the retail outlets sold the same items a lot cheaper. These details were published in local magazine popular in the coal mining belt of Madhya Pradesh and Chhattisgarh. Thereafter, the Vigilance unit instituted a formal investigation and action against the concerned officials was initiated.

Source: http://cic.gov.in/bestpractices.htm

SUCCESS STORY 6

PAYMENT OF PENSION DUES FROM RAILWAYS

"Payment of interest on arrears due on account of recomputation of pension and other retirement benefits as a result of implementation of Supreme Court's Judgment dated 25-07-1997 in CA No. 4174/88of 1995 and other tagged SLPs" Indian Railway Pensioners Association Bhavnagar Division of Western Railway, over the years, submitted hundreds of representations to GM Western Railway and DRM Bhavnagar to get the payment in the above case. 137 specific cases of non-payment were filed in the pension Adalat, but nothing happened. When, a request under RTI ACT 2005 was submitted to CPIO Western Railway for disclosing the reasons for not implementing the judgment of the Apex court, things started moving and the Western Railway accepted the liability for making payment and all the Divisions of Western Railway were advised to take immediate steps for making payment.

4.20 LANDMARK JUDGEMENTS

The need for Right to Information has been widely felt in all sectors of the country and this has also received judicial recognition through some landmark judgements of Indian courts.

A Supreme Court judgement delivered by Mr. Justice Mathew is considered a landmark. In his judgement in the State of UP vs. Raj Narain (1975) case, Justice Mathew rules: In a government of responsibility like ours, where all the agents of the public must be responsible for their conduct, there can be but few secrets. The people of this country have a right to know every public act, everything that is done in a public way by their public functionaries. They are entitled to know the particulars of every public transaction in all its bearing. Their right to know, which is derived from the concept of freedom of speech, though not absolute, is a factor which should make one wary when secrecy is claimed for transactions which can at any rate have no repercussion on public security. But the legislative wing of the State did not respond to it by enacting suitable legislation for protecting the right of the people.

The people of this country have a right to know every public act, everything that is done in a public way by their public functionaries. They are entitled to know the particulars of every public transaction in all its bearing.

According to Attorney General Soli Sorabjee - It was in 1982 that the right to know matured to the status of a constitutional right in the celebrated case of *S.P. Gupta vs. Union of India* (AIR) 1982 SC (149), popularly known as Judges case. Here again the claim for privilege was laid before the court by the Government of India in respect of the disclosure of certain documents. The Supreme Court by a generous interpretation of the guarantee of freedom of speech and expression

The Supreme Court by a generous interpretation of the guarantee of freedom of speech and expression elevated the right to know and the right to information to the status of a fundamental right.

elevated the right to know and the right to information to the status of a fundamental right, on the principle that certain unarticulated rights are immanent and implicit in the enumerated guarantees.

The court declared: The concept of an open government is the direct emanation from the right to know which seems to be implicit in the right of free speech and expression guaranteed under article 19 (1) (a).

The Supreme Court of India has emphasized in the *S.P.Gupta case* (1982) that open Government is the new democratic culture of an open society towards which every liberal democracy is moving and our country should be no exception. In a country like India which is committed to socialistic pattern of society, right to know becomes a necessity for the poor, ignorant and illiterate masses.

In 1986, the Bombay High Court followed the S.P.Gupta judgment in the well-known case *Bombay Environmental Group and others vs. Pune Cantonment Board.*

The Bombay High Court distinguished between the ordinary citizen looking for information and groups of social activists. This was considered a landmark judgment concerning access to information.

4.21 PROBLEMS DUE TO THE IMPLEMENTATION OF RIGHT TO INFORMATION ACT, 2005

Seeing the increasing trend of request for the information in the different organizations and the implementation of the RTI Act, 2005 in just four months, personal interview of the Public Information Officers (PIO) of different organizations were conducted with the objective to identify the problems (if any) faced by them due to the implementation of RTI Act, 2005 and the suggested solution. It was found that three types of organizations exist on the basis of use of information technology.

1. **Low use of Information Technology:** In these organizations most of the records are maintained manually (paper work) and computer is not used to store information.
2. **Medium use of Information Technology:** In these organizations moderate level of information technology is used. Some of the records are maintained in computer and some are maintained manually.
3. **High use of information Technology:** In Such type of organizations high level of information technology is used and the computerized records are stored at central place.

It was found that the organizations with low or medium use of information technology are facing problems due to the implementation of RTI Act, 2005. The organizations with high use of information technology are not facing difficulties due to the implementation of RTI Act, 2005 (see Table 4.3).

4.22 IMPACT OF RIGHT TO INFORMATION ON DEVELOPMENT — A PERSPECTIVE ON INDIA'S RECENT EXPERIENCES

Until 2005, an ordinary citizen had no access to information held by a public authority. Even in matters affecting legal entitlements for such subsidized services as food for work, wage employment, basic education and health care, it was not easy to seek the details of decision making process that affected or harmed him. Without access to relevant information, it was not possible for a common man to participate in a meaningful debate on political and economic options or choices available to him for realizing socio-economic aspirations. The Constitution of India has guaranteed (u/s 19) the freedom of expression and speech. Even then a citizen had no legal right to know about the details of public policies and expenditures. And, therefore, it was not possible for a common man to observe and scrutinize the public actions with a view to providing feed back for rectifying the deficiencies in policy planning and the execution of programmes.

Until 2005, an ordinary citizen had no access to information held by a public authority. Even in matters affecting legal entitlements for such subsidized services as food for work, wage employment, basic education and health care, it was not easy to seek the details of decision making process that affected or harmed him.

Under the Official Secret Act, 1923, the entire development process has thus been shrouded in secrecy. The people who voted for the formation of democratically elected governments and contributed to the huge costs of financing public activities, had no legal rights to know as to: what process has been followed in designing the policies affecting them, how the programmes have been implemented, who are the concerned officials associated with the decision making process and execution of the schemes and why the promises made for delivery of essential services to the poor have not been fulfilled?

TABLE 4.3 PROBLEMS AND SUGGESTED SOLUTIONS DUE TO THE IMPLEMENTATION OF RTI ACT, 2005

Organization	Use of IT	Problems due to RTI Act	Suggested Solution
1.	Low	• Access to information • Time constraint •Lack of fully dedicated executive as PIO	• Integration of different department through IT • Fully dedicated executive as PIO
2.	Low	• Access to information • Time constraint • Lack of co-ordination from the other department. • Lack of fully dedicated executive as PIO	• Integration of different department through IT • Fully dedicated executive as PIO
3.	Low	• Access to information • Time constraint • Lack of fully dedicated executive as PIO	• Integration of different department through IT • Fully dedicated executive as PIO
4.	Medium	• Access to information • Time constraint	• Integration of different department through IT • Fully dedicated executive as PIO
5.	Medium	• Access to information • Time constraint • Difficulties in doing routine work	• Integration of different department through IT
6.	Medium	• Access to information • Time constraint • Difficulties in doing routine work	• Integration of different department through IT
7.	High	Nil	-
8.	High	Nil	-
9.	High	Nil	-
10.	High	Nil	-

Not surprisingly, the culture of secrecy beginning from the colonial rule till the first six decades of Independence fuelled rampant corruption, in which large amount of public money was diverted from development projects and welfare schemes to private use through mis-use of power by the authorities.

Not surprisingly, the culture of secrecy beginning from the colonial rule till the first six decades of Independence fuelled rampant corruption, in which large amount of public money was diverted from development projects and welfare schemes to private use through mis-use of power by the authorities. Lack of openness in the functioning of the Government, provided a fertile ground for breeding inefficiency and lack of accountability in the working of the public authorities, which, in turn, has perpetuated all forms of poverty, including nutritional, health and educational. In order to rectify the deficiencies in the mechanisms for ensuring the reach of entitlements, particularly the basic human needs, the people in general and NGOs, in particular, demanded for a greater access to the information held by the public bodies, which was acceded to by the Government in 2005.

In this backdrop, the Right to Information Act 2005, was enacted by the National Parliament to dismantle the culture of secrecy and to change the mindset of the bureaucrats and political leaders and to create conditions for taking informed decisions. The major concern of the Act is to allow for greater probity in the functioning of the government departments so as to promote transparency and accountability in the working of the public bodies and contain the scourge of corruption, which are critical for ensuring good governance.

RTI: A Response to Paradigm Shift in Development Approach

Of the major forces which have, of late, led to a re-thinking on issues that affect economic development, at least three of them are most important.

These are:

- Sharing of knowledge and communication strategies for dissemination of information;
- Involvement of NGOs in designing of policies and implementation of schemes; and
- Adoption of citizen centric approach to development.

We may briefly outline the significance of these factors, particularly in the context of the emerging development scenario.

Democratization of Information and Knowledge

In the knowledge society, in which we live today, acquisition of information and knowledge and its application have intense and pervasive impact on productivity gains.

Information and knowledge are critical for realizing all the human aspirations, such as, improvement in quality of life. In the knowledge society, in which we live today, acquisition of information and knowledge and its application have intense and pervasive impact on productivity gains. People who have access to information and who understand how to make use of the acquired information in the processes of exercising their political, economic and legal rights become empowered, which, in turn, enable them to build their strengths and assets.

In view of this, almost every society has made endeavors for democratizing knowledge resources by way of putting in place the mechanisms for free flow of information and ideas so that people can access them without asking for it. They are thus empowered to make proper choices for participation in development process. The efforts made thus far to disseminate information and knowledge through the use of communication technologies such as radio and television, have yielded positive results. Sharing of information, for instance, about the new techniques of farming, health care facilities, hazards of environmental degradation, opportunities for learning and earning, legal remedies for combating gender biases, etc., have, overtime, made significant contributions to the well being of poor people. Every individual or section of the society, whether working in farm, industrial or services sectors, requires a wide range of information to be able to effectively function in the knowledge and technology driven economy.

Every individual or section of the society, whether working in farm, industrial or services sectors, requires a wide range of information to be able to effectively function in the knowledge and technology driven economy.

Democratization of information and knowledge, by way of creating conditions for sharing among the people, who are partners in development, is critical to the task of equalizing opportunities for development. In view of this, the RTI seeks to set up the facilitation process for free flow of information, which forms the basis for a healthy debate on issues of vital importance to every section of the society.

Increasing Demand by NGOs for Participation in Development Activities

In the backdrop of inefficient implementation of development programmes, the NGOs/self-help groups have demanded at various fora, for creating conditions for democratic governance. It has been alleged, and that not without a basis, that the implementing agencies have frequently indulged in corrupt practices leading to diversion of resources from public use to private purposes. And, that the entitlements of the poor have not been assured, mainly in respects of food grains, jobs, health care facilities, basic education, etc. Poverty of all forms has thus been perpetuated, which is a major drag on the overall development of the country.

It has been alleged, and that not without a basis, that the implementing agencies have frequently indulged in corrupt practices leading to diversion of resources from public use to private purposes.

There are umpteen numbers of cases which demonstrate that the role of NGOs in exposing corruption and in providing necessary feedback for designing policies and effective implementation of the programmes has been commendable. For instance, NGOs have exposed the inclusion of fictitious names in the list of beneficiaries, under the schemes like subsidized food grains, employment guarantee scheme for poor, domestic gas (LPG), medicines, reservation of seats in private schools for the children from the poor families, etc.

There are umpteen number of cases which demonstrate that the role of NGOs in exposing corruption and in providing necessary feedback for designing policies and effective implementation of the programmes has been commendable.

Prior to the implementation of RTI Act 2005, at least eight Indian States had enacted the laws on freedom of information since 1997. People, in these states took recourse to the various provisions of transparency norms to obtain information held by the public bodies. The NGOs also conducted social audits of the schemes, particularly the poverty alleviation programmes, the outcomes of which have resulted in appropriate reforms in governance of the projects. This forms the basis for replicating these experiences throughout the country.

In view of commendable contributions of NGOs in carrying out the programmes in partnership with the public bodies, the RTI Act has envisaged for providing a framework for promoting interface between the citizens and the Government, such that informed decisions could be taken at all levels by the functionaries of the governments. And, the projects should be executed under the sunshine to allow for reasonable scrutiny by the citizens.

4.23 CITIZEN-CENTRIC APPROACH TO DEVELOPMENT

An equally important concern of the development planners has been to evolve Citizen Centric Approach to development, as people live in diverse socioeconomic and geographic conditions. The approach to fit for all sizes, particularly in respect of poverty alleviation programmes, has failed. Without obtaining necessary feedback from the people about their socio-economic aspirations and the manner in which the accepted goals are to be realized, it is not possible to design and implement schemes that may eradicate poverty and liquidate illiteracy. The RTI therefore empowers every citizen to take charge of his life and make proper choices, on the basis of freely available information and knowledge, for effective participation in political and economic processes or activities.

Briefly, RTI has been implemented in response to the major challenges of development, mainly the urgency for democratization of information and knowledge which are vital for equalizing opportunity for development, increasing NGOs participation in decision making and democratic governance and for evolving citizen-centric approaches for addressing the concerns of every member of the society. In the following paragraphs, an attempt is made to present the salient features of the Act and to examine the extent to which the stated objectives of the RTI Act are realized.

RTI has been implemented in response to the major challenges of development, mainly the urgency for democratization of information and knowledge which are vital for equalizing opportunity for development,

Promotion of Citizen-Government Partnership

The RTI Act provides a framework for promotion of citizen-government partnership in carrying out the programmes for welfare of the people. The principle of partnership is derived from the fact that people are not only the ultimate beneficiaries of development, but also the agents of development. The stakeholders' participation leads to better projects and more dynamic development.

Under the RTI regime, citizens' participation has been promoted through—

(a) access to information and involvement of affected groups/communities in design and implementation of projects; and

(b) empowerment of local government bodies at village level through the involvement and cooperation with NGOs/self-help groups.

The proactive disclosure of information has enabled the beneficiaries, mainly through NGOs, to assume a central role in design and execution of projects. RTI has instilled a wider sense of ownership in the development activities. Besides, access to information has enabled the people to participate in economic and political processes through a dialogue between people and the government officials or public campaign on public policies. For instance, information obtained under RTI, in respect of utilization of funds allocated under rural employment guarantee scheme, has been used by NGOs for campaign in favour or against the political leaders during recent elections in some States, with a desirable impact on political process. Almost all the welfare projects, particularly at Village and Panchayat levels, are being designed and developed in cooperation and support with the NGOs or affected persons, with a view to raising the satisfaction level of people.

Lack of transparency and accountability encourage the government officials to indulge in corrupt practices, which result in lower investments due to misuse or diversion of funds for private purposes.

Reduction in Corruption

Lack of transparency and accountability encourage the government officials to indulge in corrupt practices, which result in lower investments due to misuse or diversion of funds for private purposes. As a result, the government's social spending yields no worthwhile benefits, because, for instance, the teachers do not teach, doctors and nurses do not attend health centres, ration card holders do not receive subsidized food grains and the promised jobs are not provided to the people. In the process, it perpetuates poverty and harms the poor. It creates an environment of distrust between the people and the government, which impinge upon the development and jeopardize democratic governance. Under the RTI regime, there is unprecedented transparency in the working of public departments. As a result, there is better understanding of the decision making process and greater accountability of government. This has led to reduction in corruption in the country as evident from the following:

- The Transparency International (TI) has consecutively reported in the last two years that perceived corruption in India (a score of 3.5 out of 10)has declined at the rate of about 15-20 per cent per year, due mainly to the implementation of the RTI Act.
- The Centre for Media Studies in collaboration with TI has recently accomplished an all India survey study (unpublished) of the poor below the poverty line. The views of the poor have been elicited in respect of all the flagship programmes that have been implemented for alleviation of poverty. At least 40 per cent of the respondents have reported that corruption has declined.
- It has also been observed that wherever NGOs are actively involved in the development activities, the perceived corruption is abysmally low.

Questions

Section — A Objective Type

1. State any two objectives of RTI Act, 2005.
2. State two advantages of RTI Act.
3. What is transparency as per RTI Act?
4. Who is a Information Officer as per RTI Act?
5. What are the rights of the citizens under RTI Act?
6. What are the information that are exempted from RTI Act?
7. Who is a public authority as per the RTI Act?

Section — B Analytical Type

1. Briefly explain the information that can be secured under RTI Act.
2. Explain the information that is not obtainable under the RTI Act.
3. List the powers of Public Information Officer.
4. List the functions of Public Information Officer.
5. Briefly explain the functions of Central Information Commissioner.
6. List the offences under RTI Act.
7. List the penalties under the RTI Act.

Section — C Essay Type

1. Discuss the salient features of RTI Act.
2. Discuss the important cases of RTI Act.
3. Discuss the powers and functions of Public Information Officer.
4. Explain the powers and functions of CIC.
5. Discuss the offences and penalties under RTI Act.

INDIAN CONTRACT ACT, 1872

Module Objectives

After reading this chapter, you should be able to

- Know the salient features covering essentials of contract, offer, acceptance, considerations and contingent contract.
- Understand the concepts of free consent, coercion undue influence, fraud, misrepresentation and mistake.
- Know the various modes of discharge of a contract.
- Understand the concept of breach of contract and their remedies.

THE INDIAN CONTRACT ACT, 1872

The Indian Contract Act, 1872, is the most important piece of legislation affecting business. This and the next four sub-chapters are devoted to a brief description of the general principles of the law of contract.

5.1 BRIEF HISTORY OF THE ACT

The Indian Contract Act came into force on the first day of September 1872. Prior to this there was an English Common Law which was applied to Indians indiscriminately.

The Indian Contract Act came into force on the first day of September 1872. Prior to this there was an English Common Law which was applied to Indians indiscriminately. This led to many inconveniences. To obviate this, statutes were enacted to regulate contracts where parties were Mohammedans and Hindus. If both parties were Hindus, they were regulated by the Hindu Law and in the case of Monammedans, by the laws and usage's of Mohammedans. The effect of these statutes was to supersede English Law so far as it regards Hindu and Mohammedans in the case of contracts and other matters enumerated in the status and to declare the right of Hindus and Mohammedans to their own laws and usages. The result was that in a suit on contract, for instance, between Hindus, Hindu Law of contract was applied, and the Mohammedan Law in the case of a contract between Mohammedans, and this continued upto the enactment of the Indian Contract Act.

5.2 SCOPE OF THE ACT

The Act applies to the whole of India except the state of Jammu and Kashmir. The Act does not profess to be complete code dealing with the law relating to contracts. It deals with the general principles of law of contracts and contains special contracts only. Sections 1 to 75 of Act deal with different stages in the formation of a contract, its essential features, its performance or breach, and the remedies for breach of contract* Sections 124 to 238 cover some of the special contracts, viz., indemnity and guarantee, bailment and pledge and agency. Sale of goods, forming and functioning of partnership, insurances, transfer of property and negotiable instruments are not covered by the Act, though they are also contracts. The Act defines and amends only certain parts of the law relating to contracts. A particular usage or custom is allowed to prevail and remain unaffected. However usages and customs shall not be inconsistent with the provisions of the Act. Where the Contract Law is silent on any matter, Hindu and Mohammedan Law relating to contracts shall apply. The Act is, therefore, not a complete code and is not exhaustive.

The main objective of the Contract Act is to ensure that the rights and obligations are honoured, that the expectations created by the promises of parties to an agreement are fulfilled.

It should be emphasized that wherever promises are made, Contract Act comes into picture. Promises may or may not be related to business.

5.3 OBJECTIVES OF THE ACT

The main objective of the Contract Act is to ensure that the rights and obligations are honoured, that the expectations created by the promises of parties to an agreement are fulfilled and that legal remedies are available to an aggrieved party against the party failing to honour his part of agreement.

---

* Sections 76 123 were repealed from the Act and separate Acts called the Sale of Goods Act and the Partnership Act were enacted in 1930 and 1932 respectively.

With regard to business transactions, the Contract Act lends definiteness. Naturally, the Act is of great importance to businessmen as it enables them to plan ahead with the knowledge that what has been promised to them will be performed by the promisors failing which they will be made to pay compensation for the loss suffered.

5.4 DEFINITION OF CONTRACT

Sir Federic Pollock defines a contract as "Every agreement and promise enforceable at law." It is this definition which formed the basis for defining the term contract in the Indian Contract Act. According to Section 2(h) of the Act, Contract is an agreement cnforceable at law. This crisp definition has two important components which constitute the bases for a contract. They are:

Every agreement and promise enforceable at law is contract.

(1) The existence of an agreement, and (2) its enforceability at law. These two need elaboration.

An agreement is defined as every promise and every set of promises forming consideration for each other (Sec.2(e)). A Promise is defined thus: "when the person to whom the proposal is made signifies his assent thereto, the proposal is said to be accepted. A proposal, when accepted, becomes a promise (Sec.2(b)). To sum up, it may be stated that an agreement is an accepted proposal. There must be one party to offer a proposal and another to accept the proposal. An agreement then comes into existence. Thus, agreement = Offer + Acceptance.

An agreement is defined as every promise and every set of promises forming consideration for each other.

Offer + **Acceptance** = **Contract**

Enforceability of an agreement is another requisite of a contract. An agreement becomes enforceable when it gives rise to legal obligation. Obligation is a restraint which one party exercises over another. It is by virtue of this obligation that one party can compel the other to do something or to refrain from doing something. What is important is that the obligation must be legal and not social or religious. The main distinction between legal obligation and a social or religious obligation is that the former involves money value but the latter does not. It should also be remembered that obligations arise even without agreements, as in torts or civil wrongs, Quasi contracts, judgement of courts, etc. In order to constitute a contract an agreement must create legal obligation. It is this argument which has given rise to the popular saying: *All contracts are agreements but all agreements need not be contracts.*

An agreement becomes enforceable when it gives rise to legal obligation.

The main distinction between legal obligation and a social or religious obligation is that the former involves money value but the latter does not.

Case Laws

The following illustrations are useful to appreciate the nature of obligation:

1. X agrees to sell his motorcycle to Y for Rs. 15,000. The agreement gives rise to a legal obligation on the part of X to deliver the vehicle to Y and on the part of Y to pay Rs. 15,000 to X. Failure of X to deliver the vehicle or Y to make the payment entitles the aggrieved to sue against the offender.
2. X invites for dinner in a restaurant. Y having accepted the invitation, goes to the restaurant on the stipulated date and time. X is either not there at the restaurant or even if present refuses to entertain Y. In either case, Y has no remedy against X.

3. X gives a promise to his son to give him a pocket allowance of Rs. 200 every month. If the promise is not fulfilled by X, the son cannot sue his father.

In the above illustrations only the first results in a contract. Second and third do not constitute contracts as they are only social obligations.

5.5 ESSENTIALS OF A VALID CONTRACT

A contract must have two components: (i) Existence of an agreement (ii) Its enforceability.

As was pointed out earlier, a contract must have two components, viz., (a) existence of an agreement, and (b) its enforceability. These are not the only requirements of a valid contract. There are few more essentials of a valid contract which are laid down in Sec. 10 of the Act.

According to Sec. 10, all agreements are contracts if they are made by the free consent of the parties who are competent to contract, for a lawful consideration and with a lawful object, and are not hereby expressly declared to be void. In order to become a valid contract, an agreement must have the following essential qualities (see Fig. 5.1):

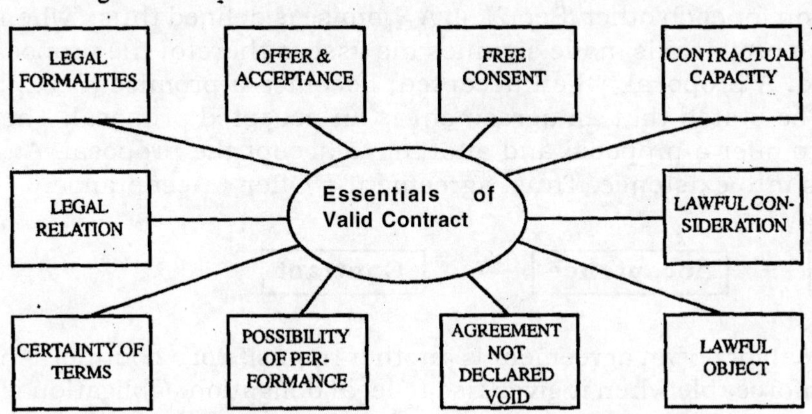

Fig. 5.1 Essentials of a Valid Contract

An offer to do or not to do a definite act or acts is made by one person who is called the offeror. The proposal is accepted by the other party who is called the offeree.

(i) Offer and Acceptance: An agreement is the result of offer or proposal and acceptance. An offer to do or not to do a definite act or acts is made by one person who is called the offeror. The proposal is accepted by the other party who is called the offeree. Thus, there are two parties to a contract.

(ii) Free Consent: An agreement, to be made enforceable, must be based on free consent. Free consent is said to exist when both the offerer and the offeree are of the same mind and upon the same subject. Free consent does not exist when it is obtained by coercion, undue influence, fraud, mistake or misrepresentation.

(iii) Contractual Capacity: The parties who enter into contract must be competent to do so. A person is said to be competent when he is (a) of the age of maturity, (b) is of sound mind, (c) and is not disqualified from entering into contract by any law to which he is subject. Incapacity arises from minority, lunacy, idiocy, drunkenness, and similar other factors. If one of the parties to the contract suffers from any incapacity the contract cannot be enforced by law.

(iv) Lawful Consideration: An agreement to become enforceable must be supported by consideration. Consideration means something given or taken for something in return. If an agreement is not supported by consideration it becomes *nudum pactum*, i.e., bare or naked agreement not enforceable by law, subject to certain exceptions specified in the Act.

(v) Lawful Object: The object of the agreement must be lawful. It is unlawful if the object is forbidden by law, immoral or opposed to public policy. Any agreement with an unlawful object cannot be enforced by law.

(vi) Not Expressly Declared Void: The agreement must not have been expressly declared to be void under any law. Void agreements cannot be enforced by law. Examples of void agreements are such as those in restraint of trade, in restraint of marriage, in restraint of legal proceedings and wagering agreement.

(vii) Possibility of Performance: The act contemplated in the agreement should be capable of performance. Agreement to perform an impossible act cannot be enforced. For example, A promises to share with B, 50 per cent of the treasure, provided the treasure is created by magic. Such an agreement cannot be enforced because of impossibility of performance.

(viii) Certainty of Terms: The terms of the agreement must be certain. Vague or uncertain terms make the agreement unforceable. For example, A company agreed with V that on the expiration of V's existing contract, the company would favourably consider a request of V for renewal of the contract. It was held that the company had no obligation to renew the contract as the agreement did not bind the company to do so. (*Monstreal Gas Company v. Vasey* (1900) A.C. 595).

(ix) Intention to Create Legal Relationship: When two parties enter into an agreement, their intention must be to create legal relationship between them. In the absence of such an intention the agreement cannot be enforced.

Case Laws
In agreements relating to business, the law will presume that the parties have the intention of legal relationship. However, such presumption have the intention of legal relationship. However, such presumption may be negated by express terms to the contrary. For example, in an agreement between R company and C company, the former was appointed as the agent of the latter. One of the clauses in the agreement read thus: "This agreement is not entered into...as a formal or legal agreement, and shall not be the subject to legal jurisdiction in the Law Courts." It was held that the agreement was not enforceable as there was no intention to create legal relations. (**Rose and Frank Co**. v. Crompton Bros. (1925) A.C. (445).

(x) Legal Formalities: One aspect of legal formalities is whether the agreement must be written or it can be oral. A contract can be both. But it is in the interest of both the parties that they must reduce the contract into writing because "an oral contract is the refuge of Scoundrels. Registration is another aspect of legal formalities. Registration is again optional, though it is compulsory in cases like gift and mortgages. Similarly, in some cases the documents containing agreements, besides being in writing, need to be stamped and attested too.

5.6 CLASSIFICATION OF CONTRACTS

Contracts may be classified on the basis of their (a) enforceability, (b) validity, or (c) performance (see Fig. 5.2).

Contracts

A. Formation	B. Validity	C. Performance
— Express contracts	— Valid contracts	— Executed contracts
— Implied contracts	— Void contracts	— Executory contracts
— Quasi contracts	— Void agreements	OR
	— Voidable contracts	— Unilateral contracts
	— Illegal contracts	— Bilateral contracts
	— Unforceable contracts	

Fig. 5.2 Classification of Contracts

A. Classification According to Formation

Express Contract

In an express contract, the terms are made clear in writing or orally at the time of entering into an agreement.

Express Contracts: In an express contract, the terms are made clear in writing or orally at the time of entering into an agreement.

An express contract is one that is explicitly set forth in words, either spoken or written. It does not arise from actions or implications of the parties.

In an implied contract, the terms are not made clear but the acts, conduct or dealing of the parties lend themselves to form a contract.

Implied Contract: In an implied contract, the terms are not made clear but the acts, conduct or dealing of the parties lend themselves to form a contract. Sometimes individuals may not actually express in specific language their intent to enter into a contract. The implied-in-fact contract is entered into based on the conduct of the parties. If you accept services from another and those services are usually paid for, you will be expected to pay the individual who performs that service, if you hire a gardener to take care of your lawn, you will be expected to pay him. An implied contract is formed and the gardener could enforce the agreement if you refused to pay. In this case, the gardener is expected to be paid for his services, and you intended to pay him when you asked him to take care of your lawn.

Basically, in an implied contract, neither party will use words of promise or explicit words indicating that a contract has been formed. However, by nature of your conduct in calling the gardener and his conduct in performing the work, a valid contract will be implied. In this case, the court would look at the facts and circumstances surrounding the transaction to determine whether both parties intended to enter into an agreement.

Quasi Contract: There are certain transactions which cannot be strictly called contracts but which create peculiar obligations. Such obligations are :

(i) Supplier of necessaries to minors, lunatics, married woman etc.,

(ii) Person paying money owned by another,

(iii) Person enjoying benefit of non-gratuitous act of Quantum Meruit,

(iv) Person receiving money or goods belonging to another under mistake or under coercion,

(v) Finder of goods.

Now, in all the above cases the person receiving the benefit has an obligation to compensate the person paying the benefit. Law recognizes this obligations as a contract though there is no explicit agreement between giver and receiver of benefit. Contracts of this nature are called Quasi contracts.

A **contract** which was valid when it was first entered into but subsequently becomes unenforceable due to impossibility of performance, change of law or other reasons, is called void contract.

B. Classification Based on Validity

Valid Contract: A contract which satisfies all the legal requirements laid down in Sec. 10 of the Act is known as a valid contract. These requirements were explained earlier.

Void Contract: A contract which was valid when it was first entered into but subsequently becomes unenforceable due to impossibility of performance, change of law or other reasons, is called void contract. Example is a contract to import goods from a foreign country. If war breaks out between countries, it becomes impossible to import goods. The contract, therefore, cannot be enforced.

Void Agreement: Void agreement is an agreement not enforceable by law. An agreement with a minor, an agreement in restrain of trade, etc., are examples of void agreements.

It is widely argued that void contract must be rightly called void agreement because when the contract is void, it is no contract at law. The terms 'void' and 'contract' apparently cannot go together.

Void agreement is an agreement not enforceable by law. An agreement with a minor, an agreement in restrain of trade.

A **voidable contract** is the one that can be set aside at the option of one of the parties to the contract.

Voidable Contracts: A voidable contract is the one that can be set aside at the option of one of the parties to the contract. The party who can rescind the contract is the aggrieved. The other party who causes wrong cannot set aside the contract.

It may so happen that a party may obtain the consent of the other party by force, undue influence, fraud or misrepresentation. The party whose consent is so obtained is the aggrieved party who can set aside the contract. The right of rescission must, however, exercised within a reasonable time and before a third party acquires the rights of the contract. Otherwise the contract will be binding on the aggrieved party. It may be stressing the obvious, but it needs to be stated that the voidable contract remains valid until set aside by the aggrieved party.

Illegal Contract: As in voidable contract, the terms 'illegal' and 'contract' cannot go together. What is illegal or against law cannot be enforced. More appropriate expression, therefore, would be 'illegal agreement.' An illegal agreement then is an agreement, the consideration or object of which (I) is forbidden by law, (ii) defeats the provisions of any law, (iii) is fraudulent, (iv) involves or implies injury to the person or property of another, or (v) the court regards it as immoral, or opposed to public policy. Needless it is to say that illegal agreement cannot be enforced by law.

An unenforceable contract is valid but for certain technical reasons such as want of proof, expiry of the period within which enforceable, insufficiency of stamp, and the like.

An executed contract is the one which is wholly performed. Both the parties to the contract have discharged their respective obligations and there remains nothing to be performed by either party.

Are void agreements and illegal agreements one and the same? The answer is no. An illegal agreement is forbidden by law but not void agreement. Thus every illegal agreement is void but every void agreement is not unenforceable.

Unenforceable Contract: An unenforceable contract is valid but for certain technical reasons such as want of proof, expiry of the period within which enforceable, insufficiency of stamp, and the like, it becomes necessarily illegal.

C. Classification According to Performance

Executed Contracts: An executed contract is the one which is wholly performed. Both the parties to the contract have discharged their respective obligations and there remains nothing to be performed by either party. For example,

A agrees to paint picture for B for Rs. 100. When A paints the picture and B pays Rs. 100 the respective obligations are performed, and the contract is executed.

It is possible that a contract may be executed but its effect may remain. For example, when a person buys a bun for a penny and subsequently breaks his tooth due to a stone in it, he has a right to recover damages from the seller [*Chaproniere v. Mason* (1905) 21, T.L.R.633].

Unlike in executed contract, parties to an executory contract have not performed their respective obligations.

Executory Contract: Unlike in executed contract, parties to an executory contract have not performed their respective obligations. In the example quoted above, A has neither painted the picture nor B has paid Rs. 100.

A contract may be both executed and executory. In other words, the contract is partly performed and partly not. To continue the same example, B has paid Rs. 100 but A has not yet painted the picture.

Another way of classifying contracts, on the basis of performance, is unilateral and bilateral contracts.

Unilateral Contract: Here one party has already performed his part of obligations at the time of or before forming the contract. Only the other party has to fulfil his obligation. These contracts are also called contracts with executed consideration.

Bilateral Contract: Here, both the parties to the contract have to fulfill their respective obligations. In effect, bilateral contracts are executory contracts and are also known as contracts with executory consideration.

5.7 OFFER AND ACCEPTANCE

In the previous chapter it was pointed out that offer and acceptance are essential to make a valid contract. In this sub-chapter it is proposed to discuss the two concepts, viz., offer and acceptance in greater detail.

Offer or Proposal

"when one person signifies to another his willingness to do or to obtain from doing anything, with a view to obtain the assent of that other to such act or abstinence, he is said to make a proposal."

Proposal or offer is the starting point in the process of making an agreement. Sec. 2(1) defines a proposal thus: "when one person signifies to another his willingness to do or to obtain from doing anything, with a view to obtain the assent of that other to such act or abstinence, he is said to make a proposal."

The person who makes the proposal is called the promiser or offerer, and the person to whom the proposal is made is called the promisee or offeree.

Most contracts result from an offer and an acceptance. So our first concern is whether an offer has actually been made. In contract law, we say that an offeror is the person who makes the offer and an offeree is the person who accepts it.

Essentials of a Valid Offer

The definition of offer given in Sec.2(1) is crisp. Further elaboration is necessary to make the nature of offer clear. The following are essentials of valid offer (see Fig. 5.3):

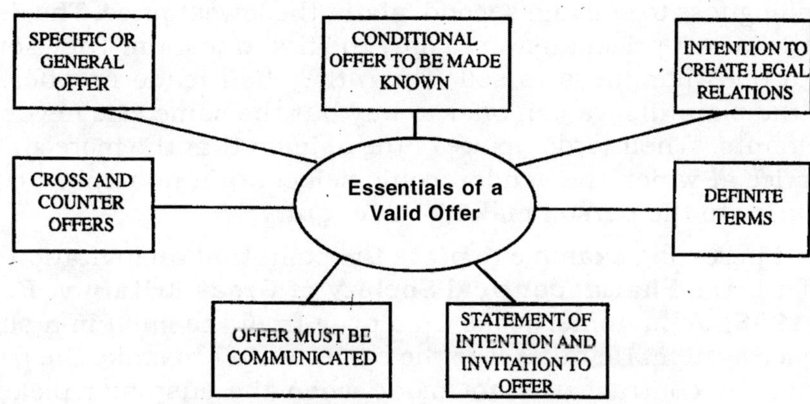

Fig. 5.3 Essentials of a Valid Offer

1. **Intention to Create Legal Relationship:** An offer must be such that when accepted it must create a valid contract. An offer with social or religious connotation, as was pointed out in the previous chapter, does not constitute a valid offer. A case to prove the validity of an offer is the **Kalai Haldar v. Sheikh (23 W.R. 217)**. A invited B for dinner. On B's failure, A filed a suit against B for the price of the non-consumed food. A's suit was dismissed on the ground that his invitation for dinner did not create legal relationship between himself and B.
2. **Terms Must be Definite and Certain:** The terms of offer must be definite and certain. Vague and ambiguous terms make the offer invalid. For example, an offer to take a house on lease for three years at 285 per annum if the house was "put into through repair and drawing rooms thoroughly decorated according to the present style" is too vague to result in a legal obligation. **Tayler v. Portington, (1855).**
3. **Statement of Intention and Invitation to Offer:** A mere statement of intention does not constitute a binding promise even though a person to whom it is made acts upon it. For example, in **Re ficus (1900)**. A father wrote to his would be son-in-law that his daughter would have a share of whatever he had left. Held that it was merely a statement of intention and not a valid offer.

Similarly, an invitation to offer does not constitute a valid offer. Price-lists, catalogues, advertisements, window displays, tenders, invitations by a company to public to subscribe to its shares and the like are merely statements of intention and hence do not constitute valid offers.

Case Laws

In **Harvey v. Facie (1839 A.C. 552)**, the plaintiffs telegraphed to the defendants thus: "will you sell us Bumper Hall Pen? Telegraph lowest cash price." The defendants replied by a telegram saying, "Lowest price for Bumper Pen, 900." The plaintiffs immediately sent their last telegram stating: " we agree to buy Bumper Hall Pen for 900 asked by you." The defendants refused to sell the Bumper Hall Pen, a plot of land, and expectedly the plaintiffs sued the defendants. The contention of the plaintiffs was that by quoting their minimum price in response to the inquiry the defendants had made an offer to sell at that price. But the Judicial committee rejected the contention. Their lordships pointed out that in their first telegram the plaintiffs had asked two questions, first, about the willingness to sell and second, about the lowest price. The defendants by quoting the lowest price, answered only the first question. They served their answer as to the willingness to sell. Thus, they had made no offer. The last telegram of the plaintiffs was an offer to buy but the same was never accepted by the defendants. "Their lordship are of the opinion that the mere statement of the lowest price at which the vendor would sell contain no implied contract to sell at that price to the person making the enquiry."

Another interesting example to prove the point that an invitation to offer is not valid offer is the **Pharmaceutical Society of Great Britain v. Boots Cash Chemists (1953)**. A customer picks up a drug from the shelf in a shop under the self-service system. He takes it to the cash counter to make the payment. It was held that the contract was not made when the customer picked up the drug. Contract would have been made if the cashier received the price. **Lord Goddard, C.J.** said : "It would be wrong to say that the shopkeeper is making an offer to sell every article in the shop to any person who might come in and that person can insist on buying any article by saying: 'I accept your offer....' In most bookshops customers are invited to go in and pick up books and look at them even they do not actually buy them, there is no contract by the shopkeeper to sell until the customer has taken the book to the shopkeeper or his assistant and said: ' I want to buy this book' and the shopkeeper says 'yes.' That would not prevent the shopkeeper, seeing the book picked up, saying, 'I am sorry, I cannot let you have that book; it is the only copy I have got and I have already promised it to another customer.' Therefore, I am of opinion — the mere fact that a customer picks up a bottle of medicine from the shelves in this case does not amount to an acceptance of an offer to sell. It is an offer by the customer to buy. And there is no sale effected until the buyer's offer to buy is accepted by the acceptance of the price."

A banker's catalogue of charges is also not an offer. An auctioneer's announcement that specified goods will be sold by auction on a specified day is not an offer to hold the auction and he will not be liable the auction. **(Spencer v. Harding, 1870)**. Even when an auction is held the bid is not an acceptance so as to entitle the highest bidder to get the goods. The highest bid is nothing more than an offer to buy which must be accepted by the auctioneer. A railway time table is in the same category.

4. **Offer must be Communicated :** An offer to be complete, must be communicated to the person to whom it is made. This is the essence of the first part of the definition of proposal. As was pointed out in the beginning of the chapter, willingness to make an offer must 'signified'. To signify means to communicate. Acceptance is not possible unless offer is brought to the knowledge of offeree. Nor acceptance, in ignorance of the offer, confer any right on the acceptor. This principle was acted upon by the Allahabad High Court in **Lalman Shukla v. Gauri Datt** (1913).

Lalman Shukla V/s. Gauri Dutt Case

It so happened that the defendant's nephew absconded from home. He sent his servant in search of the boy, when the servant had left the defendant, by handbills, offered to pay Rs. 501 to anybody discovering the boy. The servant came to know of this offer only when he had already traced the missing child. He however brought an action to recover the reward. But his action failed.

Elaborating the principal, **Bannerji J.** said: " In my opinion a suit like the present one can only be founded on a contract. In order to constitute a contract, there must be an acceptance unless there is knowledge of the offer."

Normally, an individual cannot accept an offer that was directed to someone else. You may want to sell your personal coin collection to a close friend. If you make an offer by letter to this individual, it cannot be accepted by another collector who happens to see your offer on your friend's desk. If the law were otherwise, people would find that they had made contracts with individuals that they never intended to deal with. The offeror should never be forced to accept an agreement with someone he or she does not want to do business with.

So the law takes the position that an offer has not actually been made until brought directly to the attention of the offeree. Until the offer has been communicated, the offeree does not even know that an offer was even in existence and consequently cannot accept it.

5. **An Offer can be Specific or General:** Earlier it was suggested **(Weeks v. Tybold)** that an offer must be specific. In other words it must be addressed to a specific person. But the modern position is that the offer can be made to the world at large. It can, therefore, be general offer. But the contract is not made with all the world. Contract is made only with that person who comes forward and performs the conditions of the proposal. The principle of general offer was underlined in the famous case.

Carlill v. Carbolic Smoke Ball Co. (1893)

Details of the case are: A company offered by advertisement, to pay £1000 to anyone "who contracts the increasing epidemic influenza, colds or any disease caused by taking cold, after having used the ball according to printed directions." It was added that "£1,000 is deposited with the Alliance Bank showing out sincerity in the matter." The plaintiff used the smoke balls according to the directions but she nevertheless subsequently suffered from influenza. She was held entitled to recover the promised reward.

The defendants contended that (a) there was no intention to enter into legal relations as it was simply a puffing advertisement; (b) that the offer was to made to any particular individual, and (c) that the plaintiff had not communicated her intention to accept.

The first argument was turned down by **Bowen, L.J.,** by saying :"was it intended that £100 should, if the conditions were fulfilled, be paid? The advertisement says that £1,000 is lodged at the bank for the purpose. Therefore, it cannot be said that the statement that £100 would be paid was intended to be a mere puff."

Rejecting the second argument that an offer could not be made to the world at large his Lordship observed thus: "why should not an offer be made to all the world which is ripen into contract with anybody who comes forward and performs the condition? It is an offer to become liable to any one who before it is retracted, performs the conditions, and although the offer is made to the world, the contract is made with that limited portion of the public who came forward and perform the condition on the faith of the advertisement."

His Lordship also pointed out that in cases like this communication of acceptance is not necessary.

6. **Offer with Special Conditions:** If there are special terms or conditions in an offer, these must be brought to the notice of the offeree at the time

of making a proposal. A conditional offer lapses when the condition is not accepted by the offeree.

7. **Cross Offers and Counter Offers:** When the parties make identical offers to each other, in ignorance of each other's offer, the offers are said to be cross offers. In such a case, the court will not construe one offer as the offer and the other as the acceptance and as such there can be no concluded contract.

A counter offer is a rejection of original offer. It is new offer which needs acceptance by the original promisor before a contract is made. This point was made clear in the following case:

Hyde. V. Wrench (1840)
In this case an offer to sell a form for £1,000 was rejected by the plaintiff, who offered £950 for it. This was turned by the offerer and then the plaintiff agreed to pay £1,000. Holding that the defendant was not bound by any such acceptance, the court said: "The defendant offered to sell it for £1,000, and if that had been at once unconditionally accepted, there would undoubtedly be a perfect binding contract, instead of that, the plaintiff made an offer of his own to purchase the property for £950 and thereby rejected the offer previously made to the defendant. It was not afterwards competent for him to revive the proposal of the defendant by rendering an acceptance of it, and that, therefore, there exists no obligation of any sort between the parties.

Acceptance

"When the person to whom the proposal is made signifies his assent thereto, the proposal is said to be accepted. A proposal when accepted, becomes a promise."

If an offer is the starting point of forming an agreement acceptance represents the end point of the process. In between there are formalities to be fulfilled. These formalities will be examined in the subsequent sub-chapters. Coming to the acceptance, section 2(b) defines the term thus: "When the person to whom the proposal is made signifies his assent thereto, the proposal is said to be accepted. A proposal when accepted, becomes a promise." Acceptance is, therefore, the assent given to a proposal and it has the effect of converting the proposal into a promise.

Essentials of Valid Acceptance

The essentials of valid acceptance are : (i) communication, (ii) absolute and unqualified, (iii) express or implied, (iv) definite person, (v) mode of acceptance, (vi) not mere mental acceptance, (vii) when the offer is in force, and (viii) preceded by offer (see Fig. 5.4):

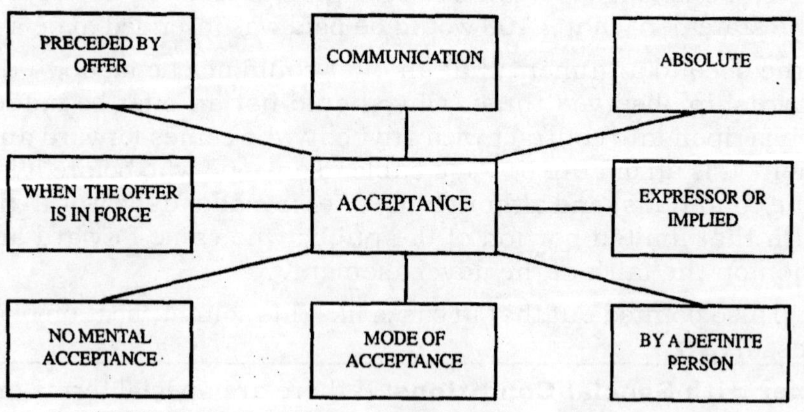

Fig. 5.4 Essentials of Valid Acceptance

1. **Acceptance Must be Communicated:** The definition of acceptance clearly requires that the assent must be signified. To signify means to communicate. If the acceptance is not communicated to the offerer, no contract is created. A case to prove this principle is the **Brogden vs. Metropolitan Railway Co. (1877)**. A draft relating to the supply of coal was sent to the manager of a Railway Company for his acceptance. The Manager wrote the word 'approved' on the agreement but, oversight the document remained in the drawer. It was held that there was no contract.
2. **Acceptance Must be Absolute and Unqualified:** Acceptance of a proposal with conditions, variations and reservations is no acceptance at all. Acceptance with variations is a counter-proposal and as was pointed out earlier, there is no contact unless this counter proposal is accepted by the original proposer. In **Neele vs. Meritt (1930)** Meritt offered land to Neele at $ 280. Neele replied accepting and enclosing $ 30 and promising to pay the balance by monthly installments of $ 50 each. As Neele accepted the proposal subject to making payment in installments, it was held that there was no contract as the acceptance was qualified.
3. **Acceptance Can be Express or Implied:** Acceptance is express when it is communicated by words, spoken or written. If the proposer prescribes any mode of acceptance, the offeree must follow the same mode. Thus, if the proposer prescribes a method of delivery of goods at a particular place, he is not bound to accept delivery at any other place.

Acceptance is implied when it is to be gathered from the surrounding circumstances or the conduct of the parties. For example, in an auction sale if the highest bidder strikes a hammer on the table, it is treated as an implied acceptance.

4. **Acceptance by a Definite Person:** Where an offer is made to a particular person, he alone must accept the proposal. Acceptance by anybody else invalidates the offer. We quote the **Boulton vs. Jones (1857)** case in support of this principle. The plaintiff had taken over the business of one Brocklehurst. The defendant used to deal with Brocklehurst and not knowing of the change sent him an order of certain goods. The defendant came to know of the change only when he received an invoice and by that time he had already consumed the goods. The defendant had a set off against Brocklehurst and, therefore refused to pay the price. The plaintiff sued him. It was held that the offer was made to Brocklehurst and it was not in the power of Boulton to step into the shoes of Brocklehurst and accept the offer. The observation made by Pollock, C.B. one of the judges, is worth quoting: "Now" said he, "the rule of law is clear, that if you propose to make a contract with A, then B cannot substitute himself for A without your consent and to your disadvantage, securing to himself all the benefit of the contract." The defendant was not held liable.

If the offer is made to world at large, one person must accept the offer. It is only then that the contract is made. The general offer is closed as soon as it is accepted by a definite person.

5. **Acceptance Must be Through Prescribed or Reasonable Mode:** If the acceptance is not according to the mode prescribed, or some usual and reasonable mode (where no mode is prescribed) the offerer may intimate to the offeree, within reasonable time, that the acceptance is not according to the mode prescribed and may insist that the acceptance must be in the

prescribed mode only. If the proposer fails to do he is said to have accepted the acceptance. For example, if the proposer says, "wire reply" and the reply is sent by telephone, there is valid acceptance if the proposer does not raise objection. If he objects, there is no valid acceptance.

6. **Mere Mental Acceptance in no Acceptance:** No contract is formed if the offeree remains silent and does nothing to show that he has accepted the offer. A mere mental determination to accept unaccompanied by an external indication will not be sufficient. In the words of **Shah J.** (afterward C.J.): "An agreement does not result from a mere state of mind: intend to accept an offer or even a mental resolve to accept an offer does not give rise to a contract. There must be ... some external manifestation of the intent by speech, writing or other act." **(Bhagavandas vs. Giridharilal (1966).**

7. **Acceptance when Offer is in Force:** Acceptance must be made before the offer lapses. If any time limit is prescribed, the offer must be accepted before the expiry of the time. If no time is prescribed, the offer must be accepted within reasonable time. M offered to take shares in a company on 8th June and received acceptance on 23rd November. M refused to take the shares. As the reasoable period of acceptance had elapsed, he was entitled to refuse to take the shares **[Ramagate Victoria Hotel Com., vs. Moantetoire (1886)].**

8. **Acceptance Must be Preceded by offer:** Offer must precede acceptance. Acceptance without offer is no acceptance. Allotment of shares previous to the application, for example, is not valid.

Revocation of Offer

Revocation of offer means withdrawing the offer before its acceptance.

According to section 6 an offer is revoked under the following ways (see Fig. 5.5):

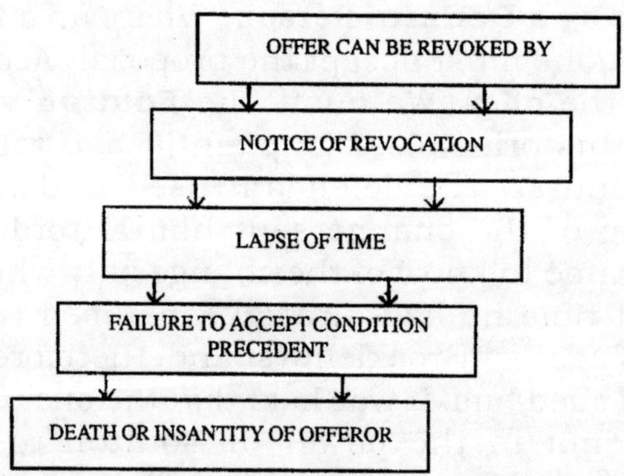

Fig. 5.5 Revocation of Offer

(i) Notice of Revocation: Offer is revoked once the offerer gives notice of revocation to the offeree. Notice must be given by the offerer anytime before its acceptence as against him.

(ii) Lapse of Time: Offer lapses if it is not accepted within prescribed time. Where definite time is stipulated, or within reasonable time where no time limit is stipulated for acceptance.

(iii) Failure to Accept Precedent: Where the offer is subject to a condition precedent thereto, it lapses on failure to accept it without fulfilling the condition.

(iv) Death or Insanity of Offeror: An offer lapses on the death or insanity of the offeror, provided that the fact comes to the knowledge of the offeree before he makes his acceptance.

Revocation of Acceptance

As in the offer, acceptance is also revocable. An acceptor may cancel his acceptance by a speedier mode of communication which will reach earlier than the acceptance itself. Section 5 is the relevant provision. The Section reads thus **"An acceptance may be revoked at any time before the communication of the acceptance is complete as against the acceptor, but not afterwards."** Thus, the communication of revocation should reach earlier than the acceptance itself. What if both acceptance and its cancellation reach the proposer at the same time ? In such a case also, the acceptance will be deemed to have been cancelled.

5.8 COMMUNICATION OF OFFER AND ACCEPTANCE

In the previous sub-chapter, it was pointed out that an offer must be communicated to the offeree for his acceptance. There can be no valid proposal unless it is communicated to the proposee. Similarly, the proposee must communicate the acceptance to the proposal to the promisor. Acceptance cannot be valid unless it is communicated to the offerer. Again where proposal or acceptance is revoked, the same should be communicated to the concerned party. Thus, communication constitutes an important aspect of a contract. It is, therefore, proposed to discuss in detail of communication in effecting an agreement.

How Communication is Effected?

The communication of proposal or its revocation and the communication or acceptance or its revocation are deemed to be made by (a) any act; or (b) omission; of the party proposing, accepting or revoking, by which he intends to communicate such proposal, acceptance or revocation, or which has the effect of communicating it (Section 3).

Communication is effected on any of the following methods:

(i) By any Act: Act includes by conduct, by words, written or oral. Communication can, therefore, be by a letter, telegram, telex, etc. it can also be by telephone. Any act by a person by which he intends to communicate or which has the effect of communication will constitute communication, for example entering into a bus or any public vehicle is communication of acceptance by act or conduct.

(ii) By Omission: Omission includes conduct or forbearance. An abstinence or forbearance on the part of one person which has the effect of communicating will constitute communication.

Implied Proposal and Acceptance

A proposal conveyed by conduct is called implied offer, and the one which is expressed by words, written or spoken, is called an "express offer.' Similarly, acceptance conveyed through conduct is said to be an 'implied' acceptance and

A proposal conveyed by conduct is called implied offer, and the one which is expressed by words, written or spoken, is called an "express offer.'

the one communicated, otherwise than through conduct, is called 'express' acceptance.

Communication of Proposal

An offer, to be made complete, must be communicated to the person to whom it is made. Acceptance is not possible unless offer is brought to the knowledge of the offeree. Nor acceptance, in ignorance of offer, confer any right on the acceptor **(Lalman Shukla vs. Gauri Dutt)**.

The communication of a proposal is complete when it comes to the knowledge of the person to whom it is made.

According to Section 4 the communication of a proposal is complete when it comes to the knowledge of the person to whom it is made. Obviously, an offer cannot be accepted unless and until it has been brought to the knowledge of the offeree.

Revocation of Offer Through Communication

A proposal may be revoked at any time before the communication of its acceptance is complete as against the proposer, but not afterwards. Therefore, in case of postings of a letter of acceptance the same can be revoked by a telegram which shall reach earlier to the letter. In case both letter of acceptance and revocation by telegram arrive simultaneously, both cancel each other, and as such, there would be no valid contract. Revocation is effective only when it comes to the knowledge of the person to whom the offer is made.

Communication of Acceptance

A proposal may be revoked at any time before the communication of its acceptance is complete as against the proposer, but not afterwards.

Acceptance of offer must be communicated to the proposer. Communication of acceptance is complete —

(i) As against the Proposer: When it is put in the course of transmission to him, so as to be out of the power of the accepter. In case of acceptance through post, the contract is complete on the date when the letter of acceptance is posted. Whether or not the letter is received by the offerer is absolutely immaterial. The offer, however, becomes bound only when a property addressed and adequately stamped letter of acceptance is posted. The contract is completed when acceptance of offer is put in the course of transmission to the offerer.

(ii) As Against the Accepter: When it comes to the knowledge of the proposer (Section 4).

Is Silence Communication?

Silence on the part of the offeree cannot be construed as his acceptance. This was underlined in the popular case **Felthouse vs. Bindlay (1862)**.

It so happened that the plaintiff offered, by means of a letter, to purchase his nephew's horse. The letter said : "If I hear no more about the horse, I consider the horse as mine at £33.15s." To this letter no reply was sent. But the nephew told the defendant, his auctioneer, not to sell the horse as it was already sold to his uncle. The auctioneer, put up the horse for auction and sold it. The plaintiff sued the auctioneer on the ground that under the contract the horse had become his property and, therefore, defendant's unauthorized sale amounted to conversion. But the action failed since according to the court "It is clear that the nephew in his own mind intended the uncle to have his horse, but he had not communicated his intention to the uncle." Thus, nephew's silence did not entitle any right on the horse to the plaintiff.

The case is also an authority for two further propositions. One of them is that the acceptance must be communicated to the offerer himself or to the person he has authorized to receive the acceptance. Communication to a stranger, like the auctioneer in this case, will not do.

Secondly, an offerer cannot impose upon the offeree the burden of refusal. The offerer cannot say that if no answer is received within a certain time, the same shall be deemed to have been accepted.

Further, acceptance of offer must be communicated by the party who has the authority to accept the offer. This is made clear in the popular case **Powell vs. Lee (1908)**. The plaintiff was an applicant for the headmastership of a school. The managers passed a resolution appointing him, but the decision was not communicated to him. One of the members, however, in his individual capacity informed him. The managers cancelled their resolution and the plaintiff sued for breach of contract. Rejecting the action the court observed; "there must be notice of acceptance from the contracting party in some way. Information by an unauthorized person is as insufficient as over-hearing from behind the door."

When Communication is not Necessary?

In two cases communication of acceptance is not necessary, viz.:

1. When there is prescribed mode of acceptance and the offeree follows it.
2. When the offerer has acquiesced in a certain conduct on the part of the offeree as equivalent to acceptance.

Revocation of Acceptance Through Communication

When can acceptance be revoked? An acceptance may be revoked at any time before the communication of the acceptance is complete as against the accepter, but not afterwards (Section 5). Thus, the communication of revocation should reach earlier than the acceptance itself. What will be the result if they reach together? The answer is that the acceptance stands revoked.

Consideration may be understood as some value given in exchange for a promise.

5.9 CONSIDERATION

Consideration is one of the essentials of a valid contract. Section 25 of Indian Contract Act opens with the declaration that "an agreement made without consideration is void." Same view is held in English Law too. What is consideration? What are the rules regarding consideration? These and other related aspects require detailed discussion. This sub-chapter is devoted for the purpose.

Definition

In simple words consideration may be understood as some value given in exchange for a promise. In **Fazalladdin vs. Panchamam Das (1957)** the Calcutta High Court observed thus, "Consideration is the price of a promisee, a return or *quid pro quo*, something of value received by the promise as inducement of the promise."

Section 2(d) of the Indian Contract Act defines consideration as follows:

"When, at the desire of the promisor, the promisee or any other person has done or abstained from doing, or does or abstains from doing, or promises to do or to abstain from doing something, such act or abstinence or promise is called consideration for the promise."

"When, at the desire of the promisor, the promisee or any other person has done or abstained from doing, or does or abstains from doing, or promises to do or to abstain from doing something, such act or abstinence or promise is called consideration for the promise."

An analysis of the definition given in Section 2(d) reveals three important components of consideration:

(i) The act or abstinence should be done at the desire of the promisor.

(ii) The act or abstinence should be done by the promisee or any other person, and

(iii) The act, or abstinence has been already done or remains to be done.

Legal Rules as to Consideration

The nature of consideration can be made more clear by analyzing the rules or essentials of lawful consideration. The rules are analyzed in the paragraphs that follow (See Fig. 5.6).

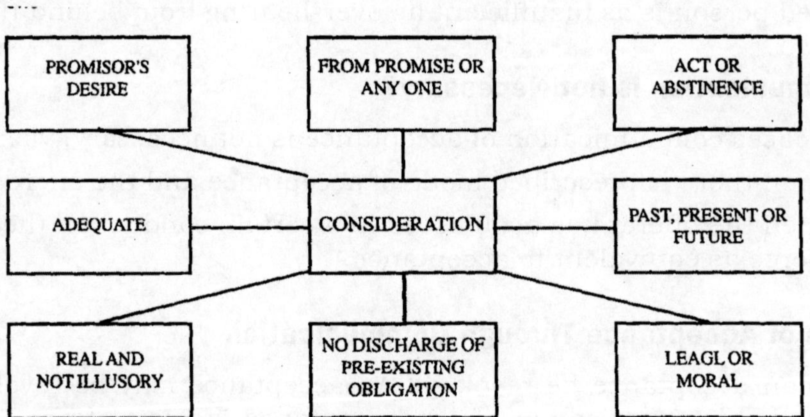

Fig. 5.6 Rules of Consideration

1. **Desire of the Promisor:** The act or abstinence must be done at the desire of the promisor. If is done at the instance of a third party or without the desire of the promisor, it is no consideration. The definition of consideration in Section 2(d) clearly emphasizes that an act or abstinence which is to be a consideration for the promise must be done or promised to be done in accordance with the desire of the promisor. In **Durga Prasad vs. Baldeo (1880)**: the plaintiff, on the order of the collector of a town, built at his own expense, certain shops in a bazaar. The shops came to be occupied by the defendants who, in consideration of the plaintiff having spent money in the construction, promised to pay him a commission on articles sold through their agency in the bazaar. The plaintiff sued for recovery of commission. Rejecting the action **Oldfield, J.** said : "The only ground for the making of the promise is the expense incurred by the plaintiff in establishing the Ganj; but it is clear that anything done in that way was not 'at the desire' of the defendants so as

to constitute consideration." The act was the result of the collector's order but not of the promise.

However, consideration need not to be to the benefit of the promisor. Even if an act done at the promisor's desire is of no personal significance or benefit to him, yet it will form a valid consideration. The decision of the Calcutta High Court in **Kedar Nath vs. Gorie Mohammed (1886)** is highly relevant in this connection.

It was thought advisable to erect a town hall at Howrah provided sufficient subscription could be mobilized for the purpose. To this end the Commissioner of Howrah municipality set out to work to obtain necessary funds by public subscription. The defendant was a subscriber to this fund for Rs. 100. He had signed for this amount in the subscription book. The plaintiff had, on the faith of the promise of the defendant, entered into a contract with a contractor for building the town hall. The defendant failed to pay the amount and contended that there was no consideration for his promise. The defendant was held liable to pay the amount as the act of the plaintiff in entering into contract with the contractors was done at the desire of the defendant (the promisor) so as to constitute consideration within the meaning of Section 2(d).

In the above case liability of the defendant arose because the promisee (the plaintiff) did something, i.e., entered into a contract. If follows, therefore, that where the promisee has done nothing, there is no consideration. This principle was underlined in *Abdul Aziz vs. Masum Ali* (1914). The defendant had promised to the secretary of a Mosque Committee to subscribe Rs. 500 to rebuild a mosque. The Committee had done nothing to repair and reconstruct the mosque. In a suit by the secretary of the Committee it was held that the defendant was not liable since, "the secretary of the committee to whom the promise was made suffered to determinent in getting the promise from the subscriber."

2. **Consideration May Move from the Promisee or any Other Person:** Consideration need not be furnished by the promisee only according to the Indian Contract Act, though the English Law consideration must move from promisee and promisee only. According to the Indian Contract Act, a promise is enforceable if there is some consideration or any other person. But the stranger to the consideration will be held to sue only if he is a party to the contract. The leading authority here is the decision of the Madras High Court in **Chinnaya vs. Ramaya 1882**.

An old lady, by deed of gift, made over certain landed property to the defendant, her daughter. By the terms of the deed, which was registered, it was stipulated that an annuity of Rs. 635 should be paid every year to the plaintiff, who was the sister of the old woman. The defendant on the same day executed in plaintiff's favour an agreement promising to give effect to the stipulation. The annuity was, however, not paid and the plaintiff sued to recover it. The reason advanced by the defendant for refusing to pay the annuity was that the promisee (the plaintiff) had not furnished any consideration. It was held the defendant was liable to pay the amount since the consideration was furnished by the old lady to her daughter. Consideration paid by a third party is a consideration, nevertheless.

But according to English Law, as pointed out above, consideration must come from promisee only. **Dunlop Pneumatic Tyre Co. Ltd., vs. Selffridge & Co. Ltd. (1915)** is the popular case to prove this principle. The defendants bought tyres from the plaintiffs on the condition that they (defendants) will not sell below company's sale price failing which the defendants will pay damages. The defendants sold the types to sub-dealer who sold them below the stipulated price. The plaintiffs sued for damages. The suit was rejected because the plaintiffs were strangers to the contract.

3. **Consideration May be an Act or Abstinence:** In the definition it was emphasized that consideration can be an act or abstinence. A person may promise to do something or not do something for a promise. To do or not to do something in return is consideration.

4. **Consideration may be past, present or future.**

   (a) **Past Consideration:** Past consideration represents the value or benefits given prior to the date of promise. For example, X renders some service to Y in January. In March Y promises to compensate X for the services rendered. The consideration of X is a past consideration.

   According to English Law past consideration is no consideration at all. But past consideration is valid according to the Indian Contract Act.

   (b) **Present Consideration:** Also called executed consideration, present consideration moves simultaneously with promise. In cash sale, for example, consideration is present or executed. For example, X receives Rs. 200 in return for which he promises to deliver goods to Y. The money X receives is present consideration for the promise he makes to deliver the goods.

   (c) **Future or Executory Consideration:** When consideration is to move at a future date, it is called future or executory consideration. For example, X promises to deliver certain goods to Y after a week. Y promises to pay the price after a fortnight. The promise of X is supported by the promise of Y. The consideration here is future or executory.

5. **Consideration Need not be Adequate:** Consideration need not be adequate nor equivalent to promise. What is important is that an agreement must be supported by consideration. Its adequacy or otherwise is the lookout of parties. The courts can hardly assume the role of settling what should be the appropriate consideration for a promise. This is the principle followed in English Law and the same is maintained in our country too. In **Devji Shivji vs. Karsandas Ramji (1954)** the transfer of the goods will and the whole of the assets of a business for a mere Rs. 1,000 has been upheld.

The Indian Contract Act further provides (Explanation 2 to Section 25) that an agreement to which the consent of the promisor is freely given is not void because the consideration is inadequate, but the inadequacy of the consideration may be taken into account by the court in determining the question whether the consent of the promisor was freely given. For example, A agrees to sell a horse worth Rs. 1,000 for Rs. 10. A denies that his consent to the agreement was freely given. The inadequacy of the consideration is a fact which the court should take into account in considering whether or not A's consent was freely given.

An agreement may be set aside provided the consideration (inadequate) is given under coercion, fraud, or mistake. **(R.B. Banerji vs. Commissioner of**

Income-Tax (1940). Here the agreement is invalidated not because of inadequacy of consideration but because of fraud or some other vitiating element. Otherwise, an agreement is held valid once a court is satisfied that a person has entered into a contract freely and with full knowledge of its purpose, not withstanding inadequate of consideration.

6. **Consideration Must be Real and Not Illusory:** Consideration must be real and be of some value in the eyes of law although it need not be adequate. It is not real when consideration is uncertain, illusory, or when it is physically or legally impossible to perform. The observation made by the Madras High Court is worth quoting in this context. In Kulasekra **Perumal vs. Pathakutty (1961)**, it was observed that "though the Indian Contract Act does not provide that consideration must be good or valuable to sustain a contract it has always been understood that consideration means something which is of some value in the eyes of law. It must be real and not illusory, whether adequate or not...so long as the consideration is not unreal it is sufficient if it be of slight value only."
7. **Discharging of a Pre-existing Obligation is no Consideration:** Consideration must be something more than what the promisee is already bound to do. A person may be bound to do something by law or by contract. Performance of a legal obligation is no consideration for a promise. This principle has been underlined in the popular case **Collins vs. Godefroy(1831).** X promised to pay, Y, who had received summons to appear at a trial in a civil suit, a certain sum being a compensation for the loss of time during his attendance. It was held that the promise was without consideration, for Y was under an obligation imposed by law to appear and give evidence.

This principle of English Law was adopted by the Madras High Court in **R. Sashannah Chetti vs. V.P. Ramaswami Chetti (1968)** even before the Indian Contract Act came into force, although the Act does not contain any provision on the point. The facts of the case are that the plaintiff had been served with summons requiring him to give evidence before a court of law. The defendant, who was a party to the case, gave him a promisory not promising to pay a sum of money for his trouble. The note was held to be void for want of consideration.

Another interesting case to prove the same point is **Ramachandra Chintaman vs. Kalu Raju (1877)**. K agreed to pay an additional sum to R if the latter succeeds in winning the case. K failed to pay the additional sum. R filed suit to recover the money. It was held that K was not liable to pay because R was already under an obligation to render his best services as a pleader.

8. **Consideration should not be Illegal or Immoral:** Consideration must not be illegal or immoral. Illegal or immoral consideration makes the agreement void.

Exceptions to the Rule "No Consideration No Contract"

To the general rule than an agreement without consideration is void. Section 25 lays down certain exceptions. Following are the exceptions and in all these case agreements without considerations are valid (see Fig. 5.7).

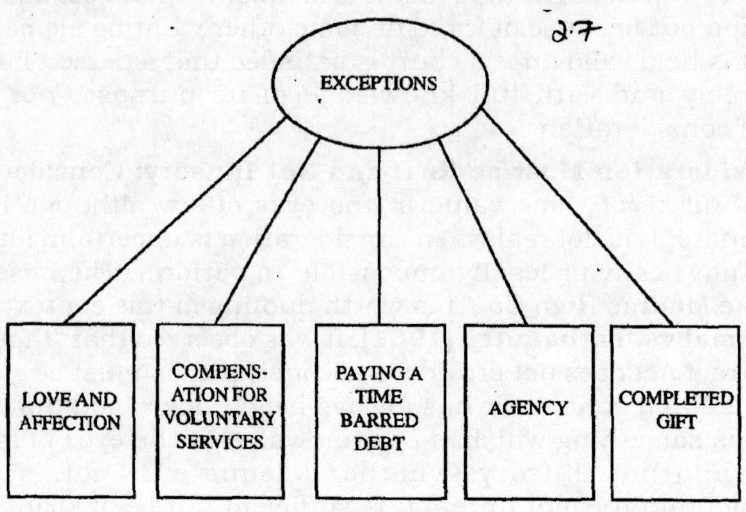

Fig. 5.7 Exceptions to Consideration

(i) An Agreement Made on Account of Natural Love and Affection: A written and registered agreement based on natural love and affection among near relatives is valid even without consideration. This is the essence of Section 25(1). To quote the relevant provision: "An agreement made without consideration is void unless it is expressed in writing and registered under the law for the time being in force for the registration of the documents and is made on account of natural love and affection between the parties standing in near relation to each other."

In **Rajlukhy Dabee vs. Bootnath Mookerji (1900)**, the defendant promised to pay his wife a fixed sum of money every month for her separate residence and maintenance. The agreement was contained in a registered document which mentioned certain quarrels and disagreements between the two. The suit by the plaintiff was rejected by the Calcutta High Court which held the view that the quarrels made the couple separate. There was, thus, no love or affection, between the parties.

Contrast this with another example where A writes to B, his son, wherein he promises to pay Rs. 10,000 to the latter without any consideration, but out of love. A is liable to pay to B Rs. 10,000.

(ii) Past voluntary Service: A promised to compensate wholly, or in part, a person who has already, voluntarily done something for the promisor is binding. In other words, a promise to pay for a past voluntary service is enforceable. For example, A writes to B, "at the risk of your life, you saved me from a serious motor accident. I promise to pay you Rs. 1,000." The agreement is valid.

In order to come under this exception, service should have been rendered voluntarily and also for the promisor. Thus, where services were rendered for a company not then in existence, a subsequent promise to pay for them will not make the contract valid **[Ahmedabad Jubilee S. & M.Co. vs Chotalal Chaganlal (1908)]**. But a promise made after attaining majority to pay for goods supplied to the promisor during minority is held valid **[Karan Chand vs. Basant Kaur (1911)]**.

(iii) Time-barred Debt: 'A' promised to pay a time-barred debt to Mr.'B' and that is enforceable by law. But the promise must be in writing and duly signed by the promisor or by his authorised agent. The promise may be to pay the whole or any part of the debt. The debt must be such "of which the creditor might have enforced payment but for the law for the limitation of suits." For example, A owed to B Rs. 5,000 but the debt is barred by limitation. A gives a letter to B promising to pay him Rs. 3,000 on account of debt. The agreement is valid.

(iv) Agency: "No consideration is necessary to create agency (Section 185).

(v) Completed Gift: According to explanation 1, Section 25 " Nothing in this section shall affect the validity, as between the donor and the donee, if any gift actually made." Thus, in the case of a gift actually made, not being an agreement to make a gift, no consideration is necessary.

5.10 CAPACITY TO CONTRACT

Legal Capacity to Contract

The term legal capacity refers to the status or attributes necessary for a person to have his or her acts legally allowed and recognised. Every individual is presumed to have legal capacity to make a contract until the contrary is proved. Among the classes, who may not have legal capacity to contract are minors, insane persons, convicts persons who are intoxicated or on drugs or aliens.

As was pointed in an earlier sub-chapter, one of the essentials of a valid contract is that the parties to the contract must be competent to contract. Competence has been defined in Section 11 thus: "Every person is competent to contract who is of the age of majority according to the law to which he is subject, and who is of sound mind, and is not disqualified from contracting by any law to which he is subject."

"Every person is competent to contract who is of the age of majority according to the law to which he is subject, and who is of sound mind, and is not disqualified from contracting by any law to which he is subject."

Going by the above definition the persons who are incompetent to contract are: (i) minors, (ii) persons of unsound mind, and (iii) persons disqualified by law to which they are subject.

Minors

A minor is a person who has not completed 18 years of age, but in the following two cases the person continues to be a minor upto 21 years of age:

(i) Where a guardian of a minor's person or property has been appointed, or

(ii) Where the superintendence or a minor's property is assumed by a Court of Wards.

Nature of Minor's Agreement

Section 10 requires that the parties to a contract must be competent and Section 11 declares that a minor is not competent. But neither section makes it clear whether, if a minor enters into an agreement, it would be voidable at his option or altogether void. These provisions had, therefore, quite naturally given rise to a controversy about the nature of a minor's agreement. The controversy was only resolved in 1903 by the Judicial Committee of the Privy Council in their well-known pronouncement in **Mohoribibi vs. Dharmodas Ghose**.

Ever since this decision it has been held that an agreement with a minor is 'absolutely void.' But in the modern circumstances of society it does not seem to be possible and much less desirable for law to adhere to the declaration that a minor's agreement is always 'absolutely void.' Minors are appearing in public life today more frequently than ever before. A minor has to travel, to get his dress tailored, or cleaned, to visit cinema halls and deposit his cycle at a stand. He has to deal with educational institutions and purchase many things for the facility of life and education. If, any one of these cases, the other party to the contract would brush aside the minor on the ground that the engagement is void, the legal protection against contractual liability would be too dear to minors. The earlier decisions have been modified and the position now is that if a guardian, on behalf of minor, enters into an agreement, it is enforceable. This was the opinion held in **Srikakulam Subramanyam vs. Kurra Subba Rao (1949)**. The facts of the case are:

In order to pay-off the promissory note and the mortgage debt of his father, the minor son and his mother sold a piece of land to the holders of the promissory note in satisfaction of the note and he was also to pay-off the mortgage debt. He paid-off the mortgage accordingly and the possession of the land was given over to him. Later the minor brought an action to recover back the land, the action was rejected on the ground that the sale of the land in question was valid as it was done by the mother for her minor son and on his behalf.

Effects of Minor's Agreements

The position of a minor as regards his agreements may be outlined as follows: (see Fig. 5.8).

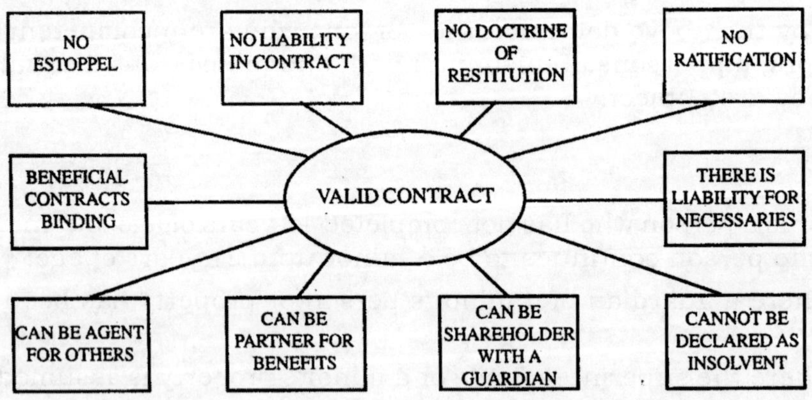

Fig. 5.8 Effects of Minor's Agreements

(i) No Estoppel Against Minor: Suppose that a minor, by misrepresenting his age, includes another to enter into an agreement with him, will he be prevented from disclosing his true age in a litigation resulting from the contract? In other words, will there be any estoppel against him? The answer is that there is no such estoppel against the minor. The reason is very simple. There can be no estoppel against a statute. One of the principles of the Law of Contract to protect persons below a statute. One of the principles of the Law of Contract to protect persons below age from contractual liability and naturally the doctrine of estoppel cannot be use to defeat the principle. The Bombay High Court overruled its earlier decisions, and held in **Gadigeppa Bhimappa Meti vs. Balangoxda Bhimangowda (1931)** that "where an infant represents frequently or otherwise that he is of age and thereby induces another to enter into a contract with him, in an action found in the contract, the infant is not estopped from setting up infancy."

(ii) No Liability in Contract or in Tort Arising out of Contract: As pointed out earlier, a minor's agreement is void. This was simply made clear in the popular case **Moharibibi vs. Dharmodas Ghose.** In this case, a minor mortgaged his house in favour of a moneylender to secure a loan of Rs. 20,000 out of which the mortgage (the money lender) paid the minor a sum of Rs. 8,000. Subsequently, the minor sued for setting aside the mortgage stating that he was still under-age when he executed the mortgage. It was held that the mortgage was void and, therefore, it was cancelled. Further, the moneylender's request for repayment of the sum advanced to the minor as part of the consideration for the mortgage was also not accepted.

With regard to a tort the position is: where the tort is directly connected with the contract and is the means of effecting it, the minor is not liable in tort. But where the tort is independent of the contract, the minor cannot escape his liability. Thus, where an infant borrowed a mare for riding only, he was held liable when he lent her to one of his friends who jumped and killed her. **(Burnard vs. Haggis (1863)).**

(iii) Doctrine of Restitution: If an infant acquires property or goods by misrepresenting his age, he can be compelled to restore it, but so long as the same is traceable in his possession. This is known as the equitable doctrine of restitution. Where the infant has sold the goods or converted them, he cannot be made to pay the value of the goods because that would amount to enforcing the void contract. Again, the doctrine of restitution is not applied where the infant has obtained cash instead of goods.

(iv) Ratification: As a minor's agreement is void there can be no question of its being ratified. Ratification refers to validation of an agreement previously entered into by a minor after his attainment of age of majority. As is well-known, minor's agreement is void *ab initio*, there can be no question of ratification of a void agreement. Of course, a fresh contract can be made on attaining majority. And a new contract will also require a fresh consideration.

(v) Beneficial Contracts: Agreements entered into by a minor for his or her benefit are valid and enforceable. Such contracts are: (a) contracts of marriage, and (b) contracts of apprenticeship.

(a) Contracts of Marriage: A contract for the marriage of a minor is *prima facie* for his or her benefit. It is customary amongst most of the communities in India for parents to arrange marriages between their minor children and the law has to adopt itself to the habits and customs of the people. It has, therefore, become well established that the contract of marriage can be enforced against the other contracting party at the instance of the minor, but the same cannot be enforced against the minor.

(b) Contracts of Apprenticeship: Contract of apprenticeship are also for the benefit of minors. The Indian Apprenticeship Act, 1850 provides for contracts in the nature of contracts for service which are binding on minors. But the act requires that the contracts be made by guardians on behalf of minors.

In English Law contracts of service and apprenticeship are treated as similar to contracts for necessaries. The popular case in this context is **Roberts vs. Gray (1913)**. The defendant, an infant, entered into a contract with the plaintiff, a famous billiard player, to go on a world tour with him. The plaintiff spent time and money in making arrangements for billiards matches but the defendant repudiated the contract before the tour began. The plaintiff succeeded in recovering damages to the tune of £1,500 for the breach of the contract. It was observed by the court that "to play in company with a noted billiard player like the plaintiff was instruction of the most valuable kind for an infant who wished to make billiard playing his occupation." Here the contract was held to be for necessaries as it was the infant's "good teaching or instruction whereby he may profit afterwards."

(vi) Liability for Necessaries: A minor is liable for necessaries supplied to him or his minor dependent by another person. This implies that a minor can make valid contract for necessaries. The law has provided the exception intentionally because if it were no so, it would be almost impossible for minors to live and feed their dependents, if any.

What is necessary for a minor? It depends on the fortune of the particular minor. Thus, article that may be considered necessaries for one may be mere conveniences for matters of taste for others. Whether an article is a necessary or not also depends upon the circumstances in which it is brought and the use for which it is put. For instance, articles purchased by a minor for his wedding may be deemed necessary, while under ordinary circumstances the same articles may not be considered so. Again, debt incurred for performing funeral obsequies of the father of a minor is necessary. So also expenses incurred on the defense of minor's property or liberty. Such expenses are considered necessaries which can be recovered from the minor's estate.

In order to render a minor's estate liable for necessaries two conditions must be satisfied: (1) the contract must be for goods reasonably necessary for his support in his station in life, and (2) he must not have already a sufficient supply of these necessaries.

(vii) Minor as an Agent: Although a minor is not entitled to employ an agent, he can be an agent himself for someone else. As an agent, he can represent the principal, and bind him for his acts done in the course of agency. But the minor is not responsible to the principal for his acts.

(viii) Minor as a Partner: According to the Partnership Act, 1932, a minor cannot make a contract of partnership though he may be admitted to its benefits with the consent of all the partners. A minor partner cannot be made personally liable for any obligation of the firm, but his share in the firm's property can be made liable.

(ix) Minor as a Shareholder: Since membership of a company arise on the basis of a contract, a minor cannot be a member of a company. However, he is not expressly forbidden by any law in force in India from holding shares in a company provided he is properly represented by a guardian who should act on his behalf. Even then, the minor does not incur any liability to pay the call money and he can always repudiate the contract even if he had fraudulently overestimated his age at the time of becoming a member, or his name appears inadvertently in the register of members.

(x) Insolvency: A minor cannot be declared insolvent as he is capable of entering into a valid contract.

Persons of Unsound Mind

An agreement with a person of unsound mind is like that of minor, is absolutely void. According to Section 12 "a person is said to have a sound mind for the purpose of making a contract if, at the time when he makes it, he is capable of understanding it and of forming a rational judgement as to its effects upon his interests." However, a person who is usually of unsound mind may make a contract when he is of sound mind. But a person who is usually of sound mind cannot make a contract when he is of unsound mind. For example, a patient in a lunatic asylum, who is at intervals of sound mind, may contract during those intervals.

"a person is said to have a sound mind for the purpose of making a contract if, at the time when he makes it, he is capable of understanding it and of forming a rational judgement as to its effects upon his interests."

Another example is that a sane man, who is delirious from fever, or who is so drunk that he cannot understand the terms of a contract or form a rational judgement as to its effect on his interests, cannot contract whilst such delirium or drunkenness lasts. A drunken person is treated in same category as a person of unsound mind.

Law relating to contractual capacity of persons of unsound mind in our country contrasts from English Law. The difference between the two is revealed in Table 5.1.

Table 5.1 Difference between Indian Law and English Law relating to Persons of Unsound Mind.

Indian Law	*English Law*
1. A person with unsound mind cannot enter into contract	1. A person with unsound mind is competent to contract
2. A contract with a person of unsound mind is absolutely void	2. Contract with a person of unsound mind is voidable at his option

Other Persons

As was explained above minors and persons of unsound are incompetent to contract. In the same category are included alien enemies, insolvents and convicts who are also incompetent to enter agreements.

Alien Enemy

An Alien enemy is a citizen of a foreign country which is at war with India. The status of an alien enemy with regard to contractual capacity depends on the timing of the contract in question. While the war is in progress the alien enemy can neither enter into a contract with an Indian subject nor can be sued in an Indian Court. He can do so only after obtaining a licence from the Central Government.

Contracts made before the war breaks out may be either suspended or dissolved. They will be dissolved if they are against public policy or if their performance would benefit the enemy. Others are suspended till the war ends and are revived provided they have not become time-barred under the law of limitation.

Insolvent

An insolvent cannot enter into a contract as his property vests in the hands of the Official Receiver or Assignee whom enters into contracts on behalf of the insolvent. This disqualification is removed when he is obsolved from insolvency.

Convict

A convict is incapable of entering into a valid agreement while undergoing imprisonment. He can, however, enter into a contract if he is lawfully at large under a licence called "ticket of leave." The disqualification comes to an end once the term of imprisonment expires or when the convict is acquitted.

5.11 FREE CONSENT

Free consent, as was pointed out earlier, is one of essentials of a valid contract. This sub-chapter is devoted to a detailed discussion of free consent.

Consent is said to exist when two or more persons agree upon the same thing in the same sense. To quote Section 13 "Two or more persons are said to consent when they agree upon the same thing in the same sense."

Consent is said to be free when it is not caused by coercion, undue influence, fraud, misrepresentation and mistake.

When the consent is obtained without coercion, undue influence, fraud, misrepresentation or mistake, it becomes free consent. To quote Section 14 consent is said to be free when it is not caused by:

1. Coercion, as defined in Section 15, or
2. Undue influence, as defined in Section 16, or
3. Fraud, as defined in Section 17, or
4. Misrepresentation, as defined in Section 18, or
5. Mistake, subject to the provisions of Sections 20, 21 and 22.

Where consent to an agreement is caused by coercion, undue influence, fraud, or misrepresentation, the agreement is a contract voidable at the option of the party whose consent was so caused. Where consent is caused by mistake, the agreement is void (see Fig. 5.9).

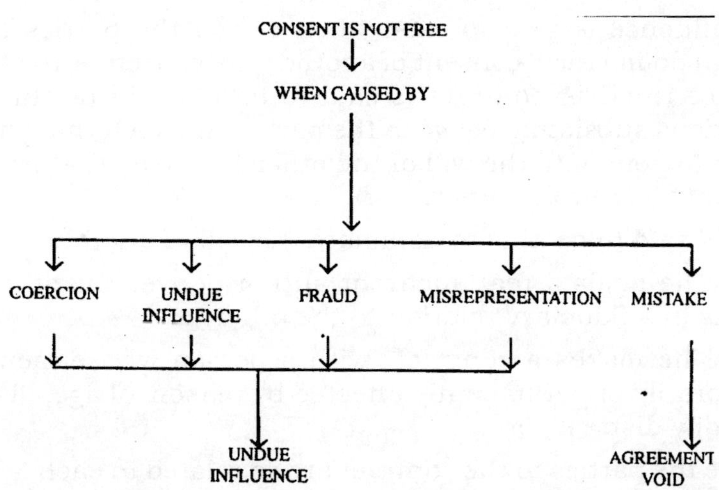

Fig. 5.9 Circumstances when Consent is not Free

Coercion

In simple terms, coercion or duress may be understood as threat or force used by one party against the other for making him enter into an agreement. According to Section 15 "coercion is the committing, or threatening to commit, any act forbidden by the Indian Penal Code, or the unlawful detaining, or threatening to detain, any property, to the prejudice or any person whatever, with the intention of causing any person to enter into agreement." The explanation to this section states that, "it is immaterial whether the Indian Penal Code is or is not in force in the place where the coercion is employed."

"Coercion is the committing, or threatening to commit, any act forbidden by the Indian Penal Code, or the unlawful detaining, or threatening to detain, any property, to the prejudice or any person whatever, with the intention of causing any person to enter into agreement."

Thus, consent is said to be caused by coercion when it is obtained by pressure exerted by either of the following techniques:

1. committing or threatening to commit any act forbidden by the Indian Penal Code; or
2. unlawfully detaining or threatening to detain any property.

And an agreement the consent to which is caused by coercion is voidable at the option of the party whose consent was so caused.

The leading case on this position is **Ranganayakamma vs. Alwar Setty (1889)**. In this case, a young Hindu girl of 13 years, who had just lost her husband, was forced to adopt a boy of their choice by her relatives who refused to remove the dead body of her husband unless she consented to the adoption. It was held that the adoption was not binding on her since her consent was not free but included by coercion in as much as any person who obstructed a dead body from being removed would be guilty of an offence as per the Indian Penal Code.

Another interesting case on the same point is **Chikkam Amiraju vs. Chikkam Seshamma (1917)**. In brief the particulars about the case are: by threat of suicide, a Hindu induced his wife and son to execute a release in favour of his brother in respect of certain properties which they claimed as their own. It was held that the threat of suicide amounted to coercion and the release was therefore voidable.

Undue Influence

" A contract is said to be induced by "undue influence" where the relations subsisting between the parties are such that one of the parties is in a position to dominate the will of the other and uses that position to obtain an unfair advantage over the other."

Undue influence is said to exist when one of the parties to the contract obtains, through dominance, consent of another party. Section 16 of the Act defines undue influence thus: "A contract is said to be induced by "undue influence" where the relations subsisting between the parties are such that one of the parties is in a position to dominate the will of the other and uses that position to obtain an unfair advantage over the other."

A person is said to be able to dominate the will of another:

(a) Where he holds a real apparent authority over the other, or where he stands in a fiduciary relation to the other; or

(b) Where he makes a contract with a person whose mental capacity is temporarily or permanently affected by reason of age, illness, or mental or bodily distress; or

(c) Where the parties to the contract are so related to each other than one of them is able to dominate the will of another.

Instances of undue influence are : Income-Tax Officer in relation to an assessee, magistrate and accused, spiritual adviser and his devotee, doctor and patient, parent or guardian and child, creditor and debtor, wife and husband, trustee and beneficiary, solicitor and client, and the like.

And as was pointed out earlier, when consent to an agreement is caused by undue influence, the contract is voidable at the option of the party whose consent was so caused.

A few leading cases are quoted below to make the meaning of undue influence more clear.

(i) Manu Singh vs. Umadat Pandey (1890): U, a spiritual guru, induced M, his devotee, to gift to him the whole of his property to secure benefits to his soul in the other world. M applied for setting aside the agreement. It was held that the agreement was improper as the consent under influence. Observed the Allahabad High Court: "Would any reasonable man, in full possession of his senses and not under unusual influence of some kind or the other, do such a thing?"

An English case of the same kind but contrasting judgement is **Alcard vs. Skinner (1887)**. The plaintiff was living with her mother in London. She was introduced to the defendant by a Parish priest Rev. Nihill. The defendant was the lady superior of the sisterhood of St. Mary at the Cross. The plaintiff also joined the sisterhood and became a sister. On becoming a sister, she took vows of obedience, poverty and chastity. In accordance with the vows of poverty, she made over to the sisterhood by a will, the whole of her property, valued at £8,500. Subsequently she became a Roman Catholic and left sisterhood. Later she used the defendant to recover the entire amount on the ground of undue influence. Rejecting the appeal, **Lindley L.J.** observed that, "There is no evidence that pressure was put upon her to enter upon the mode of life of which she adopted. She chose it as the best for herself, she devoted her life to it, heart and soul; she was to use her own expression, infatuated with the life and with the work. but though infatuated, there is no evidence to show that she was in such a state of mental imbecility as to justify the inference that she was unable to take care of herself or to manage her affairs....The result of the evidence convinces me that no pressure, except the inevitable pressure of the vows and rules, was brought to bear upon the plaintiff, that no deception was practiced upon her, that no unfair advantage was taken of her."

The learned judge felt that although the money was recoverable in principle owing to the fact she was not at liberty to consult any outsider without the leave of her superior, it was too late for the plaintiff (the plaintiff joined the sisterhood in 1868, left it in 1879, and sued for recovery of money in 1885) to invoke the assistance of the court. Her argument that she did not know of her rights earlier was not sustainable because "ignorance which is the result of deliberate choice is no ground for equitable relief."

(ii) Williams vs. Bavley (1866): A son forged his father's signature on several promissory notes and paid them into his bank account. When the truth came to light, the manager of the bank threatened prosecution of the son and "transportation" if a satisfactory solution were not found. To avert this threat, the father agreed to give an equitable mortgage to the bank on his property in return for the promissory notes. Subsequently the father sought to have this agreement cancelled on the ground that he was influenced by the threat. It was held that the agreement was voidable.

The above case underlines the point that there is active trust and confidence between the parties or the parties are not on equal footing and one of the parties takes unfair advantage of the situation.

In the case cited above, the court observed that the father agreed to give security for the promissory notes hoping it would relieve the son from the consequences of his criminal act, and the fears of the father were stimulated and operated on to an extent to deprive him of free agency, and to extort an agreement from him for the benefit of the bankers. There was inequality between the parties and one of them took unfair advantage of the situation of the other and used undue influence to force an agreement from him.

(iii) Ranee Annapurni vs. Swaminatha (1910) is another case where undue influence was proved to exist. The plaintiff, a poor Hindu widow, having no financial means, borrowed Rs. 1,500 from a moneylender and 100 per cent interest per annum for the purpose of enabling her to establish her right of maintenance. It was held that this was a clear case of undue influence and the Madras High Court allowed interest at a reduced rate of 24 per cent.

(iv) When one party can cause economic duress to the other there exists undue influence. This principle was underlined in the popular case **Llyods Bank v. Bundy (1975)**. A contractor borrowed a sum of money from a bank but could not repay it in time. The banker pressed for repayment or for security. He suggested that his father (the defendant) might mortgage the family's only residential house. The banker visited Bundy and obtained his signatures upon ready made papers. The contractor still could not pay and the banker sought to enforce the mortgage which might have meant throwing the family out from its only residence. Bundy sought to set aside the mortgage which was promptly done. Clearly the banker sought to take unfair advantage of Bundy whose bargaining position was considerably weak.

Burden of Proof

To set aside an agreement on the ground of undue influence, the plaintiff has to prove two main points. First, he must show that the other party was in a position to dominate his will, and second, the other party actually used his influence to obtain the plaintiff's consent to the contract. The law says that (a) not only must the defendant have a dominant position but, (b) he must use it.

Thus, in the cases cited above Manu Singh proved successfully that Umadat Pandey had enjoyed dominant position, being spiritual adviser as he was. He used the dominant position to obtain consent unduly from Manu Singh. But Allcard failed to prove the effect of undue influence exerted on her by Skinner, the defendant. Williams, on the other hand, proved the effect of undue influence brought on him by Bavley, the defendant. He was afraid of the prosecution of his son threatened by the bank manager. The fact that Ranee Annapurni was charged 100 per cent interest on a loan taken by her to establish her right to maintenance was enough to prove the existence of undue influence. It was not difficult for Annapurni to prove the undue influence nor it was difficult for the Madras High Court to slash interest rate to 24 per cent. But Lloyds Bank was not lucky. The fact that the Bank wanted to enforce the mortgage, the consent for which was obtained from Bundy under economic duress, turned the judgement against the Bank.

Distinction between Coercion and Undue Influence

The law draws distinction between coercion and undue influence. The distinction is shown in Table 5.2.

Table 5.2 Distinction between Coercion and Undue Influence

Coercion	*Undue Influence*
1. Consent is obatined under the theat of an offence. The person is forced to give his consent.	1. Consent is obtained by the dominant will of another. Consent is given in good belief, but under moral influence. Confidence is reposed, but betrayed.
2. Coercion is mainly of physical character. It involves use of physical or violent force.	2. Undue influence is mainly moral in character. It involves use of moral force or mental pressure.
3. Coercion attracts the provisions of of the Indian Penal Code. As such, the party exercising coercion exposes himself to criminal liability, besides an action on contract.	3. There is no criminal liability in the case of undue influence.

Misrepresentation

Sec. 18 of the Act defines misrepresentation thus: "Misrepresentation means and includes:

(i) the positive assertion, in a manner not warranted by the information of the person making it, of that which is not true, though he believes it to be true;

(ii) any breach of duty which, without any intent to deceive, gains an advantage to the person committing it, or any one claiming under him, by misleading another to his prejudice; or to the prejudice of any one claiming under him;

(iii) causing, however innocently, a party to an agreement, to make a mistake as to the substance of the thing which is the subject of the agreement."

To cut short, misrepresentation refers to misstatement of a fact material to a contract. As was pointed out in the beginning of this chapter, a contract the consent to which is induced by misrepresentation is voidable at the option of the deceived party.

Misrepresentation refers to misstatement of a fact material to a contract.

Continuing with Sec. 18, the following are the types of misrepresentation according to the section.

1. Unwarranted Statements

When a party to a contract positively asserts that a particular fact relating to the subject-matter of the agreement is true, when his information does not warrant it to be so, he is guilty of misrepresentation. In the **Oceanic Steam Navigation Co. v. Soonderdas Dharamsey (1890)**, the defendants chartered a ship from the plaintiffs. The plaintiffs stated that the ship was certainly not more than 2,800 tonnage register. In fact, the ship had never been in Bombay and it was unknown to the plaintiffs. She turned out to be of the registered tonnage of more than 3,000 tonnes. This was a clear case of misrepresentation and the defendants, were therefore, entitled to avoid the charter-party.

2. Breach of Duty

When a person commits a breach of duty without any intention to deceive the other party, and thereby gains an advantage to himself to the prejudice of the other party, the person committing the breach of duty is said to be guilty of misrepresentation. In other words, misrepresentation includes committing any breach of duty, by which the person committing it gains an advantage to the prejudice of another. There is no intent to deceive but the party representing commits a breach off duty which he owes to the other by making a negligent statement whereby the party represented is misled to his prejudice. The party representing gains an advantage.

As is well-known, there exists a duty between buyer and seller, debtor and creditor, insurer and insured, banker and customer, and landlord and tenant. Breach of duty by one party in such a relationship by making an untrue statement would definitely prejudice the other party if he acts upon it and causes gain to the party making such representation. The contract is avoidable at the option of the prejudiced party.

A popular case to be quoted in this context is the **Oriental Banking Corporation vs. John Fleming (1989)**. The plaintiff, having no time to read the contents of a deed, signed it as he was given the impression by the defendant that it contained nothing but formal matters already settled between them. The deed, however, contained a release in favor of the defendants. The plaintiff was allowed to set aside the deed. The court observed, "The defendant was under no obligation, legally or morally to communicate the contents of the deed. But the plaintiff placed confidence. It then became his duty to state fully without concealment, all that was essential to a knowledge of the contents of a document."

3. Inducing Mistake about Subject-matter

If the party to an agreement induces the other party, although innocently, to commit a mistake as to the nature or quality of the subject-matter of the agreement, he becomes guilty of misrepresentation. The subject-matter of every agreement is supposed by the parties to possess certain value or quality. If one of the parties leads the other, however innocently, to make a mistake as to the nature or quality of the subject-matter, there is misrepresentation, **Jonson vs. Crowe (1874)** is a case in the context. The defendant agreed to sell and deliver a boiler to the plaintiff at Rajghat. At the time of entering into the contract, the plaintiff made the representation that there was a road all the way to carry the boiler. The representation was innocent. In fact there was a suspension bridge on the way but the bridge was not strong enough to bear the weight of the boiler. When the defendant came to know of the fact, he abstained from delivering the boiler. In a suit by the plaintiff, it was held that the agreement was voidable at the option of the defendant.

Misrepresentation may also arise from suppression of vital facts. Suppression of a fact may amount to breach of duty or inducing the other party to commit a mistake about the subject-matter of the contract. For instance, the prospectus of a company, in **R.V. Kylsant (1932)** stated that the company was paying dividends regularly implying that it was making profits continuously. But the truth was that the company was in red for several years and dividends were paid out of war times accumulated profits. Concealment of this information was as clear as misrepresentation.

Fraud means and includes any of the following acts done with "intend to deceive" or to induce a person to enter into a contract.

Fraud is intentional or deliberate misrepresentation of facts. According to Section 17, "Frauds means and includes any of the following acts done with "intend to deceive" or to induce a person to enter into a contract."

1. The suggestions that a fact is true when it is not true and the person making the suggestion does not believe it to be true;
2. Active concealment of a fact by a person who has knowledge or belief of the fact;
3. Promise made without any intention of performing it;
4. Any other act fitted any intention of performing it;
5. Any such act or commission as the law specifically declares to be fraudulent.

Essential Elements of Fraud

An act becomes a fraud when it has the following components: (See Fig. 5.10).

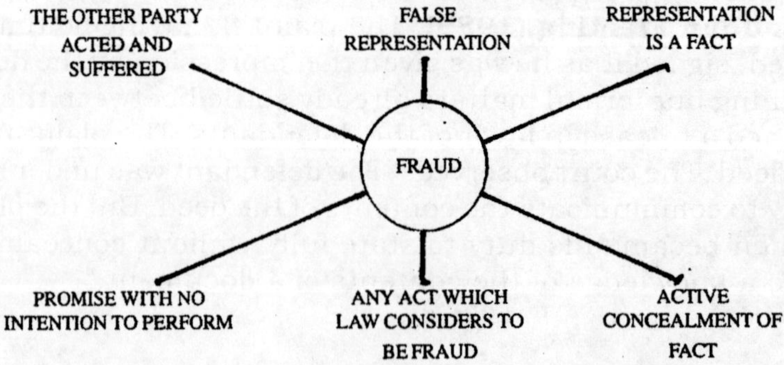

Fig. 5.10 Characteristics of Fraud

(i) There must be a representation or assertion and it must be false.
(ii) The representation must relate to a fact.
(iii) There must be active concealment of a fact of which the party has the knowledge and duty to disclose.
(iv) There must be a promise without any intention of performing it.
(v) Any act or omission which the law refers it to be fraudulent or fitted to deceive which is done with obvious intention to commit fraud.
(vi) The other party must have acted upon the false representation, and must have been deceived and must have suffered loss or damage.

The contract, the consent for which has been obtained by fraud, is voidable at the option of the party whose consent was so caused.

A leading case in this context is **Derry vs. Peek (1889)**. In this case, the company's prospectus contained a representation that the company has been authorized by a special Act of parliament to run trams by steam or mechanical power. The authority to use stream was, in fact subject to the approval of the Board of Trade, but no mention was made of this. The board refused consented consequently the company was wound up. The plaintiff, having bought some shares, sued the directors for the fraud. But the directors were not held liable as they were not held guilty of fraud. They honestly believed that once the parliament had authorized the steam the consent of the Board would automatically come forward. There was a false representation but was done believing it to be true. If representation was made deliberately, it would have amounted to fraud.

Another interesting case is the **Reese River Silver Mining Co. vs. Smith (1869)**. In this, a company issued prospectus giving false information about the unbounded wealth of Nevada. A shareholder, who has taken shares on the faith of the prospectus, wanted to avoid the contract. It was held that the shareholder could do it as the false representation in the prospectus amounted to fraud.

Is Silence Fraud?

The answer is not always. A contracting party is under no obligation to disclose the whole truth about the subject-matter to the other party. A trader is, therefore, justified in keeping silent about the change in prices. A seller who puts forth an unsound horse for sale, but says nothing about the quality, commits a fraud. Similarly, if a student does not disclose details about attendance shortage in his application though he knew it, he cannot be stopped from appearing examination. No fraud was committed by the student by not disclosing the attendance shortage. It was the duty of the University to scrutinize forms and call for explanation in case of doubts. **(Sri Krishna vs. Kurukshetra University, 1976)**.

1. **But silence cannot go too far.** It amounts to fraud in certain cases. One such case is when the party keeping silence under duty to speak. Duty to speak arises when one party responses, and the other accepts, confidence. A father selling a horse to his son, for example, has the duty to tell his son whether the horse was of unsound mind, because the son reposes confidence in his father. Duty to speak also arises when one party is utterly without any means of discovering the truth and has to depend on the good sense of the other party. In case of insurance, for example, there is no way for the insurance company to obtain full details about the life of assured. It is the duty of the assured to put the insurer

in possession of all material facts affecting the risk covered. Failure to do so amounts to a fraud, notwithstanding the certificate issued by the medical officer of the insurance corporation to the effect that the health of assured is good **(P. Sarojam vs. LIC, 1986)**. It is for this reason that the contract of insurance is called the contract of absolute good faith.

2. **Silence amounts to fraud when there is a change of circumstances.** Sometimes a representation is true when made, but may become false when acted upon by the other party, this may happen because of changed circumstances. In such cases, it is the duty of the person who made the representation to communicate the change of circumstances. In **Rajagopala Iyer vs. The South Indian Rubber Works (1942)**, a company's prospectus represented that certain persons would be directors of the company. This was true. But before the allotment took place, there were changes in the board, some directors having retired. The allotee was allowed to avoid the allotment as the change was not communicated to him in time.
3. **Finally, silence amounts to fraud when a person voluntarily makes a statement but stops half way through.** In other words, the person has disclosed only half truth. Having committed himself to disclose, he has a duty to speak out the remaining truth. Failure to do so amounts to fraud. As is wellknown, "half truth is not better than a down right falsehood."

5.12 MISREPRESENTATION AND FRAUD COMPARED

There are similarities and differences between misrepresentation and fraud. They are shown in Table. 5.3.

Mistake

An erroneous belief about something is called 'mistake.'

An erroneous belief about something is called 'mistake.' Consent caused by mistake is not free. Mistake is of various types (see Fig. 5.11).

Mistake of Law

Mistake of Law in Force in India: A contract extended into an erroneous belief as to a law is force in India is valid contract and cannot be avoided. This is based on the famous principle, "ignorance of law is no excuse."

Table 5.3 Fraud and Misrepresentation Compared and Contrasted

A. Similarities

1. Both fraud and misrepresentation render contract void.
2. There is false representation in both.
3. Consent should have been caused by fraud or misrepresentation.

B. Dissimilarities

Misrepresentation	*Fraud*
1. Person making the false statement honestly believes it to be true.	1. Person making the false statement believes it to be false, yet deliberately makes the statement.
2. There is no intention to deceive the other party.	2. There is intention to deceive the other party.

3. Contract is voidable at the option of the party whose consent was caused by misrepresentation.	3. Voidable and gives rise to an independent action in tort for damages.
4. Aggrieved party cannot avoid the contract if he had the means to discover the truth with ordinary diligence.	4. Except in fraud by silence, the contract is voidable even though the aggrieved party had the means of discovering the truth with ordinary diligence.

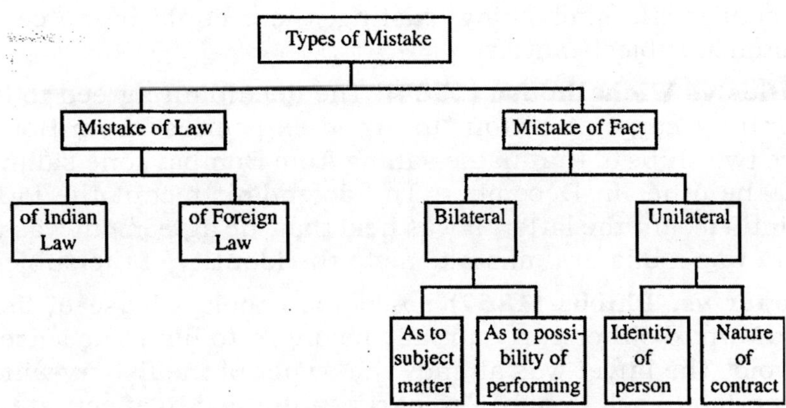

Fig. 5.11 Classification of Mistakes

Mistake of Fact

Mistake of fact may be (a) bilateral mistake, or (b) unilateral mistake as to a matter of fact essential to the contract.

a) Bilateral Mistake: Here both the parties to an agreement are under a mistake as to a matter of fact essential to the contract. The contract is void.

Examples

P, a widow, thinks that she has lost occupancy rights on account of her remarriage and as such agrees to hire the same land at enhanced rate from S, her Zamindar. The widow cannot avoid the new contract as is a mistake as to law of her own country.

Mistake of Law not in force in India: Mistake of law of a foreign country vitiates the contract. The contract becomes void. Mistake of law not in force in India is treated as a mistake of fact.

5.13 VARIATIONS OF BILATERAL MISTAKES

The various cases of bilateral mistakes are explained below:

Bilateral mistake is one where both the parties to an agreement are under a mistake relating to the subject-matter, the contract is void (Galloway vs. Galloway). Mistake relating to the subject-matter may be about (i) its non-existence, (ii) identity, (iii) title, (iv) quantity, (v) quality, (vi) price, or (vii) performance. The following examples underline the principles:

(i) Couturier vs. Hastie (1856): The defendant was employed to sell the plaintiff's cargo which was on voyage. After the defendant had sold the cargo to a third person, it was discovered that the cargo having been damaged by bad weather, had been sold at an intermediate port. The buyer repudiated the contract and the defendant, being a delcredere agent was sued for the price. But he was not held liable. It was observed that, "what the parties contemplated, those who bought and those who sold, was that there was an existing something to be sold and bought. ... The contract plainly imparts that there was something which was to be sold and was to be sold at the time of contract, and something to be purchased. No such thing existing, there could be no contract" (non-existence subject-matter).

(ii) Raffles vs Wichelhouse (1864): The defendant agreed to buy from the plaintiff a cargo of cotton "to arrive ex-peerless from Bombay." There were two ships of that name sailing from Bombay, one sailing in October and the other in December. The defendant meant the former but the plaintiff meant the latter. It was held that the agreement was void because there was a bilateral mistake as to the identity of the subject-matter.

(iii) Cooper vs. Phibbs (1867) : A person took a lease of fishery which, unknown to either party already belonged to him. The lease was held to be void. The buyer was already the owner of the fishery which the seller purported to sell to him. The parties intended to effectuate a transfer of ownership (title), which was held to be impossible.

(iv) Sheikh Bros. Ltd. vs. Ochener (1957): The appellant company, the lessor of the forest in Kenya, granted a license to the respondent to cut, process and manufacture all sisal growing in the forest. The respondent, in return, undertook to manufacture and deliver to the appellant 50 tons of sisal fibre per month. But it turned out that the leaf potential of the sisal area was of sufficient to permit the manufacture of the stipulated quantity and the respondent was sued for the breach. The agreement was held to be void. Bilateral mistake as to the quantity of the subject-matter rendered the agreement void.

(v) Bell vs. Lever Bros. (1932) : Lever Bros. appointed one Bell as a managing director for five years on an annual salary of 8,000 to manage one of their subsidiaries in Africa. Much before the expiry of this term his services of this term had to be dispensed with on account of the merger of the subsidiary with a third company. Bell agreed to retire on a compensation of 30,000. After this sum was paid, it was discovered that during his term of service, Bell had made secret profits and was, therefore guilty of breach of duty which entitled the company to dismiss him without paying compensation. The company, therefore, claimed the return of the money on the ground *inter alia* that it was paid under a mutual mistake of fact. But the action of the company failed.

In **Nicholson and Venn vs. Smith Marriott (1947)**, table napkins were sold at an auction by a description "with the crest of Charbles I and the authentic property of that monarch." In fact the napkins were Georgian. The agreement was held to be void.

Both the cases, viz., **Bell vs. Lever Bros**. and **Nicholson and Venn vs. Smith Marriott** relate to the mistake of quality regarding the subject-matter. In the former, the mistake was unilateral and, therefore, the contract was held valid. In the latter, the mistake was bilateral and this rendered the agreement void.

(vi) Webster vs. Cecil (1861): The defendant, who had rejected an offer from the Plaintiff to buy several plots of land for 2,000 made an offer to sell the plots for £1,250. Immediately after making the offer, the defendant discovered that there was a mistake in adding up the prices of the plots. The figure should have been 2,250 instead of 1,250. He informed the plaintiff of the mistake without delay, but by then, the plaintiff had accepted the offer, although he knew that his own earlier offer for 2,000 had been refused. The plaintiff filed a suit for performance of the contract which was rejected by the court. There was mutual mistake of price relating to the subject-matter of the agreement.

(vii) Griffith vs. Brymer (1903): A contract for the hire of a room for witnessing the coronation procession of Edward VII, made in ignorance of both the parties that the procession had already been cancelled, was held void on the ground of impossibility of performance.

(b) Unilateral Mistake: Unilateral mistake is the mistake of one of the parties to a contract as to its subject-matter. Unlike bilateral mistake, unilateral mistake does not cause the agreement to be void. Section 22 of the Act lays down that, "A contract is not voidable merely because it was caused by one of the parties to it being under a mistake as to a matter of fact."

Smith vs. Hughes (1871), the defendant wanted to buy old oats for his horses. The plaintiff showed him the sample of the oats he had, but said nothing about their age. The defendant kept the sample for 24 hours and then packed an order for the oats. After a portion of them as delivered to him he found that they were new and, therefore, rejected them on the ground that he was mistaken about their quality. But the court felt that the defendant could not avoid the contract.

Similarly, in **Singh vs. Union of India (1970)**, the Government sold, by auction, the right of fishery and the plaintiff offered the highest bid under the impression that the right was sold for three years, when in fact it was for one year only. The plaintiff could not avoid the contract because of unilateral mistake caused by his own negligence. He should have ascertained the tenure of fishery before bidding at the auction.

5.14 LEGALITY OF OBJECT

Legality of object is yet another requirement of a valid agreement. A contract the object of which is opposed to the law of the land may be either unlawful or simply void, depending upon the provision of the law to which it is opposed. Unlawful agreements are discussed here. The discussion of void agreements follows in the latter section in third sub-chapter.

A contract the object of which is opposed to the law of the land may be either unlawful or simply void, depending upon the provision of the law to which it is opposed.

5.15 UNLAWFUL AGREEMENTS

According to Section 23 certain considerations and objects are declared unlawful. The consideration or object of an agreement is lawful, unless:

— it is forbidden by law;
— is of such nature that, if permitted, it would defeat the provisions of any law;
— is fraudulent;
— involves injury to the person or property of another, or
— the court regards it as immoral or opposed to public policy (see Fig. 5.12).

In each of these cases the consideration or object of an agreement is said to be unlawful. And every agreement of which the object or consideration is unlawful is void.

The section covers the illegality of both the object of the contract and the consideration for it. In some cases both "object" and "consideration" may be the same, but they are usually distinct. The word "object" means purpose or design. The word "consideration", on the other had, refers to the benefit accruing to each party in a contract. In some cases consideration for an agreement may be lawful but the purpose or object for which the agreement was entered into may be unlawful. For example, if money is borrowed for the purpose of the marriage of a minor, consideration for the contract is loan which is lawful, but the object of marriage of a minor is unlawful. Such an agreement would be void. Thus, to render an agreement valid both object and consideration must be lawful, otherwise the contract is void.

5.16 ILLEGAL CONTRACTS

1. Forbidden by Law

As stated above, the object or consideration becomes unlawful when it is forbidden by law. An agreement the consideration or object of which is unlawful is void. "Law" in this connection means the law for the time being in force in India and, therefore, includes Hindu and Mohammedan Laws and also principles of unwritten law.

Examples: (i) A promises B to drop a prosecution which he has instituted against B for robbery, and B promises to restore the value of things taken. The agreement is void, as the object is unlawful.

(i) A promises to obtain for B an employment in the public service and B promises to pay Rs. 1000 to A. The agreement is void, as its consideration is unlawful.

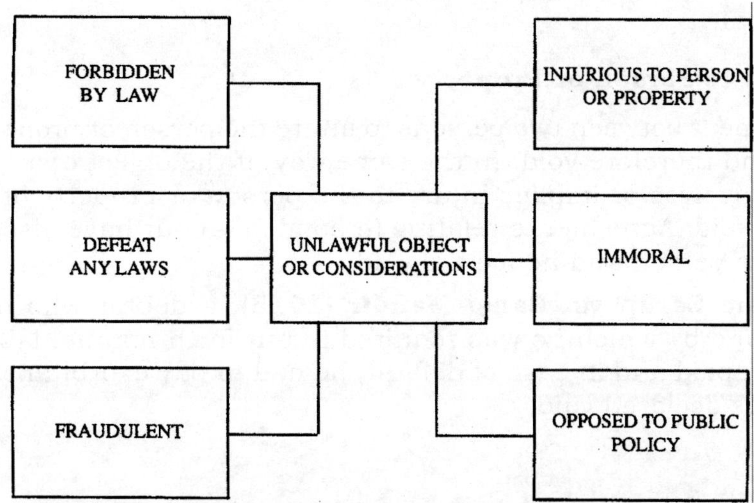

Fig. 5.12 Unlawful Objects of Consideration

(ii) In **Nandlal vs. Thomas J. Williams** the plaintiff was licensed under an Excise Act to work a liquor shop. The Act forbade the sale, transfer or sublease of the licence of the creation of a partnership to run the shop. The partnership was held void as it would defeat the policy of the law if unapproved persons could find their way into working liquor shop.

2. Defeat any Law

Sometimes the consideration for an agreement may not be directly forbidden by law, but if permitted, it might defeat the provisions of any law. Such agreement is also void. A popular case in this context is the **Fateh Singh vs. Sanwal Singh (1878).** An accused is required under the Criminal Procedure Code to furnish a surety in the sum of five thousand rupees for his good behaviour. He deposits the sum with the defendant and persuades him to become surety. After the period of suretyship is over the accused sues the defendant for the amount. The Allahabad High Court held the agreement to be void and the amount irrecoverable.

Similarly, in **Chandra Sreenivasa Rao vs K.R.R. Mohan Rao (1952)**, the Madras High Court held the view that the amount advanced under a promissory note for the purpose of celebrating a marriage contrary to the provisions of the Child Marriage Restraint Act, 1929, could not be recovered since the purpose of borrowing was of such a nature that, if permitted, would defeat the provisions of the Child Marriage Restraint Act.

3. Fraudulent

An agreement made for a fraudulent purpose is void. Where the parties agree to impose a fraud on a third person, their agreement is unlawful. Agreement to defraud creditors, or to give fraudulent preference, to a creditor or to defraud revenue authorities, or investors in a company are illegal.

Examples: (i) A, B, and C enter into an agreement for division among them of gains acquired by them, by fraud. The agreement is void, as its object is unlawful.

(ii) A being agent for a landed proprietor, agrees for money, without the knowledge of his principal, to obtain for B a lease of land belonging to his principal.

The agreement between A and B is void, as it implies fraud by concealment by A, on his principal.

4. Injurious to Person or Property

An agreement between two persons to injure the person or property of another is unlawful and therefore void. In the same way, if the object of an agreement is such that is involves or implies injury to the person or property of another, the agreement is void. Agreements relating to bonded labour have also been held to be injurious to person and hence are void.

In **Ram Sarup vs. Bansi Mandir (1915)**, a debtor who owed Rs. 100 executed a bond by which he was required to put forth manual labour until the amount was repaid and in case of default, he had to pay exorbitant interest. The agreement was declared void.

5. Immoral

Every agreement the object or consideration of which is immoral is void. Clearly the law does not allow an agreement tainted with immorality to be enforced. What is immoral is not made clear in the law and therefore if fell to the wisdom of the courts to decide, from time to time, what immorality meant. The attitude of the Courts has been based upon the premium placed by the society on the social Institution of Marriage and the concept that nothing should be done to spoil the relationship of a married couple. Thus, lending money to a lady with a promise to marry her after the death of her present husband or after she secures a divorce from him is immoral. In the same way a promise to marry by a married man to a married woman after the death of his first wife or after obtaining divorce from her is illegal.

Further, certain kinds of acts have been regarded as immoral since times immemorial and will perhaps always be so regarded. Dealings with prostitute come under this category. Thus, if articles are sold or something is hired to a prostitute for the purpose of enabling her to carry on her profession, neither the price of the articles sold not the rent of the thing hired can be recovered. Similarly, settlements in consideration of concubinage and agreements to pay money for future illicit cohabitation are considered to be immoral.

Public policy is very unruly horse and when once you get astride it, you never know where it will carry you.

An agreement is unlawful if the court regards it as opposed to public policy. What is public is not clearly defined anywhere and in the words of Justice Burrogh "public policy is very unruly horse and when once you get astride it, you never know where it will carry you."

However, in England the circumstances under which a contract can be struck down as one opposed to public policy are fairly well established. Thus, in England contract of marriage brokerage, the creation of perpetuity, a contract in restraint of trade, a gaming or wagering contract, or the assisting of the king's enemies are all unlawfulness on the ground of public policy:

In our country too the same view is held to be specific, in our country the following are held to be illegal as they are opposed to public policy.

(i) Trading with the enemy.

(ii) Inducing a public officer to act corruptly.

(iii) Interfering with the administration of justice.

(iv) Marriage brokerage contract agreement to procure the marriage of a person in consideration of a sum of money.

(v) Maintenance and champerty — agreements that tend to promote speculative litigation's.

(vi) Stifling prosecution — an agreement not to prosecute an offender.

(vii) Sale of seats in a public institution, e.g., a medical college **(N.V.P. Pandian vs. M.M. Roy (1979)**.

(viii) Consideration for the contract in the marriage expenses of minor girl.

5.17 VOID AGREEMENTS

An agreement not enforceable by law is said to be a void agreement. It is useful to make distinction between unlawful and void agreements. An unlawful or illegal agreement is one which is actually forbidden by law. A void agreement on the other hand, is not forbidden by law as in the case of a contract with a minor. But both illegal and void agreements are not enforceable. Thus, an illegal agreement is both unenforceable and forbidden but a void agreement is only unenforceable but not illegal.

The following is said to be void agreements (see Fig 5.13).

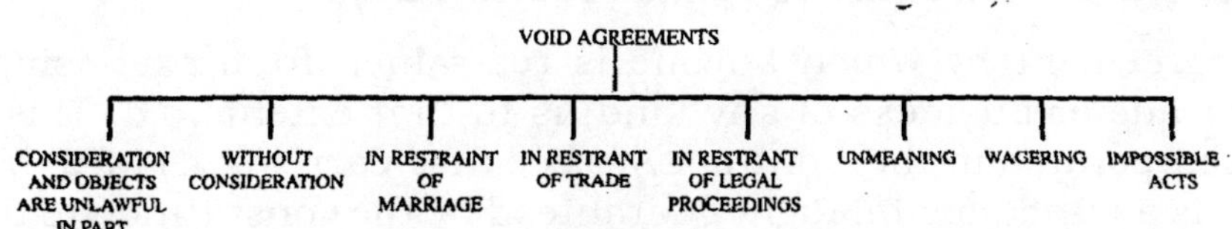

Fig. 5.13 Void Agreement

The other void agreements are those made by incompetent persons, agreements made under bilateral mistake of fact, and agreements of which consideration or object is unlawful. These were already explained in the earlier sub-chapter in this book. It is proposed to discuss here only those unenforceable agreements which are shown in Fig. 5.13.

1. Agreements in which a part of the consideration or Object is Unlawful (Section 24)

If any part of a single consideration for one or more objects or any one or any part of anyone of several considerations for a single object, is unlawful, the agreement is void. In other words, when a part of the consideration for an object or more than one object of an agreement is unlawful, the agreement is void. The whole of the agreement would be void unless unlawful portion can be separated without damaging the lawful portion.

In **Gopalrao vs. Kallappa (1901)**, a licence was granted to a person for sale of opium and ganja with a rider that he would not take any partner in the ganja business without the permission of the collector. Without such permission he admitted a partner into the whole business on receiving from him a fixed sum as his share of capital. Differences arose between them subsequently. The new entrant filed a case for dissolution and refund of his money. His claim was not allowed as it was impossible to separate the contract or to determine how much capital was advanced for the opium and how much for the ganja.

But if the legal part of an agreement is severable from illegal, the former would be valid. In **Poonoo Bibi vs. Fyaz Buksh (1874)**, a Muslim husband agreed, by a registered deed, to handover to his wife the totality of his earnings and not to do anything without her permission and if he did so, she would be at liberty to divorce him. The later part of the agreement was unlawful. It was separated from that part under which he promised to handover all earnings and this part was enforced binding him to pay only maintenance amount and not every bit that he might earn.

2. Agreements without Consideration (Section 25)

An agreement without consideration is void. This rule is subject to certain exceptions which were considered in earlier sub-chapter in this book.

3. Agreements in Restraint of Marriage (Section 26)

An agreement in restraint of marriage of any person, other than a minor, is void. It is the policy of law to discourage agreements which restraint freedom of marriage. Hence, this provision. In **Lowe vs. Peers (1768)**, P promised L only and none else and to pay a definite sum if he married someone else. P married X. It was held that L could not recover the sum as the agreement was in restrain of marriage and therefore not enforceable.

4. Agreements in Restraint of Trade (Section 27)

Every agreement by which anyone is restrained from exercising a lawful profession, trade or business of any kind, is to that extent void.

Every agreement by which anyone is restrained from exercising a lawful profession, trade or business of any kind, is to that extent void. This provision has been incorporated in the Contract Act because carrying a lawful business of one's choice is a Fundamental Right guaranteed by the constitution to the citizens of India. Courts in our country have been zealously guarding this right as a principle of common law. The principle of law is "public policy requires that every man shall be at liberty to work for himself, and shall not be at liberty to deprive himself or the state of his labour, skill or talent, by any contract that he enters into."

In **Madhub Chander vs. Rajcoomar (1874)**, the plaintiff and the defendant were rival shopkeepers in a locality in Calcutta. The defendant agreed to pay a sum of money to the plaintiff if he would close his business in that locality. The plaintiff did close the shop but the defendant refused to pay. It was held that the agreement was void.

Similarly, in **Nordenfelt vs. Maxim Nordenfelt Gun Co. (1894),** the appellant, Thorston Nordenfelt, a manufacturer and inventor of guns and ammunition had established a valuable business in England and Sweden. In 1886, he sold his business to the respondent company for £2,87,500 and entered into an agreement according to which he would not, (1) for 25 years, engage except on behalf of the company, either directly or indirectly in the trade or business of manufacture of quick firing guns, (2) or in any business competing or liable to compete in any way with that carried on by the company. He afterwards entered into an agreement with another manufacturer of guns and ammunition and the company brought an action to restrain him.

It was held that the first part of the agreement was valid being reasonably necessary for the protection of buyer's interest. But the second part of the covenant by which he was prohibited from competing with the company in any business that the company might carry on was held as unreasonable and therefore void. Lord Macnaghten laid down: The public have an interest in every person's carrying on his trade freely. So has the individual. All interference with individual liberty of action in trading, and all restraint of trade of themselves, if there is nothing more, are contrary to public policy and, therefore, void. That is the general rule. But there are exceptions. Restraints of trade...may be justified by the special circumstances of a particular case. The only justification is that the restriction should be reasonable — reasonable in reference to the interest of the parties and reasonable to the public interest. The restriction should be so framed and guarded as to afford adequate protection to the party in whose favour it is imposed while at the same time it is in no way injurious to the public.

Thus, both in our country and in England the general principle is the same, namely, that all restraints of trade whether partial or total, are void. The only difference is that in England a partial restraint of trade is valid if reasonable and not opposed to public interest. However, in our country even partial restraint is void, except if it falls in one of the exceptions that are explained below.

Exceptions

There are two kinds of exceptions to the principle of restraint of trade:

(1) exceptions created by statutes, and (2) exceptions arising from judicial interpretations of Section 27.

Statutory Exceptions

A. Sale of Goodwill: One who sells the goodwill of business may agree with the buyer to restrain from carrying on a similar business, within specified local limits so long as the buyer carries on a like business therein, provided that such limits appear reasonable to the court, regard being had to the nature of the business.

Thus, in the case of a sale of goodwill of business (a) the restraint on the seller can be in respect of carrying on a similar business within the specified local limits. (b) the restraint can be applied so long as the buyer carries on a similar business, and (c) the restraint is reasonable.

In **N.S. Golikari vs. Century Spinning and Manufacturing Co. Ltd. (1967)**, A, the owner of a motor bus entered into a contract with B carrying on a similar business plying buses between Pune and Mahabaleswar. To avoid competition, B, purchased the entire business along with its goodwill. It was agreed by A that he would not carry on similar business in the same place for three years. However, at the end of one year, 'A' started a similar business. It was held that the contract was valid as it was covered by the exception.

B. Partnership Act: The Partnership Act, 1932 provides certain exceptions with regard to the principle of restraint of trade. The trade exceptions are:

(i) A partner of a firm may be restrained from carrying on a similar business so long as he remains as a partner.

(ii) A partner may agree with his other partners that, on ceasing to be a partner, he will not carry on a similar business within a specified period and specified local limits.

(iii) Partners may, upon or in anticipation of the dissolution of the firm make an agreement that some or all of them will not carry on a business similar to that of the firm within specified local limits.

The above agreements, though in restraint of trade, are valid. But it is necessary that —

(a) the agreement should specify the local limits or the period of restraint, and

(b) the restriction imposed must be reasonable.

Judicial Interpretations

A. Trade Combinations: Traders and manufacturers in the same line of business normally form associations in order to regulate such aspects as price fixation, working hours, supply of materials, power supply and the like. These restrictions are valid even though they are in restraint of trade. Argument in support of such validity is that trade combinations are desirable in the interest of trade and for promotion of public interest. Trade combination seek, though restrictions, to carry on business in an organized way. Restrictions are imposed not to prevent the business but to carry it in an organized way. However, courts would not allow a restraint to be imposed disguised as trade regulations. Thus, an agreement between certain persons to carry on business with the members of their caste only, and an agreement to restrict the business of a sugar mill within a zone allotted to it, have been held void.

B. Exclusive Dealing Agreements: Exclusive dealing is a practice whereby a manufacturer or supplier of goods restrains his distributors from dealing in competitive goods and requires them to deal exclusively in the products manufactured and supplied by him. The distributor, in turn, may agree not to deal with the goods of any other manufacturer or supplier. Such agreements are held to be valid. Thus, an agreement by a manufacturer of dhotis to supply 1,36,000 pairs of certain description to the defendant and not to sell goods of that kind to any other person for a fixed period is valid. **[Carliles Nephews & Co. vs. Ricknanth Bucktermull (1882)].** Similarly, an agreement by a person to send all the mica produced by him to the plaintiffs, and not to send them to any other firm, nor to keep in stock is also valid **[Subha Naidu vs. Haji Badsha Sahib (1902)].** The negative stipulations of the type found in exclusive dealings do not have the effect of restraining the manufacturer. On the contrary, "he is encouraged to exercise his business because he is assured market for the products of his labour."

It may be noted that exclusive dealings invite regulatory measures under the Monopolies and Restrictive Trade Practices Act, particularly when they effect competition on the market.

C. Restraints on Employees: An agreement of service by which a person binds himself during the tenure of the agreement not to take service with anyone else, or directly or indirectly take part in any business in competition with the present employer is valid. The leading case in this context is the **Niranjan Shankar Golikari vs. Century Spinning & Manufacturing Co. Ltd. (1967).** A contract of employment for five years provided that the employee should not serve anywhere else during the five years even if he left the employment. This condition was imposed because the employee had access to technical information. The employee left the organization before the expiry of the period and joined another company for better remuneration. The former employer sought injunction and the court had no hesitation in granting it.

But an agreement to restrain an employee from competing with his employer after the termination of employment is void. In **Brahamaputra Tea Company vs. Scarth (1885),** it was held that an agreement restraining an employee from taking service or engaging in any similar business for a period of five years after termination of his services was void.

5. Restraint of Legal Proceedings (Section 28)

An agreement which prohibits a person from taking judicial proceedings, in respect of any right arising from a contract, is void. Similarly, any time limitation within which he may enforce his rights is also void.

An agreement which prohibits a person from taking judicial proceedings, in respect of any right arising from a contract, is void.

There are two exceptions to the rule laid down in Section 28. They are:

(a) a contract between two or more persons to refer to arbitration any dispute that may arise between them and to recover only the amount awarded in such arbitration in respect of the dispute so referred, and

(b) an agreement to refer to arbitration any question which has already arisen.

Agreement in restraint of legal proceedings is void.

Sec. 28 provides that any agreement which absolutely restricts a party to it from enforcing his rights under or in respect of any contract, by the usual legal proceedings in the ordinary tribunals or which limits the time within which he may thus enforce his rights is void to that extent.

This section recognizes well-known rule of English Law which prohibits an agreement ousting jurisdiction of the courts. Art. 32 of the Constitution guarantees that rights to move Supreme Court by appropriate proceedings for enforcement of rights conferred by

Part III — Fundamental Rights is guaranteed.

1. **Restriction on Jurisdiction of Courts:** Parties to an agreement may restrict the right of either party to sue in a particular court only. A mere selection of one of the two competent tribunals for disposal of disputes between the parties is not invalid. Thus is a contract between A & B of Mumbai and Bangalore respectively, it may be provided that all disputes between them should be decided by a court of Mumbai. Therefore in case B files a suit in Bangalore, A may successfully object to the jurisdiction of courts in Bangalore
2. **Restrictions on Time Limitation:** Though a term in an agreement absolutely restricting the time within which legal rights are to be enforced is not valid to that extent, law does not prohibit an agreement which does not absolutely limit the time for enforcing any rights, but only provides that failure to enforce them within a stipulated time shall operate as a release or forfeiture of such rights are outside the scope of the section and are therefore binding between the parties, **Baroda Spinning v/s Satynarayana 1914,** 38 Bombay 344.
3. **Agreement to Refer a Dispute to Arbitration:** Exception to Section 28 relates to a provision in an agreement to refer a dispute that may arise to arbitration. Such an "Arbitration Clause" is not affected. Similarly (Exception 2) where parties to a contract have agreed to refer a dispute that has already arisen to arbitration is not affected by any provision of

any law in force for the time being. Such an agreement shall not be rendered illegal.

Amendment of Section 28 (Agreement in restrain of legal proceedings, void).

A bill to amend the Indian Contract Act, 1872 was introduced in Parliament in the year 1996 for enactment of the Indian Contract (Amendment) Act, 1996. The Bill was passed by Rajya Sabha on 3-12-1996. By virtue of this amendment following part of Sec. 28 substituted:

"Every agreement, by which any party thereto is restricted absolutely from enforcing his rights under or in respect of any contract, by the usual legal proceedings in the ordinary tribunals, or which limits the time within which he may thus enforce his rights, is void to that extent."

Following text is substituted in place of the above by virtue of the amendment, namely:

"Every agreement, by which any party thereto is restricted absolutely from enforcing his rights under or in respect of any contract, by the usual legal proceedings in the ordinary tribunals, or which limits the time within which he may thus enforce his rights; or which extinguishes the rights of any party thereto, from any liability, under or in respect of any contract on the expiry of a specified period so as to restrict any party from enforcing his rights, is void to that extent."

All agreements, the meaning of which is not certain, or capable of being made certain, are void.

It is clear from the foregoing that a clause in a contract stating that failure of a party to enforce its rights within a shorter period, say 12 months. Stipulated in the contract shall be operated as release or forfeiture of such rights is also within the scope of this section and such stipulations are void to that extent.

Illustration

ABC Ltd., an Insurance Company granted a shopkeeper's insurance policy to Mr. D. As per the terms of insurance policy, Mr. D shall file suit or other legal proceedings in respect of any claim arising out of the policy within one year and failure to do so within stipulated period of 12 months will operate as a forfeiture of such rights and notwithstanding any other law or law of limitation, Mr. D is deemed to have released ABC Ltd., from any liability under the Act. Whether such a clause in a contract is valid? Such a provision in a contract was upheld earlier by courts in **Baroda Spinning v/s Satyanarayan 1914, 38 Bombay, 344** and by National Commission in **M/s Paras Textile v/s The New India Assurance Co. Ltd., 1993 (1) CPR 713 (NC)**. Amendment of Sec.28 has now changed the above legal positions. As the effect of the agreement is to discharge a party from liability on the expiry of specified period, the same is now void and the affected party is entitled to initiate usual legal proceedings in the court or ordinary tribunal.

6. Unmeaning of Uncertain Agreements (Section 29)

According to Section 29 all agreements, the meaning of which is not certain, or capable of being made certain, are void.

The reason is without certainty it is not possible for courts to give practical meaning to a contract. If the terms of the contract are not clear there is nothing that could been enforced. For example, in **Guthyng vs. Lynn (1831)**, a horse was bought for a certain price coupled with a promise to give 5 pound more if the horse proved lucky. The agreement was held to be void for want of certainty. The court has no machinery to determine what luck, bad or good, the horse had brought to the buyer. Uncertainty normally arises in agreements relating to sale of goods, particularly relating to price. Thus, where goods are sold, the price being payable subject to 'hire purchase terms or clause' or at such price as should be agreed upon between the parties, the agreement in each case was held to be void for uncertainty as to price.

7. Wagering Agreements (Section 30)

Section 30 of the Act lays down that agreements by way of wager are void, and no suit shall be brought for recovering anything alleged to be won on any wager, or entrusted to any person to abide by the result of any game or other uncertain event on which any wager is made.

A wager is an agreement between two parties by which one party has to pay money to another party on the happening or not happening of a future uncertain event. Besides uncertainty of event, a wager possesses other features. An agreement becomes a wager when it has the following features:

A wager is an agreement between two parties by which one party has to pay money to another party on the happening or not happening of a future uncertain event.

(a) Uncertain Event: As stated above, an agreement becomes a wager when it is based on the happening or not happening of a future event. A wager generally contemplates a future event, but it may relate to an event which has already happened in the past, but the parties are not aware of its result or the time of its happening.

(b) Mutual Chances of Gain or Loss: The second essential feature is that upon the happening of the contemplated event each party should stand to win or loose. If there are no such mutual chances of gain or loss, there is no wager.

(c) Neither Party to have Control Over the Event: The third essential feature is that neither party should have control over the happening of the event one way or the other. If one of the parties has the event in his own hands, the transactions lacks an essential ingredient of a wager.

(d) No Other Interest in the Event: Finally, neither party should have any interest in the happening of the event other than the sum of stake he will win or lose. If neither of the parties has any proprietary interest in the subject-matter of the agreement, the same ceases to be a wagering agreement, but becomes enforceable as a contract. It is on this basis that a wagering agreement is distinguished from a contract of insurance. Every contract of insurance requires, for its validity, the existence of insurable interest. An insurance effected without insurable interest is no more than a wagering agreement, and therefore, void. Insurable interest means the risk of loss to which the assured is likely to be exposed by the happening of the event assured against. In a wager, on the other hand, neither party is running any risk of loss out of the distinction between the two more clearly.

Table 5.4 Wagering and Insurance Contracts Distinguished

Insurance Agreements	*Wagering Agreements*
1. There is insurable interest.	1. There is no insurable interest.
2. Both parties have interest in the subject-matter.	2. Neither party has any interest in the happening or non-happening of an event.
3. These are valid contracts.	3. These are void agreements as they are opposed to public policy.
4. These are contracts of indemnity except life insurance contracts which are contingent contracts.	4. These are conditional contracts.
5. A contract is based on scientific and actuarial calculation of risks.	5. A wagering agreement is just a gamble.

Effects of Wagering Transactions

Coming to the wagering agreements, as stated above, these agreements are void. For example, in **Badridas Kothari vs Megharaj Kothari (1967),** two persons entered into wagering transactions in shares and one became indebted to another. A promissory note was executed for the payment of the debt. The note was held to be enforceable.

Exceptions

The following agreements are not held to be wagers:

(i) Horse Race: An agreement to contribute or subscribe towards any plate, prize or sum of money of five hundred rupees or more to be awarded to the winners of any horse race is a valid agreement and not a wager.

(ii) Crossword competitions: These competitions which involve the application of skill and in which an effort is made to select the best and most skilful competitor, are not wagers.

(iii) Share Market Transactions: Here there is a clear intention of give and take, and delivery of shares and bonds. Hence these are not wagers. If there is no such clear intention of give and take and if the parties are only intend to gamble on the rise or fall of share prices, the transactions become wagers.

Collateral Transactions

Though wagering agreements are void, agreements collateral, incidental or subsidiary to them are valid. It has been laid down by the Supreme Court, in **Gherulal Parekh vs. Mahadev Das (1959)** that the wager is not forbidden by law not withstanding the fact it is void and unenforceable. Hence, a wagering agreement is not unlawful under Section 23 of the Contact Act, and the transactions collateral to the main transaction are enforceable. Accordingly, an agent who pays and loses on wagering transactions can recover the amount from his principal. Similarly, a partner who has paid the loss on wagering transactions may recover proportionate indemnity from his co-partners.

8. Agreements to do Impossible Acts (Section 56)

Section 56 of the Act lays down an agreement to do an act impossible in itself is void. For example, if A agrees with B to discover treasure by magic, the agreement is void. Similarly, if A agrees with B to put life into a dead man, the agreement is void.

Sometimes the performance of a contract is quite possible when it is first entered into by parties. But some event susequently happens which renders its performance impossible or unlawful. In either case the contract becomes void. For example after making a contract of marriage one of the parties goes mad, or where a contract is made for the import of goods and the import is thereafter forbidden by a Government order or where the singer contracts to sing and becomes too ill to do so, thc agrccmcnt in each case becomes void.

DISCHARGE OF CONTRACT
(Completion of Contracts)

The rights and liabilities created by a contract subsist as long as the contract is in force. Once the contract is discharged the rights and liabilities cease to exist. A contract may be discharged in any of six ways: (i) by performance, (ii) by agreement, (iii) by impossibility, (iv) by bar of limitation, (v) by operation of law, and (vi) by breach of contract (see Fig.5.14).

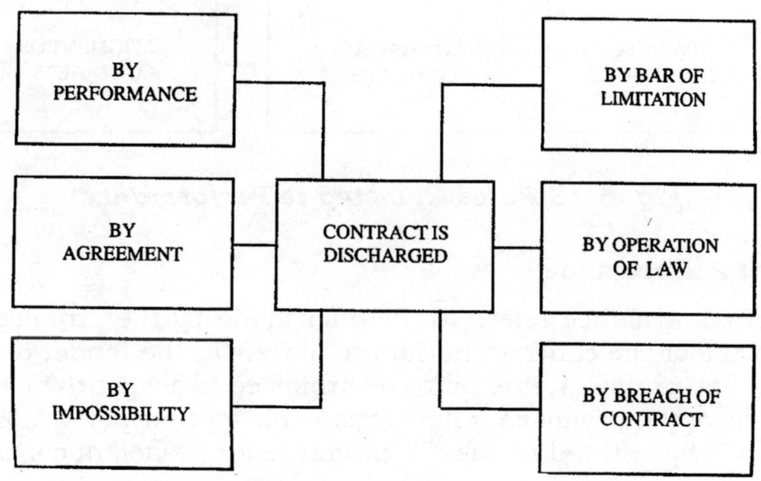

Fig. 5.14 Discharge of a Contract

The parties to a contract must either perform, or offer to perform their respective promises, unless such performance is dispensed with or executed under the provisions of this Act.

1. Performance of Contract

Section 37 lays down that the parties to a contract must either perform, or offer to perform their respective promises, unless such performance is dispensed with or executed under the provisions of this Act, or of any other law.

Promises bind the representatives of the promisor in case of the death of such promisors before performance, unless a contrary intention appears from the contract.

Illustrations

(a) A promises to deliver goods to B on a certain day on payment of Rs. 1000. A died before that day. A's representatives are bound to deliver the goods to B, and B is bound to pay Rs. 1000 to A's representatives.

(b) A promises to paint a picture for B by a certain day, at a certain price. A dies before the day. The contract cannot be enforced either by A's representatives or by B.

Rules Relating to Performance

Rules relating to performance of promises are summarized below (see Fig. 5.15):

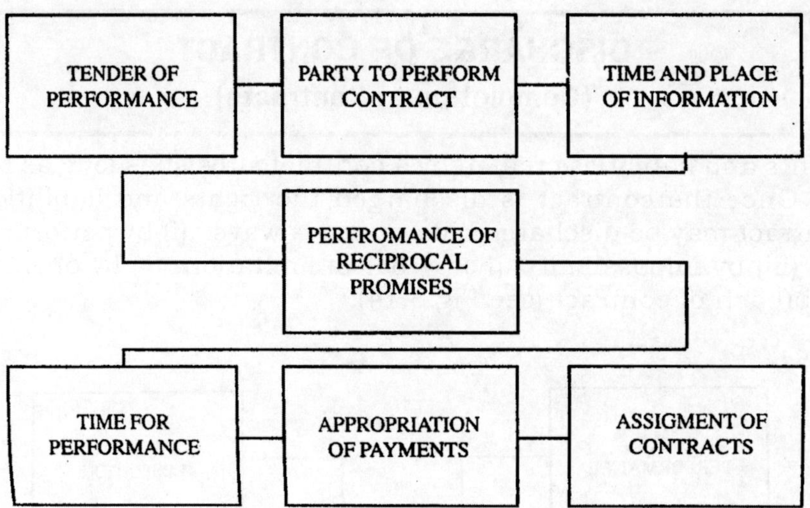

Fig. 5.15 Rules Relating to Performance

A. Tender of Performance

Tender of performance refers to the offer made by the promisor to perform his obligation under the contract to the promisee.

Tender of performance refers to the offer made by the promisor to perform his obligation under the contract to the promisee. On the tender of performance being made by the promisor, it is upto the promisee to accept the performance. If he does not accept the promisee is not responsible for non-performance. Besides, the promisor will be entitled to sue the promisee for breach of contract.

Thus, a tender of performance is equivalent to performance. This is the essence of Section 38.

Section 38 further stipulates that the tender of performance must fulfill the following situations:

(i) The tender of performance must be unconditional. It becomes conditional when it is not in accordance with the terms of the contract.

(ii) The tender must be made at a proper time and place, and under such circumstances that the person to whom it is made may have a reasonable opportunity to ascertain that the person by whom it is made is able and willing there and then to do the whole of what he is bound by his promise to do.

B. Party to Perform Contract

According to Section 40, if it appears from the nature of the case that it was the intention of the parties to any contract that any promise contained therein should be performed by the promisor himself, such promise must be performed by the promisor. This happens in cases where the use of the personal skill of the promisor is involved, for instance, the contract to paint, sing or marry, and contract of technical nature. In such cases the death of the promisor puts an end to the contract. The promise can neither be enforced against the leagel representatives, nor can they enforce the promise.

If the intention of the parties to a contract is not particular that the promisor alone should perform the promise, the promisor or his representatives may employ a competent person to perform the promise.

C. Time and Place of Performance

With regard to time and place of performance the rules are as follows:

(i) Time for Performance of Promise — no Application is to be Made and no Time is Specified: If a promisor has to perform his promise without application by the promisee, and no time for performance is specified, the engagement must be performed within a reasonable time (Section 46). What is reasonable time is, in each particular case, a question of fact. Unreasonably long delay cannot be regarded as reasonable. For example, where a person undertook to discharge the debt of another but no time for payment was fixed, it was held that the offer of payment after three years was too late.

(ii) Time and Place for Performance of Promise, where Time is Specified and no Application to be Made: When a promise is to be performed on a certain day, and the promisor has undertaken to perform it without application by the promisee, the promisor may perform it at any time during the usual hours of business on such day and at the place at which the promise ought to be performed (Section 47). In a promise, for example, to deliver goods at the buyer's warehouse, the tender of performance must be made at that place. The promisor must bring gods at that place during the usual business hours. If he brings the goods after the business hours and they are not received, it cannot be said that the promise has been performed. Where the day fixed for performance happens to be a public holiday, then under the Negotiable Instruments Act, the performance must be offered a day before. But in other cases much depends upon the usage of the particular trade. If the usage permits performance on the succeeding day, it will be reasonable to offer the performance on that day.

(iii) Application for performance on Certain Day to be at Proper Time and Place: When a promise is to be performed on a certain day, and the promisor has not undertaken to perform it without application from the promisee, it is the duty of the promisee to apply for performance at a proper place and within the usual hours of business (Section 48). The question what is proper place and time in each particular case, is the question of fact.

(iv) Place for Performance, where no Application to be Made and no Place Fixed for Performance: When a promise is to be performed without application by the promisee, and no place is fixed for the performance of it, it is the duty of the promisor to apply to the promisee to appoint a reasonable place for the performance of the promise, and to perform it at such place (Section 49). For example, A undertakes to deliver a thousand maunds of jute to B on a fixed day. A must apply to B to appoint a reasonable place for purpose of receiving it, and must deliver it to him to such place.

(v) Performance in Manner or at Time Prescribed or Sanctioned by Promise: the performance of any promise may be in any manner, or at any time which the promisee prescribes or sanctions (Section 50).

For example, B owes A Rs. 2,000. A desires B to pay the amount to A's account in a bank. B who has an account in the same Bank, orders the Bank to transfer the amount from his account to the credit of A. This was done by the bank. Before A comes to know of this the bank fails. Even so B is discharged from his liability.

D. Performance of Reciprocal Promises

When a contract consists of an exchange of promises, they are called reciprocal promises.

When a contract consists of an exchange of promises, they are called reciprocal promises. When such promises have to be performed simultaneously, the promisor is not bound to perform unless the promisee is ready and willing to perform his promise (Section 51).

For example, A and B contract that A shall deliver goods to B to be paid for by B on delivery. A need not deliver the goods, unless B is ready and willing to pay for the goods on delivery. B need not pay for the goods unless A is ready and willing to deliver them on payment.

What is the Order of Performing Reciprocal Promises? Section 52 lays down rules in this regard. According to the section, where an order for performing reciprocal promises is fixed expressly, the performance must be in that order. Where the order is not expressly fixed, the performance of promises must be in that order which the nature of the transactions requires. In Hashman vs. Lucknow Improvement Trust (1927), the defendant took a lease of land from a town municipality on condition that he pays Rs. 630 for leveling charges and possession was to be delivered after leveling. The question arose whether the sum was to be paid before or after leveling. The agreement was silent on the point. The court held that : in the ordinary course of business work is not usually paid for before it is done. It is the custom in some cases for payment to be made in installments as the work progresses but the person for whom a work is done is not expected to pay the entire cost in advance without an express agreement to that effect.

What if One Party Prevents the Other from Performing His Promises? Section 53 provides answer to this question. The section lays down the principle that where one of the parties to reciprocal promises prevents the other from performing his promise, the contract becomes voidable at the option of the party so prevented, and he is entitled for compensation from the other party for any loss which he may sustain in consequence of the non-performance of the contract. For example, A and B contract that B shall execute certain work for A for a thousand rupees. B is ready and willing to execute the work accordingly, but A prevents him from doing so. The contract is voidable at the option of B; and if he elects to rescind it, he is entitled to recover from A compensation for any loss incurred as a result of non-performance.

What happens when a promise which must be first performed is not performed? Section 54 has answer to this question. The section lays down that where the nature of the reciprocal promises is such that one cannot be performed or its performance cannot be claimed unless the other party performs his promise in the first place, then if the later fails to perform, he cannot claim performance from the other, but must make compensation to him for his loss.

For example, A contracts with B to execute certain builder's work for a fixed price, B supplying the scaffolding and timber necessary for the work. B refuses to furnish any scaffolding or timber, and the work cannot be executed. A need not execute the work and B is bound to make compensation to A for any loss caused to him by the non-performance of the contract.

How about promises to do certain legal and other things illegal? According to Section 57 where a person reciprocally promises, firstly, to do certain things which are legal, and secondly under specified circumstances, to do certain things which are illegal, the first set of promises is a contract, but the second is a void agreement.

For example, A and B agree that A shall sell B a house for Rs. 10,000, but that if B uses it as a gambling house, he shall pay A Rs. 50,000 for it. The first part, namely, sale of house for Rs. 10,000 is a contract but the second part is a void agreement.

E. Time for Performance

Sometimes the parties to a contract specify the time for its performance. Ordinarily it is expected that either party shall perform his obligation at the stipulated time. But if one of them fails to do so, the question arises what is the effect upon the contract. Section 55 provides the answer.

According to this section if the intention of the parties was that time should be the essence of the contract, then a failure to perform at the agreed time renders the contract voidable at the option of the opposite party. Time is generally considered to be of the essence of contract in the following cases:

1. Where the parties have expressly agreed to treat it as the essence of the contract.
2. Where delay operates as an injury.
3. Where the nature and necessity of the contract requires it to be so construed, for example, where a party asks for extension of time for performance.

Where time is not of the essence of the contract, failure on the part of the promisor to perform his obligation within the fixed time does not make the contract voidable, but the promise is entitled to compensation for any loss caused to him by such failure. Example of an agreement where time is not of essence is the one for the sale of immovable property.

F. Appropriation of Payments

The issue of appropriation of payment becomes relevant when a debtor owes several debts to a creditor and makes a payment which is insufficient to discharge all the debts. The question is to which debt the payment should be appropriated? The Act, in Sections 59 to 61, lays down the following three rules in this regard:

(a) Where the debtor intimates: Where the debtor intimates to which particular debts his payment must be applied, the payment should be applied accordingly (Section 59).

(b) **Where the debtor does not intimate:** Where the debtor has omitted to intimate, and there are no other circumstances indicating to which debt the payment is to be applied, the creditor may apply the payment even to a debt which is time barred (Section 60).

(c) **Where the debtor does not intimate and the creditor fails to apply:** In a situation where the debtor fails to intimate and the creditor does not use his descretion to apply to a particular debt, the law gets the right to appropriate the payment. And the law prefers to clear the debts in the order of time in which they were incurred (Section 61).

G. Assignment of Contracts

Assignment means transfer of contractual rights or liability by a party to the contract to some other person, who is not a party. Transfer may take place (a) by an act of the parties, or (b) by operation of law.

Assignment means transfer of contractual rights or liability by a party to the contract to some other person, who is not a party. Transfer may take place (a) by an act of the parties, or (b) by operation of law.

(a) Assignment by act of parties: parties, by mutual agreement and of their own accord, drop out from the performance of promise and bring in other parties to perform their part of promise. However, contracts of personal skill and ability cannot be assigned.

Benefits or rights can be assigned but not the burden of the contract except with the consent of the parties. However, if rights are personal in nature they cannot be assigned.

For example, A owes B Rs. 1,000. A cannot transfer his liability to a third person. However, if B agrees to accept C as his debtor in place of A, the liability can then be transferred from A to C.

A debtor, therefore, cannot relieve himself of his liability except by consent of the creditor and new party to whom the burden is being assigned. If the parties consent, original debtor is discharged. Notice of assignment must be given.

(b) Assignment by operation of law: (i) Upon death of a party to the contract, his rights and liabilities devolve upon his heirs and legal representatives.

But when the personal skill and abilities are involved the contractual relations are put to an end by the death of the promisor.

(ii) In case of insolvency by a party to the contract, his rights and obligations pass on to the Official Assignee or Official Receiver, as the case may be.

Contracts which Need not be Performed

Sections 62 to 67 of the Act state the following circumstances under which contracts need not be performed:

1. If the parties to a contract agree to substitute a new contract for it, or to rescind, or alter it, the original contract need not be performed (Section 62).
2. If parties to a contract agree to dispense with or remit performance of promise, technically called a remission, either wholly or in part, the original contract stands discharged (Section 63).
3. When a person at whose option a contract is voidable rescinds it, the other party thereto need not perform his promise (Section 64).
4. If any promisee neglects or refuses to afford the promisor reasonable facilities for the performance of his promise the promisor is executed by

such neglect or refusal as to any non-performance caused thereby (Section 67). For example, A contracts with B to repair B's house. B neglects or refuses to point out to A the places in which his house requires repair. A is excused for the non-performance of the contract, if is caused by such neglect or refusal.

2. Impossibility of Performance and Frustration

An agreement to do an act impossible in itself is void.

According to Section 56 an agreement to do an act impossible in itself is void. For example, A agrees with B to discover treasure by Magic. The agreement is void. Even subsequent impossibility renders a contract void. Sometimes the performance of a contract is quite possible when it is made by the parties. But some event subsequently happens which renders its performance impossible or unlawful. In either case, the contract becomes void. Where, for example, after making a contract of marriage, one of the parties goes mad, or where a contract is made for the import of goods and the import thereafter forbidden by the Government order, or where a singer contracts to sing and becomes too ill to do so, the contract in each case becomes void. The principle of subsequent impossibility is popularly called the **'doctrine of frustration.'**

Grounds of Frustration

The principle of frustration of contract is applicable to a variety of situations. The well-established grounds, however are: (i) destruction of the subject-matter, (ii) change of circumstances, (iii) non-occurrence of contemplated event, (iv) death or incapacity of party, (v) Government or legislative intervention, and (vi) intervention of war (see Fig. 5.16).

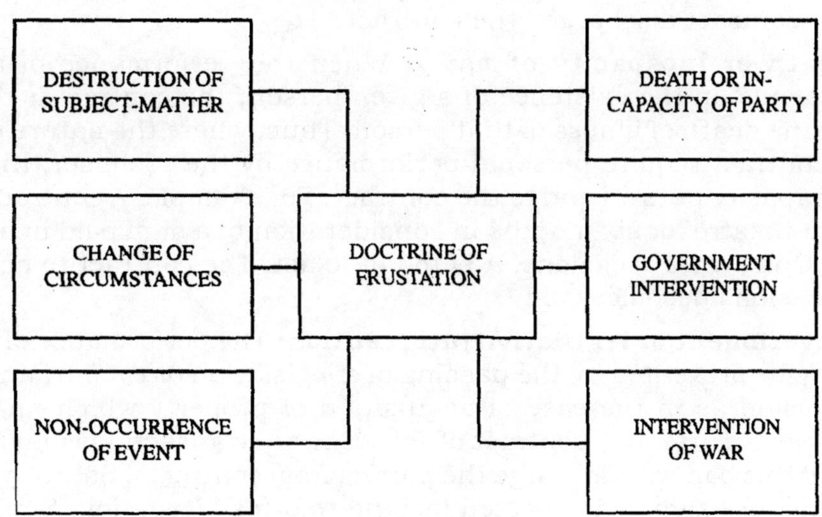

Fig. 5.16 Heads of Frustration

(i) **Destruction of subject-matter:** The doctrine of frustration applies with full force where the actual and specific subject-matter of the contract has ceased to exist. A leading case in this context is the **Taylor vs. Caldwell (1863).** In this case the defendant had agreed to let the plaintiffs, the use of their music hall between certain dates for the purpose of holding a concert there. But before the consent was given, the hall was destroyed by the fire without the fault of either party. The contract was held not to be absolute on the principle of frustration. Similarly, when a cinema hall engaged for showing a film collapsed on account of heavy rains, the contract was held to be frustrated **(V.L. Narasu vs. P.S.V. Iyer, 1953).**

(ii) Change of Circumstances: A contract will frustrate when circumstances arise which make the performance of the contract impossible in the manner and at the time contemplated. The Punjab High Court observed in **[P.D. Mehra & Sons vs. Ramachandra Omprakash (1952)]** thus: "it is clear that if there is entirely unanticipated change of circumstances, the question will have to be considered whether this change of circumstances has affected the performance of the contract to such an extent as to make it virtually impossible or even extremely difficult or hazardous. If that be the case, the change of circumstances not having been brought about by the default of either party, the court will not enforce the contracts."

(iii) Non-occurrence of a contemplated event: Sometimes, the performance of a contract is possible, but owing to the non-occurrence of the event contemplated by both parties as the reason for the contract, the value of the performance is destroyed. The leading case to be quoted here is the **Krell vs. Henry (1903).** In this case the defendant agreed to hire a flat from the plaintiff for June 26 and 27, for witnessing a coronation procession of Kind Edward VII. A part of the rent was paid in advance. But the procession have been cancelled owing to the king's illness, the defendant refused to pay the balance. He was freed from paying the balance because non-occurrence of the event, which was the basis for the contract discharged the contract.

(iv) Death or incapacity of party: When the performance of a contract depends on the existence of a given person, the contract is discharged on the death of illness of that person. Thus, where the nature of terms of a contract require personal performance by the promisor, his death or incapacity puts an end to the contract. For example, A contracts B to act at a theatre for six months in consideration of a sum paid in advance by H. On several occasions, A is too ill to act. The contract to act on those occasions becomes void.

(v) Government or legislative intervention: The performance of a contract may be prevented by the passing of a legislation or even by an executive decision as in the case of acquisition of property which might be the subject-matter of a contract of sale. Certain transactions may be banned and this ban will discharge the parties from contracts. Sale of agricultural land, for example is affected by land reforms legislation. Similarly, sale of urban land is affected by the urban land ceiling law. In **Boothalinga Agencies vs. V.T.C. Poraiswan Nadar (1969),** the defendant had a licence to import chicory for manufacturing coffee powder. The license was subjected to the condition that he would use it for his factory. He agreed to sell the whole shipload. Before the arrival of the ship, the sale of such imported goods was banned. The contact to sell was held to be frustrated because of the ban.

(vi) Intervention of war: As soon as a war breaks out, it becomes impossible to perform a contract. During the continuance of war, therefore, the contracts are suspended and may be resumed after the war is over. If continued for a longer-period the inordinate delay makes the contract void. A contract with an alien enemy is void.

Exceptions to Doctrine of Frustration

Supervening impossibility or doctrine of frustration will not discharge a contract in the following cases:

(a) Difficulty of performance: Unexpected difficulty does not excuse performance. In **Karl Ettlinger vs. Chagandas & Co. (1915)** X promised to send certain goods from Bombay to Antwerp in September. In August, war broke out and shipping space was available at very high rates. It was held that the increase of freight rates did not excuse performance.

(b) Commercial Impossibility: A contract is not discharged merely because expectation of higher profits is not realized, or the rates of materials have gone up because of outbreak of war, or there is a sudden depreciation of currency.

(c) Default of a third party: Where performance of contract is not possible because of the default by a third party, the contract is not discharged. In **Harnandrai Fulchand vs. Pragdas (1923),** A a wholesaler, entered into a contract with B for the sale of a certain type of cloth to be produced by C, a manufacturer of the cloth. It was held that A was liable to B for damages.

When the parties to a contract agree to substitute the existing contract with a new one, it is called novation.

(d) Strikes, Lockouts and civil disturbances: A strike by workers, or a lockout by an employer does not excuse performance unless there is a clause in the contract providing that in such cases that contract is not to be performed or that the time of performance is to be extended. Same logic applies to a civil disturbance too.

(e) Failure on one of the objects: When there are several purposes for which a contract is entered into, failure of one of them does not discharge the contract.

3. Discharge by Agreement

As a contract is created by means of an agreement, it may be discharged by another agreement between the same parties nullifying the previous contract. This may happen in any of the following ways (see Fig.5.17):

(a) Novation: When the parties to a contract agree to substitute the existing contract with a new one, it is called novation. With novation, the old agreement is discharged and in this place a new one comes into effect. The new agreement must be enforceable.

For example, A owes money to B under a contract. It is agreed between A, B and C that B shall henceforth accept C as his debtor, instead of A. The old debt between A and B comes to an end and the new debt from C to B has been contracted.

Remission means the acceptance of less than what was agreed for. There is no need for any consideration for remission.

(b) Remission: Remission means the acceptance of less than what was agreed for. There is no need for any consideration for remission.

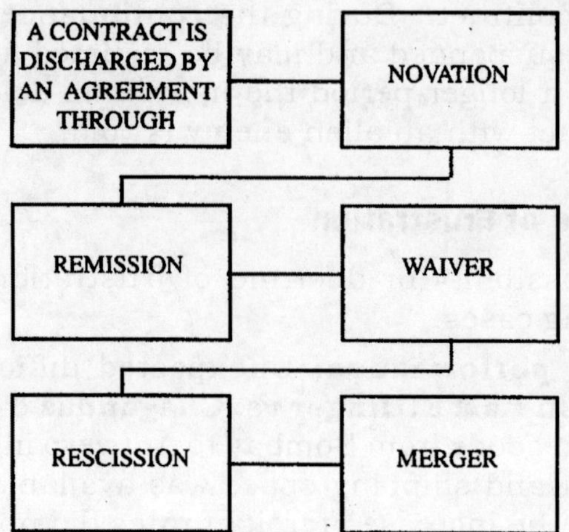

Fig. 5.17 Discharge of Agreement

Waiver means the deliberate abandonment of the rights by the parties to a contract.

(c) **Waiver:** Waiver means the deliberate abandonment of the rights by the parties to a contract. The parties are no longer bound by the terms of the contract. Consideration is not necessary for waiver.

(d) **Rescission:** Rescission of an agreement takes place when all or some of the terms of the contract are cancelled. It may occur (i) by mutual consent of the parties, or (ii) where one party fails in performing his obligation, the other party may rescind the contract without prejudice to his right to claim compensation for the breach of contract.

(e) **Merger:** Merger takes place when an inferior right accruing to a party under a contract merges into a superior right accruing to the same party under the same or some other contract.

4. Discharge by Limitation

Rescission of an agreement takes place when all or some of the terms of the contract are cancelled. It may occur (i) by mutual consent of the parties,

Since man himself is mortal, his rights and duties cannot be immortal. It is on this assumption that the Limitations Act, 1963 lays down that a contract must be performed within a specified period. The specified period is called period of limitation. Now, if the contract is not performed within the period of limitation, it stands terminated. For example, the price of goods sold without any stipulation as to credit must be paid within three years. If the debtor fails to pay within three years and if the creditor does not to sue the debtor for the recovery, the debt shall become time-barred and irrecoverable.

However, it is upto the parties to rejuvenate a contract by acknowledgements. If the promisor gives a written acknowledgement of debt before the expiry of limitation, a new period of limitation will come into force. This acknowledgements may be an endorsement on the original document or by means of a separate communication.

5. Discharge by Operation of Law

A contract is discharged by the operation of other laws. There are three ways of intervention of law: (i) death, (ii) insolvency, and (iii) unauthorized alteration.

(i) Death: Death of the promisor results in termination of the contract in cases involving personal skills or ability.

(ii) Insolvency: On a person being adjudicated insolvent, he is released from all his debts and liabilities. The rights and liabilities are transferred to an Official Assignee or an Official Receiver under the Presidency Towns Insolvency Act or Provincial Insolvency Act, as the case may be. The order of discharge gives a new lease of life to the insolvent, but not to his earlier debts and obligations.

(iii) Unauthorized Alteration: Where one of the parties to a contract alters any of its terms without seeking the consent of the other party to it, the contract stands discharged.

6. Discharge by Breach

Discharge by breach is the last way of dissolving a contract. There is a breach when one party to a contract repudiates his liability to the contract or conducts himself in such a way as to make him impossible to perform the contract. Failure to perform the promise may take place when the time for performance has arrived or even before that. Thus, breach is of two kinds, viz., (a) anticipatory breach, and (b) present or actual breach.

Anticipatory Breach: An anticipatory breach occurs when, prior to the promised date of performance, the promisor absolutely repudiates the contract. It is an announcement by the contracting party of his intention not to fulfill the contact and that he will no be no longer be bound by it.

Present or Actual Breach: Actual breach occurs when the performance is due or during the performance of the contact.

In an anticipatory breach the contract stands discharged unless the aggrieved party chooses to keep it alive till the date of performance arrives. In the present breach, the party not in breach, treats the contract as no longer binding on him. In either case, the aggrieved party has certain remedies. These remedies will be discussed in the next sub-chapter.

5.18 REMEDIES FOR BREACH OF CONTRACT

Breach and its Remedies

When all provisions of a contract have been complied with, the contract is said to have been discharged. In effect, the contract no longer exists. Sometime, however, the contract may never reach this stage, since one party may simply refuse to perform or may handle the agreement in an unsatisfactory manner. on occasion, this failure to perform may arise from changed conditions that make performance impossible, but at other times there may be no real justification.

A breach of contract is the failure, without legal excuse, to perform any promise that comprises the whole or part of a contract.

Major and Minor Breach

The courts say that whether the breach of a contract is major or relatively minor makes a significant legal difference. But the courts do not lay down hard and fast rules for deciding whether the breach is major or minor. In general, a minor breach involves a somewhat insignificant in quantity or quality — something that may be corrected or offset without serious harm. A minor breach may involve a small delay of an hour or two in performance when the time of completion is not really critical.

This does not mean that the party bargaining for a specified product or service can be cheated out of the contract specifications. The aggrieved party is entitled to damages to make up for the differences. But if the breach is minor, the damages or other remedies are limited to those caused by the breach, and the contract is said to be "substantially performed."

On the other hand, a major breach is something that goes on the very substance of the agreement. In a situation of this kind, the injured party is immediately excused from the counterperformance owing under the terms of the agreement.

Options of Injured Party

When a major breach of contract occurs, the injured party to the agreement will usually have several options:

Filing suit for monetary damages:

Asking the court for specific performance by the other party.

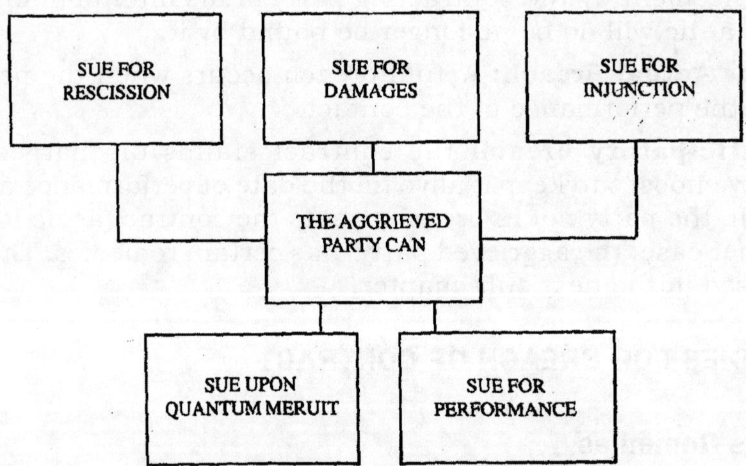

Fig. 5.18 Remedies for Breach of Contract

Instituting rescission (cancellation) and restitution.

Seeking money damages in a lawsuit not based on contract law, but rather based on tort or quasi-contract (unjust enrichment) principles.

Of these possible remedies, a request for specific performance seeks to enforce the contract, whereas the remedy of rescission requests a cancellation of the contract.

As was pointed out in the previous sub-chapter breach of a contract occurs when one of the parties to the contract refuses to perform it. When the breach occurs, the aggrieved party is entitled to the following remedies: (See Fig. 5.18).

1. Sue for rescission of the contract.
2. Sue for damages.
3. Sue for injunction.
4. Sue upon quantum meruit.
5. Sue for specific performance.

A discussion of each remedy follows.

1. Rescission of the Contract

When a contract is broken by one party, the other party may sue for rescission and refuse further performance. In such a case, he (the aggrieved) is absolved of all his obligations under the contract.

The court may grant rescission in the following two cases:

(a) Where the contract is voidable at the option of the plaintiff the court grants rescission to the plaintiff. For example, A sells a field to B. There is a right of passage over the field of which A has direct personal knowledge, but which he conceals from B. B is entitled to have the contract rescinded.

(b) Where the contract is unlawful for causes not apparent on its face and the defendant is more to blame than the plaintiff, the court may grant rescission. For example, A, an attorney, induces his client B, a Hindu widow, to transfer property to him for the purpose of defrauding B's creditors. Here the parties are not equally in fault and B is entitled to have the instrument to transfer rescinded.

The court may, on the other hand, refuse to grant rescission in the following cases:

(a) Where the plaintiff has expressly or impliedly ratified the contract;

(b) Where owing to the change of circumstances since the making of the contract, the parties cannot be restored to their original positions;

(c) Where third parties having, during the subsistence of the contract acquired rights in good faith and for value; or

(d) Where only a part of the contract is sought to be rescinded and such part is severable from the rest of the contract.

Where the party treats the contract as rescinded, he makes himself liable to restore any benefits he has received under the contract to the party from whom such benefits were received. But if the person rescinds a contract he is entitled to compensation for any damage which he has sustained through non-fulfillment of the contract by the other party.

2. Suit for Damages

The party who has aggrieved by the breach of contract may bring an action for damages. 'Damages' mean compensation payable in terms of money for the loss suffered by the aggrieved or injured party. Rules regarding damages are: (i) the principle of "remoteness of damage", (ii) compensation and not penal damages, (iii) nominal damages, (iv) mental pain and suffering, (v) duty to mitigate, (vi) liquidated damages and penalty, (vii) statutory damages, (viii) interest by way of damages, and (ix) difficulty of assessment (see Fig. 5.19).

'Damages' mean compensation payable in terms of money for the loss suffered by the aggrieved or injured party.

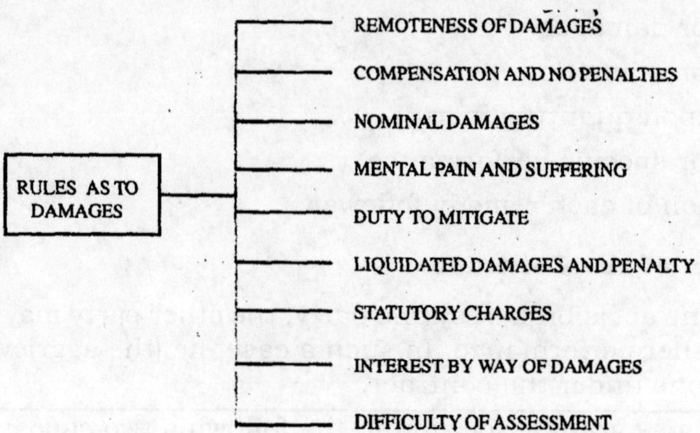

Fig. 5.19 Rules as to Damages

A brief explanation of each rule follows:

Remoteness of Damages: Every breach of contract upsets many a settled expectation on the injured party. He may feel the consequences for a long time and in a variety of ways. A person, for example, agrees to supply to a shop-keeper pure mustered oil but supplies impure stuff instead. This is a breach, prosecuted and convicted. He suffers the loss of oil, the loss of profit, the loss of his personal prestige, and the prestige of his business. Besides of course the loss of time, money and energy wasted on defense and the mental agony and torture of the prosecution.

Thus, the consequence of a breach may be endless, but there must be an end to liability. The defendant cannot be held liable for all that follows from his breach. There must be a limit to liability and beyond this damage is said to be too remote and, therefore, not recoverable. The problem is to decide the limit. The historic judgement in **Hadley v. Baxendale** (1854) provides answer to the problem. The facts of the case are:

The plaintiff were engaged in milling business at Gloucester. The mill was stopped owing to the breakage of crankshaft, which was the only one they had. They ordered a replacement from a firm by name Joyce & Co., engineers at Greenwich, who asked for the defective shaft to be sent to them as a pattern. The shaft was accordingly sent to the defendants who were a firm of common carriers, for the purpose of carrying it to Greenwich. At the time of delivery to the carriers, the plaintiff's clerk told them that the mill was stopped owing to the breakage of the shaft and hence, it must be sent immediately.

Nevertheless there was delay in delivery due to negligence on the part of the carriers, and the consequence was that the plaintiffs did not receive the new shaft for several days. During the interval, the mill remained idle and the plaintiffs, as a result, lost profit which they otherwise would have earned. Estimating the loss of profit at £300, the plaintiff sought to recover the amount from the defendants.

Alderson B. observed thus: "Where two parties have made a contract which one of them has broken, the damages which the other ought to receive in respect of such breach of contract should be such as may fairly and reasonably be considered either arising naturally , i.e., according to the usual course of things, from such breach of contract itself, or such as may reasonably be supposed to have been in the contemplation of both parties, at the time they made the contract, as the probable result of the breach of it."

On the basis of this principle the defendants were not held liable for the loss of profits. The judgement given by Alderson formed the basis for modern law of damages both in our country and in England. Sec. 73 of our Contract Act is, in fact, faced on the above judgement. To quote the section, "When a contract has been broken, the party who suffers by such breach is entitled to receive, from the party who has broken the contract, compensation for any loss or damage caused to him thereby, which naturally arose in the usual course of things from such breach, or which the parties knew, when they made the contract, to be likely to result from the breach of it.

"Such compensation is not to be given for any remote and indirect loss or damage sustained by reason of breach."

Thus, the section recognizes two types of losses, viz., (a) general damages, and (b) special damages.

General Damages: General or ordinary damages are those which arise naturally in the usual course of things from the breach itself. The defendant is liable for the reasonably foreseeable consequences of his breach. For example, A contracts to buy rice of B, at Rs. 950 per quintal, 50 quintals of rice, no time being fixed for delivery. A afterwards informs B that he will not accept the rice if tendered to him. The market price of rice on that day is Rs. 930 per quintal. B is entitled to receive from A compensation at the rate of Rs. 20 per quintal.

Special Damages: Special damages are those which arise on account of the unusual circumstances affecting the plaintiff. They are not recoverable unless the special circumstances were brought to the knowledge of the defendant so that the possibility of the special loss was in the contemplation of the parties.

Failure to bring to the knowledge of the defendant about the unusual circumstances prevented the plaintiff from recovering special damages.

One illustration is the decision of the Madras High Court in **Madras Railway Co. V. Govinda Rao (1898)**. The plaintiff, who was a tailor, delivered a sewing machine and some cloth to the defendant railway company to be sent to a place where he expected to carry on his business with special profit by reason of a forthcoming festival. Through the fault of the company's servants the goods were delayed in transmission and were not delivered until some days after the conclusion of the festival. The plaintiff had given no notice to the company of his special purpose. He claimed as damages the expenses of travelling upto the place of festival, and of staying there, and the loss of profits which he would have earned. The court held that he could not claim damages for the loss of profit since the special purpose was not known to the railway company.

Compensation and not Penal Damages: Damages for breach are given by way of compensation for the loss suffered by the plaintiff and not for the purpose of punishing the defendant for his breach. Punitive damages have no place in contract law and are not recoverable. But in the case of breach of a promise to marry, dishonour of a cheque by a banker wrongfully, and the issue of a cheque by a customer when he has no adequate balance to his credit in the bank the court may award penal damages.

Nominal Damages: Where the plaintiff suffers no loss the court may still award him nominal damages in recognition of his right. But this is the discretion of the court. The court may altogether refuse any award or award substantial damages.

Mental Pain and Suffering : In the normal circumstances damages for mental pain and suffering are not allowed. But damages are allowed in exceptional cases. For example, where "the breach was wanton or reckless and caused bodily harm" and when the defendant had reason to know that the breach would cause mental suffering "the courts would not hesitate in awarding damages."

In Diesen v. Samson (1971), a photographer who had been engaged to cover a wedding failed to turn up resulting in the absence of mementos to the parties and accordingly damages were allowed. Similarly, in **Jarvis V. Swan Tours Ltd.** (1973), a tourist agency was sued for disappointment in expectations regarding promised facilities and recreation in a conducted tour. The court observed that it was a fit case for awarding damages for mental distress caused by bitter disappointment.

Duty to Mitigate: The injured is expected to make reasonable efforts to avoid the losses resulting from the breach so that his loss is kept to the minimum. This rule is frequently applied to sale and purchase of goods. On the buyer's refusal to take delivery, the seller must resell the goods at the prevailing market rates. He may then recover the difference between the price he realizes by the sale and price he would have got had the contract been performed. If the seller fails to resell the goods and the loss aggravates, he cannot recover the enhanced loss.

The principle also finds its application in premature termination of a contract of employment. It is expected of a dismissed employee to find an alternative employment. Failure to do so will deny him the right to damages. But if the employment is for a particular period, termination of the service before the period expires, entitles the dismissed employee for damages which will be equal to the total salary he would have earned during the remaining part of the service period.

Liquidated Damages and Penalty: It is somewhat usual for the parties to a contract to state in the contract that on its breach a certain specified sum will become payable as damages. Such a sum may amount to either 'liquidated damages' or a 'penalty.' The former represents a fair and genuine pre-estimate of the probable loss that might ensure as a result of the breach. The later is a sum named in the contract and is disproportionate to the damage likely to accrue as a result of the breach. It is fixed in order to ensure performance of the contract.

The English law allows, 'liquidated damages' but relieves a party against 'penalty.' In our country no such distinction is made. The injured party is allowed only reasonable compensation.

Statutory Damages: Where damages are payable in terms of a statutory provision, the Supreme Court has held that the provision applicable would be one that is in force at the time of cause of action and not that was in force when the agreement was made.

In Padma Srinivasan v. Premier Insurance Co. Ltd. (1982), the plaintiff's husband was killed by a goods lorry which was insured with the defendant company. When the policy was taken the amount payable for loss of life, under the Motor Vehicles Act, was Rs. 20,000. By the time the accident took place, the Act was amended and the compensation was raised to Rs. 50,000. The court allowed the revised figure.

Difficulty of Assessment: Any difficulty in assessing damages shall not prevent the injured party from recovering them. The court must do its best to determine the amount of damages. In **Chaplin v. Hicks (1911),** the readers of a certain newspaper had to select 50 ladies for a beauty contest organized by the defendant. Out of the 50 selected, the defendant had to choose 12 for a theatrical job. The plaintiff was one among the 50 selected by the readers. She was not, however, given reasonable opportunity to appear at the final selection because of negligence by the defendant. Although the value of a chance of getting selected in a competition is difficult to assess, the breach by the defendant resulted in the loss of that chance to the plaintiff. Accordingly, in a suit by her against the defendant, she was awarded £100 as damages.

3. Sue for Injunction

An injunction is as order of the court directing a person to do or refrain from doing some act, which is the subject-matter of the contract and which a party undertakes to do or not to do. On breach of contract, court can restrain a party, by an order of injunction, from committing the breach. The power of the court to grant injunction is discretionary and may be granted for a temporary or an indefinite period. An injunction is, therefore, used as means of enforcing a promise or forbidding the party from committing a breach.

4. Sue upon Quantum Meruit

Quantum meruit is another remedy available for a party to a contract on its breach. Often it so happens that one party to the contract has performed part of the promise and fails to perform the remaining part because the other party has committed a breach. The first must, therefore, be compensated for the part he has performed. This is called the doctrine of quantum meruit which means 'as much as merited' or 'as much as earned or deserved.'

For example, where the author had prepared a considerable manuscript for the publisher's library but subsequently the publishers had discontinued the library, the author was held entitled to compensation for the trouble he had taken **(Plinche v. Colburn, 1931).** So also in **Clay v. Yates (1856).** The painter painted most of the picture but refused to complete it because the work was libelous, was held entitled to recover on quantum meruit.

Recovery on quantum meruit is allowed when a person has rendered services under a supposed contract which turns out to be a nullity. **In Craven Ellis v. Canons. Ltd. (1936),** the plaintiff was appointed managing director of a company. The appointment was made by the other directors who were disqualified by reason of having not taken their qualification shares. The plaintiff also did not take his qualification shares. But he continued to act as managing director and sued the company for his agreed remuneration or for a reasonable remuneration on the basis of quantum meruit. His action for agreed remuneration was rejected as the appointment was void but the court allowed reasonable remuneration on the basis of quantum meruit.

Specific Performance: As pointed out, earlier the party injured by a breach of contract may file a lawsuit asking for money damages. Or the injured party can ask for specific performance. That is, the injured party may ask the court to compel the defaulting (breaching) party to actually carry out what should have been done under the terms of the agreement. Normally, all courts recognizes that the aggrieved party can demand compensatory damages, but specific performance is up to the fairness and judgement of the court. Of course, the plaintiff cannot expect to receive both an award of damages and an order for specific performance. Such a judgement would constitute "double enrichment", as the courts term it.

Judges consistently say that no one has an absolute right to specific performance, since such relief is within the court's discretion. In many situations, however, the measure of damages that can be awarded will not be an adequate remedy.

Almost invariably a court will order specific performance of an agreement to sell a home or land, or to lease real estate of any kind. But specific performance will seldom be ordered for the sale of personal property (chattels) unless the subject matter of the sale is unique or almost impossible to obtain elsewhere. Usually, personal goods can be bought on the open market and an award of monetary damages will be considered adequate.

For example, a coin collector spent years in locating an owner who was willing to sell a specific mintage of rare penny. The collector made a contract. A court would likely order specific performance (delivery of the coin upon payment of the price). This is because the coin would not be available in comparable conditions from other coin dealers.

The courts will usually order specific performance of a contract for personal services for an actor, artist, singer, portrait painter or some one with unique talent; at the same time specific performance would not likely be ordered for a contract to paint a house. The party inuured by the default could likely obtain another house painter, swing the first for damages. In some other cases specific performance of a contract for personal services for an actor, artist, singer, portrait painter, or someone with unique talent: at the same time, specific performance would not likely be ordered for a contract to paint a house. The party injured by the default could likely obtain another house painter, suing the first for damages. In some other cases, specific performance will not be ordered because the court feels this requirement could work an undue hardship on the defaulting party. At other times the court may simply not have sufficient technical background to supervise specific performance of some matters. Thus, a judge might order specific performance of a contract to sell an office building. But would not order specific performance of a contract to build an office building.

5. Sue for Specific Performance

Sue for specific performance is the last remedy available to the aggrieved party. When damage is not an adequate remedy, the court may at its discretion, grant the specific performance of the contract, compel the party in breach to do what he promised to do. But unlike damages, specific performance cannot be claimed as a matter of right. It is a discretionary remedy allowed in limited cases.

5.19 QUASI CONTRACTS AND CONTINGENT CONTRACTS

Quasi Contracts

If the agreement involves services performed by one of the parties and the other refuses to pay thereof, the injured party may sue under a quasi contract theory. In that case, the court would allow recovery for the reasonable value of the services performed. For instance, if you hire someone to paint your house and then refuse to pay the amount due, the painter could sue under a theory of quasi contract for the reasonable value of services performed. Usually, the court requires the individual providing the service.

The Indian Contract Act contains provisions not only to cover cases of contracts but also to cover certain types of situations which are analogous to contracts. Sections 68 to 72 of the Act provide for such situations. For example, as is well-known, a minor has no contractual capacity. But when necessaries are supplied to him, the person so supplying to entitled to sue and get reimbursement from the minor's property. Similarly, a person in whose home certain goods have been left by mistake is bound to restore them to the true owner. To cover cases of this nature, a new expression, namely, quasi contracts has been invented and used widely. The Contract Act prefers to call quasi contracts as "certain relations resembling those created by contract" but avoids the words quasi contracts.

> Quasi contracts as "certain relations resembling those created by contract" but avoids the words quasi contracts.

The rationale behind quasi contract is the principle that law as well as justice should try to prevent "unjust enrichment." That is, enrichment of one person at the cost of another. A person who has received benefit from another must pay for it. Otherwise, it would be unjust for him to retain such benefit.

Quasi contract is not a contract in strict sense as it is not intentionally created by the parties to a contract. It is created only by law.

Kinds of Quasi Contracts

Sections 68 to 72 provide for five kinds of quasi contractual obligations, namely, (a) supply of necessaries, (b) payment by an interested person, (c) liability to pay for non-gratuitous acts, (d) finder of goods, and (e) mistake (see Fig. 5.20). A brief explanation of each follows:

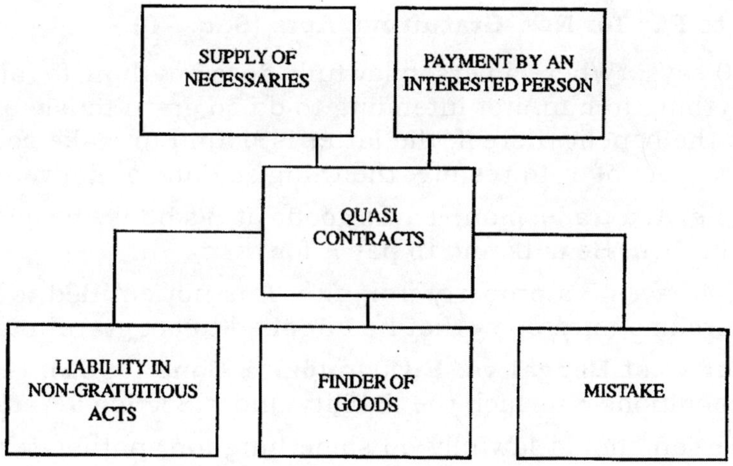

SUPPLY OF NECESSARIES

PAYMENT BY AN INTERESTED PERSON

QUASI CONTRACTS

LIABILITY IN NON-GRATUITIOUS ACTS

FINDER OF GOODS

MISTAKE

Fig. 5.20 Types of Quasi Contract

A. Supply of Necessaries (Sec. 68)

Where necessaries are supplied to a person who is incompetent to contract (for example, a minor) or to someone whom he is legally bound to support, the supplier to recover the price from the property of the incompetent person.

To quote the section: "If a person, incapable of entering into a contract or anyone whom he is legally bound to support, is supplied by another person with necessaries suited to his condition in life, the person who has furnished such supplies is entitled to be reimbursed from the property of such incapable person."

For example, A supplies B, a lunatic, with necessaries suitable to his condition in life. A is entitled to be reimbursed from B's property.

Similarly, A supplies the wife and children of B, a lunatic, with necessaries suitable to their condition in life. A is entitled to be reimbursed from B's property.

B. Payment by an Interested Person (Sec. 69)

According to Sec. 69 "a person who is interested in the payment of money which another is bound by law to pay, and who therefore, pays it, is entitled to be reimbursed by the other."

For example, B holds land in Bengal, on a lease granted by A, the Zamindar. The revenue payable by A to the Government in arrears, his land is advertised for sale by the Government. Under the revenue law the consequences of such sale will be annulment of B's lease. B to provide the sale and consequent annulment of B's lease. His own lease, pays to the Government the sum due from A. A is bound to make good to B the amount so paid.

However, in a suit under this section, the following conditions must be fulfilled:

(a) The plaintiff must be interested in making the payment. The interest which the plaintiff seeks to protect must be bonafide.

(b) It is necessary that the plaintiff should not be bound to pay. He should only be interested in making the payment in order to protect his own interest.

(c) The defendant should have been bound by law to pay the money.

C. Liability to Pay for Non-Gratuitous Acts (Sec. 70)

Section 70 says, "Where a person lawfully does anything for another person, or delivers anything to him, not intending to do so gratuitously and such other person enjoys the benefit thereof, the latter is bound to make compensation to the former in respect of or to restore, the thing so done or delivered."

For example, A, a tradesman, leaves goods at B's house by mistake. B treats the goods as his own. He is bound to pay A for them.

Similarly, A saves B's property from fire. A is not entitled to compensation from B if the circumstance show that he intended to act gratuitously.

In **State of West Bengal vs. B.K.Mondal & Sons (1962),** Gajendragadkar stated three conditions on which the liability under Section 70 arises:

(i) " a person should lawfully do something for another person or deliver something to him;

(ii) in doing the said thing or delivering the said thing he must not be intended to act gratuitously; and

(iii) the other person for whom something is done or to whom something is delivered must enjoy the benefit thereof."

D. Finder of Goods (Section 71)

Section 71 lays down the responsibility of a finder of goods. The section reads thus: "A person who finds goods belonging to another and takes them into his custody, is subject to the same responsibility as a bailee." His responsibilities are:

"A person who finds goods belonging to another and takes them into his custody, is subject to the same responsibility as a bailee."

(i) to take care of the goods, as a man of ordinary prudence would take care of his own goods;

(ii) must, with reasonable diligence, trace the true owner;

(iii) not to make any unauthorized use of goods; and

(iv) to return the goods, along with accretion to them if any, to the true owner.

For example, F picks up a diamond on the floor of S's shop. He hands it over to S to keep it till the true owner is found. No one appears to claim the diamond from S who refuses to return. S is bound to return the diamond to F who is entitled to retain the diamond against the whole world except the true owner.

E. Mistake (Section 72)

According to this section " a person to whom money has been paid, or anything delivered by mistake or under coercion, must pay or return it."

For example, A and B jointly owes Rs. 100 to C. A alone pays the amount to C, and B not knowing this fact, pays Rs. 100 over again to C. C is bound to repay the amount to B.

A contract is said to be contingent when its performance is made to depend upon the happening or not happening of a future event which is collateral to the contract.

Similarly, a railway company refuses to deliver certain goods to the consignee, except upon the payment of an illegal charge for carriage. The consignee pays a sum charged in order to obtain the goods. He is entitled to recover so much of the charge as was illegally excessive.

Money paid under mistake is recoverable whether the mistake may be of fact or of law. About mistake of law there was a controversy earlier. If a person, for example, by an error paid sales-tax, should he be earlier permitted to file a suit for its return? In Sri, **Sir Shiba Prasad Singh vs. Maharaja Srish Chandra Nandi (1949),** the judicial committee of the Privy Council declared that under Section 72 it was immaterial whether it was a mistake of fact or law. What was not legally due could be recovered as mistakenly paid.

The Supreme Court, in its decision in **Sales Tax Officer, Banaras vs. Kanhaiya Lal Mukund Lal Saraaf (1959),** has accepted his interpretation of Section 72. In this case a certain amount of sales tax was paid by the firm under the **U.P. Sales Tax Law** on its forward transactions and subsequently the **Allahabad High Court** ruled the levy of sales tax on forward transactions to be ultra vires. The firm sought to recover back the tax. Allowing the recovery, the Supreme Court observed that "section does not make any distinction between a mistake of law or a mistake of fact. The term 'mistake' has been used without any qualification or limitation whatsoever...."

Contingent Contracts

Sections 31 to 36 of the Contract Act define and illustrate contingent contracts. A contract is said to be contingent when its performance is made to depend upon the happening or not happening of a future event which is collateral to the contract.

A contingent contract is a contract to do or not to something, if some event, collateral to such contract, does or does not happen.

Section 31 of the Act defines a contingent contract thus: "A contingent contract is a contract to do or not to something, if some event, collateral to such contract, does or does not happen."

A contingent has the following features:

(i) The existence of a condition precedent which must be fulfilled before the contract can be enforced.

(ii) The condition must relate to a future event which may or by not happen.

(iii) The event does not form an essential part of the transaction but is collateral to it.

Rules Regarding Contingent Contracts

The following rules relate to contingent contracts (see Fig. 5.21).

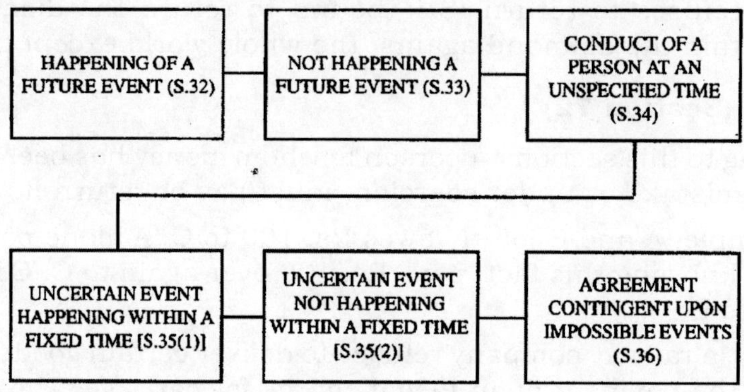

Fig. 5.21 Rules of Contingent Contracts

1. Happening of a Future Event (Section 32): The future uncertain event must happen if the contingent contracts were to be enforced. If the events become impossible, the contingent contracts become void.

For example, A makes a contract with B to buy B's house if A survives C. This contract cannot be enforced by law unless and until C dies in A's life-time.

Similarly, A contracts to pay B a sum of money when B marries C. C dies without being married to B. The contract becomes void.

2. Not happening of a future event: Section 33 lays down that "contingent contracts to do or not to do anything if an uncertain future event does not happen can be enforced when the happening of that event becomes impossible, and not before."

For example, A agrees to pay B a sum of money if a certain ship does not return. Th ship is sunk. The contract can be enforced when the ship sinks.

3. Conduct of person at an unspecified time (Section 34): According to Section 34 "if the future event on which a contract is contingent is the way in which a person will act at an unspecified time, the event shall be considered to become impossible when such person does anything which renders it impossible that he should so act within any definite time, or otherwise than under future contingencies."

For example, A agrees to pay B a sum of money if B marries C. C married D. The marriage of B to C must now be considered impossible although it is possible that D may die and that C may afterwards marry B.

4. Specified Uncertain Event Happening within a Fixed Time (Section 35 (1)): According to Section 35 (1) "contingent contracts to do or not to do anything if a specified uncertain event happens within a fixed time become void if, at the expiration of the time fixed, such event has not happened, or if, before the time fixed such event becomes impossible."

For example, A promises to pay B a sum of money if a certain ship returns within a year. The contract may be enforced if the ship returns within the year and becomes void if the ship is burnt within the year.

5. Specified Uncertain Event not Happening Within a Fixed Time: (Section 35 (2)): Section 35 (2) lays down that "contingent contract to do or not to do anything, if a specified uncertain event does not happen within a fixed time may be enforced by law when the time fixed has expired and such cvcnt has not happened or, before the time fixed has expired, if it becomes certain that such event will not happen."

For example, A promises to pay B a sum of money if a certain ship does not return within a year. The contract may be enforced if the ship does not return within a year, or is burnt within the year.

6. Agreements Contingent on Impossible Events are Void (Section 36): To quote Section 36 "contingent agreements to do or not to do anything if an impossible event happens, are void, whether the impossibility of the event is known or not to the parties to the agreement at the time when it is made."

For example, A agrees to pay B Rs. 1000 if two straight lines should enclose a space. The agreement is void.

Again, A agrees to pay B Rs. 1000 if B will marry A's daughter C. C was dead at the time of the agreement. The agreement is void.

Contingent Contracts vs. Wagering Contracts

Since a wagering contract resembles a contingent contract it is useful to distinguish the two. Table 5.5 reveals the difference.

Table 5.5 Contingent and Wagering Contracts Distinguished

Contingent Contract	*Wagering Contract*
1. A contingent contract is a contract to do or not to do something if some event colateral to such contract does or does not happen.	1. A wagering contract is an agreement between two parties to the effect that if a given event is determined one way, one of them shall pay a sum of money to the other, and in the contrary event, the latter shall pay to the former.
2. It is not necessary that there should be mutual promises.	2. There is mutual promises, each of them conditional on the happening or not happening of an unknown event.
3. Parties are interested in performing respective promises.	3. Neither party is interested in the performance of promises, but only to pay or receive the difference.
4. These are valid agreements.	4. These are void.
5. The parties are interested in the occurrence or non-occurrence of the event.	5. The parties are not interested in the occurrence or non-occurrence of the event.

6. The future event is merely collateral or incidental to the contract.	6. The future event is the sole determining factor of the contract.
7. All contingent contracts are wagers, insurance and contracts of indemnity and guarantee, for example.	7. All wagers are contingent.

5.20 THE FLIP SIDE OF THE INDIAN CONTRACT ACT, 1872

Is it possible for anyone to be acknowledgeable about laws which are almost countless? The answer is it is not possible. In fact, it is a waste of time even for lawyers, to be fully knowledgeable and to memorize all the legal rules. The reasons are obvious:

(i) There are simply too many rules.

(ii) The same rules are not applied all over the country.

(iii) Rules are constantly modified by legislators, judges, and to a limited extent by other officials.

(iv) Most rules are not simple and categorical.

But for the Contract Act, ignorance of law is no excuse.

Secondly, the contract Act is not comprehensive. It does not cover the whole of contract. In fact, the preamble to the Act in using the phrase "to define and amend certain parts of the law relating to contracts", makes it clear that it does not profess to be a complete code on contracts. Besides laying down the general principles of law of contracts such as indemnity and guarantee, bailment and pledge, and agency. It is not, however, cover such areas as partnership, sale of goods and negotiable instruments which are also contracts.

Thirdly, the Act does not override usage or custom of trace. Section 1 of the Act lays down that "nothing herein contained shall affect the provision of any statue, act or regulation not hereby expressly repealed, nor usage or custom of trade, nor any incident of any contract not inconsistent with the provisions of this Act." Accordingly, the Act does not supersede any custom of trade though it is inconsistent with the provisions of the Act.

Fourthly, contract of marriage of a minor is treated as beneficial contract according to the Contract Act. A minor can enforce a contract that is beneficial to him. The argument behind this provision is that it is customary amongst most of the communities in India for parents to arrange marriages among their minor children and the law has to adopt itself to the habits and customs of the people.

But the customs in our country is gradually changing and the marriage below 18 (girls) and 25 (boys) years of age is discouraged and is even made an offence. Under the present circumstances it would be difficult to understand why the provisions is still retained in the Act.

True, preamble to the Contract Act says that no section in the Act shall affect the provisions of any statute, act or regulations in force in the country. But a premier legislation like the Contract Act allowing minor's marriage is inconceivable to say the least.

Finally, the Act, as was mentioned in the beginning, came into force in 1872 and since then it has not been amended till today. Not that the act has been foolproof in all respects. There are a number of gaps in the Act and these gaps have been filled up by case laws. Instead of relying on case laws which may be vulnerable for subjective interpretation, it is advisable to amend the Act and incorporate the principles derived from case laws in the Act itself.

QUESTIONS

A. Objective Type

1. Define the term contract.
2. What is a void contract?
3. What is voidable contract?
4. What is an illegal contract?
5. What is quasi contract?
6. What is executory contract?
7. What is an executed contract?
8. What is a bilateral contract?
9. What is an unilateral contract?
10. What is an offer?
11. State the essentials of valid offer.
12. What is a specific offer and a general offer?
13. What is cross offer and a counter offer?
14. What is acceptance?
15. State the essentials of valid acceptance.
16. What is consideration?
17. State the essentials of valid consideration.
18. State exception to consideration.
19. What is meant by legal capacity?
20. Who is a minor?
21. What is a tort?
22. What is doctrine of restitution?
23. What does English Law say about contractual capacity of a person with unsound mind?
24. Who is an alien enemy?
25. What is a free consent?
26. What is coercion?
27. Define undue influence?
28. Define misrepresentation.
29. What is fraud ?
30. What is an unlawful agreement? Give examples.
31. What is a void agreement? Give examples.
32. What is an exclusive dealing?
33. What is an uncertain agreement?
34. What is a wagering agreement?
35. Give an example of a contract that might be struck down by the courts as against public policy.
36. What are reciprocal promises?
37. What do you mean by doctrine of frustration?
38. Give the meaning of assignment of contracts.
39. State the contracts that need no performance.
40. What is novation?
41. What is remission?
42. What is anticipatory breach of a contract?
43. What is present breach of contract?

44. What is the basic rule in the assignment of contracts?
45. State remedies available on breach of contract.
46. State the circumstances when court can refuse rescission.
47. What do you mean by remoteness of damages?
48. What are special damages?
49. What do you understand by duty to mitigate?
50. What do you understand by quantum meruit?
51. What is a quasi contract?
52. What is a contingent contract?
53. State the various quasi contracts.
54. State the rules regarding contingent contracts.

B. Analytical Type

1. "The Indian Contract Act, 1872, is not a complete code and is not exhaustive." Discuss.
2. "All agreements are not contracts, but all contracts are agreements." Discuss, pointing out essentials of a valid contract.
3. "In business transactions, the presumption is that parties intend to create legal relationship." Comment.
4. Distinguish between (a) valid, void and voidable contracts, and (b) unilateral and bilateral contracts.
5. Mr. Balfour carrying on business in Sri Lanka promised his wife Mrs. Balfour lining in England to pay her a monthly allowance so long as she cannot come over to Sri Lanka for reasons of health. Can Mrs. Balfour claim the allowance?
6. A fire broke out in P's farm. He called upon the uptown Fire Brigade to put out the fire which the latter did. P's farm did not come under the free service zone although he believed to be so. Is P liable to pay for the services?
7. X& Co. through a newspaper advertisement, announce a reduction sale of ready-made woolen garments and exhibit articles in their showroom with the original and reduced prices marked on them. B, who has read the advertisement, picks up a woolen suit marked Rs. 400 as the original price and Rs. 200 as the reduced price. B, then, offers Rs. 200 to the salesman of X & Co., who refuses to accept and hand over the suit to B. What are B's rights against the company?
8. X, an auctioneer, advertise through newspaper that the sale of office furniture will be held in Bangalore. Y, a broker from Chennai, reaches Bangalore on the stipulated date and time. X, the auctioneer, withdrew all the furniture from the auction sale. Y sues X for the loss of time and expenses. Will he succeed?
9. Why is intention to create legal relations an essential requirement of a valid contract? Give three examples of obligations arising from contracts which are not legal obligations.
10. Having accepted an order from X, Y writes a letter and posts it. A few days later Y sends a telegram expressing his inability to accept the offer. Both letter and the telegram reach X at the same time. Is Y bound by the acceptance?
11. On 28th November, 1990, B wrote to A offering to sell and deliver to him 20 bags of rice at Rs. 600 a bag. On the same day A wrote to B offering to buy 20 bags of rice at Rs. 600 a bag. The two letters crossed in post. Is A's connection tenable? Give reasons.
12. A offers to sell his scooter to B for Rs. 10,000. B offers to buy it for Rs. 8,500. A refuses to sell. B then says to A, "I accept your offer and shall purchase the vehicle for Rs. 10,000." Is A bound to sell his scooter for Rs. 10,000?
13. "A mental resolve to accept an offer does not give rise to a contract." Comment.
14. Describe in your own words, the principles you have learnt from the following cases:
    (a) Carlill vs. Carbolic Smoke Ball Co,
    (b) Harvey vs. Facie.
    (c) Lalman Shukla vs. Gauri Dutt.
    (d) Boultan vs. Jones.
15. "An agreement without consideration is void, but an agreement with insufficient consideration is valid." Comment.

16. What principles did you learn from the two cases, viz., (1) Kedar Nath vs. Gorie Mohammed, and (2) Abdul Aziz vs. Masum Ali? What is the main difference between the two?
17. What principles of contract law have learnt from: (1) Chinnaya vs. Ramaya, and (2) Dunlop Pneumatic Tyre Co. Ltd. Vs. Selgridge & Co. Ltd.?
18. Should the consideration be always at the desire of the promisor's ? Discuss.
19. A and B are friends. B treats A during A's illness. B does not accept payment from A for treatment and A promises B's son, X, to pay him Rs. 1,000. A, being in poor circumstances is unable to pay. X sues A for the money. Can X recover?
20. What do you know about contract entered into with a minor from the legal point of view in India? Are there contracts with minor that are valid? If yes, which are they?
21. What principles did you learn from the case Mororibibi vs. Dharmodas Ghose? How do they differ from those of Srikakulam Subramanya vs. Kurra Subba Rao?
22. Write, in your own words, about what you learnt from Fig. 1.8 in this book.
23. A, a minor borrows Rs. 5,000 and executes a pronote for the amount in favour of B. After attaining majority, A executes another pronote in settlement of the first pronote. Will B succeed in recovering money from A? give reason in support of your answer.
24. A minor borrows Rs. 500 on a fraudulent representation of his age as a major. Can the creditor sue for the amount?
25. What principle did you learn from the popular case, viz., Roberts vs. Gray?
26. Distinguish between fraud and misrepresentation.
27. "Mere silence to facts likely to affect the willingness of a person to enter into a contract is not fraud." Discuss.
28. "Undue influence is a subtle form of coercion." Discuss.
29. Distinguish between coercion and undue influence.
30. A, falsely representing herself as the wife of a well-known millionaire, takes a ring from a jeweler's shop for the approval of her husband. She pledges it with a pawn-broker, who in good faith and without notice of the first transaction pays her Rs. 5000. Can the jeweler recover the ring from the pawn-broker?
31. X offers to sell his factory to Y stating that the factory produces 1,500 articles every day. Y checks the amount and finds that the factory produces only 1,300 articles per day. Y accepts the offer but later on refuses to buy the factory on the ground that it products only 1,300 articles per day, while X had represented that it produces 1,500 articles per day. Give your opinion with reasons.
32. What differences do you notice between the decisions given in Bell vs. Lever Bros. And in Nicholas and Venn vs. Smith Marriott.
33. What principles of contract law have you learnt from Allcard vs. Skinner and Mannu Singh vs. Umadat Pandey?
34. "An agreement in restrain of trade is void." Examine the statement stating exceptions, if any.
35. What principles of contract law have you learnt from the two popular cases, namely:
    (a) Madhub Chander vs. Rajcoomar, and
    (b) Nordenfet vs. Maxim Nordenfelt Gun Co.? Discuss.
36. What criteria would you adopt to determine whether an agreement is a wager or not? Applying the criteria can you say that the contract of insurance is a wager?
37. Miss Kokila agreed to sing at the star theatre for a period of three months commencing from 1st January 2011. She further agreed not to sing elsewhere during this period. Is this agreement valid?
38. Ram joined a company as a manager. The management of the company obtained an agreement from Ram to the effect that he should not leave the company for a period of five years. Is the agreement valid?
39. A promises B, in consideration of Rs. 1,000, never to marry throughout his life. Is this contract valid?
40. A, who bets with B and loses, applied to C for a loan in order to pay B. C gives the loan to A to enable him to pay B. Can C recover the amount of loan from A?
41. Are concepts not to compete against a former employer valid? Explain.

42. How far are the liabilities of parties to a contract affected by supervening impossibility? Discuss.
43. "Impossibility of Performance is as a rule, not an excuse for non-performance of a contract." Discuss.
44. What principle of Contracts Act did you learn from Taylor vs. Caldwell? Or Krell vs. Henry? Or Karl Ettlinger vs. Chagandas & Co.?
45. Is the promisor discharged from his obligation in each of the following cases:
    (a) A music hall was agreed to be let out on certain dates but before those dates it was destroyed by fire.
    (b) An artist to paint a picture for a certain price but before undertaking to do so, he met with an accident and lost his eyesight.
    (c) A contracts to marry B, being already married to C, and being forbidden by the law to which he is subject to practice polygamy.
    (d) A promised B, for a valuable consideration, to put back the life of a dead relation of B by some supernatural powers but fails to keep up his promise.
    (e) A agreed to sell to B the entire crop of apples growing in his orchard. After the agreement was made a sudden frost destroyed the crop.
46. X let premises in Calcutta to Y in January 1942 at a high rent for opening a restaurant, the agreement to remain in force as long as British European troops would remain stationed in Calcutta. Although British European troops continued to be stationed in the town, the particular locality of the restaurant was declared out of bounds for the troops and thus Y lost their customer. Y refuses to pay X the dues of rent on the plea of frustration of contract. Advise X.
47. "Where there is a right, there is a remedy." Amplify this statement and briefly explain the various remedies available for breach of contract.
48. What rules of damages have you learnt from Hadly v. Buxandale? Discuss the duty of the aggrieved to mitigate damages.
49. When does a claim on quantum meruit arise? Discuss.
50. A, in Delhi, entrust 100 packages of crackers with the Railways to be carried to his branch at Allahabad and instructs the Railway authorities to deliver the same by the first week of November 1976. Due to negligence of Railways, the packages were delivered by the third week of November, after Diwali season over. A sues Railway for the loss of profit he might have earned by the sale of crackers during the Diwali season. Will A succeed?
51. A agrees to pay Rs. 100,000 to B, a contractor, after he builds A's house as per specifications. After some time the work is abandoned. B demands part payment for the work done. Will he succeed?
52. A contract was made to pay a sum of money to B on a specified day. A does not pay the money on that day. B in consequence of not receiving the money on that day, is unable to pay his debts and is totally ruined. B claims heavy damages. Will he succeed?
53. Distinguish between wagering contracts and contingent contracts.
54. X agrees to construct a building for Y for Rs. 500,000 on the terms that no payment shall be made till the completion of the work. Is it a contingent contract?
55. A agrees to pay B a sum of money if b marries C. C married D, subsequently D dies. C afterwards marries B. Is A legally bound to pay the agreed sum?
56. Critically review the operation of the Contract Act.

C. Essay Type

1. What is a contract? What are the essential of a valid contract?
2. Define the term contract. Bring out the various classes of contracts.
3. Define the term 'offer.' What are the essentials of a valid offer? When can an offer be revoked?
4. Define the term acceptance. What are the essentials of a valid acceptance? When can an acceptance be revoked?
5. What is consideration? What are the essentials of valid consideration?
6. What is the general rule regarding consideration? What are exceptions to the rule?

7. What do you understand by competence of parties? State the position of a minor in detail.
8. State briefly the law relating to competence of parties to a contract.
9. What are necessaries? When is a minor liable on a contract for necessaries?
10. Write, in your own words, summary of this sub-chapter.
11. Write, in your own words, a summary of this sub-chapter.
12. What is free consent? When is consent not free? Explain with illustrations.
13. What is coercion? Undue influence? Their impact on contracts.
14. What is fraud? Mistake? Their effect on contracts?
15. What is an unlawful agreement? State and explain the various unlawful agreements.
16. What is a void agreement? State and explain the various void agreement.
17. Write, in your own words, a summary of this sub-chapter.
18. What are the various ways in which a contract may be discharged? Explain.
19. Should noticc of an assignment be promptly given? Why?
20. Explain, with illustration, what is meant by frustration of contact ?
21. Write, in your own words, a summary of this chapter.
22. Explain the various remedies available to an aggrieved party on the breach of a contract.
23. Explain the principles on which damages are awarded on the breach of a contract.
24. What is a quasi contract? Explain the different types of quasi contracts.
25. What is a contingent contract? Explain the rules regarding contingent contracts.

SALE OF GOODS ACT, 1930

Module Objectives

After reading this chapter, you should be able to

- Know the meaning of contract of sale and their essentials
- Distinguish between sale and agreement to sell, sale and hire purchase, sale and bailment
- Bring out the differernces between condition and warranty along with different types of implied conditions
- Know the different types of sale where ownership is transferred
- Explain the different types of goods and modes of delivery
- List the rights of an unpaid seller against goods and against the buyer.

6.1 SALE OF GOODS ACT, 1930

Contracts relating to sale of goods are governed by the Sale of Goods Act, 1930. This Act codifies, in a separate enactment, the law relating to sale of goods which was contained in *Sec.* 76 *to* 123 *of the Indian Contract Act,* 1872. These sections have been repealed from the Contract Act and are embodied in the *Sale of Goods Act.* The Sale of Goods Act is based on the principle of *English Sale of Goods Act,* 1893.

Scope of the Act

Sale of Goods Act applies only to movable property other than actionable claims and money and not to immovable which are governed by the *Transfer of Property Act,* 1882.

The Act applies to the whole of India except the state of Jammu and Kashmir. It applies only to movable property other than actionable claims and money and not to immovable which are governed by the *Transfer of Property Act,* 1882.

The Act deals with rights and duties of parties to a contract of sale. The parties to the contract have unfettered freedom to agree to any terms they like relating to delivery of goods and payment of price for them. The act does not seek to fetter this freedom. Rather it seeks to balance these rights and duties of sellers and buyers of goods.

6.2 FORMATION OF THE CONTRACT OF SALE

A contract of sale *"a contract whereby the seller transfer or agrees to transfer the property in goods to the buyer for a price."*

A contract of sale, according to Sec. 4 of the Act, is *"a contract whereby the seller transfers or agrees to transfer the property in goods to the buyer for a price."*

This definition emphasises the following essential features of a sale (see Fig. 6.1).

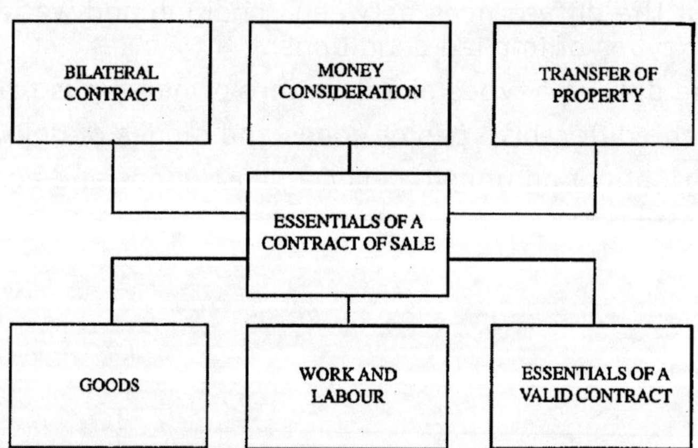

Fig: 6.1 Essentials of a Contract of Sale

(i) ***Bilateral Contract:*** The contract of sale must essentially be a bilateral contract because the property in goods should transfer from one party to another.

The two parties are seller and buyer and these must be different persons. The two must be different because a person cannot buy his own goods. In *the State of Gujarat* v. *Ramanlal* S. & *Co.* (1965) a partnership firm was dissolved and the surplus assets, including some goods, were divided among the partners, in specie. Sales Tax Officer sought to tax this. The action of the Officer was rejected on the contention that division among partners did not amount to sale as the partners themselves were the joint owners of the goods and they could not be both sellers and buyers of the goods. But law recognises the sale of goods by a partner to the firm and vice versa. Similarly, a contract of sale between one part owner and another is also recognised.

(ii) *Money Consideration:* The consideration for a sale of goods must be money, called the price. Where the property in goods is transferred for any consideration other than money, it is not sale. Thus, swap deals which are popular nowadays, are not contracts of sale in the strict sense. But where goods are sold for a definite sum and the price is paid partly in valued up goods and partly in cash, it is sale. For example, where an old car is returned to the dealer for anew one and the difference are paid in cash, it should be sale. Same logic applies to an exchange of an old TV for a new one, the difference being paid in cash. This logic is derived from the judgment in *Aldridge V. Johnson* (1857). In this case, fifty-two bullocks, valued at $ 6 a piece, were exchanged for 100 quarters of barley of $ 2 per quarter, the difference to be made up in cash. The contract was treated to be a valid sale.

The consideration for a sale of goods must be money, called the price. Where the property in goods is transferred for any consideration other than money, it is not sale.

(iii) *Transfer of Property:* Transfer of property is another essential of contract of sale. The seller must either transfer the property or agree to transfer the property in goods to the buyer. Property here means 'ownership' over the goods. What is important is that there must be a transfer of general property as distinguished from special property in goods from the seller to the buyer. If A owns certain goods, he has general property in the goods. If he pledges them with B, B has special property or interest in the goods. When it is said that the property in the goods has passed to the buyer, it means that the goods have ceased to be the property of the seller and have become the property of the buyer. Transfer of property in goods is distinct from delivery of goods. Property in goods may pass from the seller to the buyer without delivery of the goods. In other words, the buyer may become owner of the goods without possessing them.

The seller must either transfer the property or agree to transfer the property in goods to the buyer.

(iv) *Goods:* The subject-mater of the contract of sale must be goods. The term 'goods' is defined in Sec.2(7) of the Act thus: *"Goods mean every kind of movable property other than actionable claims and money; and includes stocks and shares, growing crops, grass, and things attached to or forming part of the land which are agreed to be severed before sale or under the contract of sale."*

The subject-mater of the contract of sale must be goods.

Thus, every kind of movable property except actionable claims and money is regarded as 'goods.' To be specific, things like goodwill, copyright, trademark, patents, water, gas, electricity, ships, standing trees, grass; shares and stock, etc., are 'goods' for the purpose of this section.

Every kind of movable property except actionable claims and money is regarded as 'goods.'

Things like goodwill, copyright, trademark, patents, water, gas, electricity, ships, standing trees, grass; shares and stock, etc., are 'goods' for the purpose of this section.

Actionable claim is understood as a "thing in action." Thing in action is where a person has not the enjoyment of the thing, but merely a right to recover it by a suit or action. A debt is a thing in action or actionable claim. A debt cannot be goods because it can only be assigned under the Transfer of Property Act but cannot be sold.

"Money" means current money. Current money is not 'goods.'

"Money" means current money. Current money is not 'goods.' Money is legal tender and is an essential aspect of every sale because the price of goods has to be expressed in terms of money. Money itself, therefore, cannot be the subject-mater of sale. However, old and rare coins, which have ceased to be legal tender and which have become objects of curiosity may be bought and sold. Foreign currency may also be bought and sold.

(v) ***Sale and Contract of Work and Material:*** Contract for painting of a portrait, contract for providing and fixing windows according to specifications, contract for fabrication and installation of shutters according to specifications and supply of meals in a hotel are not contract of sale for the purpose of this Act. But contracts to take and supply photographs, to build ships and to prepare medical prescription, have been held to be contracts of sale. The former are not held to contracts of sale because they are agreements involving the exercise of skill or labour on some material. A contract of sale must be distinguished from a contract of work and labour. The Sale of Goods Act applies to contracts of sale and not to contracts of labour and work.

The Sale of Goods Act applies to contracts of sale and not to contracts of labour and work.

(vi) ***Essentials of Valid Contract:*** It is only stressing the obvious that all the essentials of a valid contract must be present in the contract of sale also.

All the essentials of a valid contract must be present in the contract of sale also.

How is Contract of Sale Made?

A contract of sale, like any other contract, is made by an offer and its acceptance. It may be made in writing or a word of mouth; it may also be implied from the conduct of the parties or the course of business between the parties. Thus, if a person goes into a shop and selects an article exposed for the sale in the shop and takes it away, it is a purchase of the article at the price fixed to it or at a reasonable price, if no price is fixed.

The contract of sale may provide for the immediate delivery of the goods or immediate payment of the price or both or for the delivery or payment by instalments, or delivery or payment or both may be postponed.

"Where under a contract of sale the property in the goods is transferred from the seller to the buyer the contract is called a sale, but where the transfer of the property in the goods is to take place at a future time or subject to some condition thereafter to be fulfilled, the contract is called an agreement to sell."

Some Distinctions

It is useful to make distinction between a sale and an agreement to sell, between a sale and a hire-purchase and sale and bailment. These differences help us understand the nature of sale more clearly.

A sale must be distinguished from an agreement to sell. The legal implications of the two are vastly different. The basic difference between the two is brought out by Sec.4(3) of the Act. Thus, according to the Section "Where under a contract of sale the property in the goods is transferred from the seller to the buyer the contract is called a sale, but where the transfer of the property in the goods is to take place at a future time or subject to some condition thereafter to be fulfilled, the contract is called an agreement to sell." Table contains differences between a sale and an agreement to sell more specifically.

Table 6.1 Sale Distinguished from Agreement to Sell

Sale	*Agreement to Sell*
1. Property or ownership of goods is transferred immediately to the buyer.	1. Ownership is to be transferred at a future time or subject to certain conditions to be fulfilled.
2. A sale makes the buyer owner of goods. He can exercise all the proprietary rights in respect of them, such as an action for conversion or detenue. If the seller refuses to deliver the goods, the buyer may sue for recovery of the goods.	2. An agreement to sell does not entitle the buyer to sue for recovery of goods, it only entitles him to sue for damages for breach and not for recovery of goods. Buyer's right is against the seller and against goods.
3. If the buyer fails to pay for the goods, the seller may sue for the price.	3. If the buyer fails to accept and pays for the goods, the seller can only sue for damages and not for price.
4. If the goods are destroyed, the loss falls upon the buyer (unless otherwise agreed) even though the goods have never come into his possession.	4. If the goods are destroyed, the loss falls on the seller, unless otherwise agreed.
5. The seller (in possession of goods after sale) cannot resell goods because the property on goods vests with the buyer, if the seller sells, the second buyer cannot acquire a better title to the goods if he is aware of the previous sale.	5. The seller can resell the goods because their ownership continues to stay with him. The first buyer can only sue the seller for damage, the second buyer gets a goods title to the goods even if he is aware of the previous agreement to sell.
6. When seller is declared insolvent, buyer is entitled to receive the goods from the Official Assignee or Receiver.	6. Buyer has to prove the amount he has paid to seller. He is entitled to receive a ratable dividend, he cannot compel the Official Assignee or Receiver to deliver the goods.
7. If the buyer becomes insolvent before he pays for the goods, the seller, in the absence of a lien over the goods, must return them to the Official Receiver or Assignee. He can only claim a ratable dividend for the price of the goods.	7. If the buyer becomes insolvent and has not yet paid the price, the seller need not part with the goods until paid for.
8. A sale is an executed contract.	8. An agreement to sell is an executory contract.

6.3 SALE AND HIRE-PURCHASE AGREEMENT

A hire-purchase agreement is a contract whereby the seller of the goods agrees to transfer the property in the goods to the hire-purchaser after a fixed number of instalments of price are paid by the buyer. If the hirer fails to pay any particular instalment, the seller has every right to terminate the contract and take away the goods. The instalments paid so far are assumed to be hire charges paid by the hirer for use of goods. The following Table brings out the distinction more clearly:

A hire-purchase agreement is a contract whereby the seller of the goods agrees to transfer the property in the goods to the hire-purchaser after a fixed number of instalments of price are paid by the buyer.

Table 6.2 Sale distinguished from Hire-Purchase

Sale	*Hire-purchase*
1. Ownership of goods is transferred to the buyer immediately.	1. Ownership is transferred to the hirer only after the last instalment has been paid.
2. Buyer cannot terminate the contract. He is bound to pay the price.	2. Hirer is at liberty to terminate the agreement at any stage. He cannot be forced to pay his remaining instalments.
3. When the buyer becomes insolvent, the seller takes the risk of any loss.	3. When the hirer becomes insolvent the seller does not run the risk of any loss. He can take back the goods.
4. A sale is subject to the implied conditions and warranties provided under the Sale of Goods Act, 1930.	4. A hire-purchase agreement is not subject to such implied conditions and warranties. It is, however, subject to the implied conditions provided under the hire-purchase agreement.
5. A sale is subject to levy of sales tax at the time of contract of sale.	5. Sales tax is not leviable on hire-purchase until it finally converts into sale.
6. If the payment is made by the buyer in instalments, the amount payable by the buyer to the seller is reduced, for the payment made by the buyer is towards the price of the goods.	6. The instalments paid by the hirer are regarded as hire charges and not at payments towards the price of the goods till the option to purchase the goods is exercised.
7. Sale is governed by the Sale of Goods Act, 1930.	7. Hire-purchase is governed by the Hire-purchase Act, 1972.

6.4 NATURE OF A BAILMENT

Personal property may not always remain under the owner's care and control. A variety of legal rights and claims may come into play when personal property is loaned, sent for repairs, stored, or otherwise placed in the custody of someone other than the owner — a type of transaction known as a bailment.

Bailment Defined

A bailment is a delivery of possession of goods or personal property to another for temporary custody, care, repair, or use by the recipient.

A bailment is a delivery of possession of goods or personal property to another for temporary custody, care, repair, or use by the recipient. The subject of a bailment transaction is always personal property. The person turning over the property is called the bailor, and the person taking custody of the property is known as the bailee. Under appropriate circumstances the concept of bailment may include many types of transaction, among them the deposit, storage, rental, loan, checking, pledge, or repair of property or the holding of lost property. Bailments are sometimes divided into several classes by the courts, according to who is to benefit. These courts impose a greater degree of care on those who benefit most.

The bailor of property is usually the owner, but not necessarily. A thief who checks a stolen briefcase at a parcel checkroom is a bailor, even though the thief does not have title. A friend who borrows a set of golf clubs becomes a bailor when the clubs are left at a repair shop.

A bailee is never one who has title to the property or who is expected to gain title. If the intent of the parties is for the receiver to gain title, then the transaction is a sale or barter (a variation of a sale) rather than a bailment.

Title is to remain with the owner in every bailment.

As one of the requirements of a bailment, it is expected that the identical goods will be returned to the bailor. The courts say that "bailment is characterized by a transfer of possession, as distinguished from a change in ownership."

It is often part of the bailment arrangement, however, that the property will be returned in altered form. For example, a broker watch may be returned in working condition; soiled laundry may be returned as clan; milk may be returned as cheese; or wheat may be ground and returned as flour.

A bailment is usually regarded by the courts as a contract arrangement.

Basic Requirements for a Bailment

The courts sometimes list three requirements for a bailment:

Title to personal property is not transferred.

Temporary possession and control is given to and accepted by the bailee.

Possession eventually reverts back to the bailor or to someone designated by the bailor.

Sale and Bailment

While in a sale, the property to the goods is transferred from seller to buyer for a price, in a bailment only the possession of goods is transferred from one person (bailor) to another (bailee). The bailee is expected to return the goods to the bailor or dispose of as directed, after the purpose for which the goods were bailed, is served. The differences between sale and bailment are outlined in the Table 6.3.

While in a sale, the property to the goods is transferred from seller to buyer for a price, in a bailment only the possession of goods is transferred from one person (bailor) to another (bailee).

6.5 SUBJECT-MATTER OF CONTRACT OF SALE

As was pointed earlier, goods constitute the subject-matter of contract of sale. Since goods are an important element, it is proposed to discuss in detail the types of goods and the effect of destruction of goods.

Table 6.3 Sale Distinguished from Bailment

Sale	*Bailment*
1. Property in goods is transferred from seller to buyer.	1. Only possession of goods is transferred from bailor to bailee.
2. Consideration for a sale is the price in terms of money only.	2. Consideration may be in money or in kind.
3. Buyer can deal with the goods as he likes because he is the owner of them.	3. Bailor must return or dispose of goods as directed by bailor after the purpose is served.
4. Goods once sold normally cannot be returned.	4. Goods must be returned to bailor after the specified purpose is accomplished.

Goods include every kind of movable property other than actionable claims and money. Goods may be either existing or future goods.

1. *Existing Goods:* Existing goods are owned and possessed by the seller at the time of sale. Existing *goods* themselves are of three types, namely, (i) specific goods, (ii) ascertained goods, (iii) unascertained or generic goods.

Specific goods are identified and agreed upon at the time a contract of sale is made. *Ascertained goods* are those which become ascertained subsequent to the formation of the contract of sale.

As the expression itself suggests, *specific goods* are identified and agreed upon at the time a contract of sale is made. *Ascertained goods* are those which become ascertained subsequent to the formation of the contract of sale. In nature, ascertained goods resemble specific goods. But there is difference. Specific goods are identified at the time of forming the contract, whereas ascertained goods are ascertained after the contract has been formed. *Generic goods* or unascertained goods are not identified at the time of forming a contract but are defined by description and may form part of a lot.

2. *Future Goods:* Future goods represent goods to be manufactured or acquired by the seller after forming a contract. These goods are not therefore, in the possession of seller at the time of entering into the contract of sale.

Effect of Destruction of Goods

Future goods represent goods to be manufactured or acquired by the seller after forming a contract.

In a contract for sale of specific goods may perish before sale is gone through. Such a contingency may arise in any of the following two stages:

A. *Goods Persisting Before Forming Contract (Sec.27):* Where there is a contract for the sale of specific goods, the contract is void if the goods without the knowledge of the seller have, at the time when the contract is made, perished or so damaged as no longer to answer to their description in the contract.

In order that the contract may be valid the following conditions must be complied with:

(a) The goods must be specific goods. This action does not apply to unascertained goods.

(b) The goods must have perished or so damaged as no longer to answer to their description in the contract.

(c) The goods must have been so damaged or finished without the knowledge of the seller.

(d) The goods must have been so damaged or finished before forming the contract.

In *Barrow Lane & Ballard V Phillips (1929)*: There was a contract for the sale of a parcel of 700 bags of Chinese groundnuts. Unknown to the seller, 10 bags had been stolen at the time of the contract. The seller delivered the remaining 591 bags and, on the buyer's refusal to take them, bought-an action for the price. It was held that the buyers were not liable to take or pay for the goods. The buyers had contracted to buy a specific quantity and to ask them to take less would be to compel them to do what they had not contracted to do. The contract had accordingly become void by reason of the loss of goods.

B. *Goods Perishing After Agreement to Sell (Sec.8):* Where there is an agreement to sell specific goods, and subsequently the goods without any fault on the part of either seller or buyer perish or become so damaged as no longer to answer to their description in the agreement before the risk passes to the buyer, the agreement becomes void.

In order for this section to operate, the following essentials must be present:

(a) the goods must be specific goods.

(b) the goods must have perished or damaged before the risk passes to the buyer.

(c) the goods must be perished or damaged without the fault of seller or buyer.

In *Howell V. Coupland* (1876), the defendant agreed to sell to plaintiff 200 tonnes of regent potatoes to be grown on the land belonging to the defendant. the defendant sowed sufficient land to grow more than 200 tonnes, but without any fault in him, a disease attacked the crop, and he was able to deliver only about eight tonnes. The agreement was held to have become void.

6.6 CONDITIONS AND WARRANTIES

A contract contains some stipulations or terms some of these terms may be essential to the contract and others are incidental or collateral to it. The former are hard core of the contract and their non-fulfillment may seem to upset the very basis of the contract. They may be so vital to the contract that their breach may seem to be breach of the contract itself. Such terms are known as conditions of the contract and their breach entitles the innocent party to repudiate the contract. A stipulation which is collateral to the contract is called a warranty. Its breach does not lead to repudiation, but only to damages for the breach. This distinction between a condition and a warranty is not universal. Whether a stipulation is a condition or a warranty depends on the construction of each contract. A stipulation may be a condition though called a warranty to the contract. To quote the relevant sections of the Act, "a condition is a stipulation essential to the main purpose of contract, the breach of which gives rise to a right to treat the contract as repudiated" (Sec. 12(2)).

> May seem to upset the very basis of the contract. They may be so vital to the contract that their breach may seem to be breach of the contract itself. Such terms are known as conditions of the contract.
>
> A stipulation which is collateral to the contract is called a warranty.
>
> A condition is a stipulation essential to the main purpose of contract, the breach of which gives rise to a right to treat the contract as repudiated.

"A warranty is a stipulation collateral to the main purpose of the contract, the breach of which gives rise to a claim for deranges but not to a right to reject the goods and treat the contract as repudiated" (Sec.12(3)).

6.7 NATURE OF A WARRANTY

Legal Definitions of Warranty

In legal terminology, a guarantee made by a seller is called a warranty may be defined as "Any affirmation of fact or promise made by the seller to the buyer which relates to the goods and becomes part of the basis of the bargain.... That the goods shall conform to the affirmation or promise."

In slightly different language, the courts frequently define a warranty as: An assurance by one party to a contract of the existence of a fact upon which the other party may rely and amounts to a promise to indemnify [repay] the promisee for any loss if the fact warranted proves untrue.

Generally when there is a breach of warranty, the buyer can go back on the seller in a lawsuit. The ability to hold the seller to the warranty is a distinct legal right, separate from the right to sue for breach of contract.

Condition and Warranty Distinguished

The difference between a condition and a warranty is shown in Table.

Table 6.4 Distinction between a Condition and a Warranty

Condition	*Warranty*
1. Essential to the main purpose of the contract.	1. Only collateral or subsidiary to the main purpose of the contract.
2. Breach entitles the innocent party to repudiate the contract.	2. Breach entitles the innocent party to sue for damage.
3. A breach of condition may be treated as a breach of warranty.	3. A breach of warranty cannot be treated as a breach of condition.

When can Breach of Condition be treated as a Breach of Warranty?

Sec. 13 of the Act entitles the buyer to treat breach of condition as breach of warranty though the former enables him to repudiate the contract. In the following three cases breach of condition may be treated as breach of warranty:

(i) Where the buyer elects to treat breach of condition as breach of warranty, i.e., he prefers to claim damages instead of repudiating the contract;

(ii) Where the buyer waives the condition. Once the buyer has waived his right, he cannot, afterwards insist on its fulfillment. Waiver may be express or implied; and

(iii) Unless there is an express or implied contract to the contrary —

(a) Where a contract of sale is not severable and the buyer has accepted the goods or part thereof; or

(b) Where contract is for specific goods, the property in which has passed to the buyer.

Express or Implied Conditions and Warranties

Conditions and warranties may be expressly stated or implied from the circumstances. It is open to the parties to a contract to include any number of express conditions and warranties. But in addition to what the contract may provide the law implies into every sale of goods a number of conditions and warranties. They are read into every contract of sale unless excluded and are known as implied conditions and warranties. Sections 14 to 17 contain implied conditions and warranties.

Implied Conditions

Implied conditions (see Fig. 6.2) are explained the paragraphs that follow:

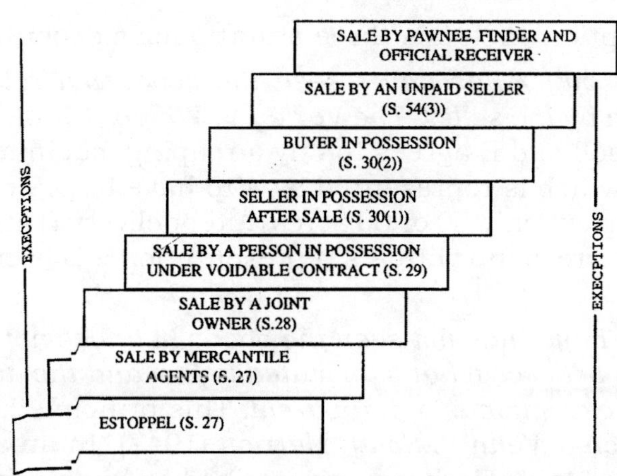

Fig. 6.2 Implied Conditions

1. *Conditions as to Title:* Sec. 14 declare that in contract of sale, unless the circumstances of the contract are such as to show a different intention there is:

(a) an implied condition on the part of the seller that, in the case of a sale, he has a right to sell the goods; and

(b) that in the case of an agreement to sell, he will have a right to sell the goods at the time when the property is to pass.

'Right to sell' means that the seller has lawful ownership of goods he wants to sell. If his title to goods is defective he cannot transfer property to buyer. And transfer of property is the essence of contract of sale. That is why the law reads into every sale the implied conditions that the seller has the right to sell.

'Right to sell' means that the seller has lawful ownership of goods he wants to sell.

In *Rowland V. Divall* (1923), R bought a secondhand car from D and used it for some months. It was subsequently seized by the police as a stolen car. Here there was a breach of implied conditions regarding the title, R was entitled to recover full price from the seller.

'Right to sell' means not mere possession of defect-free title to goods. It also means that the seller should not infringe on trade mark of other seller. This principle was underlined in *Niblett V. Confectioners Materials Co.* (1921), it so happened that the defendant sold to the plaintiff 3,000 tins of condensed milk. On their arrival in England from New York it was found that 1,000 tins were labelled 'Nissy Brand.' Another manufacturer of the condensed milk under the brand name of 'Nestle' claimed that this was an infringement of his trade-mark. The plaintiff had to remove all the labels in order to obtain the goods and subsequently sold them at a reduced value. He sued the sellers for the breach of the conditions as to title. It was held that the plaintiff had the right to reject the goods or to recover as damages the loss caused by the sale at a reduced price.

2. *Sale by Description (Sec.* 15): This section lays down that "where there is a contract of sale of goods by description, there is an implied condition that the goods shall correspond with description."

"Where there is a contract of sale of goods by description, there is an implied condition that the goods shall correspond with description."

The sale by description is a condition which goes to the root of the contract and the breach of it entitles the buyer to reject the goods. However, the buyer can invoke this section provided (i) there is a sale by description, and (ii) goods sold do not correspond to the description.

'Sale by description' includes three situations as described below:

(a) *Where the buyer has never seen the goods but relies entirely on their description by the seller: The Varley V. Whipp* (1900), is a case in point. A agrees to sell and B agrees to buy a reaping machine which B has never seen and which is represented by A to have been new the previous year and used to cut only 50 or 60 acres. After delivery B finds that the machine does not correspond with A's representations. B is entitled to return the machine.

(b) *Where the buyer has not seen the goods but does not rely on what he has seen — he believes what was stated to him and the deviation of the goods from the description is not apparent:* This principle has been underlined in *Nicholson* & *Venn V. Smith Marriott* (1947). In an auction sale a set of napkins and table cloths were described as "dating from the seventeenth century." The plaintiffs, who were dealers in antiquities, saw the set and bought it. They subsequently found it to be an eighteenth century set and sought to reject it. It was held that they could do so. The plaintiffs relied on description and the deviation of quality from description could not have been noticed with casual examination.

(c) *Packing of goods may sometimes be a part of the description: In Moore* & *Co.V. Landauer* & *Co.,* (1921), M Sold to L 300 tins of Australian fruits packed in cases, each containing 30 tins. M tendered a substantial portion in cases containing 24 tins. The method of packing was held to be a part of description and, therefore, the buyers were entitled to reject the entire lot.

Sale by Sample as well as Description: bulk of the goods correspond with the sample. They must correspond with the description as well.

3. *Sale by Sample as well as Description:* If the sale is by sample as well as by description, it is not sufficient that the bulk of the goods correspond with the sample. They must correspond with the description as well. If goods correspond with sample but not with description, the condition is breached, and the buyer is entitled to reject the goods.

In *Nichol V. Godts* (1854), the plaintiff sold to the defendant some oil described as 'foreign refined rape oil, warranted only equal to sample.' The oil delivered was equal to sample but contained a mixture of hemp oil. It was held that the defendant was entitled to reject, because the goods, though correspondent with sample, did not correspondent with the description.

4. *Exceptions to the Principle of Caveat Emptor (Sec.16):* *Caveat Emptor* is a Latin expression, which when translated into English, means 'let the buyer beware.' In the context of sale of goods, caveat emptor means that the seller is not bound to supply goods which should be fit for any particular purpose or which should possess any particular quality. It is the duty of the buyer to select goods of his requirement. He must 'take care' but not 'take chance' while selecting goods. This principle has been incorporated into the Sale of Goods Act. The opening words of Sec. 16 of the Act reads thus: "Subject to the provisions of this Act and of any other law for the time being in force, there is no implied warranty or conditions as to the quality or fitness of for any particular purpose of goods supplied under a contract of sale.... "

The principle of *caveat emptor* was applied in *Ward V. Hobbs* (1878). The plaintiff bought some pigs in an auction from the defendant who knew that the pigs were suffering from swine fever. He did not disclose this fact to the plaintiff, and the pigs were sold 'with all faults.' Subsequent to the purchase, all pigs, except one, die of fever. They also infected a few of the plaintiff's own pigs. Rejecting the plaintiff's claim for damages, it was observed that "although a vendor is bound to employ no artifice or disguise for the purpose of concealing defects in the article sold, since that amount to a positive fraud on the vendor, yet under the general doctrine of a *caveat emptor,* he is not ordinarily bound to disclose every defect of which he may be cognisant, although his silence may operate virtually to deceive the vendee."

The principle of *caveat emptor* appears to have had its origin in those days when sale of goods in the open market was common. The buyer and the seller came face to face, the seller exhibited his wares, the buyer examined them and bought them if he liked. This practice is no more possible nowadays. Most sale deals are not effected through correspondence. Besides, because of the complex nature of the present day goods, it is only the seller who can assure the structure and quality of the goods. It is because of these reasons that it became necessary to restrict the rule of *caveat emptor* by imposing certain exceptions to it. The exceptions to the rule of *caveat emptor* have now become more prominent than the rule itself.

Doctine of *Caveat Emptor* is not practicable because of the complex nature of the present day goods, it is only the seller who can assure the structure and quality of the goods. It is because of these reasons that it became necessary to restrict the rule of *caveat emptor* by imposing certain exceptions to it.

Exceptions: There are four exceptions to the rule, viz.: (i) Fitness for buyer's purpose, (ii) merchantable quality, (iii) implied conditions of trade, and (iv) express terms. In these exceptions the rule of caveat emptor will not apply. The seller will be held liable for breach of any of these four exceptions. The exceptions are explained below:

(i) Fitness for buyers purpose, (ii) merchantable quality, (iii) implied conditions of trade, and (iv) express terms. In these exceptions the rule of caveat emptor will not apply.

***(i) Fitness for Buyers Purpose* (Sec. 16(1)):** (a) The rules in this context are: (a) Where the goods are ordered for a specific purpose, (b) the seller is made aware of it, (c) the buyer relies on the skill or judgment of the seller, and (d) the goods must be of a description dealt in by the supplier, whether he be the manufacturer or not.

These four conditions must co-exist. And in any routine purchase these conditions are implicitly satisfied. For example, in *Grant V. Australian Knitting Mills* (1936), the plaintiff, a doctor, bought two woolen underpants from a retailer. The pants were manufactured by the defendants. Next day, after wearing one of them he became ill. His illness was diagnosed as dermatitis caused by a chemical irritant which the defendants had negligently omitted to remove in the process of manufacture. It was held that the sale was within the exception and the implied conditions of fitness for the buyer's purpose was broken. The doctor was, therefore, entitled to succeed.

Fitness of buyers purpose: (a) Where the goods are ordered for a specific purpose, (b) the seller is made aware of it, (c) the buyer relies on the skill or judgment of the seller, and (d) the goods must be of a description dealt in by the supplier, whether he be the manufacturer or not.

The purpose for which goods are required is implied if goods are purchased from a specialised dealer, buying a TV set from a dealer in electronics, for example. If the goods turn out to be unfit for the purpose intended, they can be rejected. Particular purpose must be disclosed when goods are used for more than one purpose.

However, where the sale of a specific article is under its patent or trademark, there is no implied condition as to its fitness for a specific purpose the doctrine of caveat emptor will apply. The buyer here relies more on the brand than on the skill and judgment of the seller and it is "manifestly unjust to burden the seller with responsibility for fitness." For example, B writes to A the owner of a patent invention for cleaning cotton, "send me your patent cotton-cleaning machine at my factory." A sends the machine according to order. There is no implied condition or warranty on the part of A that the machine is fit for the particular purpose of cleaning the cotton at B's factory.

The dealer who sells goods by description is bound to deliver goods of merchantable quality.

***(ii) Merchantable Quality* (Sec. 16(2):** The second exception to the doctrine of caveat emptor is that the dealer who sells goods by description is bound to deliver goods of merchantable quality. Merchantable quality means:

(a) goods must be marketable under the description by which they are known in the market at their full value.

(b) goods are not merchantable when they possess some defects rendering them unfit to serve their intended purposes.

(c) goods must be such that their sale does not violate any statute in force in the country. For example, a boiler must satisfy the requirements of the Boilers Act.

(d) packing of goods is also an important consideration in judging the merchantability of goods.

A few cases may be cited wherein implied condition as to merchantability was breached and the seller was held liable.

In *Godley V. Perry* (1960), a toy dealer displayed in his shop window some plastic toy catapults. A child of six was attracted by them and bought one. While he was using it, the catapult broke off and entered his left eye which had to be removed. The seller was held liable.

In *Jones V. Just* (1868), a firm of Liverpool merchants contracted to buy from a London merchant a number of bales of Manilla hemp to arrive from Singapore. The hemp arrived wetted by sea water and it was so much damaged that it would not pass in the market as Manilla hemp. Consequently it had to be sold at about five per cent of original price. It was held that the goods were not of merchantable quality and the seller was bound to make good the loss caused by selling at the reduced price.

In *Priest V. Last* (1903), the plaintiff bought a hot water bottle which is ordinarily used for application of heat to human body. The bottle burst scalding the plaintiff's wife, the seller was held liable.

In *Morelli V. Pitch and Gibbons* (1928), the plaintiff bought a bottle of Stone's Ginger Wine. When he attempted to draw its cork with a corkscrew and with due care, the neck of the bottle broke off, the bottle fell to the ground cutting the plaintiff's hand. The seller was held responsible for damages.

In *Jackson V. Rota Motor and Cycle Co.* (1920), the sellers who were manufacturers of motor horns, sold 600 horns to the defendant. Of these, 364 were defective as they were dented, badly polished and were of faulty manufacture. The buyer rejected these and accepted the remaining. Rejecting the seller's suit for the price, the court observed that 'there was here a substantial failure on the part of the seller to deliver goods of merchantable quality and the buyers were entitled to treat this as one contract and to reject the goods. They were not bound to go picking and choosing. The seller cannot say pick out the various portions which are good and pay for those.

Examination by the Buyer

Implied conditions as to merchantability, is however, subject to a provision. According to this provision, if the buyer has examined the goods, there shall be no implied conditions as regards defects which such examination ought to have revealed. Thus, *in Thrnett and Fehr V. Beers and Sons* (1919), a buyer contracted to buy a quantity of glue. The goods were contained in casks which were lying in the seller's godown. The seller took the buyer to the godown and offered to show him the glue. But being pressed for time, the buyer did not ask that any of the casks should be opened. He contended himself with looking at the casks. The glue turned to be defective and not of merchantable quality. The seller was not held responsible. The buyer's contention that he did not examine the goods was dismissed by the court.

***(iii) Conditions implied by Trade Usage (Sec.* 16(3)):** An implied condition or warranty as to quality or fitness for a particular purpose may be annexed by the usage of trade. Where the trade usage makes the purpose of the article explicit, the buyer need not tell the seller the purpose for which he buys the goods. For example, in *Dr. Baretto V. T.R. Price* (1939), A bought a set of false teeth from a dentist. The set did not fit into A's mouth. It was held that A could reject the set as the purpose for which anybody would buy it was known to the seller, the dentist. Similarly, a watch that will not keep time, a pen that will not write, and a tobacco that will not smoke do not satisfy the implied condition as to trade usage.

***Conditions implied by Trade Usage (Sec.* 16(3)):** If a buyer makes clear for which he needed the goods, the seller should sell the goods of such quality and quantity to fit the purpose of the buyer.

However, a custom should not be unreasonable. An unreasonable custom will not affect the parties' contract. Similarly, the custom should not be inconsistent with the express terms of the contract.

***(iv) Express Terms (Sec.* 16(4)):** The parties to a contract have liberty to include any express condition(s) and/or warranty(s) in their contract. But an express warranty or condition does not contradict a warranty or a condition implied by the Act unless the express terms are inconsistent with the implied conditions.

Except in the above cases, doctrine of caveat emptor shall apply and the seller will not be held liable for any penalty if the goods purchased turn out to be unfit. The buyer may, however, protect himself by express warranty or condition.

***5. Sale by Sample (Sec.* 17):** A sale by sample is a contract for sale by sample where there is a term in the contract, express or implied, to that effect (Sec. 17(1)). In the case of a contract for sale by sample, there is an implied condition:

In a sale by sample the bulk shall correspond with the sample in quality.

(a) that the bulk shall correspond with the sample in quality.

(b) that the buyer shall have a reasonable opportunity of comparing the bulk with the sample.

(c) that the goods shall be free from any defect, rendering them unmerchantable, which would not be apparent on a reasonable examination of the sample (Sec. 17(2)).

Breach of any of these implied conditions will entitle the buyer to reject the goods unless he has accepted them, or, in the case of a contract relating to specific goods, the property in the goods has passed to him. In these cases, the buyer is entitled to damages only.

6. Implied Condition as to Wholesomeness: In the case of eatables and provisions, in addition to the implied conditions as to merchantability, there is another implied condition — the goods must be wholesome. For example, P bought milk from D. The milk contained typhoid germs. P's wife took the milk and got infection as a result of which she died. P was entitled to recover the damages (*Frost* v. *Aylesbury Dairy Co. Ltd.* (1905)).

Wholesomeness means without any defects.

Similarly, P bought a bun containing a stone which broke one of P's teeth. It was held that P could recover damages *(Chaproiere* v. *Manson* (1905)).

6.8 EXPRESS AND IMPLIED WARRANTIES

An express warranty is a statement made in express, or specific words by the seller.

Warranties are of two kinds, either express or implied. An express warranty is a statement made in express, or specific words by the seller. An express warranty may be either written or oral, so long as the seller writes or orally describes some specific fact, quality, or feature of the thing being sold. A printed newspaper advertisement is, of course, an express warranty.

When an express warranty is given by a salesperson in a store, a subsequent dispute could come down to the word of the consumer (buyer) against the word of the salesperson. To the protected, the buyer may want to obtain a brief written warranty from the sales clerk. This need not be lengthy or greatly detailed. For example, the clerk could be asked to write across the fact of the sales ticket: "This sweater is 100% wool."

In some instances a warranty may be implied from the seller's failure to deny certain facts when specifically questioned about the quality or properties of merchandise.

If the seller has made an express warranty of items being offered for sale, almost all courts agree that the buyer is not under the necessity of making an inspection as to hidden or latent defects that may later come to light. The warranty relieves the buyer of the burden of making the inspection and the buyer does not assume the risk of defects that an examination might reveal.

If the buyer knows of defects at the time the purchase is made, the courts differ about whether the buyer must accept known defects.

"Opinion" or "Sales Talk"

Generally, the courts hold that a warranty must relate to or be a statement of fact and not one of opinion. As stated in the following:

An affirmation merely of the value of the goods or a statement purporting to be merely the seller's opinion or commendation of the goods does not create a warranty.

The courts usually distinguish mere words of description.

From a warranty, if a merchant agrees to sell a housewife some green window curtains, the contract would not be met by delivering tan curtains or a green sofa cover. The buyer is under no obligation to take either, since she would not be getting that for which she bargained. Legally, the furnishing of tan curtains would be a breach of contract, permitting the buyer to back out of the purchase. Many courts, however, allow the buyer in a situation of this kind to treat the improper delivery as a breach of an express warranty. Under either interpretation the buyer would be protected.

The courts have always given the seller considerable leeway in "puffing" of goods in an attempt to sell them. Expressions of opinion and words of praise are consistently regarded as mere sales talk. The legal definition of "mere sales talk" is never easily drawn. Courts often differ in their interpretations among cases.

To illustrate these differences, a statement that "this sweater in cashmere" is a warranty. So, too, is a salesman's claim that "these suits are 100% wool."

But the courts usually consider the following claims as mere puffery: "This coat is worth at least twice what we are asking for it!"

The courts ordinarily make the legal point that sale puffery may include expressions that are somewhat extravagant so long as they do not misrepresent some specific quality or feature of the article being sold.

For example, the seller could inform a lady looking at a fox fur coat that "you will never be in better style than when you wear this cape." However, had the salesman misrepresented the item as a more expensive mink, then the seller could have been held to the higher quality.

A warranty, then, is a legally binding representation by the seller that specifies the quality or condition of the goods offered for sale. There is no magic in the word "warranty" standing alone. In fact the term may be used in a document that is not actually a warranty. Similarly, a statement that does not contain the word "warranty" may still operate as a warranty.

Implied Warranties

The following the implied warranties in a contract of sale (see Fig. 6.3)

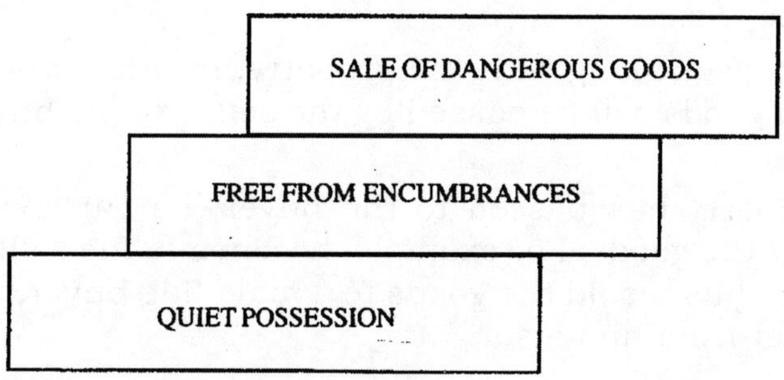

Fig. 6.3 Implied Warranties.

(1) *Quiet Possession: (Sec.14(b)):* In every contract of sale, unless there is some agreement to the contrary, there is an implied warranty that the buyer shall have and enjoy quiet possession of the goods. It is a warranty that nobody, including the seller, shall interfere with the quiet enjoyment of the vendee. If the right of enjoyment or possession of the buyer is disturbed by the seller or any other person, the buyer is entitled to sue the seller for damages.

(2) *Free from Encumbrances (Sec 14(c)):* The second implied warranty is that "the goods shall be free from any charge or encumbrance in favour of any third party not declared or known to the buyer before or at the time when the contract is made." If for example, a person has pledged his goods and, having taken them from the pledge under some excuse, sells them, the goods being subject to an encumbrance, this warranty is broken and the buyer may recover compensation if his possession is disturbed by the pledge.

(3) *Sale of Dangerous Goods:* In the case of a sale of goods, which to the knowledge of the seller, are dangerous or likely to be dangerous and if the buyer is ignorant of the same, there is an implied warranty that the seller shall warn the buyer about the danger. Failure to do so will entitle the buyer to claim damages if he incurs any loss consequent to the occurrence of the danger.

In every contract of sale, there is an implied warranty that the buyer shall have and enjoy quiet possession of the goods.

"the goods shall be free from any charge or encumbrance in favour of any third party not declared or known to the buyer before or at the time when the contract is made."

The goods which are dangerous or likely to be dangerous there is an implied warranty that the seller shall warn the buyer about the danger.

Exclusion of Implied Terms (Sec. 62)

Implied terms to a contract of sale (discussed till now) may be negative or varied by (a) express agreement between the parties, (b) the course of dealing between the parties, or (c) the custom or usage of trade. Sec. 62 lays down that "where any right, duty or liability would arise under a contract of sale by implication of law, it may be negatived or varied by express agreement or by the course of dealing between the parties, or by usage, if the usage is such as to bind both parties to the contract."

6.9 TRANSFER OF PROPERTY AND TITLE

Transfer of Property

Transfer of property is, therefore, the essence of a contract of sale.

As was pointed out in chapter 17, a contract of sale of goods is a contract whereby the seller transfers or agrees to transfer property in goods to the buyer for a price. Transfer of property is, therefore, the essence of a contract of sale. The most important question in the contract of sale naturally is when does the property (ownership) in the goods pass from the seller to the buyer? The determination of the time when ownership passes to the buyer is important for atleast four reasons, viz.:

(i) The risk passes along with the property. In other words, risk of loss or damage of goods will be passed by the seller to the buyer along with the property.

(ii) When property has passed to the buyer, he can exercise proprietary rights over the goods. For example, he can sue the seller for delivery and if the seller has resold the goods to a mala fide buyer, the original buyer can recover from him also.

(iii) The seller cannot sue for the price unless the goods have become the property of the buyer.

(iv) In the event of insolvency of the seller or the buyer, the question whether the Official Receiver can take over the goods or not depends on whether the property in the goods has passed from the seller to the buyer.

Property Passes when Intended to Pass (Sec.19)

The intention of the parties is significant to determine the transfer of property. In fact, the question of property transfer centers around the intention of the parties to the effect.

Sec.19 provides that "where there is a contract for the sale of specific or ascertained goods the property in them is transferred to the buyer at such time as the parties to the contract intend it to be transferred."

For the purpose of ascertaining the intention of the parties regard shall be had to (i) the terms of the contract, (ii) the conduct of the parties, and (iii) the circumstances of the case.

Where the intention of the parties is not apparent from their contract, the intention will be ascertained according to the rules laid down in Secs. 18 and 20 to 24. These sections deal with three types of situations: (a) sale of specific goods, (b) sale of goods on approval, and (c) sale of unascertained goods (see Fig.)

A. Sale of Specific Goods (Sec. 20-22)

Rules regarding sale of specific goods are summarised as follows:

(i) Passing of Property at the Time of Contract: According to Sec. 20 "where there is an unconditional contract for the sale of specific goods in a deliverable state, the property in the goods passes to the buyer when the contract is made, and it is immaterial whether the time of payment of the price of the delivery of the goods, or both, is postponed."

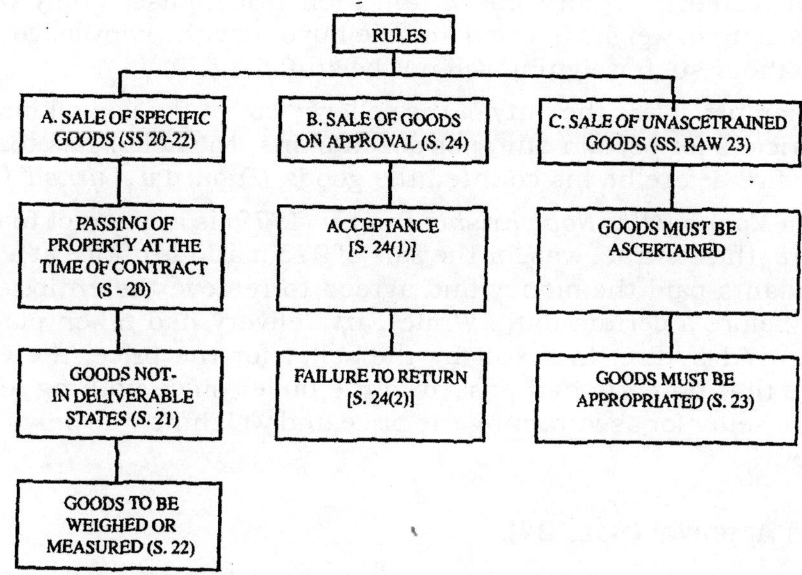

Fig. 6.4 Rules Regarding Transfer of Title

Thus, in the case of specific goods, property in them passes to the buyer at the time of making the contract, provided the goods are in a deliverable state, and the contract is unconditional. The fact that the time of delivery or the time of payment (or both) is postponed does not prevent the property from passing at once.

In the case of specific goods, property in them passes to the buyer at the time of making the contract, provided the goods are in a deliverable state, and the contract is unconditional.

Deliverable state means such a state that the buyer would, under the contract, be bound to take delivery of them (Sec. 2(3)).

For example, in *Tarling V. Baxer* (1827), A, on the 4th Jan. agreed to sell to B, a stack of hay to be paid on the 4th Feb. till then the stack to be allowed to stand in A's premises until 1st of May. A stipulated that the hay should not be cut until it was paid for. The hay was destroyed before being cut. It was held that the ownership had passed to B on the making of the contract and he was liable for the loss.

(ii) Goods not in Deliverable State (Sec. 21): According to Sec. 21 "where there is a contract for the sale of specific goods and the seller is bound to do something to the goods for the purpose of putting them into a deliverable state, the property does not pass until such thing is done and the buyer has notice thereof." Thus, if anything remains to be done on the part of the seller, until this is done the property is not transferred to the buyer.

In *Rugg v. Minett* (1809), there was a sale of the whole of turpentine oil lying in a cistern. The oil had to be filled by the seller in casks, which was partly done in the buyer's presence, but before he could remove the casks the whole oil was consumed by fire. It was held that the buyer had to bear the loss for the casks which had been filled up because the seller did everything that was necessary to put the oil in deliverable state.

Property in the goods, which are to be measured, weighed or tested, in order to ascertain their price, passes only when they are actually measured, weighed, tested and the buyer has the knowledge of it.

***(iii) Goods to be Weighted or Measures* (Sec. 22):** Where the specific goods are in deliverable state "but the seller is bound to weigh, measure, test or do some other act or thing with reference to the goods for the purpose of ascertaining the price, the property does not pass until such act or thing is done and the buyer has notice thereof." Thus, property in the goods, which are to be measured weighed or tested, in order to ascertain their price, passes only when they are actually measured, weighed, tested and the buyer has the knowledge of it. Symbolic delivery without such weighing will not be sufficient.

For example, if it is the duty of the seller to count the goat skins in each bale, and the price is for certain sum per dozen skins, the seller has to bear the loss caused by fire before he his counted the goods *(Zagury v. Furnell* (1809)).

Shoshi Mohun Pal v. Nobo Krishto Poddar (1979) is a contract to the case cited above. Here, the contract was for the sale of 975 maunds of rice at a certain price. The defendants paid the money and agreed to remove the entire quantity after weighing, before a certain date. While part delivery had taken place, the goods were destroyed by fire. In a suit by the seller for the price, the Calcutta High Court held that property had passed to the buyer since nothing remained to be done by the seller for ascertaining the price and weighing was only for the buyer's satisfaction.

B. Sale on Approval (Sec. 24)

The question of transfer of property in goods sent on approval or on 'sale or return' basis is answered by Sec. 24. According to the section property in such goods passes to the buyer "(a) when he signifies his approval or acceptance to the seller or does any other act adopting the transaction; (b) if he does not signify his approval or acceptance to the seller but retains the goods without rejection, then, if a time has been fixed for the return of the goods on the expiration of such time, and, if no time has been fixed, on the expiration of a reasonable time."

The essence of the section is that the property passes either by acceptance or failure to return. Rules regarding these two situations are summarised below:

When goods are sent on approval, sale or return, or on trial, the transaction is merely an agreement to sell, and the property and the risk remain in the seller until the buyer gives his acceptance.

(i) Acceptance (Sec. 24(i)): When goods are sent on approval, sale or return, or on trial, the transaction is merely an agreement to sell, and the property and the risk remain in the seller until the buyer gives his acceptance. The acceptance may be express or implied from conduct. An implied acceptance takes place when the buyer deprives himself of the power of return of the goods. Thus, if goods are sent on sale or return and the buyer pledges them to a third person, he has adopted the transaction and the property passes to him. This principle is underlined *in Kirkham* v. *Attenborough* (1897). The plaintiff delivered some jewellery to one Winter on "sale or return." Winter pledged the Jewellery with the defendant, Atten Borough, a pawnbroker. Winter failed to pay the price. The plaintiff sued the pawnbroker for the price. It was held that the plaintiff should have sued Winter for the price and not the defendant, who had acquired a good title from Winter. Winter, by pledging the goods, had adopted the transaction and the property did pass to him.

***(ii) Failure to Return (Sec.* 24(2)):** Failure on the part of the buyer to return the goods send to him on approval, may take place after expiration of specified time, or if no time is fixed, after expiry of a reasonable time. Till the expiry of such time the goods remain the property of the seller. To illustrate this principle we have the popular case, viz., *Elphick* v. *Barnes* (1880). In this case, a horse was delivered to the defendant on terms that he should try it for eight days and then return it if he did not like it. The horse died on the third day without the fault of the defendant. The seller could not recover the price from the defendant as the horse, being still his property when it died.

Property will pass to the buyer if he fails to return the goods sent to him after expiry of specified time. Seller can then sue the buyer for price. Where no time is fixed the buyer must return the goods after reasonable time, or else, they become the property of the buyer. What is reasonable time is a question of fact in each case. In *Poole* v. *Smith's Car Sales Ltd.* (1962) the plaintiff delivered, in August, a secondhand car to the defendants on "sale or return." No time was fixed for return of the car. It was not returned till October. Plaintiff subsequently wrote to the defendant that if the car was not returned by Nov. 10, it would be deemed to have been sold to them. Even so it was not returned till November end and that too in a very bad condition, the car having been damaged by the defendant's employees. It was held that reasonable time did elapse between August and November and the plaintiff was entitled to recover the price.

Property will pass to the buyer if he fails to return the goods sent to him after expiry of specified time. Seller can then sue the buyer for price.

C. Sale of Unascertained Goods (Sec. 18 and 23)

Rules regarding passing of property in unascertained goods are summarised as follows:

(i) Goods Must be Ascertained (Sec.18): According to this section "where there is a contract for the sale of unascertained goods, no property in them is transferred to the buyer unless and until the goods are ascertained."

"where there is a contract for the sale of unascertained goods, no property in them is transferred to the buyer unless and until the goods are ascertained."

In *Commissioner of Sales Tax, Nagpur* v. *Adamji & Co.*(1959), A entered into a contract with B for the supply of sawar logs during 1947-48 season. The goods to be supplied under contract were to be dispatched by A from railway stations in the Central Provinces. They were to be measured under supervision of B's/factory manager on arrival of goods at the factory. The price of the logs to be supplied were specified as "F.O.R. Ambernath." It was held that the contract was for sale of unascertained goods and consequently property in them could not, under Sec. 18, pass unless and until goods were ascertained.

(ii) Goods Must be Appropriated (Sec.23): Mere ascertainment is not enough - the goods must be appropriated. Sec. 23 contains provision to this effect. To quote the section: "Where there is a contract for the sale of unascertained or future goods by description and goods of that description and in a deliverable state are unconditionally appropriated to the contract, either by the seller with the assent of the buyer or by the buyer with the assent of the seller, the property in the goods thereupon passes to the buyer."

"Where there is a contract for the sale of unascertained or future goods by description and goods of that description and in a deliverable state are unconditionally appropriated to the contract."

The distinction between 'ascertainment' and 'appropriation' is interesting. Ascertainment means identification of the goods to be delivered under the contract. Appropriation, on the other hand, refers to the intention of both the parties to use the goods in performance of the contract. Another distinction is that ascertainment can be unilateral act. The seller along may set apart the goods. But appropriation involves consensus of both the seller and the buyer.

In *Rhode* v. *Thwaites* (1827), there was a sale of 20 hogheads of sugar out of larger quantity. Four hogheads were filled and taken away by the buyer.

Subsequently the seller filled 16 more hogheads and informed the buyer who promised to take them away, but before he could do so the goods were lost. It was held that the property had passed to the buyer. There was clear appropriation of goods when the seller filled up the 16 bags and the buyer promised to take delivery of the 16 bags.

Another point that needs emphasis is that the appropriation must be unconditional. It is unconditional when the seller does not resume himself the right of disposal of the goods. The appropriation, as pointed out above, may be done by the seller with the buyer's assent. Such assent may be express or implied, and may be given either before or after the appropriation is made.

Delivery of goods by seller to a common carrier is a mode of extending unconditional appropriation to the goods (Sec.23(2)). But it is necessary that delivery to the carrier must show to which particular buyer the goods are appropriated, otherwise the property does not pass.

Reservation of Right of Disposal (Sec. 25)

The property in goods does not pass if the seller reserves right to disposal, even if the goods are appropriated or delivered to the buyer, to a carrier or to a bailee for transmission to the buyer.

Apart from an express reservation of the right of disposal, the seller is deemed to reserve the right where —

(a) the goods are shipped or delivered to a railway for carriage, and by the bill of lading or railway receipt they are deliverable to the order of the seller or his agent.

(b) the seller sends to the buyer a bill of exchange for the price together with the bill of lading or railway receipt. The property does not pass to the buyer until the buyer accepts the bill of exchange. The buyer must return the bill of lading or railway receipt if he does not accept the bill of exchange. If he wrongfully retains the bill of lading or railway receipt, the property in the goods does not pass to him.

Transfer of Title

Where goods are sold by a person who is not the owner thereof and who does not sell them under the authority or with the consent of the owner, the buyer acquires no better title than the seller had "no one can give that which he possesses not."

Where goods are sold by a person who is not the owner thereof and who does not sell them under the authority or with the consent of the owner, the buyer acquires no better title than the seller had (Sec. 27). As a general rule, no one can sell the goods and give a good title thereof unless he is the owner thereof. This general rule is expressed by the maxim — *Nemo dat quod non habet* which means "no one can give that which he possesses not." The seller cannot give to the buyer of the goods a better title to the goods than he himself has. The rule is the same, even if the sale is accompanied by a transfer of a bill of lading, delivery order, warrant, or similar other documents. Such documents are not negotiable instruments and their transfer does not guarantee better title to the buyer.

Exceptions

There are eight important exceptions to the rule that no seller of goods can give to the buyer a better title than himself, namely:

1. Estoppel.
2. Sale be mercantile agent.
3. Sale by joint owner.
4. Sale by person in possession under voidable contract.
5. Seller in possession after sale.
6. Buyer in possession.
7. Sale by an unpaid seller.
8. Other exceptions (see Fig.) A brief explanation of each follows:

***1. Estoppel (Sec. 27)*:** Section 27 lays down that the owner of the goods is, by his conduct, precluded from denying the seller's authority to sell. For example, where a person sells his mother's goods in her presence and if she raises no objection, she cannot subsequently be permitted to deny her son's authority to sell and the sale will be binding on her.

2. Sale by Mercantile Agent (Sec. 27, Proviso): A mercantile agent is an agent who, in the customary course of his business, has authority to sell, consign, or buy goods, or raise money on the security of goods.

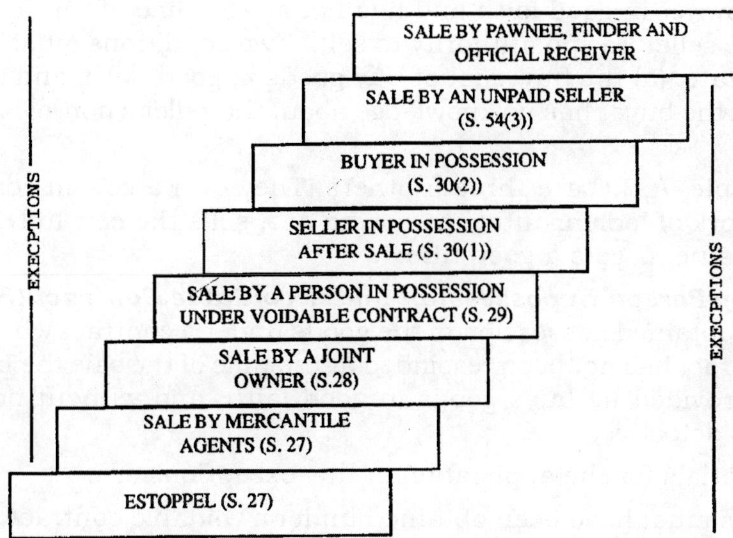

Fig: 6.5 Exceptions to Nemo Dat Quod – Non Habet

If a mercantile agent is, with the consent of the owner, in possession of the goods or of a document to title to the goods, then any sale made by him shall be binding on the owner (Sec.27(2)). This rule is, however, subject to the following conditions:

If a mercantile agent is, with the consent of the owner, in possession of the goods or of a document to title to the goods, then any sale made by him shall be binding on the owner.

(a) the agent is in possession of the goods or of the document of title to the goods,

(b) he is in possession of the goods as mercantile agent with the consent of the owner,

(c) the agent sells the goods in the ordinary course of his business as mercantile agent,

(d) the buyer acts in good faith, and

(e) the buyer has no notice, at the time of contract of sale, that the agent has no authority to sell.

In *Folks* v. *King* (1923), Folks, the owner of a car, delivered it to A, a mercantile agent for sale, stipulating that the car should not be sold for less than $ 575. The mercantile agent, however, sold the car to the king for $ 340 and misappropriated the amount. Folks could not recover his car from king who got a good title to the car.

If the mercantile agent obtains possession of goods without the consent of the owner, for example, by theft, the agent cannot give a good title to the goods. It must be noted that a person who is merely in possession of goods will not become a mercantile agent. Thus, a caretaker, a servant, a friend, a lawyer and a carrier are not mercantile agents. Therefore, to constitute a mercantile agent, he must not only be in possession of the goods or the documents of title to the goods, but he must be in a such a possession as a mercantile agent with the consent of the true owner of the goods and must be given authority to sell the goods in the ordinary course, of his business as such agent.

3. Sale by a Joint Owner (Sec.28): This section lays down that "if one of several joint owners of goods has the sole possession of them by permission of the co-owners, the property in the goods is transferred to any person who buys them of such joint owner in good faith and has not at any time of the contract of sale, notice that the seller has no authority to sell." Two conditions must be fulfilled for Sec.28 to operate: (a) the buyer must buy goods in good faith, and (b) at the time of the contract the buyer has no knowledge about the seller's non-existent authority to sell.

For example, A,B,C are three brothers. They own a cow in common. B & C entrust the work of looking after the cow to A. A sells the cow to D. D Purchases bonafide for value. D gets a good title.

***4. Sale by Person in possession under voidable Contract* (*Sec 29*):** When the seller has obtained possession of the goods under a contract which is voidable, and if the contract has not been rescinded at the time of the sale the buyer acquires a good title provided he buys goods in good faith, and without notice that the seller's title is defective.

The essentials for the application of this exceptions are:

(a) goods must have been obtained under a voidable contract as opposed to a void contract.

(b) contract must have not been rescinded at the time of sale.

(c) buyer must buy goods in good faith, and

(d) at the time of sale the buyer must have no knowledge of seller's defective title to goods.

In *Phillips V. Brooks* (1919), a fraudulent person posed himself to be a respectable person and obtained from a shopkeeper a valuable ring by issuing a worthless cheque. Before the fraud could be discovered the rouge had pledged the ring with a bonafide pledgee. It was held that the pledgee obtained a good title.

5. Seller in Possession after Sale [Sec.30(i)] : Where a seller having sold goods continues in possession of them, and sells them again to another person the buyer gets a good title provided he receives them in good faith and without notice of the previous sale.

In order to enable the seller to pass a good title the following conditions must be satisfied:

(a) the seller must continue in possession of the goods or of the documents of title to the goods. Possession as a hirer of the goods from the buyer after the delivery of the goods to him will not do.

In *Staffs Motor Guarantee Ltd. V. British Wagon Co. Ltd.* (1934), the owner of a lorry sold it to the defendants and took it back on hire-purchase. He then resold it to the plaintiffs. The later could not get a good title because the seller was not in possession 'as seller' but as a bailee under a hire-purchase agreement.

(b) the goods must have been delivered to the buyer or the documents of title must have been transferred to him. A mere agreement for sale, pledge or other disposition will not do.

(c) good faith and absence of notice of the previous sale on the part of the second buyer.

***6. Buyer in Possession (Sec.* 30(2)):** This section deals with converse case of sale or other disposition by the buyer of the goods in which the property has not yet passed to him. The section says that if the buyer obtains possession of the goods before the property in them has passed to him, with the consent of the seller, he may sell pledge or otherwise dispose of the goods in good faith and without notice of any lien or other right of the original seller in respect of the goods, he will get a good title to them.

In *Marten V. Whale* (1917), the plaintiff agreed to buy a plot of land from one T in return for a car subject to the condition that his solicitor approved the title to the land. Before anything was done in this connection, the plaintiff gave possession of his car to T who sold it to the defendant acquired a good title.

***7. Sale by an Unpaid Seller (Sec.* 54(3)):** Where an unpaid Seller, who has exercised his right of lien or stoppage in transit resells the goods the buyer acquires a good title to the goods as against the original buyer.

8. Other Exceptions: The other exceptions to the general rule *Nemo dat quod non habet* are:

(a) Sale by the finder of lost goods, Sec. 169 of the Contract Act.

(b) Sale by Pawnee, Sec. 176 of the Contract Act.

(c) Sale by an Official Receiver or Assignee according to the Civil Procedure Code.

6.10 PERFORMANCE OF THE CONTRACT

In the contract of sale performance means the delivery of goods by the seller and acceptance and payment for the same by the buyer. Both these duties are to be performed in accordance with the terms of the contract of sale. According to Sec.31 "it is the duty of the seller to deliver the goods and of the buyer to accept and pay for them in accordance with the terms of the contract of sale."

Performance means the delivery of goods by the seller and acceptance and payment for the same by the buyer.

Delivery of the goods and payment of the price are concurrent conditions. Concurrent conditions mean that they must be performed simultaneously, that is to say, the seller must be ready and willing to give delivery in exchange for the price, and the buyer must be ready and willing to pay the price in exchange for possession of the goods. The principle of simultaneous performance is underlined in Sec.32. To quote the section, "unless otherwise agreed, delivery of the goods and payment of the price are concurrent conditions, that is to say, the seller shall be ready and willing to give possession of the goods to the buyer in exchange for the price, and the buyer shall be ready and willing to pay the price in exchange for possession of the goods."

6.11 DELIVERY

Since delivery of goods is an important element in the performance of the contract of sale, it is useful to discuss, in detail, the nature, mode, and rules of delivery.

'Delivery', "means voluntary transfer of possession from one person to another."

'Delivery', according to Sec.2(2) of the Act "means voluntary transfer of possession from one person to another." Voluntary transfer is important and anything transferred by force, by theft, for example, does not constitute delivery.

Section 33 of the Act provides for the mode of delivery. To quote the Section, "Delivery of goods sold may be made by doing anything which the parties agree shall be treated as delivery or which has the effect of putting the goods in the possession of the buyer or of any person authorised to hold them on his behalf.

Following are the Modes or Delivery

Actual delivery takes place when the seller transfers the physical possession of the goods to the buyer.

Symbolic Delivery: "anything which the parties agree shall be treated as delivery."

(a) Actual Delivery: This is the most common method of delivery. Actual delivery takes place when the seller transfers the physical possession of the goods to the buyer or to a person authorised to hold them on his behalf.

(b) Symbolic Delivery: Sec.33 recognises even symbolic delivery when it says "anything which the parties agree shall be treated as delivery." Symbolic delivery takes place when, for example, the seller hands over to the buyer the key of the godown where the goods are stored. Symbolic delivery is accepted when the goods are ponderous, bulky and heavy.

(c) Constructive Delivery: This happens when the goods are in the custody of a third person who, in accordance with the seller's order, acknowledges to hold them on the buyer's behalf and the buyer has assented to it, or accepts rents for the goods from the buyer.

Rules as to Delivery

"Apart from any express contract, the seller of goods is not bound to deliver them until the buyer applies for delivery."

Rules regarding delivery are summarised below (see Fig. 6.6):

1. Demand for Delivery: Though it is the duty of the seller to deliver the goods to the buyer, the seller is not bound to do so unless demanded by the buyer. Sec.35, which is a reproduction of Sec.93 of the Contract Act, underlines this principle. The Section reads thus: "Apart from any express contract, the seller of goods is not bound to deliver them until the buyer applies for delivery."

The place at which the delivery of goods is to take place must be stated in the contract.

2. Place of Delivery (Sec.36 (**1)]:** The place at which the delivery of goods is to take place must be stated in the contract. Where it is done, the goods must be delivered at the place (stated in the contract) during business hours on a working day. Where there is no specific mention about the place, the goods must be delivered at the place at which they are at the time of sale. In the case of an agreement to sell, the goods are to be delivered at the place, where they are at the time of the agreement, or the goods are not then in existence, at the place where they are manufactured or produced.

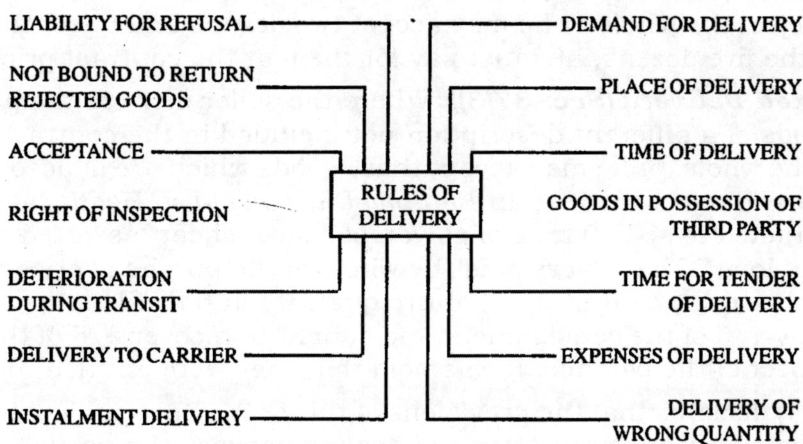

Fig.: 6.6 Rules Regarding Delivery of Goods

3. *Time of Delivery (Sec.36(2)):* If the seller is bound to send the goods as per the terms of the contract, but the contract does not contain any time, the seller must send the goods within reasonable time. What is reasonable time is a question of facts (Sec.63). If the seller fails to do so he shall be guilty of breach even if the delivery is subsequently prevented by the intervention of war or some Government order.

Seller is bound to send the goods as per the terms of the contract, but the contract does not contain any time, the seller must send the goods within reasonable time.

4. *Goods in Possession of a Third Party (Sec.36(4)):* Where the goods are in the possession of a third person, there is no delivery unless and until such third person acknowledges to the buyer that he holds goods on his (buyer) behalf. Once the third person does this, it amounts to delivery to the buyer, and, therefore, the third person cannot afterwards refuse to deliver on the ground that the goods have to be paid for or that the buyer has become insolvent.

5. *Time for Tender of Delivery (Sec.36(4)):* Goods sold must be demanded by the buyer at reasonable hour. Similarly, the seller must tender them at a reasonable hour. What is the reasonable hour is a question of fact.

6. *Expenses of Delivery (Sec.36(5)):* Expenses of and incidental to delivery are, as a general rule, to be borne by the seller. The parties may, however, agree otherwise.

7. *Delivery of Wrong Quantity (Sec.37):* Delivery of quantity will be wrong when the quantity supplied is less than, more than stated quantity or when it is mixed delivery.

(i) Delivery of Goods less than Contracted for (Sec.37(i)): "Where the seller delivers to the buyer a quantity of goods less than he contracted to sell, the buyer may reject them. But, if the buyer accepts the goods so delivered he shall pay for them at the contract rate."

For example, A agrees to sell and deliver to B 500 quintals of rice, but only 420 are delivered. B has the rice weighed and he accepts the quantity sent. B cannot afterwards object that the whole of 500 quintals was not delivered, and he must pay for the 420 quintals accepted by him at the contract rate.

(ii) Excess Delivery (Sec.37(2)): Where the seller delivers a quantity larger than he contracted to sell, the buyer may accept the goods included in the contract and reject the rest, or he may reject the whole lot. He is not bound to accept the contract quantity and reject only the excess.

For example, A orders B two dozen bottles of wine. B sends five dozen. A is entitled to reject the whole or he may accept two dozens and reject the rest. If he accepts all the five dozens, he must pay for them at the contract price.

(iii) Mixed Delivery (Sec. 37(3)): Where the seller delivers the goods mixed with the goods of a different description not included in the contract, the buyer may reject the whole, or he may accept those goods which are in accordance with the contract and reject the rest. In *Ebrahim Dawood Ltd.* v. *Heath Ltd.* (1961), the sellers contracted to sell 50 tons of galvanised steel sheet "assorted over 6, 7, 8, 9 and 10 feet long." The buyers paid the whole of the purchase price in advance. The sellers, however, delivered the entire quantity in 6 feet lengths. The buyers accepted only 1/5 of the consignment and sought to recover 4/5 of the purchase price in respect of the balance. It was held that they were entitled to do so.

Sec.37(4) declares that the provisions of this section are subject to any usage of trade, special agreement or course of dealing between the parties.

8. Instalment Delivery (Sec.38): Unless otherwise agreed, the buyer of goods is not bound to accept delivery thereof by instalments (Sec.38(i)). It follows, therefore, that instalment deliveries can be made or demanded only if the contract so provides. The contract to make instalment deliveries may be express or implied.

If the parties have agreed to deliver and accept goods in instalments and the price to be paid in the same manner, the problem arises as to what should happen if the seller fails to deliver an instalment and delivers defective goods in one instalment or the buyer refuses to take or pay for an instalment? Sec.(38(2) provides answer to the problem. To quote the section, "It is a question in each case, depending on the terms of the contract and the circumstances of the case, whether the breach of contract is a repudiation of the whole contract, or whether it is a severable breach giving rise to a claim for compensation, but not to a right to treat the whole contract as .repudiated." Thus, the section leaves the whole matter to be determined on the merits of each case.

Maple Flock Co. Ltd. v. *Universal Furniture Products (Wembley) Ltd.* (1933) is a case which lays down definite principles on the above issue. The facts of the case are -the sellers contracted to sell 100 tonnes of rag flock by instalments, at the rate of three weekly instalments of one and a half tonnes each. The first 15 deliveries were satisfactory but the 16th instalment contained much more chlorine than was permitted. The subsequent four deliveries were, however, satisfactory. This showed that there was no probability of the default being repeated, yet the buyers sought to repudiate the entire contract.

It was held that they were not entitled to do so. The court felt that two tests are necessary to be applied in a situation such as the one contemplated in sub-section (2). The first is "the ratio quantitatively which the breach bears to the contract as a whole and secondly, the degree of probability or improbability that such a breach will be repeated."

9. Delivery to a Carrier or Wharfinger (Sec.39): Where the seller is authorised or is required as per the term of the contract, to send the goods to the buyer, delivery of goods to a carrier for the purpose of transmission to the buyer, or to a wharfinger for safe custody, is *prima facie* deemed to be a delivery to the buyer (Sec.39(i)).

It is also the duty of the seller, unless otherwise agreed to enter into suitable agreement with the carrier or wharfinger on behalf of the buyer considering the nature of the goods and other circumstances of the case. The purpose of this duty is to secure entitlement for the buyer to sue the carrier in case the goods are lost. If the seller fails to make such a contract the buyer may refuse to treat the delivery to the carrier as delivery to himself or may hold the seller liable for damages. In *Thomas Young & Sons Ltd. v. Hobson & Partner (1949),* fourteen electric machines were sold, which, it was agreed should be sent to the buyers by sail. The sellers despatched them "at owner's risk" and not "at company's risk." There was no difference in the freight rates. The only difference was that before accepting at "company's risk" the company would have inspected their packing and required the machines to be properly secured in the wagons. "At owner's risk", they did not bother about these things. The machines were lying loose in the wagons and shunting damaged them. It was held that the sellers had not secured a contract which the nature of goods required them to do. The buyers could reject the goods and were not bound to pay the price.

Where goods are sent by the seller to the buyer a route involving sea transit, the seller shall give notice to the buyer to the effect as to enable him to insure the goods during the sea transit. If the seller fails to do so, the goods shall be deemed to be at his risk during such sea transit (Sec.39(3)).

10. Deterioration during Transit (Sec.40): "Where the seller of goods agrees to deliver the goods at his own risk at a place other than that where they are when sold, the buyer shall nevertheless, unless otherwise agreed, take any risk of deterioration in the goods necessarily incidental to the course of transit." For example, A agrees to sell hoop iron to B to be sent from post X to post Y. The iron is clean and bright when despatched, but is rusted to a certain extent before it reaches post Y. The rusting is no more than what would necessarily occur in the course of transit. The seller is not responsible if the iron becomes unmerchantable to that extent.

The section also applies to animals sent for human food from one place to another.

This rule is based on the: following passage in the judgment in *Bull v. Robinson (1854):* "A manufactured article at a distant place, must indeed stand the risk of any extraordinary or unusual deterioration, but the vendee is bound to accept the article if only deteriorated to the extent that it is necessarily subject to in its course of transit from one place to another."

11. Buyers Right of Inspection (Sec.4I): Where goods are delivered to the buyer which he has not previously examined, he is not deemed to have accepted them unless and until he has had reasonable opportunity of examining them for the purpose of ascertaining whether they are in conformity with the contract (Sec.41(1)).

When the seller tenders delivery of goods to the buyer, he is bound, on request, to afford the buyer a reasonable opportunity of examining the goods to ascertain whether they are in conformity with the contract. This provision operates unless otherwise agreed upon (Sec.41(2)).

12. Acceptance (Sec.42): A buyer is deemed to have accepted the goods in the following circumstances:

(a) When he intimates to the seller that he has accepted the goods.

(b) When the goods have been delivered to him and he does any act in relation to them which is inconsistent with the ownership of the sellers.

(c) When, after the lapse of a reasonable time, he retains the goods without intimating to the seller that he has rejected them.

In *Hardy* & *Co.* v. *Hillerns* & *Fowler* (1923), a quantity of wheat arrived on c.i.f. terms. The buyers, without making proper inspection, resold various parcels to sub-buyers. Three days later the buyers found that the wheat was not of contract quality and therefore sought to reject it. But they were not allowed to do so.

13. Buyer not Bound to Retum Rejected Goods (Sec.43): Where a buyer rejects goods as not being of the contract description, it is not his duty to send them back to the seller; it is enough for him to give a clear notice that they are not accepted, and then they are at the seller's risk. He is not bound to take the trouble of returning the goods and bear expenses incidental to it. It is the seller's business to take away the goods if he is so minded. This principle applies when the rejection is rightful and there is no agreement to the contrary.

14. Buyer's Liability for Refusal (Sec.44): If the property in the goods has passed to the buyer, he is liable to the seller for any loss occasioned by his (buyer's) refusal to take delivery of the goods. He is also liable to the seller for a reasonable charge for the case and custody of the goods. Conversely, if the seller delays delivery, and the buyer notwithstanding the delay accepts delivery, the seller is liable for any loss occasioned by the delay.

6.12 RIGHTS AND DUTIES OF BUYER

The rights and duties of buyer are as follows:

Rights

1. to have delivery of the goods as per contract.
2. right to repudiate contract if the seller commits any breach.
3. to have reasonable opportunity to examine the goods.
4. to sue the seller for damages for non-delivery of the goods.
5. to recover price paid if the seller has failed to deliver the goods.
6. to sue the seller for specific performance of the contract.
7. to reject the goods.
8. to receive notice of insurance.
9. to sue the seller for damages for breach of warranty.

Duties

1. to pay for the goods and take delivery thereof.
2. to apply for the delivery of goods as the seller is not bound to deliver the goods until the buyer applies for delivery.
3. to compensate the seller for any loss occasioned by his neglect or refusal to take delivery of the goods and also for reasonable charge for care and custody of the goods.
4. to accept instalment delivery of goods and pay for the same.
5. to accept risk of deterioration in course of transit.
6. to intimate the seller if the goods are rejected.

Rights and Duties of Seller

The rights and duties of the seller are summarised below:

Rights

1. to receive the price of the goods.
2. to receive compensation or sue for damages for any loss occasioned by neglect or refusal of the buyer to take delivery of the goods.
3. to receive reasonable charge for case and custody of the goods.
4. if he is an unpaid seller
   (i) to exercise right of lien.
   (ii) to exercise right of stoppage in transit.
   (iii) to exercise right of resale.
5. to recover interest, from the buyer if there is a specific agreement to that effect or charge interest on the price when it becomes due.
6. to sue for the price of the goods.
7. to sue for damages on buyer repudiating the contract.

Duties

1. to deliver the goods when the buyer demands.
2. to compensate the buyer for any breach of contract.
3. to give unreasonable opportunity to the buyer to examine the goods.
4. to refund price paid by the buyer in case he fails to deliver the goods.
5. to compensate the buyer in case of delivery of wrong quantity of goods.

6.13 RIGHTS OF UNPAID SELLER AGAINST THE GOODS

Who is an Unpaid Seller?

The seller of goods is deemed to be an 'unpaid seller' when (i) the whole of the price has not been paid or tendered, (ii) when a bill of exchange or other negotiable instrument has been received as conditional payment, and the condition on which it was received has not been fulfilled by reason of the dishonour of the instrument or otherwise (Sec.45(1), (iii) when even a part of the price has not been paid.

The seller in this context is any person who is in the position of a seller, as, for instance, an agent of the seller to whom the bill of lading has been endorsed or a consignor or agent who has himself paid or is directly responsible for the price (Sec.45(2)).

Explanation of the term 'seller' is important because the Act offers protection to any person who is in the position of seller and who is unpaid either full or part of price.

Rights of an Unpaid Seller

Unpaid seller has rights both against the goods as well as against the buyer. Rights against the goods are discussed in this chapter. The next chapter deals with the rights against the buyer.

The unpaid seller's rights against goods can be studied under two headings, viz., (a) where property in the goods has passed to the buyer, and (b) where the property in the goods has not passed to the buyer.

Where property has passed, the seller's rights against goods are:

(i) a lien on the goods for the price while he is in possession of them;

(ii) if the buyer becomes insolvent before payment, a right to stop the goods in transit after he has parted with the possession of them;

(iii) a right of re-sale, which implies that he is in possession of goods. (Sec.46(i))

The seller's rights, where the property in the goods has not passed to the buyer, are:

(i) Withholding delivery of the goods when they are in his possession.

(ii) Stoppage in transit when goods are not in his possession (Sec.46(2)) (see Fig. 6.7)

These rights are elaborated in the paragraphs that follow:

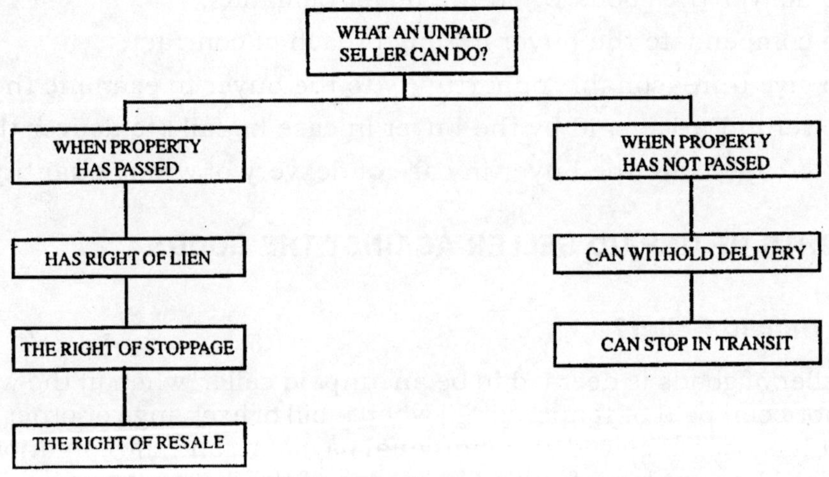

Fig: 6.7 Rights of an Unpaid Seller Against Goods

Where the Property in Goods has Passed to the Buyer

Right of lien means right to retain the possession of goods until certain charges due in respect of them are paid.

1. Right of Lien (Sec.47)*:* Right of lien means right to retain the possession of goods until certain charges due in respect of them are paid. The unpaid seller has the right to retain the goods until tender or payment of the price. Sec.47 provides lien to the unpaid seller in the following cases, namely:

(a) Where the goods have been sold without any stipulation as to credit;

(b) Where the goads have been sold on credit, but the term of credit has expired;

(c) Where the buyer becomes insolvent.

Rules regarding lien are as follows:

(i) The right of lien is linked with possession not with title. It is not affected even if the documents of title to the goods are transferred to the buyer.

(ii) The seller may exercise his right of lien notwithstanding that he is in possession of the goods as agent or bailee for the buyer (Sec.47(2)).

(iii) The right of lien exists only for the price of the goods. The seller is not entitled to lien for any other charges like storage, because the goods are stored against the buyer's will. For these charges the seller has only personal remedy against the buyer.

(iv) Right of lien may be exercised even if the seller has delivered to the buyer a part of the goods. Lien may be exercised on the remainder, unless such part delivery has been made under such circumstances as to show an agreement to waive the lien.

(v) If goods are, at the time of sale, in the custody of a third person, they are considered to be in the seller's possession for the purpose of his lien until the third person attorns to the buyer and thereby becomes a bailee for the buyer.

(vi) The unpaid seller of goods, having a lien thereon, does not lose his lien by reason only that he has obtained a decree for the price of the goods.

(vii) Termination of lien:

The lien is lost in any of the following four cases:

(a) When he delivers the goods to a carrier or other bailee for the purpose of transmission to the buyer without reserving the right of disposal of the goods. For example, in *Valpy v. Gibson* (1847), the goods sold were delivered to the buyer's shipping agents who had put them on board a ship. But the goods were returned to sellers for repacking. While they were still with the sellers on this mission the buyer became insolvent and the sellers, being still unpaid, claimed to retain the goods in exercise of their right of lien. It was held that they were not entitled to do so.

This right consists in stopping the goods while they are in the possession of a carrier.

(b) When the buyer or his agent lawfully obtains possession of the goods.

(c) By waiver thereof (Sec.49). The waiver may be express or implied. It is express waiver if the seller shall not be entitled to retain possession until payment of the price.

The lien is waived by implication:

(i) When goods have been sold on credit, during the currency of the credit, but the lien revives on the expiry of the credit;

(ii) When the seller takes a bill for the price payable at a future day, during the currency of the bill, but the lien revives if the bill is dishonoured;

(iii) If the seller assents to a sub-lease;

(iv) If the seller parts with the documents of title so as to exclude his title by estoppel;

(v) If the seller wrongfully refuses to deliver the goods, such a refusal being a repudiation of the contract;

(vi) By tender of price — 'when the buyer tenders price for the goods, the seller ceases to be an unpaid seller and therefore loses the right of lien.

2. Right of Stoppage in Transit (Sec.50): This is the second right of an unpaid seller. This right consists in stopping the goods while they are in the possession of a carrier or lodged at any place in the course of transmission to the buyer. The seller can resume possession of the goods and retain them until the price is tendered or paid.

To exercise the right of stoppage in transit four conditions must be satisfied, namely:

(i) the seller must be unpaid,

(ii) the buyer must be insolvent,

(iii) the seller must have parted with the possession of the goods, and

(iv) the buyer must not have acquired possession of the goods, in other words, the goods must be in transit.

When the transit of goods begins and ends is made clear in Sec.51.

Duration of Transit (Sec.51)

(i) Goods are deemed to be in course of transit from the time they are delivered to a carrier or other bailee for the purpose of transmission to the buyer, until the buyer or his agent takes delivery of them from the carrier or bailee.

For example, B, living at Chennai, orders goods of A, at Patna, and directs that they shall be sent to Chennai. The goods are sent to Kolkata, and there delivered to C, a wharfinger to be forwarded to Chennai. The goods, while in possession of C, are in transit.

(ii) The transit of goods comes to an end if the buyer not his agent obtains delivery of the goods before their arrival at the appointed destination. It may be wrongfully for the carrier to deliver the goods to the buyer before their arrival at the appointed destination and the carrier may be held liable in damages for depriving the seller of his opportunity, but the transit, nevertheless, comes to an end.

(iii) When the goods have arrived at their appointed destination and the carrier acknowledges to the buyer or his agent that he is now holding the goods on his behalf, the transit comes to an end, and it is immaterial that the goods are still with the carrier or that the buyer has indicated a further destination. It requires a very clear acknowledgement to put an end to the original contract of carriage.

(iv) The transit comes to an end when the goods are rejected by the buyer and the carrier continues in possession of them. This is so even if the seller has refused to take the goods back.

(v) Where the goods are delivered to a ship chartered by the buyer, it is a question depending on the circumstances of the particular case, whether the carrier is acting independently or as agent of the buyer. If the circumstances show that the carrier is acting as agent of the buyer, the transit comes to an end as soon as the goods are loaded on board the ship. For example, B a merchant of London, orders 100 bales of cotton of A, a merchant at Mumbai. B sends his own ship to Mumbai for the cotton. The transit is at an end when the cotton is delivered on board the ship.

(vi) Where the carrier of other bailee wrongly refuses to deliver the goods to the buyer or his agent, the transit is deemed to be at an end. But if the carrier or bailee rightfully refuses to deliver the goods, the transit is not at an end.

(vii) Where the goods have been delivered in part, the seller may stop remainder of the goods unless such part delivery shows an agreement to give up the possession of the whole.

How Stoppage is Effected? (Sec.52)

The unpaid seller may exercise his right of stoppage in transit either –

(a) by taking actual possession of the goods, or

(b) by giving notice of his claim to the carrier or other bailee in whose possession the goods are. Such notice may be given either to the person in actual possession of the goods or to his principal.

The unpaid seller may exercise his right of stoppage in transit either –
(a) by taking actual possession of the goods, or
(b) by giving notice of his claim to the carrier or other bailee in whose possession the goods are. Such notice may be given either to the person in actual possession of the goods or to his principal.

When notice of stoppage in transit is given by the seller to the carrier or other bailee in possession of goods, he shall redeliver the goods to the seller. If he refuses to do so, he is guilty of conversion. The expenses of redelivery shall be borne by the seller.

Distinction between Right of Lien and Right of Stoppage in Transit

Below Table brings out the distinction between right of lien and right of stoppage.

Table 6.4 Right of Lien and Right of Stoppage Distinguished

Right of Lien	*Right of Stoppage*
1. Right of lien arises on default of the buyer whether he is solvent or insolvent.	1. Right of stoppage arises when the buyer is only insolvent.
2. Lien is exercisable as long as the seller is in possession of goods.	2. Right of stoppage is execisable when the goods are in transit.
3. Lien ends where right of stoppage commences.	3. Right of stoppage commences where lien ends.
4. Lien is the right to retain possession.	4. Right of transit is to regain possession.

Transfer by Buyer and Seller (Sec.53)

Suppose the buyer, without paying the whole of the price, sells the goods or pledges them to another person. Does the sub-sale or pledge affect the seller's right of lien or right of transit? If yes, to what extent? Sec.53 provides answers to these questions.

According to Sec.53(i) the unpaid seller's right of lien or stoppage in transit is not affected by any sale or other disposition of the goods which the buyer may have made. For example in *Mordaunt Brothers v. British Oil and Cake Mills (1910)*, an oil merchant sold a quantity of oil to B, without appropriating any particular oil to the contract, B sold some of it to C and gave him a delivery order. C lodged the delivery order with the merchant requesting him "to await his orders." Meanwhile B failed to pay the merchant, who therefore, became unpaid seller. And his right of lien on the goods was upheld.

But in two circumstances the unpaid seller's right is defeated (a) where seller has given consent to the buyer's sale or disposition of goods, and (b) where the seller has issued to the buyer documents of title to the goods and he had sold or pledged the goods by transferring the documents of this.

In *Ant. Jurgens Margarine Fabrieken v. Louis Dreyfus & Co.* (1914), the defendants sold 2,649 bags of mowva seed to one F & Co., from out of a consignment of 6,400 bags and gave them delivery orders. F & Co., paid the defendants by cheque for the price. F & Co. sold the goods to the plaintiffs by endorsing to them the delivery orders. The cheque was dishonoured. Consequently the defendants became unpaid sellers and claimed lien on the goods. It was held that their lien on goods was lost when the delivery orders issued by them were transferred to *bona fide* buyers for value.

Similarly, in *G.T:P. Railway Co. v. Hanumandas* (1889), goods were sent by the seller to the buyer through the G. T.P. Railway Co. At the place of destination the railway company delivered the goods to the buyer who had loaded them on his cart. Before the cart left the station compound, the railway company received a telegram from the seller to stop delivery, as the buyer had become insolvent. The railway company did not act upon the telegram, and hence, was sued by the seller in damages. Since the railway receipt was already transferred to the defendant, it was held that the seller could not exercise the right of stoppage in transit.

An unpaid seller who has exercised his right of lien or stoppage in transit is also empowered to resell the goods.

3. Right of Re-sale (Sec.54): An unpaid seller who has exercised his right of lien or stoppage in transit is also empowered to resell the goods. This right is known as right of 'resale' since the goods are already sold once and the property therein was also transferred.

Sec.54 lays down that the contract of sale is not rescinded when the seller exercises his right of lien or stoppage in transit. In other words, the contract is still in force and it is upto the buyer to claim delivery of the goods on tendering the price. The property having passed to the buyer cannot be reverted to the seller. At the same time the seller cannot wait indefinitely till the buyer tenders the price. The seller is, therefore, given a limited right to resell the goods. The right is applicable in two cases, namely:

(i) Where the goods are perishable in nature, the seller can resell them without even giving notice to the buyer.

(ii) If the goods are not of perishable nature, and the buyer does not pay the price within reasonable time, the seller can resell the goods.

It is, however, necessary for the seller to given notice of resale to the defaulting buyer.

Where notice of resale is given, the unpaid seller can recover from the defaulting buyer any loss occasioned by the resale. In case of profit the unpaid seller can keep it with himself. Where notice of resale is not given, the loss caused by resale shall be borne by the unpaid seller. At the same time any profit arising out of resale goes to the defaulting buyer.

Where the Property in Goods has not Passed to the Buyer?

1. Right to Withhold: where the property in the goods has not passed to the buyer, an unpaid seller has, in addition to his other remedies, a right of withholding delivery similar to and co-extensive with his right of lien and stoppage in transit where the property has passed to the buyer (Sec.46(2)).

Where the property in the goods has not passed to the buyer, and the buyer becomes insolvent before paying the price, the seller can have no such right as lien because a man cannot have lien on his own goods. But he has the right to withhold delivery of goods. This right is analogous to a lien, and is often called a quasi-lien.

2. Right of Stoppage (Discussed earlier).

6.14 SUITS FOR BREACH OF THE CONTRACT

As was pointed out in the previous chapter the unpaid seller enjoys remedies against the buyer besides exercising his rights against the goods. Sections 55, 56, 60 and 61, provide for the unpaid sellers' remedies against the buyer (see Fig.) The rights are explained in the paragraphs that follow.

***1. Suit for Price* (*Sec.* 55):** Where under a contract of sale the property in the goods has passed to the buyer and the goods have actually come into his possession, the seller is entitled to sue for the price, if the buyer wrongfully neglects or refuses to pay for the goods.

For breach of contract, the seller may sue for *price*, Damages as to non-acceptance, Damages for repudiation sue for special damages.

Even if the property in the goods has not passed to the buyer, the seller may maintain an action for the price if the price is payable on a certain day irrespective of delivery.

***2. Damages for Non-Acceptance* (*Sec. 56*):** This section lays down that if the buyer wrongfully neglects or refuses to accept and pay for the goods, the seller may sue him for damages for non-acceptance. Damages are assessed in accordance with the principles laid down in Sections 73 and 74 of the Contract Act. Where there is a ready market for the goods in question, the principle applicable is that the buyer has to pay the loss that the seller has sustained on reselling the goods on the day of breach. If the seller does not resell, the difference between the market price and the contract price on the day of breach is adopted as the measure of damages. If the contract price and the market price are same, the seller can recover only nominal damages.

If the buyer wrongfully neglects or refuses to accept and pay for the goods, the seller may sue him for damages for non-acceptance.

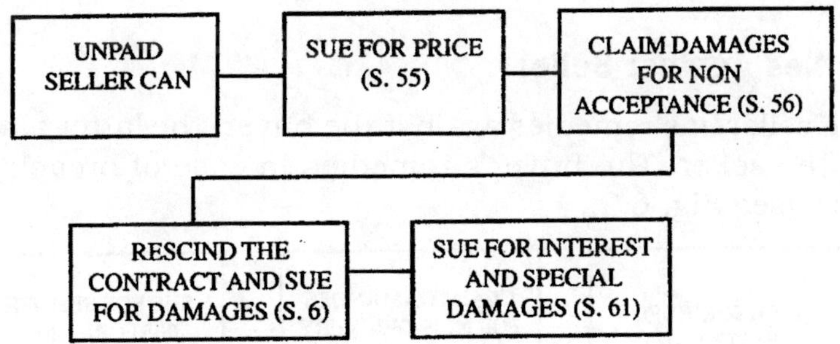

Fig. 6.8 Rights of the unpaid seller against the buyer

In *WL Thompson v. Robinson (Gunmakers) Ltd.* (1955), the plaintiff, who were car dealers, contracted to sell a motor car to the defendants. On the defendants' refusal to take delivery of the car, the plaintiffs returned the car to the manufacturers and claimed damages from the defendants for the loss of profit on sale. Their claim was upheld.

In *Charter v. Sullivan* (1957), the plaintiff agreed to sell to the defendant, a Hillman Minx motor car for $ 773-15-0, the retail price fixed by the manufacturers. On the defendant's failure to pay the price, the plaintiff, resold the car to a third party and claimed damages of $ 95-15-0 which was the loss of profit he would have made had he sold the car to the defendant and a similar car to the third party. The plaintiff was allowed to claim damages of 40 sh. only as he failed to prove the loss of profit.

Contrast the above two cases with *Lazenby Garages Ltd. v. Wright* (1976). Here, the plaintiffs bought a second hand car for $ 1,325 and agreed to sell the same to the defendant for $ 1,670. On the defendant's refusal to take delivery of car, it was sold to a third party for $ 1,770. The plaintiffs sought an action against the defendant to recover $ 345 as damages, being the difference between the purchase price and the resale price to the defendant. The action was rejected since the plaintiffs suffered no loss because of the defendant's refusal to take delivery of the car.

Where the goods are deliverable by instalments, and the buyer refuses to accept one or all the instalments, the difference in prices is to be reckoned on the day that a particular instalment was to be delivered. In the *Union of India v. Kesar Singh* (1978), when the military authorities refused to accept further supplies of cots in breach of their contract, the *J & K. High Court* allowed Rs. 4 per cot to supplier as damages being the profit which the supplier would have earned under his contract of supply.

3. Damages for Repudiation **(Sec. 60):** Where the buyer repudiates the contract before the date of delivery, the seller may either treat the contract as subsisting and wait till the date of delivery, or he may treat the contract as rescinded and sue for damages for the breach.

This is called the principle of anticipatory breach of contract laid down in Sec. 39 of the Contract Act.

4. Suit for Interest and Special Damages: Sec. 61 of the Act entitles the seller to recover from the buyer, special damages and interest from the date on which the amount become payable.

Buyer's Remedies Against Seller

Just as the seller has remedies against the buyer, the latter also enjoys certain rights against the seller. The buyer's remedies in case of breach of contract are explained below (see Fig. 6.9).

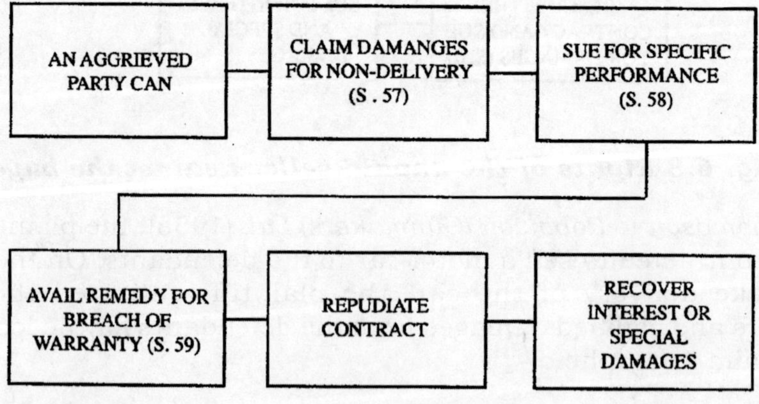

Fig. 6.9 Buyer's Remedies

***1. Damages for Non-delivery (See.* 57):** Where the seller wrongfully neglects or refuses to deliver the goods to the buyer, he may sue the seller for damages for non-delivery. The measure of damages will be on the following lines:

(a) Where there is an available market for the goods in question, the measure of damages is to be ascertained by the difference between the contract price and the market price on the date of the breach.

(b) Where there is no such market, the measure of damages is the estimated loss directly or indirectly resulting in the ordinary course of events from the breach of the contract.

Where the seller wrongfully neglects or refuses to deliver the goods to the buyer, he may sue the seller for damages for non-delivery.

***2. Remedy for Specific performance (Sec.* 58):** In any suit by the buyer for breach of contract to deliver specific or ascertained goods the court may, on application by the buyer, direct the seller to deliver the goods in terms of contract instead of permitting him to retain the goods on payment of damages. This remedy is allowed to the buyer subject to two conditions, namely —

(a) the contract must be for the sale of specific goods.

(b) the power of the court to order specific performance of the contract is subject to the provisions of the Specific Relief Act, 1877. This Act empowers the court, in its discretion, to order specific performance whenever damages would not be an adequate remedy.

In any suit by the buyer for breach of contract to deliver specific or ascertained goods the court may, on application by the buyer, direct the seller to deliver the goods in terms of contract.

***3. Remedy for Breach of Warranty (Sec.* 59):** Where the seller commits breach of a condition, the buyer is entitled to reject the goods and treat the contract as repudiated. But where there is a breach of warranty or where the buyer elects or is compelled to treat the breach of a condition as a breach of warranty, the buyer cannot reject the goods. He can set-up the breach of warranty in extinction or diminution of the price payable by him and if the loss suffered by him is more than the price, he may sue the seller for damages. If he has already paid the price, his only remedy is an action for damages.

Where the seller commits breach of a condition, the buyer is entitled to reject the goods and treat the contract as repudiated.

4. Repudiation of Contract: Repudiation of the contract by the seller before the date of delivery entitles the buyer to treat the contract as rescinded and sue the seller for damages.

***5.* Recovery of Interest (Sec. 61):** This section gives a right to the buyer to recover interest or special damages from the seller. The same remedy is available for the unpaid seller too.

Some Observations on the Act

It may be said to the credit of the Sale of Goods Act that it has been regulating the activities relating to sale and purchase of goods which are the very basis of business. One of the requirements of smooth functioning of sale and purchase is the determination of the time when ownership over the subject-matter of sale passes from the seller to the buyer. The Act lays down elaborate guidelines to determine the time of the transfer of property.

One of the requirements of smooth functioning of sale and purchase is the determination of the time when ownership over the subject-matter of sale passes from the seller to the buyer.

Secondly, the Sale of Goods Act has been protecting the interests of consumers by applying certain principles of implied conditions and warranties and imposing exceptions to the maxim caveat emptor. In fact, this was one legislation which was protecting consumer interests by the MRTP Act and the Consumer Protection Act came into force.

Sale of Goods Act was one legislation which was protecting consumer interests prior to enactment of the MRTP Act and the Consumer Protection Act came into force.

Having said these, let us point out certain anomalies of the Act. Sec. 62 of the Act say that "where any right, duty or liability would arise under a contract of sale by implication of law, it may be negatived or varied by an express agreement." This provision may give rise to peculiar problems. For example, you go to a retail shop dealing in sports goods to buy a throw-ball. You are not knowledgeable about sports and are not, therefore, in a position to differentiate between a throw-ball and a soccer-ball. The shopkeeper gives you a soccer-ball and you accept it out of ignorance. Next day you go to the shop to exchange it for a throw-ball. But the shop-keeper refuses to oblige you invoking the statement "goods sold cannot be taken back or exchanged" prominently printed at the bottom of the receipt.

One of the implied conditions of the Act is that the goods must fit buyer's purpose.

True, one of the implied conditions of the Act is that the goods must fit buyer's purpose (Sec. 16(i)) This implied right of the buyer may be negatived by an express statement as the one mentioned above. The result is that you must keep the soccer ball with you though it may not serve your purpose. In the alternative you must seek redressal under the Consumer Protection Act, 1986.

Secondly, the most obnoxious provision of the Sale of Goods Act is Sec.16. According to this section there is no implied warranty or condition as to the quality or fitness for any particular purpose of goods under a contract of sale.

This is a statement of the principle of *Caveat Emptor:* "Under the general doctrine of *caveat emptor,* he (seller) is not ordinarily bound to disclose every defect of which he may be cognisant, although his silence may operate virtually to deceive the vendee" *(Ward v. Hobbs).*

The principle of caveat emptor is totally outdated and unacceptable nowadays. True, Sec. 16 of the Act provides for several exceptions which have become more prominent than the rule.

The principle of caveat emptor is totally outdated and unacceptable nowadays. True, Sec. 16 of the Act provides for several exceptions which have become more prominent than the rule. But unfortunately each exception is subject to so many 'ifs' and 'buts' and one is not sure when an exception really operates. It is time that Sec. 16 is withdrawn from the Act.

Thirdly, the Act has given scope for certain contradicting interpretations. For example, providing food in a restaurant is considered to be a sale for the purpose of the Act according to the judgement in *Locket v A.M. Charles Ltd.* (1938). But in *Northern 1ndia Caterers (India) Ltd v. Ltd. Governor of Delhi* (1978), service of food in restaurants is treated as service and not a transaction of sale.

Finally, extending the demand for repeal of Sec. 16 of the Act, it may be suggested that the entire Act may be merged with the Consumer Protection Act, the Consumer Protection Act is consumer-oriented, unlike the Sale of Goods Act which is more seller-oriented. We have too many legislations in our country. By merging the Sale of Goods Act with the Consumer Protection Act, the problem of multiple legislations can be solved to some extent.

QUESTIONS

Section — A. Objective Type

1. What do you understand by the term 'goods'?
2. What do you mean by actionable claim?
3. What are specific goods?
4. What are generic goods?
5. What is the legal position if goods perish before forming a contract?
6. What is a condition? What is the legal consequence of its breach?
7. What is a warranty? What is the legal consequence of its breach?
8. State the circumstances when a condition becomes a warranty.

9. What is sale by description?
10. What is sale by sample?
11. What is merchantable quality?
12. What is the essence of Sec. 19 of the Act?
13. What is the essence of Sec. 20 of the Act?
14. State exceptions to the rule *"Nemo dat quod non habet."*
15. Who is a mercantile agent?
16. What do you mean by performance of the contract of sale of goods?
17. What do you mean by delivery of goods?
18. What do you understand by symbolic delivery of goods?
19. What is constructive delivery of goods?
20. Who is unpaid seller?
21. What is the right of lien?
22. When can the right of stoppage in transit be exercised?
23. How can the stoppage effected?
24. Why is the right of resale so-called?
25. State the rights of the unpaid seller against the buyer.
26. State the remedies of buyer against the seller.
27. When can the unpaid seller sue the buyer for price?

B. Analytical Type

1. Distinguish between a sale and an agreement to sell, and a sale and a bailment.
2. Distinguish between a sale and a hire-purchase agreement.
3. Discuss the legal effect of destruction of goods.
4. What principle of sale of goods have you learnt from the famous case, namely, the *State of Gujrath V. Ramanlal & Co.?*
5. X delivered on OX to Y on a trial basis for 8 days agreeing that if found suitable for intending buyer's purpose, the bargain then would be absolute. The OX died within 8 days without any fault of either party. Was it a valid contract of sale? Who will bear the loss in such case?
6. Discuss the legal rules regarding implied conditions.
7. "Exceptions to caveat emptor are more prominent than the rule itself." Comment.
8. Discuss the legal rules regarding implied warranties.
9. A hirer, who obtains possession of a car from its owner under a hire-purchase agreement, sells the car to a buyer who buys in good faith and without notice of the right of the owner. Does the buyer get a good title to the car? Discuss.
10. N agreed to buy rice from S on inspection. He accepted part delivery of the goods and later refused to accept the remaining quality on the ground that the rice was of inferior quality. Was N entitled to do that?
11. A seller undertakes to supply 1,000 tons of Java Sugar warranted equal only to the sample. The sample when supplied corresponds to the sample but is not Java Sugar. Has the buyer any remedy against the seller?
12. There is a contract between A and B for the supply for 1000 articles to be packed in 200 containers of five pieces each. But the seller sends 150 containers of eight pieces each. What are the rights of the buyers?
13. "Determination of the time when ownership passes from seller to buyer is significant." Elucidate.
14. "Where the intention of seller and buyer is about the transfer of property is not clear from their contract, the intention will be ascertained according to the rules laid down in Sec. 18 and 20 to 24." Discuss.
15. "There are eight exceptions to the rule that no seller of goods can give to the buyer a better title than himself." Discuss.
16. A agreed to purchase 200 tons of wheat from B out of a large stock. A sent his men with sacks and 150 tonnes of wheat were put into the sack. Then there was a sudden fire and the entire stock was gutted. Who will bear the loss and why?

17. There is a contract for the sale of timber standing at B's land. It is the duty of the buyer A to the timber and take it away in his own transport. After making the contract, the standing timber, is destroyed by a sudden fire. Who will suffer the loss and why?
18. A hirer, who obtains possession of a car from its owner under a hire-purchase agreement, sells the car to a buyer who buys in good faith and without notice of the right of the owner. Does the buyer get a good title to the car? Discuss.
19. A and B jointly purchased a cycle for Rs.1500. It was agreed that each of them would keep the cycle in his possession for a period of one month by rotation. While the cycle was in possession of A, he without the consent of B, sold it to C who bought it in good faith. Does C get a good title? Give reasons for your answer.
20. A finds a costly ring and after making reasonable efforts to discover the owner, sells it to B, who buys without knowledge that A was merely a finder. Can the true owner recover the ring from B?
21. "Delivery does not amount to acceptance of goods." Discuss when a buyer can be said to have accepted the goods.
22. What rights and liabilities flow in case of part-delivery of goods. Of wrong delivery of goods?
23. What are the liabilities of the buyer for rejecting the goods or neglecting or refusing delivery of goods?
24. X contracts with Y to buy 50 copies of Business Law authorised by A. Y supplies 25 copies of the book written by A, and 15 copies written by B and 10 copies written by C. Advise X.
25. A of Bangalore orders certain goods from B of Mumbai. B sends the goods, not ordered, along with them. What should A do?
26. X sells to Y 200 bags of cement which are locked up in a godown. X hands over to Y the key of the godown. Is there delivery of goods?
27. "The unpaid seller has the right to retain the goods until tender or payment of price." Discuss.
28. Distinguish between the right of lien and the right of stoppage in transit.
29. A, an unpaid seller, sends goods to B by Railway. B becomes insolvent and A sends a telegram to Railway authorities not to deliver goods to B. B goes to the Railway, presents the Railway Receipt and takes delivery of the goods and starts putting them on his cart. Meanwhile, the station master comes running with the telegram in hand and takes possession of the goods from B. Discuss the rights of A and B to the goods in possession of Railway authorities.
30. X sells goods to Y. Y pays X through a cheque. Before y could obtain delivery of goods, the cheque has been dishonoured by the bank. X therefore, refuses to give delivery of the goods until paid. Is X's action justified?
31. A sells to B a quantity of sugar which is in A's warehouse. It is agreed that B shall get two months' credit. B allows the sugar to remain in A's warehouse. B becomes insolvent before the expiry of the two months, and the official receiver demands delivery of the sugar without offering to pay. What are the rights of A?
32. A consigns certain goods to B and sends him the bill of lading. a is still an unpaid seller. While the goods are in transit B becomes insolvent. B assigns the bills of lading for cash to C who is unaware of B's insolvency. Can A stop the goods in transit?
33. Critically examine the operation of the Sale of Goods Act.
34. X, a dealer in cars, bought a second hand car for Rs.50,000 and agreed to sell it to Y for Rs.60,000. On Y's refusal to take delivery, X sold the car to Z for Rs.65,000 and sought to recover Rs.10,000 as damages from Y. Can X succeed?

C. Essay Type

1. What is contract of sale? Explain its essentials.
2. Explain, in detail, the implied conditions. What happens when any implied condition is breached?
3. What is a warranty? Explain the implied warranties.
4. Explain the rules regarding transfer of property and of title to goods.

5. What do you understand by the transfer of property in goods? Why it is important? Explain the rules regarding transfer of property in (a) specific goods, and (b) unascertained goods.
6. What is delivery of goods? Explain the rules regarding delivery of goods.
7. What are the rights and duties of buyer? Of seller?
8. Who is an unpaid seller? What are his rights against goods?
9. What do you understand by stoppage in transit? In what circumstances has the unpaid seller the right to sell and the right to recover the damages for loss?
10. Explain the rights of an unpaid seller against buyer and of the buyer's remedies against the seller.

CONSUMER PROTECTION ACT, 1986

Module Objectives

After reading this chapter, you should be able to

- Know the terms consumer, consumer dispute, defect and deficiency
- Understand all about District Forum, State Commission, and National Commission
- Comprehend the treatment of complaint of goods and services
- Diagonise the leading consumer case laws of India, USA, UK and Australia

THE CONSUMER PROTECTION ACT, 1986

7.1 INTRODUCTION

The population in our country is ever increasing. But goods and services are lacking. The buyers in the sellers' market have low bargaining power. A consumer in India does not pursue his complaint against cheap quality and high priced goods, because of more cost and time consuming court process.

The Government enacted a number of laws to protect the interest of the consumers. Some of the acts are: The Essential Commodities Act, Trade and Merchandise Marks Act, Drug (Control) Act, Indian Standard Institution (Certification Mark) Act, etc. But the sections of most of these laws are not directly helpful to a single consumer.

It marks the growth of consumer movement in our country. It has the law relating to consumer protection. It provides simple, speedy and less expensive remedy to consumers' grievance.

Hence, the Consumer Protection Act 1986 was enacted by the Government. It marks the growth of consumer movement in our country. It has the law relating to consumer protection. It provides simple, speedy and less expensive remedy to consumers' grievance.

Objects of the Act

The main objects of the act (are briefly given below):

1. To protect the interest of the consumer.
2. To protect the rights of the consumers regarding
   (a) Marketing of goods or services
   (b) Quality of goods and
   (c) Price of the goods and services.
3. To protect the consumer against unfair trade practices.
4. To set up consumer protection council at the centre and state level.
5. To provide speedy and simple redressal to consumer disputes by
   (a) giving reliefs and
   (b) compensation to consumers.

Definitions

1. Consumer Section 2(1)(d)

"Consumer" means any person who —

(i) buys any goods for a consideration which has been paid or promised or partly paid and partly promised, or under any system of deferred payment and includes any user of such goods other than the person who buys such goods for consideration paid or promised or partly paid or partly promised, or under any system of deferred payment when such use is made with the approval of such person, but does not include a person who obtains such goods for resale or for any commercial purpose; or

(ii) hires or avails of any services for a consideration which has been paid or promised or partly paid and partly promised, or under any system of deferred payment and includes any beneficiary of such services other than the person who 'hires or avails of the services for consideration paid or promised, or partly paid and partly promised, or under any system of deferred payment, when such services are availed of with the approval of the first mentioned person but does not include a person who avails of such services for any commercial purposes.

2. Consumer dispute

It means a dispute, where the person against whom a complaint has been made, denies or disputes the allegation contained in the complaint [Section 2(1)(e)].

3. Defect

Defect means any fault, imperfection (or) shortcoming in the quantity, quality, purity and potency in the nature and performance of contract which are required to be maintained under any law for the time being in force, under by contract, express or implied. [Section 2(1)(f)]

4. Deficiency

It means any fault, imperfection, shortcoming or inadequacy in the quality, nature and manner of performance, which is required to be maintained under any law for the time being on force. [Section 2(1)(g)]

5. Service

It means service of any description which is made available to potential users. It includes the provision of facilities like (a) banking, (b) financing, (c) insurance, (d) transport, (e) processing, (f) supply of electrical and other energy, (g) boarding or lodging or both, (h) house construction, (i) entertainment or supplying of news or other information. [Section 2(1)(o)]

It excludes any service done free of charge or personal service.

7.2 CONSUMER PROTECTION COUNCIL

There are two consumer protection council one at central level (called control council) another at state level (called state council).

I. Central Consumer Protection Council (Section 4 to 8)

Constitution: The central government by notification may form a council, known as central consumer protection council (i.e., central council).

Composition: It shall have 150 members namely:

1. The central Minister in charge of consumer affairs shall be the chairman.
2. The Minister of state in the department of civil supplies (without independent charge) shall be vice chairman.
3. 8 MPs (5 from Lok Sabha and 3 from Rajya Sabha).
4. The commissioner for SC and ST.
5. 20 Representative of the central government departments concerned with consumer interest.
6. At least 20 representative of the consumer(s)(organisation).
7. At least 10 representatives of women.
8. 20 Representatives of farmers, trade and industries.
9. 15 members capable of representing consumer interest.
10. The Secretary in the Department of civil supplies shall be also the secretary of the central council.

Meeting of the Central Council (Section 5)

The council shall meet at least once in every year. The place and time of meeting may be decided by the chairman.

Objects (Sect. 6)

The central councils object shall be to promote and protect the different consumer rights. Such rights are:

1. The right against marketing of hazardous goods and services.
2. The right against unfair trade practices.
3. The right to get various goods and services at competitive prices.
4. The right to be heard to ensure that the consumer's interest receives due consideration at different forums.
5. The right to be redressed against unfair trade practices.

II. The State Consumer Protection Council (Section 7-8)

Constitution: The state government may also set up by notification a council known as state consumer protection council (ie., state council).

Composition: It will have the state minister in charge of consumer affairs as the chairman and members nominated by the state government.

Meeting: It shall meet at least twice in every year. The time and place of the meeting is decided by the chairman.

Objects: The object of the state council is to promote and protect the consumer rights (under Sect.6) within the state.

7.3 CONSUMER REDRESSAL AGENCIES (Section 9-27)

Section 9: Under the act 3 consumer dispute redressal agencies can be set up. One at District level, one at State level and one at National level. They are:

1. A District Forum: (set up by the state government in each district by notification).

2. A State Commission: (set up by the state government) and

3. A National Commission: (set up by the central government, by notification).

CONSUMER DISTRICT REDRESSAL FORUM (The District Forum) (Section 10-15)

Constitution: It is set up by the state government one at each district.

Composition: It shall have a president and 2 members, one of whom must be a woman.

Appointment: They are appointed by state government on the recommendation of a selection committee, of 3 persons.

This selection committee has a chairman and 2 members. The chairman is the president of the state commission. One member is the secretary in the law department of the state and another member is the secretary of consumer affairs of the state.

Qualification: The president of a District Forum must be a qualified district judge and the other 2 members must have the ability and integrity and have enough knowledge, and experience in economics, commerce, accountancy, law, industry and public affair.

Period of office: Every member of the district forum shall hold office for a period of 5 years, and there shall be no re-appointment.

Terms of Service: The salary, and terms and conditions of the members may be prescribed by the state government.

Jurisdiction (Section 11): Its jurisdiction is based on the amount of compensation. This Forum will have jurisdiction when the amount of compensation claimed is up to Rs.20 lakhs. The complaint must be given to that district forum in the district in which opposite party (the person answering the complaint) has thc business or the branch office or works for gain.

Who shall give complaint (Section 12): A complaint may be filed with a district forum by:

(a) the consumer to whom such goods are sold or service rendered.

(b) any recognised consumer association (i.e., consumer association registered under Companies Act 1956).

(c) the Central or State Governments.

Treatment of Complaint (Section 13)

(A) Complaint Regarding the Goods: When the district forum receives a complaint about any goods, it will send a copy of complaint to the opposite party mentioned in the complaint. The opposite party must give reply within 30 days. It may be extended by another 15 days.

When the district forum receives a complaint about any goods, it will send a copy of complaint to the opposite party mentioned in the complaint. The opposite party must give reply within 30 days. It may be extended by another 15 days.

When the complaint alleges a defect in the goods (if it can't be decided without Lab test) the District Forum will receive a sample and fix lab charges from the complainant and seal it. Then the sample so sealed may be sent to Laboratory for a test along with the charges. The laboratory must submit its report of the test within 45 days from the date of receiving the complaint.

After receiving the report from the laboratory the District forum shall send a copy of the report to the opposite party. If the opposite party disputes over the correctness of the report, he must give in writing his objection to the District Forum.

Issuing order: The district forum shall issue an appropriate order after giving a reasonable opportunity of hearing to both the parties, (i.e., the complainant and the opposite party) and considering laboratory report and objection to it.

(B) Complaint Regarding the Services: When the District Forum receives a complaint about any services, it will send a copy of the complaint to the opposite party and he shall give his reply within 30 days (may be extended by another 15 days).

The district forum shall issue an appropriate order after giving a reasonable opportunity of hearing to both the parties, (i.e., the complainant and the opposite party) and considering laboratory report and objection to it.

It will examine the evidences given by both parties in support of their claim. And after giving an opportunity of hearing to both parties, it shall pass an appropriate order.

Powers: The order given by the District Forum shall be the final. It shall have the power of a civil court under the code of civil procedure 1908. The proceedings of the District Forum is equal to a judicial proceeding under Sect.193 and 228 of IPC.

Section 14: It can issue an order to the opposite party on one or more of the following steps:

1. to replace the goods with new goods.
2. to remove the defect in the goods or services pointed by the lab report.
3. to repay the price to the complainant.

4. to pay compensation to the consumer for any loss suffered due to the negligence of the opposite party.
5. to discontinue unfair trade practices.
6. to stop the sale of hazardous goods.

This order of the district forum shall be signed by its president and the members who conducted the proceedings.

Any person aggrieved by the order of District Forum can go for an appeal, against such order in the state commission with 30 days from the date of the order.

Appeal (Section 15): Any person aggrieved by the order of District Forum can go for an appeal, against such order in the state commission with 30 days from the date of the order.

CONSUMER DISPUTES REDRESSAL COMMISSION (The State Commission)(Sect.16-19)

Constitution: It is set up by the state government by notification.

Composition (Section 16): It shall have a president and 2 members one of whom must be a woman.

Appointment: The president is appointed in consultation with the chief justice of the High Court.

They are appointed by the state government on the recommendation of a selection committee of 3 persons (composition of the selection committee is the same as referred under District Forum).

Qualification: The president of the state commission must be a Judge of a High Court, and he is appointed by the state government. The qualification of the 2 members is the same as in case of members of District Forum.

Period of office: Same as in case of District Forum.

Terms of service: It is also prescribed by the state government as in case of District Forum.

Jurisdiction (Section 17): The jurisdiction of the state commission is limited to the extent of compensation value of above Rs.5 lakhs and upto Rs.one crore and appeals against the orders of any District Forum in the state.

Treatment of complaint: The rule of Section 12, 13 and 14 and procedure explained under District Forum may be applicable to the state committee also.

Power: It has the powers of a civil court. It can call for the records and issue an appropriate order in any consumer dispute pending before it and also the disputes decided by any District Forum within the state. It can issue an order to the opposite party directly to do one or more thing referred under Sect.14.

Appeal (Section 19): The aggrieved party can appeal against the order of the state commission within 30 days from the date of the order in the National Commission.

NATIONAL CONSUMER DISPUTES REDRESSAL COMMISSION (National Commission) (Section 20-23)

Constitution: It is set up by the Central Government by notification.

Composition (Section 20): It shall have a president and 4 members, one of whom must be a woman.

Appointment: The president is appointed in consultation with the Chief Justice of India and the other members are appointed by the recommendation of a selection committee.

This selection committee has one chairman, and 2 members. The chairman is a judge of the supreme court (nominated by the chief justice of India) and one member is the secretary in the Department of Law in the Government of India and another member is the secretary of the Department of Consumer Affairs in the Government of India.

Qualification: The president of the National Commission is the judge of the Supreme Court and he is appointed by the central government and the other 4 members must have the ability and integrity and have enough knowledge and experience in economics, commerce, accountancy, law, industry and public affair.

Period of office: Same as in case of state commission.

Terms of service: The salary and terms and conditions of the service of the members of National Commission is prescribed by the Central Government.

Place of office: The office of this commission must be in the state of Delhi.

Jurisdiction (Section 21): Its jurisdiction is limited to the extent of compensation value of above Rs.one crore and appeals against the orders of any state commission.

Treatment of complaint: Is the same as in case of District Forum.

Power (in form of procedure) Section 22: It has the powers of a civil court. It can call for the records and issue an appropriate order in any consumer dispute pending before it and also on the disputes decided by any district commission within the country. It can issue an order to the opposite party directly to do one or more thing referred under Sect.14.

Appeal Section 23: Any person aggrieved by the order of National Commission, may appeal against such order in the Supreme Court within 30 days from the date of the order.

Prevention of Action taken in Good Faith (Section 28)

The actions taken in good faith by the 3 members of the District Forum, the state commission or the national commission cannot be challenged in any court of law. And also the actions of the officers who acted under their direction.

Power to remove difficulties (Section 29): If any difficulties arise in implementing the provisions of the Act, the central can remove such difficulties by an order in the official Gazette within 2 years from the commencement of this act.

Power to make rules (Section 30): Under the act both the central government and the state government can make necessary rules for implementing the provisions of this act by Notification.

7.4 LEADING CONSUMER CASE LAWS — INDIA

The consumer forum cannot absolve its responsibility and refer to Civil Court just because the case requires scrutiny of voluminous records and examination of witnesses.

Case – 1

Chambers Co-operative Housing Society Ltd. (CCI) Vs. Development Credit Bank Ltd. 2003.

The Consumer Forum cannot absolve its responsibility and refer to Civil Court just because the case requires scrutiny of voluminous records and examination of witnesses. The leading case in this regard was *Chambers Co-operative Housing Society Ltd. (CCI) Vs. Development Credit Bank Ltd. 2003.* The facts of the case was that a Bank wrongly debited an amount of Rs. 75,30,352/- in the account of the society, which alleged that the cheques bore forged signatures and in some of the cheques the figures had been altered. As many as 72 cheques were issued on such dates when one of the two persons purportedly drawing the cheques was already dead. The other one denied his signatures and such disputed signatures did not at all tally with the standard specimen signatures. Suspicion was raised against an official of the Bank.

Consumer Forum under the Act cannot shut the orders to the aggrieved person merely on the ground that the matter required scrutiny of voluminous records and examination of witnesses etc.

Since numerous documents including about 150 cheques were required to be proved, the experts were to be requisitioned for proof of the signatures and writings where in the figure in cheques had been altered and also the matter was to be examined within a set frame of time, the National Commission returned the complaint to the society to knock the doors of Civil Court. Hence the Society filed an appeal before the Hon'ble Supreme Court of India.

The Supreme Court by setting aside the order of the National Commission and subsequently the case was referred back to the National Commission for hearing afresh. The Supreme Court held that forum under the Act cannot shut the orders to the aggrieved person merely on the ground that the matter required scrutiny of voluminous records and examination of witnesses etc.

Further SC noticed that the Fora under the Act are specifically empowered to follow such procedure what may not require more time or delay the proceedings.

"Merely because it is mentioned that the Commission or Forum is required to have summary trial would hardly be a ground for directing the consumer to approach the Civil Court." So observed by the Hon'ble Justice R.C. Lahoti of Supreme Court of India while allowing the appeal filed by appellant society.

Case – 2

Indian Medical Association v. Santha

Theservices rendered by medical practitioner or at hospitals or nursing homes if are deficient then such deficiency has to be judged by applying the test of reasonable skill and care which is applicable in action for damages for negligence.

Inclusion of 'Health' as a 'Service' within the purview of the Consumer Protection Act, 1986 was taken up in a landslide case of Indian Medical Association Vs. Santha , the Facts and Judgment of the case that the consumer Protection Act, 1986 or subsequent amendment carried out in it in 1993, did not incorporate 'health as a service within the purview of the Act. However, Supreme Court in *Indian Medical Association v. Santha*, held that remedy against medical malpractice or negligence is available under the Act to affected persons as consumers. The three judges bench of Kuldip Singh, Agarwal and Hansaria JJ held that medical hospitals, government or private are covered by the main part of the definition of 'service' subject to the exclusion of definition like 'free of charge' and 'contract of personal service.' The learned judges said, that services rendered by medical practitioner or at hospitals or nursing homes if are deficient then such deficiency has to be judged by applying the test of reasonable skill and care which is applicable in action for damages for negligence.

Though the decision is welcome one because of its new dimension given to 'health service' as came to be read in Consumer Protection Act, 1986, but at the same time the exclusion of 'free service' and 'contract of personal service' needs reconsideration.

Whatever was done by the apex court in Santha's Case was undone by it in *Achutrao Haribhau Khodwa v. State of Maharastra.* The division bench comprising S.P. Bharucha and B.N. Kripal JJ refused to hold either doctor or government liable for a death caused due to negligence on the part of the doctor.

Case – 3
Achutrao Haribhau Khodwa Vs. State of Maharashtra

Death of a patient amounts to medical negligence where 'reasonable care' expected of from the doctor *Achutrao Haribhau Khodwa Vs.State of Maharashtra.* The facts and judgment in the instant case was that a doctor left towel inside abdomen while conducting sterilization operation in hospital, which caused pus. By second operation performed by another surgeon to ascertain cause of aliment the towel was removed but the patient died thereafter. The court held that neither doctor nor government is liable unless it is proved that the death was caused due to leaving towel inside the abdomen. It was again submitted with great respect that leaving towel inside the abdomen was itself an act of negligence on the part of a doctor concerned and which ultimately resulted in causing pus. Therefore, the further inquiry sought by the judges whether death was caused due to leaving towel inside abdomen was an unwarranted and uncalled for.

Death of a patient amounts to medical negligence where 'reasonable care' expected of from the doctor.

Professional and particularly doctors have to perform their duties with utmost care and caution. It is also not only a duty of care but 'reasonable care' expected from doctor wherein in the instant case he was failed to take the same. Therefore, liability ought to have been imposed on doctor/government for negligent conduct, which ultimately cost patient's life.

Case – 4
Spring Meadows Hospital Vs. Harjot Ahluwalia

'Parents are Consumers.' This was articulated in a famous case of *Spring Meadows Hospital Vs. Harjot Ahluwalia.* The Supreme Court took a very progressive and dynamic step in *Spring Meadows Hospital v. Harjot Ahluwalia,* and held that when a young child was taken to a private hospital by parents and treated by doctors, then not only child but his parents are also be treated as 'consumers.' Hence, when child suffered damage due to the hospital, nurse and doctor, both the child and parents could claim compensation under the Consumer Protection Act, 1986. These cases display some dynamism on the part of the judges to give 'live' interpretation to the Act to do justice to consumers.

'Parents are Consumers'

Case – 5
Smt. Savita Garg v. Director, National Heart Institute

A More important case from the point of view of consumer is: *Smt. Savita Garg v. Director, National Heart Institute.* Non-Impleading of Particular Doctor Would Not Absolve the Hospital of Its Responsibilities *Smt. Savita Garg v. Director, National Heart Institute* In this case the wife, children and brother of A.K. Garg, the deceased, filed a consumer complaint against the National Heart Institute alleging negligence and deficiency in service on part of the Institute and its doctors who had been treating him in the Institute. This original complaint was dismissed by the National Commission holding that it was not maintainable since the doctors who treated him were not impleaded as party.

Non-Impleading of Particular Doctor Would Not Absolve the Hospital of Its Responsibilities.

On an appeal before the Supreme Court the question was whether the non-impleadment of the doctors who treated the deceased as a necessary party could result in the dismissal of the original petition?

In a justice savvy tone the Supreme Court observed that the consumer forum is primarily meant to provide better protection to the interests of the consumers and not to short-circuit the matter or to defeat the claim on technical grounds.

The Supreme Court further held that, if the hospital failed to discharge its duties through their doctors, it was the hospital which had to justify the same and non-impleading of particular doctor would not absolve the hospital of its responsibilities.

With these observations the order was set aside by the Supreme Court and the original petition was remitted to the National Commission to be decided in accordance with law.

The decision has not only lightened the burden of proof on the aggrieved patients or their kin in case of medical negligence, but also has put the hospitals on the alert to take better care of the patients through the doctors employed by them.

A Sensational Judgment in medical negligence was pronounced on 6th August 2004, by the Apex Court.

Case – 6

Dr. Suresh Gupta Vs. Government of NCT New Delhi and another

If a patient dies due to an error of judgment committed by the doctors, then he is not criminally liable though he could be held liable to pay damages

If a patient dies due to an error of judgment committed by the doctors, then he is not criminally liable though he could be held liable to pay damages in *Dr. Suresh Gupta Vs. Government of NCT New Delhi and another.* The decision came as relief for the entire medical fraternity, the Supreme Court ruled that if a patent dies due to an error of judgment committed by the doctors, then he is not criminally liable though he could be held liable to pay damages. The facts of the case is that on 18th April 2004, Dr. Suresh Gupta of Delhi had conducted an operation to remove nasal deformity, but the patient died on the same day. According to the post-mortem report conducted after three days, the cause of the death was "Blockage of respiratory passage by aspirated blood consequent upon surgically incised margin of nasal septum." The cause of action in this case is that the prosecution laid against the surgeon was that there was negligence in "not putting a cuffed endo-tracheal tube of proper size" and in a manner so as to prevent aspiration of blood blocking the respiratory passage. Thus Dr. Suresh Gupta was facing charges under Section 304A of the Indian Penal Code for causing death of the Patient.

This judgment was given by a Bench comprising Justice Y.K.Sabharwal and Justice D.M. Dharmadhikari while quashing criminal proceedings against a plastic surgeon who faced trial of criminal changes for causing the death of a person who had wanted to remove a minor deformity in his nose. Held that "Where a patient's death results merely from error of judgment or an accident, no criminal liability should be attached to it. Mere inadvertence or some degree of want of adequate care and caution might create civil liability but would not suffice to hold him criminally liable." For fixing criminal liability on a doctor or surgeon, the court laid down that the standard of negligence required to be proved should be as high as could be described as "gross negligence" or "reckless."

This Judgment brought a great relief to Doctors. If the doctor had made criminally liable in this case, then the doctors would be scared of taking the cases, which will finally result in the death of poor patients in India.

Case – 7

Pravat Kumar Hospital and others v. Ruby General Hospital

Doctors cannot insist and wait for fees when death is knocking the doors of the patient.

Doctors cannot insist and wait for fees when death is knocking the doors of the patient as held in *Pravat Kumar Hospital and others v. Ruby General Hospital.* The case involves unfortunate death of a young boy, Sri Sumanta Mukhejee, a student of second year B. Tech, Electrical Engineering, was seriously injured in an accident, in which a bus of the Calcutta Tramway Corporation dashed with the motor cycle driven by the deceased. The deceased was brought to the Ruby General Hospital, Kolkata, which was close the place of accident. The treatment, discontinued after 45 minutes due to failure on part of persons who brought him to hospital to deposit Rs. 15,000/- which resulted in denial of treatment and consequential death of young boy.

It was contended by the hospital, since no consideration was paid by the deceased or complainant,

It was held by the National Commission that persons belonging to "poor class" who are provided services free of charge are beneficiaries of services which is hired or availed of by "paying class" and status of "emergency or critically ill patient" would be same as "persons belonging to poor class", since both are not in position to pay further it was held that free services would also be services and recipient would be consumer under the Act.

In this case it was proved by expert evidence that discontinuance of treatment hastened the death of patient which itself deficiency in service and it was decided that there was serious negligence and laxity on part of hospital by refusing admission and treatment facility to youth who almost in dying condition, defying all medical ethics and gross violation of Clinical Establishment Rules and Act of 1950 as amended in 1998, obvious reason is recovery of fee can wait but not the death nor the treatment for trying to save the life. Compensation of Rs. 10 lakhs awarded for mental pain and agony to the parents of the deceased.

Case – 8

Secretary, Thirumurugan Co-operative Agriculture Credit Society v. M.Lalitha(Dead) through her L.R. and Others.

the CPA Act attempts to remove the helplessness of a consumer which he faces against powerful, influential and well-organised sectors of manufacturers and traders.

Whether consumer has the option of seeking relief in the consumer forum/ commission by avoiding the arbitration clause ? in a case of *the Secretary, Thirumurugan Co-operative Agriculture Credit Society v. M.Lalitha(Dead) through her L.R. and Others.* The Facts and Judgment is that when a potential consumer goes to buy some goods, he may be required to sign on an agreement paper in which an arbitration clause is also appended. In case a dispute arise out of the transaction, whether he has the option of seeking relief in the Consumer Forum/ Commission by avoiding the arbitration clause.

Recently in *Secretary Thirumurugan Co-operative Agriculture Credit Society v. M.Lalitha(Dead) through L.R. and Others,* the Apex Court gave the reasoning for the non-ouster of jurisdiction of Consumer Disputers Redressal Agencies in spite the presence of non-obstante clause in the Arbitration and Concilliation Act of 1996. It observed that the remedies that are available to an aggrieved party under the CPA Act of 1986 are wider. For instance, in addition to granting a specific relief the Forums under the Act of 1986 have jurisdiction to award compensation for the mental agony, suffering, etc., which possibly could not be given under other statutes. Confirming its decision in *State of Karnataka v.*

Vishwabharathi House Building Coop Society and Ors, the SC opined that the CPA Act attempts to remove the helplessness of a consumer which he faces against powerful, influential and well-organised sectors of manufacturers and traders.

The forums under this benevolent legislation supplements and supplants the jurisdiction of the civil courts or other statutory authorities, therefore, an arbitration clause in a contract cannot debar an aggrieved consumer from knocking the door of the District Forum or the State/National Commission as the case may be and seek shelter under the Act enacted specially and exclusively to protect him.

Case – 9

Unnikrishanan v. State of Andhra Pradesh

Imparting education has never been treated as a trade or business in this country since time immemorial. It has been treated as a charitable activity.

Education is not Commerce but inherent charity of this Nation — Accountability of Educational Institutions and the Consumer Protection Act, 1986 was held in *Unnikrishanan v. State of Andhra Pradesh.* Imparting of education is the nature of a mission or a noble vocation. A teacher educates children, he moulds their character, builds up their personality and makes them fit to become a reasonable citizen. Children grow under the care of teachers, as held by the Supreme Court in *Academy Educational Society v. Gorary Kumar.*

In *Unnikrishanan v. State of Andhra Pradesh,* the Supreme Court observed that, Education has never been commerce in this country. Making it one is opposed the ethos and traditions and sensibilities of this nation. The argument to the contrary has an unholy ring to it. Imparting education has never been treated as a trade or business in this country since time immemorial. It has been treated as a charitable activity.

Case – 10

S. Somasundaram v. International Matriculation Academy, Tamil Nadu.

Parents of school going children are consumers.

Parents of school going children are consumers — says Supreme Court in *S. Somasundaram v. International Matriculation Academy, Tamil Nadu*. The petitioner S. Somasundram had moved the State Forum alleging that his three-and-a half year old daughter Brinda, who was admitted to the school in upper kg, died after she had fallen down in an open septic tank near the toilet in the school premises on 2nd December 1993, and claimed Rupees Five lakhs as compensation from the school authorities. Describing the negligence of the school authorities as 'shocking.'

The State Commission while holding the school responsible for deficiency in service had awarded only Rs. 10,000 as compensation to be paid by the school authorities to parents.

Aggrieved by the decision of the State Commission regarding low amount of compensation the petitioner filed an appeal to the National Commission.

National commission in a landmark judgment allowing an appeal against State Commission of Tamil Nadu, The National Commission held that "there clearly has been deficiency in service. Further held that in the present case there are two consumers, one the child and the other the parents. Not only the child suffered, parents have suffered as well for loss and injury to the child. They are entitled to damages and has directed a private school in Tamilnadu to cough off about Rs. 2.9 lakhs as compensation for negligence which had resulted in the death of three-and-half year old child in 1993.

Case – 11

Sumathidevi v. Union of India

11. Traveling on the train by the passengers, the Railway Authorities responsibilities exists right from boarding the train and alighting of the destination by the passengers.

Traveling on the train by the passengers, the Railway Authorities' responsibilities exists right from boarding the train and alighting at the destination by the passengers in *Sumathidevi v. Union of India,* the petitioner Sumati Devi M. Dhanwatay traveled by first class air-conditioned berth from Nagpur to Bombay by Hawrah-Bombay Mail on 4th December 1991. She was carrying her luggage which included gold, pearl, silver and diamond jewelery and other valuables valued at Rs. 1,11,756.

While she was traveling, she was assaulted by some unauthorized passengers and her valuables were taken away forcibly. Many people entered into the compartment and assaulted the passengers, the crowd committed so many other illegal acts of assaulting the bonafide passengers, they molested the women and even raped the young girl passengers, Sumathi Devi pulled the alarm chain thrice, as a result of which, the train stopped at Igatpuri station. She, along with other bonafide passengers got down at that station. She approached the railway authorities for protection but they did not get any assistance. On reaching Bombay she lodged a complaint with the police about the incident. She approached the consumer disputes redressal commission, Maharastra State. By filing a complaint claiming compensation of Rs. 9,32,256 against the railway administration.

The State Commission, after considering the material that was placed before it, allowed the claim of the appellant partly awarding total compensation of Rs 1,41,756.

The Railway administration, not satisfied with the said order filed an appeal before the National Consumer Disputes Redressal Commission, the National Commission set aside the order made by the State Commission. Hence, the petitioner filed this appeal in the Supreme Court contending that the Railway administration failed to take precaution and preventive measures and there had been a deficiency in service on the part of the railway administration.

Supreme Court held that, there is a breach of common law duty of reasonable care, which lies upon all carriers including railways. The standard of care must be high and strict. It is not a case where the omission on the part of railway officials can be said to be wholly unforeseen or beyond their control.

This being the position, in our view, the impugned order passed by the National Commission cannot be sustained. Accordingly the appeal was allowed.

Case – 12

R.P. Jain v. Sahara India Airlines

Chicken Curry Served to Vegetarian in *R.P. Jain v. Sahara India Airlines.* By an oversight Chicken-curry was served to a vegetarian airlines passenger. There was no complaint of vomiting or food poisoning. The Passenger contended that his religious sentiment had been hurt. The opposite party Sahara Airlines tendered apology. Since the mistake was not malicious and no physical injury has been caused, no compensation was allowed to the passenger.

Case – 13

Udayaram v. Rajasthan S.R.T. Corporation

Bus booked for marriage not reached in *Udayaram v. Rajasthan S.R.T. Corporation.* The complainant booked a bus of the Opposite Party for carrying marriage party. Advance of Rs. 3,000 had been paid. The bus did not reach and the complainant had to book another bus by paying Rs.4100. For this marriage a Brass Band had also been booked for Rs. 3000 for availability at the specified time. The marriage programme was considerably delayed causing lot of loss and embarrassment to complainant. The Opposite Party was directed by the State Commission to pay compensation of Rs. 8000 apart from the refund of Rs. 3000 paid as advance, to the complainant for deficiency in service. The opposite party was free to recover Rs. 8000 from the employee guilty of the default.

Case – 14

Pravath Kumar Mukharjee Vs. Ruby General Hospital and others

In an medial emergency or a critical case, it is the implicit duty of a noble profession to treat the injured person without waiting either for consent or for fees. The refusal to give treatment would even be violative of the provisions of the Code of Medical Ethics and would constitute a deficiency in service.

"Can treatment be refused because an accident results in a medico-legal case" — the National Commission, Mumbai says, "first treat then ask for fee" in *Pravath Kumar Mukharjee Vs. Ruby General Hospital and others.* On the judgment of the Supreme Court in the case of Paramanand Katara Vs. Union of India and others, the National Commission held that preservation of Human Life is of paramount importance. Hence an injured citizen for medical treatment should be instantaneously given medical aid to preserve life. This is also in consonance with the provisions of the Code of Medical Ethics.

Can treatment be refused because of non-payment of fees ? the commission held that recovery of fees can wait but the treatment trying to save a life cannot be delayed or neglected. A person who agrees to pay also enjoys the status of a Consumer. Besides, the Supreme Court has laid down that in a hospital which has two categories of patients — those who pay and those who are treated free — the free patients also acquire the status of consumer because it is deemed that their treatment is being met by the paying patients *(Indian Medical Association Vs. V.P. Shantha and others).*

This same analogy can be extended to emergency cases of critically injured persons who cannot pay. Hence even in the absence of payment, the complainant would be considered a 'consumer.'

Can a doctor refuse to treat in an emergency for want of consent ? The Commission held that in an emergency or a critical case, it is the implicit duty of a noble profession to treat the injured person without waiting either for consent or for fees. The refusal to give treatment would even be violative of the provisions of the Code of Medical Ethics and would constitute a deficiency in service.

Would the inevitable certainty of death be a factor for refusal to treat ? On merits the hospital claimed there was no evidence suggest that the failure to give treatment resulted in Kolkata Youth Sumantha Mukharjee's death. On the contrary, in such a serious accident, death was inevitable, and the post mortem established this fact. The commission disagreed with the hospital's stand, and held that it was contrary to established principles of Medical Jurisprudence. It observed that present day medical sciences believes in treatment till the last breath and for some time thereafter by resuscitation. Doctors do not say that as the death is inevitable they will stop treatment. Hence the imminent certainty of death was irrelevant and of no help to the hospital.

On the issue of compensation, the commission observed that there was gross negligence on the part of the hospital and doctors. Hence, the compensation must not only served to recompense the individual, but also aim at bringing about the qualitative change in the attitude of the service provider. Accordingly he Hospital and the doctors were directed to pay Rs. 10 lakh to the complainant.

This judgement is a milestone. Hospitals will no longer be able to turn away accident patients and will be severely penalized if they do so.

Case – 15

New India Assurance Co.Ltd., v. Goel Exports

Issues within the knowledge of the Insurance Company before Insurance and dispatch of Consignment : Repudiation wrong.

Issues within the knowledge of the Insurance Company before Insurance and dispatch of Consignment : Repudiation wrong in **New India Assurance Co.Ltd., v. Goel Exports.** Respondent lodged a claim for Rs. 1213600 which was not settled by the petitioner. Respondent filed the complaint before State Commission. After filing the complaint petitioner repudiated the claim on the basis of exclusion clause of International Chamber of Commerce. Complaint allowed.

Pre-dispatch investigation report clinches the issue and now the insurance company can not raise issues of insufficiency nature of packaging. The commission felt that there was deficiency of service by insurance company who raised many contentions only after the damage occurred. Although all these issues were within their knowledge before the consignment was insured and dispatched under the above circumstances. The commission finds that repudiation of the claim by the insurance company is not correct.

Case – 16

Gurudeep Kaur v. Body and Care, Bangalore

Consumer forum pulls up firm for weight loss advertisements.

Consumer Forum pulls up firm for weight loss advertisements in *Gurudeep Kaur v. Body and Care, Bangalore.* The petitioner Gurudeep Kaur of Rajaajinagar, Bangalore had approached body care on Sankey Road after seeing an advertisement in News Paper, 'claimed to help loss of weight upto 20 kgs' in one month. The firm also promised the complainant that she could lose 17 kgs without any dieting and diet supplement without any side effect. After paying Rs. 10,000 the complainant was given a list of diet requirements and also was asked to walk every day for an hour. She was even told to buy massage oil costing Rs. 550.

Before starting the programme on December 10, 2004 the complainant weighed 73.4 kgs. Seven months later after nearly 70 sessions she had lost only five kgs.

Responding to the complaint by Gurudeep Kaur, the third Addl. Bangalore Urban District Consumer Disputes Redressal Forum said it is a great disappointment for a person having paid the money to the firm and undergone inconvenience of time and effort, while directing the respondent firm to refund the entire programme amount along with Rs. 25,000 as litigation cost to the victim. The forum observed, "advertisements are made to attract attention and generally tend to exaggerate the products and promises which can mislead people."

Frivolous and vexatious complaint - deserved award of costs under section 26 of Consumer Protection Act, 1986

Case – 17

Y.S. Varma Vs. Union of India

Frivolous and vexatious complaint — deserved award of costs under section 26 of Consumer Protection Act, 1986 in (a) **Y.S. Varma Vs. Union of India.** The complainant booked a telephone under Own-Your-Telephone (OYT) scheme by depositing Rs. 8,000. He filed a complaint alleging that no telephone connection was issued to him while others were given telephone connections. The allegations were found to be false and the complaint was found to be frivolous and vexatious which resulted in harassment of the respondent. The complaint was dismissed and the complainant was ordered to pay the Opposite Party the cost of Rs. 500 within one month and in (b) **Biharilal Thavait v. Doctor Prakash Ladekar** case, the complainant, Biharilal, who was a polio patient was operated upon by the Opposite Party free of cost in November 1988 and the calipers and walkers were also provided to him free of cost.

He filed a complaint in 1996 which was time barred and also alleged that fraud had been committed by the Opposite Party. Since the treatment had been done free of cost it was held that the question of fraud did not arise.

The complaint was held to be frivolous and vexatious and the costs under section 26 deserved to be awarded. However, looking to the poverty and disability of the complainant no costs were in fact awarded.

The burden of proof is not discharged by the LIC, by proving that the act of repudiation of the policy is not bonafide, there is no error of law warranting interference in exercise of revisional jurisdiction.

Case – 18

Life Insurance Corporation v. S. Hymavathi

Suppression of material facts in LIC policy — burden of proof vests on LIC in **Life Insurance Corporation v. S. Hymavathi.**

If the LIC alleged that the policy holder made the statement fraudulently that is knowing that the same was false and he deliberately concealed material facts, the burden of proof was on the LIC. The burden of proof is not discharged by the LIC, by proving that the act of repudiation of the policy is not bonafide, there is no error of law warranting interference in exercise of revisional jurisdiction.

Purchasing of a machinery by a customer for commercial purposes can not come under the purview of 'Consumer' as defined under Consumer Protection Act, 1986.

Case – 19

Abbay Chemicals Pvt. Ltd. v. Kanti Bhai D. Patel

Purchasing of a machinery by a customer for commercial purposes can not come under the purview of 'Consumer' as defined under Consumer Protection Act, 1986. Hence no compensation for defective machines purchased for manufacturing activities in **Abbay Chemicals Pvt. Ltd. v. Kanti Bhai D. Patel.** In the present case, the National Commission held that no compensation could be awarded in respect of defects of a machine worth more than Rs. 10 lakhs, purchased for use in large scale manufacturing activity, since the purchase would be for a commercial purpose and the buyer in such case would not be a consumer under the Consumer Protection Act. Similar decision was given in the case of **Synco Textiles Pvt. Ltd. v. Greaves Cotton & Co. Ltd.**

Case – 20

Y. N. Gupta v. DESU

Highly inflated electricity bills and defective electricity meter amounts to willful and reckless deficiency of service was noticed in Y N Gupta v. DESU. The Highly inflated electricity bills and defective electricity meter, the National Commission, New Delhi considered a complaint regarding the inflated electricity bills served by DESU on the complainant. In this case, DESU did not raise bills in keeping with the cycle normally adopted. It also did not replace the defective meter. However, it slapped the bill for over Rs. 1.06 lacs for a period from 21st December, 1988 to 25th March, 1990. The power connection was also disconnected but restored after making a complaint to the General Manager. The National Commission ruled that it was difficult to envisage a situation where the consumer could have utilised over 1 lakh units of electricity and the expect a poor consumer to pay bills of over a lakh. The National Commission ruled that the bills were casually prepared. DESU did not have the authority to raise bills upon a defective meter beyond six months under the Electricity Act, 1910. In these circumstances, the National Commission concluded that there was deficiency in services on the part of DESU and awarded a compensation of Rs.30000 and costs of Rs. 5,000.

Highly inflated electricity bills and defective electricity meter amounts to willful and reckless deficiency of service was noticed.

Case – 21

P. Goel v. Collector of Stamps

Government servants not doing any service for consideration but a statutory function in **P. Goel v. Collector of Stamps.** In the above case, it was held that a government official does not render any service in the course of doing his statutory duties. Hence, no remedy can be granted under the CPA. In this case, the complainant presented before the Sub-Registrar a document claiming it to be a will for registration. The Sub-registrar did not register the document claiming it to be a deed of conveyance and hence not adequately stamped. He impounded the document and sent it to the Collector of Stamps for action. Despite several notices issued to him by the Collector, the appellant did not appear before him. When the appellant appeared before the Collector he was asked to furnish certain other documents. In the meantime, however, the appellant filed a complaint before the District Forum under the Consumer Protection Act alleging harassment by the Sub-Registrar and Collector and had prayed for compensation being awarded to him.

Government servants not doing any service for consideration but a statutory function.

The District Forum held the view that the appellant having paid registration fees, he shall be treated to have hired the services of the Sub-Registrar and the Collector and since the Collector had not taken any decision as to the nature of the document for about six years, allowed compensation to be paid to the complainant.

On appeal by the Collector, the State Commission, upheld the order of the District Forum and enhanced the compensation to Rs. 5,000.

On the revision petition filed by the Collector, the National Commission held the view that the appellant was not a "consumer" under the CPA. because there was no hiring of services by the complainant for consideration and because a government official doing his duty as functionary of the State under law could not be said to be rendering a service to the complainant. It stated that assuming the Collector was discharging a service, he was doing the same as a functionary of the Government under the authority of the statute and for the benefit of the revenue for which he was being paid by the Government and not by the complainant.

The Supreme Court upheld the order of the National Commission on appeal.

Case – 22

Consumer Protection Act, 1986 in J.K. Puri Engineers v. Mohan Breweries & Distilleries Ltd.

Maintenance of Guest house – Not for commercial purpose – Service rendered by the Air Conditioning Company falls under the scope of **Consumer Protection Act, 1986.**

Maintenance of Guest house - Not for commercial purpose - Service rendered by the Air Conditioning Company falls under the scope of Consumer Protection Act, 1986 in **J.K. Puri Engineers v. Mohan Breweries & Distilleries Ltd.** In the instant case, it was held that a guest house maintained for company officials is not for commercial purposes and hence benefit under the CPA can be availed of.: The company maintained a guest house for use of its managing director and other executives. It entered into a contract with the appellants for the installation of a central air-conditioning system. The company alleged that the system installed did not properly, developed snags, and that there was leakage of water from the ducting system. The appellant having failed to make good the defects, the complainant appointed a consultant and obtained from him a report on the working of the system which pointed out a number of defects. The State Commission held that the complainant was a consumer under the CPA and that the air-conditioning system had not been installed for a commercial purpose because the guest house was not maintained for a commercial purpose. The National Commission upheld the decision of the State Commission.

Case – 23

S.P. Dhavaskar v. Housing Commissioner, Karnataka Housing Board & Vice Versa

Failure to deliver houses by the housing board is deficiency in service.

Failure to deliver houses by the housing board is deficiency in service in **S.P. Dhavaskar v. Housing Commissioner, Karnataka Housing Board & Vice Versa.** In the above case, the complainant had made a deposit of Rs. 1.66 lakhs with the Housing Board for a house proposed to be built by the Board. He was told that the construction be completed within two years from March, 1987. In March, 1992 he was informed that the construction was not upto the expected level because of the use of low cost technology and that the houses constructed developed distress and might not long and suggested that the complainant might take back the amount of deposit without interest or opt for a new house in lieu of the house already allotted. The complainant made a claim of Rs. 4.65 lakhs which was rejected. The State Commission held that the act of the Housing Board amounted to a deficiency in service and returning deposit amount without interest was unreasonable and ordered payment of interest at 18% p.a. In appeal, the National Commission upheld the order of the State Commission.

Case – 24

Sashikant Krishnaji Dole v Shikshan Prasarak Mandali

Failure to provide basic safeguards in the swimming pool amounted to deficiency in service.

Failure to provide basic safeguards in the swimming pool amounted to deficiency in service. **Sashikant Krishnaji Dole v Shikshan Prasarak Mandali.** The National commission held that failure to provide basic safeguards in the swimming pool amounts to deficiency in service. A school owned a swimming pool and offered swimming facilities to the public on payment of a fee. The school conducted winter and summer training camps to train boys in swimming and for this purpose engaged a trainer/coach. The complainants had enrolled their only son for learning swimming under the guidance of the coach. It was alleged that due to the negligence of the coach, the boy drowned and died. The school denied any responsibility on its part. The coach claimed that he had considerable experience in coaching young boys in swimming. When the deceased was found to have been drowned, the coach immediately took him out of the water and removed the water from his stomach and gave him artificial respiration and thereafter took him to a doctor. The doctor advised that the boy be taken to the nearest hospital where the boy died. The State Commission held the school and the coach deficient in rendering service to the deceased. On appeal, the order was upheld by the National Commission.

Case – 25

Indian Airlines v. Dr. Jiteswar Ahir

Removal of ladder of an aircraft while disembarking by the passenger amounts to deficiency in service. Station Manager in **Indian Airlines v. Dr. Jiteswar Ahir.** The National Commission held that removal of ladder while a passenger was disembarking, leading to injury to the passenger amounted to deficiency in service. The complainant after he was seated on the plane, was intimated by announcement that part of his luggage was lying on the ground unidentified. He moved towards the door and finding that the ladder was in place, tried to get down. But before he could get his entire body on the ladder, the ladder was moved as a result of which of which he fell to the ground and sustained injuries. The passenger demanded compensation of Rs. 10 lakhs from the Airline. The Airline was willing to pay Rs. 40000/- which was the maximum amount payable under the Carriage by Air Act, 1972. The State Commission ordered a compensation of Rs. 4 lakhs and Rs. 1 lakh for mental agony and distress plus costs. The order of the State Commission was upheld by the National Commission.

Removal of ladder of an aircraft while disembarking by the passenger amounts to deficiency in service.

Case – 26

Poonam Verma v. Ashwin Patel

Homeopathic Doctor is restrained from treating the patient with Allopathic Medicines in **Poonam Verma v. Ashwin Patel.** It was held that a doctor qualified under the homeopathic system of medicines treats a patient with allopathic medicines, he is guilt of negligence and compensation is due if the patient dies on such account.

Homeopathic Doctor is restrained from treating the patient with Allopathic Medicines.

Case – 27

Union of India v. Nathmal Hansaria

Passenger Passing through the different interconnected compartments of a train falls due to deficiency in providing a error free intercepting plate in **Union of India v. Nathmal Hansaria,** in this case, the deceased while traveling from Delhi to Gohati was going from one compartment to other through interconnecting passage. The passage being unfenced, she fell down from the train and died by being run over by the train. It was held to be deficiency in service on the part of the Railways. The parents of the deceased girl were awarded compensation of Rs. 2,25,000/-.

Passenger Passing through the different interconnected compartments of a train falls due to deficiency in providing a error free intercepting plate.

The judicial pronouncements meticulously discussed in the above instances ranging from Housing, Health, Education, Fast Moving Consumer Goods, Consumer Durables, Insurance, Air Travel to a host of services, highlight one thing in common that is defects in goods or deficiency in the services rendered. The legal remedy for these laxes was met in one of the Consumer Dispute Redressal Forums either in the original jurisdiction or in the First and Second Appeal. The landmark judgments given by National Commission and the Supreme Court of India have changed the entire paradigms in respect of Consumer Protection and safeguarding their interests and rights in our country. The judiciary is fully active in this regard through its activism doctrine.

7.5 CONSUMER PROTECTION LEADING CASE LAWS — UNITED STATES OF AMERICA

Case – 1

Macperson v. Buick Motor Co.

A car manufacturer had to compensate a consumer who had been injured when one of the car wheels collapsed because of a defect. The liability was fixed.

A car manufacturer had to compensate a consumer who had been injured when one of the car wheels collapsed because of a defect. The liability was fixed in **Macperson v. Buick Motor Co.** case. In New York Court of Appeal, it was held that a car manufacturer had to compensate a consumer who had been injured when one of the car wheels collapsed because of a defect.

The Court held that the manufacturer had been negligent because the defect could have been discovered by reasonable inspection.

This decision helped in bringing out manufacturer's liability to compensate injured consumers and to try to encourage manufacturers to take steps to prevent defective products getting into market.

Case – 2

Tesco Stores Ltd. v. Pollard

Personal Injury Arising Out Of Dishwasher Powder from a Plastic Bottle – Negligence of Service.

Personal Injury Arising Out Of Dishwasher Powder from a Plastic Bottle — Negligence of Service was held in **Tesco Stores Ltd. v. Pollard.** The appellants (T) appealed against a decision granting judgment in favour of the respondent (C) in a personal injury action. C, who was 13 months old at the time, was injured when he ingested dishwasher powder from a plastic bottle. The powder had been purchased from the first appellant, but the bottle had been manufactured by the second appellant. The claim against T was that the bottle and cap had been defective so that the cap was easier to detach than it should have been. The cap was a child resistant closure (CRC) cap. T joined C's mother (P) to the action on the basis of their claim that she had left the bottle in a place where C could see and reach it, and had left the cap off or not properly screwed up. The judge found T liable and acquitted P of any negligence.

Allowing the appeal and dismissing the cross appeal, that (1) this was a case of breach of statutory duty or nothing. One aspect of the factual scenario which, having exonerated P, the judge accepted, was that it was surely not reasonably foreseeable that this injury would happen as he found it did. In a case such as the instant, any calculation of foreseeability had to assume that the child's parents would take steps in the home to prevent the child having access to the bottle. Every case must be judged by the colour of its own facts and, in the instant case, foreseeability could not be got out of the fact that it proved possible for C to open the bottle coupled with the fact that the British Standard certificate was not met. Accordingly, the case turned upon whether there was a breach of the 1987 Act. (2) The test as to whether a product had a defect under the 1987 Act was what persons generally were entitled to expect. Persons were generally entitled to expect that the bottle in the instant case would be more difficult to open than if it had an ordinary screwtop. Anything more specific, as a test of public expectation, ran into difficulties. The bottle was more difficult to open than an ordinary screw top, though not as difficult as it would have been if the British Standard torque measure had been complied with. Thus, there was no breach of the 1987 Act.

Case – 3

Marianne T. CAULFIELD, et al., Appellants v. Howard A. STARK, M.D., et al., Appellees

Claims for Fraud, Unlawful Trade Practices to Perform Colonoscopy was held in **Marianne T. CAULFIELD, et al., Appellants v. Howard A. STARK, M.D., et al., Appellees.** The Patient brought action against gastroenterologist and employer to recover for negligence, fraudulent misrepresentation, and unlawful trade practices in connection with failure to perform colonoscopy and detect colon cancer. The Superior Court, District of Columbia, Anna Blackburne-Rigsby, J., granted defendants' motion for judgment as a matter of law (JMOL) on claims for fraud, unlawful trade practices, and punitive damages and entered judgment on jury verdict for defendants on negligence claim. Patient appealed. The Court of Appeals, Ferren, Senior Judge, held that:

Claims for Fraud, Unlawful Trade Practices to Perform Colonoscopy.

- gastroenterologist did not engage in fraud;
- performance of medical services is a "trade practice" under the Consumer Protection Procedures Act (CPPA);
- with respect to some alleged misrepresentations, patient could not recover damages for personal injury under former version of CPPA;
- gastroenterologist did not violate CPPA with regard to code and diarrhea diagnosis on billing form; and
- patient could not recover punitive damages.

Appeal allowed.

Case – 4

National City Home Loan Services, Inc. ("National"), Jr. Creditor v. In re Thaddeus Rudolph JONES, Jr. Debtor.

Bankruptcy Abuse Prevention and order in favour of Judgment Creditor was held in **National City Home Loan Services, Inc. ("National"), Jr. Creditor v. In re Thaddeus Rudolph JONES, Jr. Debtor.** Repeat Chapter 13 filer brought adversary proceeding for determination that, under provision of the Bankruptcy, Abuse, Prevention and Consumer Protection Act (BAPCPA) purporting to limit duration of automatic stay in successive bankruptcy cases commenced by certain repeat filers, stay terminated 30 days after petition date only as to actions against debtor, and not as to actions against debtor's property or property of the estate.

Bankruptcy, Abuse, Prevention and order in favour of Judgment Creditor.

The Bankruptcy Court, A. Thomas Small, J., held that phrase "with respect to the debtor," as used in section of the Bankruptcy, Abuse, Prevention and Consumer Protection Act (BAPCPA) providing that, 30 days after commencement of successive bankruptcy cases by certain repeat filers, automatic stay will terminate "with respect to the debtor," had to be interpreted as providing for automatic termination of stay with respect to actions against the debtor or against property of the debtor, but not with respect to actions taken against property of the estate. So ordered.

Case – 5

Myracle, Deceased, Appellant, v. Gary McMICKLE, Individually and d/b/a Creative Capital, Inc., McMickle Associates, Inc., and Creative Capital, Inc., Appellees

Medical Malpractice, Violations of Deceptive Trade Practices–Consumer Protection Act (DTPA).

Medical Malpractice, Violations of Deceptive Trade Practices—Consumer Protection Act (DTPA). In **Myracle, Deceased, Appellant, v. Gary McMICKLE, Individually and d/b/a Creative Capital, Inc., McMickle Associates, Inc., and Creative Capital, Inc., Appellees** Decedent's estate sued attorney who had represented decedent in settlement of medical malpractice action, and annuity broker, alleging negligence, breach of fiduciary duty, violations of Deceptive Trade Practices—Consumer Protection Act (DTPA), and fraud, relating to purchase, with portion of settlement proceeds, of deferred, life-only annuity without guaranteed refund of premium. The County Court at Law No. 1, Wichita County, David Cleveland, J., granted summary judgment to annuity broker and later granted broker's motion to sever. Estate appealed.

The Court of Appeals, Dixon W. Holman, J., held that:

- annuity broker did not have duty of care to minor's mother, as minor's next friend, because mother had been replaced as personal representative by guardian ad litem, and
- evidence did not show false representation.

Affirmed / Appeal Allowed

Case – 6

Melrose Hotel Company, Plaintiff, v. ST. Paul Fire And Marine Insurance Company

Commercial General Liability of the Insurer under Telephone Consumer Protection Act.

Commercial General Liability of the Insurer under Telephone Consumer Protection Act. In **Melrose Hotel Company, Plaintiff, v. ST. Paul Fire And Marine Insurance Company,** Defendant Insured hotel company brought state-court action seeking declaration that commercial general liability (CGL) insurer had duty to defend and indemnify insured against class action brought under Telephone Consumer Protection Act (TCPA) by recipients of insured's mass facsimile advertisements. Insurer removed action on basis of diversity, and parties cross-moved for summary judgment.

The District Court, Schiller, J., held that:

- insured's alleged violation of TCPA was outside "right to privacy" clause of CGL policy's advertising injury coverage;
- recipients' complaint against insured alleged "property damage" potentially within CGL coverage; but
- property damage alleged was not result of accident and thus was outside CGL policy's property damage coverage provision; and
- CGL policy's "expected or intended" exclusion also applied.

Insurer's motion granted.

Case – 7

Power & Telephone Supply Company, Inc., Plaintiff-Appellant, v. Suntrust Banks, INC.; SunTrust Bank; SunTrust Bank--Atlanta; SunTrust Bank — Nashville, N.A.; SunTrust Equitable Securities Corporation; SunTrust Capital Markets, Inc., Defendants-Appellees.

"swap" Agreements and Variable Interest Rates Power & Telephone Supply Company, Inc., **Plaintiff-Appellant, v. Suntrust Banks, INC**.; SunTrust Bank; SunTrust Bank—Atlanta; SunTrust Bank— Nashville, N.A.; SunTrust Equitable Securities Corporation; SunTrust Capital Markets, Inc., Defendants-Appellees. Commercial borrower brought action against financial services companies to recover $6 million in costs incurred under two derivative interest rate "swap" agreements which were to act as hedge against increases in variable interest rate on its syndicated lines of credit. Defendants counterclaimed seeking indemnification for attorney fees and costs incurred in defending action. The United States District Court for the Western District of Tennessee, Jon Phipps McCalla, J., 2005 WL 1329851, granted judgment for defendants. Borrower appealed.

The Court of Appeals, Ralph B. Guy, Jr., Circuit Judge, held that:

- borrower could not wait to file suit under Tennessee Consumer Protection Act (TCPA) until after all of injurious effects or specific type of legal claim were known;
- representations made to induce borrower to work with companies generally were not fraudulent;
- companies did not owe borrower legal duty to advise it on appropriateness of interest rate swap transactions;
- commitment letter's attorney fees provision applied to litigation associated with credit agreement;
- indemnity clause in commitment letter was not superseded by allegedly narrower indemnity clause found in restated credit agreement; and
- companies were collectively entitled to single recovery from commercial borrower of total reasonable attorney fees and costs incurred.

Affirmed / Appeal Allowed.

In America, it is not the question of protecting Consumer rights and interests that matter, what really happening in that country is the concept of self regulation by the organizations supplying goods or rendering services. The organizations adopts the famous adage that is prevention is better than cure. In that the corporates take all proactive measures to restrain the consumer in approaching the Hon'ble Court. Approaching the courts in America by the consumer and the subsequent verdict by the courts will prove to be a costly affair for the corporates. This speaks of the regulation and protection given to the consumers in USA.

7.6 CONSUMER PROTECTION LEADING CASE LAWS — UNITED KINGDOM

Case – 1

Donoughue v. Stevenson

In **Donoughue v. Stevenson** the first leading case of this world relating to consumer rights came before the court of England in the year 1932 in an interesting way. In this case a person went to a restaurant with a women friend and bought one bottle of ginger-beer manufactured by the defendants. The women consumed part of the contents but when the remainder was poured into the tumbler the decomposed body of a snail floated out of the ginger-beer. The ginger-beer bottle being opaque and sealed, the presence of snail could not have been observed earlier.

The women brought an action against the manufacturer for negligence and alleged that by taking a part of the contaminated drink, she had contracted serious illness.

The House of Lords held that the manufacturer owed her a duty to take care that the bottle did not contain noxious matter injurious to health. The court said that every manufacturer owes a duty towards every ultimate consumer, of its product even though there is no contract between them.

Case – 2

R v. Birmingham City Council, ex parte Ferrero Ltd.

Every manufacturer owes a duty towards every ultimate consumer, of its product even though there is no contract between them.

R v. Birmingham City Council, ex parte Ferrero Ltd. The respondents manufactured chocolate eggs, each of which contained a plastic capsule which itself contained a kit which could be assembled to make a small toy representing well-known cartoon characters, one of which was known as the 'Pink Panther.' In October 1989 a little girl accidentally swallowed part of a 'Pink Panther' toy and died from asphyxiation as a result. The appellant local authority, through its trading standards officer, issued a suspension notice under s 14a of the Consumer Protection Act, 1987 prohibiting the supply of eggs containing the 'Pink Panther' toy for a period of six months. Despite attempts by the respondents to persuade it to do so, coupled with offers of undertakings, the local authority declined to withdraw it, contending, inter alia, that the council had acted unfairly in failing to consult them before issuing the suspension notice. The judge granted the relief sought. The local authority appealed, contending, *inter alia*,

The Act aimed at withholding goods from the public if there was reasonable suspicion that they were unsafe and that the suspension prohibiting supply was to remain in force until the goods were cleared of danger even if the process by which the enforcement authority reached its flawed.

(1) that the judge had erred in entertaining the respondents' application and granting the relief sought when they had a statutory right of appeal under Section 15b of the 1987 Act, which provided that a person having an interest in any goods in respect of which a suspension notice was in force could apply to a magistrates' court for an order for setting aside the notice, and

(2) that the local authority had not acted unfairly in failing to consult the respondents before issuing the notice.

The Court of Appeal, Civil Division Bench held, where there was an alternative remedy and especially where Parliament had provided a statutory appeal procedure it was only exceptionally that judicial review would be granted. In determining whether an exception should be made and judicial review granted it was necessary for the court to look carefully at the suitability of the statutory appeal in the context of the particular case.

It further held that, the statutory emphasis under the 1987 Act was on consumer safety, that the Act aimed at withholding goods from the public if there was reasonable suspicion that they were unsafe and that the suspension prohibiting supply was to remain in force until the goods were cleared of danger even if the process by which the enforcement authority reached its flawed. The respondents should have been left to pursue their appeal under 15 of Consumer Protection Act, 1987. The local authority's appeal would therefore be allowed and the judge's decision to grant judicial review reversed.

Case – 3

R v. Secretary of State for Health, exparte US Tobacco International Inc.

R v. Sccretary of State for Health, exparte US Tobacco International Inc In 1984 the applicants, a United States corporation which imported oral snuff products into the United Kingdoms, were encouraged by the Department of Trade and Industry to set up a manufacturing plant in the United Kingdom and were provided with government incentive grants to build a factory in Scotland. The factory commenced operation in 1985 and the applicants become the sole manufacturer in the United Kingdom of oral snuff products. However, in January 1986 a committee of experts set up to advise the government on the carcinogenicity of chemicals in food, consumer products and the environment reported that there was a causal link between snuff and oral cancer, which caused the government to negotiate voluntary agreements with the applicants not to market oral snuff to persons under 18 and to publish a health warning on their product.

There was a causal link between snuff and oral cancer, which caused the government to negotiate voluntary agreements with the applicants not to market oral snuff to persons under 18 and to publish a health warning on their product.

On 17th June 1986 the committee advised the government to ban oral snuff and on 26th February 1988 the Secretary of State for health announced that he proposed to make regulations under S 10a of the Consumer Protection Act 1987 banning oral snuff.

The applicants, who until then had been given no indication that their product might be banned, were invited in accordance with s 11(5)(a)(b) of the 1987 Act to make representation by 26th May 1988. The applicants asked for the evidence relied upon by the Secretary of State in deciding to propose the regulations but were not informed until 27th October 1988 that the government's proposals were based upon the advice of the committee in 1986. The secretary of State refused to disclose the test of the committee's advice and on 13th December 1989 he made the Oral Snuff (Safety) Regulations 1989, which came into force on 13th March 1990.

The Applicants applied for judicial Review of the Secretary of State's decision to make the regulations, contending, interalia, that the regulations were ultra Vires because the Secretary of State's power to make regulations under the Act was restricted to making regulations concerned with consumer protection and safety in connection with defective products and not with matters of health, and he had unfairly withheld the text of the committee's advice in 1986 from the applicants.

The Secretary of State's power to make regulation under Section 11 of Consumer Protection Act, 1987, included power to make regulations such as the 1989 regulations since the purpose of the regulations was to protect the consumer and the safety of the consumer, which included protection from the risk of death or personal injury to any person whatsoever furthermore, the decision to make regulation was not so disproportionate to the perceived risk to health as to be irrational and the applicants had no legitimate expectation that the Secretary of State would not change his policy notwithstanding the government's previous encouragement to the applicants to set up a factory, since the Secretary of state could not fetter a discretion conferred on him by statute and provided he acted rationally and fairly he was entitled to change his policy, and given that the change in policy resulting in the banning or oral snuff had been made in the public interest, his discretion could not be fettered by any moral obligation owned to the applicants.

However, the secretary of State's duty to consult affected parties under sec. 11(5)(a) required him to show a high degree of fairness and candor to the applicants because, as the sole manufacturers and packagers of oral snuff in the United Kingdoms, they were the only persons affected by the ban, in those circumstances the Secretary of State had acted unfairly in concealing from the applicants the scientific advice given to him in 1986 which directly let to the ban and an order to certiorari would issue to quash the regulations.

Case – 4

West Yorkshire Metropolitan Country Council v. MFI Furniture Central Ltd. and another appeal

Misleading advertisement are barred under CPA.

West Yorkshire Metropolitan Country Council v. MFI Furniture Central Ltd and another appeal. A furniture company inserted two advertisements in the press. One stated that it was selling a Six-drawer chest at $24.95 which it described as a 'bargain price' and 'Britain's lowest price.' The other stated that it was selling a Welser dresser at $69.95, which it described as a 'special clearance price.' The Company was charged and convicted in respect of both advertisements as contravening art 2(1)(a)a and 3(1)(b)b of the Price Marking (Bargain offers) Order 1979 by indicating that the price of the goods was 'lower than... the amount of another price for the sale of goods of the same description.' The company appealed to the Crown Court, contending:

(a) that in the first advertisement the words 'bargain price' and 'Britain's lowest price' did not inevitably imply that the goods are cheaper than elsewhere, and

(b) that in the second advertisement the words 'special clearance price' did not contravene art 3(1)(b) because they merely invited comparison between the advertised price of the goods and another price for the sale of other goods of the same description. The Crown Court allowed the appeals because in respect of the first advertisement it was not satisfied beyond reasonable doubt that an ordinary shopper would understand from the advertisement that he was getting a preferential price and not just a bargain, i.e., good value for money, and in respect of the second advertisement it had not been established that the words 'special clearance price' contravened the terms of art 3(1)(b). The prosecutor appealed.

1. The court would not interfere with the Crown Court's decision regarding the first advertisement, the words 'bargain price' and Britain's 'lowest price' contravened art 2 and 3 of the 1979 order, and the Crown Court had adopted the correct approach of looking at the advertisement through the eyes of an ordinary shopper and applying the criminal standard of proof. The appeal in respect of the first advertisement would accordingly be dismissed.

2. The second advertisement infringed the terms of art 3(1)(b) of the 1979 order, because on the true construction of the article the words 'goods of the same description' included a particular item of goods which was marked down as against itself. The appeal in respect of the second advertisement would accordingly be allowed.

Case – 5
Allen v. Redbridge London Borough Council

Allen v. Redbridge London Borough Council. The appellant owned a pharmacy which also sold perfumes and cosmetics most of which were kept in locked glass cabinets with their price labels being displayed either on the back or underside of the individual items. Any person interested in the items could ascertain their price by asking the appellant or a member of his staff to unlock the cabinet and remove the items for closer examination. The appellant was charged with failing to indicate the selling prices of those goods in accordance with art 3a and 8b of the Price Marking Order 1991, contrary to s 7 of and the schedule to the Prices Act 1974. Article 3 of the 1991, order provided that any goods to be sold by retailer were required to have the selling price thereof indicated in writing and art 8 provided that any goods to be sold by retail were required to have the selling price thereof indicated in writing and art 8 provided that the indication of price had to be unambiguous, easily identifiable and clearly legible to a prospective purchaser and marked on the goods or their container or on a ticket or notice in close proximity to the goods. The appellant was convicted on the basis that a 'prospective purchaser' included someone who could ascertain the price of goods without seeking the assistance of the shopkeeper or his staff and that as the price labels could not be viewed from the front of the cabinet they did not comply with art 8. The appellant appealed.

It was held by the Queen's Bench that the 1991 order did not lay down the precise method by which a shopkeeper had to bring the prices of his goods to the notice of the public, but left it open to the shopkeeper how it should be done. Furthermore, art 8 of the order was not directed at any person who walked into a shop but was specifically aims at a prospective purchaser. Accordingly, it was sufficient for the purpose of art 8 if it was clearly stated on or alongside of the particular article a price indicator which unmistakably related to it and if the price could not be seen from outside a locked cabinet it did not matter that the shopkeeper or one of his staff had to be asked to produce the article from the cabinet for inspection.

The shopkeeper was not required either to put a label on the front of the article or to put the article in a position where it could be handled by a customer a proper opportunity of seeing the price on the article. It followed that the appellant had not contravened art 3 and 8 of the 1991 order. The appeal would therefore be allowed and the convictions quashed.

Case – 6
Warwickshire Country Council v. Johnson

Warwickshire Country Council v. Johnson, the appellant was employed as the branch manager of a retail electrical goods shop. With the authority of the owners he placed a free-standing notice outside the shop stating 'We will beat any TV HiFI and Video price by $ 20 on the spot.' While the notice was displayed a customer saw a television set offered for sale elsewhere in the area at a price of $159.95. He took the appellant to see the set and then sought to purchase an identical set at the appellant's shop for $139.95, but although the appellant had one in stock he refused to sell it at the reduced price.

The customer reported the matter to the respondent council's trading standards department, which preferred an information against the appellant under S. 20(1) a of the Consumer Protection Act, 1987 alleging that the appellant had 'in the course of a business of his' given to the customer a misleading indication by means of the notice as to the price at which the television set was offered in that it was not $20 less than the price at which it was offered by another shop in the area. After preliminary appeals the appellant appealed to the House of Lords, where the issues were —

(i) whether a notice which was not misleading on its face could subsequently become misleading by a refusal to honour its term and

(ii) whether for the purposes of S.(20) the words 'in the course of a business of his' could include an employee.

The House of Lords held that: (1) the notice was continuing offer and therefore whether it was misleading or not could only be tested by somebody taking up the offer. Accordingly, since the appellant had refused to honour the terms of the notice by beating 'any Hifi, Video price by $ 20 on the spot' the notice was a misleading indication as to the price at which the goods were offered, contrary to S. 20(2)(1) of indication as the price at which the goods were offered.

(2) However, the words 'in the course of any business of his' in S. 20(2)(a) of the 1987 Act meant any business of which the defendant was whether the owner or in which he had a controlling interest, since the 1987 Act was directed against employers, i.e., the corporate body standing behind the misleading price indication, rather than the individual employees. Accordingly, since the appellant was only a manager of the shop he was not guilty of the offence charged and the appeal would therefore be allowed.

The Consumer protection in UK can be treated in the same footing as that of USA. The stringent product liability clause and other consumer related laws adequately protects the consumer besides redressing their problems in real time.

7.7 CONSUMER PROTECTION LEADING CASE LAWS — AUSTRALIA

Case – 1

John L. Proprietary Limited Appellant; and The Attorney-General for the State of New South Wales Respondent

John L. Proprietary Limited Appellant; and The Attorney-General for the State of New South Wales Respondent Section 32(1) of the Consumer Protection Act 1969 (NSW) provided that a person who, to promote the supply of goods or services, published a statement "to his knowledge false or misleading in any material particular" committed an offence. Section 56(1) provided that proceedings for offences against the Act might be taken "only by a person acting with the authority in writing of the Minister" and disposed of before magistrates or "the Supreme Court in its summary jurisdiction." Section 56(4) required the proceedings to be commenced by information.

John L. Pty. Ltd. ("the company"), a dealer in motor vehicles, published a newspaper advertisement offering quantities of free petrol to every customer buying a car over a nominated price during a limited period. The Department of Consumer Affairs considered that the advertisement, being intended to promote the supply of goods or services, was knowingly false or misleading in a "material particular" and that its publication was an offence against S. 32(1) of the

Consumer Protection Act 1969 (NSW). John Michael Clayton, an officer of the Department so authorized by the Minister for Consumer Affairs, laid in his own name an information under that Act to the Supreme Court of New South Wales. It was entertained in pursuance of S. 5C of the Criminal Appeal Act 1912 (NSW). Objections to competency were overruled, the complaint was allowed. The company appealed, by special leave, to the High Court.

The High Court Held that in the present case the information identified the time, place and manner in which the present appellant was alleged to have contravened S. 32(1) of the Consumer Protection Act. It failed to specify the respect in which the advertisement was false or misleading. It is true that S. 32(1) of the Act makes it an element of the offence created by that sub-section that a person publish a statement which is, to his knowledge, false or misleading in any material particular. But it was held that information or application that sets out the statement, identifying the time, place and manner of publication, and then alleges that the statement was false or misleading in a material particular, without identifying the particular, is bad in substance. Certainly the material particular should have been identified and would be ordered by way of particulars; nevertheless, in my view, the information or application is not defective by reason of the omission. It is legally sufficient, to borrow the words of Evatt J. in **Davies v. Ryan**. The distinction is an important one to maintain even though statutory provisions may render it of little practical importance at times.

For these reasons, it is unnecessary to deal with the appellant's submission that S. 6 of the Supreme Court (Summary Jurisdiction) Act is limited to an application, order or warrant and does not extend to an information under S. 56(4) of the Consumer Protection Act. The appeal should be dismissed.

Case – 2
Colgate Palmolive Pty Ltd v Rexona Pty Ltd

Colgate Palmolive Pty Ltd v Rexona Pty Ltd. The applicant held sixty per cent of the toothpaste market in Australia. The respondent sought to capture ten to twenty per cent of the Australian toothpaste market. The respondent commenced a massive advertising campaign to obtain a market share for a new toothpaste known as "Aim." Aim toothpaste included an ingredient known as "citraden." The applicant claimed that the respondent had been guilty of false, misleading or deceptive conduct by its advertising of Aim. It sought interlocutory injunctions pursuant to Ss. 52, 53 (a), (b), (c) and 55 of the Trade Practices Act 1974.

Misleading and deceptive conduct via advertisement resulted in interlocutory injunctions.

It was held that the interlocutory injunctions were granted for the following reasons: (1) The applicant had established a *prima facie* case of false, misleading or deceptive conduct in that the court was satisfied that the respondent had made false claims in its advertising falling within one or more of the following categories — that Aim with citraden reduced decay in teeth or that Aim was better than other toothpastes in reducing decay.

Case – 3
Effem Foods Ltd v. Pamela Nicholls

Effem Foods Ltd v. Pamela Nicholls. Shortly before the evening meal on the day in question the opponent decided to eat one of these bars, and having selected this one from a kitchen cupboard she tore the wrapping across the top

Goods not of merchantable quality, supplying of defective goods by manufacture held liable for injuries caused to consumer.

and down one side. She then pushed the bar partly out of what remained of the wrapping and bit off a substantial portion. As she began to chew the bar she felt a hard object at the back of her tongue which caused momentary pain that led her to spit what was in her mouth onto a nearby coffee table. She went to the bathroom, washed out her mouth, and became aware of the taste of blood. She rejoined her husband and discovered that the material she had spat out included an open safety pin with a badly bent pin.

Since the opponent's tongue had been penetrated she was given a tetanus injection which unfortunately produced an allergic reaction. Subsequently she was tested for the presence of the HIV and Hepatitis B and C viruses. She developed an obsessive condition which manifested itself in poor appetite and disturbed sleep.

The opponent brought an action in the District Court against the manufacturer for breach of ss 74D and 75AD of the Trade Practices Act 1974. The trial Judge (Phegan DCJ) held that the plaintiff had proved a *prima facie* breach of S. 74D(1) because the bar was not of merchantable quality, and a *prima facie* breach of S. 75AD because the defendant, in trade and commerce, had supplied defective goods manufactured by it which had injured the plaintiff. The manufacturer appealed against the trial judge's finding.

Mr. Hoeben J., while acknowledging that the liability of a manufacturer under these provisions was strict, submitted, correctly, that it was not absolute. He asked, rhetorically, what more could a manufacturer be expected to do to discharge the onus under these provisions than was done in this case. His point is valid, so far as it goes, but the manufacturer has to establish these defences on the balance of probabilities and speculation and proof of mere possibilities are not enough. This does not mean that a manufacturer's liability is absolute. There is scope for these defences where an examination of the product after the accident establishes that it has been deliberately tampered with. Examples that come to mind include the sabotage of car tyres or brake fluid lines or the presence of poison in a glass of soft drink. A manufacturer is not required to lead direct evidence to support these defences and a case based on circumstantial evidence is capable of discharging the onus

It was held that (1) Under the statutory defenses the manufacturer had to establish on the civil onus that the defect occurred after the bar had left its control and did not exist when it was supplied by the manufacturer; (2) It had only proved that deliberate sabotage in the retailer's shop was a possibility; (3) Since any such act would be a criminal offence the presumption of innocence applied. Hence Appeal was dismissed.

Case – 4

Grace Bros Pty Limited v Magistrates of the Local Courts of New South Wales and Another

Grace Bros Pty Limited v Magistrates of the Local Courts of New South Wales and Another

In a summons returnable before the Local Court it was stated that the appellant, Grace Bros, had, in contravention of Sec. 32 of the Consumer Protection Act 1969 (NSW), caused to be published a statement which was intended to promote the supply of certain specified goods which, to its knowledge, was false in a material particular.

Section 32(1) of the Consumer Protection Act provided for a penalty for publishing or causing to be published any false advertisement to promote the supply of goods if it was published with knowledge of its false and misleading nature.

Section 53 of the Trade Practices Act 1974 (Cth) prohibited the making in trade or commerce, in connection with the promotion of the supply or use of goods or services, of false representations of the kind specified in pars (a) to (g) thereof. Certain defences were provided by S. 85 of the Act. False representations other than those specified were not dealt with by the Commonwealth Act.

The alleged inconsistency was that the Commonwealth Act allowed the making in trade of a wilfully false statement if it was not of the specified kind, whereas the State Act prohibited the publication in trade of every false statement unless it was innocently made. The application of Grace Bros was dismissed at first instance and they went in appeal.

It was held that (1) The court had jurisdiction to hear the application pursuant to s 163A of the Trade Practices Act. The subject matter of the appellant's application was that by the combined operation of S. 109 of the Constitution and certain provisions of the Trade Practices Act the relevant provisions of the Consumer Protection Act were invalidated. This was thus a matter arising under 1969 the Commonwealth Act because the operation of that statute was a necessary ingredient in the constitutional process of the invalidation of the State law.

(2) The appellant failed to establish any constitutional inconsistency. Just because the federal legislation was aimed at certain defined conduct only, did not mean that the Commonwealth Act was intended to create legal immunity in respect of other conduct which was not made an offence. Appeal dismissed.

Case – 5

Australian Communications Authority v Viper Communications Pvt. Ltd.

Australian Communications Authority v Viper Communications Pvt. Ltd. Section 128 of the Telecommunications (Consumer Protection and Service Standards) Act 1999(Cth) (the Service Standards Act) and its predecessor, s 246 of the Telecommunications Act 1997(Cth), required "eligible carriage service providers" to enter into the Telecommunications Industry Ombudsman scheme (the TIO scheme), which was established by Pt 10 of the Telecommunications Act and continued by Pt 6 of the Service Standards Act. The TIO scheme was operated by Telecommunications Industry Ombudsman Limited (TIO Ltd) and the Telecommunications Industry Ombudsman (the TIO). The scheme provided for the investigation and determination of complaints by consumers about carriage services. TIO Ltd. was a corporation registered in the ACT, the members of which were the eligible carriage service providers. Clause 6.1 of the Constitution of TIO Ltd. provided that the TIO could, after investigating a complaint, resolve the complaint in various ways, including "by making a determination that the member the subject of investigation pay compensation to a complainant" not exceeding $10,000. Clause 6.1 also provided that determinations made under it "shall be automatically binding upon members." The costs of the TIO scheme were borne *381 by the members of the scheme pursuant to Art 4 of the Memorandum and Articles of TIO Ltd.

The applicant sought to recover pecuniary penalties from the respondents, who were internet service providers who had failed to enter the TIO scheme.

The respondents alleged they had no obligation to join the scheme, but that question was resolved against them in proceedings in **Australian Communications Authority v Viper Communications Pty Ltd.** The respondents also challenged the constitutional validity of Section 128 of the Service Standards Act. This was heard as a separate question. The grounds of challenge were that Section 128 invalidly conferred the judicial power of the Commonwealth on the TIO, a non-judicial body, and that Section 128 imposed taxation on eligible carriage service providers otherwise than in conformity with Section 55 of the Constitution of the Commonwealth (the Constitution).

It was held that (1) The decision-making functions conferred on the TIO by or under the authority of s 128 of the Service Standards Act do not constitute exclusive and inalienable exercises of judicial power contrary to Ch III of the Constitution.

Determinations made by the TIO are not automatically enforceable. Although expressed to be binding on a service provider, they can only be enforced by proceedings taken in a court. Thus an independent exercise of judicial power is required to give effect to a determination. Nor does s 128 require the TIO to resolve complaints by making determinations on the basis of the application of principles of law to the facts as found. The TIO is free to create norms to resolve a particular dispute or class of dispute. Petition allowed.

In Australia, similar to UK and USA the consumer protection laws are comprehensive, contemporary and relevant. The infringement of consumer rights in any form is dealt with stringently by the consumer protection laws. Also the law courts in that country is very serious on the defects of goods and deficiency of service of any form.

Questions

Section — A Objective Type

1. State the objectives of consumer protection Act, 1986.
2. Define "consumer" as per CPA, 1986.
3. Define "consumer dispute" as per CPA, 1986.
4. What is the difference between "defect" and "deficiency"?
5. Who shall give complaint against unfair trade practices in consumer court?

Section — B Analytical Type

1. State the rights of consumer as per CPA, 1986.
2. Write a note on control consumer protection council as per CPA, 1986.

Section — C Essay Type

1. Explain the District Forum State Commission and National Commission as consumer disputes redressal agencies.
2. Narrate any two case studies of consumer disputes.
3. Bring out any five decided cases under Consumer Protection Act, 1986.

INDIAN PATENT LAWS AND WTO PATENT RULES

Module Objectives

After reading this chapter, you should be able to:

- Know the meaning of Intellectual Property (IP), IP law, and moral rights
- Understand Intellectual Capital (IC), segments of IP, the difference between Intellectual capital, intellectual Assets and I P
- Discuss the Provisions of Patent Act, 1970
- Interpret the various aspects included in International Intellectual Property Organizations, their treaties and agreements especially WIPO — World Intellectual Property Organization

8.1 What is intellectual property?

Is it 'intellectual' ? Is it 'property'?

The ordinary common-sense description of intellectual property is that it simply comprises all those things that are 'intellectual' because they emanate from the use of the human brain.

To this question there are two answers, one is based on an ordinary colloquial understanding of the literal meanings of the words 'intellectual' and 'property'; the other is legal. The ordinary common-sense description of intellectual property is that it simply comprises all those things that are 'intellectual' because they emanate from the use of the human brain, for example Lara Croft, websites, mobile phones, lists of names and addresses, the way to make genuine Coca-Cola or a suitable seductive name for a new brand of perfume.

Some may take pedantic exception to the stipulation that it is specifically from the brain that intellectual property must be taken to originate; what, for example, of the computer which exercises its own 'intellect' in printing out the results of its own calculations, or of the hypothetical monkey shackled eternally to a presumably indestructible PC, hammering the keyboard at random until it writes the next Harry Potter book? Are these also intellectual property? If the answer to this question is answered in the affirmative, it is not because of any inherent vice in the definition offered above, but rather because of a subtle appreciation that there is a low level of human intellectual activity which we are inclined to regard as enjoying the status of 'property.' After all, not only activities of monkeys or computers but also the programming of the intelligent computer, the cunning juxtaposition of monkey and typewriter can be regarded as part of the process of intellectual endeavour. But there is a level below which intellectual activity is not capable of being treated as 'property.' Thus the decision to play Dwight Yorke up front alongside Andy Cole in the Manchester United football team may be the result of an intellectual process but most people would not consider the result of that process as being 'property.'

The legal description of intellectual property differs from the colloquial in that it focuses upon the rights which are enjoyed in the produce of the mind, rather than upon that produce itself.

The legal description of intellectual property differs from the colloquial in that it focuses upon the rights which are enjoyed in the produce of the mind, rather than upon that produce itself. In legal terms we call a piece of land, a painting or a motor car 'property' not because it is a solid, physical thing in itself but because individuals or legal entities such as companies can assert a right in it against some or all other persons. The word 'property' itself comes from the Latin word proprius, which means 'one's own.' If we bear this in mind, we can take the expression 'intellectual property' to mean the legal rights which may be asserted in respect of the product of the human intellect, for example, Channel's Right to stop people filling bottles with home made concoctions and selling them on the street corner as CHANNEL NO 5. It is also convenient to treat as intellectual property the rights and powers which one may enjoy over another's work, such as the manufacturer's right to be allowed to use someone else's invention where a patent for that invention has been granted to that another person but has not been industrially exploited.

Legal rights which may be asserted in respect of the product of the human intellect.

The intelligent observer of human behaviour will have spotted that the fruits of exercise of human intellect would exist even if they enjoyed no legal protection-in the same way as a plot of land or of chocolate would exist even if no one could claim the legal right to own or possess it; but it is the existence of such a right to do so which entitles us to refer to such physical things as 'property.' The ordinary words which form the component parts of our day-to-day conversation are not generally regarded as intellectual property, even if a great deal of thought went into their being coined: words such as 'chair', 'banana' and 'Tarzan' do not exist in nature—they have all been created by the use of the human intellect—but we do not regard them as 'property' because the law does not provide a right to prevent their expropriation. The opposite is true of words such as "Pepsi', 'champagne' or 'Darth Vader', all of which are carefully guarded items of property notwithstanding the frequency with which they find their way out of people's mouths. Confusingly, some words are sometimes property and sometimes not, for example 'aspirin', 'marigold' and 'Pocahontas.'

What is Intellectual Property Law?

The intelligent and logical reader may regard this question as superfluous once the phrase 'intellectual property' has been defined in legal terms. Can he not safely conclude that intellectual property law is the aggregate of rights and duties which pertain to the control of intellectual property? This assumption would be incorrect, because the demands of practical reality have supplanted the strict rules of logic. On reading this book, our logical reader will reference to rules and remedies that appear to have no relevance whatsoever to ownership or control of the product of the human intellect. For example, intellectual property law as widely understood by its devotees includes such topics as whether the London and Provincial Law Assurance Society could stop the London and Provincial Joint Stock Life Assurance Company from trading under that name, whether a manufacturer of wine in the Champagne region of France could stop a British manufacturer of a non-vinous substance from advertising it as 'Babycham', the genuine 'Champagne Perry' or whether a mild roundsman employed by a dairy could be prevented from soliciting his employer's customers prior to his leaving the dairy's employment.

There are two explanations as to why such apparently irrelevant or extraneous legal material is traditionally included within the corpus of intellectual property law. The first is that the traditional manner of protecting the owner of intellectual property against encroachment by others is the grant by the state of an exclusionary, and in some cases exclusive, right to the exploitation, for a limited duration, of the creative output of the intellect. The owner of such rights naturally seeks to derive the greatest benefit from them. One effective means of doing this is by finding other legal means of extending the limited duration of his rights.

> The traditional manner of protecting the owner of intellectual property against encroachment by others is the grant by the state of an exclusionary, and in some cases exclusive, right to the exploitation, for a limited duration, of the creative output of the intellect.

Thus as inventor normally has a maximum legal monopoly of just twenty years of the right to stop others making a product protected as a patented invention; but if he can find an attractive name for that product people may continue to buy it from him, even though others can compete with him in the manufacture and sale of it after his patent has expired. Accordingly the law of marks and names as applied to goods and services and to the companies that market them is of great importance to the person who wishes to exploit his intellectual produce; the overall legal control of monopolies (whether generated by statute or not) will be important when it is considered whether the intellectual owner can sustain his market dominance even once his patent or copyright has expired.

> Inventor normally has a maximum legal monopoly of just twenty years of the right to stop others making a product protected as a patented invention.

Second, whether a person enjoys a monopoly over his intellectual property or not, he knows that his exploitation of it will be free from the terrors of unwanted competition if he can persuade his likeliest competitors not to compete against him, or if he can persuade his employees, most intimately acquainted with his trade secrets and practices, not to leave him and work instead for a competitor. Both of these aims are capable of being achieved by means of the law of contract.

Thus the making of contracts, with regard to the result of intellectual endeavour, and the validity of those contracts once made, inevitably becomes subjects of interest to the intellectual property lawyer.

Is Intellectual Property Law an Important Subject?

Universities and colleges vie with each other for the privilege of offering the most attractive IP programmes, which exist in ample supply for both graduates and undergraduates. Advertisements in lawyer's magazines and on the Internet proclaim the many rewards bestowed even relatively junior specialists in the art.

Devotees of intellectual property law can take comfort in the fact that their subject is no longer perceived as a niche, an arcane professional craft of no genuine significance. While the topic was scarcely known as late as the beginning of the 1980s, it has finally assumed its position as the jewel in the crown of legal practice. Universities and colleges vie with each other for the privilege of offering the most attractive IP programmes, which exist in ample supply for both graduates and undergraduates. Advertisements in lawyer's magazines and on the Internet proclaim the many rewards bestowed even relatively junior specialists in the art. No fewer than three professions—lawyer, patent agent and trade mark attorney—exist to serve the burgeoning and lucrative demands of clients. Intellectual property is a benign patent; it feeds the hungry, occupies the idle and neglects the needs of none of its children.

This is the age of satellite and cable transmission, of broadcast, of interactive media, of computers and the internet, of data creation and transfer, of entertainment and education, fact and fancy; all of this is intellectual property.

The reason for this is not hard to find. Intellectual property is the currency of our time. The production of commodities was replaced by the supply of services as the dynamo that propels the engine of the economy, now the supply of services has itself been superseded by the provision of information. This is the age of satellite and cable transmission, of broadcast, of interactive media, of computers and the internet, of data creation and transfer, of entertainment and education, fact and fancy; all of this is intellectual property. While a minority of the UK's population consists of home-owners, virtually everyone owns some intellectual property. Traders pick their way warily through the myriad trade mark monopolies that govern the import and sale of goods and the supply of services in this land. Literally hundreds of millions of copyright works are created daily; many are infringed. Our feet may be planted on the ground but our heads are in cyberspace.

An important function of intellectual property law that it encourages (if such is possible) the creation of ideas and inventions, their disclosure for the benefit of all, not to mention their commercial exploitation so as to facilitate the greatest potential exploitation of their practical or concrete embodiments.

Even if one chooses to dismiss as insignificant a claim for greater teaching of intellectual property law which is based on practical professional expediency, one should not treat so lightly the claim that intellectual property law plays a vital part in the physical well-being of the individual and in the commercial vitality of the economy. For it is an important function of intellectual property law that it encourages (if such is possible) the creation of ideas and inventions, their disclosure for the benefit of all, not to mention their commercial exploitation so as to facilitate the greatest potential exploitation of their practical or concrete embodiments. The positive, as well as potential negative, effects of intellectual property on global well-being appear to be recognized in Art 16.5 of the Convention on Biological Diversity, which states:

> 'The Contracting Parties, recognizing that patents and other intellectual property rights may have an influence on the implementation of this Convention, shall cooperate in this regard subject to national legislation and international law in order ensure that such rights are supportive of and do not run counter to its objectives.'

Where land is purchased, the purchaser can often derive immense financial advantage without actually doing anything to, with or under the land he buys. In contrast, a person who acquires an intellectual property right can derive no financial benefits from it except by using it commercially. If he secures, for example, a patent for a new product, he will gain advantage only by making that product and selling it, or by charging others who wish to exploit his patent. This use is capable of benefiting more than merely the patent's owner. For example, a patent's user may derive profit through his use of it, the consumer will benefit through the ability to acquire a product manufactured under it, members of the country's available workforce will gain employment, the government will take its taxes and all will (in theory) be happy.

If a person who creates intellectual property subsequently derives some benefit from its use, he will (in theory) be encouraged to endeavour to repeat the process by which the pleasure of that benefit was previously obtained. An economy which is incapable of creating its own intellectual property must import it. It is thus imperative for economic well-being of any country that it guard against a massive outflow of funds by providing a commercial environment in which the creation of intellectual property is rewarded; and it is this which has been perhaps the most important function of intellectual property law.

A person who acquires an intellectual property right can derive no financial benefits from it except by using it commercially.

Intellectual Property and Moral Rights

Apart from its practical and economic aspects, intellectual property law fulfils functions which have a purely moral content; for it is ideally capable of providing

(i) that no one other than the inventor, author or other intellectual creator is falsely described as being such;

(ii) that the creator of a work may make legal objection to the distortion of his work by others; and

(iii) that the author who has changed his mind about the validity of his intellectual product can retract it prior to the embarrassment he incurs by reason of its publication by any other person.

The rights described above are sometimes referred to as moral rights, since they protect the creator's moral rather than his pecuniary interest in his work. In those countries which share with the UK a common law heritage these rights are often vestigial or non-existent, but the intellectual property laws of many other countries (notably those influenced by civil law principles) accord them a good deal of jurisprudential content. In principle, moral rights are the author's non-transferability is wise if one considers that their function is to protect the creator's integrity as a human being, which is not an appropriate subject of sale. It is only necessary to reflect upon the plot of The Phantom of the Opera appreciate the benefits which can accrue from such rights, and the distress resulting from their absence.

Intellectual Property Means and Ends

The Universal Declaration of Human Rights would appear to depend upon intellectual property law for the realization of at least some of its objects. For example, no one is to be subject to arbitrary interference with his or her privacy, and everyone has a right to own property and to make a living. Professor C. G. Weeramantry, however, in The Slumbering Sentinels, lists' intellectual property in scientific knowledge' as a source of possible denigration of the right to share in scientific advancement and its benefit. Whether on takes this assertion seriously or not (and intellectual property rights are characteristically circumscribed by rules relating to the protection of the public interest), it does indicate that intellectual property rights — in common with all other legal rights — are capable

Intellectual property law is not a sacred cow; it is merely a body of laws which is intended to act as a means of achieving a particular set of ends.

of abuse or, more accurately, of use in a manner which may be regarded as prejudicial either to competing private interests or to the public interest. This is no mere hypothetical matter. In **Service Corpn International Ptc v Channel Four Television Corpn Lightman J** based a decision not to grant an injunction to suppress alleged an infringement of copyright on a direct application of the European Convention on Human Rights' commitment to freedom of speech.

It is proper to emphasize the importance of intellectual property law as an academic discipline and as a driving force in the economic life of the new millennium. However, it must be recognized that, despite its importance, intellectual property law is not a sacred cow; it is merely a body of laws which is intended to act as a means of achieving a particular set of ends. Where such laws do not achieve their stipulated ends, or the price which is paid for their doing so exceeds the value of achieving those ends, then intellectual property law is as much an object of scrutiny, criticism, amendment or repeal as is any other set of normative or distributive rules.

In the UK at any rate, each brand of intellectual property law evolved as a result of essentially practical consideration; those same considerations could lead to its death. In many foreign jurisdictions, in contrast, intellectual property rights are not dependent upon consideration of practical utility but are superior (and possibly anterior) to them. At the time of writing, the shifting sands of necessity and the adoption of policies of international harmony have brought British intellectual property laws close to those of other countries; whether this state of affairs is purely temporary, or not, is a matter for speculation beyond the covers of this book, which has been written with the British reader particularly in mind. Where subsequent chapters review and examine the law, they will therefore give more scope to the investigation of their relation to the ends achieved than to the irresoluble question of their metaphysical link between man, his creation and his relations with others.

8.2 INTELLECTUAL CAPITAL

— Comprises the sum total of all knowledge in an enterprise

— It is what every one in a firm knows, and what therefore gives the firm its competitive advantage

IC – includes

— the knowledge and skills of employees;

— the processes, ideas, designs, inventions, and technologies utilised by the Firm

— the relationships it has developed with both customers and suppliers

— Software, business methods, manuals, reports, publications, and databases

— patents, trademarks, copyrights, Internet domain names, and the like

Intellectual capital is the sum total of all knowledge in an enterprise, as it resides in the minds of its employees, which can be leveraged to create wealth.

Intellectual capital is what is left of an enterprise after it has been stripped of all its tangible assets, such as land, buildings, machinery, inventory and cash

IC — enterprise value — value of all hard assets

IC — cannot exist outside the context of a particular Enterprise or independent of its strategy

IC — clearly defined strategy can separate useful knowledge from informational noise and disparate facts

> Like a magnet attracts iron filings, strategy and purpose create the discernable Informational patterns that we call knowledge
>
> Purpose → strategy → information → knowledge

IC — is the cornerstone of the modern business enterprise

— much of it (IC) is tacit knowledge that reside in the minds of its employees

— when an employee leaves the organization so does the IC that resides in the employee — his knowledge, experience, skills creativity and relations with others

IC — is what walks out the door at the end of the day

— obviously, there is a risk that it won't walk back in tomorrow

Moreover,

— even while an employee is working for an organization, his or her knowledge cannot be most effectively utilized unless it is identified, documented, and shared with others.

The Principal Objectives of Intellectual Capital Management (ICM)

— To identify, capture and document IC

— To make it accessible to others in the organization

> Intellectual Capital that has been so captured, preserved, catalogued, and made available for sharing is known as Intellectual Assets

In the best of the enterprise, it should encourage its employees to disclose and record this Intellectual capital

Intellectual capital Management process Flow:

Search out→Identify→Capture→Document→Index→Store→Augment→Replicate

Intellectual Property (IP)

Intellectual Assets legally protected under applicable laws are called Intellectual Property. A typical example of Intellectual property is a patent that is protected by the patent law.

Figure 8.1 OVERLAPPING INTELLECTUAL PROPERTY

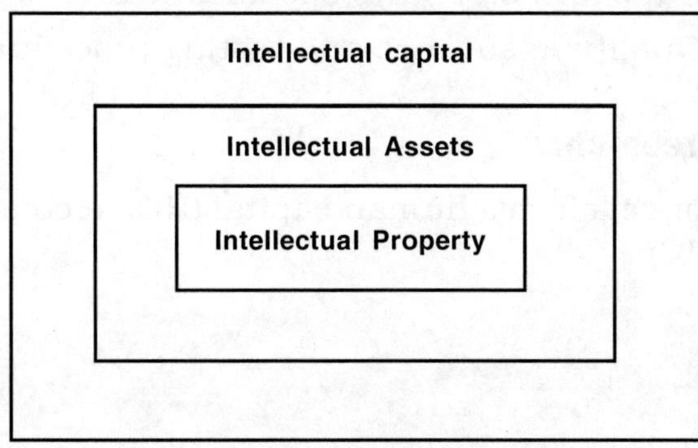

— IPs form a more valuable subset of IC
— IP forms an even more valuable subset of IAs

The goal of Management is to produce Intellectual Property (see Figure 4.1)

Segments of Intellectual Property (IP)

I. According to well-defined "classical" or statutory assets
   — patents, trademarks, and copyrights (the trinity)
   — mask works and registered designs

Mask Works

— stencils used for semiconductor chip manufacturing
— semiconductor chips, the heart and soul of the electronic age, are produced by a chemical etching process that utilizes a stencil known as mask work

(these chips, which may be very costly to develop, are surprisingly inexpensive to fabricate. This situation positively cries out for copying — known as piracy to chip developers and free enterprise to chip copiers)

Current pace of technological advancement is such that chips are often obsolute

II. According to the less definite contractual or "common low assets" (IP)
   — Trade secrets
   — know-how
   — non-competition Agreements
   — Confidential Disclosure Agreements (Industrial espionage)

Trade Secrets

A trade secret is information that is not generally available and that confers a competitive advantage on its possessor.

For example, a chemical formula
a manufacturing process
a machine design or
a business method

Know-how

Comprises a body of information, the components of which may be individually known, but the compilation of which has competitive value

For example, Supplier lists, parts specifications
Quality Assurance and testing procedure

Non-competition Agreements

Employees comprise a firm's human capital (HC), a constituent ingredient of Intellectual Capital (IC)

— Deporting employees deplete a firm's stock of intellectual capital worse, they may convey a firm's IC to a competitor

A non-competition Agreement is a contractive undertaking b/w an employee and his or her employer. The agreement limits the right of the employee, upon departure, to accept employment with a competitor of his or her former employer.

Confidential Disclosure Agreements

An agreement that the recipient of specified information will use that information only for a specified purpose and will maintain it in confidence.

These agreements are designed to protect the Intellectual capital of the employer.

8.3 INTELLECTUAL PROPERTY

Patents

A patent conveys to its owner (Inventor) the right to prevent others from making, using, selling, offering for sale, or importing the patented invention, patents are national in nature, having effect only within the territory of the issuing country.

Patent is the legal right, for a limited term, to exclude others from using, selling, or making an invention or discovery as described in the patent claims

Conditions

In order to qualify for a patent, an invention must be

Useful → that is, it has some purpose

Novel → that is, it differs in some way from the publicly known or existing knowledge in the field

Non-obvious → that is, person working in the field would not consider the invention obvious

KINDS OF PATENTS

1. Utility Patent

Legal protection granted for inventions or discoveries that are categorized as machines, processes, compositions, articles of manufacture, or new uses of any of these.

2. Design Patent

Protects new, original, and ornamental designs for useful objects. The design patent protects only the appearance of an article, not its structure or utilitarian features.

Design patents have been granted for stained-glass windows, Adidas shoes, and the shape of an electric guitar.

3. Plant Patent

Protects distinctive plants reproduced asexually (i.e., by means other than seeds) plant patents have been granted for new variations of tulips, roses, and tomatoes.

Copyright

The legal right to exclude others for a limited time, from copying, selling, performing, displaying, or making derivative version of a work of authorship.

The legal right to exclude others for a limited time, from copying, selling, performing, displaying, or making derivative version of a work of authorship.

Copyright protects only the expression of an idea, not the idea being expressed.

Copyrights are generally associated in the common mind with —

— Literature
— Movie scripts
— Music
— Song lyrics
— Product manuals
— Instruction booklets
— Training materials
— Marketing & sales publication
— Computer software

Lasts for the life of the author + 70 years

Trademark

A trademark is any word, symbol, design, logo, or slogan that identifies and distinguishes one product or service from another.

A trademark is any word, symbol, design, logo, or slogan that identifies and distinguishes one product or service from another.

e.g.: Kodak trademark distinguishes Kodak film from other brands.

The trademark also informs consumers that a product has certain quality or reliability, this consumer connection, known as goodwill, strengthens the trademark's value.

The owner of a trademark can exclude others from using a similar trademark on similar or related goods or services if it is likely that consumers will be confused by the use.

The following tables 4.1, 4.2 and 4.3 give detailed information about different components of IP, what is protected, length of protection with examples.

Table 8.1 IP Protection and Length of Protection

	What is Protected?	*Examples*	*Length of Protection*
Patent	Machines, compositions, plants, processes, articles of manufacture, ornamental designs	Digital camera; chemical fertilizer; Luther Burbank's hybrid peach: process of manipulating genetic traits in mice (and the resulting mice); ironing board; design of Bo Diddley's box-shaped guitar	17 years* from the date the patent is issued, for utility and plant patents filed before June 8, 1995; 20 years from the date of filing, for utility and plant patents filed after June 7, 1995; 14 years for design patents
Copyright	Books, photographs, music, recordings, fine art, graphics, videos, film, choreography, architecture, computer programs	*Interview with the Vampire* (book and movie); Andy Warhol print; Alanis Morrisette's *Jagged Little Pill* (music recording, compact disc, artwork, and videos); architectural plans for the Trump Tower; *Microsoft Windows* computer program	Life of the author plus 70 years (for works created by a single author). Other works may be protected for 120 years from date of creation of 95 years from first publication**
Trademark	Word, symbol, logo design, slogan, or device that identifies and distinguishes products or services	*Coca-Cola* name and distinctive "wave" logo; *Good Housekeeping* seal; Pillsbury doughboy character	For as long as the business continuously uses the trademark in connection with goods or services
Trade Secret	Formula, method, device, or compilation of facts or any information that is maintained in confidence and gives a business an advantage over competitors	*Coca-Cola* formula; survey methods used by professional pollster; buying habits of ethnic groups; new invention for which patent application has not been filed	For as long as information remains confidential and functions as a trade secret

Table 8.2 Comparative Table of Intellectual Properties

	Utility Patent	*Design Patent*	*Trademark/ Service mark*	*Copyright*	*Trade Secret*	*Mask Work*	*Registered Design*
Protects	Products devices, processes, business methods	Industrial design	Words, phrases, or symbols that identify the source of goods or service	Expressions of creative works, such as pictures, novels, music performance advertising copy, etc.	Condifential information that is maintained secret	Mask work stencils used for semi-conductor chip manu-facturing	Industrial designs
Term (in years)	20	14	Perpetual, so long as used	70 minimum	Perpetual, as long as secret is maintained	10	10
Registration required	Yes	Yes	No	No	No	Yes	Yes
Examined	Yes	Yes	Yes	No	N/A	No	No
Cost to Obtain and Maintain	High	Medium	Low	Low	Low	Low	Low

Table 8.3 Intellectual Property Protection Table

	Utility Patent	*Design Patent*	*Trademark/ Service mark*	*Copyright*	*Trade Secret*	*Mask Work*	*Registered Design*
Article of Manufacture	Yes	Yes			Possibly		Yes
Manufacturing Process	Yes				Possibly		
Computer Software	Yes			Yes	Possibly		
Business Method	Yes				Possibly		
Brand Name			Yes				
Product Manual				Yes			
Training Manual				Yes	Yes		
Semi-conductor Chip						Yes	
Corporate Logo			Yes				
Chemical Compound	Yes				Possibly		
Fabric Print Pattern		Yes					Yes
Photograph				Yes			
Novel				Yes			
Movie Script				Yes			
Musical Performance				Yes			
Series of Movements in Sports	Yes						
Web page		Yes		Yes			Yes
Internet Domian			Possibly				

8.4 PATENT ACT, 1970

Introduction: Patent is an official document giving an exclusive right to the inventor of a new thing or new manufacturing process for a fixed no. of years to use or sell his invention. After the fixed period is over, it become" "Public Juris" (public right), i.e., any person can manufacture the article. On which patent is granted by the Govt.

The law relating to patents in India is governed by Patents Act 1970. It is based on the English Patents Act 1949. This Act is applied to the whole of India.

Objects of the Act (Also consider it as Advantages)

The main object of the act is to strengthen and amend the law relating to patents.

The Other Advantages of Patents

It gives the exclusive right to the patentee to use his invention.

It helps the patentee to sue the persons who wrongly use (infringe) his patent.

It helps the patentee to sell his patent or give licence to others to use it and thereby earn money. (when he could not use (work) the patent himself).

It helps the patentee to get "Patent of Addition" when he makes improvement or modification in the main invention.

Invention. (Sect. 2 [j])

Patent is granted to an invention. Invention means any new and a set of useful:

(a) art, process method of manufacture.

(b) a machine, instruments or other articles.

(c) substance produced by manufacture.

It also includes new improvements in any of the above items. Hence the 3 basic requirements of an invention are:

(1) Method of Manufactures. (2) Novelty and (3) Utility.

When patent rights are not given (Sect. 3)

For certain works patent right may not be given in the public interest. Hence **certain items are not inventions**:

They are

(1) invention which is against matural law. (Tripling invention)

(2) invention which are for unlawful use or harmful to public health.

(3) discovery of a scientific principle.

(4) a simple discovery of any new property or new use for a old substance.

(5) a substance obtained by a mere Admixture (mixing something).

(6) mere arrangement or re-arrangement or duplication of known devices.

(7) a method for increasing efficiency.

(8) a method of Agriculture or horticulture.

(9) any medical, surgical or other treatments of human beings or any other methods used for similar treatment of animal or plants.

Note: For any invention relating to atomic energy patent right shall not be given.

Grant of Patent

Certain procedures for the Grant of Patent are laiddown in the act. These procedures are briefly explained here.

(1) Who should apply: (Sect. 6): The first inventor of the (invention or) work who claims to be the true and first owner or his legal representative.

(2) Condition: For each invention separate application for a patent shall be made.

(3) Application form (Sect. 7): The true and first owner shall apply in Form I and legal Rep. of true owner shall apply in Form II.

(4) Filing of Specification (Sect. 9): A complete specification shall be filled with a fee of Rs. 50/- within 12 months from the date of filing of application. It may be extended by another 3 months.

Note: In provisional and complete specification.

Provisional specification gives the same particulars about the nature of invention without drawings and statement of claim. But complete specification gives all the details about the invention with drawings. Until the complete specification is filed, a provisional specification may be filed with fees.

Examination of application (Sect. 12): The application along with specification, will be referred (sent) to the examiner by the controller of patent to find out whether the application is submitted according to the requirements of the act.

Report of the Examiner: The examiner will make a report of the examination and return the application to the controller along with the report.

Refusal of the application (Sect. 15): When the application submitted does not comply with the requirement of the act, the controller may either refuse the application or ask the applicant to amend the details in the application.

Acceptance of application (Sect. 22): When the submitted application along with complete specification filed has satisfied the requirement of the act (in satisfying the conditions imposed by under Sect. 21 of the act by the controller) the controller may accept the application and complete specification.

Advertising the acceptance of complete specification (Sect. 23):

The fact that the complete specification has been accepted must be advertised in the official Gazette. Then the application and complete specification with drawings shall be kept open to the public inspection.

Opposition to Grant of Patent (Sect. 25): Within 4 months from the date of advertisement (of acceptance of a complete specification) only person may give notice of opposition to the grant of patent to the controller. This period of 4 months may be extended by the controller by another 1 month.

The Grant of the Patent may be opposed by anyone on the following grounds

(a) When the applicant for the patent **wrongly obtained** the patent.

(b) **When the alleged invention claimed by the applicant has** been **previously published** in India before any specification filed.

(c) When the so-called invention claimed by the applicant **was publicly used** in India.

(d) When the so-called invention claimed by the applicant **does not involve any inventive step**.

(e) When the subject given in the complete specification is **not really an invention** as per the act.

(f) When the complete specification does not **clearly describe** the invention or the method of its performance.

Opportunity of hearing: After the notice of opposition is duly given, both the parties shall be given opportunity to be heard before deciding the case.

Grant and Sealing of Patent

After the application for a patent along with a complete specification has been accepted or after the opposition has been decided finally in favour of the applicant, the controller shall grant the patent to applicant and the patent will be sealed with the seal of the patent office and the date on which it is sealed, shall be entered in the register. It is only after the patent is sealed the patentee can sue infringers for infringement.

Note on patent of Addition: When patentee makes any **improvement** or **modification to the main patent** (or to his earlier invention), he will be issued a special type of patent called "Patent of Addition."

Restoration of Lapsed Patent

Application for Restoration: When the patent fails to pay any renewal fee within the prescribed time (or extend period the patent may not have the effect (ceased to have the effect).

Then the patentee or his legal rep. may apply for the restoration of the patent, within one year from the date on which the patent ceased to have effect.

The patentee must give the reasons for not having paid the prescribed fee in the prescribed manner.

If the controller *prima facie* is satisfied that (1) the failure to pay the renewal fee unintentional and (2) no undue delay was caused in applying for restoration then he shall **advertise the application** in the prescribed manner.

Any person (interested) may give notice opposition (to the application) to the controller disproving the above said 2 reasons within the prescribed time. The controller shall send the notice of opposition to the applicant. Then he gives opportunity to both parties to be heard before deciding the case.

If no notice of opposition is received by the controller, then he may decide it in favor of the applicant (i.e., he shall restore that patent which has lost the effect) after the payment of any unpaid renewal fees.

Note: The patentee **can't sue** any infringer for infringement of patent between the **date on which the patent ceased to have effect** and **the date of advertisement** of the application for restoration of lapsed patent.

Surrender of Patent

Under the act the patentee can surrender the patent. The steps involved for surrender of the patent are briefly given below:

(1) Notice of offer to the controller: The patentee may give a notice in the prescribed manner to the controller offering to surrender the patent.

(2) Advertisement of the offer: The controller shall advertise such offer in the prescribed manner and notify to those persons whose name appear in the register as persons interested in the patent.

(3) Opposition to surrender: Any person interested shall give notice of opposition to the controller. The controller shall notify the patentee of such notice.

(4) Revocation of offer: After hearing both the parties, if the controller is satisfied that, the patent, may be surrendered he may accept the offer and revoke the patent by order.

INFRINGEMENT OF PATENT

If the invention is used by any other person, without a license from patentee, it leads to infringement of patent.

Meaning: A patent granted to a person (patentee) gives him a bundle of exclusive rights to use the invention for a fixed period under the act. If the invention is used by any other person, without a licence from patentee, it leads to infringement of patent. This infringement means **violation or misuse of the exclusive right of the patentee.**

Remedies for infringement: The remedies are available to patentee in case of infringement. They are:

(1) Suit for an injunction (to stop future and infringement) and

(2) Suit for damages or an account for profit.

The patentee shall go to District court having jurisdiction to try the suit. But when the defendants make counter-claim for the revocation of the patent, then it shall be transferred to the High Court.

Right of Licencee: When a patentee gives licence to another person to use his invention, then that another person is called licensee. In case of infringement, the licencee shall ask the patentee to take proceeding to prevent any infringement of the patent. If the patentee refuses or fails to do so within 2 months, then the licencee may file a suit for Infringement in his own name as if he is the patentee.

Note: Scientific Adviser: He is an independent scientific adviser appointed by the court to assist the court in any suit for infringement. He will conduct enquiry into any such questions of fact or of opinion and submit a report to the court. His remuneration is fixed by the court itself.

Intellectual Property rights: Intellectual property includes patent, copyright, design Property and trade mark. They require intellectual effort. A person spends considerable amount of time, energy and effort to produce something new. The law gives an exclusive right to the owner to use his invention (or work) in the way he likes for a certain period. This exclusive right protects the interest of the inventor and prevents the other person from misusing the invention for a profit.

PATENTS (AMENDMENT) ACT, 2005: MAIN PATENT PROVISIONS

- Exclusive Marketing Rights (EMRs) to be granted for 5 years for pharma and agro-chemical products.
- A Mail Box will be kept in which all applications for pharmaceutical and agro-chemical products will be kept.
- Three conditions for grant of EMRs : the new chemical entity should be filed after January 1, 1995, the product should not have been marketed earlier in India and compulsory licensing, wherein the government could reserve the right to allow to four companies to licence and manufacture the same product in case of a major demand-supply shortage.
- Restrictions on application for patents abroad, for inventions made in India, removed.
- The government can sell or distribute products for which EMRs have been granted for non-commercial use, in the public interest.
- Government to have discretion in determining the price of the product for which EMR has been granted in the public interest and for reasons to be stated.
- Exclusive right to sell or distribute will not be granted to articles based on Indian system of medicine which is already in public domain.

WTO and Patent Act

As per WTO agreement, Indian Patent Act, needs to be amended to have product patent for 20 years, the Patent Act (2005) is designed to address the issues of patent rights in India.

8.5 INTERNATIONAL INTELLECTUAL PROPERTY ORGANIZATIONS

Intellectual property refers to creations of the mind: inventions, literary and artistic works, and symbols, names, images and designs used in commerce.

Intellectual property refers to creations of the mind: inventions, literary and artistic works, and symbols, names, images and designs used in commerce.

Intellectual property is divided into two categories: Industrial property, which includes inventions (patents), trademarks, industrial designs, and geographic indications of source; and Copyright, which includes, literary and artistic works such as novels, poems and plays, films, musical works, artistic works such as drawings, paintings, photographs and sculptures, and architectural designs. Rights related to copyright include those of performing artists in their performances, producers or phonograms in their recordings, and those of broadcasters in their radio and television programs.

WIPO: The World Intellectual Property Organization (WIPO) is an international organization dedicated to promoting the used and protection of works of the human spirit. These words, — intellectual property — are expanding the bounds of science and technology and enriching the world of the arts. Through its work, WIPO plays an important role in enhancing the quality and enjoyment of life, as well as creating real wealth for nations.

With headquarters in Geneva, Switzerland, WIPO is one of the 16 specialized agencies of the United Nations system of organizations. It administers 23 international treaties dealing with different aspects of intellectual property protection. The organization counts 182 nations as member states.

Activities and Services

The World Intellectual Property Organization (WIPO) is an international organization dedicated to promoting the used and protection of works of the human spirit.

WIPO carries out a wide variety of activities and services in its work. These includes establishing international standards for intellectual property laws and practices and providing registration services that allow patents, trademarks and designs to be protected in many countries. WIPO also extends various technical and legal assistance to developing countries, facilitates resolution of intellectual property disputes, and explores new issues arising in the global intellectual property arena. In all these activities, the latest information technologies are employed to promote efficiency and facilitate the electronic exchange of information on intellectual property.

International Classifications

Anyone applying for a patent or registering a trademark or design, whether at the national or international level, is required to determine whether their creation is new or is owned or claimed by someone else. To determine this, huge amounts of information must be searched. WIPO treaties (listed below) created classification systems which organize information concerning inventions trademarks, and industrial designs into indexed, manageable structures for easy retrieval. Regularly updated to include changes and advances in technology and commercial practices, the classification systems are used voluntarily by many countries which are not member States of the related agreements.

WIPO administers four treaties establishing international classifications, the texts of which are also available:

- the Strasbourg Agreement Concerning the International Patent Classification (IPC);
- the Nice Agreement Concerning the International Classification of Goods and Services for the Purposes of the Registration of Marks;
- the Locarno Agreement Establishing the international Classification for Industrial Designs;
- the Vienna Agreement Establishing the International Classification of the Figurative Elements of Marks.

International Agreements

The major International agreements on intellectual property are: the Paris Convention for the Protection of Industrial Property:

- — the Berne convention for the Protection of Literary and Artistic Works
- — the Universal Copyright Convention
- — the Patent Cooperation Treaty
- — the European Patent Convention
- — Agreement on Trade-related Aspects of Intellectual Property Rights — one of the Annexes of the World Trade Organization (1994 GATT)
- — Common regulations under the Madrid Agreement Concerning the International Registration of Marks and the Protocol relating to that Agreement; adopted by the Assembly of the Madrid Union with effect from April1, 1996.

What is Arbitration?

Arbitration is a procedure in which a dispute is submitted by agreement of the parties, to one or more arbitrators who make a binding decision on the dispute.

Arbitration is a procedure in which a dispute is submitted by agreement of the parties, to one or more arbitrators who make a binding decision on the dispute in choosing arbitration, the parties opt for a private dispute resolution procedure instead of going to court.

Its principal characteristics are:

Arbitration is Consensual

An Arbitration can only take place if both parties have agreed to it. In the case of future disputes arising under a contract, the parties insert an arbitration clause in the relevant contract. An existing dispute can be referred to arbitration by means of a submission agreement between the parties. In contrast to mediation, a party cannot unilaterally withdraw from an arbitration.

The Parties Choose the Arbitrator(s)

Under the WIPO Rules, the parties can select a sole arbitrator together, if they choose to have a three-member arbitral tribunal, each party appoints one of the arbitrators; those two persons then agree on the presiding arbitrator. Alternatively the Center can suggest potential arbitrators with relevant expertise or directly appoint members of the arbitral tribunal. The Center maintains an extensive roster of arbitrators ranging from seasoned dispute resolution generalists to highly specialized practitioners and experts covering the entire legal and technical spectrum of intellectual property.

Arbitration is Neutral

In addition to the selection of neutrals of an appropriate nationality, parties are able to choose such important elements as the applicable law, language and venue of the arbitration. This allows them to ensure that no party enjoys a home court advantage.

Arbitration is a Confidential Procedure

The WIPO Arbitration Rules specifically protect the confidentially of the existence of the arbitration, any disclosures made during that procedure, and the award in certain circumstances, the WIPO Rules allow a party to restrict access to trade secrets or other confidential information that is submitted to the arbitral tribunal or to a confidentiality advisor to the tribunal.

The decision of the arbitral tribunal is final and easy to enforce

Under the WIPO Rules, the parties agree to carry out the decision of the arbitral tribunal without delay, International awards are enforced by national courts under the New York Convention, which permits them to be set aside only in very limited circumstances. More than 130 States are party to this Convention.

The following table explains the common features of intellectual properties disputes, court litigation and arbitration procedure.

Common features of many IP disputes	*Court litigation*	*Arbitration*
International	Multiple proceedings under different laws, with risk of conflicting results	A single proceeding under the law determined by parties
	Possibility of actual or perceived home court advantage of party that litigates in its own country	Arbitral procedure and nationality of arbitrator can be neutral to law, language and institutional culture of parties
Technical	Decision maker might not have relevant expertise	Parties can select arbitrator(s) with relevant experties
Urgent	Procedures often drawn-out	Arbitrator(s) and parties can shorten the procedure
	Injunctive relief available in certain jurisdictions	WIPO Arbitration may include provisional measures and does not preclude seeking court-ordered injunction
Require finality	Possiblity of appeal	Limited appeal option
Confidential/ trade secrets and risk to reputation	Public proceedings	Proceedings and award are confidential

8.5 DECIDED CASE ON BASMATI RICE, TURMERIC, AND PHARMA PRODUCTS

(A) BASMATI RICE PATENT ISSUE

In September 1997, a Texas company called RiceTec won a patent (U.S. Patent No. 5,663,484) on "basmati rice lines and grains." The patent secures lines of basmati and basmati-like rice and ways of analyzing that rice. RiceTec, owned by Prince Hans-Adam of Liechtenstein, faced international outrage over allegations of biopiracy. It had also caused a brief diplomatic crisis between India and United States with India threatening to take the matter to WTO as a violation of TRIPS which could have resulted in a major embarrassment for the United States. Both voluntarily and due to review decisions by the United States Patent Office, RiceTec has lost most of the claims of the patent, including, most importantly, the right to call their rice lines "basmati." This was a huge victory for Indian farmers who could have faced enormous economic losses from the patent.

(B) DECIDED CASES ON TURMERIC

The turmeric patent is a landmark case in the area of Intellectual property rights. This was the first time a patent based on the Traditional Knowledge of a developing country was challenged successfully and Unite States Patent and Trademark Office (USPTO) revoked the patent.

In 1995, two non-resident Indians, Suman K. Das and Hari Har P. Cohly, associated with the University of Mississippi Medical Centre, Jackson, USA obtained patent for Use of turmeric in wound healing. As turmeric has been used by all Indian families as a traditional wound healer in India for thousands of years for healing wounds and rashes.

Indian Council of Scientific and Industrial Research (CSIR) were entrusted with the responsibility of challenging the patent. CSIR challenged the patent on the ground that it lacked novelty. CSIR could locate 32 references (some of them being more than one hundred years old, in Sanskrit, Urdu and Hindi), which showed that this finding was well-known in India prior to filing of this patent. The formal request for re-examination of the patent was filled by CSIR at USPTO on 28 October 1996. The first re-examination result rejected all the six claims based on the references submitted by CSIR on the ground of 'anticipated references'

University of Mississippi Medical Centre, decided not to pursue the case and transferred the rights to the inventors. Inventors Mr. Suman K. Das and Mr. Hari Har P. Cohly decided to file Objections to the re-examination results. The inventors argued that the powder and paste form of Turmeric had different physical properties which helps wound healing, i.e., bio-availability and absorbability, and therefore, one of the ordinary skills in the art would not expect, with any reasonable degree of certainty, that a powdered material would be useful in the same application as a paste of the same material. The inventors, further, mentioned that oral administration was available only with honey and honey itself was considered to have wound healing properties.

In the second re-examination it was observed that the paste and the powder forms were equivalent for healing wounds in view of the cited material by CSIR. the examiner rejected all the claims once again and upheld the contentions raised by CSIR. Turmeric patent case is the fist successful case in the area of intellectual property violation.

(C) DECIDED CASES ON PHARMA PRODUCTS

Novartis AG vs. Union of India (The Glivec Case)

Novartis, a Swiss pharmaceutical MNC filed an application for a patent on the beta crystalline form of Imatinib Mesylate, marketed by the company under the brand name of Glivec/ Gleevec in several countries. Glivec is a drug used to treat chronic myeloid leukaemia. The Chennai patents office rejected the application on the grounds that the drug was a new form of an old drug and therefore was not patentable under Indian Law (Section 3(d) of the Indian Patents Act 2005).

Novartis filed two lawsuits against Government of India. The first case appeals rejection of patent application. The second case challenges Section 3(d) of the Patents Act 2005, the provision that seeks to prevent evergreening of patents.

Novartis contended before the Chennai High Court that Section 3(d) is vague, ambiguous and arbitrary. It is violative of Art 14 which guarantees right to equality and non-discrimination. The Swiss MNC also claimed that section does not comply with TRIPS agreement of the WTO which mandating a strict patent regime which India has signed.

The Court ruled that it had no jurisdiction to decide whether Indian patent laws comply with TRIPS; and that Section 3(d) does not suffer from vagueness, ambiguity and arbitrariness and contains reasonable in-built protection for patent applicants. The Chennai High Court accordingly dismissed the petitions by Novartis AG and its Indian subsidiary.

Implications of the Case

Over 30000 cases of chronic myeloid leukaemia (CML), a form of cancer of the blood cells are reported in India every year. Novartis introduced Glivec in 2001 in India. It proved to be a really useful drug producing remission in over 90 percent of cases. Glivec has to be taken lifelong and the treatment for the Novartis version costs Rs 1.2 lakh a month. On the other hand, nine Indian Companies were making and marketing it at a price of about Rs.8000 per month.

If patent would have been granted to Novartis, it would have prevented generic competition as domestic companies cannot produce the drug. Treatment cost would make the drug unaffordable and inaccessible for those who need it the most. Thus a patent enabled drug monopoly would have proved harmful for the majority.

Fulfilling public interest requires a regular stream of safe, effective and innovative medicines for all those who need them. This requires a balance between protecting intellectual property rights and safeguarding public health. Internationally agreed safeguards like the Doha Declaration are in place to ensure this balance but these safeguards will serve their true purpose only when they are respected and uphold.

CONCLUSION

The most practicable solution to the problem which at the same time allows for TRIP compliance would be granting of dual licences. This would mean that the patent would be partly product patent and after a reasonable time being given to the inventor to make a reasonably large profit it would be converted to a process patent whereby the patented drug can be manufactured by competing manufacturers using an alternative process. This would solve the problem of excessive hike in prices and would render the drugs more accessible to the millions suffering. Collaboration with the MNCs on various fronts such as research and development, manufacturing and marketing will help Indian Pharma companies make profitable breakthroughs.

Section 3(d) is one of the strongest aspects of our Patents Act. Complete compliance with TRIPS agreement will prove to be prejudicial to our national interests. It should be remembered that pharmaceutical industry owes a moral responsibility towards society. The monopoly granted by patents to the Drug companies should not be exercised without responsibilities.

As far as Indian pharmaceutical industry is concerned, various options are possible in the WTO regime. But ultimately, the path currently being followed by international standards for patent protection moves inevitably toward a clash between public health and intellectual property. Despite the Doha Declarations affirmation of public health as the paramount concern, it is not clear how such an objective would be achieved, because generic substitution is so instrumental in the effort to improve drug accessibility. Stringent intellectual property protection for pharmaceuticals would only retard public health initiatives in the coming years. Given the rapid evolution of the AIDS crisis throughout the world, with more than 35 million cases alone in India , a twenty-year term of market exclusivity for new treatments is not reasonable if we expect to make real progress in containing the disease. It might well be appropriate for a governing body to clearly define a list of essential medicines, such as antiretroviral (ARV) agents, that would be subject to somewhat more relaxed patent protection compared to other drugs.

INDIA BEATS US BID TO PATENT ASHWAGANDHA

A wonder herb, it has been used in traditional medicines for ages.

India has foiled a major bio-piracy bid on the use of Ashwagandha India's wonder plant in the treatment of a range of illnesses including depression, diabetes, insomnia, convulsions and gastritis.

On March 25,the European Patent Office (EPO) decided to withdraw American multinational company Natreon Incs patent applications on the plants medicinal properties after India submitted documented proof confirming how medicinal formulations using Ashwagandha were being used in India as far back as in the 12th century. Called the Indian ginseng, Ashwagandha is used extensively in Ayurveda, Siddha and Unani Indias traditional systems of medicine. But Natreon on July 27,2006 filed patent applications in the EPO on Ashwagandhas (Withania somnifera) ability to treat anxiety induced stress, depression, insomnia, gastric ulcers and convulsions. Shocked, head of India's Traditional Knowledge Digital Library (TKDL) Dr V K Gupta shot off a letter to EPO on July 6,2009 submitting evidence to confirm that Ashwagandhas medicinal properties against the mentioned conditions were long known.

Interestingly, India's protest letter also contained 15 pieces of evidence and documents dating back to the 12th century. Excerpts from age-old texts of Ayurveda, Unani and Siddha where such formulations were mentioned were also attached.

Council of Scientific and Industrial Researchs letter to EPO in 2009 said, the patent application number EP 1906980 titled method of treatment or management of stress may kindly be referred to wherein treatment of anxiety induced stress, depression induced stress, sleep deprivation induced stress, thermic change induced stress and gastric ulcer induced stress with Withania somnifera has been claimed to be as novel.

The letter added, but in TKDL, several references are there, wherein Withania somnifera is used for treatment of depression, insomnia, gastritis, gastric ulcer and convulsions since long. Hence, there does not seem to be any novelty or inventive step involved in the claims made in the above patent application. As a result of this third party submission, a notice was issued to the American company concerning the patentability of the invention and was directed to comment on it.

Source : Times of India, p19, March 27, 2010

Questions

Section — A Objective Type

1. What is Intellectual Property?
2. What is Intellectual Property Law?
3. What Intellectual Property comprises of?
4. What are the principal objectives of Intellectual Capital Management?
5. What is Intellectual Capital?
6. Name the segments of Intellectual Property.
7. What are Mask works?
8. What are Trade Secrets?
9. What is know-how?
10. What is a patent?
11. What is utility patent?
12. What is design patent?
13. What is plant patent?
14. What is copyright?
15. What is Trademark?
16. Differentiate between Licensce and Assignment.
17. What is Voluntary Licensce?
18. What is Compulsory Licensce?
19. Name the remedies available for Infringement of copyright.
20. What are the objectives of Trade and Merchandise Mark Act, 1958?
21. Name any two features of a trademark.
22. What is deceptively similar trademark?
23. What is certification of trademark?
24. Who is a registered user of a trademark?
25. Name the two advantages of obtaining patent.
26. What is Invention as per Patent Act?
27. What is Infringement of Patent?
28. Expand WIPO.
29. What is Arbitration?
30. What is passing off under Trademarks Act?

Section — B Analytical Type

1. What is Intellectual Property Law?
2. Is Intellectual Property Law an important subject?
3. Write a note on Intellectual Property and Moral Rights.
4. Briefly explain the Intellectural Capital Management Process flow.
5. Explain different kinds of Patents.
6. Distinguish between Licensce and Assignment.
7. Briefly explain the remedies of Infringement for copyright.
8. Distinguish between Trademark and Copyright.
9. Distinguish between Deception and Confusion.
10. Write a note on Infringement of Trademark.

11. List the advantages of obtaining a patent.
12. What are inventions? And What are not inventions as per the Patent Act, 1970?
13. What is the procedure for grant of patent?
14. When the grant of patent may be opposed? List the grounds.
15. When patent lapses? How to restore it?
16. What is surrender of Patent? Narrate the procedure.
17. Explain the salient features of Patent Amendment Act, 2005.
18. Write a note on Infringement of patent.
19. Write a note on WIPO.
20. Name the Major International Agreements on Intellectual Property.

Section — C Essay Type

1. Write a note on Intellectual Property, Intellectual Assets and Intellectual Capital.
2. What is patent? Explain the procedure to obtain patent.
3. Briefly explain the salient features of Copyright Act, 1957.
4. Explain the salient features of Trade and Merchandise Mark Act, 1958.
5. Write a note on Patent Act, 1970 including Amendment Act, 2005.
6. Discuss in great detail the Basmati Rice Case as IPR.
7. Explain the facts of the case in relation to turmeric as Patent Right.
8. Bring out the decided cases of Pharma Products in India as WTO-TRIPS paradigm.

FOREIGN EXCHANGE MANAGEMENT ACT, 1999 AND THE PREVENTION OF MONEY LAUNDERING ACT, 2002

Module Objectives

After reading this chapter, you should be able to:

- Understand the important terms like Authorised person, Foreign exchange and Foreign security
- Know the regulation and management of Foreign exchange
- Learn the contraventions and penalties under FEMA
- Deliberate on the power and functions of Director of Enforcement
- Know the meaning and objectives of Money laundering
- List the stages and forms of Money laundering operations
- Chart out the problems and solutions of Money laundering and Hawala transactions.

FOREIGN EXCHANGE MANAGEMENT ACT (FEMA), 1999

FEMA is an Act to consolidate and amend the law relating to foreign exchange with the objectives of facilitating external trade and payments and for promoting the orderly development and maintenance of foreign exchange market in India.

9.1 OBJECTS OF THE FEMA

This is an Act to consolidate and amend the law relating to foreign exchange with the objectives of facilitating external trade and payments and for promoting the orderly development and maintenance of foreign exchange market in India.

This Act extends to the whole of India and applies to all branches, offices and agencies outside India owned or controlled by a person resident in India and also to any contravention thereunder committed outside India by any person to whom this Act applies.

Important Terms

The Act defines certain important terms, which are as follows:

Authorised person means an authorized dealer, money changer, offshore banking unit or any other person for the time being authorized under Section 10 (1) to deal in foreign exchange or foreign securities.

Authorised person: means an authorized dealer, money changer, offshore banking unit or any other person for the time being authorized under Section 10 (1) to deal in foreign exchange or foreign securities.

Capital account transactions: means a transactions which alters the assets or liabilities, including contingent liabilities, outside India of persons resident in India or assets or liabilities in India of persons resident outside India, and includes transactions referred to in Section 6 (3).

Currency: includes all currency notes, postal notes, postal orders, cheques, drafts, travellers cheques, letter of credit, bill of exchange and promissory notes, credit cards or such other similar instruments, as may be notified by the Reserve Bank.

Currency notes: means and includes cash in the form of coins and bank notes.

Current account transactions: means a transaction other than capital account transaction and without prejudice to the generality of the foregoing such transactions include:

1. payments due in connection with foreign trade, other current business, services, and short-term banking and credit facilities in the ordinary course of business.
2. payments due as interest on loans and as net income from investments.
3. remittances for living expenses or patents, spouse and children residing abroad, and
4. expenses in connection with foreign travel education and medical care of parents, spouse and children.

Export: means—

1. the taking out of India to a place outside India any goods
2. provision of services from India to any person outside India

Foreign Currency: means any currency other than Indian currency.

Foreign Exchange: means foreign currency and includes—

1. deposits, credits and balances payable in any foreign currency.
2. drafts, travelers cheques, letter of credit or bills of exchange, expressed or drawn in Indian currency but payable in any foreign currency.
3. drafts, travelers cheques, letter of credit or bills of exchange drawn by banks, institutions or persons outside India, but payable in Indian currency.

Foreign Security: means any security, in the form of shares, stocks, bonds, debentures or any other instrument denominated or expressed in foreign currency and includes securities expressed in foreign currency, but where redemption or any form of return such as interest or dividends is payable in Indian currency.

Import: with its grammatical variations and cognate expressions means bringing into India any goods or services.

Indian currency: means currency which is expressed or drawn in Indian rupees but does not include special bank notes and special one rupee notes issued under Section 28 A of the RBI Act, 1934.

Person: Includes

1. an individual
2. a Hindu undivided family
3. a company
4. a firm
5. an association of persons or body of individuals, whether incorporated or not.
6. every artificial juridical person, not falling within any of the preceding sub-clauses, and
7. any agency, office or branch owned or controlled by such person.

Person — resident in India: means—

1. a person residing in India, for more than 182 days during the course of the preceding financial year but does not include—
   (A) a person who has gone out of India or who stays outside India; in either case—
      (a) for or on taking up employment outside India, or
      (b) for carrying on outside India a business or vacation outside India, or
      (c) for any other purpose, in such circumstances as would indicate his intention to stay in India for an uncertain period.
   (B) a person who has come to or stays in India, in either case, otherwise than—
      (a) for or on taking employment in India, or
      (b) for carrying on in India a business or vocation in India, or
      (c) for any other purpose, in such circumstances as would indicate his intention to stay in India for an uncertain period.
2. any person or body corporate registered or incorporated in India
3. an office, branch or agency in India owned or controlled by a person resident outside India.

4. an office, branch or agency outside India owned or controlled by a person resident in India.

Person Resident Outside India: means a person who is not resident in India.

Repatriate to India: means bringing into India the realized foreign exchange and —

(i) the selling of such foreign exchange to an authorized person in India in exchange for rupees; or

(ii) the holdings of realized amount in an account with an authorized person in India to the extent notified by the Reserve Bank.

And includes use of the realized amount for discharge of a debt or liability denominated in foreign exchange and the expression "repatriation" shall be construed accordingly.

Security: means shares, stocks, bonds and debentures, Government securities as defined in the Public Debt Act, 1944, saving certificates to which the Government Savings Certificates Act, 1959, applies deposit receipts in respect of securities and units of the Unit Trust of India established under Section 3 (1) of the UTI Act, 1963 or of any mutual fund and includes certificates of title to securities, but does not include bills of exchange or promissory notes other than Government promissory notes or any other instruments which may be notified by the Reserve Bank as security for the purposes of this Act.

Service: means service of any description which is made available to potential users and includes the provisions of facilities in connection with banking, financing, insurance, medical assistance, legal assistance, chit fund, real estate transport, processing, supply of electrical or other energy, boarding or lodging or both, entertainment, amusement or the purveying of news or other information, but does not include the rendering of any service free of charge or under a contract of personal service.

Transfer: includes sale, purchase, exchange, mortgage, pledge, gift, loan or any other form of transfer of right, title, possession or lien.

9.2 REGULATION AND MANAGEMENT OF FOREIGN EXCHANGE

Dealings in Foreign Exchange

As per Act, no person shall—

(a) Deal in or transfer any foreign exchange or foreign security to any person not being an authorized person.

(b) Make any payment to or for the credit of any person resident outside India in any manner.

(c) Receive otherwise through an authorized person, any payment by order or on behalf of any person resident outside India in any manner.

(d) Enter into any financial transaction in India as consideration for or in association with acquisition or creation or transfer of a right to acquire, any asset outside India by any person.

Section 3 seeks to prohibit dealings in foreign exchange except through an authorized person.

Holdings of Foreign Exchange

Section 4 describes the provisions in relation to acquisition, holding etc., of foreign exchange, foreign security or immovable property situated outside India.

As per this section, no person resident in India shall acquire, hold, own, possess or transfer any foreign exchange, foreign security or any immovable property situated outside India.

Current Account Transactions

Section 5 stipulates that sale or drawal for all current account transactions shall qualify for drawal of foreign exchange from authorized persons. It also empowers the Central Government to prescribe, in public interest and in consultation with the Reserve Bank, the restrictions for such transactions as may be considered reasonable.

Any person may sell or draw foreign exchange to or form an authorized person if such sale or drawal is a current account transaction.

Provided that the Central Government may, in public interest and in consultation with the Reserve Bank, impose such reasonable restrictions for current account transactions as may be prescribed.

Capital Account Transactions

Sub-section (1) of Section 6 provides that subject to certain conditions and limitations any person may sell or draw foreign exchange to or from any authorized person for capital account transaction. Sub-section (2) thereof enables the Reserve Bank, in consultation with the Central Government; to specify the permissible class of such transactions and the limits up to which foreign exchange shall be admissible for such transactions. Sub-section (3) further enables the Reserve Bank to prohibit, restrict or regulate the specific transactions, mentioned therein by regulations framed under the Act. Sub-sections (4) and (5) incorporate the existing policy with respect to the person resident in India acquiring, etc. foreign assets outside India and a non-resident acquiring etc., assets in India while he was resident in India. Sub-section (6) empowers the Reserve Bank to regulate the setting up of branches or office in India by foreign firms.

(1) Subject to the provisions of Sub-section (2) of Section 6, any person may sell or draw foreign exchange to or from an authorized person for a capital account transaction.

(2) The Reserve Bank may, in consultation with the Central Government, specify—

  (a) Any class or classes of capital account transactions which are permissible;

  (b) The limit up to which foreign exchange shall be admissible for such transactions.

Provided that the Reserve Bank shall not impose any restriction on the drawal of foreign exchange for payments due on account of amortization of loans of for depreciation of direct investments in the ordinary course of business.

(3) Without prejudice to the generality of the provisions of sub section (2), the Reserve Bank may, by regulations prohibit, restrict or regulate the following:

(a) transfer or issue of any foreign security by a person resident in India;

(b) transfer or issue of any security by a person resident in India;

(c) transfer or issue of any security or foreign security by any branch, office or agency in India of a person resident outside India;

(d) any borrowing or lending in foreign exchange in whatever form or by whatever name called is required;

(e) any borrowing or lending in rupees in whatever form of by whatever name called between a person resident in India and a person resident outside India;

(f) deposits between persons resident in India and persons resident outside India;

(g) export, import or holding of currency or currency notes;

(h) transfer of immovable property outside India, other than a lease not exceeding five years, by a person resident in India;

(i) acquisition on transfer of immovable property in India, other than a lease not exceeding five years, by a person resident outside India;

(j) giving of a guarantee or surety in respect of any debt, obligation or other liability incurred—

(i) by a person resident in India and owed to a person resident outside India; or

(ii) by a person resident outside India.

(4) A person resident in India may hold, own, transfer or invest in foreign currency, foreign security or any immovable property situated outside India if such currency, security or property was acquired, held or owned by such person when he was resident outside India or inherited from a person who was resident outside India.

(5) A person resident outside India may hold, own transfer or invest in Indian currency, security or any immovable property situated in India if such currency, security or property was acquired, held or owned by such person when he was residing in India or inherited from a person who was resident in India.

(6) Without prejudice to the provisions of this section, the Reserve Bank may, by regulation, prohibit, restrict, or regulate establishment in India of a branch, office or other place of business by a person resident outside India, for carrying on any activity relating to such branch, office or other place of business.

Export of Goods and Services

Section 7 provides for control over repatriation of sale proceeds of exported goods. The section preserves the Reserve Bank's existing powers to direct an exporter to comply with the requirements as deemed fit for the purpose of ensuring that the export value of the goods is received without any delay.

(1) Every exporter of goods shall—

(a) Furnish to the Reserve Bank or to such other authority a declaration in such form and in such manners as may be specified, containing true and correct material particulars, including the amount representing the full export value or, if the full export value of the goods is not ascertained at the time of export, the value which the exporter, having regard to the prevailing market conditions, expects to receive on the sale of the goods in a market outside India.

(b) Furnish to the Reserve Bank such other information as may be required by the Reserve Bank for the purpose of ensuring the realization of the export proceeds by such exporter.

(2) The Reserve Bank may, for the purpose of ensuring that the full export value of the goods or such reduced value of the goods as the Reserve Bank determines, having regard to the prevailing market conditions, is received without any delay, direct any exporter to comply with such requirements as it deems fit.

(3) Every exporter of services shall furnish to the Reserve Bank or to such other authorities a declaration in such form and in such manner as may be specified, containing the true and correct material particulars in relation to payment for such services.

Realization and Repatriation of Foreign Exchange

Section 8 casts certain obligations on persons resident in India having any amount of foreign exchange due or acquired in his favour. Save as otherwise provided in this Act, where any amount of foreign exchange is due or has accrued to any person resident in India, such person shall take all reasonable steps to realize and repatriate to India such foreign exchange within such period in such manner as may be specified by the Reserve Bank.

Exemption from Realization and Repatriating in Certain Cases

Section 9 seeks to provide for exemptions in respect of realization and repatriation is the case specified therein. Most of the transactions specified therein are present in terms of various notifications of the Reserve Bank.

The provisions of Section 4 and 8 shall not apply to the following, namely:

(a) possession of foreign currency or foreign coins by any person up to such limit as the Reserve Bank may specify;

(b) foreign currency account held or operated by such person or class of persons and the limit up to which the Reserve Bank may specify;

(c) foreign exchange acquired or received before the 8th day of July, 1947, or any income arising or accruing thereon which is held outside India by any person in pursuance of general or special permission granted by the Reserve Bank;

(d) foreign exchange held by a person resident in India upto such limit as the Reserve Bank may specify, if such foreign exchange was acquired by way of gifts or inheritance from a person referred to in clause (c), including any income arising therefrom;

(e) foreign exchange acquired from employment, business, trade, vocation, services, honorarium, gifts, inheritance or any other legitimate means upto such limit as the Reserve Bank may specify; and

(f) such other receipts in foreign exchange as the Reserve Bank may specify;

9.3 AUTHORISED PERSON

Section 10 empowers the Reserve Bank to authorize persons to deal in foreign exchange or in foreign securities. The authorization can also be granted for dealing in foreign securities besides foreign exchange. The Reserve Bank may specify the conditions in the authorization and may also revoke the same in the public interest in the case of any contravention of the provisions of the Act or failure to comply with the conditions in the authorization.

The rules relating to 'Authorised person' are as follows:

(1) The Reserve Bank may, on an application made to it in this behalf, authorize any person to be known as authorized person to deal in foreign exchange or in foreign securities, as an authorized dealer, money changer or offshore banking unit or in any other manner as it deems fit.

(2) An authorization under this section shall be writing and shall be subject to the conditions laid down therein.

(3) An authorization granted under sub-section (1) may be revoked by the Reserve Bank at any time if the Reserve Bank is satisfied that—

   (a) it is in public interest so to do; or

   (b) the authorized person has failed to comply with the condition subject to which the authorization was granted or has contravened any of the provisions of the act or any rule, regulation, notification, direction or order made thereunder: provided that no such authorization shall be revoked on any ground referred to in clause (b) unless the authorized person has been given a reasonable opportunity of making a representation in the matter.

(4) An authorized person shall, in all his dealings in foreign exchange or foreign security, comply with such general or special directions or orders as the Reserve Bank may, from time to time, think fit to give, and except with the previous permission of the Reserve Bank, an authorized person shall not engage in any transaction involving any foreign exchange or foreign security which is not in conformity with the terms of his authorization under this section.

(5) An authorized person shall, before undertaking any transaction in foreign exchange on behalf of any person, require that person to make such declaration and to give such information as well reasonably satisfy him that that transaction will not insolve, and is not designed for the purpose of any contravention or evasion of the provisions of this Act or of any rule, regulation, notification, direction or order made thereunder, and where the said person refuses to comply with any such requirement or makes only unsatisfactory compliance therewith, the authorized person shall refuse in writing to undertake the transaction and shall, if he has reason to believe that any such contravention or evasion as aforesaid is contemplated by the person, report the matter to the Reserve Bank.

(6) Any person, other than an authorized person, who has acquired or purchased foreign exchange for any purpose mentioned in the declaration made by him to authorized person under sub-section (5) does not use it for such purpose or does not surrender it to authorized person within the specified period or uses the foreign exchange so acquired or purchased for any other purpose for which purchase or acquisition of foreign exchange is not permissible under the provisions of the Act or

Reserve Bank's Powers to Issue Directions to Authorized Person

Section II empowers Reserve Bank to issue directions to authorized persons and impose penalty if the direction given by the Reserve Bank is contravened by any authorized person.

(1) The Reserve Bank may, for the purpose of securing compliance with the provisions of this Act, and of any rules, regulations, notifications or directions made thereunder, give to the authorized persons any direction in regard to making of payment or the doing or desist from doing act relating to foreign exchange or foreign security.

(2) The Reserve Bank may, for the purpose of ensuring the compliance with the provisions of this Act of any rule, regulation, notification, direction or order made there under, direct any authorized person to furnish such information in such manner, as it deems fit.

(3) Where any authorized person contravenes any direction given by the Reserve Bank under this Act or fails to file any return as directed by the Reserve Bank, the Reserve Bank may, after giving reasonable opportunity of being heard, impose on the authorized person a penalty which may extended to ten thousand rupees and in the case of continuing contravention with an additional penalty which may extend to two thousand rupees for every day during which such contravention continues.

Power of Reserve Bank to Inspect Authorized Person

Section 12 empowers the Reserve Bank to inspect the authorized person who shall have to produce such books, accounts, and other person who shall have to produce such books, accounts and other documents etc., as may be required by the other person making the inspection.

(1) The Reserve Bank may, at any time, cause an inspection to be made, by any officer of the Reserve Bank specially authorized in writing by the Reserve Bank in this behalf, of the business of any authorized person as may appear to it to be necessary or expedient for the purpose of—

(a) verifying the correctness of any statement, information or particulars furnished to the Reserve Bank;

(b) obtaining any information or particulars which such authorized person has failed to furnish on being called upon to do so;

(c) securing compliance with the provisions of this Act or of any rules, regulations, directions or orders, made thereunder.

(2) It shall be the duty of every authorized person, and where such person is a company or a firm, every director, partner or other officer of such company or firm, as the case may be, to produce to any officer making an inspection under

Sub-section (1), such books, accounts and other documents in his custody or power and to furnish any statement or information relating to the affairs of such person, company or firm as the said officer may require within such time and in such manner as the said officer may direct.

9.4 CONTRAVENTION AND PENALTIES

Penalties

Section 13 deals with the contravention as civil offences and the adjudicating officers are empowered to impose penalties.

(1) If any person contravenes any provision of this Act, or contravenes any rule, regulation, notification, direction or order issued in exercise of the powers under this Act, or contravenes any condition subject to which an authorization is issued by the Reserve Bank, he shall, upon adjudication, be liable to a penalty upto thrice the sum involved in such contravention where such amount is quantifiable, or upto two lakh where the amount is not quantifiable, and where such contravention is a continuing one, further penalty which may extend to five thousand for every day after the first day in which the contravention continues.

(2) Any Adjudicating Authority adjudging any contravention under Sub-section (1), may, if he thinks fit in addition to any penalty which he may impose for such contravention direct that any currency, security or any other money or property in respect of which the contravention has taken place shall be confiscated to the Central Government and further direct that the foreign exchange holdings, if any of the persons committing the contraventions or any part thereof, shall be brought back into India or shall be retained outside India in accordance with the directions made in this behalf.

Explanation: For the purpose of this Sub-section, "Property" in respect of which contravention has taken place, shall include—

(a) deposits in a bank, where the said property is converted into such deposits;

(b) Indian currency, where the said property is converted into that currency, and

(c) Any other property which has resulted out of the conversion of that property.

Enforcement of the Orders of Adjudicating Authority

Section 14 lays down the procedure for payment of penalty and the consequences of civil imprisonment for failure to make full payment of the penalty within the specified period. It provides that the detention order shall be executed like a warrant of arrest.

(1) Subject to the provisions of Sub-section (2) of Section 19, if any person fails to make full payment of the penalty imposed on him under Section 13 within a period of ninety days from the date on which the notice for payment of such penalty is served on him, he shall be liable to civil imprisonment under this section.

(2) No order for the arrest and detention in civil prison a defaulter shall be made unless the Adjudicating Authority has issued and served a notice upon the defaulter calling him to appear before him on the date specified in the notice and

to show cause why he should not be committed to the civil prison, and unless the Adjudicating Authority, for reasons in writing is satisfied—

(a) that the defaulter, with the object or effect of obstructing the recovery of penalty, has after the issue of notice by the Adjudicating Authority, dishonestly transferred, concealed, or removed any part of his property, or

(b) that the defaulter has, or has had since the issuing of notice by the Adjudicating Authority, the means to pay the arrears or some substantial part thereof refuses or neglects or has refused or neglected to pay the same.

(3) Notwithstanding anything contained in Sub-section (1), a warrant for the arrest of the defaulter may be issued by the Adjudicating Authority if thc Adjudicating Authority is satisfied, by affidavit or otherwise, that with the object or effect of delaying the execution of the certificate the defaulter is likely to abscond or leave the local limits of the jurisdiction of the Adjudicating Authority.

(4) Where appearance is not made pursuant to a notice issued and served under Sub-section (1), the Adjudicating Authority may issue a warrant for the arrest of the defaulter.

(5) A warrant of arrest issued by the Adjudicating Authority under Sub-section (3) or Sub-section (4) may also be executed by any other Adjudicating Authority within whose jurisdiction the defaulter may for the time being been found.

(6) Every person arrested in pursuance of a warrant of arrest under this section shall be brought before the Adjudicating Authority issuing the warrant as soon as practicable and in any event within twenty-four hours of his arrest (exclusive of the time required for the journey).

Provided that, if the defaulter pays the amount entered in the warrant of arrest as due and the costs of the arrest of the officer arresting him, such officer shall at once release him.

Explanation: For the purposes of this Sub-section, where the defaulter is a Hindu undivided family, the Karta thereof shall be deemed to be the defaulter.

(7) When a defaulter appears before the Adjudicating Authority pursuant to a notice to show cause or is brought before the Adjudicating Authority under this section, the Adjudicating Authority shall give the defaulter an opportunity showing cause why he should not be committed to the civil prison.

(8) Pending the conclusion of the inquiry, the Adjudicating Authority may, in his discretion, order the defaulter to be detained in the custody of such officer as the Adjudicating Authority may think fit or release him on his furnishing the security to the satisfaction of the Adjudicating Authority for his appearance as and when required.

(9) Upon the conclusion of the inquiry, the Adjudicating Authority may make an order for the detention of the defaulter in the civil prison and shall in that event cause him to be arrested if he is not already under arrest:

Provided that in order to give a defaulter an opportunity of satisfying the arrears, the Adjudicating Authority may, before making the order of detention, leave the defaulter in the custody of the officer arresting him or of any other officer for a specified period not exceeding fifteen days, or release him on his furnishing security to the satisfaction of the Adjudicating Authority for his appearance at the expiration of the specified period if the arrears are not satisfied.

(10) When the Adjudicating Authority does not make an order of detention under Sub-section (9), he shall, if the defaulter is under arrest, direct his release.

(11) Every person detained in the civil prison in execution of the certificate may be so detained—

(a) where the certificate is for a demand of an amount exceeding rupees one crore, up to three years, and

(b) in any other case, up to six months:

Provided that he shall be released from such detention on the amount mentioned in the warrant for this detention being paid to the officer in charge of the civil prison.

(12) A defaulter released from detention under this section shall not, merely by reason of his release, be discharged from his liability for the arrears, but he shall not be liable to be arrested under the certificate in execution of which he was detained.

Power to Compound Contravention

Section 15 seeks to vest in the Directorate of Enforcement the powers to compound offences. This power is to be exercised in accordance with the provisions of the rules framed by the Central Government.

(1) Any contravention under Section 13 may, on an application made by the person committing such contravention, be compounded within one hundred and eighty days from the date of receipt of application by the Director of Enforcement or such other officers of the Directorate of Enforcement and officers of the Reserve Bank as may be authorized in this behalf by the Central Government in such manner as may be prescribed.

(2) Where a contravention has been compounded under Sub-section (1), no proceeding or further proceeding, as the case may be, shall be initiated or continued, as the case may be, against the person committing such contravention under that section, in respect of the contravention so compounded.

9.5 ADJUDICATION AND APPEAL

Section 16 provides for appointment of Central Government officers as Adjudicating Authorities for holding an inquiry for the purpose of imposing any penalty. It also provides for the procedure for taking cognizance by the Adjudicating Authority and confer powers of a civil court on the said Authority.

(1) For the purpose of adjudication under Section 13, the Central Government may, by an order published in the official Gazette, appoint as many officers of the Central Government as it may think fit, as the Adjudicating Authority for holding an inquiry in the manner prescribed after giving the person alleged to have committed contravention under Section 13, against whom a complaint has been made under sub-section (2) (herein after in this section referred to as the said person) a reasonable opportunity of being heard for the purpose of imposing any penalty:

Provided that where the Adjudicating Authority is of opinion that the said person is likely to abscond or is likely to evade in any manner, the payment of penalty; if levied, it may direct the said person to furnish a bond or guarantee for such amount and subject to such conditions as it may deem fit.

(2) The Central Government shall, while appointing the Adjudicating Authorities under Sub-section (1), also specifies in the order published in the official Gazette, their respective jurisdictions.

(3) No Adjudicating Authority shall hold an enquiry under Sub-section (1) except upon a complaint in writing made by an officer authorized by a general or special order by the Central Government.

(4) The said person may appear either in person or take the assistance of a legal practitioner or a chartered accountant of his choice for presenting his case before the Adjudicating Authority.

(5) Every Adjudicating Authority shall have the same powers of a civil court which are conferred on the Appellate tribunal under Sub-section (2) of Section 28 and —

(a) all proceedings before it shall be deemed to be judicial proceedings within the meaning of Sections 193 and 228 of the Indian Penal Code (45 of 1860);

(b) shall be deemed to be a civil court for the purposes of Sections 345 and 346 of the Code of Criminal Procedure, 1973 (2 of 1974).

(6) Every Adjudicating Authority shall deal with the complaint under Sub-section (2) as expeditiously as possible and endeavour shall be made to dispose of the complaint finally within one year from the date of receipt of the complaint:

Provided that where the complaint cannot be disposed of within the said period the Adjudicating Authority shall record periodically the reasons in writing for not disposing of the complaint within the said period.

Appeals of Special Director (Appeals)

Section 17 provides for appeals to the Special Director (Appeals) from the orders made by the Adjudicating Authority being an Assistant Director of Enforcement or Deputy Director of Enforcement.

(1) The Central Government shall, by notification, appoint one or more Special Directors (Appeals) to hear appeals against the orders of the Adjudicating Authorities under this section and shall also specify in the said notification the matter and places in relation to which the Special Director (Appeals) may exercise jurisdiction.

(2) Any person aggrieved by an order made by the Adjudicating Authority, being an Assistant Director of Enforcement or a Deputy Director of Enforcement, may prefer an appeal to the Special Director (Appeals).

(3) Every appeal under Sub-section (1) shall be filed within 45 days from the date on which the copy of the order made by the Adjudicating Authority is received by the aggrieved person and it shall be such form, verified in such manner and be accompanied by such fee as may be prescribed.

Provided that the Special Director (Appeals) may entertain an appeal after the expiry of the said period of 45 days, if he satisfied that there was sufficient cause for not filing it within that period.

(4) On receipt on an appeal under Sub-section (1), the Special Director (Appeals) may after giving the parties to the appeal an opportunity of being heard, pass such order thereon as he thinks fit confirming, modifying or setting aside the order appealed against.

(5) The Special Director (Appeals) shall send a copy of every order made by him to the parties to appeal and to the concerned Adjudicating Authority.

(6) The Special Director (Appeals) shall have the same powers of a civil court which are conferred on the Appellate Tribunal under Sub-section (2) of Section 28 and —

(a) all proceedings before him shall be deemed to be judicial proceedings within the meaning of Sections 193 and 228 of the Indian Penal Code (45 of 1860);

(b) shall be deemed to be a civil court for the purposes of Sections 345 and 346 of the Code of Criminal Procedure, 1973 (2 of 1974).

Establishment of Appellate Tribunal

Section 18 provides for establishing of an Appellate Tribunal and appointment of Special Director (Appeals) to hear appeals against the orders of the Adjudicating Authority.

The Central Government shall, by notification, establish an Appellate Tribunal to be known as the Appellate Tribunal for Foreign Exchange to hear appeals against the orders of the Adjudicating Authorities and the Special Director (Appeals) under this Act.

Appeal to Appellate Tribunal

Section 19 provides for preferring or appeal before the Appellate Tribunal against the order made by the Adjudicating Authority and the Special Director (Appeals), period for filing the appeal, conditions of delay for sufficient cause and the period for disposal of appeal.

(1) Save as provided in Sub-section (2), the Central Government or any person aggrieved by an order made by an Adjudicating Authority other than those referred to in Sub-section (1), of Section 17, or the Special Directors (Appeals), may prefer an appeal to the Appellate Tribunal:

Provided that any person appealing against the order of the Adjudicating Authority or the Special Director (Appeals) levying any penalty, shall while filing the appeal, deposit the amount of such penalty with such authority as may be notified by the Central Government.

Provided further that where in any particular case, the Appellate tribunal is of the opinion that the deposit of such penalty would cause undue hardship to such person, the Appellate Tribunal may dispense with such deposit subject to such conditions as it may deem fit to impose so as to safeguard the realization of penalty.

(2) Every appeal under Sub-section (1) shall be filed within a period of 45 days from the date on which a copy of the order made by the Adjudicating Authority or the Special Director (Appeals) is received by the aggrieved person or by the Central Government and it shall be in such form verified in such manner and be accompanied by such fee as may be prescribed:

Provided that the Appellate Tribunal may entertain an appeal after the expiry of the said period of 45 days if it is satisfied that there was sufficient cause for not filing it within that period.

(3) On receipt of an appeal under Sub-section (1), the Appellate Tribunal may after giving the parties to the appeal an opportunity of being heard, pass such orders thereon as it thinks fit, confirming, modifying or setting aside the order appealed against.

(4) The Appellate Tribunal shall send a copy of every order made by it to the parties to the appeal and to the concerned Adjudicating Authority or the Special Director (Appeals), as the case may be.

(5) The appeal filed before the Appellate Tribunal under Sub-section (1), shall be dealt with by it as expeditiously as possible and endeavour shall be made by it to dispose of the appeal finally within one hundred and eighty days from the date of receipt of the appeal.

Provided that where any appeal could not be disposed of within the said period of one hundred and eighty days, the Appellate Tribunal shall record its reason in writing for not disposing of the Appeal within the said period.

(6) The Appellate Tribunal may, for the purpose of examining the legality, propriety or correctness of any order made by the Adjudicating Authority under Section 16 in relation to any proceeding, on its own motion or otherwise, call for the records of such proceedings and make such order in the case as it thinks fit.

Composition of Appellate Tribunal

Section 20 to 23 provide for the composition of the Appellate Tribunal, the qualifications for appointment of the Chairperson, other Members of the Appellate Tribunal and the Special Director (Appeals), the term of office of the Chairperson and other Members and the Special Director (Appeals) and their salary allowances and other conditions of service.

Composition of Appellate Tribunal (Sec. 20)

1. The Appellate Tribunal shall consist of a Chairperson and such number of Members as the Central Government may deem fit.

2. Subject to the provisions of this Act—

(a) The jurisdiction of the Appellate Tribunal may be exercised by Benches thereof;

(b) A Bench may be constituted by the Chairperson with one or more Members as the Chairperson may deem fit;

(c) The Benches of the Appellate Tribunal shall ordinarily sit at New Delhi and at such other places as the Central Government may, in consultation with the chairperson, notify;

(d) The Central Government shall notify the areas, in relation to which each Bench of the Appellate Tribunal may exercise jurisdiction.

(3) Notwithstanding anything contained in Sub-section (2), the Chairperson may transfer a Member from one Bench to another Bench.

(4) If at any stage of the hearing of any case or matter it appears to the Chairperson or a Member that the case or matter is of such a nature that it ought to be heard by a Bench consisting of two Members, the case or matter may be, referred to him for transfer, to such Bench as the Chairperson may deem fit.

Qualifications for Appointment of Chairperson, Member and Special Director (Appeals) (Section 21)

(1) A person shall not be qualified for appointment as the Chairperson or member unless he —

(a) In the case of Chairperson, is or has been, or is qualified, to be a Judge of a High Court; and

(b) In the case of a Member, is or has been, or is qualified to be, a District Judge.

(2) A person shall not be qualified for appointment as a Special Director (Appeals) unless he —

(a) Has been Member of the Indian Legal Service and has held a post in Grade I of the Service; or

(b) Has been a Member of the Indian Revenue Service and has held a post equivalent to a Joint Secretary to the Government of India.

Term of Office

The Chairperson and every other Member shall hold office as such for a term of 5 years from the date on which he enters upon his office:

Provided that no Chairperson, or other member shall hold office as such after he has attained —

(a) In the case of the Chairperson, the age of 65 years;

(b) In the case of any other Member, the age of 62 years.

Terms and Conditions of Service

The salary and allowances payable to and the other terms and conditions of service of the Chairperson, other Members and the Special Director (Appeals) shall be such as may be prescribed:

Provided that neither the salary and allowances nor the other terms and conditions of service of the Chairperson or a Member shall be varied to his disadvantages after appointment.

Procedures and Powers of Appellate Tribunal and Special Director (Appeals)

Section 28 enables the Appellate Tribunal and the Special Director (Appeals) to adopt its own procedure. The proceedings of the Appellate Tribunal and the Special Director (Appeals) shall be deemed to be judicial proceedings.

(1) The Appellate Tribunal and the Special Director (Appeals) shall not be bound by the procedure laid down by the Code of Civil Procedure, 1908 (5 of 1908), but shall be guided by the principles of natural justice and, subject to the other provisions of this Act, the Appellate Tribunal and the Special Director (Appeals) shall have powers to regulate its own procedure.

(2) The Appellate Tribunal and the Special Director (Appeals) shall have, for the purpose of discharging its functions under this Act, the same powers as are vested in a civil court under the Code of Civil Procedure, 1908 (5 of 1980) while trying a suit in respect of the following matters, namely:

(a) Summoning and enforcing the attendance of any person and examining him on oath;

(b) Requiring the discovery and production of documents;

(c) Receiving evidence on affidavits;

(d) Subject to the provisions of Section 123 and 124 of the Indian Evidence Act, 1872, requisitioning any public record or document or copy of such record or document from any office;

(e) Issuing commissions for the examinations of witness or documents;

(f) Reviewing its decisions;

(g) Dismissing a representation of default or deciding it exparte;

(h) Setting aside any order of dismissal of any representation for default or any order passed by it exparte; and

(i) Any other matter, which may be prescribed by the Central Government.

(3) An order made by the Appellate Tribunal and the Special Director (Appeals) under this Act shall be executable by the Appellate Tribunal or the Special Director (Appeals) as a decree of civil court and, for this purpose, the Appellate Tribunal and the Special Director (Appeals) shall have all the powers of a civil court.

(4) Notwithstanding anything contained in the Sub-section (3), the Appellate tribunal or the Special Director (Appeals) may transmit any order made by it to a civil court having local jurisdiction and such civil court shall execute the order as if it were a decree made by that court.

(5) All proceedings before the Appellate Tribunal and the Special Director (Appeals) shall be deemed to be judicial proceedings within the meaning of Sections 193 and 228 of the Indian Penal Code (45 of 1860) and the Appellate Tribunal shall be deemed to be a civil court for the purposes of Sections 345 and 346 of the Code of Criminal Procedure, 1973 (2 of 1974).

Distribution of Business Amongst Benches

Section 29 provides for distribution of business of the Appellate Tribunal amongst the benches.

Where Benches are constituted, the Chairperson may, from time to time, by notification, make provisions as to the distribution of the business of the Appellate Tribunal amongst the Benches and also provide for the matters, which may be dealt with by each Bench.

Decision to be by Majority

Section 31 provides that the decision of the Appellate Tribunal shall be by majority.

If the Members of a Bench consisting of two Members differ in opinion on any point, they shall state the point or points on which they differ, and make a reference to the Chairperson who shall either hear the point or points himself or refer the case for hearing on such point or points by one or more of the other Members of the Appellate Tribunal and such point or points shall be decided according to the opinion of the majority of the Members of the Appellate Tribunal who have heard the case, including those who first heard it.

Right of Appellant to the assistance of legal practitioner or Chartered Accountant and of Government, to appoint presenting officers.

Section 32 provides that the appellant may take the assistance of a legal practitioner or a chartered accountant to present his case before the Appellate Tribunal and the Special Director (Appeals).

Civil court not to have jurisdiction

Section 34 bars the jurisdiction of the civil court in respect of matters to be dealt with by Adjudicating Authority or by the Appellate Tribunal or the Special Director (Appeals).

Appeal to High Court

Section 35 provides for filing an appeal to the High Court against the decision or order of the Appellate Tribunal on a question of law arising out of such decision or order.

Any person aggrieved by any decision or order of the Appellate Tribunal may file an appeal to the High Court within 60 days from the date of communication of the decision or order of the Appellate Tribunal to him on any question of law arising out of such order:

Provided that the High Court may, if it is satisfied that the appellant was prevented by sufficient cause from filing the appeal within the said period, allow it to be filed within a further period not exceeding 60 days.

Explanation: in this section "High Court" means —

(a) The High Court within the jurisdiction of which the aggrieved party ordinarily resides or carries on business or personally works for gain; and

(b) Where the Central Government is the aggrieved party, the High Court within the jurisdiction of which the respondent, or in a case where there are more than one respondent, any of the respondents, ordinarily resides or carries on business or personally works for gain.

9.6 DIRECTOR OF ENFORCEMENT

Directorate of Enforcement (Sec. 36)

1. The Central Government shall establish a Directorate of Enforcement with a Director and such other officers or class of officers as it thinks fit, who shall be called officers of Enforcement, for the purposes of this Act.

2. Without prejudice to provisions of Sub-sections (1), the Central Government may authorize the Director of Enforcement or an Additional Director of Enforcement or a Special Director of Enforcement or a Deputy Director of Enforcement to appoint officers of Enforcement below the rank of an Assistant Director of Enforcement.

3. Subject to such conditions and limitations as the Central Government may impose, an officer of Enforcement may exercise the powers and discharge the duties conferred or imposed on him under this Act.

Appointment of Officers of Enforcement

The Central Government has established the Directorate of Enforcement, vide Notification No. S.O.534 (E) dt. 1.6.2000, comprising the following officers as 'Officers of Enforcement', namely—

(a) Director of Enforcement,

(b) Special Director of Enforcement,

(c) Additional Director of Enforcement,

(d) Deputy Director of Enforcement,

(e) Deputy Legal Advisor,

(f) Assistant Director of Enforcement, and

(g) Assistant Legal Advisor.

Further, the Director of Enforcement has been empowered to appoint Chief Enforcement Officer, Enforcement Officer and Assistant Enforcement Officer, vide Notification No. S.O.536 (E), dt.1.6.2000.

Power of Search, Seizure etc. (Sec. 37)

1. The Director of Enforcement and other officers of Enforcement, not below the rank of an Assistant Director, shall take up for investigation the contravention referred to in Section 13.

2. Without prejudice to the provisions of sub-section (1), the Central Government may also, by notification, authorize any officer or class of officers in the Central Government, State Government or the Reserve Bank, not below the rank of an Under Secretary to the Government of India to investigate any contravention referred to in Section 13.

3. The officers referred to in sub-section (1) shall exercise the like powers which are conferred on Income-tax authorities under the Income Tax Act, 1961 (43 of 1961) and shall exercise such powers, subject to such limitations laid down under the Act.

Sections 36 to 38 provide for establishment of a Directorate of Enforcement, powers to be exercised by the officers of the Directorate of Enforcement and other officer authorized by the Central Government in respect of search, seizure, etc.

Sub-section (1) of Section 40 empowers the Central Government in the public interest and by notification to suspend or relax the provisions of the Act in certain circumstances. Sub-section (3) Provides that notification issued for suspension of relaxation shall be laid before each House of Parliament.

Contravention by Companies

Section 42 provides that where contravention of any of the provisions of this enactment is committed by a company, the person responsible for the conduct of its business shall be deemed to be guilty of the contravention.

(1) Where a person committing a contravention of any of the provisions of this Act or of any rule, direction or order made thereunder is a company, every person who, at the time the contravention was committed, was in charge of, and was responsible to, the company for the conduct of the business of the company

as well as the company, shall be deemed to be guilty of the contravention and shall be liable to be proceeded against and punished accordingly:

Provided that nothing contained in this Sub-section shall render any such person liable to punishment if he proves that the contravention took place without his knowledge or that he exercised all due diligence to prevent such contravention.

(2) Notwithstanding anything contained in Sub-section (1), where a contravention of any of the provisions of this Act or of any rule, direction or order made there under has been committed by a company and it is proved that the contravention has taken place with the consent or connivance or, is attributable to any neglect on the part of, any director, manager, secretary or other officer of the company, such director, manager, secretary or other officer shall also be deemed to be guilty of the contravention and shall be liable to be proceeded against and punished accordingly.

Explanation: For the purpose of this section—

(1) "Company" means any body corporate and includes a firm or other association of individuals; and

(2) "Director", in relation to a firm, means a partner in the firm.

Bar of Legal Proceedings

Section 44, bars the prosecution or legal proceedings against the officers of the Central Government or the Reserve Bank or any other person exercising any powers or discharging any functions or performing any duties under the provision of this enactment for anything done in good faith.

9.7 MONEY LAUNDERING WITH DECIDED CASES

Introduction

Money laundering refers to the practice of moving illegally acquired cash through financial and other systems so that it appears to be legally acquired.

Money laundering refers to the practice of moving illegally acquired cash through financial and other systems so that it appears to be legally acquired. Financial institutions such as banks, insurers, and securities and futures firms are usually considered the frontline in the war against illicit money movements. Money Laundering refers to the conversion or "Laundering" of money, which is illegally obtained, so as to make it appear to originate from a legitimate source. Money Laundering is being employed by launderers worldwide to conceal criminal activity associated with it such as drug / arms trafficking, terrorism and extortion. As per an estimate of the International Monetary Fund, the aggregate size of money laundering in the world could be somewhere between two and five percent of the worlds gross domestic product.

Money Laundering involves financial transactions, to conceal the identity, source, and/or destination of money. It is the main operation of underground economy.

Money Laundering involves financial transactions, to conceal the identity, source, and or destination of money. It is the main operation of underground economy. The Interpol General Secretariat Assembly in 1995 defines money laundering as, any act or attempted act to conceal or disguise the identity of illegally obtained proceeds, so that they appear to have originated from legitimate sources. The conversion of criminal incomes to forms that allows the offender unfettered spending and investment has been an ongoing concern to the law enforcement agencies.

After the attack on the twin towers in the U.S., the world has focused its attention on the entire concept of money laundering and has recognized it as a source of funding of terrorist activities. This could be between $800 billion to $2 trillion each year. Thereby, all over the world, the need has been recognized to control this form of illegal activity, which involves the misuse of financial systems all around the world.

Money laundering is a process by which criminals give the color of legality and legitimacy to slush funds. Ignoring economic vandalism, most crime is economic crime. In Black's Law of Lexicon the term laundering is being referred to as investment or other transfer of money flowing from racketeering, drug transactions and other sources (illegal sources) into legitimate channels so that its original source cannot be traced. Apart from the traditional activities of drugs, racketeering, kidnapping, gambling, procuring women and children, smuggling (alcohol, tobacco, medicines), armed robbery, counterfeiting and bogus invoicing, tax evasion and misappropriation of public funds, new markets are also flowering. These include smuggling, illegal labour and refugees, computer piracy, trafficking in works of art and antiquities, in stolen cars and parks, in protected species and human organs, forgery in arms, toxic and nuclear products etc.

> Money laundering is a process by which criminals give the colour of legality and legitimacy to slush funds.

Money Laundering as a Part of Organized Crime

The characteristics of organized crime are quite evident in money laundering as it is a group activity which is long-term and continuing; a criminal activity which is carried out often by more than one person; an activity which is carried out irrespective of national boundaries at large scale; and generates proceeds, which are often made available for illicit use. Criminals involved in money laundering commit three basic types of crimes, i.e., Crimes of passion or honour; Crimes of violence or vandalism; and Economic crimes — crime committed to make money. Most often crimes are committed for two reasons; for kicks (to prove that they can get away with it and for unscrupulous greed for quick money (they think that they can make more money from the crime than they can from the same amount of legitimate endeavours).

> Criminals involved in money laundering commit three basic types of crimes i.e. Crimes of passion or honor; Crimes of violence or vandalism; and Economic crimes.

Money Laundering: Basic Concept

Money laundering is the process, by which, large amounts of illegally obtained money is given the facade of having a legitimate source. Earlier the concept of money laundering was associated with organized crime alone. However, in recent times, the ambit of money laundering operations has dramatically increased.

The concept of money laundering originated in the U.S.A. It started with the attempt to disguise the ill-gotten wealth, obtained from trading in alcoholic beverages. American mobster Meyer Lansky transferred funds from small casinos to overseas accounts, especially Swiss banks, the term used for such activity is, 'capital flight'. The first reference to the term, 'Money Laundering' itself appeared during the Watergate scandal. Here illegal funds obtained for the president re-election were moved to Mexico and then brought back through a company to Miami. In this context the British newspaper coined the term 'Laundering.'

> The concept of money laundering originated in the U.S.A. It started with the attempt to disguise the ill-gotten wealth, obtained from trading in alcoholic beverages.

Negative Economic Effects of Money Laundering

The negative economic effects of money laundering on economic development are difficult to quantify, yet it is clear that such activity damages the financial sector institutions that are critical to economic growth, reduces productivity in the economy's real sector by diverting resources and encouraging crime and corruption, which slow down economic growth, and can distort the economy's external sector — international trade and capital flows — to the detriment of long-term economic development. Developing countries' strategies to establish offshore financial centers (OFCs) as vehicles for economic development are also impaired by significant money-laundering activity through OFC channels. Effective anti-money-laundering policies, on the other hand, reinforce a variety of other good governance policies that help sustain economic development, particularly through the strengthening of the financial sector.

OBJECTIVES OF MONEY LAUNDERING

The most important objective of Money Laundering activities are covering up of the factual ownership of illegitimately procured money and placement, layering and integration of such funds. Through money laundering, the launderer transforms the monetary proceeds derived from criminal activity into funds with an apparently legal source.

Objectives of Money Laundering and Rules for Bankers

The major objectives of Money Laundering activities are:

1. Concealing the true ownership of illegally-obtained money and
2. Placement, layering and integration of such funds
3. Two cardinal rules that are to be invariably observed by bank officials for steering clear of the Money Laundering Trap, are:
4. Know your customer (KYC) and,
5. Know your employee.

Money Laundering can be traced back to the Hawala Mechanism, which facilitated the conversion of money from black into white.

Stages in Money Laundering

There are three independent steps or stages in Money Laundering as shown below:

(1) Placement: It refers to the physical disposal of bulk cash proceeds derived from illegal activity.

(2) Layering: This term refers to the separation of illicit proceeds from their source by creating complex layers of financial transactions. Layering conceals the audit trail and provides anonymity.

(3) Integration: It refers to the re-injection of the laundered proceeds back into the economy in such a way that they re-enter the financial system as normal business funds.

Money laundering is thus a substantial effort and obscures the illegal source of money. Launderers for starters, find a bank in a foreign country which does not have very strict banking laws. They strike deals with such banks and then obtain some property discreetly. Later on, the funds are re-routed back to the country as legal money. Nowadays wire transfer systems are being used to make risk free transfers of money from one country to the other. Such money is basically used to prop up illegal activities such as smuggling, terrorist activities etc.

Thus it has been seen that banks have become a chief end of Money Laundering operations and monetary crime because they are endowed with a range of services and instruments that can be used to cover up the source of money. With their refined, coherent and beguiling behaviour, Money Launderers attempt to make bankers relax their guard so as to accomplish their purpose.

There can be different sources of laundering and hiding the source of money. Most countries require, transactions above a certain limit to be reported by the banks or financial institutions or organizations. If a person earns money in small change, but above the limit that needs to be reported, he can use a person already involved in heavy cash transactions to deposit his amount and not get caught in the process. Another method involves establishing a business whose cash inflow cannot be monitored, and funneling the small change into this business and paying taxes on it.

FORMS OF MONEY LAUNDERING OPERATIONS

The different methods which can be termed suspicious and indicative of money laundering operations include:

1. Crooked / Doubtful Transactions related to Money Laundering — Customers depositing cash through a large number of cash deposit slips into the similar account or customers having plentiful accounts into which large cash deposits are made. Each deposit is such that the quantity thereof is not noteworthy but the collective of all credits is ample. This is known as "smurfing."
2. A considerable boost in earnings in a sleeping account or large cash withdrawals from a formerly sleeping or immobile account, or from an account that has received an unforeseen large credit from abroad
3. Receipt or payment of big sums of cash, which have no clear rationale or connection to the account holder and / or his business
4. Disinclination to offer standard information when opening an account or providing negligible or untrue information
5. Depositing high value third party cheques authorized in favour of the customer or other transactions on behalf of non-account holders
6. Abrupt amplification in cash deposits of an entity with no explanation
7. Employees leading sumptuous ways of life that do not match their known sources of income

Money Laundering today, poses a major challenge to countries all over the world and thereby there have been international attempts to curb this problem of money laundering.

International Attempts to Curb Money Laundering

Keeping in mind the gravity of the problem, the Committee on Banking Regulations and Supervisory Practices was formulated at a meeting in Basle in Switzerland, in December 1988. It evolved a set of principles to address the dangers posed by Money Launderers. These principles deal with the prevention of criminal use of the banking system for the purpose of Money Laundering. Recommendations for banks and other financial institutions have been set out in the Basle Principles so that these institutions can protect themselves against Money Laundering. The

Basle Statement of Principles covers all aspects of laundering through the banking system.

Policies and Procedures to Curb Money Laundering
The Basle Principles suggest policies and procedures in four areas to curb Money Laundering as shown below: • *Customer Identification:* This re-emphasizes the wise saying 'Know Your Customer'(KYC). KYC necessitates that banks should make sensible pains to settle on the customers true identity, and must set up successful measures for verifying the *bona fides* of new customers. • *Compliance with Laws*: The rules and regulations pertaining to financial transactions as performed in different Banking related statutes, must be experimented. Banks should not tender services or make available dynamic aid in case of transactions where they have superior reason to assume that these are linked with Money Laundering activities. • *Cooperation with Law Enforcement agencies:* Banks should combine forces fully with national law enforcement authorities to the degree permitted by precise local regulations regarding Customer privacy. • *Adherence to the Statement*: Holding fast to the Statement entails that banks need to adopt policies that are unswerving with the Statement and guarantee that all staff members are well-versed of the bank's policy in this regard. Some chief factors in supporting loyalty to the Statement of Principles are staff training and putting into practice definite procedures for customer identification and keeping hold of in-house records of transactions. The Basle Principles set out an effective guideline for what banks and financial institutions should do to cope with Money Laundering.

Money Laundering in India: The Problem and Solutions

(a) Money Laundering and Drug Trafficking: In India, money laundering is largely connected with drug trafficking. The alternate remittance systems such as the Hawala transactions are used effectively for this very purpose. Offenders ensure that money does not reach the banking systems at all, so that they can escape being caught or discovered. The easy route here is usually the underground banking system which leaves no paper trial. These systems are based on trust and the fear of retribution. Such systems are based on family and gang alliances and have been found to be difficult to penetrate. People here deposit money in one country and are given a 'chit' or a 'seal.' On production of this 'chit' or 'seal' money is remitted to the person concerned.

(b) Liberalisation of Indian Economy: Moreover now with the liberalization of the Indian economy and the dismantling of various regulations, increasingly the risk of money laundering via banks has increased tremendously. The impact of money laundering in India is substantial, the Union Revenue Department recently unearthed 900 bank accounts, with a pooled deposit of nearly Rs. 1,000 crore being run with fabricated names of companies and persons in two dozen banks of Delhi alone. According to a KPMG study money laundered in India is approximately 2% to 3% of the country's GDP.

(c) Political Declaration and Global Programmes: While adopting the political declaration and global programme of action of the Resolution S-17.2 of 1990 and political declaration to adopt the national money laundering legislation and programme in 1998 by the General Assembly of United Nation, India enacted Prevention of Money Laundering Act, 2002. The Money Laundering Act defines the offence of money laundering as any activity connected with the 'proceeds of crime' which in turn is defined as any property or value of such property derived as a result of criminal activity relating to a 'Scheduled offence.' The schedule to the Act is in two parts. Part A lists waging of war against the government of India (Sections 121 and 121A of Indian Penal Code) and several offences under the Narcotics Drugs and Psychotropic Substances Act, 1985. Offences listed in Part B have now been subjected to a monetary limit of Rs. 3 million or more which was not there in the original Bill.

The Money Laundering Act defines the offence of money laundering as any activity connected with the 'proceeds of crime' which in turn is defined as any property or value of such property derived as a result of criminal activity relating to a'Scheduled offence.'

There has been much concern about the terror funds coming into country. In addition to that it is also widely believed that the stock market can also be potential investment destination for terrorist groups. In absence of the adequate laws and enforcement mechanism in place, it is difficult to trace the source of money coming into the country and going outside from the country. Given the above context, anti-money laundering laws and regulations assume utmost significance.

Prevention of Money Laundering (amendment) Bill, 2008 (PMLA) is yet another milestone in the wide spectrum of anti-money laundering initiatives by government of India. This Bill introduces new category of offences that have cross-border implications for fighting terrorism. Insider trading and market manipulation will be treated as a laundering offence and invite stricter punishment. Offences related to human trafficking, smuggling of migrants, piracy and environmental crimes, over invoicing and under invoicing under customs are also punishable under PMLA. With the passing of Prevention of Money Laundering (Amendment) Act, all casinos, payment gateways like Mastercard, Visa and Western Union and even Credit Card deals will be monitored by law. These organizations will be required to report details of all suspected transactions to the government.

The substantive law aspect of the act seems less well developed, compared to the US Patriot Actor the EU Directives, the crimes included under the money laundering are fewer. Significant omissions in the Schedule of Money Laundering Act to the new law are lack of any references to offences relating to tax evasion, smuggling, foreign trade law violations and foreign exchange manipulations on account of these offences. Proceeds of crime relating to these offences, therefore, will remain outside the scope of the Money Laundering Act. It will be the case also with Schedule B offences if the amount involved in a case is less than Rs.3 million.

It is also somewhat incongruous that large-scale manipulations of foreign exchange, let us say arising out of tax evasion or import/export violations, will be mere civil offences under FEMA and will attract no penalty under the anti-money laundering law, yet the same can lead to preventive detention under COFEPOSA. Though the Money Laundering Act has been passed, but the rules to effect its operations are yet to come.

In India, a number of Acts have existed which played the role of prevention of money laundering, though these were not so named. However, in India, we have certain statutes, as given below that incorporate measures which attempt to address the problems of money laundering:

The Conservation of Foreign Exchange and Prevention of Smuggling Activities Act, 1974; The Income Tax Act, 1961, The Benami Transactions (Prohibition) Act, 1988, The Indian Penal Code and Code of Criminal Procedure, 1973, The Narcotic Drugs and Psychotropic Substances Act, 1985, The Prevention of Illicit Traffic in Narcotic Drugs and Psychotropic Substances Act, 1988.

RBI Role in Curbing Money Laundering

The RBI too has played an important role in curbing the menace of money laundering. The RBI issued the Know-Your-Customers (KYC) Guidelines — Anti Money Laundering Standards on 16th August 2005. The Government has also established a Financial Intelligence Unit-India (FIU-IND), in rank with FATF recommendations. The FIU would be given the Suspicious Activity Reports from all FIs and would study them before passing them to the Enforcement Directorate for investigation and prosecution. The RBI has asked all the banks to put the policy with the sanction of their boards, within the next three months. The RBI has stressed that banks can successfully control and decrease their risks only if they have an understanding of the normal and practical activity of the customer so that they have the means of spotting transactions that fall outside the standard model of activity.

In the context of internet banking, there is always a danger that being extremely mobile, these transactions shall remain undetected. Thereby such banks have been asked to open accounts only after proper physical introduction and substantiation of the customer. The online banking systems are also required to keep a record of all the transactions or series of transactions taking place within a month, the character and worth of which may be set by the Central Government. This will sufficiently guard in opposition to any abuse of the Internet banking services for the intention of money laundering.

The RBI's know your customer standards are important in the context of controlling money laundering. As per these standards Banks must outline their KYC policies slotting in the following four key fundamentals:

- Customer Acceptance Policy;
- Customer Identification Procedures;
- Monitoring of Transactions; and
- Risk management.

Despite the various measures that have been undertaken it has to be understood that India's anti-money laundering regime is still in its early stages and banks need to put in place, better systems to ensure they do not fall prey to misuse. Banks can effectively reduce the risks of banking transactions if they identify transactions that fall outside the regular pattern of consumer's activities. Banks need to have an effective anti-money laundering technology system. These have yet to be effectively implemented in the country.

Money Laundering and Global Financial System

Money laundering is a serious threat to global financial system and good governance. It is also boosting international crimes and terrorist activities. Governments in various countries today have come up with different legislations to deal with this menace. However more needs to be done in this regard. Black money in India, it is estimated accounts for around 40% of India's GDP. Moreover it is politicians in India, who are high risk customers who indulge in this activity.

In times of globalization, Indian financial institutions and banks would like to become important players in the financial setup. This could be achieved only by ensuring that proper prevention of money laundering norms are in place and have been setup effectively. In the absence of these norms it is likely that the indigenous institutions and banks shall be black listed by the foreign countries.

Thereby there is a need to not only effectively implement the anti-money laundering operations, but also to ensure that there is a constant review of the anti-money laundering (AML) programme and timely upgradation as well. Banks need to strictly adhere to the Know Your Customer (KYC) Guidelines, setup by the RBI.

Anti-Money Laundering and Combating Terrorist Financing

Need for Money Laundering Low

Every year, huge amounts of funds are generated from illegal activities. These funds are mostly in the form of cash. The criminals who generate these funds need to bring them into the legitimate financial system. Over $1.5 trillion of illegal funds are laundered each year.

Consequences of Money Laundering

Finances Terrorism: Money laundering provides terrorists with funds to carry out their activities.

Undermines rule of law and governance: Rule of Law is a precondition for economic development — Clear and certain rules applicable for all.

Affects macro economy: Money launderers put money into unproductive assets to avoid detection.

Affects the integrity of the financial system: Financial system advancing criminal purposes undermines the function and integrity of the financial system.

Reduces Revenue and Control: Money laundering diminishes government tax revenue and weakens government control over the economy.

The Prevention of Money Laundering Act, 2002

Money Laundering Act is an endorsement of various international conventions to which India is a party, and it seeks to declare laundering of monies carried through serious crimes a criminal offence. The Act also lists modalities of disclosure by financial institutions regarding reportable transactions, confiscation of the proceeds of crime, declaring money laundering as an extraditable offence and promoting international cooperation in investigation of money laundering.

The Act allows for confiscation of property derived from or involved in money laundering. Co-operative banks, non-banking financial companies, chit funds and housing financial institutions come under its ambit.

The Act also makes it mandatory for banking companies, financial institutions and intermediaries to maintain a record of all transactions of a prescribed value and to furnish information whenever sought within a prescribed time period. Thus, these entities are required to maintain the record of the transactions for 10 years.

The minimum threshold limit for certain categories of offences under the Indian Penal Code and other legislations has been fixed at Rs.30 lakh in the Bill. This limit is further likely to be reduced to Rs.10 lakh.

Objective of the Act

An Act to prevent money laundering and to provide for confiscation of property derived from, or involved in, money laundering and for matters connected therewith or incidental thereto.

Important Terms in the Act

Attachment means prohibition of transfer, conversion, disposition or movement of property by an order issued under Chapter III;

Proceeds of Crime means any property derived or obtained, directly or indirectly, by any person as a result of criminal activity relating to a scheduled offence or the value of any such property;

Property means any property or assets of every description, whether corporeal or incorporeal, movable or immovable, tangible or intangible and includes deeds and instruments evidencing title to, or interest in, such property or assets, wherever located;

scheduled Offence means—

- the offences specified under Part A of the Schedule; or
- the offences specified under Part B of the Schedule if the total value involved in such offences is thirty lakh rupees or more;

Transfer includes sale, purchase, mortgage, pledge, gift, loan or any other form of transfer of right, title, possession or lien;

Value means the fair market value of any property on the date of its acquisition by any person, or if such date cannot be determined, the date on which such property is possessed by such person.

Offence of Money-laundering

Offence of money-laundering: Whosoever directly or indirectly attempts to indulge or knowingly assists or knowingly is a party or is actually involved in any process or activity connected with the proceeds of crime and projecting it as untainted property shall be guilty of offence of money laundering.

Punishment for money-laundering: Whoever commits the offence of money-laundering shall be punishable with rigorous imprisonment for a term which shall not be less than three years but which may extend to seven years and shall also be liable to fine which may extend to five lakh rupees: Provided that where the proceeds of crime involved in money-laundering relates to any offence specified under paragraph 2 of Part A of the Schedule, the provisions of this section shall have effect as if for the words "which may extend to seven years", the words "which may extend to ten years" had been substituted.

9.8 ATTACHMENT, ADJUDICATION AND CONFISCATION

Attachment of property involved in money-laundering, where the Director, or any other officer not below the rank of Deputy Director authorised by him for the purposes of this section, has reason to believe (the reason for such belief to be recorded in writing), on the basis of material in his possession, that

- any person is in possession of any proceeds of crime;
- such person has been charged of having committed a scheduled offence; and
- such proceeds of crime are likely to be concealed, transferred or dealt with in any manner which may result in frustrating any proceedings relating to confiscation of such proceeds of crime under this Chapter, he may, by order in writing, provisionally attach such property for a period

not exceeding ninety days from the date of the order, in the manner provided in the Second Schedule to the Income-tax Act, 1961 (43 of 1961) and the Director or the other officer so authorised by him, as the case may be, shall be deemed to be an officer under sub-rule (e) of rule 1 of that Schedule:

The Director, or any other officer not below the rank of Deputy Director, shall, immediately after attachment under Sub-section (1), forward a copy of the order, along with the material in his possession, referred to in that Sub-section, to the Adjudicating Authority, in a sealed envelope, in the manner as may be prescribed and such Adjudicating Authority shall keep such order and material for such period as may be prescribed.

Every order of attachment made under Sub-section (1) shall cease to have effect after the expiry of the period specified in that Sub-section or on the date of an order made under Sub-section (2) of Section 8, whichever is earlier.

Nothing in this section shall prevent the person interested in the enjoyment of the immovable property attached under Sub-section (1) from such enjoyment.

The Director or any other officer who provisionally attaches any property under Sub-section (1) shall, within a period of thirty days from such attachment, file a complaint stating the facts of such attachment before the Adjudicating Authority.

Adjudicating Authorities, Composition, Powers, etc.

The Central Government shall, by notification, appoint one or more Adjudicating Authorities to exercise jurisdiction, powers and authority conferred by or under this Act.

An Adjudicating Authority shall consist of a Chairperson and two other Members: Provided that one Member each shall be a person having experience in the field of law, administration, finance or accountancy. A person shall, however, not be qualified for appointment as Member of an Adjudicating Authority,—

(a) in the field of law, unless he

- is qualified for appointment as District Judge; or
- has been a member of the Indian Legal Service and has held a post in Grade I of that service;
- in the field of finance, accountancy or administration unless he possesses such qualifications, as may be prescribed.

(4) The Central Government shall appoint a Member to be the Chairperson of the Adjudicating Authority.

(5) Subject to the provisions of this Act,—

- the jurisdiction of the Adjudicating Authority may be exercised by Benches thereof;
- a Bench may be constituted by the Chairperson of the Adjudicating Authority with one or two Members as the Chairperson of the Adjudicating Authority may deem fit;
- the Benches of the Adjudicating Authority shall ordinarily sit at New Delhi and at such other places as the Central Government may, in consultation with the Chairperson, by notification, specify;

- the Central Government shall, by notification, specify the areas in relation to which each Bench of the Adjudicating Authority may exercise jurisdiction.

Notwithstanding anything contained in Sub-section (5), the Chairperson may transfer a Member from one Bench to another Bench.

If at any stage of the hearing of any case or matter it appears to the Chairperson or a Member that the case or matter is of such a nature that it ought to be heard by a Bench consisting of two Members, the case or matter may be transferred by the Chairperson or, as the case may be, referred to him for transfer, to such Bench as the Chairperson may deem fit.

The Chairperson and every Member shall hold office as such for a term of five years from the date on which he enters upon his office: Provided that no Chairperson or other Member shall hold office as such after he has attained the age of sixty-two years.

9.9 OBLIGATIONS OF BANKING COMPANIES, FINANCIAL INSTITUTIONS AND INTERMEDIARIES

Banking companies, financial institutions and intermediaries to maintain records.

Every banking company, financial institution and intermediary shall—

- Maintain a record of all transactions, the nature and value of which may be prescribed, whether such transactions comprise of a single transaction or a series of transactions integrally connected to each other, and where such series of transactions take place within a month;
- Furnish information of transactions referred to in clause (a) to the Director within such time as may be prescribed;
- Verify and maintain the records of the identity of all its clients, in such manner as may be prescribed.

Provided that where the principal officer of a banking company or financial institution or intermediary, as the case may be, has reason to believe that a single transaction or series of transactions integrally connected to each other have been valued below the prescribed value so as to defeat the provisions of this section, such officer shall furnish information in respect of such transactions to the Director within the prescribed time.

The records referred to in sub-section (1) shall be maintained for a period of ten years from the date of cessation of the transactions between the clients and the banking company or financial institution or intermediary, as the case may be.

No civil proceeding against banking companies, financial institutions, etc., in certain cases — Save as otherwise provided in Section 13, the banking companies, financial institutions, intermediaries and their officers shall not be liable to any civil proceedings against them for furnishing information under clause (b) of Sub-section (1) of Section 12.

9.10 SUMMONS, SEARCHES AND SEIZURES, ETC.

Search and seizure — (1) Where the Director, on the basis of information in his possession, has reason to believe (the reason for such belief to be recorded in writing) that any person —

- has committed any act which constitutes money-laundering, or
- is in possession of any proceeds of crime involved in money-laundering, or
- is in possession of any records relating to money-laundering, then, subject to the rules made in this behalf, he may authorise any officer subordinate to him to
  - — enter and search any building, place, vessel, vehicle or aircraft where he has reason to suspect that such records or proceeds of crime are kept;
  - — break open the lock of any door, box, locker, safe, almirah or other receptacle for exercising the powers conferred by clause (a) where the keys thereof are not available;
  - — seize any record or property found as a result of such search;
  - — place marks of identification on such record or make or cause to be made extracts or copies therefrom;
  - — make a note or an inventory of such record or property;
  - — examine on oath any person, who is found to be in possession or control of any record or property, in respect of all matters relevant for the purposes of any investigation under this Act.

9.11 HAWALA TRANSACTIONS

*"**Hawala**"* is an Arabic word meaning the transfer of money or information between two persons using a third person. The system dates to the Arabic traders as a means of avoiding robbery. It predates western banking by several centuries. The Hawala Mechanism left virtually no paper trail, which would attract investigations. The profits generated from Hawala were surreptitiously invested in real estate, gilt edged securities etc., to launder them.

*"**Hawala**"* is an Arabic word meaning the transfer of money or information between two persons using a third person.

> A Hawala transaction simply means that you pay rupees over here in India and in return get dollars abroad. For instance, if you want to do a hawala transaction from Mumbai to Dubai, then by paying Rs.1 lac in Mumbai, you can transfer 8000 dirhams in Dubai.

The Uses: A hawala transaction is an illegal transaction, which is carried out by businessmen, people who want to show bogus exports and even importers. Importers indulge in such hawala transactions by sending a part of the money abroad through this route and thus bringing the goods into the country at much lower rates. By showing lower rates for the goods they are able to save on the import duty. Also, individuals who have surplus black money indulge in such transactions by paying cash over here and getting dollars from abroad. These are also shown as gifts received by some relatives living abroad. Exporters benefit greatly by this route since the export income is 100 per cent tax-free and can help them to convert their black money into official income. The Benefits Profits derived from export of software (including some of the infotech-enabled services) are exempt from Income Tax under Section 80HHE of the Income Tax Act.

A hawala transaction is an illegal transaction, which is carried out by businessmen, people who want to show bogus exports and even importers. Importers indulge in such hawala transactions by sending a part of the money abroad through this route and thus bringing the goods into the country at much lower rates.

An Interesting Case of Hawala Transaction

An Example: Let us take a simple example to prove our case. Assume there is an existing BSE-listed company, which is closed and is not trading at all. Today, there are over 7000 companies listed on the BSE, of which more than 4500 companies are in the B2B category and are hardly traded. Many of these companies may have even closed down and are mostly based in places like Ahmedabad, Chennai and Hyderabad. It can happen that two or three people get together and take over such a company changing its name to an infotech company. It is even possible that the existing promoters of the company simply change the name of their company to a software company. By installing a few computers, modems, data transmission lines and other equipment, a software company is born.

Some computer literate staff is also hired to show some kind of activity present in the office. Such companies do not even be having the requisite infrastructure or the requisite personnel required for running a software company forget aside any export orders. The next step is to set up a subsidiary abroad by renting a place or just even employing a person to conduct the operations. Most of the exports are done to duty free ports such as Hong Kong, Singapore or Dubai where the money can be remitted back. After that, the promoters conduct hawala transactions by paying cash over here and getting dollars from abroad through the subsidiary. The same dollars transferred from abroad are shown as software exports in the company's books. In this way the company is able to report decent sales figures in its balance sheet by the way of export income.

The next step is to catch a flamboyant market operator through whom rumours about the company can be floated in the market. The operator then spreads stories such as the company has got big software orders or tie-ups and is going to report excellent profits. Naturally, the bogus export income drives up the net profit reflecting a healthy Earnings Per Share for the company. Since, the P/E of the company appears to be quite low in comparison with the industry standards; the stock appears to be an excellent buy.

The market operators start providing liquidity in the counter and consequently the volumes in the counter start rising. Many of the deals take place between two or three operators itself who start creating a demand for the stock. The stock price of the company is jacked up touching three to five upper circuits in succession. The promoters taking advantage of this situation start dumping their own stock to the small investors who in turn enter to buy. In the end we have the small investors who are left holding the stock which they have purchased at the high prices.

Thus the promoters are able to benefit in two ways. Firstly they are able to get a good price for the dead stocks of their company, which were not being traded at all and secondly are able to convert their cash into official export income at a low premium without paying any income tax.

However, the question which authority is responsible to check whether the companies are actually engaged in and whether their exports are genuine or not? If no one is then somebody or authority has to be appointed who can monitor the activities of these companies. This is necessary so that the investors can be more enlightened about such companies before putting their hard-earned money into them. This is the magic of technology !

How Hawala Works

An initial transaction can be a remittance from a customer (CA) from country A, or a payment arising from some prior obligation, to another customer (CB) in country B. A hawaladar from country A (HA) receives funds in one currency from CA and, in return, gives CA a code for authentication purposes. He then instructs his country B correspondent (HB) to deliver an equivalent amount in the local currency to a designated beneficiary (CB), who needs to disclose the code to receive the funds. HA can be remunerated by charging a fee or through an exchange rate spread. After the remittance, HA has a liability to HB, and the settlement of their positions is made by various means, either financial or goods and services. Their positions can also be transferred to other intermediaries, who can assume and consolidate the initial positions and settle at wholesale or multilateral levels.

The settlement of the liability position of HA vis-a-vis HB that was created by the initial transaction can be done through imports of goods or "reverse hawala." A reverse hawala transaction is often used for investment purposes or to cover travel, medical, or education expenses from a developing country. In a country subject to foreign exchange and capital controls, a customer (XB) interested in transferring funds abroad for, in this case, university tuition fees, provides local currency to HB and requests that the equivalent amount be made available to the customer's son (XA) in another country (A). Customers are not aware if the transaction they initiate is a hawala or a reverse hawala transaction. HB may use HA directly if funds are needed by XB in country A or indirectly by asking him to use another correspondent in another country, where funds are expected to be delivered. A reverse hawala transaction does not necessarily imply that the settlement transaction has to involve the same hawaladars; it could involve other hawaladars and be tied to a different transaction. Therefore, it can be simple or complex. Furthermore, the settlement can also take place through import transactions. For instance, HA would settle his debt by financing exports to country B, where HB could be the importer or an intermediary.

> A reverse hawala transaction is often used for investment purposes or to cover travel, medical, or education expenses from a developing country.

The 'Hawala' mechanism is amongst the original sources of money laundering. 'Hawala' is an Arabic word connoting the transfer of money or information involving two persons using a third person. Hawala is an effective, efficient system of remitting money. It implies more profit to the parties involved. A hawala transaction can be completed within a day or two and is free of bureaucratic control and other hassles. Essentially the system is based on trust, and proper links and connections between people. The third party in this transaction has to be trusted in order to make such transactions a success. The Hawala system offers better opportunities for placement, integration and layering of illegally earned money and hence is usually considered to be a better system of money laundering. It has been usually found that such a system is impossible to trace.

> Hawala is an effective, efficient system of remitting money. It implies more profit to the parties involved. A hawala transaction can be completed within a day or two and is free of bureaucratic control and other hassles.

Hawala Transactions with Decided Cases

Even today after the big burst of the Dotcom bubble almost "EVERY" investor dreams of owning stocks of technology companies looking at their high growth potential and fantastic returns they provide. Since, many of the infotech stocks are out of reach of the small investor considering their phenomenal prices; they rush for the smaller and the relatively cheap infotech stocks. But every company is not TCS or Infosys. Some of them are the shell companies which have the only business of laundering the money. Many techies have started investing in the shares and they look for the attractive growth prospects. How do such companies operate and show decent earnings is the main question? There seems to be a kind of nexus between the export earnings of some technology companies and money laundering transactions.

Many of these so-called software companies were known to be using the Hawala route in order to show income from software exports. Getting the knowledge about these transactions was not a big deal. It is provided to these companies by the CA's, Lawyers and other professionals who knows the transactional loopholes.

When income-tax authorities busted a Delhi-based software company that was doing business with a blue chip IT company, they found to their horror that there were no computers in the office premises. The ones that were there were still packed. The son of the software company owner told one investigator, "My father does not even know what a mouse of a computer is, let alone the meaning of software." Shell-shocked investigators realized that this Delhi-based company had already transacted business worth Rs.500 crore with the blue chip company. It was only later that they discovered no business had been transacted; only money had been rolled over to improve valuation. When the income tax officials took up the matter with finance ministry officials, they were told to keep quiet as it could hurt India's image as an IT destination.

Questions

Section — A Objective Type

1. State the objects of the FEMA.
2. Define currency as per FEMA.
3. What is Current account Transaction?
4. What are Capital Account Transactions?
5. Who is an Authorised person as per FEMA?
6. What is Foreign Exchange?
7. What is Foreign Security as per FEMA?
8. Expand – NRI and PIO.
9. Name the composition of Directorate of Enforcement.
10. Name the composition of Appellate Tribunal as per FEMA.
11. What is money laundering?
12. What is Hawala Transaction?

Section — B Analytical Type

1. What are the objectives of FEMA?
2. What are the powers of Appellate Tribunal and Special Director (Appeals) as per FEMA?
3. Discuss the contravention and penal provisions of FEMA.
4. Write a note on Directorate of Enforcement under FEMA.
5. Briefly explain the different forms of money laundering.
6. Explain the different modes of Hawala transactions.

Section — C Essay Type

1. Discuss in brief the Salient features of FEMA.
2. Discuss the decided cases on money laundering in India.
3. Bring out the leading decided cases of Hawala transactions applicable to India.

INDIAN COMPANIES ACT, 2013

Module Objectives

After reading this chapter, you should be able to:

- Know the meaning of the terms company and types of company
- Know all about Memorandum of Association and Articles of Association
- Understand the concept and process of Initial Public Offer (IPO), book building
- Distinguish between private and public company
- Understand different kinds of meeting, agenda, quorum and resolutions
- Know the different methods of winding up of the companies

10.1 THE COMPANIES ACT, 2013

Any person desirous of running a large business needs huge funds and resources, which generally he is not able to contribute himself. He, therefore, wants some others to join him either in partnership or in a company. A partnership firm is generally suitable for small to medium size businesses, but for a large enterprise, company is often preferred. We shall study the nature, advantages and procedure of forming a company.

Administration

The Companies Act is administered by the Central Government through Department of Company Affairs and the Offices of Registrar of Companies, Official Liquidators, Public Trustee, Company Law Board, Director of Inspection, etc. The Registrar of Companies controls the task of incorporation of new companies and the administration of running companies.

Meaning and Definition of a Company

"Company" means a company formed and registered under this Act or an existing company as defined in the Act.

"Existing Company" means a company formed and registered under any of the previous companies law (i.e., Act of 1866, 1882 and 1913).

Company is a voluntary association of persons formed for the purpose of doing business, having a distinct name and limited liability. It is juristic person having a separate legal entity distinct from the members who constitute it, capable of rights and duties of its own and endowed with the potential of perpetual succession.

The Indian Companies Act, 1956 defines joint stock company as *"a company limited by shares having a permanent paid up or nominal share capital of fixed amount divided into shares also of fixed amount, held and transferable as stock and formed on the principle of having in its members only the holders of those shares or stocks and no other persons."*

Characteristics of a Company

1. **Separate Legal Entity:** A company is a distinct legal entity, different from its members or shareholders. The company may hold property, make contracts, employ persons, sue or be sued in its own name.
2. **Limited Liability of Members:** The liability of the members of a company is limited to the amount remaining unpaid on the shares subscribed by them. Thus, in case of fully paid-up share, the members cannot be asked to contribute any further if the company goes into liquidation.
3. **Perpetual Succession:** In case of partnership firm, the partnership comes to an end on the death, insolvency or retirement of any partner or admission of new partner. The partners may agree to continue the same business, but under a new partnership agreement. Whereas a company enjoys continuous existence, members may come and go, the shareholders may change on account of transfer or transmission of shares, but the company survives, till wound up.

4. **Common Seal:** A company has a common seal, which is the signature of that company. The company's seal is affixed on all documents executed for and on its behalf.
5. **Separate Property Ownership:** A company may own and dispose of its property in its own name. The property of the company is not the property of its shareholders. Shareholders are not co-owners of the assets of a company.
6. **Transferable Shares:** Shares held in a company are movable property and are freely transferable. Shareholders may transfer their shares to another person and this does not affect the funds of the company, its capital remains intact. A private company may impose certain restrictions on the transfer of its shares.
7. **Capacity of sue and being sued:** A company is capable of entering into contracts and enforcing its rights under the contracts. It can sue and be sued in its own name.

10.2 KINDS OF COMPANIES

We can classify companies broadly into three types based on the mode of incorporation. They are:

1. Chartered Companies,
2. Statutory Companies, and
3. Registered Companies.

Chartered Companies: Companies incorporated under a special Royal charter issued by the King or Queen are called "Chartered Companies." They are regulated by the provisions of that charter. Such companies were generally started in the 17th and 18th centuries. The East India Company, Bank of England are some examples of chartered companies. In India Chartered Companies are not in existence now, because there is no monarchy.

Statutory Companies

Companies incorporated under the Special Act of Parliament or legislature are called "Statutory Companies". For example, The Reserve Bank of India, The State Bank of India, Life Insurance Corporation, The Indian Airlines and The State Trading Corporation of India. The activities of Statutory Companies are governed by the special act under which they are established.

A company not having any limit on the liability of its members is called an unlimited company.

Registered Companies: Companies incorporated through registration with the Registrar of Companies under the provisions of the Companies Act, 1956 are called "Registered Companies." They are also called 'Incorporated Companies.' Registered Companies are of the following types:

Based on the liability of the members, registered companies are:

1. Unlimited companies;
2. Companies limited by guarantee; and
3. Companies limited by shares.

1. Unlimited Companies

A company not having any limit on the liability of its members is called an unlimited company. The members of unlimited companies are like a sole proprietor or partners of a firm, liable for its debts without any limit. The concept of unlimited liability does not conform to corporate concept, which necessarily postulates limited liability. Hence, unlimited companies are rare but not extinct.

2. Companies Limited by Guarantee

Companies limited by guarantee are formed to promote art, culture, science, religion, trade and sports. A guarantee company may be formed with or without share capital.

Companies limited by guarantee are formed to promote art, culture, science, religion, trade and sports. A guarantee company may be formed with or without share capital. Where the company is without share capital, it raises needed funds through entrance fees and subscriptions. Where the company has share capital, the liability of members, in addition to the shares held by them, is extended to certain additional amount guaranteed by them to pay company's debts in the event of winding up. The additional amount to be paid is laid down in Memorandum or Articles of Association.

3. Companies Limited by Shares

In a limited company, the liability of the members is limited to the amount of the shares held by them. In the event of its winding up, a shareholder can be called upon to pay only the unpaid amount (if any) on shares held by him, and not even a paise more, whatever may be the debts of the company.

In a limited company, the liability of the members is limited to the amount of the shares held by them.

The companies limited by shares and guarantees may be classified into two types:

(a) Private limited companies.

(b) Public limited companies.

(a) Private Company

A company having a minimum paid-up share capital of one lakh rupees or such higher paid-up share capital as may be prescribed, and which by its articles, —

(i) restricts the right to transfer its shares;

(ii) except in case of One Person Company, limits the number of its members to two hundred:

Provided that where two or more persons hold one or more shares in a company jointly, they shall, for the purposes of this clause, be treated as a single member:

Provided further that — (A) persons who are in the employment of the company; and (B) persons who, having been formerly in the employment of the company, were members of the company while in that employment and have continued to be members after the employment ceased, shall not be included in the number of members; and

(iii) Prohibits any invitation to the public to subscribe for any securities of the company.

(b) Public Company

Public company means a company which—

(a) is not a private company;

(b) Has a minimum paid-up share capital of five lakh rupees or such higher paid-up capital, as may be prescribed:

Provided that a company which is a subsidiary of a company, not being a private company, shall be deemed to be public company for the purposes of this Act even where such subsidiary company continues to be a private company in articles.

The other forms of company ownership are:

1. Government Companies
2. Foreign Companies
3. Holding and Subsidiary Companies.

1. Government Companies

Section 617 of Companies Act, defines a Government Company as one in which not less than fifty one percent of the paid up capital is held by the Central Government, or by any State Governments, or partly by the Central Government and partly by one or more State Governments, and includes a company which is a subsidiary of a Government Company.

2. Foreign Companies

Companies falling under the following two classes are called foreign companies, namely:

(a) Companies incorporated outside India which, after the commencement of this Act, establish a place of business within India; and

(b) Companies incorporated outside India, which have, before the commencement of this Act, established a place of business within India and continue to have an established place of business within India at the commencement of this Act.

In brief, a foreign company is one, which is registered outside India but has a place/s of business in India. The operations of these companies (in the territory of India) are governed by the regulations laid down by the Indian Companies Act.

3. Holding and Subsidiary Companies

A holding company is one which holds more than 50 percent of the nominal value of the equity share capital of another company or which controls the composition of the Board of Directors of another company. Such other company is known as subsidiary company. In other words, a subsidiary company is one whose majority of shares is over 50 percent are held by the holding company.

4. Associate Company

Associate company, in relation to another company, means a company in which that other company has a significant influence, but which is not a subsidiary company of the company having such influence and includes a joint venture company.

Explanation—

For the purposes of this clause, "significant influence" means control of at least twenty per cent of total share capital, or of business decisions under an agreement.

5. One-person Company

The 2013 Act introduces a new type of entity to the existing list, i.e., apart from forming a public or private limited company, the 2013 Act enables the formation of a new entity, a 'one-person company' (OPC). An OPC means a company with only one person as its member [Section 3(1) of 2013 Act].

6. Small Company

A small company has been defined as a company, other than a public company.

(i) Paid-up share capital of which does not exceed 50 lakh INR or such higher amount as may be prescribed which shall not be more than five crore INR.

(ii) Turnover of which as per its last profit and loss account does not exceed two crore INR or such higher amount as may be prescribed which shall not be more than 20 crore INR.

As set out in the 2013 Act, this section will not be applicable to the following:

1. A holding company or a subsidiary company
2. A company registered under section 8
3. A company or body corporate governed by any special Act [Section 2(85) of 2013 Act]

7. Dormant Company

The 2013 Act states that a company can be classified as dormant when it is formed and registered under this 2013 Act for a future project or to hold an asset or intellectual property and has no significant accounting transaction. Such a company or an inactive one may apply to the ROC in such manner as may be prescribed for obtaining the status of a dormant company [Section 455 of 2013 Act].

8. Banking Company

Banking company means a banking company as defined in clause (c) of Section 5 of the Banking Regulation Act, 1949.

Distinction between a Private Company and a Public Company

Private Company	*Public Company*
1. Requires minimum paid-up capital of *one lakh rupees*	1. Requires minimum paid-up capital of *five lakh rupees*
2. Requires minimum two members	2. Requires minimum seven members
3. Maximum limit of 200 members	3. No maximum limit
4. Atleast two directors	4. Atleast three directors required
5. Consent of directors need not be filed with the Registrar	5. Consent of directors is to be filed with the Registrar

6. Raises capital by private arrangement, public subscription is not allowed	6. Raises capital by inviting public subscription or by private arrangement
7. Shares not transferable except for provisions in the Articles	7. Shares are freely transferable, and may be even quoted on Stock Exchange
8. No restriction on managerial remuneration	8. Restrictions on total managerial remuneration
9. The words 'Private Limited' are added to the company's name	9. The word 'Limited' is added to the company's name

Conversion of a Private Company into Public Company

A private limited company is converted into public limited company, by any of the three modes, namely, by default, by operation of law and by an act of violation.

Conversion by Default

Private company imposes three characteristics restrictions, namely:

(a) restriction on transfer of shares;

(b) restrictions on public invitation to subscribe to its shares and debentures and

(c) restriction on the maximum number of its members, which should not exceed 200.

If default is made in complying with any of these restrictions, the company, shall cease to be a private company and all provisions applicable to public company shall apply to that company.

The company Law Board may, however, on an application grant relief in committing the default, and from the date of such order, the company will again be entitled to all the privileges and exemptions available to a private company.

Conversion by Operation of Law

A Private company is deemed to be a public company, in following cases:

(a) when 25% or more of its paid up share capital is held by one or more bodies corporate;

(b) when its average annual turnover (during the last 3 years) exceeds Rs.10 crores;

(c) when it holds 25% or more of the paid up share capital of a public company; or

(d) when it accepts or renews deposits from the public after making an invitation by an advertisement.

Within 3 months after any of the above contingency arises, the fact should be notified to the Registrar.

The Registrar then makes necessary amendments in records and documents of the company, the word 'private' is deleted from the name of the company, a new certificate of incorporation is issued, the company makes necessary amendments in its memorandum and articles, and the company is deemed to be a public company.

Conversion by an Act of Violation

A private company may get itself voluntarily converted into a public company by following the procedure given below:

1. Convene a Board Meeting and decide the time, place and agenda for convening a General Meeting to alter the name and Articles of Association or to adopt a new set of Articles applicable to a public company.
2. Send notice for the General Meeting proposing the Special Resolutions along with Explanatory Statement.
3. Ensure that the quorum is fulfilled at the General Meeting and the Special Resolutions are passed to the following effect:
   (i) to delete the articles applicable to a private company only and insert new articles that shall be necessary for a public company.
   (ii) To delete the word 'private' from the name of the company.
   (iii) To permit raising of capital from public.
4. Prepare and file a Prospectus/Statement in lieu of Prospectus, in the prescribed form, within 30 days of passing the above resolutions.
5. File the Special Resolutions passed and the Explanatory Statement, in the prescribed form along with prescribed fee, within 30 days of their passing.
6. Apply to the Registrar, for issue of a fresh certificate of incorporation, after deleting the word 'private' from its name.
7. The number of directors should be raised to a minimum of three, if necessary.

Conversion of a Public Company into Private Company

The procedure for conversion of a public company into private company is similar to that for voluntary conversion of a private company into public company, except for the following:

(i) The articles shall be suitably amended to include the three basic restrictions applicable on a private company, and other provisions necessary thereto.

(ii) The name of the company shall be amended to include the word 'private' on all documents.

It may be noted that no resolution amending the articles, which has the effect of converting a public company into a private company, shall be effective unless it has been approved by the Central Government.

After such alteration has been approved, a printed copy of the Articles as altered shall be filed with the Registrar within one month of the date of receipt of the order of approval.

10.3 FORMATION OF COMPANIES

The formal steps involve in the formation of a company include finding a suitable name for the company, determining the location of the registered office of the company, drawing up the Memorandum of Association and Articles of Association, submitting the necessary documents to the Registrar of

Companies, and finally getting the company registered with him. Once a company is registered, it emerges as a legal entity.

From the point of view of ownership mainly two types of companies can be formed — private company and public company. The promoters have to decide whether it should be a private company or a public company considering the nature of business to be carried on, capital requirements and the liability of members. People who take all these steps are known as 'promoters.' They do all necessary preliminary work incidental to the formation of a company.

Therefore, the term 'promotion' refers to a series of processes or stages by which a company is brought into existence.

The stages of formation are:

1. Promotion stage
2. Selection of name
3. Incorporation stage
4. Raising of share capital stage
5. Commencement stage

We discuss each stage in detail:

1. Promotion Stage

This is the first stage in which the promoters conceive the idea of bringing a company into being and take the necessary steps to constitute promotion stage. This includes—

(a) Discovery of a business opportunity

(b) Detailed investigation

(c) Assembling

(d) Financing the proposition

Discovery of a Business Opportunity

Promoters should develop various business opportunities in a new field which has not been commercially exploited or in some existing business lines of manufacture or trade.

Detailed Investigation

The promoters need to make a detailed investigation of the different business opportunities to find out whether it is worthwhile to enter the field or not. Investigation should be in respect of the capital requirements, place of location, size of the unit, market opportunities, threats, cost of production, probable return on investment and the like. This will help the promoters to know the profitability or otherwise of a particular opportunity.

Assembling

On satisfaction of the profitability of the proposed business, the promoters take steps to assemble the necessary requirements of the proposed business, i.e., arranging for purchase of plant and machinery, land and building, patents, power supply, appointments, the required personnel, consent of other persons willing to act as directors or founder members and preparing the necessary documents for registration.

Financing the Proposition

After assembling the requirements, the promoters prepare financial schemes for securing the finance required for the business. The financial schemes include the type of securities, such as shares and debentures to be issued to the public for raising the required finance, entering into contracts with underwriters for the subscription of shares and debentures, and preparation of the project reports for getting loan from the financial institutions.

2. Selection Stage

Every company should have a name by which it will be identified for legal and business purposes. The name selected should not be similar to or identical with the name of an existing company. For this purpose the promoters submit an application containing a few names to the company law administration, Government of India, through the Registrar of Companies for approval. The promoters can then adopt any name from the list of approved names. The name of the company should end with the word 'Limited' in case of public companies and 'Private Limited' in case of private companies. If a company is formed to promote science or culture, the Central Government may permit the company to drop the word 'limited.'

3. Incorporation Stage

A company is said to be incorporated when it fulfills the formalities of registration and obtains the certificate of incorporation from the Registrar of Companies in the concerned state where the registered office is situated. The following documents, duly signed by a minimum of seven members in case of a public company and a minimum of two members in case of a private company are to be filed with the Registrar of Companies for incorporation of company.

1. Memorandum of Association.
2. Articles of Association.
3. Written consent of all the directors to act as directors duly signed by each director along with a written undertaking to take the prescribed qualification shares.
4. A list of persons who have agreed to become directors of the company with their names, addresses and occupations.
5. A statutory declaration by an advocate or an attorney or a chartered accountant practicing in India, or by a person named as director, manager or secretary of the company, stating that all the legal requirements with respect to incorporation have been duly complied with.
6. The address of the registered office of the company should be filed within 30 days of incorporation.

The Memorandum of Association and the Articles of Association must bear stamp duty as per the Indian Stamp Act.

On receipt of the above documents and the required registration fee, the Registrar examines these documents and if in order, he issues the Certificate of Incorporation. The Certificate of Incorporation is a conclusive evidence that the company has come into being.

A Private limited company can commence its operations immediately after incorporation. A public company to do so, should raise the required capital and obtain another certificate known as a certificate to commence the business.

4. Raising of Capital Stage

Next stage in the formation of a company is to raise capital. A public company raises its capital by inviting public to subscribe for its capital. The steps involved in raising capital are:

(a) Entering into agreement with the underwriters.

(b) Applying to the stock exchange for listing of shares.

(c) Issuc of prospectus inviting public to subscribe for share capital.

(d) Allotting shares.

After receiving the applications for shares towards the share capital, a public company can proceed with the work allotment provided the following conditions are fulfilled:

1. Minimum subscription as stated in the prospectus has been collected along with applications.
2. Not less than 5% of the nominal value of share has been received as application money.
3. The application money received has been deposited in a scheduled bank.
4. If prospectus has not been issued, statement is lieu of prospectus is made and delivered to the Registrar atleast three days before the first allotment.
5. Listing of shares in a stock exchange if stated in the prospectus and Articles of Association.

If the minimum subscription is not received from the public within 120 days from the date of issue of prospectus, allotment should not be made. Application money should be returned to the applicants within 130 days from the date of issue of prospectus, if not, the directors of the company will be jointly and severally liable to return the application money along with interest at 6% per annum.

Minimum Subscription

The minimum subscription is the minimum amount of capital, which is required to commence business. The prospectus and articles of association generally mention the amount of minimum subscription. If the amount is not so mentioned, the whole of the capital issued will be considered as minimum subscription. The amount of minimum subscription is fixed taking the following factors into consideration:

1. Purchase price of any property bought or to be bought;
2. Preliminary expense including underwriters, commission payable;
3. Repayment of any money borrowed for the above purposes;
4. Working capital; and
5. Any other expenditure.

Allotment of Shares

Allotment of shares means the distribution of securities in accordance with or in proportion to applications from subscribers. The Board of Directors at their meeting decide the basis of allotment and pass a formal resolution for allotment. The letters of allotment are then sent to the subscribers and a return of allotment is submitted to the Registrar of Companies.

5. Commencement Stage

A public company in order to commence its business has to obtain a '*Certificate of Commence of Business*' from the Registrar of Companies by submitting the following further statements:

1. A declaration that a copy of the prospectus is filed with him.
2. A declaration that minimum subscription has been received.
3. A declaration that the directors have taken up the qualification shares and have paid for, like others.
4. A statutory declaration by the Secretary or one of the Directors that the above requirements have been compiled with.

The Registrar of Companies will scrutinise all these documents and if satisfied, he then issues a certificate to commence business.

Before a company commences its business, a team of people who can manage the company must be constituted. Management is entrusted to directors, who are collectively called 'Board of Directors.' The first directors are appointed by the promoters. In its absence, signatories to the Memorandum of Association, will act as directors. The first directors shall hold office till the first general body meeting, at which the new directors are elected by shareholders.

We have studied that in the process of formation of a company, the promoters are required to prepare and file with the Registrar of Companies, a number of documents. Of these the most important, which are considered to be basic documents are Memorandum of Association, Articles of Association and prospectus.

Who can Promote a Company?

The promotion of a company comprises the preparatory steps leading to its incorporation. A promoter brings together the persons interested in setting up an enterprise, procures the subscribers and sets in motion the machinery which leads to the formation itself. A promoter forms a company with reference to a given project and takes necessary steps to accomplish that purpose.

Any person capable of entering into a contract can be a promoter. Minor, undischarged insolvent, a non-resident without the general or special permission of the Reserve Bank of India, partnership firm, HUF persons working in professional capacity, cannot be a promoter.

Duties of a Promoter

Promoters are neither agents nor trustees of the company they promote, the reason being that no one can be an agent or trustee for a company, which does not exist since a company comes into existence only on incorporation.

Yet, the promoter's role in the formation of a company is the one of considerable skill, energy and ingenuity. The promoters have a duty to ensure—

(i) that the acquisition of any property or business for the proposed company is on justifiable terms;

(ii) that the capital base and the financial structure of the proposed company is appropriate;

(iii) that the proposed directors and other executive officers are persons of integrity, competence and eminence;

(iv) that the memorandum and articles of association are properly framed; and

(v) that necessary assistance from banks or financial institutions has been obtained.

Pre-incorporation Contracts

Pre-incorporation contracts are the contracts made by the promoters purportedly on behalf of the company, before its incorporation, such as, for acquisition of a property or a business, or for drafting and printing of memorandum and articles, etc., though such contracts are vital for the very birth of the company yet the company is not bound by such contracts, since the company is non-existent before its incorporation and does not have the capacity to contract. The company can neither sue nor be sued in respect of such contracts. The company cannot even ratify or adopt such contracts after incorporation. Thus, the promoters remain personally liable on such contracts.

In order to avoid the personal liability of the promoters, following clauses may be included in pre-incorporation contracts.

(i) If the company, after its incorporation, adopts the contract, the liability of the promoter shall cease with immediate effect;

(ii) If the company, after its incorporation, fails to adopt the contract, within a certain time either party may rescind the contract.

Further, as soon as the company is incorporated, a fresh contract should be made between the company and the third party, in terms of the old contract.

Objects of the Company

The promoters have to decide the main, incidental and other objects of the company. A company can be incorporated for a lawful purpose only. Thus, the objects of the company must not be forbidden by law or opposed to public policy.

Registered Office of the Company

The promoters have to take yet another important decision as to the place of registered office of the proposed company. The state wherein the registered office shall be situate is to be specified in the application for availability of name in Form 1A and in the Memorandum. Besides, the documents of registration shall be filed with the Registrar of Companies, having territorial jurisdiction over the state.

The exact location of the registered office is to be informed to the Registrar within 30 days of the incorporation.

Application for Availability of Name

A company is known by its name. The promoters may select any suitable name, but it must not be identical with or resembling to the name of another registered company. The name may suggest the main objects of the proposed company.

The promoters should select three to five different names, and apply in prescribed form to the Registrar of Companies having Jurisdiction, along with a filing fee.

If the Registrar is satisfied and finds no objection to the proposed name, he informs the promoters of the name approved for incorporation of the company. The promoters should then complete all other formalities and get the company registered within 6 months from the date of approval of name by the Registrar.

10.4 MEMORANDUM OF ASSOCIATION

The Memorandum of Association is the fundamental document of the company containing the basic conditions on which the company is incorporated. It lays down the objects of the company and specifies the limit within which the company can operate.

Format and Content: A memorandum for a company limited by shares, should be in the format given in Table B of Schedule I to the Act, or as near thereto as circumstances admit.

A memorandum contains the following clauses:

The Memorandum of Association is the fundamental document of the company containing the basic conditions on which the company is incorporated. It lays down the objects of the company and specifies the limit within which the company can operate.

(a) Name Clause: Containing the name as approved by the Registrar, along with the words 'private limited' or 'limited' as the case may be.

(b) Registered office clause: Specifying the state wherein the registered office of the company shall situate.

(c) Object clause: Specifying the activities which the company proposes to and is authorised to undertake. It contains the three sub-clauses:

(i) Main objects, which are pursued by the company immediately after its incorporation.

(ii) Objects incidental or ancillary to the attainment of main objects, which are carried out only to the extent necessary for the attainment of the main objects.

(d) Liability clause: Stating that the liability of the members is limited to the extent of the unpaid amount with reference to the shares held by them (or to the extent of the amount undertaken to be contributed in the event of winding up, in case of a company limited by guarantee).

(e) Capital clause: Stating the authorized capital up to which the company can issue its shares.

(f) Association clause: Is the subscriber's declaration that they desire of being formed into company and agree to take the specified number of shares in the company's capital.

Alteration of Memorandum of Association of a Company

As per Section 2(3) of the Companies Act, 2013 (the Act) "alter" and "alteration" shall include the making of additions, omissions and substitutions.

Change in Name

A company desiring to change its name may do so in accordance with the provisions of Section 13 read with Section 4 of the Act by passing **Special Resolution** and the name approved by the Ministry of Corporate Affairs (MCA) on prescribed application. The power of the Central Government under Section 13(2) to approve change in name has been delegated to Registrar of Companies (ROC).

However, if the change required is the addition thereto or deletion therefrom, of the word "Private", consequent upon conversion of a public company into a private company or vice versa, no such approval of Central Government is required.

Alteration of Authorized Capital

A company seeking to issue shares by way of Private Placement or Rights Issue or by any other prescribed methods, has to check the Authorized Capital, as the issue cannot exceed the amount of Authorized Capital. Thus, in the view of the above, a company may alter its Authorized Capital, i.e., Capital Clause by virtue of Section 13 read with Section 61 by passing an **Ordinary Resolution.**

The Capital Clause will be altered by prescribed process as per the applicable rules and payment of relevant stamp duty as may be applicable and levied by concerned state in which the registered office of the company is situated.

Change in Objects

A company may change its objects as enshrined in its MOA in accordance with the provisions of Section 13 of the Act. Accordingly, any alteration of MOA with respect to the objects of the company is permitted through **Special Resolution.**

However, Section 13(8) **restricts** the change in object of a company which has raised money from public through prospectus and still has any unutilised amount out of the money so raised unless a special resolution is passed by the company and the details of such resolution shall be published in one vernacular language and one English language newspaper in circulation at the place of registered office of the company as well as on the website of the company indicating the justification for such change in the object.

Shift in Registered Office

As per Section 12 of the Act, every company shall have a registered office at all times, to which all communications and notices may be addressed.

Every company **within 30 days** of its incorporation or any change in the address of its registered office shall furnish a verification of registered office in **INC-22.**

A company is permitted to change its registered office from its existing location to another location—

- Within the local limits of the same city, town or village (e.g., Bandra, Mumbai to Andheri, Mumbai)

- Outside the local limits of the same city, town or village but:
  - ❖ within same state under jurisdiction of same ROC
  - ❖ under jurisdiction of another ROC within same state (e.g., Mumbai to Pune)

Stamp Duty and Witness

The memorandum is to be stamped by affixing stamps of the prescribed value. The memorandum should be signed and dated by all the subscribers and witnessed by any one person.

Doctrine of Ultra Vires

The objects stated in the memorandum define the field of industry within which the company must confine its activities. When a company acts beyond its objects, it exceeds its legal capacity and its powers under the memorandum; such an action is stated to be ultra vires the memorandum is void. The company cannot even ratify such act by amending its memorandum.

The implications of ultra vires acts are:

1. Any member can get an injunction restraining the company from acting *ultra vires*.
2. The directors become personally liable to the company and must make good any loss incurred by the company under such Act.
3. The directors shall be personally liable to the third party for any loss incurred by him, where such third party was incited by the directors to contact with the company in a matter that was *ultra vires*.

Exceptions: The doctrine of *Ultra Vires* does not apply to-

(a) where an act is ultra vires the powers of the directors only, it can be ratified by the shareholders.

(b) where an act is ultra vires the Articles of the company, the act can be ratified by amending the articles.

(c) where company's money has been spent ultra vires on purchasing some property, the company's right over that property are not affected.

10.5 ARTICLES OF ASSOCIATION

Articles of Association is the second constitutional document, which lays down the rules and regulations for the conduct of internal affairs of the company. The Articles constitute a contract between the company and its members and between the members themselves.

Articles of Association is the second constitutional document, which lays down the rules and regulations for the conduct of internal affairs of the company. The Articles constitute a contract between the company and its members and between the members themselves. The Articles are subordinate to the Memorandum, and should not therefore; contain any regulation, which is contrary to the Memorandum.

Articles may be drafted in one of the forms given in Tables F, G, H, I or J of Schedule I to the Act, as may be applicable or in a form as near thereto as the circumstances admit.

The articles of private company having share capital must:

(a) restrict the right to transfer its shares;

(b) limit the maximum number of members to 200; and

(c) prohibit invitation to public to subscribe for any of its shares or debentures.

Articles usually provide for the following matters:

(i) Exclusion wholly or in part of Table F.

(ii) Common seal, its use and safe custody.

(iii) Alteration of capital — how and to what extent.

(iv) Borrowings — the mode and the limit.

(v) General Meetings — notice required, resolutions, voting rights, proxies etc.

(vi) Directors – their appointment, qualification, remuneration, powers, duties and removal, names of first directors, minimum and maximum number of directors.

(vii) Dividend and reserve funds.

(viii) Accounts and audit.

(ix) Manager or Secretary — appointment and remuneration.

(x) Adoption of contracts entered into by the promoters.

(xi) Remuneration to promoters.

(xii) Special provision for amalgamation, etc.

(xiii) Winding up.

Stamp Duty and Witness

The Articles are to be signed by all the subscribers, duly stamped and witnessed, as in case of Memorandum.

Doctrine of Constructive Notice

Any person, who enters into a contract with a company, is expected to have knowledge of the power and position of the company and its directors, and is presumed to have gone through its memorandum and articles. This is popularly called the 'doctrine of constructive notice.' Thus, no person who binds himself to the company can later plead that he had no knowledge of the contents of its Memorandum and Articles.

Doctrine of Indoor Management

Though an outsider is bound to have constructive notice of the contents of Memorandum and articles of the company, he cannot be expected to know the internal affairs of the company or to inquire into the regularity of its internal proceedings. He is entitled to presume that the internal management of the company is regular. This is known as, 'Doctrine of Indoor Management' or Turguand's Rule. For example, where the directors have the authorities to bind the company for certain debts, but prior consent of the shareholders is required to be obtained by special resolution, before that power is exercised. The person extending the credit is not entitled to presume that the directors are acting lawfully.

Exceptions: The rule of indoor management does not apply in following cases:

(i) where the affected has the knowledge of the irregularity;

(ii) where the circumstances surrounding the contract are suspicious and therefore invite inquiry;

(iii) in the case of forgery;

(iv) where the affected party does not have, in fact, knowledge of the existence of the power of delegation, he cannot rely upon its suggested exercise;

(v) where the act of a director/other officer of the company is such that it would ordinarily be beyond powers of such an officer.

Distinction between Memorandum and Articles of Association

The distinction between the two is as follows:

1. The Memorandum is the charger of the company setting out its Constitution, Status and the relationship of the company with the outside world. Articles on the other hand, contain the rules and regulations of the company for the conduct of its internal administration. They define the rights, duties and powers of directors, shareholders and officers.
2. The Memorandum states the objects and purpose for which the company is established, whereas the Articles prescribe the regulations for the establishment of these objectives.
3. A company prepare and file a Memorandum for incorporation with the Registrar of companies, whereas the preparation of Articles is not compulsory for a public company — it can adopt Table 'A' of the Companies Act, 1956 which contains model rules and regulations.
4. Any alteration to Memorandum requires consent of the Company Law Board. Whereas, members themselves can make alterations to the Articles of Association.
5. Acts of the company outside the scope of Memorandum is void and incapable of ratification. However, acts which are *ultra vires* the articles, i.e., beyond the scope of articles, but *intra vires* (within) the Memorandum are not void and can be ratified by the company by a special resolution.
6. The Memorandum of Association is governed by the Companies Act, 1956. But the Articles of Association are governed by the Memorandum of Association and the Companies Act.

Certificate of Incorporation

On the receipt of the necessary documents and on payment of the necessary fees, the Registrar will issue the 'Certificate of Incorporation' if he is satisfied that the requirements of the Companies Act have been complied with. He will enter the company's name in the Register. The company comes into existence. A private limited company can commence its operations immediately after incorporation. A public company, to do so, should raise the required capital and obtain another certificate known as certificate of commencement of business.

10.6 PROSPECTUS

A company may raise funds either by private placement with friends and relatives or by making public issues. A company may raise funds by various instruments, viz., shares, debentures, bonds or deposits. The procedure of raising share capital is being discussed in the following paragraphs. The procedure for other instruments is also the same.

'Prospectus' is the basic document for raising funds from the public. Prospectus means any document described or issued as a prospectus inviting deposits from the public or inviting offers from the public for the subscription or purchase of any shares in, or debentures of the company. Thus, a prospectus is a general invitation to the public to subscribe to the capital of the company on the conditions specified in the application form.

A prospectus is a general invitation to the public to subscribe to the capital of the company on the conditions specified in the application form.

Private companies are prohibited from inviting any public subscription in shares or debentures and as such they cannot issue any prospectus.

Every public company having share capital is required to issue on its formation a prospectus, or to file with the Registrar a statement in lieu of prospectus, where the company does not invite public subscription.

Essential Contents of Prospectus

Every prospectus shall state the matters specified in Schedule II of the Act, viz., —

(i) Date of prospectus which is generally the date of its publication.

(ii) Name and registered office of the company.

(iii) Consent of the Central Government for the present issue / compliance with SEBI Guidelines.

(iv) Names of stock exchange where application made for listing of present issue.

(v) Punishment for fictitious applications.

(vi) Refund of the issue if minimum subscription of 90% is not received within 90 days from issue closure.

(vii) Issue of allotment letters/refunds within a period of 10 weeks and interest on delayed funds.

(viii) Date of opening and closing and the earliest closing date.

(ix) Name and address of auditors and lead managers.

(x) Name and address of trustee under debenture trust deed.

(xi) Credit rating from CRISIL (The Credit Rating Information Services of India Limited) or other rating agency for the proposed debenture/ preference shares issue.

(xii) Terms of underwriting.

(xiii) Capital structure of the company, size of present issue, paid up capital after present issue or after conversion of debentures.

(xiv) Terms and particulars of the issue.

(xv) Main objects of the company, promoters, names, addresses and occupation of manager, managing director and other directors, details of the project, its implementation and prospects.

(xvi) Stock market data for shares/debentures, high/low price in the last three years and monthly high/low during the last six months.

(xvii) Particulars of any previous issue by the company and other companies under the same management.

(xviii) Management perception of risk factors.

(xix) General information as to consent of directors, auditors, solicitors, managers, to the issue, Registrar of issue, bankers to the company, bankers to the issue, names and addresses of the company secretary, legal adviser, lead managers, auditors, co-managers etc.

(xx) Financial information of the company.

(xxi) Minimum subscription expenses of the issue, underwriting, commission and brokerage.

(xxii) Rights of members as to voting, dividend, lien on shares, forfeiture of shares, etc.

(xxiii) Restriction on transfer and transmission of shares/debentures.

(xxiv) Material contracts and inspection of documents, etc.

Registration of Prospectus

A copy of the prospectus must be submitted to the Registrar for his approval, before it is printed for mass circulation. Every person who is named in the prospectus as a director or a proposed director, should consent and sign the prospectus.

Within ninety days from the date on which a copy delivered for registration, the prospectus will be issued by the company to the public.

Statement in Lieu of Prospectus

A public company not raising its share capital from general public, need not issue a prospectus. However, it should file a 'statement in lieu of prospectus' (which contain almost the same particulars) with the Registrar.

SEBI Guidelines for Public Issues

The Securities and Exchange Board of India (SEBI) has issued elaborate guidelines on public issues, including first public issue to be made by an existing private or closely held company after its conversion into a public company.

10.7 POWERS OF SECURITIES AND EXCHANGE BOARD OF INDIA

The matters relating to issue and transfer of securities and non-payment of dividend by listed public companies and those public companies which intend to get their securities listed on any recognized Stock Exchange in India will be administered by the Securities and Exchange Board of India and all powers relating to all other matter including the matters relating to prospectus, statement in lieu of prospectus, return of allotment, issue of shares and redemption of irredeemable preference shares will be exercised by the Central Government, Company Law Board or the Registrar of Companies, as the case may be.

Shelf Prospectus

"Shelf Prospectus" means a prospectus issued by any financial institution or bank for one or more issues of the securities or class of securities specified in that prospectus.

As per the Act—

(1) Any public financial institution, public sector bank or scheduled bank whose main object is financing shall file a shelf prospectus.

(2) A company filing a shelf prospectus with the Registrar shall not be required to file prospectus at every stage of offer of securities by it within a period of validity of such shelf prospectus.

(3) A company filing a shelf prospectus shall be required to file an information memorandum on all material facts relating to new charges created, changes in the financial position as have occurred between the first offer of securities, previous offer of securities and the succeeding offer of securities within such time as may be prescribed by the Central Government, prior to making of a second or subsequent offer of securities under the shelf prospectus.

(4) An information memorandum shall be issued to the public along with shelf prospectus filed at the stage of the first offer of securities and such prospectus shall be valid for a period of one year from the date of opening of the first issue of securities under that prospectus:

Provided that where an update of information memorandum is filed every time an offer of securities is made, such memorandum together with the shelf prospectus shall constitute the prospectus.

Here "financing" means making loans to or subscribing in the capital of a private industrial enterprise engaged in infrastructural financing or, such other company as the Central Government may notify in this behalf.

"Shelf Prospectus" means a prospectus issued by any financial institution or bank for one or more issues of the securities or class of securities specified in that prospectus.

CRIMINAL LIABILITY FOR MIS-STATEMENT IN PROSPECTUS

If a prospectus includes any untrue statement, every person who authorized the issue of prospectus is punishable with imprisonment for a term which may extend to two years, or with fine which may extend to fifty thousand rupees, or with both unless he proves either that the statement was immaterial or that he had reasonable ground to believe, and did, up to the time of the issue of the prospectus believe, that the statement was true.

If a prospectus includes any untrue statement, every person who authorized the issue of prospectus is punishable with imprisonment for a term which may extend to two years, or with fine which may extend to fifty thousand rupees, or with both.

Initial offer of securities to be in dematerialized form in certain cases

Every listed company, making initial public offer of any security for a sum of rupees ten crore or more, should issue the same only in dematerialised form by complying with the requisite provisions of the Depositories Act, 1996 and the regulations made thereunder.

10.8 OFFER OF INDIAN DEPOSITORY RECEIPTS

Notwithstanding anything contained in any other law for the time being in force, the Central Government may make rules applicable for—

(a) the offer of Indian Depository Receipts;

(b) the requirement of disclosures in prospectus or letter of offer issued in connection with Indian Depository Receipts;

(c) the manner in which the Indian Depository Receipts shall be dealt in a depository mode and by custodian and underwriters;

(d) the manner of sale, transfer or transmission of Indian Depository Receipts.

[by a company incorporated, or to be incorporated outside India, whether the company has or has not been established or, will or will not establish any place of business in India.]

10.9 KINDS OF SHARES

Share capital of a company is divided into certain indivisible units of a fixed amount. These units are called shares. 'Share' means share in the capital of a company.

Share capital of a company is divided into certain indivisible units of a fixed amount. These units are called shares. 'Share' means share in the capital of a company. The person owning a share or shares of a company is called a shareholder. He is a part owner and risk bearer of the company. He gets income on his investment in shares in the form of dividends from the company. Dividend is that part of the profits of the company, which is distributed among the shareholders for the shares held by them.

A public joint stock company can issue two classes of shares, they are:

(a) Preference shares, and
(b) Equity shares.

Preference Shares

Preference shares are those, which have preferential right to the payment of dividend during the life-time of the company, and a preferential right to the return of capital when the company is wound up.

Preference shares are those, which have preferential right to the payment of dividend during the life-time of the company, and a preferential right to the return of capital when the company is wound up.

Preference shares have the following characteristics:

(i) The dividend on them is fixed by the Articles of the company;
(ii) Preference shareholders get their fixed rate of dividend before any dividend is distributed among the other class of shareholders;
(iii) At the time of winding up of the company, the preference shareholders must be paid back their capital before anything is paid to ordinary shareholders.

Kinds of Preference Shares

1. ***Cumulative preference shares:*** The cumulative preference shares are entitled to fixed dividends whether there are profits or no profits. If profits are not sufficient to pay dividends in a particular year, the dividends are accumulated and paid in the succeeding year as profits become available for distribution.
2. ***Non-cumulative preference shares:*** Unlike the cumulative preference shares, these shares cannot claim arrears of dividends of any year out of the profits of subsequent years.
3. ***Participating preference shares:*** In the case of the participating preference shares, shareholders receive a fixed rate of dividend in priority to ordinary shares and, further, the right to participate in the balance of profit in an agreed proportion together with ordinary shareholders.
4. ***Non-participating preference shares:*** These shares are entitled to only a fixed rate of dividend; they have no claim in the surplus profit, which belongs to ordinary shareholders.
5. ***Redeemable preference shares:*** These are shares, which can be purchased back by the company. The company reserves its right to call back or purchase these shares at any time, subject to the provisions of its Articles.

6. ***Irredeemable preference shares:*** These are shares that cannot be purchased back by the company.

Equity Shares

All shares, which are not preference shares are equity shares, also called ordinary shares. Unlike the preference share, equity shares do not have a fixed rate of dividend. Equity shareholders are entitled to dividends only after the dividend claims of the preference shareholders have been met. Similarly, at the time of the winding up of the company, equity shareholders get back their capital only after the capital of the preference shareholders has been paid back. Equity shares are always irredeemable and their holders have normal voting rights.

New Issues of Share Capital to be only of two kinds

The share capital of a company limited by shares shall hereafter be of two kinds only, namely:

(a) Equity share capital

(i) with voting rights; or

(ii) with differential rights as to dividend, voting or otherwise in accordance with such rules and subject to such conditions as may be prescribed.

(b) Preference share capital.

Sweat Equity

"Sweat equity shares" means equity shares issued by the company to employees or directors at a discount or for consideration other than cash for providing know-how or making available rights in the nature of intellectual property rights or value additions, by whatever name called.

"Sweat equity shares" means equity shares issued by the company to employees or directors at a discount or for consideration other than cash for providing know-how or making available rights in the nature of intellectual property rights or value additions, by whatever name called.

A company may issue sweat equity shares of a class of shares already issued if the following conditions are fulfilled, namely:

(a) the issue of sweat equity shares is authorised by a special resolution passed by the company in the general meeting;

(b) the resolution specifies the number of shares, current market price, consideration, if any, and the class or classes of directors or employees to whom such equity shares are to be issued;

(c) not less than one year has, at the date of the issue, elapsed since the date on, which the company was entitled to commence business;

(d) the sweat equity share of a company, whose equity shares are listed on a recognised stock exchange, are issued in accordance with the regulations made by the Securities and Exchange Board of India in this behalf.

Provided that the case of a company whose equity shares are not listed on any recognised stock exchange, the sweat equity shares are issued in accordance with the guidelines as may be prescribed.

Recent Developments

Convertible cumulative preference shares: In 1985, Government of India introduced a new type of preference share, namely, convertible cumulative preference (CCP) share. The entire issue of CCP shares shall be converted to equity any time the third and fifth year of issue. Since conversion to the equity is compulsory, the CCP shares cannot be redeemed at any stage. The CCP shareholders enjoy the same voting rights as the cumulative preference shareholders. For calculation of debt equity ratio, CCP shares are treated as part of equity. However, for calculation of preference-equity ratio, CCP shares are totally excluded from both categories.

10.10 COMPANIES (AMENDMENT) ACT, 1988

The above Act inserted a new sub-section, 80A, to the Companies Act, 1956. According to this sub-section:

(a) Irredeemable preference shares issues before the commencement of this Amendment Act shall be redeemed by the company within a period of five years from the commencement of this Amendment.

(b) Preference shares which are not redeemable before expiry of 10 years from the date of issue and which had not been redeemed before the commencement of this Amendment Act, shall be redeemed on the due date or within a period of 10 years from the commencement of the Amendment, whichever is earlier.

Where a company is not in a position to redeem any such share within the period aforesaid and to pay the dividend, if any, due thereon, it may, with the consent of the Company Law Board (CLB) issue further redeemable preference shares equal to the amounts due (including the dividend) in respect of the unredeemed preference shares, and on the issue of such further redeemable preference shares, the unredeemed shares shall be deemed to have been redeemed.

Issue of Bonus Shares

Bonus shares are the shares allotted to existing equity shareholders without any consideration being received from them, in cash or in kind. They are issued to capitalise profits of the company.

Bonus shares are the shares allotted to existing equity shareholders without any consideration being received from them, in cash or in kind. They are issued to capitalise profits of the company. Bonus shares can be issued only if Articles of Association permit such an issue. For such an issue, sanction of SEBI is also required. The Central Government has prescribed certain guidelines for the issue of bonus shares. The sanction of SEBI can be obtained only if these guidelines have been followed. For example, the issue can be made only out of free reserves built out of the genuine profits and share premium collected in cash, reserves created by revaluation of assets cannot be used for the purpose. Development Rebate Reserve and Investment Allowance Reserve cannot be used for issue of bonus shares. The residual reserves remaining after the issue of the bonus shares should be atleast 40% of the paid-up capital after the bonus shares. On issue of bonus shares, reserves used for such an issue are debited and Bonus to equity shareholders Account is credited with the amount for which bonus shares are issued.

Rights Issue

When a company which has already issued shares wants to make a further issue of shares, it is under a legal obligation to first offer the fresh issue to the existing shareholders unless the company has resolved otherwise by a special resolution. The right of existing shareholders to buy shares from the company in this manner is transferable. If the market price of the shares is higher than the amount at which the company has offered new shares, the right to buy shares from the company will carry a price. Suppose a company offers to its equity shareholders the right to buy one equity share of Rs. 100 each at Rs. 120 for every equity of Rs. 100 each held. Suppose the market value of one equity share is Rs. 180. Then the value of the right will be calculated as follows:

Market value of 4 equity shares Rs. 180 × 4	= Rs. 720
Add: Issue price of 1 new equity share	= Rs. 120
Total price of 5 shares	= Rs. 840
Value of one share = Rs.840/5	= Rs. 168
The value of right = Rs.180 – Rs.168	= Rs. 12

The whole process can be expressed in the form of the following formula also:

$$\text{Value of rights} = \frac{\text{New shares}}{\text{Total shares}} \times (\text{cum right price} \times \text{New issue price})$$

Thus, if we apply the formula in the above-mentioned example, we will get

Value of right = 1/5 × (180–120)
= Rs.1/5 × 60
= Rs.12

It gives us the value of right attached to each share held. But in order to buy the share from the company, a person will have to buy 4 such rights because the company will issue one share against four shares held.

Right Issue

When a company which has already issued shares wants to make a further issue of shares, it is under a legal obligation to first offer the fresh issue to the existing shareholders unless the company has resolved otherwise by a special resolution.

Debentures

The term debenture is defined as "a document under the company's seal which provides for the payment of a principal sum and interest thereon at regular intervals which is usually secured by a fixed or floating charge on the company's property or undertaking which acknowledges a loan to the company."

Debenture is defined as a document under the company's seal which provides for the payment of a principal sum and interest thereon at regular intervals which is usually secured by a fixed or floating charge on the company's property or undertaking which acknowledges a loan to the company.

Kinds of Debentures

1. *Redeemable and Irredeemable:* From the point of view of redemption, debentures are classified into redeemable and irredeemable. Redeemable debentures are those that will be repaid by the company at the end of a specified period, or on demand; or by instalments. Irredeemable debentures are those that are not repayable during the life-time of the company. Irredeemable debentures are also called perpetual debentures.

2. *Mortgage and Simple:* From the point of view of security, debentures are classified into mortgage and simple or naked debentures. Mortgage debentures, also called secured debentures, are those which are secured by a charge on the assets or property of the company, whereas simple debentures are those that are not secured by any charge on the assets of the company.

3. *Registered and Bearer:* From the point of view of records, debentures may be classified into registered and bearer debentures. Registered debentures are those in respect of which the names, addresses and particulars of the holdings of debenture holders are entered in the Register of Debenture holders. The transfer of registered debenture cannot be effected without the execution of a regular transfer deed. As against this, the company keeps no such records of bearer debenture holders. Bearer debentures are negotiable by mere delivery of the document.

4. *Convertible and unconvertible:* In case of convertible debentures, the holders have the option to convert their debenture holdings into equity shares of the company at a specified rate after a specified period.

Debenture Trust Deed

(1) A trust deed for securing any issue of debentures shall be in such form and shall be executed within such period as may be prescribed.

(2) A copy of the trust deed shall be open to inspection to any member or debenture holder of the company and he shall also be entitled to obtain copies of such trust deed on payment of such sum as may be prescribed.

(3) If a copy of the trust deed is not made available for inspection or is not given to any member or debenture holder, the company and every officer of the company who is in a default, shall be punishable, for each offence, with fine, which may extend to five hundred rupees for every day during which the offence continues.

Appointment of debenture trustees and duties of debenture trustees

(1) No company shall issue a prospectus or a letter of offer to the public for subscription of its debentures, unless the company has, before such issue, appointed one or more debenture trustees for such debentures and the company has, on the face of the prospectus or the letter of offer, stated that the debenture trustee or trustees have given their consent to the company to be so appointed:

Provided that no person shall be appointed as a debenture trustee, if he —

(a) beneficially holds shares in the company;

(b) is beneficially entitled to moneys which are to be paid by the company to the debenture trustee;

(c) has entered into any guarantee in respect of principal debts secured by the debentures or interest thereon.

(2) Subject to the provisions of this Act, the functions of the debenture trustees shall generally be to protect the interest of holders of debentures (including the creation of securities within the stipulated time) and to redress the grievances of holders of debentures effectively.

(3) In particular, and without prejudice to the generality of the foregoing functions, a debenture trustee may take such other steps as he may deem fit —

(a) to ensure that the asset of the company issuing debentures and each of the guarantors are sufficient to discharge the principal amount at all times;

(b) to satisfy himself that the prospectus or for letter of offer does not contain any matter which is inconsistent with the terms of the debentures or with the trust deed;

(c) to ensure that the company does not commit any breach of covenants and provisions of the trust deed;

(d) to take such reasonable steps to remedy any branch of the covenants of the trust deed or the terms of issue of debentures;

(e) to take steps to call a meeting of holders of breach as and when such meeting is required to be held.

(4) Where at any time the debenture trustee comes to a conclusion that the assets of the company are insufficient or are likely to become insufficient to discharge the principal amount as and when it becomes due, the debenture trustee may file a petition before the Company Law Board and the Company Law Board may, after hearing the company and any other person interested in the matter, by an order, impose such restrictions on the incurring of any further liabilities as the Company Law Board think necessary in the interests of holders of the debentures.

Liability of Company to Create Security and Debenture Redemption Reserve

(1) Where a company issues debentures after the commencement of this Act, it shall create a debenture redemption reserve for the redemption of such debentures, to which adequate amounts shall be credited, from out of its profits every year until such debentures are redeemed.

(2) The amounts credited to the debenture redemption reserve shall not be utilised by the company except for the purpose aforesaid.

(3) The company shall pay interest and redeem the debentures in accordance with the terms and conditions of their issue.

(4) Where a company fails to redeem the debentures on the date of maturity, the Company Law Board may, on the application of any or all the holders of debenture shall, after hearing the parties concerned, direct, by order, the company to redeem the debentures forthwith by the payment of principal and interest due thereon.

(5) If default is made in complying with the order of the Company Law Board, every officer of the company who is in default, shall be punishable with imprisonment which may extend to three years and shall also be liable to a fine of not less than five hundred rupees for everyday during which such default continues.

Distinction between Debentures and Shares

The following are the points of distinction between debentures and shares:

1. ***Creditorship security v/s Ownership security:*** Whereas a debenture is a creditorship security, a share is an ownership security. It means that a debenture holder is a creditor of the company, while a shareholder is a part-owner of the company. It is the fundamental distinction between a debenture and a share.
2. ***Certainty of return:*** A debenture holder is certain of return on his investment. The company has to pay interest on debentures at the fixed rate agreed upon at the time of issue even if it suffers heavy losses. A shareholder cannot get dividends if the company does not earn profits. As a matter of fact, even when a company earns a profit, its Directors may decide to plough back the profits and not declare a dividend. Thus, there is no certainty of return on investment in shares.
3. ***Order of repayment on winding up:*** In case of winding up of a company, the amount of debentures will be repaid before any amount is paid to shareholders to return share capital.

4. ***Restrictions on issue at a discount:*** There are no restrictions on issue of debentures at a discount, but there are legal conditions which have to be fulfilled to issue shares at a discount.
5. ***Mortgage:*** There can be mortgage debentures. It means that assets of the company can be mortgaged in favour of debenture holders by way of security. But there can be no mortgage shares.
6. ***Convertibility:*** Debentures which can be converted into shares at the option of debenture holders can be issued. But shares convertible into debentures cannot be issued.

Share Capital

Share capital means the capital raised by a company by the issue of shares. In this connection the meaning of the following terms should be understood:

(i) ***Nominal or authorised capital:*** This is the nominal or face value of the shares which the company is authorised to issue by its Memorandum of Association. This is the maximum capital, which a company can have without altering the capital clause of the Memorandum of Association for an increase in its Authorised Capital.

(ii) ***Issued capital:*** It is the nominal value of shares, which are offered to the public for subscription. It cannot be more than the authorised capital.

(iii) ***Subscribed capital:*** It is the nominal value of the shares taken up by the public. If all the shares offered to the public are taken up by the public, subscribed capital will be equal to issued capital. But sometimes, all the shares, which are offered to the public for subscription are not taken up by public. In such a case, only that part of the issued capital, which is taken up by the public, will be called subscribed capital.

(iv) ***Called up capital:*** This is that part of the subscribed capital which has been called up. If the Board of Directors has called up the total amount payable in the shares, the called up capital will be equal to subscribed capital.

(v) ***Paid-up capital:*** This is that part of the called up capital which has been paid up by the shareholders or which is credited by the company as paid-up on the shares. If all the called up capital has been received, paid-up capital will be equal to called up capital. That part of the called up capital which has not yet been received is called "calls in Arrear" thus, called up capital – calls in Arrear = paid up capital.

Transfer of Shares

Shares are movable property transfer-able by delivery and endorsement, in ac-cordance with the articles of associa-tion.

Shares are movable property transferable by delivery and endorsement, in accordance with the articles of association. The instrument of transfer, i.e., transfer deed is executed both by the transferor and the transferee, and the transferor endorses his signature on the back of the share certificate and delivers it to the transferee. A company shall register transfer of shares only when a proper instrument of transfer duly stamped and executed, alongwith the share certificate or (letter of allotment) is lodged with the company. Thereafter, the transferee's name is entered into the register of members, and the transferor's name is either struck off or his holding is reduced by the number of shares transferred.

Transmission of Shares

Transmission of shares means transfer of property or title in shares by law. Under this case the shares of the deceased member may be transferred to his legal representatives. In case of bankrupt member the shares may be transferred to his official Receiver, in case of lunatic member shares are transferred to his administrator (appointed by the Court).

Transmission of shares means transfer of property or title in shares by law.

There are two alternatives open to a legal representative (1) the legal representative may himself become the member and/or (2) he may transfer the shares to some other person.

If the legal representative does not opt for any alternative, the company sends a notice for his decision. If no reply is received within 90 days, the Directors may withhold the payment of dividend and bonus payable on these shares. If the legal representative wants to become the member of the company, he will have to request for the same with the company, in that case the share certificates and the succession certificate have to be enclosed with the application. On being satisfied with the documents, the company will delete the name of the deceased member and in that place enter the name of the legal representative in the Register of Members, then a new share certificate will be issued to the legal representative in his name.

If the legal representative opt to transfer the shares he will have to follow the usual procedures of transfer of shares. The one difference is that the legal representative should attach one more document, i.e., the succession certificate with the instrument of transfer.

Share Certificates

Share certificates are issued by a company to its shareholders, as an evidence of the title to the shares. A share certificate is a declaration that the person whose name is written on that certificate is legal owner of the number of shares specified therein. A share certificate is transferable by delivery and endorsement.

A share certificate is a declaration that the person whose name is written on that certificate is legal owner of the number of shares specified therein.

Share Warrant

A share warrant entitles the bearer to the shares specified in that warrant and the shares may be transferred to him on delivery of the warrant. A public company may issue share warrants with respect to its fully paid-up shares, if authorised by its Articles and with prior approval of the Central Government.

Difference between Transfer and Transmission of Shares

Transfer of Shares	*Transmission of Shares*
1. It is a voluntary one.	1. It happens according to the operations of law.
2. A duly executed instrument of transfer is essential.	2. There is no need to have such instrument of transfer, but a letter of request with succession certificate should be enclosed.

3. Consideration is essential.	3. No consideration is essential.
4. Shares are transferred irrespective of the happening of events like death, bankruptcy or lunacy of a member.	4. It happens only on the happening of events like death, bankruptcy or lunacy of a member.
5. Stamp duty is necessary.	5. Stamp duty is not necessary.

Dividend on Shares

The shareholders get the return on their share investment in the company in the form of dividend. Dividend can only be paid out of the profit and not out of capital.

Normally, dividend is recommended by the Board of Directors on the basis of the profits earned by the company and are paid to the shareholders after it is declared at the Annual General Meeting. The shareholders have a right to declare dividend or adopt as it is recommended by the directors but they have no right to increase the dividend.

The Board of Directors may pay an interim dividend, if so authorised by the Articles, if they feel satisfied that the current year's profits are sufficient for paying interim dividend.

10.11 COMPANY MANAGEMENT

A company is, though a legal person, but has no body or mind of its own. It carries out its functions and manages its affairs through some managerial personnel, which are basically of following types:

1. Directors, Managing Director, Chairman and Board of Directors,
2. Manager, and
3. Secretary.

Directors

The directors are the brain of the company, who generally control the company's functions and management.

The directors are the brain of the company, who generally control the company's functions and management. The directors may be described as agents and trustees of the company who act on behalf of the company.

A private company must have a minimum of two directors. The maximum number of directors is generally fixed by its articles.

Any individual who is not suffering from any disqualification mentioned u/s 274 of the Act or under the articles can be appointed as a director of a company.

Appointment

The first directors of a company are appointed by the subscribers to the memorandum or the subscribers themselves, who are individuals, are deemed as first directors of the company.

The subsequent directors are appointed by passing an ordinary resolution at the general meeting of the company. The directors shall hold office in accordance with the provisions of the articles. In the absence of any specific provision in the articles, all the directors shall retire at the end of next annual general meeting. A private company may appoint all permanent directors, if the articles so provide.

Qualifications

1. To hold the prescribed number of qualification shares within two months of his appointment. The value of qualification shares cannot exceed Rs.5,000 except the nominal value of one share exceeds that amount.
2. To be free from following disqualifications:
   (a) person certified to be of unsound mind,
   (b) person being an undischarged insolvent,
   (c) person against whom an insolvency petition is pending,
   (d) person sentenced to imprisonment for not less than six months for any offence involving moral turpitude and five years have not elapsed from the expiry of the sentence,
   (e) person whose calls are in arrears for six months,
   (f) person guilty of offence for fraudulent promotion, formation, management or winding up of a company.
   (g) any other disqualification provided in the articles of a private company.

Maximum Number of Directorship

A person cannot be a director of more than 20 companies at the same time. This will include appointments held as Managing Director. This rule applies to public companies and a private company, which is a subsidiary of a public company.

Duties of Directors

1. To act honestly in good faith for the benefit of the company and not to make secret profit.
2. To act within the powers conferred by Memorandum and Articles.
3. To attend personally to the business of the company with reasonable care and diligence.
4. To attend Board meetings. If a director absents himself from three consecutive meetings or from all meeting during 3 consecutive months, without obtaining leave of absence from the Board, he shall cease to be a director.
5. Not to delegate his functions unless and to the extent authorised by the articles.
6. To disclose to the Board, his interest in any transaction with the company.

Liabilities of Directors

(a) The directors are liable to pay on the shares held by them like any other shareholder.

(b) If a director acts *ultra vires* the company, he will be liable to indemnity the company for any loss or damage and also the third party for breach of warranty of authority.

(c) If a director acts dishonestly, he will be liable to the company for breach of trust or misfeasance.

(d) A director shall be liable to the company for negligence in the exercise of his powers and duties.

(e) A director is liable for statutory penalties for non-compliance with certain requirements, viz:

  (i) Failure to inform the Registrar when a private company becomes a public, the fine imposable is upto Rs.500 for every day of default.

  (ii) Failure to deposit share application money in a separate bank account, fine imposable upto Rs.5,000.

  (iii) Failure to submit annual return, fine imposable upto Rs. 50 per day.

  (iv) For accepting directorship in more than 20 companies, fine imposable upto Rs. 5,000 in respect of each excess directorship.

(f) Besides, a director may incur criminal liability with respect to certain duties such as, concealing name of creditor, default in distributing dividend, non-maintenance of proper books of account, failure to supply balance sheet at the annual general meeting, or an information to the auditor, supplying wrong information to the Government, improper grant of loan to directors, fraudulently obtaining credit for the company, etc.

Loans to Directors

No company (except a private company which is not a subsidiary of a public company) can give loans, without the previous approval of the Central Government, to any director, his partner or relative, any firm in which a director is a partner, any private company in which a director is a member, any body corporate in which a director or directors control 25 per cent of voting power or any company under the same management.

'Managing Director' is a director who, by virtue of an agreement with the company or of a resolution passed by the company in a general meeting or by its Board of Directors or by virtue of its memorandum or articles of association, is entrusted with substantial powers of management, which would not otherwise be exercisable by him.

Remuneration to Directors

Remuneration payable to directors is determined either by the Articles of the company or by a resolution of the company in general meeting. Besides, salary, bonus and commission, the remuneration may be paid by way of sitting fees, rent free accommodation, perquisites made available from the company funds, expenditure incurred for any obligatory service, expenditure incurred to insure life, to provide any gratuity or pension.

In case of a public company and a 'private company', which is subsidiary of a public company, the remuneration of directors is subject to the restrictions laid down in Sections 198 and 309.

Managing Director

'Managing Director' is a director who, by virtue of an agreement with the company or of a resolution passed by the company in a general meeting or by its Board of Directors or by virtue of its memorandum or articles of association, is entrusted with substantial powers of management, which would not otherwise be exercisable by him.

Every public company or a private company which is a subsidiary of a public company having paid-up share capital of Rs.5 crore or more, must have a Managing Director or whole-time director or a manager. In such companies the managing director can be appointed for a maximum term of five years at a time.

A person may be appointed managing director of any number of private companies, none of which is a subsidiary of a public company. However, a person cannot be appointed managing director in more than two companies, if anyone company is a public company or a private company, which is subsidiary of a public company.

For qualifications, duties, liabilities, remuneration of and loans to a managing director, refer under 'Directors.'

Chairman

'Chairman' is the head of the company's Board of Directors and supervises and controls the work of all directors and managing director. The company may, however, appoint the same person as its Chairman and the Managing Director.

'Chairman' is the head of the company's Board of Directors and supervises and controls the work of all directors and managing director.

Board of Directors

All the directors of the company jointly constitute the 'Board.' The directors must act jointly and concurrently. For this purpose, it is essential that company's decisions are taken jointly by the Board, at the Board Meeting. The decisions are generally taken by majority and sometimes under power of the Chairman.

All the directors of the company jointly constitute the 'Board.'

The Board of Directors must meet atleast once in every three months, and atleast four such meetings to the provisions of the articles. The proceedings of every meeting should be recorded in a 'Minutes Book.'

Manager

'Manager' is an individual who, subject to the superintendence, control and direction of the Board of Directors, has the responsibility for management of the whole or substantially the whole of the affairs of a company. Manager may be one of the directors or any other person appointed under a contract of service.

'Manager' is an individual who, subject to the superintendence, control and direction of the Board of Directors, has the responsibility for management of the whole or substantially the whole of the affairs of a company.

The provisions relating to the appointment, disqualifications term of appointment and remuneration of a manager are similar to those for managing director.

Secretary

A secretary is an officer of the company appointed to perform the duties which may be performed by a Secretary under the Act and other managerial or administrative duties. Thus, a firm or body corporate cannot be appointed as a Secretary.

Every company having a paid-up share capital of Rs.25 lakhs or more shall have a whole-time secretary. Where the paid-up capital of a company is Rs.50 lakhs or more, the Secretary must be a qualified member of the Institute of Company Secretaries of India.

Where the Board of Directors comprises of only two directors, neither of them shall be the Secretary of the company unless he is qualified company Secretary.

The primary duties of a Secretary are:

1. To superintend, direct and control his department.
2. To sign documents and proceedings requiring authentication by the company.
3. To do all such acts as are authorised by the Board of Directors.
4. To carry out all the functions of the company as required under the Act or Rules, or as directed by the Central Government, Company Law Board, Registrar or the Court.
5. To ensure proper filing of documents with the Registrar and the Central Government.
6. To attend all the meetings and to ensure that all requirements as to holding of meetings are carried out.

A secretary is an officer of the company appointed to perform the duties which may be performed by a Secretary under the Act and other managerial or administrative duties. Thus, a firm or body corporate cannot be appointed as a Secretary.

10.12 INITIAL PUBLIC OFFER (IPO)

DEFINITIONS OF INITIAL PUBLIC OFFERING
• A corporation's first offer to sell stock to the public.
• Initial public offering (IPO), also referred to simply as a "public offering" or "flotation," is when a company issues common stock or shares to the general public.
• When a privately held company-owned, for example, by its founders and its venture capital investors-offers shares of its stock to the public.
• A process of taking a private company to public by offering the shares of the company to the public market via a stock exchange.
• The first public issuance of stock from a company that has not been publicly traded before.
• The first sale of a company's securities to the general public.
• A company's first sale of stock to the public. Companies making an IPO are seeking outside equity capital and a public market for their stock.
• Is the initial offering to the public of a company is securities. After the initial offering, the securities are said to trade in the secondary market.
• The process of going public through an offering of securities by a corporation to the public and filing and seeking effectiveness of a stock.
• The first issue of shares by an existing or a newly-formed firm to the general public.
• The sale or distribution of a stock of a portfolio company to the public for the first time.

- The first fund-raising from the general public. It generally results in a listing on a stock exchange.
- The "flotation" of a company through the open sale of its shares in a stock market — the conventional exit route for early investors such as à business angle and a venture capital funds
- The initial sale of stock in a public corporation. The dot-com boom of the late 1990s coincided with the mainstreaming of open source software, leading to some over-rated IPO's for open source companies.

Thus an Initial Public Stock Offering (IPO) referred to simply as an "offering" or "flotation," is when a company, called the issuer, issues common stock or shares to the public for the first time. They are often issued by smaller, younger companies seeking capital to expand, but can also be done by large privately-owned companies looking to become publicly traded.

Corporate may raise capital in the primary market by way of an initial public offer, rights issue or private placement. An Initial Public Offer (IPO) is the selling of securities to the public in the primary market. This Initial Public Offering can be made through the fixed price method, book building method or a combination of both.

An Initial Public Stock Offering (IPO) referred to simply as an "offering" or "flotation," is when a company, called the issuer, issues common stock or shares to the public for the first time.

A company that is planning an IPO appoints lead managers to help it decide on an appropriate price at which the shares should be issued. There are two ways in which the price of an IPO can be determined: either the company, with the help of its lead managers, fixes a price or the price is arrived at through the process of book building.

In case the issuer chooses to issue securities through the book building route then as per SEBI guidelines, an issuer company can issue securities in the following manner:

(a) 100% of the net offer to the public through the book building route.

(b) 75% of the net offer to the public through the book building process and 25% through the fixed price portion.

(c) Under the 90% scheme, this percentage would be 90 and 10 respectively.

TYPES OF INITIAL PUBLIC OFFER / PUBLIC ISSUE

Public issue of common shares is essentially carried out in two ways:

- Fixed price method, and
- Book-building method.

Fixed price issues are issues in which the issuer is allowed to price the shares as he wishes. The basis for the price is explained in an offer document through qualitative and quantitative statements. This offer document is filed with the stock exchanges and the registrar of companies.

Book-building is a process of price discovery used in public offers. The issuer sets a base price and a band within which the investor is allowed to bid for shares. Take the recent, Yes Bank IPO, the floor price was Rs. 38 and the band was from Rs. 38 to Rs. 45.

The investor had to bid for a quantity of shares he wished to subscribe to within this band. The upper price of the band can be a maximum of 1.2 times the floor price. Every public offer through the book-building process has a Book Running Lead Manager (BRLM), a merchant banker, who manages the issue. Further, an order book, in which the investors can state the quantity of the stock they are willing to buy, at a price within the band, is built. Thus the term 'book-building.' An issue through the book-building route remains open for a period of 3 to 7 days and can be extended by another three days if the issuer decides to revise the floor price and the band.

The two types of Initial Public Offer or Public Issue characteristics are presented in the following table 10.1.

Table 10.1

ISSUE TYPE	OFFER PRICE	DEMAND	PAYMENT	RESERVATIONS
Fixed Price Issues	Price at which the securities are offered and would be allotted is made known in advance to the investors	Demand for the securities offered is known only after the closure of the issue	100 % advance payment is required to be made by the investors at the time of application.	50 % of the shares offered are reserved for applications below Rs. 1 lakh and the balance for higher amount applications.
Book Building Issues	A 20 % price band is offered by the issuer within which investors are allowed to bid and the final price is determined by the issuer only after closure of the bidding.	Demand for the securities offered , and at various prices, is available on a real time basis on the BSE website during the bidding period..	10 % advance payment is required to be made by the QIBs along with the application, while other categories of investors have to pay 100 % advance along with the application.	50 % of shares offered are reserved for QIBs, 35 % for small investors and the balance for all other investors.

METHODS OF IPO SALE

The sale (that is, the allocation and pricing) of shares in an IPO may take several forms. Common methods include:

- Best efforts contract
- Firm commitment contract
- All-or-none contract
- Bought deal
- Dutch auction
- Self distribution of stock

A large IPO is usually underwritten by a "syndicate" of investment banks led by one or more major investment banks (lead underwriter). Upon selling the shares, the underwriters keep a commission based on a percentage of the value of the shares sold (called the gross spread). Usually, the lead underwriters, that is the underwriters selling the largest proportions of the IPO, take the highest commissions — up to 8 percent in some cases.

Multinational IPOs may have as many as three syndicates to deal with differing legal requirements in both the issuer's domestic market and other regions. For example, an issuer based in the E.U. may be represented by the main selling syndicate in its domestic market, Europe, in addition to separate syndicates or selling groups for US/Canada and for Asia. Usually, the lead underwriter in the main selling group is also the lead bank in the other selling groups.

Because of the wide array of legal requirements, IPOs typically involve one or more law firms with major practices in securities law, such as the Magic Circle firms of London and the white shoe firms of New York City.

Usually, the offering will include the issuance of new shares, intended to raise new capital, as well the secondary sale of existing shares. However, certain regulatory restrictions and restrictions imposed by the lead underwriter are often placed on the sale of existing shares.

Public offerings are primarily sold to institutional investors, but some shares are also allocated to the underwriters' retail investors. A broker selling shares of a public offering to his clients is paid through a sales credit instead of a commission. The client pays no commission to purchase the shares of a public offering; the purchase price simply includes the built-in sales credit.

The issucr usually allows the underwriters an option to increase the size of the offering by up to 15 percent under certain circumstance known as the greenshoe or over allotment option.

PROCEDURE TO INVEST IN IPO

An initial public offering (IPO) occurs when a company first sells common shares to investors in the public. Generally, the company offers primary shares this way, although sometimes secondary shares are also sold as IPOs. For a company to offer IPOs, they need to hire a corporate lawyer as well as an investment banker to underwrite the offer. The actual sale of the shares is generally offered by stock exchange or by regulators. When the company starts to offer IPOs, they are usually required to reveal financial information about the company so that investors know whether the company is a good investment or not.

Reasons for Issuing IPOs

In general, companies offer IPOs in order to raise money that they need for business expansion and new business opportunities. By offering shares to investors, a company stands to bring in a lot of money. They can then use this money to grow their business. The more their business grows, in turn, the higher the share prices grow and the more money is generated by investors purchasing shares. Unlike business loans, which need to be repaid with interest, IPOs do not have this disadvantage. It is investors who take the risk — although also a potential gain — buying shares. If the company loses money and they will not have to repay their investors, although investors in general demand high accountability from a company they are buying stocks from.

Many companies simply see offering IPOs as the next stage in business growth. Since public companies often enjoy larger profits and can draw on a larger capital base than private businesses, IPOs seem like the logical way to grow a company for many CEOs.

PARTIES IN INITIAL PUBLIC OFFER

Public investors can purchase IPOs through their regular investment channels, although they will need to act fast to take advantage of the initial low IPO costs. Businesses can take advantage of IPOs simply by offering public shares on the market. To do this, they require a corporate lawyer, transparent business and financial practices, and an investment banker. They also need a medium — usually a stock exchange -- to actually sell the shares. Most businesses additionally hire marketers or someone who can advertise or market the stock.

Benefits of IPOs

For businesses, stocks and shares are a fast way to raise revenue for business expansion and growth. They also can take a business to the next level. By becoming a publicly traded company a business can take advantage of new, larger opportunities and can start working towards incorporation and even worldwide expansion. IPO gives a company fast access to public capital. Even though public offering can be costly and time consuming, the tradeoffs are very appealing to companies. IPOs are also a relatively low risk for businesses and have the potential for huge gains and for huge opportunities. The more investors wish to invest in a company, the more the company stands to or from IPOs and other stock offerings.

For the investor, IPOs are attractive mainly because they may be undervalued. Initially, to make IPOs more attractive, many companies will offer their initial public offering at a low rate. This helps to encourage investors, and investors will often buy IPOs, thinking that the new company or the newly public company will be the next big thing with a huge profit margin. As prices grow and demand for the IPOs grows, early investors stand to make a lot of profit — and very quickly.

ADVANTAGES OF INITIAL PUBLIC OFFER

1. No Cost of Capital

It does not need to pay interest on the capital raised from Public. Even it doesn't need to repay the capital. Only in case of liquidation/bankruptcy it needs to pay the residual amount after paying bank loans, debentures, preferential shares etc.

2. Huge Amounts can be Raised

It can raise huge amount of capital by going to public which may not be possible otherwise.

3. Brand Value

Company's brand value will get increased because people come to know about the company very well.

4. Correct Valuation

Since the share price reflects the company's financial healthiness it would become easy to arrive at a price in case of mergers and acquisitions.

DISADVANTAGES OF INITIAL PUBLIC OFFER

1. Disclosure of Information

Once a company opens to public it has to disclose so much information to public on regular intervals. This includes share holding pattern, quarterly and annual financial statements, profiles of directors etc. Because of this restriction companies will always be under pressure to perform and show profits in every quarter. This, some times, doesn't allow the management to take bold steps which may yield long-term benefits but less profits in short-term.

We have seen some companies in recent times going bankrupt because the share prices fell down as the investors' scrutiny increased a lot. Some of them would have come out of this situation if they weren't public limited companies.

2. Decisions take Time

Implementation of any key decision is subjected to the approval by the board of directors elected by share holders. This process may take more time.

Cost of IPO

The cost of the process is very high, though it is one-time expenditure. The investment banker/underwriter charges heavily for doing this activity.

NO. OF COMPANIES WHICH HAVE ISSUED IPO IN THE LAST 5 YEARS IN INDIA

- YES Bank IPO through book building
- Industrial & Commercial Bank of China $21.6B in 2006
- NTT Mobile Communications $18.4B in 1998
- Visa Inc. $17.9B in 2008
- AT&T Wireless $10.6B in 2000
- Rosneft $10.4B in 2006

10.13 BOOK BUILDING

Introduction

Corporates may raise capital in the primary market by way of an initial public offer, rights issue or private placement. An Initial Public Offer (IPO) is the selling of securities to the public in the primary market. This Initial Public Offering can be made through the fixed price method, book building method or a combination of both.

Book Building is essentially a process used by companies raising capital through Public Offerings — both Initial Public Offers (IPOs) and Follow-on Public Offers (FPOs) to aid price and demand discovery. It is a mechanism where, during the period for which the book for the offer is open, the bids are collected from investors at various prices, which are within the price band specified by the issuer. The process is directed towards both the institutional as well as the retail investors. The issue price is determined after the bid closure based on the demand generated in the process.

Book Building is essentially a process used by companies raising capital through Public Offerings — both Initial Public Offers (IPOs) and Follow-on Public Offers (FPOs) to aid price and demand discovery.

Thus, Book Building is basically a capital issuance process used in Initial Public Offer (IPO) which aids price and demand discovery. It is a process used for marketing a public offer of equity shares of a company. It is a mechanism where, during the period for which the book for the IPO is open, bids are collected from investors at various prices, which are above or equal to the floor price. The process aims at tapping both wholesale and retail investors. The offer/issue price is then determined after the bid closing date based on certain evaluation criteria.

Book building is a technique used for marketing a public offer of equity shares of a company. In broad terms, the process is as follows:

- Decision is taken by the company on the quantum of funds to be raised from the market, by way of equity shares, and the likely timing;
- Merchant banker is associated, and a draft prospectus, excepting issue price, is prepared and placed with SEBI;
- The draft placed with SEBI also indicates that the issue price is to be decided through the book-building process;
- Bids are invited from prospective investors (which is indicative of price range) as to the likely number of shares that they would be ready to subscribe and `the price' at which they will take up subscription;
- A time-period is determined during which the bids will be received;
- After expiration of time period, these bids are evaluated and a price is determined;
- The issue price is then decided and SEBI kept informed;
- Twenty-five per cent of the total issue is offered to the public (an element of reservation is also possible);
- The balance 75 per cent can be covered by accepting the bids received at the evaluated price.

The book-building process allows for price and demand discovery. Also, the costs of the public could be kept at minimum, and the time taken for completing the process is relatively shorter than a normal public issue. In a normal public offering, the demand for shares, that is, how many shares will be subscribed for, would not be known in advance.

The likely demand for shares (as also the likely price) can be estimated more realistically under book-building, and if there were to be no bids, the issue can even be deferred.

The Process of Book Building

- The Issuer who is planning an IPO nominates a lead merchant banker as a 'book runner.'
- The Issuer specifies the number of securities to be issued and the price band for orders.
- The Issuer also appoints syndicate members with whom orders can be placed by the investors.
- Investors place their order with a syndicate member who inputs the orders into the 'electronic book.' This process is called 'bidding' and is similar to open auction.
- A Book should remain open for a minimum of 5 days.
- Bids cannot be entered less than the floor price.
- Bids can be revised by the bidder before the issue closes.
- On the close of the book building period the 'book runner evaluates the bids on the basis of the evaluation criteria which may include —
  - — Price Aggression
  - — Investor quality
  - — Earliness of bids, etc.

- The book runner and the company conclude the final price at which it is willing to issue the stock and allocation of securities.
- Generally, the number of shares are fixed, the issue size gets frozen based on the price per share discovered through the book building process.
- Allocation of securities is made to the successful bidders.
- Book Building is a good concept and represents a capital market which is in the process of maturing.

Guidelines for Book Building

Rules governing Book building are covered in Chapter XI of the Securities and Exchange Board of India (Disclosure and Investor Protection) Guidelines 2000.

BSE's Book Building System

- BSE offers a book building platform through the Book Building software that runs on the BSE Private network.
- This system is one of the largest electronic book building networks in the world, spanning over 350 Indian cities through over 7000 Trader Work Stations via leased lines, VSATs and Campus LANS.
- The software is operated by book-runners of the issue and by the syndicate members, for electronically placing the bids on line real-time for the entire bidding period.
- In order to provide transparency, the system provides visual graphs displaying price versus quantity on the BSE website as well as all BSE terminals.

Retail Individual Investor is an investor who applies for stocks for a value of not more than Rs.1,00,000.

TYPES OF INVESTOR IN BOOK BUILDING ISSUE

There are three kinds of investors in a book-building issue. The Retail Individual Investor (RII), the Non-Institutional Investor (NII) and the Qualified Institutional Buyers (QIBs).

Retail Individual Investor (RII)

Retail Individual Investor is an investor who applies for stocks for a value of not more than Rs.1,00,000. Any bid exceeding this amount is considered in the NII category.

Non-Institutional Investors (NIIs)

Non-Institutional Investors are commonly referred to as High Net-Worth Individuals.

Qualified Institutional Buyers (QIBs)

Qualified Institutional Investors are Institutional Investors who possess the expertise and the financial muscle to invest in the securities market. Mutual funds, financial institutions, Scheduled Commercial Banks, insurance companies, provident funds, State Industrial Development Corporations and the like fall under the definition of being a QIB.

Qualified Institutional Investors are Institutional Investors who possess the expertise and the financial muscle to invest in the securities market.

Each of these categories is allocated a certain percentage of the total issue. The total allotment to the RII category has to be at least 35% of the total issue. RIIs also have an option of applying at the cut-off price. This option is not available to other classes of investors. NIIs are to be given at least 15% of the total issue.

And the QIBs are to be issued not more than 50% of the total issue. Allotment to RIIs and NIIs is made through a proportionate allotment system. The allotment to the QIBs is at the discretion of the Book Running Lead Manager (BRLM).

Lately there have been some complaints by the QIBs of Book Running Lead Managers resorting to favouritism while allocating shares. The Securities and Exchange Board of India (SEBI) is in the process of reviewing this mechanism.

Cut-off Price

The cut-off price is the price discovered by the market. It is the price at which the shares are issued to the investors.

Once the issue period is over and the book has been built, the Book Running Lead Manager (BRLM) along with the issuer arrives at a cut-off price. The cut-off price is the price discovered by the market. It is the price at which the shares are issued to the investors.

Investors bidding at a price below the cut-off price are ignored. So those investors who apply at a price higher than the cut-off price have a higher chance of getting the stock. So the question that arises is: How is the cut-off price fixed?

The cut-off price is arrived at by the method of Dutch auction. In a Dutch auction the price of an item is lowered, until it gets its first bid and then the item is sold at that price.

Let us suppose, A Ltd., makes an offer for 200,000 shares. The issue is oversubscribed that is there is demand for more shares than the issuer plans to issue. Further, a minimum allotment of 100 shares is to be made for every investor.

The cut-off price has been decided and now the allotments are to be made. In the RII category, 1,500 applicants have applied for 100 shares each, that there is a demand for 150,000 shares.

A Ltd., plans to issue 35% of the total issue to this category, that is 70,000 shares. In the NII category, 200 applicants have applied for 500 shares each, that is 100,000 shares. A Ltd., plans to issue 15% of the total issue to this category, that is 30,000 shares.

The cut-off price has already been decided, so adjusting the quantity remains the only way of reaching the equilibrium. Applying the proportionate allotment system each investor in the RII category will get 46.67 shares [(70,000/ 150,000) x 100]. But the minimum allotment has to be 100 shares.

So through a lottery, 700 investors are chosen and allotted 100 shares each, making a total of 70,000 shares. In the NII category every investor will get 150 shares [(30,000/100,000) x 500]. And that is how equilibrium is reached.

Green shoe option

In case, the issue has been oversubscribed, as was the case with A Ltd., the company has to exercise a green shoe option to stabilize the post-listing price. When a particular issue is oversubscribed the appetite of investors for the stock has not been satisfied and once it gets listed they tend to pick up the stock from the secondary market.

Since the demand is greater than supply the prices tend to rise way beyond what the fundamentals of the stock would justify. So in order to stabilise the post-issue price of the stock, the issuer has to issue more shares in case of oversubscription.

These shares are taken from the pre-issue shareholders or promoters and are issued to the investors who have come in through the public offer on a prorata basis. The green shoe option can be a maximum of 15% of the public offer.

ADVANTAGES AND DISADVANTAGES AND EXAMPLES

- This process will help to discover the demand and the price of the shares.
- The costs of public issue are much reduced.
- The time taken for completion of the entire process is much less than in the normal public issue.

10.14 MEETINGS AND RESOLUTIONS

Meetings

A company functions through its directors, who hold meetings and decide on matters concerning the company's business. Besides, the shareholders also meet annually to take important decisions giving policy guidelines to the directors on various matters. Meetings are therefore, of great significance with regard to decision-making on company affairs.

Company meetings are of four types — Board Meeting, Statutory Meeting, Annual General Meeting and Extra Ordinary General Meeting.

Board Meetings

In order that the Board of Directors should meet at regular intervals, it is essential that a Board Meeting be held atleast once in every three months and atleast four times in a year.

Proper notice of the meeting should be given to every director.

The quorum for a Board Meeting is one-third of the total number of directors on the Board, or two directors, whichever is higher. If the quorum is not present, the board cannot transact any business and the meeting shall stand adjourned for the same day in the next week, at the same time and place.

The Chairman of the Board presides over the meeting. If the Chairman is not present, the directors present shall appoint one of themselves as the Chairman, who shall then preside.

At 'a Board meeting', the matters generally taken up for consideration include making calls on shares, issuing debentures or other borrowings, investment of company's funds and extending loans, delegation of certain powers to a director or a committee of the Board, filling a casual vacancy in Board, appointment of a managing director or manager, etc.

Statutory Meeting

Statutory meeting is the first general meeting of the members of the company. It is held by public limited companies within a period of not less than one month and not more than 6 months, from the date it is entitled to commence business. The meeting is held for discussing the matters relating to the formation of the company and matters arising out of the statutory report.

Annual General Meeting

Annual General Meeting (AGM) is the meeting of the members of a company. It is to be held by every company — public or private.

The first AGM must be held within 18 months of the date of incorporation of the company. One AGM must be held in every calendar year. The time gap between two successive annual general meetings should not exceed 15 months (which may be extended by the Registrar, as on application by another 3 months).

AGM must be held at the registered office of the company or at any other place in the city where the registered office is situated and not elsewhere. The meeting must be held during business hours and on a working day.

The company must give a notice of atleast 21 clear days to its members. A shorter notice can be given if all the members agree to it unanimously.

The notice must specify the place, day and hour of the meeting and the business to be transacted thereat. Besides, a copy of the balance sheet, profit and loss account, auditors and documents attached thereto, shall be sent alongwith the notice. It is also accompanied by an 'explanatory statement' setting out the material particulars regarding 'special business' to be transacted at the meeting. 'Special business' means any business other than 'ordinary business.' And ordinary business transacted at an AGM includes:

1. Consideration and adoption of accounts, report of directors and auditors,
2. Declaration of dividend,
3. Appointment of directors in place of those retiring by rotation, and
4. Appointment of auditors and fixation of their remuneration.

Quorum

Minimum number of members required to constitute a valid meeting and to transact business is called quorum.

Minimum number of members required to constitute a valid meeting and to transact business is called quorum. If no quorum is present, there can be no meeting and no business can be transacted.

Unless the Articles provide for a larger number, quorum for a public company shall be five members present personally and for a private company shall be two members present personally. Proxies are not counted for the purpose of quorum.

If within half an hour from the time appointed for holding the meeting, the quorum is not fulfilled, the meeting shall stand adjourned to the same day of the next week at the same time and place, or such other day, time and place as the Board may determine.

Minutes: A brief summary of the proceedings of the meeting, is to be recorded in the Minutes Book.

Extraordinary General Meeting

A general meeting other than the annual general meeting is called an extraordinary general meeting (EGM). An EGM is convened when some special and urgent business is to be transacted and which must be transacted before the next annual general meeting. Besides, members holding 1/ 10th of paid-up capital carrying voting rights may also require the Board of Directors to convene an EGM.

The requirements of notice, quorum, minutes etc., shall be the same as mentioned with regard to AGM.

Voting

Voting is a means of determining the sense or opinion of a meeting, i.e., whether the meeting approves or disapproves of the proposals placed before it. A proposal is also known as a motion. After discussion the motion is put to vote, and if it is favoured by the requisite majority, it is adopted as a resolution.

Voting is a means of determining the sense or opinion of a meeting, i.e., whether the meeting approves or disapproves of the proposals placed before it.

Voting may be conducted either by show of hands or by poll. On a show of hands, one member has one vote, the number of members who raise their hands in favour and those against the motion, are counted and the motion is declared carried or lost, as the case maybe. Proxy votes are not counted on a show of hands unless the Articles provide otherwise.

Proxy

Any member entitled to attend and vote at a general meeting may appoint another person, whether a member or not, to attend and vote as his proxy. A proxy has no right to speak at the meeting or vote on a show of hands. He can vote only on poll, unless the articles provide otherwise.

Resolutions

At a general meeting, all decisions are taken in the form of resolutions. Resolutions may be ordinary or special.

An ordinary resolution is one which requires a simple majority, i.e., more than 50 per cent of the votes cast in person or by proxy in favour of the resolution.

A resolution is said to be 'special resolution', where:

1. The intention to propose the resolution as special resolution is specified in the notice of the general meeting.
2 It requires atleast 75 per cent of the votes cast, either by show of hands or on poll in person or proxy, in favour of the resolution.

A special resolution shall be required in matters such as, altering the objects clause in the memorandum, changing the registered office from one state to another, changing the name of the company, alteration of the Articles, paying interest out of capital, reduction in share capital, determining the remuneration of any director or managing director. voluntary winding up of the company, commencement of new business, further issue of shares to persons other than the existing shareholder, etc.

Any member entitled to attend and vote at a general meeting may appoint another person, whether a member or not, to attend and vote as his proxy.

Certain resolutions can be considered at a general meeting only when a 'Special Notice' is given by the proposer. The proposer must give a notice to the company, signifying his intention to move the resolution, atleast 14 days before the date of the meeting. After receipt of notice, the company shall give atleast 7 days' notice to all its members, either by advertisement or by any other mode. Special Notice is required for resolutions for appointment of a director other than a retiring director, or for appointment of an auditor other than the retiring auditor, or for removal of an auditor.

Passing of Resolution by Postal Ballot (Sec. 192)

(1) Notwithstanding anything contained in the foregoing provisions of this Act, a listed public company may, and in the case of resolutions relating to such business as the Central Government may, by notification, declare to be conducted only by postal ballot, shall, get any resolution passed by means of a postal ballot, instead of transacting the business in general meeting of the company.

(2) Where a company decides to pass any resolution by resorting to postal ballot, it shall send a notice to all the shareholders, along with a draft resolution explaining the reasons therefore, and requesting them to send their assent or dissent in writing on a postal ballot within a period of thirty days from the date of posting of the letter.

(3) The notice shall be sent by registered post acknowledgement due, or by any other method as may be prescribed by the Central Government in this behalf, and shall include with the notice, a postage pre-paid envelope for facilitating the communication of the dissent of the shareholder to the resolution within the said period.

(4) If a resolution is assented to by a requisite majority of the shareholders by means of postal ballot, it shall be deemed to have been duly passed at a general meeting convened in that behalf.

(5) If a shareholder sends under Sub-section (2) his assent or dissent in writing on a postal ballot and thereafter any person fraudulently defaces or destroys the ballot paper or declaration of identity of the sharheolder, such person shall be punishable with imprisonment for a term which may extend to six months or with fine or with both.

(6) If a default is made in complying with Sub-sections (1) to (4), the company and every officer of the company, who is in default shall be punishable with fine which may extend to fifty thousand rupees in respect of each such default.

Explanation: For the purposes of this section, "postal ballot" includes voting by electronic mode.

10.15 RECONSTRUCTION AND AMALGAMATION

In the case of reconstruction of a company, the company's business and undertaking are transferred to another company formed for that purpose so that substantially same business is carried on and the same persons are interested in it as in the case of the old company. A reconstruction may be done to effectuate material alterations of the rights of a class of shareholders or creditors.

On the other hand, amalgamation occurs when two or more companies are joined to form a new entity. The effect is to wipe out the amalgamating companies and to fuse them into a new one. The new amalgamated company comes into existence with all the propriety rights and powers and subject to all the duties and obligations, of both or all the constituent companies.

Conditions prohibiting reconstruction or amalgamation of company

Where any provision in the memorandum or articles of a company, or in any resolution passed in general meeting by, or by the Board of Directors of the company, or in an agreement between the company and any other person, whether made before or after the commencement of this Act, prohibits the reconstruction of the company or its amalgamation with any body corporate or bodies corporate, either absolutely or except on the condition that the managing director or manager of the company is appointed or reappointed as managing director or manager of the reconstructed company or of the body resulting from amalgamation, as the case may be, shall become void with effect from the commencement of this Act, or be void, as the case may be.

10.16 ACCOUNTS, AUDIT AND RETURNS

Account Books

The companies are required to keep proper books of accounts in respect of:

(a) all sums of money received and expended by the company;

(b) all sales and purchases of goods by the company;

(c) all assets and liabilities of the company; and

(d) in case of company engaged in production, manufacturing, processing or mining activities, particulars relating utilisation of material or labour or other items of cost as prescribed by the Central Government.

Thus, the usual books of account maintained by a company are cash book, petty cash book, general ledger, sales book, purchases book, journal, bills receivable ledger, bills payable ledger, bank book, etc. The ledger is sometimes divided into Creditors' Ledger, Debtors' Ledger, Assets' Ledger and Expenses Ledger, etc.

The books of account must be kept either at the registered office of the company or at any other place as the Board of Directors may decide. Account books together with vouchers of previous 8 years should be preserved.

Accounts relating to a branch office should be maintained at the branch itself and summarised accounts should be forwarded to the registered office at an interval of three months.

The accounts must give a true and fair view of the state of company's affairs and must be kept on accrual basis (and not cash basis) and according to double entry system of accounting and Indian Accounting Standards (IAS).

Balance Sheet and Profit and Loss Account

The Balance Sheet and Profit and Loss Account should be drawn at the end of every financial year, and presented in the form laid down in Part I and Part II of Schedule VI of the Act.

Statutory Books and Registers

Besides the usual accounts, a company is statutorily required to maintain following books and registers:

1. Register of Investments in shares or securities not held on company's name.

2. Copy of every instrument creating any charge on assets.
3. Register of charges.
4. Register of members.
5. Index of members where their number is more than 50.
6. Register of debenture-holders.
7. Index to debenture-holders where their number is more than 50.
8. Foreign register of members and debenture-holders.
9. Copies of annual returns.
10. Minute book of Board Meetings.
11. Minute book of General Meetings.
12. Register of contracts, companies and firms in which the directors are interested.
13. Register of directors, managing director, manager and secretary.
14. Register of director's shareholders.
15. Register of loans made to companies under the same management.
16. Register of investments in shares and debentures.
17. Register of particulars of contracts.
18. Register of fixed assets.
19. Register of deposits.

Statistical Books

A company often maintains certain statistical books, which facilitate the working of the company such as:

(i) Share application and allotment book.
(ii) Share certificate book.
(iii) Register of share transfer.
(iv) Register of shareholders address.
(v) Dividend Register.
(vi) Director attendance book.
(vii) Seal book, etc.

Inspection

The books of account should be kept open for inspection by the Registrar or by any authorised officer, during business hours. It is the duty of every director, officer or employee of the company to give all assistance for inspection.

Besides, every director has the right to inspect the books of accounts during business hours.

Audit

A company is required to get its accounts audited by a qualified Chartered Accountant in practice or a firm of Chartered Accountants and obtain an audit report.

No person should hold audit of more than 20 companies at a time.

The first auditors of the company are appointed by the Board of Directors of the Company, who hold office till the conclusion of the first annual general meeting. Subsequent auditors are appointed by the shareholders at every annual general meeting who hold office till the conclusion of the next annual general. meeting.

The auditor is required to submit his report on the accounts of the company to its shareholders. The auditor's report should state:

(i) whether the accounts are kept in accordance with the provisions of the Act,

(ii) whether the accounts give a true and fair view of the state of affairs of the company,

(iii) whether he has obtained all the information and explanation which to be best of his knowledge and belief were necessary for the purpose of audit,

(iv) whether the company's final accounts are in agreement with the books of account and returns, and

(v) whether he has received report/returns on the accounts of any branch office.

Besides, the auditor is also required to inquire into and report on matters specified in Section 227(IA) and the MAOCAR Order, 1988.

Directors' Report

The Board of Directors must every year lay before the members in annual general meeting,

(i) Balance Sheet,

(ii) Profit and Loss Account, and

(iii) Report by the Company's Board of Directors.

The directors report should give the following particulars:

(i) state of company affairs;

(ii) amount proposed to be carried to reserves;

(iii) dividend recommended;

(iv) material changes and commitments affecting the financial position of the company;

(v) the conservation of energy, technology absorption, foreign exchange earning and outgo.

(vi) names of company's employees whose remuneration was not less than Rs.3,00,000 per financial year or Rs.25,000 p.m. during the year;

(vii) particulars of employees who have financial state in the company are in receipt of remuneration in excess of that drawn by managerial personnel; and

(viii) whether any employee mentioned in (vii), is a relative of any director or manager of the company, and if so the name and other particulars of such director, etc.

(ix) Corporate Governance Report and other compliance statements.

Annual Returns

Three copies of the balance sheet, profit and loss account and other documents to be attached therewith must be filed with the Registrar within 30 days of the annual general meeting.

A company should also file with the Registrar an annual return in the form as given in Schedule V, within 60 days of the annual general meeting.

10.17 EVALUATION OF COMPANY FORM OF OWNERSHIP

After examining the meaning and nature, different types of companies and their formation, it is desirable to discuss the merits and demerits of company form of ownership. Advantages and limitations of a private company were already examined. The following are additional points distinct to company, including private company form of ownership.

Advantages

1. Limited Liability of the Shareholders: A member buys only a specified amount of ownership by subscribing to a definite number of shares of the total share capital. Therefore a shareholder's liability extends only to the amount he or she has paid for that shares. If the company fails, owners lose only the amount they have invested. They are not required to pay any of the company's debts.

2. Greater Size: As there is no restrictions on membership, many members may furnish capital for the company. On account of this, company form of organisation can usually become larger than the proprietorship or the partnership. Not only can companies grow large because of their access to capital, but they can also hire large number of employees.

3. Perpetual Existence: A company being a legal entity, its life does not depend on the lives of its members. Unlike in sole proprietorship and partnership, life of the company is not affected by death, retirement, or insolvency of members. Likewise, the death or retirement of Board of Directors or officers does not affect the life of a company. The life of a company is also not affected by the transfer of ownership. The company has an existence apart from its owners and enjoys perpetual existence.

4. Ease of Expansion: Company form of ownership attracts a large number of potential investors, because of the limited liability feature. If a company needs additional capital to expand its operations, diversify its activities, it can issue more shares to secure the required capital (subject to a maximum number specified in its Memorandum).

5. Managerial Efficiency: Separation of ownership from management gives ample scope for division of labour and specialisation in the company management. Most large companies have professional managers like production engineer, sales manager, financial manager, personnel manager, chief accountant and the like. This helps the company form of ownership to face formidable challenges of today's business.

6. Transferability of Ownership: Shares of a company are easily transferable. A shareholder can easily sell or transfer his shares/stock to others through a stock broker. And stock brokers are many.

7. Adaptable to Large and Small Firms: The word company sounds big. But not always. There are companies, specially private limited companies, whose turnover hardly exceeds a few lakhs of rupees. Titan Paper Tubes Co.(Pvt.) Ltd., Ankleshwar, for example had a turnover of just Rs.50 lakhs during 1982-83. There are companies whose turnover exceeds a few hundred crores of rupees. The Indian Oil Corporation (IOC), a Government company registered a turnover of Rs.7,833 crores in 1982-83 and Tata Iron and Steel Company had sales of Rs.781 crores in 1983-84.

Not only a company lends itself to different sizes it is adjustable to different business also. A company is suitable for manufacturing, trading, banking, insurance, transportation, healthcare, construction, consultancy, agency or any other activity.

8. Financial Strength: A public company is in a better position to raise funds. Its members are many and they all contribute to its capital. Financial institutions willingly lend money to the compay because of its big size, professional management and sure repayment. Financial strength stands the company in a good stead.

9. Diffusion of Risk: Risk is shared by many but not by one or two shareholders. Moreover, sharing of risk can be avoided if shareholders are desirous to do so by transfering shares to others.

10. Discipline, the Company Law: Company is governed by the Companies Act, 1956. The discipline of the company law, right from its incorproation till its winding up, protects the interests of shareholders. A large number of articles, a large number of sections of the Companies Act, prescribe discipline, breach of any of which exposes the director to penal action under the law. These disciplines are very healthy in the interests of the investors, financial institutions, creditors, government and general public.

11. Best fit for developing Countries: Most developing countries are known to possess rich and vast resources. They need enterprising business persons to come forward to start business and exploit the available resources for speedy development of the economies. The complexities of todays business changing business environment; globalisation; crumbling trade barriers; global flow of capital and technology; intensity of market competition make the company form of ownership best fit for developing countries.

Limitations

The company form of ownership has certain limitations.

1. Government Restrictions: The company is subject to several restrictions. Government has passed a number of legislations for regulating companies. Some important legislations are:

The Companies Act, 1956.

The Industrial (Development and Regulation) Act, 1951 (IDR Act).

The Foreign Exchange Management Act, 1999 (FEMA).

The Monopolies and Restrictive Trade Practice Act, 1969 (MRTP).

The Competition Act, 2002.

These and other legislations will decide such important matters as:

Who should own what business?

Where the company should be located?

How much the company should produce or sell?

At what price goods should be sold?

What should happen to profits earned?

Because of too many legislations and several restrictions, in forming and running a company is too frustrating to its owners and managers.

2. Difficulty and Expense of Formation: Forming a company can be a relatively complex and costly process. The use of services of an attorney, chartered accountant, financial expert, management consultant to complete the legal formalities, appointment of Bankers for the Issue, Underwriter commission. Further cost of incorporation, cost of preparation of documents to be filed can amount to thousands of rupees. The company is subject to several restrictions, in contrast to a proprietory or partnership firm.

3. Lack of Secrecy: Companies are required to submit financial reports to shareholders, government and the public. They cannot keep their operations confidential. This is more relevant to a public company.

4. Lack of Personal Interest: Often the shareholders of a company have little personal interest in its management. it is managed by directors. Their only interest may be a return on their investment. Day-to-day management is looked after by the salaried executives who do not have any personal interest in the company. Such a situation can lower the employee's morale and motivation.

5. Unethical Practices: Companies are known to indulge in unethical practices like pollution, under weight, brand imitations, price-cuts to eliminate marginal competitors, stock-cornering and failure to deliver the product within a specified date though advance payment is accepted long before and abuse of advertisement. Some of these are practised by other forms of ownership also. But companies are worst culprits.

6. Reckless Speculation: Successful companies are centres of attraction for speculators. What is unfortunate is that several non-speculators become speculators because they believe that there is scope for making big money in speculation in shares.

7. Delay in Decision Making: All important decisions are taken by either the Board of Directors or shareholders in their meetings. These meetings must be properly convened as per the provisions of the Companies Act and the articles of the company concerned. This process is time consuming. Delay in decision making may result in loss of business opportunities.

8. Neglect of Minority Interest: Majority group of shareholders rules the company through their elected representatives. The minority shareholders will have no voice and their interest is often neglected.

9. Formation of Bogus Companies: Chance of bogus companies being formed are more which can go against the interest of the investors, economy of the country, the government and the general public.

10. Fraudulent Management: The directors and chief executives may manage the company in their own selfish interests. They may misuse company resources and bring losses to the company.

GOVERNMENT UNDERTAKINGS

Nature of Government Undertakings

Public sector, born as the outcome of the conscious policy of the government to speed up the industrialisation of the country with a view to give added impetus to economic growth as well as to achieve certain socio-economic goals as enunciated in Industrial Policy Resolutions of the Government. These undertakings today cover a wide spectrum of activities in basic and strategic industries like steel, coal, minerals and metals, petroleum, heavy engineering, chemicals, pharmaceuticals and fertilizers, on the one hand and consumer goods, trading and marketing activities, transportation services, contract and consultancy service, tourist services, financial services and development of small scale industries on the other. While some of these enterprises are operative under monopoly/near-monopoly conditions, there are others working under competitive conditions. There in is yet another segment of public enterprises, viz., sick units taken over from the private sector in order to protect employment.

Government undertakings are also called State Enterprises or Government Enterprises or Public Sector Undertakings (PSUs).

Meaning and Definition

Government undertakings are also called State Enterprises or Government Enterprise or Public Sector Undertakings (PSUs). These constitute a major segment of industrial activity in our country.

Definition

In simple terms a public sector enterprise is an industrial, commercial or other economic activity owned and managed by the central or state government or jointly by both. A comprehensive definition of a public sector unit is given by experts at the International Centre for Public Enterprises (ICPE) Yugoslavia. To quote the Centre:

- "A public enterprise is an organisation which is:
- owned by public authorities including central, state or local authorities to the extent of 50 per cent or more;
- the right to appoint top management and to formulate critical policy decisions are under the top management control;
- is established for the achievement of a defined set of public purposes, which may be multi-dimensional in character;
- and is consequently placed under a system of public accountability;
- is engaged in activities of a business character;
- involves the basic idea of investment and returns;
- and which markets its outputs in the shape of goods and services."

A public sector enterprise is an industrial, commercial or other economic activity owned and managed by the central or state government or jointly by both.

Objectives of Government Undertakings

The following are the objectives of public enterprises:

(i) Help in the rapid economic growth and industrialisation of the country and create the necessary infrastructure for economic development;

(ii) Earn returns on investments and thus generate resources for development;

(iii) Promote redistribution of income and wealth;

(iv) Create employment opportunities;

(v) Promote balanced regional development;

(vi) Assist the development of small-scale and ancillary industries;

(vii) Promote import substitution, save and earn foreign exchange for the economy;

(viii) Act as a countervailing force and put up an effective competition to undertakings in the private sector; and

(ix) Gain control over the commanding heights of the economy.

Origin of Government Undertakings

Though public sector was started with greater vigour only after 1947, their origin may be traced back to the period of Chola Kings (11th and 12th centuries). In South India great dams and anicuts were built across the river Cauvery by the Chola Kings. They are magnificent testimonials to the wisdom and foresight of the Cholas. There was a good deal of such economic development by the state, directed towards sustaining the life of the community. And these dams and anicuts which were set up by the great Chola Kings. Public sector went through periods of steady expansion. After 1947, Public Sector became inevitable as the Government realised that rapid economic development could be achieved only through state intervention in economic activities. The Industrial Policy Resolution of 1948 and 1956 clearly reflect the need for expanding public sector.

Ownership Pattern of Public Enterprises

Though owned by the government, public sector units are organised differently for purposes of management and control. They include:

1. Ministry
2. Departmental Undertakings
3. Statutory Corporation
4. Central Boards
5. Companies.

1. Ministry: These are undertakings which are managed by a whole ministry of the Government, which is accountable to parliament. The ministry has its own budget which is debated and approved by parliament. Indian railways are an example. The management is vested with the Board added by a Chairman. The Board has three members and a financial commissioner. These five persons enjoy the status of Secretary to the Government of India.

2. Departmental Undertakings: These undertakings are directly subordinate to a ministry. Yet these units are self-contained, and each has management responsible for its activities. The need for secrecy, strategic importance and similar conditions make the departmental form the most suitable organisation in certain areas, defence being one example. Chittaranjan Locomotive Works, Integral Coach Factory, Post and Telegraphs and Defence production units are run as departmental undertakings.

Characteristics of Departmental Undertakings

The following are the main features of departmental undertakings:

1. A departmental undertaking is managed and administered by a separate government department, attached to the concerned ministry.
2. The affairs of a departmental undertakings are managed and is under the direct control of the officials and the minister of the concerned ministry.
3. Yet these units are self-contained and each has management responsible for its activities.
4. A departmental undertaking is financed by annual budget allotments made and approved by the parliament.
5. The revenues of a departmental undertaking is required to be paid into the government treasury.
6. The activities of departmental undertakings are subject to strict Government regulations and control, such as accounting and audit controls.

Advantages of Departmental Undertakings

1. The departmental undertakings are managed and fully controlled by the government. This enables the government to realise its socio-economic objectives.
2. Departmental undertakings provide essential services at a reasonable price.
3. The activities of departmental undertakings are subject to budgetary, accounting and audit control. This ensures the proper use of public funds. The risk of misuse is comparatively less.
4. Departmental undertakings have greater accountability to the parliament.

Limitations of Departmental Undertakings

1. Departmental undertakings are subject to political interference. Ministers, political leaders and chief government officers come in the way of effective functioning of government undertakings.
2. Departmental undertakings are managed by ministers and government officials. These have neither leadership qualities nor business acumen. Obviously the management of public sector units is generally ineffective.
3. The paid officials who are incharge of the departmental undertakings have no personal interest in their affairs and they do not care for the consumer's needs.
4. Officials of departmental undertakings have to work according to the laid down procedures. This may cause undue delay in making and implementing important decisions.
5. There is lack of flexibility of operations as the officials cannot adopt and adjust plans and programmes to the changing circumstances.
6. Departmental undertakings suffer from running losses which are not taken seriously and no corrective measures initiated.

7. Departmental undertakings lack continuity of policies, because of frequent change of government officials including the ministry itself.

3. Statutory Corporations: The Life Insurance Corporation, Air India, Industrial Finance Corporation, Reserve Bank of India, Employees' State Insurance Corporation, Oil and Natural Gas Commission and National Textile Corporation are examples of statutory corporations, also called public corporations.

A corporation is a body corporate created by a separate law, independently financed and vested with autonomy in managing its affairs. The corporation is answerable to parliament which has created it (the corporation).

Characteristics of Statutory or Public Corporation

The main characteristics of a public corporation are:

1. It is a body corporate. It has a separate legal entity.
2. Its powers, duties and privileges are defined by the special act.
3. It is created by a special Act of parliament or state legislature.
4. It can sue and be sued in its own name.
5. Its share capital is wholly contributed by either the central government or the concerned state government.
6. In addition the share capital contributed by the government, it can borrow funds from the public.
7. Unlike departmental undertakings, public corporations can retain its revenues and use them for running the corporations.
8. The management of public corporations is vested in the hands of Board of Directors nominated by the government.
9. The employees of the public corporations are not government employees. Their employment conditions are in accordance with the service conditions of the corporation.
10. The prime objective of public corporation is to render service to general public.

Merits of Public Corporations

Public corporations have the following merits to their credit:

1. Public corporations are autonomous institutions. They have freedom in administrative matters. Power, duties and privileges of corporation are defined by the special act, under which they come into existence.
2. Interference by ministers, political leaders and Government officials is comparatively less.
3. If they have free hand in administrative matters, they can take quick decisions and prompt actions.
4. Public corporations enjoy flexibility of operations. They can change their policies and practices according to the circumstances.
5. They are accountable to the parliament.

Demerits of Public Corporations

1. Public corporations, though said to be autonomous in principle practically they are subject to interference by the ministers, political leaders and top government officials. Political interference come in the way of smooth functioning of public corporations.
2. Public corporations lack flexibility of operations. Any change in administrative policies, power and functions require an amendment to the act under which they are incorporated. But the act can be amended only by the parliament. Amendment is a lengthy procedure and time consuming.
3. The formation of public corporations takes a long time, as they require the passing of a special act in the parliament or legislature.
4. They are not suitable for small and medium size industries.

4. Central Boards: These are common in river valley projects which involve huge capital investment. Set-up jointly by the central government and concerned State governments, the Central Boards are charged with the responsibility of executing big projects. Such boards were set up for Bhakra Nangal, Hirakud and Nagarjuna Sagar. A similar board is now being set up to clean the river Ganga.

5. Government Companies: Companies are more common and particularly preferable for commercial and industrial activities.

The Companies Act, 1956, defines a government company as "any company in which not less than 51 per cent of the share capital is held by the central government or by any state government or partly by central government and partly by one or more state governments and includes a company which is a subsidiary of a government company as thus defined."

An enterprise becomes a government company when it has the following characteristics:

(a) It is created under the provisions of the Companies Act, 1956.
(b) It has most of the features of a private limited company.
(c) Major portion of the capital (more than 51%) is held by central government.
(d) All the directors or a majority of them are appointed by the government.
(e) Funds are obtained from the government and in some cases, from private shareholders and through revenues derived from the sale of goods or services.

Advantages of Government Companies

The main advantages of a government company are:

1. Government companies can be easily formed, with minimum legal formalities being followed.
2. Government companies enjoy a greater operational flexibility when compared to departmental undertakings.
3. Prompt decisions and quick actions could be made as they enjoy operational flexibilities and formalities are limited.

4. The working of government companies are subject to discussion in the parliament or legislature. This makes the officials to be alert, active and efficient.

Disadvantages of Government Companies

1. The directors and other officials of government companies are mere paid officials. They do not have any stake in the business. They may not take active interest in the management of the company.
2. The directors of government companies are not answerable to the parliament or legislature. Directors and executives may misuse their powers and indulge in activities which may go against public interest.
3. Government companies are also not free from political interference.

Advantages and Limitations of Government Undertakings

Government undertakings (of all types) have, over the years, proliferated in terms of numbers, turnover, number of people employed, investment involved and areas of activities covered. They have the following advantages:

1. Balanced Regional Development: Public sector units have a vital role to play removing regional disparities. While deciding the location of PSUs, due considerations are given to the backwardness of various regions, subject to the overriding consideration of techno-economic feasibility. They have greatly reduced imbalances in regional development and have laid a strong base for the rapid development of our economy. The number of enterprises rose from five in 1951 to 246 in 1992.

2. Transformation of the Country's Economy: Government undertakings have greatly contributed to the transformation of our so called poor and traditional economy into a fast developing and fairly industrialised (we now rank among the top 20 industrialised countries in the world) country. It is worth noting that some of our government undertakings have earned reputation for excellence at the international level. Some names to be quoted in this context are HMT, HMT International, ONGC and Air India. And some giant among public sector units, i.e., Indian Oil Corporation, Steel Authority of India and Oil and Natural Gas Commission figure in Fortune International's 500 large companies outside the United States.

3. Employment Generation and Employee Satisfaction: Public enterprises have done remarkably well in acting as a model employer. According to the study conducted by the Centre for Monitoring Indian Economy, public sector units in the country accounted for 71 per cent of the total employment generated in the country in 1989. There are over two million employees in government undertakings and the average emoluments per annum amount to more than Rs.40,000. PSUs assure job security, good working conditions, attractive incentive schemes, participative management, high degree of safety and adequate training facilities.

4. Contribution to the Exchequer: An enterprise's contribution to national exchequer comprises dividend payments, tax payments and payments of others such as customs and excise duties. These contributions will help finance country's economic developmental activities. During 1990-91, such contributions amounted to Rs.19,446 crores as against Rs.18,264 crores during 1989-90, Rs.49,186 crore in 2002-03.

5. Export Earnings: PSUs have greatly contributed to the export earnings of our country, thus easing the balance of payment position. During 1990-91, export earnings of public enterprises amounted to Rs.7,095-81 crores as against Rs.6,365.84 crores during 1989-90, recording an annual increase of 11.47 per cent over the previous year.

6. Contribution to the Country's Economy: Public sector has come to occupy a key position in the nation's economy in several sectors, specially in the production of fuel, basic metal industries, non-ferrous metal industries and fertilisers. Percentage of public enterprises' contribution to National Production in respect of the above items during 2001-02 was more than 76 per cent.

7. Industrialisation and Economic Development: Industrialisation, as is well known, is a *sine qua non* for economic development. Thc rolc of public enterprises in achieving industrialisation is considerable. Our country has attained several break- throughs through the public sector enterprises. The Fertiliser Corporation of India, for instance, is one of the few organisations in the world to develop and produce a complete range of fertiliser catalysts. Similarly, the quality control laboratories of Hindustan Antibiotics are equipped with full-fledged units for all chemical, pharmacological and toxicity tests. Discoveries of new antibiotics in the laboratories have attracted international interest.

8. Encouragement to Ancillary Industries: The role of public enterprises in promoting ancillary industries is noteworthy. The Bureau of Public Enterprises has been monitoring the progress of ancillary development in the central Public enterprises to find proper direction to the ancillary growth and the needed thrust. The bureau, initially in 1971 and later in 1974 and 1978 issued guidelines on the public enterprises on the growth of ancillaries. As a result of those efforts, there has been a significant progress both in terms of numbers as well as services rendered by the ancillary sector to the public sector enterprises. Small scale and ancillary units encouraged and assisted by the SAIL, alone numbered about 700 which provide employment to about 6,300 persons. The value of purchases made annually was of the order of Rs.21 crores. Similarly, ITI, Bangalore has more than 1,000 ancillary units providing employment to thousands of employees.

9. Equitable distribution of National Income: PSUs contribute to more equitable distribution of national income and greater diffusion of wealth.

Limitations: In spite of their phenomenal growth and dynamic role, PSUs have the following shortcomings:

1. Recurring Losses: Nearly 50 per cent of public sector units are incurring losses. According to latest reports, as many as 44 PSUs have been referred to the BIFR. The public enterprises survey for 1991-92 shows that as many as 61 enterprises have shown negative net worth for two successive years, latest reports indicate that 102 units are in the sick list.

2. Political Interference: Political interference is a problem faced by PSUs. Interference by political leaders is coming in the way of effective functioning of Government undertakings.

3. High Cost of Delay: No public sector unit (except Kudremukh) is completed as per schedule. The consequences of delay are the costs of output and employment foregone during the period of delay, the cost of inter-sector imbalances which strained production and investment, above all, the impact of inflation triggered by cost escalation and its financing. The reasons for delay are: delay in the acquisition of land, supply of critical equipment and material, approval procedure of foreign aid agencies, law and order disturbances, forest clearance and difficult geological conditions. Some of these reasons together with problems of power supply delayed 11 central coal projects.

4. Ineffective Management: The management of public sector units is generally ineffective. This is because of the fact that bureaucrats, often with neither leadership qualities nor business acumen, are the chief executives. Added to this is the uncertainty of tenure faced by the top executives. This problem is now solved as the tenure is made for five years to start with to be renewed in the case of proven efficiency.

5. Bad Industrial Relations: The public sector units are over-manned. Overstaffing had led to multiple trade unions resulting in inter and intra union rivalry and at unions fighting against the management. Singareni Coal Co. Ltd., is probably the ultimate in spoilt industrial relations. The company maintained its track record in spoiled industrial relations. In 1990-91 there were 445 strikes followed by heavy absenteeism. The company suffered a loss of production of 3.12 million tonnes and 34.19 lakh man days were lost.

6. Unimaginative Production and Unfavourable Pricing Policies: The products produced by many public sector units are unrelated to market demand. Yet products are sold because their products enjoy virtual monopoly. The pricing practice reveals a lot of variations from the suggested norms.

7. Nepotism and Corruption: Executives of many PSUs indulge in nepotism and corruption. Nepotism is manifest, among others, through ancillarisation. The kith and kin of the executives are encouraged to set up ancillary units and favours are shown to them.

8. Delay in Appointment of Top Executives: Non-appointment or delay in appointment of people to the top position in many undertakings is yet another problem faced by PSUs. By end of March 1988 as many as 24 chief executives' positions and 52 directors posts were lying vacant for nearly one year.

9. Underutilisation of Capacity: Underutilisation of capacity is another problem faced by government undertakings. During 1990-91, 4 per cent of the units recorded capacity utilisation less than 75 per cent. Only 54 per cent registered capacity utilisation of more than 75 per cent. The loss due to underutilisation of capacity in 1990-91 was Rs.14,496 crores which was Rs.175 crores above the previous year's loss.

10. Others: Wrong choice of locations, uncertainty about financial allocations, inefficient inventory control, and consumer discontentment due to ever increasing prices of end products, and poor quality are the other problems of public sector units.

Whatever the critics point out, the fact remains that public undertakings have, as mentioned above, vastly contributed to India's ranking as one of the fast developing countries. Nor should anybody deny the fact that public sector units are singularly responsible for laying a strong foundation for the further development of our economy.

COMPANIES AMENDMENT ACT 2013 (WITH HIGHLIGHT AND SALIENT FEATURES)

Highlights

Companies Act, 2013 is an Act of the Parliament of India which regulates incorporation of a company, responsibilities of a company, directors, dissolution of a company. The 2013 Act is divided into 29 chapters containing 470 Sections as against 658 Sections in the Companies Act, 1956 and has 7 Schedules. The Act has replaced The Companies Act, 1956 (in a partial manner) after receiving the assent of the President of India on 29 August 2013.

The Act comprises of 29 Chapters, 470 Clauses with 7 Schedules as against 658 Sections and 14 Schedules in the Companies Act, 1956.

Need for the New Law

The changing national and international economic environment

- Exponential growth of the Indian economy
- Changes in the stakeholders' expectations
- Manifold increase in number of companies

Year	**No. of Companies**
1956	30,000 approx.
2013	11,00,000 approx.

STRUCTURAL COMPARISON WITH COMPANIES ACT 1956 TO COMPANIES ACT 2013

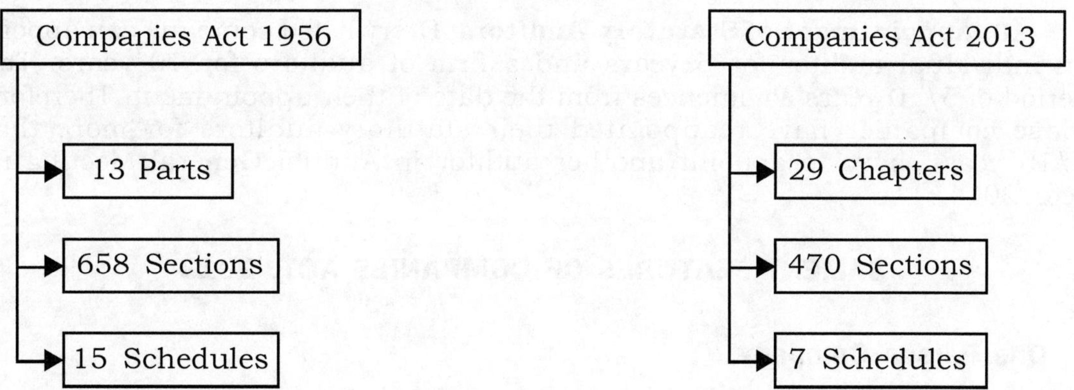

1. Immediate Changes in letterhead, bills or other official communications, as if full name, address of its registered office, Corporate Identity Number (21 digit number allotted by Government), telephone number, fax number, email ID, website address, if any.

2. One Person Company (OPC): It's a Private Company having only one Member and at least One Director. No compulsion to hold AGM. Conversion of existing private companies with paid-up capital up to Rs. 50 lakhs and turnover up to Rs. 2 crores into OPC is permitted.

3. Woman Director: Every Listed Company/Public Company with paid-up capital of Rs. 100 crores or more/Public Company with turnover of Rs. 300 crores or more shall have at least one Woman Director.

4. Resident Director: Every company must have a director who stayed in India for a total period of 182 days or more in previous calendar year.

5. Accounting Year: Every company shall follow uniform accounting year, i.e., 1st April to 31st March.

6. Loans to Director: The company cannot advance any kind of loan/ guarantee/security to any director, Director of holding company, his partner, his relative, firm in which he or his relative is partner, private limited in which he is director or member or any bodies corporate whose 25% or more of total voting power or Board of Directors is controlled by him.

7. Articles of Association: In the next General Meeting, it is desirable to adopt Table F as standard set of Articles of Association of the company with relevant changes to suit the requirements of the company. Further, every copy of Memorandum and Articles issued to members should contain a copy of all resolutions/agreements that are required to be filed with the Registrar.

8. Disqualification of Director: All existing directors must have Directors Identification Number (DIN) allotted by Central Government. Directors who already have DIN need not take any action. Directors not having DIN should initiate the process of getting DIN allotted to him and inform companies. The company, in turn, has to inform registrar.

9. Financial Year: Under the new Act, all companies have to follow a uniform Financial Year, i.e., from 1st April to 31st March. Those companies which follow a different financial year have to align their accounting year to 1st April to 31st March within 2 years. It is desirable to do the same as early as possible since most the compliances are on financial year basis under the new Companies Act.

10. Appointment of Statutory Auditors: Every listed company can appoint an individual auditor for 5 years and a firm of auditors for 10 years. This period of 5/10 years commences from the date of their appointment. Therefore, those companies have reappointed their statutory auditors for more than 5/10 years, have to appoint another auditor in Annual General Meeting for year 2014.

SALIENT FEATURES OF COMPANIES ACT, 2013

1. One Person Company

The 2013 Act introduces a new type of entity to the existing list, i.e., apart from forming a public or private limited company, the 2013 Act enables the formation of a new entity 'one person company' (OPC). An OPC means a company with only one person as its member [Section 3(1) of 2013 Act]. The draft rules state that only a natural person who is an Indian citizen and resident in India can incorporate an OPC or be a nominee for the sole member of an OPC.

Features of One Person Company (OPC)

1. Only One Shareholder:

Only a natural person, who is an Indian citizen and resident in India shall be eligible to incorporate a One Person Company. Explanation: The term "Resident in India" means a person who has stayed in India for a period of not less than 182 days during the immediately preceding one calendar year.

2. Nominee for the Shareholder:

The shareholder shall nominate another person who shall become the shareholders in case of death/incapacity of the original shareholder. Such nominee shall give his/her consent and such consent for being appointed as thc nomincc for the sole shareholder. Only a natural person, who is an Indian citizen and resident in India shall be a nominee for the sole member of a One Person Company.

3. Director:

Must have a minimum of One Director, the Sole Shareholder can himself be the Sole Director. The company may have a maximum number of 15 directors.

Terms and Restrictions of OPC

- A person shall not be eligible to incorporate more than a One Person Company or become nominee in more than one such company.
- Minor cannot shall become member or nominee of the One Person Company or can hold share with beneficial interest.
- An OPC cannot be incorporated or converted into a company under Section 8 of the Act [Company Not for Profit].
- An OPC cannot carry out Non-Banking Financial Investment activities including investment in securities of any body corporate.
- An OPC cannot convert voluntarily into any kind of company unless two years have expired from the date of incorporation of One Person Company, except threshold limit (paid-up share capital) is increased beyond Rs. 50 lakhs or its average annual turnover during the relevant period exceeds Rs. 2 crores, i.e., if the paid-up capital of the company crosses Rs. 50 lakhs or the average annual turnover during the relevant period exceeds Rs. 2 crores, then the OPC has to invariably file forms with the ROC for conversion into a Private or Public Company, within a period of six months on breaching the above threshold limits.

Steps to Incorporate One Person Company (OPC)

1. Obtain Digital Signature Certificate [DSC] for the proposed director(s).
2. Obtain Director Identification Number [DIN] for the proposed director(s).
3. Select suitable Company Name, and make an application to the Ministry of Corporate Office for availability of name.
4. Draft Memorandum of Association and Articles of Association [MOA and AOA].

5. Sign and file various documents including MOA and AOA with the Registrar of Companies electronically.
6. Payment of Requisite fee to Ministry of Corporate Affairs and also Stamp Duty.
7. Scrutiny of documents at Registrar of Companies [ROC].
8. Receipt of Certificate of Registration/Incorporation from ROC.

2. Memorandum of Association

Content: The 2013 Act specifies the mandatory content for the memorandum of association which is similar to the existing provisions of the 1956 Act and refers *inter alia* to the following:

- Name of the company with last word as limited or private limited as the case may be
- State in which registered office of the company will be situated
- Liability of the members of the company

However, as against the existing requirement of the 1956 Act, the 2013 Act does not require the objects clause in the memorandum to be classified as the following:

1. The main object of the company
2. Objects incidental or ancillary to the attainment of the main object
3. Other objects of the company [Section 4(1) of 2013 Act]

The basic purpose in the 1956 Act for such a classification as set out in Section 149 of the 1956 Act, is to restrict a company from commencing any business to pursue 'other objects of the company' not incidental or ancillary to the main objects except on satisfaction of certain requirements as prescribed in the 1956 Act like passing a special resolution, filing of declaration with the ROC to the effect of resolution.

Reservation of Name: The 2013 Act incorporates the procedural aspects for applying for the availability of a name for a new company or an existing company in Sections 4(4) and 4(5) of 2013 Act.

3. Articles of Association

The 2013 Act introduces the entrenchment provisions in respect of the articles of association of a company. An entrenchment provision enables a company to follow a more restrictive procedure than passing a special resolution for altering a specific clause of articles of association. A private company can include entrenchment provisions only if agreed by all its members or, in case of a public company, if a special resolution is passed [Section 5 of 2013 Act].

Alteration of Memorandum

The 2013 Act imposes additional restriction on the alteration of the object clause of the memorandum for a company which had raised money from the public for one or more objects mentioned in the prospectus and has any unutilised money. The 2013 Act specifies that along with obtaining an approval by way of a special resolution, a company would be required to ensure following if it intends to alter its object clause:

- Publishing the notice of the aforesaid resolution stating the justification of variation in two newspapers
- Exit option can be given to dissenting shareholders by the promoters and shareholders having control in accordance with the regulations to be specified by the Securities and Exchange Board of India (SEBI) [Section 13 of 2013 Act].

4. Incorporation of Company

The 2013 Act mandates inclusion of declaration to the effect that all provisions of the 1956 Act have been complied with, which is in line with the existing requirement of 1956 Act.

Additionally, an affidavit from the subscribers to the memorandum and from the first directors has to be filed with the ROC, to the effect that they are not convicted of any offence in connection with promoting, forming or managing a company or have not been found guilty of any fraud or misfeasance, etc., under the 2013 Act during the last five years along with the complete details of name, address of the company, particulars of every subscriber and the persons named as first directors.

The 2013 Act further prescribes that if a person furnishes false information, he or she, along with the company will be subject to penal provisions as applicable in respect of fraud, i.e., Section 447 of 2013 Act [Section 7(4) of 2013 Act; Also refer the chapter on other areas].

5. Formation of a Company with Charitable Objects

An OPC with charitable objects may be incorporated in accordance with the provisions of the 2013 Act. New objects like environment protection, education, research, social welfare, etc. have been added to the existing object for which a charitable company could be incorporated.

As against the existing provisions under which a company's licence could be revoked, the 2013 Act provides that the licence can be revoked not only where the company contravenes any of the requirements of the section but also where the affairs of the company are conducted fraudulently or in a manner violative of the objects of the company or prejudicial to public interest. The 2013 Act, thus, provides for more stringent provisions for companies incorporated with charitable objects [Section 8 of 2013 Act].

6. Commencement of Business, etc.

The existing provisions of the 1956 Act as set out in Section 149 which provide for requirement with respect to the commencement of business for public companies that have a share capital would now be applicable to all companies.

The 2013 Act empowers the ROC to initiate action for removal of the name of a company in case the company's directors have not filed the declaration related to the payment of the value of shares agreed to be taken by the subscribers to the memorandum and that the paid-up share capital of the company is not less than the prescribed limits as per the 2013 Act, within 180 days of its incorporation and if the ROC has reasonable cause to believe that the company is not carrying on business or operations [Section 11 of 2013 Act].

7. Registered Office of Company

Where a company has changed its name in the last two years, the company is required to paint, affix or print its former names along with the new name of the company on business letters, bill heads, etc. However, the 2013 Act is silent on the time limit for which the former name needs to be kept [Section 12 of 2013 Act].

8. Subsidiary Company Not to Hold Shares in its Holding Company

The existing provision of Section 42 of the 1956 Act which prohibits a subsidiary company to hold shares in its holding company continues to get acknowledged in the 2013 Act. Thus, the earlier concern that if a subsidiary is a body corporate, it may hold shares in another body corporate which is the subsidiary's holding company continues to apply [Section 19 of 2013 Act].

9. Small Company

What is a Small Company?: It means a company, other than a public company, paid-up share capital of which does not exceed fifty lakh rupees or such higher amount as may be prescribed which shall not be more than five crore rupees; or turnover of which as per its last profit and loss account does not exceed two crore rupees or such higher amount as may be prescribed which shall not be more than twenty crore rupees. The 2013 Act provides exemptions to Small Companies primarily from certain requirements relating to board meeting, presentation of cash flow statement and certain merger process.

10. Dormant Company

Section 455 of Companies Act, 2013 talks about a New Provision Calls "DORMANT COMPANY". This concept was not there in Companies Act, 1956.

A Dormant Company offers excellent advantage to the promoters who want to hold an asset or intellectual property under the corporate shield for its usage at a later stage. For instance: if a promoter wants to buy lands now for its future project at a comparatively lesser price, he may do the same through dormant company so that he can use the land for its future project. Thus, dormant company status is a new phenomenon in the Companies Act 2013 and is an excellent tool for keeping assets in the company for its future usage. A dormant company may be either a public company or a private company or a one person company.

Certain companies, due to the nature of their business, may not be able to start any business, for a long time from the date of incorporation as for instance any business for creation of intellectual property or for a future project and has no significant accounting transaction. Such a company may be an "Inactive company". Construction Companies/Real Estates Companies/ Incorporate New Companies to Hold Land/ Properties for future projects. This concept is beneficial for them. By this concept, they can Incorporate Company and Purchase Property/Land in that company and get status of Dormant Company. If a company get status of dormant company, there are less compliance in dormant company in comparison of active company. It will help to save cost of compliances for inactive companies.

Bare Act Language: According to Section 455 of the Companies Act 2013, where a company is formed and registered under this Act for a future project or to hold an asset or intellectual property and "has no significant accounting transaction", such a company or an Inactive Company may make an application to the Registrar in such manner as may be prescribed for obtaining the status of a dormant company.

Before applying for Status of Dormant Company, following conditions are required to be fulfilled: ü No inspection, inquiry or investigation has been ordered or taken up or carried out against the company; ü The company is neither having any public deposits which are outstanding nor is the company in default in payment thereof or interest thereon; ü No prosecution has been initiated or pending against the company under any law; ü The company has not defaulted in the payment of workmen's dues; ü The company does not have any outstanding statutory taxes, dues, duties, etc. payable to the Central Government or any State Government or local authorities etc.; ü The application has not been made with an objective to deceive the creditors or to defraud any other person; ü The securities of the company are not listed on any stock exchange within or outside India; ü The company is not having any outstanding loan, whether Secured and Unsecured – But if company has any Outstanding Unsecured Loan, then the company may apply for status of DORMANT only after obtaining NOC from the lender. Such NOC required to be attached in the Form which require to file with ROC. ü There is no dispute in the management or ownership of the company; A certificate in this regard required to be taken from Management. Such Certificate required to be attached in the Form which require to file with ROC.

How to Apply for a Dormant Company Status?

Step 1: The company must pass a special resolution in the general meeting of the company or after issuing a notice to all the shareholders of the company and obtaining consent of at least 3/4th shareholders (in value) for the purpose of obtaining dormant company status.

Step 2: A company can get a status of dormant company by filing an application before the MCA in Form MSC-1.

Step 3: If the registrar finds that application by the company fulfills all the conditions, it can give company a certificate of Dormant Company.

It is important to note that the registrar has the power to strike off the name of the company from the register if the Company remains dormant for **five consecutive years.**

11. Prospectus

The 2013 Act has introduced a new section [Section 23] to explicitly provide the ways in which a public company or private company may issue securities. This section explains that a public company may issue securities in any of the following manners:

- To public through prospectus
- Through private placement
- Through rights issue or a bonus issue.

For private companies, this section provides that it may issue securities through private placement, by way of rights issue or bonus issue.

Section 23 also provides that compliance with provisions of Part I of Chapter III is required for the issue of securities to public through prospectus. For private placement, compliance with the provisions of Part II of Chapter III are required.

The 2013 Act also introduces certain changes with respect to prospectus and public offers aimed at enhancing disclosure requirements as well as streamlining the process of issuance of securities.

1. Issue of Prospectus

Currently, the matters and reports to be included in the prospectus are specified in Parts I and II of Schedule II of the 1956 Act. In the 2013 Act, the information to be included in the prospectus is specified in Section 26 of 2013 Act. The 2013 Act mandates certain additional disclosures:

- Any litigation or legal action pending or taken by a government department or a statutory body during the last five years immediately preceding the year of the issue of prospectus against the promoter of the company
- Sources of promoter's contribution

The 2013 Act has also relaxed the disclosure requirements in some areas. Examples of certain disclosures not included in the 2013 Act are as follows. Particulars regarding the company and other listed companies under the same management, which made any capital issues during the last three years

- Export possibilities and export obligations
- Details regarding collaboration

The 2013 Act states that the report by the auditors on the assets and liabilities of business shall not be earlier than 180 days before the issue of the prospectus [Section 26(1)(b)(iii) of 2013 Act]. The 1956 Act currently requires that the report will not be earlier than 120 days before the issue of the prospectus.

2. Variation in Terms of Contract or Objects

The 2013 Act states that a special resolution is required to vary the terms of a contract referred to in the prospectus or objects for which the prospectus was issued [Section 27(1) of 2013 Act]. The 1956 Act currently requires approval in a general meeting by way of an ordinary resolution. The 2013 Act also requires that dissenting shareholders shall be given an exit offer by promoters or controlling shareholders [Section 27(2) of 2013 Act].

3. Offer of Sale of Shares by Certain Members of the Company

The 2013 Act includes a new section under which members of a company, in consultation with the board of directors, may offer a part of their holding of shares to the public. The document by which the offer of sale to the public is made will be treated as the prospectus issued by the company. The members shall reimburse the company all expenses incurred by it [Section 28 of 2013 Act].

4. Shelf Prospectus

The 2013 Act extends the facility of shelf prospectus by enabling SEBI to prescribe the classes of companies that may file a shelf prospectus. The 1956

Act currently limits the facility of shelf prospectus to public financial institutions, public sector banks or scheduled banks [Section 31(1) of 2013 Act].

5. Global Depository Receipts (GDRs)

The 2013 Act includes a new section to enable the issue of depository receipts in any foreign country subject to prescribed conditions [Section 41 of 2013 Act]. Currently, the provisions of Section 81 of the 1956 Act relating to further issue of shares are being used in conjunction with the requirements mandated by SEBI for the issuance of depository receipts. In several aspects across the 2013 Act, it appears that the 2013 Act supplements the powers of SEBI by incorporating requirements already mandated by SEBI.

6. Private Placement

The 2013 Act requires that certain specified conditions are complied with in order to make an offer or invitation of offer by way of private placement or through the issue of a prospectus.

- The offer of securities or invitation to subscribe securities in a financial year shall be made to such number of persons not exceeding 50 or such higher number as may be prescribed [excluding qualified institutional buyers, and employees of the company being offered securities under a scheme of employees stock option in a financial year and on such conditions (including the form and manner of private placement) as may be prescribed]. This provision of the 2013 Act is in line with the existing provision of the 1956 Act.
- The allotments with respect to any earlier offer or invitation may have been completed.
- All the money payable towards the subscription of securities shall be paid through cheque, demand draft or any other banking channels but not by cash.
- The offers shall be made only to such persons whose names are recorded by the company prior to the invitation to subscribe, and that such persons shall receive the offer by name.
- The company offering securities shall not release any advertisements or utilize any media, marketing or distribution channels or agents to inform the public at large about such an offer [Section 42 of 2013 Act].

12. Shares and Share Capital

Shares, Debentures and Deposits

- Shares, other than sweat equity, cannot be issued at a discount.
- Reduction of share capital is subject to the approval of Tribunal.
- A company may issue preference shares redeemable after 20 years for infrastructure projects as may be specified and redeemed as may be prescribed on an annual basis at the option of such preference shareholders.
- Buyback provisions eased. Companies can buy back its shares even if it has defaulted in repayment of deposit or interest payable thereon,

redemption of debentures or preference shares or payment of dividend to any shareholder or repayment of any term loan or interest payable thereon to any financial institution or bank, provided that such default has been remedied and three years have lapsed after such default ceased to subsist. This was not the case in the Companies Act, 1956.

- Debenture trustee to be appointed only when a company issues prospectus or makes an offer or invitation to the public or to its members exceeding five hundred for subscription to its debentures.

Acceptance of Deposit by Companies:

- NBFCs not to be covered by the provisions relating to acceptance of deposits. They will be governed by the Reserve Bank of India rules on acceptance of deposits.
- Deposit insurance is required to be provided as prescribed.
- Deposits can be secured and unsecured.
- The concept of small depositors is dispensed with.
- The Tribunal may allow further time taking into consideration the financial condition of the company to issue directions for repayment of the deposits or interest thereon in case of default in such repayments.

13. Directors of Company

Appointment and Variations regarding Directors and Key Managerial Personnel:

- **Appointment**
  - Certain companies, as may be prescribed, to mandatorily appoint company secretary.
  - Appointment of at least one women director on the board of prescribed classes of companies has been made mandatory.
  - Appointment of at least one director resident in India, i.e., a director who has stayed in India for at least 182 days in the previous calendar year, is made mandatory for all companies.
- **Key Managerial Personnel**
  - Company Secretary included within the definition of Key Managerial Personnel.
  - No company can have both Managing Director and Manager at the same time.
  - Every company belonging to such class or description of companies as may be prescribed, to have managing director, or chief executive officer or manager and in their absence, a whole-time director, company secretary and chief financial officer.
  - Individual limits for remuneration enhanced in the Act
- **Status of Independent Director**
  - Nominee director cannot be regarded as Independent Director.
  - Maximum term of Independent Director has been restricted to five years at once subject to a maximum of two such terms.

- The independent director is not entitled to stock option and may receive remuneration by way of fee and profit related commission as approved by members.
- Role or functions of independent directors is expanded.

- **Directorships**
  - Maximum number of directors has been increased from twelve (12) to fifteen (15) directors. Further no Central Government approval is required to increase the maximum number of directors beyond fifteen (15). Shareholders of companies may do so by passing a special resolution.
  - A person can hold directorship of up to 20 companies, of which not more than 10 can be public companies.

Eligibility Age to Become Managing Director or Whole-time Director: The eligibility criteria for the age limit has been revised to 21 years as against the existing requirement of 25 years.

Number of Directorships Held by an Individual: Section 165 provides that a person cannot have directorships (including alternate directorships) in more than 20 (twenty) companies, including ten (ten) public companies. It provides a transition period of one year from 1 April 2014 to comply with this requirement

All Existing Directors must have Directors Identification Number (DIN) allotted by Central Government. Directors who already have DIN need not take any action. However, Directors not having DIN should initiate the process of getting DIN allotted to him and inform the respective companies on which he is a director. The company, in turn, has to inform the registrar of companies (ROC).

Independent Directors: The 2013 Act defines the term "Independent Director". In case of listed companies, one-third of the board of directors should be independent directors. There is a transition period of 1 (one) year from 01 April 2014 to comply with this requirement. The 2013 Act also provides additional qualifications/restrictions for independent directors as compared to the 1956 Act.

Section 150 enables manner of selection of independent directors and maintenance of databank of independent directors and enables their selection out of data bank maintained by a prescribed body

Resident Director: Every company must have atleast one director who has stayed in India for a total period of 182 days or more in previous calendar year. For existing companies, the compliance need to be made before 31st March 2015.

Loans to Director: The company cannot advance any kind of loan/ guarantee/security to any director, director of holding company, his/her partner/s, his/ her relative/s, firm in which he or his relative is partner, private limited in which he is director or member or any bodies corporate whose 25% or more of total voting power or Board of Directors is controlled by him.

14. Woman Director

The following class of companies shall appoint at least one woman director—

- Every listed company;
- Every other public company having paid-up share capital of one hundred crore rupees or more; or turnover of three hundred crore rupees or more.
- Listed companies and certain other public companies shall be required to appoint atleast 1 (one) woman director on its board.
- Companies incorporated under Companies Act 2013 shall be required to comply with this provision within 6 (six) months from date of incorporation. In case of companies incorporated under Companies Act 1956, companies are required to comply with the provision within a period of 1 (one) year from the commencement of the Act.

While the mandatory requirement for appointment of women directors is expected to bring diversity on to the boards, companies may find it difficult to be in compliance with Companies Act 2013 unless they have already identified or internally groomed women candidates that are qualified to be appointed to the board.

15. Appointment of Managing Director, Whole-time Director or Manager Section 196 of 2013 Act]

The reappointment of a managerial person cannot be made earlier than one year before the expiry of the term instead of two years as per the existing provision of Section 317 of the 1956 Act. However, the term for which managerial personnel can be appointed remains as five years. Further, the 2013 Act lifts the upper bar for age limit and thus an individual above the age of 70 years can be appointed as key managerial personnel by passing a special resolution.

16. Key Managerial Personnel (KMP)

The provisions relating to appointment of KMP includes: (i) the Chief Executive Officer (CEO) or the Managing Director (MD) or the manager, (ii) the Company Secretary (iii) the Whole-time Director; (iv) the Chief Financial Officer (CFO); and (v) such other officer as may be prescribed is applicable only for Public Limited Companies having paid-up capital more than Rs. 10 crores and Private Limited Companies are exempted from appointment of KMPs.

Attending Board Meetings: As per Section 167 of the Act, a Director shall vacate his/her office if he/she absents himself from all the meetings of the Board of Directors held during a period of 12 (twelve months) with or without seeking leave of absence of the Board. Simply speaking, attending at least one Board Meeting by a director in a year is a must else he has to vacate his/her office.

17. Secretarial Audit

- All listed companies to annex secretarial audit report obtained from a Practicing Company Secretary to the Board's report.
- Board to respond to qualifications, made by the Secretary, in the Board's report.

18. Meetings of Company

Meetings:

(a) One Person Company is not required to hold any Annual General Meeting

(b) Noticc of general meeting need to be sent to all the directors of the Company

(c) For special business to be transacted in the General Meeting, explanatory statement should comprise of specified information

(d) Company should follow that secretarial standards are filed while making minutes

Meeting of Board and its Powers:

- A notice of not less than 7 days in writing is required to call a board meeting. The notice of meeting to be given to all directors, whether he is in India or outside India by hand delivery post or electronic means.
- Certain powers which earlier can be exercised by the Board with the approval of general meeting by way of ordinary resolution under section 293 of the Companies Act 1956, shall now to be passed by special resolution.
- Every Listed Company and such other company as may be prescribed shall have an Audit Committee.
- The Central Government permission under Section 295 and Section 372A of Companies Act, 1956 is dispensed with.
- Following committees of the Board made mandatory for listed and prescribed classes of companies:
  - Audit Committee
  - Stakeholder Relationship Committee
  - Nomination and Remuneration Committee
  - Corporate Social Responsibility Committee

Board Meetings: At least 7 days notice to be given for Board Meeting. The Board need to meet at least 4 times within a year. There should not be a gap of more than 120 days between two consecutive meetings.

19. Accounts and Audit

- Books of accounts can be kept in electronic form also.
- The term balance sheet and profit and loss accounts are collectively termed as financial statement.
- The Act provides for reopening or recasting of Books of Accounts at the instance of regulatory authorities. The financial statements can be revised at specified situations.

- No listed companies shall appoint an individual as auditor for more than one term of five consecutive years, and an audit firm as auditor for more than two terms of five consecutive years.
- Shareholders are at liberty to decide by passing resolution that audit partner and the audit team, be rotated every year.
- Auditor shall not provide directly or indirectly the specified services to the company, its holding and subsidiary companies.
- No approval of Central Government is required for appointment of cost auditor.
- Financial year will be uniform for all companies, i.e., April to March.

Related Party Transactions:

- Scope of related party transactions has been widened and definition of relatives has also been enlarged and replaced with definition of "related party".
- Clause 188 of the Act which carries provisions regarding related party transactions, combines existing Sections 297 and 314.
- Central Government Approval has been done away with. Every related party transaction to be disclosed in Board's report along with the justification.
- Approval in the Board is mandatory and also require prior shareholders 'approval for specified share capital and prescribed amounts.

Inspection and Investigation:

- The provision for establishment of Serious Fraud Investigation Office (SFIO) by the Central Government is another significant feature of the Act.
- SFIO is empowered to arrest in respect of certain offence involving fraud.

Annual Documents:

(a) Requirement of compliance certificate done away with and in its place scope of annual return has been enlarged.

(b) The annual return, filed by a listed company or, by a company having such paid-up capital and turnover as may be prescribed, shall be certified by a company secretary in practice in the prescribed form, stating that the annual return discloses the facts correctly and adequately and that the company has complied with all the provisions of this Act.

(c) Director's responsibility statement shall include additional statement related to compliance to all applicable laws and in case of listed companies, it shall include statement related to internal financial control.

(d) Benefit of private companies to file their balance sheet and profit and loss account separately has been withdrawn.

20. Appointment of Statutory Auditors

Every listed company can appoint an individual auditor for 5 years and a firm of auditors for 10 years. This period of 5/10 years commences from the date of their appointment. Therefore, those companies who have reappointed their statutory auditors for more than 5/10 years, have to appoint another auditor in their Annual General Meeting for year 2014.

Other specialized services which cannot be provided by Statutory Auditors: The Statutory Auditor of the company cannot give following specialized services directly or indirectly to the company—

- Accounting and book keeping services
- Internal audit
- Design and implementation of any financial information system
- Actuarial services
- Investment advisory services
- Investment banking services
- Rendering of outsourced financial services
- Management and/or any other services as may be prescribed

Rotation of Statutory Auditors:

Rotation of Statutory Auditor is required after transition period of 3 years from applicability of Companies Act 2013. Following companies are under the obligation to rotate the statutory auditors after 5 years or 10 years:

- All unlisted public companies having paid-up share capital of rupees ten crore or more;
- All private limited companies having paid-up share capital of rupees twenty crore or more;
- All companies having paid-up share capital of below threshold limit mentioned in (i) and (ii) above, but having public borrowings from financial institutions, banks or public deposits of rupees fifty crores or more.

21. Financial Year

The Companies Act 1956 Act provided companies to elect financial year. The Companies Act 2013 Act eliminates the existing flexibility in having a financial year different than 31 March. The 2013 Act provides that the financial year for all companies should end on 31 March, with certain exceptions approved by the National Company Law Tribunal. Companies should align the financial year to 31 March within two years from 01 April 2014.

22. Dividend

Dividend is a payment made by a company to its shareholders out of distributable profit.

Declaration of Dividend (Section 123):

A company shall declare dividend and pay it, only out of profit of the company for the financial year or out of undistributed profit of any previous financial year or out of both.

In case of any guarantee given by any Government (Central or State), the company may declaare dividend out of money provided by that government for payment of dividend.

Before declaration of dividend, a company may transfer a portion from the profit to the reserves of the company. The company is free to decide the percentage for such transfer to the reserve.

Where a company has no adequate profit or any profit in a financial year or any accumulated profit to distribute as dividend, it may declare dividend out of reserves in accordance with the rules made by the government. The company may pay dividend only from free reserves, not from any other reserves.

For the purpose of calculation of distributable profit, depreciation shall be calculated as per Schedule II.

Interim Dividend:

The Board of Directors may declare interim dividend during financial year out of surplus in profit and loss account. In case, a company is incurring loss as per financials of latest quarter, interim dividend shall not be higher than average dividend declared by the company during last three financial years.

Dividend Account in Bank:

The amount of dividend and interim dividend shall be deposited in a separate account in a Scheduled Bank within five days from the date of declaration of such dividend.

The dividend shall be paid to shareholder or to his banker in cash not otherwise. However, issue of bonus shares out of distributable profit or free reserve is permitted and not be deemed to be a violation of this rule. Making a partly paid share, fully paid through payment from distributable profit and free reserve is permitted.

Any dividend payable in cash may be paid by cheque or warrant or in any electronic mode to the shareholder.

Prohibition on Dividend:

A company which has default under Section 73 and 74 related to deposit and repayment of deposit or interest thereon may not declare dividend.

23. National Company Law Tribunal (NCLT)

- NCLT replaces the High Court, CLB. The same shall consists of Judicial and Technical members, as Central Government may deem necessary, to exercise and discharge the powers and functions conferred including approval of merger, corporate reorganization, capital reduction, extension of financial year, etc.
- Every proceeding presented before the Tribunal shall be dealt with and disposed of within 3 months from the date of commencement of proceeding before the tribunal.

The National Company Law Tribunal (NCLT), which would replace the Company Law Board, is likely to be operational by April next year, with the principal bench based in the national capital.

The tribunal is to be set up under the Companies Act, 2013. The legislation is being implemented by the Corporate Affairs Ministry.

The plan is to have about 12 to 13 NCLT benches in different parts of the country but a final decision is yet to be taken, according to a source.

To begin with, the existing benches of Company Law Board would be converted into NCLT ones. Then, in due course, new benches would be created.

The tribunal would have a President, judicial and technical members. The President should be a person who is or has been a High Court judge for at least five years.

To become a judicial member at NCLT, an individual is or should have been a High Court judge or district judge for at least five years or with a minimum of ten years experience as an advocate of a court.

Meanwhile, among others, chartered accountants or cost accountants or company secretaries having at least 15 years of experience are eligible to be technical members.

The appeals against NCLT orders would be heard by the proposed National Company Law Appellate Tribunal, which would have a chairperson, judicial and technical members.

24. Corporate Social Responsibility (CSR)

- Formation of CSR Committee has been made mandatory for a company having net worth of Rs. 500 crore or more, or turnover of Rs. 1,000 crore or more or net profit of Rs. 5 crore or more during any financial year.
- Such company shall spend, in every financial year, at least 2 per cent of the average net profits of the company made during three immediately preceding financial years, in pursuance of its Corporate Social Responsibility Policy (CSRP).

Corporate Social Responsibility (CSR) – The company has to constitute a CSR committee of the Board and 2 per cent of the average net profits of the last three financial years are to be mandatorily spent on CSR activities by an Indian company if any of the following criteria is met:

- Net worth of Rs. 500 crores or
- Turnover of Rs. 1000 crores or more or
- Net profit of Rs. 5 crores or more

Contributing to Incubators, which has been notified by the Government of India, is eligible for spending under CSR. This is a prosperous time for incubators and entrepreneurs and can really change the entrepreneurial ecosystem in India.

As per Section 135 of the Act, companies with a specified net worth or turnover or net profit are required to mandatorily spend 2 per cent of its average net profit towards specified CSR activities.

- Every company having net worth of INR 500 crore or more, or turnover of INR 1000 crore or more or net profit of INR 5 crore or more during any financial year will have to comply with the CSR provisions as laid down under the Act.
- If any of the above financial strength criteria is met, the qualifying company is mandatorily required to spend at least 2 per cent of the average net profit of past three financial years on specified CSR activities.

- While the threshold limit of net worth criteria and the turnover criteria are kept higher, the net profit threshold limit of mere INR 5 crore will bring majority of companies under the CSR net.

Under the draft CSR rules, net profit is defined to mean 'net profit before tax' as per books of accounts and shall not include profits arising from branches outside India.

What Constitutes Eligible CSR?

Spend Activities which may be considered as eligible CSR spend are provided in Schedule VII of the Act. The specified activities are as under:

- Environment sustainability
- Empowering women and promoting gender equality
- Education
- Poverty reduction and eradicating hunger
- Social business projects
- Reducing child mortality and improving maternal health
- Improvement of health
- Imparting of vocational skills
- Contribution towards Central and State Government funds for socioeconomic development and relief
- Such other matters as may be prescribed

The companies shall give preference to the local area and area around it where it operates for spending the amounts earmarked for CSR activities.

The draft CSR rules further provide following guidelines/manner in which the company can undertake CSR activities and incur CSR spend:

- The company can setup a not-for-profit organization in the form of trust, society or non-profit company to facilitate implementation of its CSR activities. However, the contributing company shall specify projects/programs to be undertaken by such an organization and the company shall establish a monitoring mechanism to ensure that the allocation to such organization is spent for intended purpose only.
- A company may also implement its CSR programs through not-for-profit organizations that are not set up by the company itself.
- Such spends may be included as part of company's prescribed CSR spend only if such organizations have an established track record of at least 3 years in carrying on activities in related areas.
- Companies may also collaborate or pool resources with other companies to undertake CSR activities.
- Only CSR activities undertaken in India would be considered as eligible CSR activities.
- CSR activities may generally be conducted as projects or programmes (either new or ongoing), however, excluding activities undertaken in pursuance of the normal course of business of a company.
- CSR projects/programs may also focus on integrating business models with social and environmental priorities and processes in order to create shared value.

- CSR activities shall not include activities exclusively for the benefit of employees and their family members.

25. E-Governance under New Companies Act

Forms and Certification:

- E-Governance proposed for various company processes like maintenance and inspection of documents in electronic form, option of keeping of books of accounts in electronic form, financial statements to be placed on company's website, holding of board meetings through video conferencing/other electronic mode; voting through electronic means.
- For all the companies (except one person companies and small companies) with prescribed paid-up capital and turnover, whether private or public, listed or unlisted, annual return has to be signed by a company secretary in practice.

In this age of well-developed information technology and telecommunications, the Electronic Governance of all business-related activities, administrative activities, and managerial functions of the corporate world, can certainly be very convenient, efficient, transparent, and fully accountable and responsible. Therefore, undoubtedly, e-governance in the corporate sector is an imperative and highly prudent requirement in every country of the world, inevitably including India. As India is one of the major, fast-progressing, and highly influential economies of the world. Thus, e-governance is absolutely essential and beneficial to Indian corporate world, especially in present-day world of cut-throat corporate competition, and ever-increasing need for greater transparency and accountability in the corporate sector. Considering these highly significant facts and business scenarios, the Government of India has rightly promulgated the provisions for e-governance in the corporate sector of the country, in its latest Companies Act of 2013.

E-Governance or Electronic Governance is basically proper and efficient utilization of the technologies of the information technology and telecommunications, for performing various functions and activities by an organization. Such use of Information and Communication Technologies [ICTs] can preferably be made at all levels of a business corporation also, in order to obtain faster and more efficient business activities, greater customer satisfaction, more accountable and transparent corporate administration and management, better profits and satisfaction of the shareholders, and the best possible progress and growth of the corporation.

MAJOR E-GOVERNANCE PROVISIONS UNDER COMPANIES ACT 2013

(A) Maintenance, Security, and Inspection of Books and Records in Electronic Form

Regarding the account keeping and maintenance of records and books related with the business activities of a company, and the well-rounded security and efficient and transparent inspection of these documents, the new Companies Act of India has proper provisions, suggestions, and recommendations. These prudent provisions and recommendations are provided in the Section 120 of the Indian Companies Act of 2013, and the

Companies (Management and Administration) Rules of 2014. The Section 120 facilitates that a company must keep a safe account of all business and management related documents, records, registers, minutes, etc., preferably in the electronic forms, in such a manner that these could easily be inspected or reproduced whenever necessary. Again, the Rules ranging from Rule 27 to Rule 29 of the Indian Companies (Management and Administration) Rules of 2014, further clarify things in this context, as follows:

- As per Rule 27, every listed company, or any other company with 1000 or more shareholders and security holders, must maintain its all such secretarial records and documents preferably [but not necessarily or mandatorily] in the electronic form. The Ministry of Corporate Affairs [MCA] vide its Notification dated 24th July, 2014, has substituted the word 'shall' by the word 'may' in Rule 27 of Companies (Management and Administration) Rules of 2014, and thereby, the task of maintaining such records strictly in the electronic form has been made optional, for time being. However, it will be wise to convert these data and records to the electronic form [from the physical form] as quickly as possible.
- The Rule 28 dictates that the MD, CS, or any other Director or Officer of the company shall be made responsible for proper and safe keeping of all records and documents of the company in electronic or physical form.
- While the Rule 29 provides provision for inspection of all electronic records and reproduction of these as per requirements, the charge for any such reproduction shall not be more than ten rupees per page.

MAPPING OF E-FORMS PRESCRIBED UNDER THE COMPANIES ACT, 2013 WITH E-FORMS PRESCRIBED UNDER COMPANIES ACT, 1956

S. No.	*e-Form (Companies Act, 2013)*	*Correspon-ding e-Form (Companies Act, 1956)*	*Purpose of Form as per Companies Act, 2013*
1.	INC-1	1A	Application for reservation of name
2.	INC-2	New form	Form for Incorporation and nomination (One Person Company)
3.	INC-3	New form	Form for consent of nominee of One Person Company
4.	INC-4	New form	Form for change in member/nominee of One Person Company
5.	INC-5	New form	Form for intimation of exceeding threshold of One Person Company
6.	INC-6	New form	Application for Conversion
7.	INC-7	1	Application for Incorporation of Company (Other than One Person Company)
8.	INC-18	New form	Application to Regional Director for conversion of Section 8 company into any other kind of company
9.	INC-20	New form	Intimation to Registrar of revocation or surrender of license issued under section 8
10.	INC-21	19	Declaration prior to the commencement of business
11.	INC-22	18	Notice of situation or change of situation of registered office and verification

12. INC-23	1AD, 24AAA	Application to Regional director for approval to shift the registered office from one state to another state or from jurisdiction of one registrar to another within the state
13. INC-24	1B	Application for approval of Central Government for change of name
14. INC-27	1B, 62	Conversion of public company into private company or private company into public company
15. INC-28	21	Notice of order of the Court or other authority
16. PAS-3	2	Return of allotment
17. SH-7	5	Notice to Registrar for alteration of share capital
18. SH-8	New form	Letter of offer
19. SH-11	4C	Return in respect of buy back of securities
20. CHG-1	8	Application for registration of creation, modification of charge (other than those related to debentures) including particulars of modification of charge by Asset Reconstruction Company in terms of Securitization and Reconstruction of Financial Assets and Enforcement of Securities Interest Act, 2002 (SARFAESI)
21. CHG-4	17	Particulars for satisfaction of charge
22. CHG-6	15	Notice of appointment or cessation of receiver or manager
23. CHG-9	10	Application for registration of creation or modification of charge for debentures or rectification of particulars filed in respect of creation or modification of charge for debentures
24. MGT-6	22B	Form of return to be filed with the Registrar
25. MGT-14	23	Filing of Resolutions and agreements to the Registrar under section 117
26. DIR-3	DIN1	Application for allotment of Director Identification Number
27. DIR-6	DIN4	Intimation of change in particulars of Director to be given to the Central Government
28. DIR-11	New form	Notice of resignation of a director to the Registrar
29. DIR-12	32, 32AD	Particulars of appointment of directors and the key managerial personnel and the changes amongst them
30. MR-1	25C	Return of appointment of managing director or whole time director or manager
31. MR-2	25A	Form of application to the Central Government for approval of appointment or reappointment and remuneration or increase in remuneration or waiver for excess or over payment to managing director or whole time director or manager and commission or remuneration to directors
32. URC-1	37, 39	Application by a company for registration under section 366
33. FC-1	44	Information to be filed by foreign company
34. FC-2	49, 52	Return of alteration in the documents filed for registration by foreign company
35. FC-3	52	List of all principal places of business in India established by foreign company
36. FC-4	PTII	Annual Return
37. GNL-1	61	Form for filing an application with Registrar of Companies
38. GNL-2	62	Form for submission of documents with Registrar of Companies
39. GNL-3	1AA	Particulars of person(s) or director(s) or charged or specified for the purpose of section 2(60)
40. ADJ	New form	Memorandum of Appeal
41. MSC-1	New form	Application to ROC for obtaining the status of dormant company
42. MSC-3	New form	Return of dormant companies

43.	MSC-4	New form	Application for seeking status of active company
44.	RD-1	24A	Form for filing application to Regional Director
45.	RD-2	24AAA	Form for filing petitions to Central Government (Regional Director)
46.	CG-1	65	Form for filing application or documents with Central Government
47.	–	66	Form for submission of compliance certificate with the Registrar
48.	–	5INV	Statement of unclaimed and unpaid amounts
49.	–	14LLP	Form for intimating to Registrar of Companies of conversion of the company into limited liability partnership (LLP).
50.	–	20B	Form for filing annual return by a company having a share capital with the Registrar
51.	–	21A	Particulars of annual return for the company not having share capital
52.	–	23AC	Form for filing balance sheet and other documents with the Registrar
53.	–	23ACA	Form for filing Profit and Loss account and other documents with the Registrar
54.	–	23ACA-XBRL	Form for filing XBRL document in respect of Profit and Loss account and other documents with the Registrar
55.	–	23AC-XBRL	Form for filing XBRL document in respect of balance sheet and other documents with the Registrar
56.	–	23C	Form of application to the Central Government for appointment of cost auditor
57.	–	23D	Form for Information by Cost Auditor to Central Government
58.	–	35A	Information to be furnished in relation to any offer of a scheme or contract involving the transfer of shares or any class of shares in the transferor company to the transferee company
59.	–	A-XBRL	Form for filing XBRL document in respect of compliance report and other documents with the Central Government
60.	–	FTE	Application for striking off the name of company under the Fast Track Exit (FTE) Mode
61.	–	I-XBRL	Form for filing XBRL document in respect of cost audit report and other documents with the Central Government
62.	–	Refund	Application for requesting refund of fees paid
63.	–	Bank ACC	Application for simplifying bank account opening process as user shall not be required to submit any physical application form.
64.	–	Investor Complaint Form	Form for filing complaint(s) against the company
65.	–	67AD	Clarification

Questions

Section — A Objective Type

1. What is a joint stock company?
2. Define joint stock company.
3. What are registered companies?
4. What do you understand by companies limited by guarantee?
5. What are unlimited companies?
6. Give the meaning of companies limited by shares.

7. Define a government company.
8. What do you understand by foreign companies?
9. What is a holding company?
10. Give the meaning of subsidiary company.
11. Define a public company.
12. Define a private company.
13. What is prospectus?
14. What is Memorandum of Association of a company?
15. What do you understand by Articles of Association?
16. State the stages in the formation of a company.
17. What is certificate of incorporation?
18. Who is a promoter?
19. What is minimum subscription?
20. What is allotment of shares?
21. What is statement in lieu of prospectus?
22. What is compulsory winding up?
23. What is voluntary winding up?
24. What is winding up subject to court's supervision?
25. What are public sector enterprises?
26. Mention any two objectives of government undertakings.
27. State the ownership pattern of public enterprises.
28. What is a departmental undertaking?
29. What is a government company?
30. What are statutory corporations?
31. What are central boards?
32. What is Initial Public Offer (IPO) ?
33. What is Book Building ?
34. What is floor price ?
35. Name the two advantages of issuing IPO.
36. List the companies that issued IPO recently.

Section — B Analytical Type

1. State the features of a joint stock company.
2. Distinguish between Memorandum of Association and Article of Association.
3. Briefly explain the promotion stage.
4. State the contents of a prospectus and what purpose does it serve?
5. What are Articles of Association? Mention its content.
6. What is minimum subscription? Bring out its importance.
7. What are the conditions of allotment?
8. What is compulsory liquidation? Under what circumstances compulsory liquidation shall take place?
9. Differentiate between compulsory liquidation and voluntary liquidation.
10. Explain the nature of government undertakings.
11. What are the objectives of government undertakings?
12. State the features of state enterprises.
13. Explain the origin of government undertakings.
14. State the features of departmental undertakings.
15. State the features of public corporation.
16. State the features of government company.
17. State the suitability of state enterprises.
18. Explain the merits of issuing IPO.
19. Explain the demerits of issuing IPO.

Section — C Essay Type

1. Define a joint stock company. What are its characteristics? Explain briefly.
2. What are the stages in the formation of a limited company?
3. What is prospectus? State contents.
4. Discuss the contents of the Articles of Association.
5. Distinguish between a private company and a public company.
6. Distinguish between a partnership firm and a joint stock company.
7. Explain the restrictions imposed on a private company.
8. State the advantages and disadvantages of a joint stock company.
9. State the advantages and disadvantages of private company.
10. Explain the different kinds of companies.
11. How can a private limited company be converted into a public limited company?
12. Explain the various types of liquidating a joint stock company.
13. Explain the ownership pattern of public enterprises.
14. Explain the advantages and limitations of government undertakings.
15. Explain the working of departmental undertakings. Also explain their advantages and limitations.
16. What are statutory corporations? Explain their merits and limitations.
17. What are government companies? What are their advantages and limitations?
18. Discuss the merits and demerits of issuing IPO.

WOMEN AND HUMAN RIGHTS AT WORKPLACE

Module Objectives

After reading this chapter, you should be able to:

- Know the concepts — Gender Equality, harassment of women in organisation, and types of workplace.
- List the fundemental rights of Women in India.
- Understand the nature of human rights, NHRC, UN Protocol on human right.
- Know job reservation issues in private sector
- Understand the concepts of discrimination, whistle blowing, their merits and demenrits plus Supreme Court judgement on protecting women's rights at workplace.

WOMEN AND HUMAN RIGHTS AT WORK PLACE

11.1 INTRODUCTION TO WORKING WOMEN

The status of women in India has been subject to many great changes over the past few millennia. From a largely unknown status in ancient times through the low points of the medieval period, to the promotion of equal rights by many reformers, the history of women in India has been eventful.

Contrary to the common perception, a large percent of women in India work. The National data collection agencies accept the fact that there is a serious under-estimation of women's contribution as workers. However, there are far fewer women in the paid workforce than there are men. In urban India Women have impressive number in the workforce. As an example at software industry 30% of the workforce is female. They are at par with their male counterparts in terms of wages, position at the work place.

India has the world's largest number of professionally qualified women.

India has more female doctors, surgeons, scientists and professors than the United States.

- India has the world's largest number of professionally qualified women.
- India has more female doctors, surgeons, scientists and professors than the United States.
- India has more working women than any other country in the world. This includes female workers at all levels of skill — from the surgeon and the airline pilot to bus conductors and menial laborers.

Women Legislation

Laws Related to Working Women in Formal Sector

India has witnessed many social changes post independence. Today, women have come out of homes and established an identity of their own in different areas of work. Though most Indian adult women make an economic contribution in one form or another (including housework, working in family land etc.), much of their work is not documented. This is because majority of women workforce is employed in the unorganized sector and working for family is considered as responsibility which should not be counted. The Economic survey data for 2008-09 reveals that the overall percentage share of female participation in work was comparatively low as compared to that of male.

Owing to cultural restrictions and family responsibility, women participation in the formal economy is limited. Some other concerns that affect working women relate to gender discrimination, quantum of payment, safety at work place, working hours and conditions of employment that are sensitive to cultural and religious bondages as well as family responsibilities. Indian legislature has been active on this front. Its main focus is on reducing inequality of any sort, and thereby promoting a fair, non-discriminatory and safe work environment.

Indian political and administrative structure is multi-layered. At the apex is the central government, under which there are states and local self bodies. Responsibilities for legislation are also divided accordingly, so that autonomy of states is protected. In labour legislation, both center and states have powers to enact suitable legislations.

The overall development in the country can be seen in the fact that women form an integral and important part of the work place. They contribute heavily in all areas towards the economic well-being of the nation. Unfortunately, for the most part, their interests are not always safe-guarded. They must contend with gender discrimination — and even more deplorable, sexual harassment. It is alarming to note that sixty per cent of working women have faced sexual harassment at some point of time in their careers. And, it must be remembered that for every woman who raises an outcry, there are numerous others who grin and bear their plight! If their positions become unbearable, they are even forced to quit their jobs or ask for transfers.

However, now there is a marked trend for women to fight against such harassment and assert their rights. Sadly, however, a great deal more awareness must be generated so that women are not victimized in any way while they are working to earn a livelihood.

Certain legislations that are already in place definitely underline the dignity and protection that must be accorded to women in the work place. For instance, the Maternity Benefit Act ensures that sufficient paid leave is given to the mother, both before as well as soon after the birth of the child. The Act gives effect to the constitutional requirement of making special provisions for the benefit of the women.

However, sexual harassment often plagues women who work. Sexual harassment can be defined as harassment in subtle as well as in blatant ways. It may range from sexual innuendoes and inappropriate sexual gestures to pinching, hugging, patting, brushing against and touching. Sexual harassment becomes more heinous when sexual favours are expected in return for employment or even advancement. Harassment often reaches such proportions that it interferes with the individual's work performance and even creates an intimidating or hostile work environment.

11.2 INTRODUCTION TO HUMAN RIGHTS

Human rights define the value and worth of each person and their relationship to government and society. They identify standards regarding the quality of life that each of us can expect to enjoy.

> Human rights define the value and worth of each person and their relationship to government and society.

Human Rights have the following Qualities:

- **Human rights are inherent:** human rights do not have to be given to us by a government to exist. They are our birthright and belong to us simply because we exist as human beings.
- **Human rights are inalienable:** human rights cannot be given away or taken away.
- **Human rights are universal:** human rights belong to everyone, irrespective of their sex, race, colour, religion, national or social origin or other status.

The United Nations (UN) has enshrined many human rights in international human rights instruments. The Universal Declaration of Human Rights, adopted in 1948, forms the basis of these documents. Its Preamble says, in part, that the 'recognition of the inherent dignity and of the equal and inalienable rights of all members of the human family is the foundation of freedom, justice and peace in the world.'

Women's Rights are Human Rights

Due to some social structures, traditions, stereotypes and attitudes about women and their role in society, women do not always have the opportunity and ability to access and enforce their rights on the same basis as men.

The UN Convention on the Elimination of All Forms of Discrimination Against Women (CEDAW) is the key international human rights document that seeks to ensure the enforcement of the human rights of women on an equal basis with men. CEDAW deals with rights including the right to vote and stand for election, equal rights to education, protection from discrimination in the work place and equality before the law.

11.3 GENDER DISCRIMINATION

Gender Inequalities refers to the obvious or hidden disparities among individuals based on the performance of gender.

Gender Inequalities refer to the obvious or hidden disparities among individuals based on the performance of gender. This problem in simple term is known as Gender Bias which in simple terms means the gender stratification or making difference between a girl and a boy that is a male or a female. In making biasness among the gender India has 10th rank out of 128 countries all over the world which is shameful for us. But this problem is increasing although government has banned the pre-natal sex examination. In India (in the older times) this problem is mainly seen in the rural areas because many rural people think that the girl child is burden on them. But now this is also being seen in the urban areas, i.e., in offices, institutions, schools and in society. The afflicted world in which we live is characterized by deeply unequal sharing of the burden of adversities between women and men. Gender Inequality exists in most part of the world, from Japan to Morocco, or from Uzbekistan to United States of America (as stated earlier).

The UN Convention on the Elimination of all Forms of Discrimination Against Women (CEDAW) is the key international human rights document that seeks to ensure the enforcement of the human rights of women on an equal basis with men. This package focuses on women's rights as human rights in the context of CEDAW. It focuses on the reality of women's lives and the experiences they have specifically because of their gender. CEDAW deals with rights including the right to vote and stand for election, equal rights to education, protection from discrimination in the work place and equality before the law.

Types of Gender Inequalities

There are many kinds of gender inequality or gender disparity which are as follows:

1. **Natality inequality:** In this type of inequality a preference is given for boys over girls that many male-dominated societies have, gender inequality can manifest itself in the form of the parents wanting the newborn to be a boy rather than a girl. There was a time when this could be no more than a wish (a daydream or a nightmare, depending on one's perspective), but with the availability of modern techniques to determine the gender of the foetus, sex-selective abortion has become

common in many countries. It is particularly prevalent in East Asia, in China and South Korea in particular, but also in Singapore and Taiwan, and it is beginning to emerge as a statistically significant phenomenon in India and South Asia as well.

2. Professional or Employment inequality: In terms of employment as well as promotion in work and occupation, women often face greater handicap than men. A country like Japan and India may be quite egalitarian in matters of demography or basic facilities, and even, to a great extent, in higher education, and yet progress to elevated levels of employment and occupation seems to be much more problematic for women than for men. The example of employment inequality can be explained by saying that men get priority in seeking job than women.

3. Ownership inequality: In many societies the ownership of property can also be very unequal. Even basic assets such as homes and land may be very asymmetrically shared. The absence of claims to property can not only reduce the voice of women, but also make it harder for women to enter and flourish in commercial, economic and even some social activities. This type of inequality has existed in most parts of the world, though there are also local variations. For example, even though traditional property rights have favoured men in the bulk of India.

4. Household inequality: There are often enough, basic inequalities in gender relations within the family or the household, which can take many different forms. Even in cases in which there are no overt signs of anti-female bias in, say, survival or son-preference or education, or even in promotion to higher executive positions, the family arrangements can be quite unequal in terms of sharing the burden of housework and child care. It is, for example, quite common in many societies to take it for granted that while men will naturally work outside the home, women could do it if and only if they could combine it with various inescapable and unequally shared household duties. This is sometimes called "division of labour," though women could be forgiven for seeing it as "accumulation of labour." The reach of this inequality includes not only unequal relations within the family, but also derivative inequalities in employment and recognition in the outside world. Also, the established fixity of this type of "division" or "accumulation" of labour can also have far-reaching effects on the knowledge and understanding of different types of work in professional circles.

5. Special opportunity inequality: Even when there is relatively little difference in basic facilities including schooling, the opportunities of higher education may be far fewer for young women than for young men. Indeed, gender bias in higher education and professional training can be observed even in some of the richest countries in the world, in India too. Sometimes this type of division has been based on the superficially innocuous idea that the respective "provinces" of men and women are just different.

Discrimination against women regardless of their religion is a matter of grave concern. The days of patriarchy are at an end. Today women are taking their rightful place in all walks of life. After the Second World War, we made a transition to a world of human rights. The United Nations Charter proclaims that all human beings are born free and equal. Contrast this with the American constitution, which proclaimed that all men are born free and equal. The Beijing Declaration also proclaims women's rights as human rights.

Women's Rights and Wrongs

The All India Muslim Personal Law Board proclaims that triple talaq is a social evil, but it is equally assertive that this social evil should not be removed by legislative reform. There is no question of banning the practice. The Muslim Personal Laws are based on divine inspiration and triple talaq comes from the same inspiration, that is, Shariat. The Muslims have no powers to amend or abolish it. So the triple talaq is irrevocable. It is difficult to understand how what is divine can at the same time be evil.

Among Hindus, polygamy too was rampant. Yet it was abolished first in Bombay State by the Bombay Prevention of Hindu Bigamous Marriages Act, 1946. Later, the Hindu Marriage Act, 1955, put an end to polygamy throughout the country. Marriage among Hindus had been held to be sacrosanct, something that could not be dissolved — yet the Hindu Marriage Act, 1955, provides for dissolution of marriage both by husband and wife on the grounds stated in the Hindu Marriage Act. The Indian Divorce Act has also been recently amended to do away with inequality between women and men in matters of divorce among Christians. Untouchability, yet another social evil, was outlawed by Article 17 of our Constitution.

Social and legal reforms must move together to ensure that all social evils are banished. It is often said that personal laws are outside the purview of challenge under Article 13 of the Constitution of India. But this has no constitutional or legal basis. The fact is that what is inhuman is both unconstitutional and illegal. A very interesting answer to the argument of the Muslim Personal Law Board lies in the fact that in several Muslim countries triple talaq has been banned or restricted. There are several countries where there is a uniform law of divorce, for all citizens irrespective of their religion. The power to legislate on marriage and divorce is specifically conferred in entry 5, List III, Schedule VII of our Constitution.

11.4 GENDER EQUALITY

Man and woman are both equal and both plays a vital role in the creation and development of their families in particular and the society in general. Indeed, the struggle for legal equality has been one of the major concerns of the women's movement all over the world. In India, since long back, women were considered as an oppressed section of the society and they were neglected for centuries. During the national struggle for independence, Gandhi gave a call of emancipation of women. He wrote "I am uncompromising in the matter of women's rights. The difference in sex and physical form denotes no difference in status. Woman is the complement of man, and not inferior." Thus, the first task in post-independent India was to provide a constitution to the people, which would not make any distinctions on the basis of sex. The preamble of constitution promises to secure to all its citizens: "Justice- economical, social, and political."

Gender equality also known as gender equity, gender egalitarianism, or sexual equality is the goal of the equality of the genders or the sexes, stemming from a belief in the injustice of myriad forms of gender inequality.

Gender equality also known as gender equity, gender egalitarianism, or sexual equality is the goal of the equality of the genders or the sexes, stemming from a belief in the injustice of myriad forms of gender inequality.

World bodies have defined gender equality as related to human rights, especially women's rights, and economic development. UNICEF defines gender equality as "levelling the playing field for girls and women by ensuring that all children have equal opportunity to develop their talents."

Gender Equity has gained prominent importance in the recent past. The third item of the Millennium Development Goals (MDGs) of United Nations describes 'promoting gender equality and empower woman.' Gender equity is giving boys and girls, women and men equal opportunities in the utilization of personal capabilities to realize full human rights.

The woman are still waiting to get the due respect and recognition in India. Unlike ancient times, women face physical, mental harassment and violence in and outside the family throughout their lives. Police records are the mute evidence of the poor state of woman. A woman is molested in the country every 26 minutes and raped every 34 minutes. Every 42 minutes, an incident of sexual harassment takes place. Every 43 minutes, a woman is kidnapped. A woman is killed every 93 minutes.

Gender equity is giving boys and girls, women and men equal opportunities in the utilization of personal capabilities to realize full human rights.

Causes of Poor Social and Economic Condition of Women

The biased mindset of men and, surprisingly enough, women is mainly accountable for the prevailing condition of gender equity in India. The boy child has always been given preference over the girl child. But the sex ratio was maintained even after this step behaviour by the society. The advent of ultrasound technology worsened. To contain the declining sex ratio and for curbing the evil practice of female feticide, the Government brought into force the Pre-Natal Diagnostic Techniques (Regulation and Prevention of Misuse) Act on September 20, 1994. A survey of ultrasound centers was undertaken during 2004-05 in those states where the number of centers registered under the Act is more and decline in child sex ratio is also significant to know the number of untrained doctors, both allopathic and non-allopathic disciplines, using ultrasound machines and the purpose for using the same.

The women are the one who eat the least and at the last in families particularly in rural India. Their health and nutrition is not taken care of that subsequently results in the poor health of the new born babies.

Health and Nutrition

The women are the one who eat the least and at the last in families particularly in rural India. Their health and nutrition is not taken care of that subsequently results in the poor health of the new born babies. Though the life expectancy rate of woman is better than their male counterparts, the maternal mortality ratio seems to be another foul player for the low female-male ratio.

Women and children are more vulnerable to ill health and diseases. Ill health of women is mainly due to poor nutrition due to gender discrimination, low age at marriage, risk factors during pregnancy, unsafe, unplanned and multiple deliveries, limited access to family planning methods and unsafe abortion services.

From Wide to Wider

The sex ratio is one of the key indicators of the status of women in a society. The child sex ratio for the age group of 0-6years has shown a continuous decline over the decades. It has come down significantly from 976 in 1961 to 927 in 2001. During the decade 1991-2001, more than 50 points decline has been observed in the States / UTs of Punjab, Haryana, Chandigarh, Himachal Pradesh. Declining trend in the child sex ratio has been a matter of concern for all. Some of the reasons commonly put forward to explain the consistently low levels of sex ratio are: son preference; neglect of the girl child resulting in higher mortality at younger age; female infanticide; female foeticide; maternal mortality; and male bias in enumeration of population.

The sex ratio is one of the key indicators of the status of women in a society.

India, among few leading countries, had been a land where woman had been given the right to vote. There is no question of any less efficiency, ability and productivity in women than men. A country cannot realize its dream of becoming super power by ignoring the better half of the humanity. Researches have proved that a country where there are more employment opportunities for woman tend to provide better and honest governance.

11.5 HARASSMENT OF WOMEN IN ORGANISATIONS

Sexual Harassment at Work Defined

Supreme Court defines sexual harassment as and includes such unwelcome sexually determined behaviour such as —

- Physical contact
- A demand or request for sexual favours
- Sexually coloured remarks
- Showing pornography
- Any other unwelcome physical, verbal or non-verbal conduct of a sexual nature that is Leering, dirty jokes, sexual remark about a person's body and the like.

The Supreme Court directive has provided a legitimate space for surfacing of hidden realities of sexual harassment at work place in which earlier only victim-blaming, witch-hunting and black-mailing flourished.

No woman employee at a work place shall be subjected to sexual harassment including unwelcome sexually determined behaviour, physical contact, advances.

No woman employee at a work place shall be subjected to sexual harassment including unwelcome sexually determined behaviour, physical contact, advances, sexually coloured remarks, showing pornography, sexual demand, request for sexual favours or any other unwelcome conduct of sexual nature whether verbal, textual, physical, graphic or electronic or by any other actions, which may include—

- implied or overt promise of preferential treatment in employment; or
- implied or overt threat of detrimental treatment in employment; or
- implied or overt threat about the present or future employment status;
- conduct which interferes with work or creates an intimidating or offensive or hostile work environment; or
- humiliating conduct constituting health and safety problems.

Work Place Harassment Defined

Work place harassment is when someone harasses a worker while he or she is doing his or her job, or on his or her way to or from work.

Work place harassment is when someone harasses a worker while he or she is doing his or her job, or on his or her way to or from work. A harasser can be anyone the worker come in contact with because of his or her work. That person might be a:

- boss;
- supervisor;

- manager;
- member of your board of directors;
- coworker;
- customer;
- patient;
- delivery person;
- person in the union.

Harassment can happen anywhere in the work place:

- in the lunchroom;
- in rest and washroom areas;
- in staff rooms;
- on the production line;
- in an office.

The worker might also be harassed outside of his or her work place. It can happen at a party, on a business trip or at a meeting at someone's home. Harassment is not always work place harassment. It depends on the situation, and the relationship to the harasser. If a boss is in the worker's home and demands that the worker has sex with him, it is still work place harassment. The worker's boss has power over the worker. He could make things hard for the worker at work if worker says no. If the same thing happens with a coworker who has no power over the worker at work, it might not be work place harassment. However, if the coworker harassed the worker at work later, it would be work place harassment. The employer would be responsible for stopping it.

The employer is responsible for any form of harassment that affects the work place, and the work.

> I saw one of the instructors at our school fondle a female instructor at a Christmas party. He grabbed her on the buttocks and pinched her breasts. She clearly did not want him to do this. I considered it sexual harassment. I urged the woman to complain. She did not. Two other women and I reported what we saw. The man was in a position of responsibility and trust, and the school considered that the incident showed that he was not fit to carry out his duties. He was demoted.
>
> — Anonymous, USA

This judgment was used with profit in the case of Apparel Export Promotion **Council v. A. K. Chopra** in which disciplinary proceedings for sexual harassment leading to dismissal from service were upheld by the Supreme Court. In this case on the allegation of sexual harassment an employee was charge-sheeted and was eventually dismissed from service. The Court observed that the behaviour of the delinquent employee of sitting close to a female subordinate and touching her amounted to molestation and not simply attempt to molest. In this judgment also the Court has drawn strength from the **International Labour Organisation Seminar held in Manila in 1993** where sexual harassment was recognised as a form of gender discrimination. The Court has also drawn on CEDAW, 1979 and the subsequent Beijing Declaration. It has observed that "the courts were under an obligation to give due regard to international conventions and norms for considering domestic laws, more so, when there is no inconsistency between them and there is a void in the domestic laws."

The Court laid down a scheme which provided that the machinery should be in place in every organisation employing men and women so as to immediately take care of any incidence of sexual harassment.

Noteworthy complaints of Sexual Harassment at Work place in India
• IAS officer in Chandigarh Rupan Deo Bajaj against the Super Cop K.P.S. Gill • An activist of All India Democratic Women's Association against Environment Minister in Dehradun • An airhostess against her colleague Mahesh Kumar Lala in Mumbai • An IAS officer in Thiruvanathpuram against the state minister

Before 1997, women experiencing sexual harassment at work place (SHW) had to lodge complaint under the Indian Penal Code Section 354 that deals with 'criminal assault of women to outrage women's modesty' and Section 509 that punishes an individual/individuals for using 'word, gesture or act intended to insult the modesty of a woman.' These sections left interpretation of 'outraging women's modesty' to the discretion of the police officer.

In 1997 the Supreme Court passed the landmark judgment in the **Vishakha case** laying down guidelines to be followed by establishments in dealing with complaints of sexual harassment. The Court stated that these guidelines were to be implemented until legislation is passed to deal with the issue.

Pursuant to this, the Government of India requested the National Commission of Women (NCW) to draft the legislation. A number of issues were raised regarding the NCW draft produced, and ultimately a Drafting Committee was set up to make a fresh draft. A number of women's organisations are part of this Committee, including, from Mumbai, Majlis. Majlis was asked to make the draft. Some women's organisations and women lawyers associated with Trade Unions in Mumbai have collectively worked on the draft with Majlis. Particular concerns while drafting have been to include the unorganized sector and to incorporate provisions of labour law.

Is This Harassment?

There are many clear cut examples of harassment. Racist and homophobic insults are harassment. When a boss demands that an employee have sex or lose her job, it is clearly harassment, and it is against the law. But there are many less obvious examples. Many people are not sure if what they are experiencing is harassment.

Here are some examples of work place behaviour:
• a man puts his arm around a woman at work.;   • someone tells an offensive joke;   • someone says "You look great," or "Your hair looks terrific," or "Did you get any last night?"

These may or may not be examples of harassment. It depends on the situation. Where two people are friends, a comment like "your hair looks terrific" could be a compliment. If the same comment is made by a stranger on the street, it feels very different. If fcmale worker's boss leans over her desk and whispers the comment in her ear while she is working, it feels different again. The important questions are: does she feel comfortable with this person making this comment? and does he has any reason for believing that his comments are acceptable and welcome?

Law on Harassment

There is more than one definition of harassment under the law. Some forms of harassment are clearer than others. More work has been done on sexual and racial harassment than on other forms.

The courts have decided:

- when employers are responsible for workers being harassed ?
- what is and is not acceptable behaviour ?
- to recognize the seriousness of the effects of harassment on women.

In India, this problem is mainly in work places, i.e., related to Sexual Harassment and Wage Payment and related to inheritance. Although, judiciary decided in favour of the deceased, i.e., the suffered parties. There are many landmark and famous cases of gender discrimination in work place like that of **Vishaka v. State of Rajasthan** it was held that a woman was brutally gang raped in the village of Rajasthan. The incident reveals the hazards to which a working woman may be exposed and the depravity to which sexual harassment can degenerate; and the urgency for safeguards by an alternative mechanism in the absence of legislative measures. In the absence of legislative measures, the need is to find an effective alternative mechanism to fulfil this felt and urgent social need. So, a writ of Mandamus was filed in Supreme Court under Article 32 of the Indian Constitution. Later the Supreme Court decided to direct that certain guidelines and norms would be strictly observed in all work places for the preservation and enforcement of the right to gender equality of the working women. These directions would be binding and enforceable in law until suitable legislation is enacted to occupy the field.

Right to a Safe Work Environment

The worker has the right to work in an environment that is free from harassment. Employers are responsible for providing this to all workers. The worker has the right to expect the employer to take her concerns seriously. It is against the law for anyone she come in contact with on the job to harass. It is against the law for female worker's supervisor to promise her a raise or job perks in return for sexual favours.

The law also says that she has the right to work in an environment that is not "poisoned" by harassment. The worker cannot help but be affected by what is happening in the work place. Her employer cannot expect her to work if people around her are making sexual, racial or homophobic jokes or comments, or putting graffiti and pinups on the wall. All of these things can make it hard to work. They are bad for your mental wellbeing. They affect your work just as if the harassment were directed at her.

The worker has the right to ask her employer, her union, or an outside agency like the Human Rights Commission to take action against harassment.

Is Work Place Harassment Against the Law?

Sometimes it is. If someone's behaviour is making the female worker uncomfortable, she should not keep it to herself, she may not choose to do anything else, but tell someone about it.

At some time in one's lives, everyone has to put up with people he or she does not like very much. Some bosses are not very good at managing staff. They can make the work place unpleasant or even miserable. That does not always mean their behaviour is against the law.

Effects of Sexual Harassment on Organizations
• Decreased productivity and increased team conflict • Decrease in success at meeting financial goals (because of team conflict) • Decreased job satisfaction • Loss of staff and expertise from resignations to avoid harassment or resignations/firings of alleged harassers; loss of students who leave school to avoid harassment • Decreased productivity and/or increased absenteeism by staff or students experiencing harassment • Increased health care costs and sick pay costs because of the health consequences of harassment • The knowledge that harassment is permitted can undermine ethical standards and discipline in the organization in general, as staff and/or students lose respect for, and trust in, their seniors who indulge in, or turn a blind eye to, sexual harassment • A company's or school's image can suffer Legal costs if the problem is ignored and complainants take the issue to court.(Boland 1990)

THE PROTECTION OF WOMEN AGAINST SEXUAL HARASSEMENT AT WORK PLACE ACT, 2007

Objective of the Act

To provide for prevention and redressal of sexual harassment of women at work place and for matters connected therewith or incidental thereto.

Important Terms in the Act

Aggrieved woman means any woman employee against whom any act of sexual harassment is alleged to have been committed;

Employee means a person employed at a workplace for any work on regular, temporary, ad-hoc or daily wage basis, either directly or by or through an agent, including a contractor, with or without the knowledge of the principal employer, whether for remuneration or not, or working on a voluntary basis or otherwise, whether the terms of employment are express or implied and includes a domestic worker, a co-worker, a contract worker, probationer, trainee, apprentice or by any other name called;

Employer means (i) in relation to any department, organisation, undertaking, establishment, enterprise, institution, office, branch or unit of the appropriate Government or a local authority, the head of that department, organisation, undertaking, establishment, enterprise, institution, office, branch or unit or such other officer as the appropriate Government or the local authority, as the case may be, may by an order specify in this behalf; (ii) in any work place not covered under clause (i), any person responsible for the management, supervision and control of the work place;

Local Committee means the Local Complaints Committee constituted under section 6;

Work Place Means,

- any department, organisation, undertaking, establishment, enterprise, institution, office, branch or unit which is established, owned, controlled or wholly or substantially financed by funds provided directly or indirectly by the appropriate Government or the local authority or a Government company or a corporation or a co-operative society;
- any private sector organisation or a private venture, undertaking, enterprise, institution, establishment, society, unit or service provider carrying on commercial, professional, vocational, educational, industrial or financial activities including production, supply, sale, distribution or service;
- a house or dwelling place;
- and includes any place visited by the employee arising out of, or during and in the course of, employment;
- "Unorganized Sector" which shall come within the meaning of "workplace", means all private unincorporated enterprises including own account enterprises engaged in any agriculture, industry, trade and/or business and includes sectors as mentioned in the schedule, being illustrative.

SALIENT FEATURES OF THE PROTECTION OF WOMEN AGAINST SEXUAL HARASSEMENT AT WORKPLACE ACT

Chapter 1 : It extends to the whole of India. Short title, extent and commencement.

Chapter 02 : Constitution of Committees, Internal Complaint Committee,

Chapter 03 : Complaint of sexual harassment, conciliation,

Chapter 04 : Enquiry into complaint, action during pendency of enquiry, enquiry report, Punishment for false or malicious complaint and false evidence, Determination of compensation, Appeal.

Chapter 05: Duties of the employer,

Chapter 06: Miscellaneous, Committee to submit annual report, Employer to include information in annual report,

GENDER INEQUALITY IN THE WORK PLACE

Women are, and have been, entering the work place in rapid numbers. Although some women may face work place discrimination, evidence shows that middle- and upper-class women are prospering.

When talking about women in the work place, often the term "glass ceiling" is used. It refers to the imaginary career barrier that seemingly impedes a woman's ability to rise to the top ranks of her profession, while men effortlessly continue up in the ranks.

11.6 TYPES OF HARASSMENTS

Sexual harassment is any unwanted attention of a sexual nature, like remarks about one's looks or personal life. Sometimes these comments sound like compliments, but they make you feel uneasy. Sexual harassment can include:

- degrading words or pictures (like graffiti, photos, or posters);
- physical contact of any kind;
- sexual demands.

Sexual harassment includes such unwelcome sexually determined behaviour as physical contacts and advances, sexually coloured remarks, showing pornography and sexual demands, whether by words or actions. Such conduct can be humiliating and may constitute a health and safety problem; it is discriminatory when the woman has reasonable grounds to believe that her objection would disadvantage her in connection with her employment, including recruiting or promotion, or when it creates a hostile working environment. Effective complaints, procedures and remedies, including compensation, should be provided.

Racial harassment is any action that expresses or promotes racial hatred and stereotypes. It can be obvious or subtle. It can include:

- spoken or written putdowns;
- gestures;

- jokes;
- other unwanted comments or acts.

THE PROTECTION OF WOMEN AGAINST SEXUAL HARASSEMENT AT WORK PLACE ACT, 2007

11.7 FUNDAMENTAL RIGHTS RELATING TO WOMEN

Sexual harassment in India is termed "Eve teasing" and is described as: unwelcome sexual gesture or behaviour whether directly or indirectly as sexually coloured remarks; physical contact and advances; showing pornography; a demand or request for sexual favours; any other unwelcome physical, verbal/non-verbal conduct being sexual in nature. The critical factor is the unwelcomeness of the behaviour, thereby making the impact of such actions on the recipient more relevant rather than intent of the perpetrator. According to India's constitution, sexual harassment infringes the fundamental right of a woman to gender equality under Article 14 of the Constitution of India and her right to life and live with dignity under Article 21 of the Constitution. Although there is no specific law against sexual harassment at work place in India but many provisions in other legislations protect against sexual harassment at workplace, such as Section 354, IPC deals with assault or criminal force to a woman with the intent to outrage her modesty, and Section 509, IPC deals with word, gesture or act intended to insult the modesty of a woman.

Constitutional Provisions for Indian Women

- Equality before the law. Article 14
- No discrimination by the State on the grounds only of religion, race, caste, sex, place of birth or any of these. Article 15(1)
- Special provisions to be made by the State in favour of women and children. Article 15(3)
- Equality of opportunity for all citizens in matters relating to employment or appointment to any office under the State. Article 16
- State policy to be directed to securing for men and women equally, the right to an adequate means of livelihood. Article 39(a)
- Equal pay for equal work for both men and women. Article 39(d)
- Provisions to be made by the State for securing just and humane conditions of work and for maternity relief. Article 42
- To promote harmony and to renounce practices derogatory to the dignity of women. Article 51(A) (e)

11.8 NATURE OF HUMAN RIGHTS

According to the Protection of Human Right Act, 1993 "**human rights**" means the rights relating to life, liberty, equality and dignity of the individual guaranteed by the Constitution or embodied in the International Covenants and enforceable by courts in India. It is necessary and expedient for employers in work places as

"Human Rights" means the rights relating to life, liberty, equality and dignity of the individual guaranteed by the Constitution or embodied in the International Covenants and enforceable by courts in India.

well as other responsible persons or institutions to observe certain guidelines to ensure the prevention of sexual harassment of women as to live with dignity is a human right guaranteed by our constitution.

It has been laid down by the Supreme Court that it is the duty of the employer or other responsible persons in work places or other institutions to prevent or deter the Commission of acts of sexual harassment and to provide the procedure for the resolution, settlement or prosecution of acts of sexual harassment by taking all steps required.

11.9 NATIONAL HUMAN RIGHTS COMMISSION

The National Human Rights Commission (NHRC) of India is an autonomous statutory body established on October 12, 1993, under the provisions of The Protection of Human Rights Act, 1993 (TPHRA). The Commission is in conformity with the Paris Principles — a broad set of principles agreed upon by a number of nations for the promotion and protection of human rights, in Paris in October 1991.

Over the past eleven years the Commission has endeavoured to give a positive meaning and a content to the objectives set out in the Protection of Human Rights Act, 1993. It has moved vigorously and effectively to use the opportunities provided to it by the Act to promote and protect human rights in the country. While undertaking the tasks set out in the Protection of Human Rights Act, 1993, the Commission has noticed several lacunae in the Act over the years. This has been mentioned in earlier reports and it is emphasized, once again, that there is a need to review and amend the Act for the proper and effective functioning of the Commission.

The Universal Declaration of Human Rights adopted by the General Assembly on 10th December, 1948, was followed by two Covenants — International Convention on Economic, Social and Cultural Rights (ICESCR) and International Convention on Civil and Political Rights (ICCPR) in 1966. India signed both these International Conventions in 1979.

The UN Committee on Economic, Social and Cultural Rights (CESCR) is taking a robust attitude towards the practical implementation of these rights under the ICESCR. This was recognized by the United Nations in 1986 when it acknowledged the right to development as a human right. The right to development as formulated in the 1986 U.N. Declaration is a synthesis of the two sets of rights.

In democratic societies fundamental human rights and freedoms are put under the guarantee of law and therefore, their protection becomes an obligation of those who are entrusted with the task of their protection. These rights are broadly classified into civil and political rights on the one hand and economic, social and cultural rights on the other. While the former are more in the nature of injunction against the authority of the State from encroaching upon the inalienable freedoms of an individual, the latter are demands on the State to provide positive conditions to capacitate the individual to exercise the former. The object of both sets of rights is, to make an individual an effective participant in the affairs of the society. Unless both sets of rights are available, neither full development of the human personality can be achieved nor true democracy can be said to exist.

The Commission, consistent with its mandate, took up issues involving human rights that are of significance, either suo motu, or when brought to its notice by the civil society, the media, concerned citizens, or expert advisers. Its primary focus is to strengthen the extension of human rights to all sections of society, in particular, the vulnerable groups.

Functions of NHRC

The Protection of Human Rights Act mandates the National Human Rights Commission to perform the following functions:

- Proactively or reactively inquire into violations of human rights or negligence in the prevention of such violation by a public servant
- Intervene in any proceeding involving any allegation of violation of human rights pending before a court
- Visit any jail or other institution under the control of the State Government, where persons are detained or lodged for purposes of treatment, reformation or protection, for the study of the living conditions of the inmates and make recommendations
- Review the safeguards provided by or under the Constitution or any law for the time being in force for the protection of human rights and recommend measures for their effective implementation
- Review the factors, including acts of terrorism that inhibit the enjoyment of human rights and recommend appropriate remedial measures
- Study treaties and other international instruments on human rights and make recommendations for their effective implementation
- Undertake and promote research in the field of human rights
- Spread literacy among various sections of society and promote awareness of the safeguards available for the protection of these rights through publications, the media, seminars and other available means
- Encourage the efforts of NGOs and institutions working in the field of human rights
- Such other function as it may consider it necessary for the protection of human rights.

Composition and Appointment

Sections 3 and 4 of The Protection of Human Rights Act lay down the rules for appointment to The National Human Rights Commission. The Chairperson and members of the national human rights commission are appointed by the President of India, on the recommendation of a committee comprising of—

- The Prime Minister: Chairperson
- The Speaker of the House of the People: Member
- The Minister-in-charge of the Ministry of Home Affairs in the Government of India: Member

- The Leader of the Opposition in the House of the People: Member
- The Leader of the Opposition in the Council of States: Member
- The Deputy Chairman of the Council of States: Member

The National Human Rights Commission consists of:

- A Chairperson who has been a Chief Justice of the Supreme Court of India
- One Member who is, or has been, a Judge of the Supreme Court of India
- One Member who is, or has been, the Chief Justice of a High Court
- Two Members to be appointed from among persons having knowledge of, or practical experience in, matters relating to human rights

Controversy

A report concerning the manner of which the Shivani murder controversy case was rejected, a case which involved high ranking officials being implicated in the murder of a journalist, opened the organisation up to questioning over the usefulness of human rights commissions setup by the government at the national and state levels.

National Human Rights Commission moved the Supreme Court in Best Bakery case. Transfer application also moved in respect of 4 other serious cases.

In response to repeated requests from representatives of the print and electronic media regarding the action being taken by the Commission in the Best Bakery case, the Commission would like to state the position which is as follows:

Deeply concerned about the damage to the credibility of the criminal justice delivery system and negation of human rights of victims, the National Human Rights Commission, on consideration of the report of its team which was sent to Vadodara, has today filed a Special Leave Petition under Article 136 of the Constitution of India in the Supreme Court with a prayer to set aside the impugned judgement of the Trial Court in the Best Bakery case and sought directions for further investigation by an independent agency and retrial of the case in a competent court located outside the State of Gujarat.

The NHRC has, inter-alia, contended in the Special Leave Petition that, the concept of fair trial is a constitutional 'imperative and is explicitly recognized as such in the specific provisions of the Constitution including Articles 14, 19, 21, 22 and 39A of the Constitution as well as the various provisions of the Code of Criminal Procedure 1973 (Cr.P.C).

The right to fair trial is also explicitly recognized as a human right in terms of Article 14 of the International Covenant on Civil and Political Rights (ICCPR) which has been ratified by India and which now forms part of the statutory legal regime explicitly recognized as such under Section 2(1)(d) of the Protection of Human Rights Act, 1993.

Violation of a right to fair trial is not only a violation of fundamental right under our Constitution but also violative of the internationally recognized human rights as spelt out in the ICCPR to which India is a party.

Whenever a criminal goes unpunished, it is the society at large which suffers because the victims become demoralized and criminals encouraged. It therefore, becomes duty of the Court to use all its powers to unearth the truth and render justice so that the crime is punished.

It is, therefore, imperative in the interests of justice for the Hon'ble Supreme Court, in exercise of its powers under Article 142 of the Constitution, to lay down guidelines and directions in relation to protection of witnesses and victims of crime in criminal trials which can be adhered to both by the prosecuting and law enforcement agencies as well as the subordinate judiciary. This is essential in order to enhance the efficacy of the criminal justice delivery system.

Article 142 of the Constitution, to lay down guidelines and directions in relation to protection of witnesses and victims of crime in criminal trials which can be adhered to both by the prosocuting and law enforcement agencies as well as the subordinate judiciary.

The Commission has also filed a separate application under Section 406 Cr.P.C. before the Supreme Court for transfer of four other serious cases, namely, the Godhra incident, Chamanpura (Gulburga society) incident, Naroda Patiya incident and the Sadarpura case in Mehsana district, for their trial outside the State of Gujarat.

11.10 UN CONVENTIONS ON HUMAN RIGHTS

The morals and values of human rights can be traced through the history of religious beliefs and cultures around the world. European philosophers of the Age of Enlightenment developed theories of natural law that influenced the adoption of documents such as the Bill of Rights of England, the Bill of Rights in the United States, and the Declaration of the Rights of Man and of the Citizen in France.

National and International pressure for an international bill of rights had been building throughout World War II, In his 1941 State of the Union address US president Franklin Roosevelt called for the protection of what he termed the "essential" Four Freedoms: freedom of speech, freedom of conscience, freedom from fear and freedom from want, as its basic war aims. This has been seen as part of a movement of the 1940s that sought to make human rights part of the conditions for peace at the end of the war. The United Nations Charter "reaffirmed faith in fundamental human rights, and dignity and worth of the human person" and committed all member states to promote "universal respect for, and observance of, human rights and fundamental freedoms for all without distinction as to race, sex, language or religion."

When the atrocities committed by Nazi Germany became public knowledge around the world after World War II, the consensus within the world community was that the United Nations Charter did not sufficiently define the rights it referenced. A universal declaration that specified the rights of individuals was necessary to give effect to the Charter's provisions on human rights.[6]

The morals and values of human rights can be traced through the history of religious beliefs and cultures around the world.

Drafting

Drafting of the Universal Declaration of Human Rights

Canadian John Peters Humphrey was called upon by the United Nations Secretary-General to work on the project and became the Declaration's principal drafter. At the time Humphrey was newly appointed as Director of the Division of Human Rights within the United Nations Secretariat. The Commission on Human Rights, a standing body of the United Nations, was constituted to undertake the work of preparing what was initially conceived as an International Bill of Rights. The membership of the Commission was designed to be broadly representative of the global community with representatives of the following countries serving: Australia, Belgium, Byelorussian Soviet Socialist Republic, Chile, China, Cuba, Egypt, France, India, Iran, Lebanon, Panama, Philippines, United Kingdom, United States, Soviet Union, Uruguay and Yugoslavia.

Adoption

The Universal Declaration was adopted by the General Assembly on 10 December 1948 by a vote of 48 in favor, 0 against, with 8 abstentions (all the Soviet Bloc States, Byelorussia, Czechoslovakia, Poland, Ukraine, USSR, as well as Yugoslavia, South Africa and Saudi Arabia).

The following countries voted in favour of the Declaration: Afghanistan, Argentina, Australia, Belgium, Bolivia, Brazil, Burma, Canada, Chile, China, Colombia, Costa Rica, Cuba, Denmark, the Dominican Republic, Ecuador, Egypt, El Salvador, Ethiopia, France, Greece, Guatemala, Haiti, Iceland, India, Iran, Iraq, Lebanon, Liberia, Luxembourg, Mexico, Netherlands, New Zealand, Nicaragua, Norway, Pakistan, Panama, Paraguay, Peru, Philippines, Thailand, Sweden, Syria, Turkey, United Kingdom, United States, Uruguay and Venezuela.

Despite the central role played by Canadian John Humphrey, the Canadian Government at first abstained from voting on the Declaration's draft, but later voted in favour of the final draft in the General Assembly.

Structure

The underlying structure of the Universal Declaration was introduced in its second draft which was prepared by Rene Cassin. Cassin worked from a first draft prepared by John Peters Humphrey. The structure was influenced by the Code Napoleon, including a preamble and introductory general principles. Cassin compared the Declaration to the portico of a Greek temple, with a foundation, steps, four columns and a pediment. Articles 1 and 2 are the foundation blocks, with their principles of dignity, liberty, equality and brotherhood. The seven paragraphs of the preamble, setting out the reasons for the Declaration, are represented by the steps.

The main body of the Declaration forms the four columns. The first column (articles 3-11) constitutes rights of the individual, such as the right to life and the prohibition of slavery. The second column (articles 12-17) constitutes the rights of the individual in civil and political society. The third column (articles 18-21) is concerned with spiritual, public and political freedoms such as freedom of religion and freedom of association. The fourth column (articles 22-27) sets out social, economic and cultural rights.

In Cassin's model, the last three articles of the Declaration provide the pediment which binds the structure together. These articles are concerned with the duty of the individual to society and the prohibition of use of rights in contravention of the purposes of the United Nations.[12] With regard to the Communist block's abstentions, the December 9th Velodrome d'Hiver meeting of 20,000 Parisiens at the invitation of World Citizen Garry Davis and his "Conseil de Solidarité" who had interrupted a General Assembly session on November 22 to call for a world government, provoked its abstention rather than voting against the human rights document. Eleanor Roosevelt in her column "My Day" wrote on December 15 that "Garry Davis, the young man who in Paris as a citizen of the world...has succeeded in getting the backing of a few intellectuals and even has received a cablegram from Albert Einstein telling him, from Professor Einstein's point of view, that the United Nations has not yet achieved peace. The United Nations, of course, is not set up to achieve peace. That the governments are supposed to do themselves. But it is expected to help preserve peace, and that think, is it doing more effectively day by day. During a pleneary session in the General Assembly, this young man tried to make a speech from the balcony on the subject of how incompetent the United Nations is to deal with the questions before it. How much better it would be if Mr. Davis would set up his own governmental organization and start then and there a worldwide international government. All who would join him would learn that they had no nationality and, therefore, not being bothered by any special interest in any one country, everyone would develop...a completely cooperative feeling among all peoples and a willingness to accept any laws passes by this super government."

Preamble of the Universal Declaration on Human Rights

The Universal Declaration begins with a preamble consisting of seven paragraphs followed by a statement "proclaiming" the Declaration.

Each paragraph of the preamble sets out a reason for the adoption of the Declaration. The first paragraph asserts that the recognition of human dignity of all people is the foundation of justice and peace in the world. The second paragraph observes that disregard and contempt for human rights have resulted in barbarous acts which have outraged the conscience of mankind and that the four freedoms: freedom of speech, belief, freedom from want, and freedom from fear — which is "proclaimed as the highest aspiration" of the people. The third paragraph states that so that people are not compelled to rebellion against tyranny, human rights should be protected by rule of law. The fourth paragraph relates human rights to the development of friendly relations between nations. The fifth paragraph links the Declaration back to the United Nations Charter which reaffirms faith in fundamental human rights and dignity and worth of the human person. The sixth paragraph notes that all members of the United Nations have pledged themselves to achieve, in cooperation with the United Nations, the promotion of universal respect for and observance of human rights and fundamental freedoms. The seventh paragraph observes that "a common understanding" of rights and freedoms is of "the greatest importance" for the full realization of that pledge.

These paragraphs are followed by the "proclamation" of the Declaration as a "common standard of achievement" for "all peoples and all nations", so that "all individuals" and "all organs of society" should by teaching and education, promote respect for these rights and freedoms and by progressive measures, national and international, secure their universal and effective recognition and observance.

The Preamble is:

- Whereas recognition of the inherent dignity and of the equal and inalienable rights of all members of the human family is the foundation of freedom, justice and peace in the world,
- Whereas disregard and contempt for human rights have resulted in barbarous acts which have outraged the conscience of mankind, and

the advent of a world in which human beings shall enjoy freedom of speech and belief and freedom from fear and want has been proclaimed as the highest aspiration of the common people,

- Whereas it is essential, if man is not to be compelled to have recourse, as a last resort, to rebellion against tyranny and oppression, that human rights should be protected by the rule of law,
- Whereas it is essential to promote the development of friendly relations between nations,
- Whereas the peoples of the United Nations have in the Charter reaffirmed their faith in fundamental human rights, in the dignity and worth of the human person and in the equal rights of men and women and have determined to promote social progress and better standards of life in larger freedom,
- Whereas Member States have pledged themselves to achieve, in co-operation with the United Nations, the promotion of universal respect for and observance of human rights and fundamental freedoms,
- Whereas a common understanding of these rights and freedoms is of the greatest importance for the full realization of this pledge,
- Now, Therefore THE GENERAL ASSEMBLY proclaims THIS UNIVERSAL DECLARATION OF HUMAN RIGHTS as a common standard of achievement for all peoples and all nations, to the end that every individual and every organ of society, keeping this Declaration constantly in mind, shall strive by teaching and education to promote respect for these rights and freedoms and by progressive measures, national and international, to secure their universal and effective recognition and observance, both among the peoples of Member States themselves and among the peoples of territories under their jurisdiction.

Human Rights set out in the Declaration

The following reproduces the articles of the Declaration which set out the specific human rights that are recognized in the Declaration.

Article 1

All human beings are born free and equal in dignity and rights. They are endowed with reason and conscience and should act towards one another in a spirit of brotherhood.

Article 2

Everyone is entitled to all the rights and freedoms set forth in this Declaration, without distinction of any kind, such as race, colour, sex, language, religion, political or other opinion, national or social origin, property, birth or other status. Furthermore, no distinction shall be made on the basis of the political, jurisdictional or international status of the country or territory to which a person belongs, whether it be independent, trust, non-self-governing or under any other limitation of sovereignty.

Article 3

Everyone has the right to life, liberty and security of person.

Article 4

No one shall be held in slavery or servitude; slavery and the slave trade shall be prohibited in all their forms.

Article 5

No one shall be subjected to torture or to cruel, inhuman or degrading treatment or punishment.

Article 6

Everyone has the right to recognition everywhere as a person before the law.

Article 7

All are equal before the law and are entitled without any discrimination to equal protection of the law. All are entitled to equal protection against any discrimination in violation of this Declaration and against any incitement to such discrimination.

Article 8

Everyone has the right to an effective remedy by the competent national tribunals for acts violating the fundamental rights granted him by the constitution or by law.

Article 9

No one shall be subjected to arbitrary arrest, detention or exile.

Article 10

Everyone is entitled in full equality to a fair and public hearing by an independent and impartial tribunal, in the determination of his rights and obligations and of any criminal charge against him.

Article 11

1. Everyone charged with a penal offence has the right to be presumed innocent until proved guilty according to law in a public trial at which he has had all the guarantees necessary for his defence.
2. No one shall be held guilty of any penal offence on account of any act or omission which did not constitute a penal offence, under national or international law, at the time when it was committed. Nor shall a heavier penalty be imposed than the one that was applicable at the time the penal offence was committed.

Article 12

No one shall be subjected to arbitrary interference with his privacy, family, home or correspondence, nor to attacks upon his honour and reputation. Everyone has the right to the protection of the law against such interference or attacks.

Article 13

1. Everyone has the right to freedom of movement and residence within the borders of each state.
2. Everyone has the right to leave any country, including their own, and to return to their country.

Article 14

1. Everyone has the right to seek and to enjoy in other countries asylum from persecution.
2. This right may not be invoked in the case of prosecutions genuinely arising from non-political crimes or from acts contrary to the purposes and principles of the United Nations.

Article 15

1. Everyone has the right to a nationality.
2. No one shall be arbitrarily deprived of his nationality nor denied the right to change his nationality.

Article 16

1. Men and women of full age, without any limitation due to race, nationality or religion, have the right to marry and to found a family. They are entitled to equal rights as to marriage, during marriage and at its dissolution.
2. Marriage shall be entered into only with the free and full consent of the intending spouses.
3. The family is the natural and fundamental group unit of society and is entitled to protection by society and the State.

Article 17

1. Everyone has the right to own property alone as well as in association with others.
2. No one shall be arbitrarily deprived of his property.

Article 18

Everyone has the right to freedom of thought, conscience and religion; this right includes freedom to change his religion or belief, and freedom, either alone or in community with others and in public or private, to manifest his religion or belief in teaching, practice, worship and observance.

Article 19

Everyone has the right to freedom of opinion and expression; this right includes freedom to hold opinions without interference and to seek, receive and impart information and ideas through any media and regardless of frontiers.

Article 20

1. Everyone has the right to freedom of peaceful assembly and association.
2. No one may be compelled to belong to an association.

Article 21

1. Everyone has the right to take part in the government of their country, directly or through freely chosen representatives.
2. Everyone has the right of equal access to public service in their country.
3. The will of the people shall be the basis of the authority of government; this will shall be expressed in periodic and genuine elections which shall be by universal and equal suffrage and shall be held by secret vote or by equivalent free voting procedures.

Article 22

Everyone, as a member of society, has the right to social security and is entitled to realization, through national effort and international co-operation and in accordance with the organization and resources of each State, of the economic, social and cultural rights indispensable for his dignity and the free development of his personality.

Article 23

1. Everyone has the right to work, to free choice of employment, to just and favourable conditions of work and to protection against unemployment.
2. Everyone, without any discrimination, has the right to equal pay for equal work.
3. Everyone who works has the right to just and favourable remuneration ensuring for himself and his family an existence worthy of human dignity, and supplemented, if necessary, by other means of social protection.
4. Everyone has the right to form and to join trade unions for the protection of his interests.

Article 24

Everyone has the right to rest and leisure, including reasonable limitation of working hours and periodic holidays with pay.

Article 25

1. Everyone has the right to a standard of living adequate for the health and well-being of himself and of his family, including food, clothing, housing and medical care and necessary social services, and the right to security in the event of unemployment, sickness, disability, widowhood, old age or other lack of livelihood in circumstances beyond his control.
2. Motherhood and childhood are entitled to special care and assistance. All children, whether born in or out of wedlock, shall enjoy the same social protection.

Article 26

1. Everyone has the right to education. Education shall be free, at least in the elementary and fundamental stages. Elementary education shall be compulsory. Technical and professional education shall be made generally available and higher education shall be equally accessible to all on the basis of merit.

2. Education shall be directed to the full development of the human personality and to the strengthening of respect for human rights and fundamental freedoms. It shall promote understanding, tolerance and friendship among all nations, racial or religious groups, and shall further the activities of the United Nations for the maintenance of peace.
3. Parents have a prior right to choose the kind of education that shall be given to their children.

Article 27

1. Everyone has the right freely to participate in the cultural life of the community, to enjoy the arts and to share in scientific advancement and its benefits.
2. Everyone has the right to the protection of the moral and material interests resulting from any scientific, literary or artistic production of which he is the author.

Article 28

Everyone is entitled to a social and international order in which the rights and freedoms set forth in this Declaration can be fully realized.

Article 29

The adoption of the Universal Declaration is a significant international commemoration marked each year on 10 December and is known as Human Rights Day or International Human Rights Day.

1. Everyone has duties to the community in which alone the free and full development of his personality is possible.
2. In the exercise of his rights and freedoms, everyone shall be subject only to such limitations as are determined by law solely for the purpose of securing due recognition and respect for the rights and freedoms of others and of meeting the just requirements of morality, public order and the general welfare in a democratic society.
3. These rights and freedoms may in no case be exercised contrary to the purposes and principles of the United Nations.

Article 30

Nothing in this Declaration may be interpreted as implying for any State, group or person any right to engage in any activity or to perform any act aimed at the destruction of any of the rights and freedoms set forth herein.

Commemoration: International Human Rights Day

Human Rights Day

The adoption of the Universal Declaration is a significant international commemoration marked each year on 10 December and is known as Human Rights Day or International Human Rights Day. The commemoration is observed by individuals, community and religious groups, human rights organisations, parliaments, governments and the United Nations. Decadal commemorations are often accompanied by campaigns to promote awareness of the Declaration and human rights. 2008 marked the 60th anniversary of the Declaration and was accompanied by year long activities around the theme "Dignity and justice for all of us".

Significance and Legal Effect of Human Rights

Significance

In the preamble, governments commit themselves and their peoples to measures to secure the universal and effective recognition and observance of the human rights set out in the Declaration. Eleanor Roosevelt supported the adoption the UDHR as a declaration, rather than as a treaty, because she believed that it would have the same kind of influence on global society as the United States Declaration of Independence had within the United States. In this she proved to be correct. Even though not formally legally binding, the Declaration has been adopted in or influenced most national constitutions since 1948. It also serves as the foundation for a growing number of international treaties and national laws and international, regional, national and sub-national institutions protecting and promoting human rights.

Legal Effect

While not a treaty itself, the Declaration was explicitly adopted for the purpose of defining the meaning of the words "fundamental freedoms" and "human rights" appearing in the United Nations Charter, which is binding on all member states. For this reason, the Universal Declaration is a fundamental constitutive document of the United Nations. Many international lawyers, in addition, believe that the Declaration forms part of customary international law and is a powerful tool in applying diplomatic and moral pressure to governments that violate any of its articles.

The 1968 United Nations International Conference on Human Rights advised that it "constitutes an obligation for the members of the international community" to all persons. The declaration has served as the foundation for two binding UN human rights covenants, the International Covenant on Civil and Political Rights and the International Covenant on Economic, Social and Cultural Rights and the principles of the Declaration are elaborated in international treaties such as the International Convention on the Elimination of All Forms of Racial Discrimination, the International Convention on the Elimination of Discrimination Against Women, the United Nations Convention on the Rights of the Child, the United Nations Convention Against Torture and many more. The Declaration continues to be widely cited by governments, academics, advocates and constitutional courts and individual human beings who appeal to its principles for the protection of their recognised human rights.

Reaction

Praise

The Universal Declaration has received praise from a number of notable people. Charles Malik, Lebanese philosopher and diplomat, called it "an international document of the first order of importance," while Eleanor Roosevelt, first chairwoman of the Commission on Human Rights (CHR) that drafted the Declaration, stated that it "may well become the international Magna Carta of all men everywhere." 10 December 1948. In a speech on 5 October 1995, Pope John Paul II called the UDHR "one of the highest expressions of the human conscience of our time." And in a statement on 10 December 2003 on behalf of the European Union, Marcello Spatafora said that "it placed human rights at the centre of the framework of principles and obligations shaping relations within the international community.

Censorship

The Cuban government has been accused of ordering copies of the Universal Declaration of Human Rights to be burned or otherwise destroyed.

Criticism

Islamic Criticism

Some Islamic countries have criticized the Universal Declaration of Human Rights for its perceived failure to take into the account the cultural and religious context of Islamic countries. In 1982, the Iranian representative to the United Nations, Said Rajaie-Khorassani, articulated the position of his country regarding the Universal Declaration of Human Rights, by saying that the UDHR was "a secular understanding of the Judeo-Christian tradition", which could not be implemented by Muslims without trespassing the Islamic law. On 30 June 2000, Muslim nations that are members of the Organization of the Islamic Conference officially resolved to support the Cairo Declaration on Human Rights in Islam, an alternative document that says people have "freedom and right to a dignified life in accordance with the Islamic Shari'ah."

Education

Some proponents of alternative education, particularly unschooling, take issue with the right to compulsory education stated in Article 26.[25] In the philosophies of John Holt and others, compulsory education itself violates the right of a person to follow their own interests:

No human right, except the right to life itself, is more fundamental than this. A person's freedom of learning is part of his freedom of thought, even more basic than his freedom of speech. If we take from someone his right to decide what he will be curious about, we destroy his freedom of thought. We say, in effect, you must think not about what interests you and concerns you, but about what interests and concerns us.

— John Holt, Escape from Childhood

Others, such as the European Students Union (ESU), suggest that access to education is a human right and should be accessible to all free of any tuition charge.

Property Rights Criticism

Some Libertarians have criticized the Declaration for its inclusion of positive rights that they believe must be provided by other's through forceful extraction (for example taxation) thereby negating others rights. Libertarian natural law theorist Frank Van Dun said of the document:

The UD's distinctive "rights" are incompatible with that doctrine [of natural rights]. Enforcement of one person's economic, social, or cultural rights necessarily involves forcing others to relinquish their property, or to use it in a way prescribed by the enforcers. It would, therefore, constitute a clear violation of their natural right to manage and dispose of their lawful possessions without coercive or aggressive interference by others. It would also deny a person the right to improve his condition by accepting work for what he (but perhaps no one else) considers an adequate wage.

— Frank Van Dun, Human Dignity: Reason or Desire?

The Right to Refuse to Kill

Groups such as Amnesty International and War Resisters International have advocated for "The Right to Refuse to Kill" to be added to the UDHR. War Resisters International has stated that the right to conscientious objection to military service is primarily derived from, but not yet explicit in, Article 18 of the UDHR: the right to freedom of thought, conscience and religion.

Steps have been taken within the UN to make this right more explicit (see Conscientious Objector); but those steps have been limited to secondary, more "marginal" UN documents. That is why Amnesty International would like to have this right brought "out of the margins" and explicitly into the primary document, namely, the UDHR itself.

To the rights enshrined in the Universal Declaration of Human Rights one more might, with relevance, be added. It is "The Right to Refuse to Kill."

— Assistant Secretary General of the United Nations, and Nobel Peace Laureate, Sean MacBride, 1974 Nobel Lecture

Bangkok Declaration

In the Bangkok Declaration adopted by Ministers of Asian states meeting in 1993 in the lead up to the World Conference on Human Rights, Asian governments reaffirmed their commitment to the principles of the United Nations Charter and the Universal Declaration of Human Rights. They stated their view of the interdependence and indivisibility of human rights and stressed the need for universality, objectivity and non-selectivity of human rights.

The Universal Declaration of Human Rights (UDHR) is a declaration adopted by the United Nations General Assembly on December 10, 1948 at the Palais de Chaillot in Paris. The Declaration has been translated into over 300 languages and dialects, making it the most widely translated document in the world. The Declaration arose directly from the experience of the Second World War and represents the first global expression of rights to which all human beings are entitled.

It consists of 30 articles which have been elaborated in subsequent international treaties, regional human rights instruments, national constitutions and laws. The International Bill of Human Rights consists of the Universal Declaration of Human Rights, the International Covenant on Economic, Social and Cultural Rights, and the International Covenant on Civil and Political Rights and its two Optional Protocols. In 1966 the General Assembly adopted the two detailed Covenants, which complete the International Bill of Human Rights.

What is an International Human Rights Treaty?

An international human rights treaty (sometimes called a 'convention') is a collection of human rights standards that has been put into the form of an agreement between different countries.

An International Human Rights Treaty (sometimes called a 'convention') is a collection of human rights standards that has been put into the form of an agreement between different countries.

To be bound by a treaty, a government must take formal steps to become a 'party' to it. This will generally either be a two-step process (comprising signature, followed by ratification), or a single-step process, called 'accession'. Both processes ultimately make the country 'a party' to the treaty, and bind the government to the treaty's terms.

Governments agree to ensure that all people living within their jurisdiction are able to access and enforce the rights outlined in the treaty. This often involves becoming subject to UN scrutiny. Scrutiny might be by special committees set up under the treaty, other governments, the community sector, or individuals who also monitor a government's actions and pressure them to protect the rights outlined in the treaty.

Australia's signing a human rights treaty does not automatically make the human rights it contains part of our domestic law. Further legislative steps must be taken to give a treaty legal force in Australia, including the enactment, prior to ratification or accession, of any domestic legislation necessary to implement the treaty.

The Australian Government is responsible for becoming party to treaties and participating in UN processes. Australian, State and Territory governments do not participate directly in these processes, however, they are often instrumental in giving effect to the human rights contained in treaties to which Australia is a party.

Implementing Human Rights

Even though human rights exist as a birthright, to be effective they need to be supported by law and able to be used in practice. This happens in many ways: through the UN, through our governments, the police, our employers, our families, our friends and through us as individuals. Our own awareness and support for human rights is one of the most important ways to enforce them. Governments however remain accountable for ensuring the implementation of convention obligations within their countries.

Governments can implement an international human rights treaty in a range of ways. Creating new laws, while critical, does not always lead directly to change in the social practices and attitudes which underpin human behaviour and lead to human rights violations. Governments aim to reduce violations in the following ways:

- creating laws that make human rights violations illegal under Australian law
- adopting policies and programs to ensure people have access to their human rights
- ensuring that human rights are properly enforced, including providing resources and assistance, access to courts and appropriate punishment for violations
- providing education and awareness raising programs about human rights.

Convention on the Elimination of All Forms of Discrimination Against Women (CEDAW)

Ultimately we have to be judged not by our highest ambitions and achievements, but by our ability to raise from the lowest level those whose needs that are greatest. That is the way I would like Australia, and every other country, to be judged in the United Nations. [Australia's Justice Elizabeth Evatt — Member of the CEDAW Committee 1984-92, Chair of the CEDAW Committee 1989-90 — highlighting the importance of CEDAW to developed countries.]

The Convention on the Elimination of All Forms of Discrimination Against Women (CEDAW) was adopted in 1979 by the UN General Assembly and entered into force on 3 September 1981. Australia has been a party to CEDAW since 17 August 1983.

CEDAW has often been described as an 'international bill of rights' for women. Enshrined within its preamble and 30 Articles are key principles of equality and an agenda for national action to end discrimination against women. It is based on the belief that basic human rights include the true equality of men and women. As of November 2008, 185 countries are parties to CEDAW.

The rights enshrined in CEDAW broadly cover many aspects of women's lives. Rights include political participation, health, education, employment, marriage, family relations and equality before the law.

Rights contained in CEDAW

CEDAW defines discrimination against women as:

any distinction, exclusion or restriction made on the basis of sex which has the effect or purpose of impairing or nullifying the recognition, enjoyment or exercise by women, irrespective of their marital status, on a basis of equality of men and women, of human rights and fundamental freedoms in the political, economic, social, cultural, civil or any other field. (Article 1)

In becoming party to CEDAW, Australia committed itself to being a society that promotes policies, laws, organisations, structures and attitudes that ensure women are given the same rights as men. CEDAW facilitates this by promoting non-discriminatory practices in the following areas:

Law, Policy and Prejudices

Article 2 of CEDAW urges parties to CEDAW to work towards eradicating discrimination against women, including by introducing new laws or policies, changing existing discriminatory laws and providing sanctions for discrimination where appropriate.

Article 3 of CEDAW requires parties to promote actively women's full development and advancement, so they can enjoy human rights and fundamental freedoms on the same basis as men.

Article 4 of CEDAW allows temporary special measures that favour women, on the basis that they are designed to speed up achievement of equality.

Article 5 of CEDAW requires parties to address and change social and cultural patterns that reinforce the stereotyping of women and traditional gender roles, or that promote the relative superiority or inferiority of either of the sexes.

Trafficking and Exploitation of Prostitution

Article 6 of CEDAW requires parties to take all appropriate measures to suppress all forms of trafficking of women and exploitation of prostitution of women. It does not intend to prohibit prostitution but to address problems of exploitation of women through prostitution.

Politics and Public Life

Article 7 of CEDAW sets out women's right to vote, to stand for election, to be involved in formulating government policy and to actively participate in non-government organisations (NGOs) and other bodies concerned with the public and political life of the country, such as political parties and lobby groups.

Article 8 of CEDAW states that women should have the same opportunities as men to represent their countries internationally and be involved in the work of international organisations.

Nationality

Article 9 of CEDAW requires that women have the same rights as men to acquire, retain or change their nationality and the nationality of their children. It provides that neither marriage to an alien nor a change of nationality by the husband during marriage will automatically change the nationality of the wife, make her stateless or force upon her the nationality of the husband. Article 9 also provides that women have the same rights as men regarding the nationality of their children.

Education and Training

Article 10 of CEDAW urges parties to ensure that women have the same opportunities as men in all aspects of education and training — from kindergarten to tertiary education. Women and girls should have access to the same curricula, professional staff and programs, especially those aimed at reducing any existing gender gaps within education, and opportunities to benefit from the same scholarships and study grants as men. Governments are required to ensure that all education is free from stereotypical concepts of the roles of men and women.

Employment

Article 11 of CEDAW requires parties to eliminate discrimination in employment so as to ensure that women have the right to work, the right to the same training and employment opportunities as men and the right to receive equal pay for work of equal value. Women must also have access to the same benefits, compensatory schemes, and allowances as men, especially in relation to retirement and incapacity to work.

This Article further requires that parties prohibit discrimination in the workplace on the basis of marriage, pregnancy and maternity, and introduce paid maternity leave without loss of benefits or career opportunities, and encourage provision of supporting social services to allow parents to combine family obligations with work responsibilities.

Health

Article 12 of CEDAW requires parties to take all appropriate measures to eliminate discrimination against women in the field of health care to ensure women and men have equal access to health services including family planning.

This Article further requires that parties provide appropriate health services in relation to pregnancy and post-natal care, and to grant free services where necessary.

Economic Life, Sport and Culture

Article 13 of CEDAW expressly requires that women have equal access to family benefits, forms of financial credit, including bank loans and mortgages, and the same rights as men to participate in recreational activities, sports and cultural life.

Women Living in Remote and Rural Areas

Article 14 of CEDAW requires all parties to take all appropriate measures to ensure that the particular needs of rural women are met and to ensure rural women have access to health care services, training and employment opportunities, and social security schemes.

Equality Before the Law

Article 15 of CEDAW requires parties to treat women and men equally in all matters relating to the law, including civil matters, contractual matters, and property ownership.

Family Relations

Article 16 of CEDAW requires parties to ensure women and men have equal rights to freely choose a spouse and enter into marriage; the same rights and responsibilities as men within marriage and upon divorce, especially with regard to choosing a family name, a profession, and the rights of ownership of property; and equal rights in all matters relating to birth, adoption and raising of their children.

Violence Against Women

Gender-based violence is a serious form of discrimination. While CEDAW does not contain an explicit reference to violence against women, the CEDAW Committee has issued a General Recommendation which states that violence directed against a women because she is woman or violence that affects women disproportionately is recognised and addressed as discrimination under the convention.

Parties to CEDAW therefore have an obligation under CEDAW to take positive steps to eliminate all forms of violence against women. The CEDAW Committee asks countries to provide information in their regular reports about legislation and other measures it uses to protect women from violence, as well as the support services available to women.

Reservations

When signing or ratifying an international treaty, a country can make a reservation to a particular provision or provisions of that treaty. This is a unilateral statement which effectively excludes the country from any obligation in regards to that provision. It is always open to any country to remove reservations to CEDAW when it wishes to commit to those rights.

Australia has two reservations to CEDAW; the provision of paid maternity leave or a 'comparable social benefit' and women's participation in direct, armed combat.

Paid Maternity Leave

When the Australian Government ratified CEDAW in 1984, it placed a reservation to CEDAW Article 11(2). This Article stipulates that countries who are party to CEDAW must introduce paid maternity or comparable social benefits which ensure that women do not lose employment, seniority or social benefits.

11.11 JOB RESERVATIONS IN PRIVATE SECTOR

"Economic empowerment of the poor, in particular the Scheduled Castes and Scheduled Tribes, as is enjoined under Article 46, is a constitutional objective as basic human and fundamental right to enable the labourer, Scheduled Castes and Scheduled Tribes to raise their economic empowerment."

For sometime past there has been a persistent demand from Dalits that law should provide reservation for scheduled castes and scheduled tribes in business enterprises and in works funded by the Governments and Public Sector.

This question has assumed urgency because of undesirable haste by which public sector is being dismantled, with the inevitable consequence of loss of opportunities for employment for large segment of Dalits.

It is no longer in dispute that because of the caste system large portion of the population in our country have been deprived of equal opportunity in various walks of life. Pt. Nehru even in 1930 wrote "therefore, not only must equal opportunities be given to all, but special opportunities for educational, economic and cultural growth must be given to backward groups so as to enable them to catch up with those who are ahead of them."

Our Supreme Court has emphasized that the Preamble of the Constitution which directs the State to secure to all citizens justice will remain a myth unless first economic justice is guaranteed to all.

In this context, it should not be forgotten that hitherto for centuries, there have been cent per cent reservations in practice in all fields, in favour of the high castes and classes, to the total exclusion of others. It was a purely caste and class-based reservation.

The employment — whether private or public - thus, is a means of social leveling. A deliberately conscious attempt to secure it to those who were designedly denied the same in the past, is an attempt to do social and economic justice to them as ordained by the Preamble of the Constitution and also the mandate of Article 16 of the Constitution.

Our Supreme Court has held that "economic empowerment of the poor, in particular the Scheduled Castes and Scheduled Tribes, as is enjoined under Article 46, is a constitutional objective as basic human and fundamental right to enable the labourer, Scheduled Castes and Scheduled Tribes to raise their economic empowerment."

A look around will show the horrendous deprivation in the matter of employment, notwithstanding the constitution providing for reservation for Dalits and backward classes. The backlog of vacancies for Dalits even after over 50 years of the Constitution is appalling — thus there is 70% in Group A jobs and even 45% in D group the lowest job of peons, khallasis etc. In the public sector it is more shocking being 88%. The backlog of appointments of S.C. and S.T. is reported to be about a million in various govt. services.

Even now in many places the country tea shops have two tumblers outside, and Dalit is expected to wash his own tumbler.

Such humiliating inhuman behaviour is done because Dalits do not possess the financial clout to assert their constitutional rights to equality and non-discrimination. Poverty is so enveloping amongst Dalits that of agricultural labour about 49% are Dalits, thus being denied dignity because without land ownership there is no respect in rural areas.

It is for this reason that it is time when similar legislation like USA is essential so as to give status in society to Dalits.

It is essential to ensure social justice and democratise wealth.

Social justice is the bedrock of any democracy. A society shaped and controlled by the ideology of caste militates against the concept of social justice. A fair society is possible only when hierarchies conceived and nurtured by the caste system are destroyed.

Social justice is the bedrock of any democracy. A society shaped and controlled by the ideology of caste militates against the concept of social justice. A fair society is possible only when hierarchies conceived and nurtured by the caste system are destroyed. Reservations in the fields of education and employment for people who have been on the wrong end of the caste hierarchy is a constitutional means to do it.

All this while, the provision for affirmative action in the form of reservations has been employed only in the public sector. With the State increasingly receding from the spheres of education and employment generation, it is time the policy of affirmative action is introduced in the private sector occupying the space. Or else, the old social order where the upper castes controlled wealth as well as the means of production and the lower castes took care of jobs that essentially facilitated the status quo will continue to hold fort in the future too.

A total destruction of caste is possible only when both the ideology as well as the economic order it created are defeated. Job reservations are a must for the latter. They are an integral part of the process of democratising the distribution of wealth.

In today's world, the caste that historically had access to education, power and wealth is at an advantage. That is why one can rarely find a dalit or an adivasi among professionals, be it in the infotech sector or any other private sector industry.

In today's world, the caste that historically had access to education, power and wealth is at an advantage. That is why one can rarely find a dalit or an adivasi among professionals, be it in the infotech sector or any other private sector industry.

A level playing field in the Indian context necessitates the creation of unequal opportunities favourable to the lower castes. What-happens-to-merit is only an argument that seeks to maintain the *status quo* in favour of the upper castes.

It is also preposterous to argue that merit is the dominant criterion for employment in the private sector.

Social linkages, including caste and family ties, matter a lot in a sector where an overwhelming amount of businesses are family-run. There is no evidence yet of merit being hereditary.

What the private sector in India needs to do is to take the cue from the developed world. Companies such as Microsoft and Intel have called for affirmative action in admissions to educational institutions as well as hiring in the US.

Rather than wait for the state to legislate, the industry should take the initiative to seek diversity among its workforce. That is how the private sector could play a role in creating a more democratic society in the country.

Protectionism, including that of private (read caste) interests, goes against the spirit of democracy as well as capitalism.

Is job reservation in private sector is a Charity or a Social Necessity?

At the outset, the main purpose of the reservation policy was to ensure social and economic justice; thereby realize the goal of the empowerment of the dalits and tribals. It can address certain social inequalities that pervade Indian society for so long. For, these social inequalities leave the so-called low castes deprived in everything from education to economy. Thus, the policy of job reservations intends to bring about proportional representation, as it is a mode of distributing benefits based on the proportion of population that is 15 percent for the Schedule Castes (SCs) and 7.5 percent for Scheduled Tribes (STs).

> Thanks to Dr. B.R. Ambedkar's instrumental role in the constitution making, the governments are bound to implement them on the basis of the principle of distributive justice and compensation for past disadvantages.

Thanks to Dr. B.R Ambedkar's instrumental role in the constitution making, the governments are bound to implement them on the basis of the principle of distributive justice and compensation for past disadvantages. But then, that was confined to only the public sector that had been shrinking over a period of time. At a time when the number of educated among these unprivileged classes is increasing in geometrical progression, their share of jobs in the public sector is dwindling on end. This is more so since the last decade and half, all in the name of so-called globalisation and till date.

Now that there is some political consensus, as is evident from the latest conclave of national leaders of all parties including the Left ones in Delhi recently, emerging from several quarters, the Central government of all nomenclatures is under the obligation to implement the job reservations in the private sector too. Of course, there were several Ambedkar organizations and Dalit-based parties raised this issue of private reservations for the past decade or so. Since the Upper class-oriented business class was adamant to concede this measure, no political party was willing to bulldoze its decision on the private sector. However, thanks to vote-bank politics, the political parties of all hues are compelled to consider the serious nature of this demand and thereby echoed with the aspirations of the underprivileged classes.

> Ever since the present United Progressive Alliance (UPA) Government at the Centre promised to introduce job reservations in the private sector, there were acrimonious reactions from some quarters.

Ever since the present United Progressive Alliance (UPA) Government at the Centre promised to introduce job reservations in the private sector, there were acrimonious reactions from some quarters. In fact, as part of its Common Minimum Programme (CMP), the Congress-led political coalition provided this measure in the election manifesto more than one year ago. While there were no serious objections raised from the very private sector since then, certain sections are at great pains to digest it. As usual, a section of media has always been biased against the downtrodden and dalit communities in this country. Thus, it evoked sharp reaction from such vested interests in the media and elsewhere.

Incidentally, the so-called experts who seldom supported for the job reservations in the public sector for so long are also the ones who raised objections to the same this time in the private sector. As a result, the UPA promise (Reservations in Private Sector) has created many a controversy on the subject. That in turn was responsible to raise certain pertinent questions. For instance, whether dalits and downtrodden should be given some preference in the employment sector? Whether this preference based on their mere birth in a particular caste or community is justified? Why is this to be given to certain people? These are some serious questions that deserve attention.

This concept of 'Reservations' aimed at ensuring the betterment of underprivileged and deprived sections of society was sabotaged from 'within' in the initial days. Thus, these reservations were being renewed decade after decade. Even though constitutional obligations are binding upon all the government departments, not more than ten percent of reservations were ever implemented. It is only in the last few years, owing to the efforts of some dalit leaders and their movements that there was some improvement in this direction. The fact that several governments both at the centre and in states and public sector units were found to be advertising, the 'backlog vacancies' in the name of special-drives, so as to recruit members from these reserved categories vindicate the above proposition.

This concept of 'Reservations' aimed at ensuring the betterment of underprivileged and deprived sections of society was sabotaged from 'within' in the initial days. Thus, these reservations were being renewed decade after decade.

Even then, none of the departments could ever claim that required vacancies were filled up. More than the case of lack of availability of suitable candidates in these communities for the prescribed positions, it is the employers' biased attitude against such candidates that is largely responsible for the prevailing situation. However, except in the top-level central services, the jobs in the other categories are still unoccupied by the dalit candidates. Of course, some court cases in the Supreme Court a couple of years ago, filed by the of All India Confederation SC & ST Organizations, could help the community in securing some justice in terms of revising the orders of promotion among other benefits.

This is long-awaited measure and of course welcomed by all sections of society. Obviously, even a section of the business class is willing to implement it, how so difficult it may appear to be as far as its feasibility is concerned. For, there are certain apprehensions expressed by several persons cutting across all castes and communities. Not just because the very security of private job is at the mercy of the management, but also because the government does not have any role in protecting the private employee. Since the government plays or intends to play the role of best spectator in the operations of private sector, private job aspirants, be they from general category or from others, have to merely dependent on none other than themselves!

In any case, this concept of private reservation cannot be considered as charity, but a right from a government that exposed its hollowness. Further, it is a necessity as the government failed to create jobs to its qualified aspirants. In other words, the nature of private job is such that there is hardly any guarantee (in terms of pay and period) to that job! It is so insecure that one should continue searching for jobs as usual, of course till a government job is secured. Then, why should there be such hue and cry about the 'reservations in private sector'?

In any case, this concept of private reservation cannot be considered as charity, but a right from a government that exposed its hollowness.

11.12 WHITSLE BLOWING

Origins of Term

The term whistleblower derives from the practice of English police officers, who would blow their whistles when they noticed the commission of a crime. The whistle would alert other law enforcement officers and the general public of danger. One who reveals wrongdoing within an organization to the public or to those in positions of authority.

Definition

Refers to the process by which insiders `go public' with their claims of malpractices by, or within, organisations - usually after failing to remedy the matters from the inside, and often at great personal risk to themselves.

The term `whistle blowing' is a relatively recent entry into the vocabulary of public and corporate affairs, although the phenomenon itself is not new. It refers to the process by which insiders `go public' with their claims of malpractices by, or within, organisations - usually after failing to remedy the matters from the inside, and often at great personal risk to themselves. It is this willingness to stand up for a principle and court risk openly that distinguishes whistle blowing from such related practices as in-house criticism, anonymous leaks, and the like. The whistleblower is considered a hero or a traitor, a do-gooder or a crank, a role model or a non-conformist troublemaker - depending on one's point of view. Whistle blowing is a universal phenomenon. India has also had its share of prominent whistleblowers from V. P. Singh to Manoj Prabhakar to P. Dinakar.

It is true that under normal circumstances, an organisation is entitled to total loyalty and confidentiality from its employees. But when there is serious malpractice or when people's lives are at stake — as in corruption and fraud in defence procurement; deaths in `encounter' of innocent persons; toxic leaks from a chemical factory; non-adherence to flight safety standards by an airline; creative accounting and false declarations by a company; cheating and plagiarism in scientific research, for example - the overriding public interest may lie in protecting the public's right to be told, and the whistleblower's right not to be punished for doing so. Without whistleblowers, we may not get to learn about problems until it is time to mourn the consequences.

No doubt, audit, ombudsman, vigilance commissions, regulating agencies, the media, civil society, and courts all play a role in deterring government and corporate transgressions to some extent. But however formidable their investigative skills, that initial inside information provided by a whistleblower is crucial. Even a powerful Freedom of Information Act, which discloses information without the need for leaking, offers only a partial solution. As the journal Index on Censorship (1995) put it: "Users would have to specify what they wanted to know. But where there is no reason to suspect that something is amiss, no one may bother to ask."

Types of Whistle Blowers

Report misconduct to a fellow employee or superior within their company.

Most whistle blowers are internal whistle blowers, who report misconduct to a fellow employee or superior within their company. One of the most interesting questions with respect to internal whistle blowers is why and under what circumstances people will either act on the spot to stop illegal and otherwise unacceptable behaviour or report it. There is some reason to believe that people are more likely to take action with respect to unacceptable behaviour, within an organization, if there are complaint systems that offer not just options dictated by the organization, but a choice of options for individuals, including an option that offers near absolute confidentiality.

External whistle blowers, however, report misconduct to outside persons or entities. In these cases, depending on the information's severity and nature, whistleblowers may report the misconduct to lawyers, the media, law enforcement or watchdog agencies, or other local, state, or central government.

External whistle-blowers, however, report misconduct to outside persons or entities.

Protecting Whistle Blowers in India

During the past decade, scams, swindles, and rip-offs have become a regular feature of the Indian political and corporate landscape, costing taxpayers, investors and banks thousands of crores of rupees. Enactment of a Whistle Blowers Protection Act is even more necessary for India than it was for the U.K. and the U.S. Together with the Freedom of Information Act it can be a potent tool for promoting good governance in the country. What we lack at the moment are public interest groups like the Government Accountability Project and the National Whistle Blower Centre in the U.S., and the Public Concern At Work in the U.K., to lobby for whistle blowers' rights and defend employees against retaliation.

Whistle Blowing and Competitive Advantage

Whistle blowing involves a conflict between two competing duties, to protect the public and to be loyal to the organization. However, given no real mechanism to deal fully with ethical concerns, an employee may be left with a 3-way choice: shut up (and take a hard knock on your conscience); get out (on the grounds of conflicting values); or blow the whistle (and pay for the heavy consequences). The inadequacies of law fail to give support.

Although there are ways to tackle it, there might still be limitations. If at all there should be a situation where an employee does not have to blow the whistle then the organization should ensure such procedures that minimize potential whistle blowing situations. There is ethical justification of whistle blowing. The need of the hour is the protection of the whistle blower. At the moment, those who do blow the whistle are ill-supported and ultimately pay a heavy price for being the conscience of us all.

The role of whiste blowing is also important with respect to ethical behaviour as long as there is no mechanism to reduce the need for whistle blowing. If there is no mechanism, then the encouragement of whistle blowing, seen in the right perspective, will bring about a positive image of the organization and will be applauded by the public. This is the beginning of the road to competitive advantage. This is because the issue of ethics is placed in the forefront of the organization. On the other hand, unethical practices in organizations will in all probability lead to its end.

Whistle Blowing A Casualty

Hundreds of people are murdered every day all over India. What makes the death of Satyendra Dubey so very special? It is surely a combination of a number of factors.

There is, first of all, the heart-breaking story of Dreams Unfulfilled: the young Dubey was the bright son every lower middle-class family prays for. He was, in the best sense of the term, their ticket to the future, their only means to fulfil their aspirations. And Satyendra Dubey seemed to be all that, a bright, young man with a bright, young intelligence who went to the Indian Institute of Technology and came out with idealism intact. All children carry their parents hopes; the Satyendras of the world carry even more. So the early loss of a child, which is terrible enough, is made even worse.

Then there is idealism factor. Why was **Satyendra Dubey** killed? Because he did something all of us should do, but don't. Which is not to just be appalled at the loot and villainy around us (all of us are upset by corruption), but do something about it. Whistle blower isn't exactly a felicitous term, but all of us understand what it means: someone who is an insider, wanting to expose the rot within the system. It needs courage to do that because you are risking the wrath of people you work with and much else. Like vindictiveness from the system leading to possible victimisation; the loss of job, career and livelihood.

Or, as in the case of Satyendra Dubey, even the loss of one's own life.

The third factor which makes Dubey's death so tragically special is that it exposes, once again, the callousness of our nation's administrative system.

It is now well established that Dubey's letter to the Prime Minister giving details of the corruption in the Golden Quadrilateral highway project, was routinely circulated. This in spite of the writer's earnest request that his name should not be disclosed as he feared vengeful reaction from the people involved in the scam. As it happens, Dubey's courage was not foolhardy: he anticipated trouble and wrote a second letter, again requesting anonymity. That too was ignored. Whether the Prime Minister's Office (PMO) did this deliberately or just through the usual carelessness isn't established, but the net result was that the whistle-blower's name fell into the hands of the very people against whom the whistle was being blown. With what consequences we all know. The callousness doesn't end there. We know that the Golden Quadrilateral is the Prime Minister's own dream project, as important to him personally as Indo-Pakistan relations. We also now know that Satyendra Dubey's killing has evoked a huge response all over the country. Yet the PM has said not a word about it.

No condemnation of the killers, no promise of swift justice, no anger at PMO officials, not even a letter of condolence to the Dubey family. The Dubey killing to the Prime Minister and the Prime Minister's Office is just another statistic, although it is anything but routine to the rest of the country.

This response, or rather the lack of it, is not an aberration. This is the way of the government. And when that is said, it isn't aimed particularly at the Bharatiya Janata Party (BJP) or the National Democratic Alliance (NDA), or for that matter, any political party. That's because a government formed by any political party will behave the same way, which is to ignore injustice and corruption, look the other way and hope that public indignation will be short-lived.

The obvious reason why all parties tacitly acquiesce in this convenient blindness is that politicians across party lines have much to hide. Look at the Telgi fake stamp paper scandal. It went on for years, crossed State boundaries, deprived the government of hundereds of crores of rupees and would have continued to do so hadn't it been for a whistle-blower (in the Pune police department) and an activist with a conscience and a Gandhian approach (Anna Hazare).

This is precisely why governments of all idealogies rush through acts like the Prevention of Terrorism Act (POTA), which gives the police powers of arbitrary detention of "other people", while ignoring proposed legislation like the Public Interest Disclosure (Protection of Informers) Bill (PIDB).

Significantly, both POTA and PIDB were drafted by the same man at the same time. Former Supreme Court Justice B.P. Jeevan Reddy submitted both drafts two years ago. The response to POTA was a rare joint session of Parliament; the response to PIDB was the usual dusty shelf. If the Protection of Informers Bill had been made into law, Satyendra Dubey might still have been alive today. All governments rely on public memory being short. It generally is because we move on to the next scandal and to yet another scam. Perhaps that's what the PMO hopes will happen here too. But it ignores one vital difference.

Some newspapers have taken on the Dubey murder as a campaigning issue to ensure that public interest does not die out. More than that, the medium of the internet, with its instant access and its rapid multiplier effect, has come into its own in this case, and the protest signatures have begun to mount in very large numbers every day, and show no sign of abating.

Could this be the beginning of a new phase in our democracy? Our middle-class has felt emasculated because the vote — democracy's most potent weapon - has meant very little to it because of the weight of numbers. But the internet gives it a chance to make its voice heard. Maybe, just maybe, this voice will now get louder. Satyendra Dubey should not have died but in his death he may have begun a revolution.

Whistle Blowing is a Deadly Affair

Mr. Satyendra Dubey and Mr. S. Manjunath both IIT/IIM graduates, when they decided to favour the decrepit public sector in India. They exposed corruption during their work for which both have paid dearly with their lives. Dubey exposed a huge swindle in the expensive national highway project, and he was killed in Bihar. Manjunath refused to take bribe to give consent to the adulteration of petrol at an IOC booth of which he was an employee. These are the new martyrs of independent India — an India where governance is free from foreign control, but where the people are still slaves to a corrupt bureaucracy.

Corruption is an accepted facet of life for most Indians — be it bribing the police, the council head, the hospital nurse or the school clerk. But whistle blowing is an honourable technique against corruption — by exposing the malpractices in one's marketplace.

Only some months back, after Satyendra Dubey's murder, that the Indian Govt. enacted a law protecting whistle blowers and giving them unprecedented rights. Dubey was honoured posthumously and the Indian Press rattled with his news for a few weeks after his unjust murder.

PROS AND CONS OF WHISTLE BLOWING

Merits

- An effectively communicated statement of responsibility.
- A clearly defined procedure for Reporting well-trained personnel to receive and investigate reports.

- A commitment to take appropriate action
- A guarantee against retaliation
- There are several statutes and legislations that protects Whistle blowing
- Open right to abuse — disgruntled employees can use it to get back at employees

Demerits

- Loss of jobs
- Damaging repercussions on profession, marriage, and family life
- Encroaches on traditional rights of organizations to run their business
- Persecution of whistle blowers has become a serious issue in many parts of the world. Although whistle blowers are often protected under law from employer retaliation, there have been many cases where punishment for whistle blowing has occurred, such as termination, suspension, demotion, wage garnishment, and/or harsh mistreatment by other employees. Many whistle blowers report there exists a widespread "shoot the messenger" mentality by corporations or government agencies accused of misconduct and in some cases whistle blowers have been subjected to criminal prosecution in reprisal for reporting wrongdoing. (Example Sathyendra Dubey and Manjunath).

WHISTLE BLOWING

SATYENDRA DUBEY MURDER: THREE GET LIFE IMPRISONMENT

Three persons were sentenced to life imprisonment by a special CBI court for murdering NHAI engineer Satyendra Dubey, the young whistleblower who had exposed corruption in the Golden Quadrilateral highway project in Bihar, in 2003.

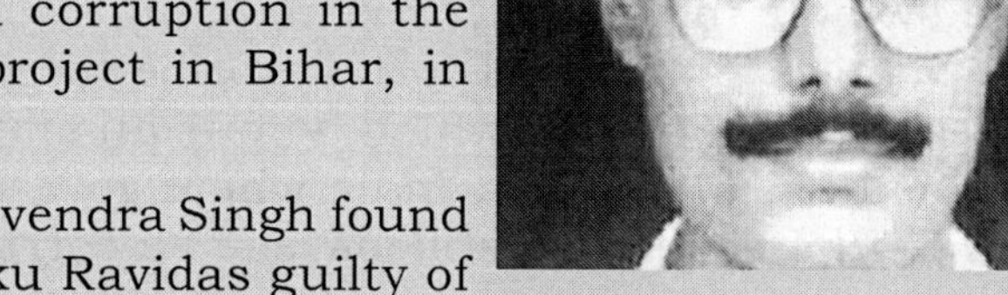

Special CBI court judge Raghvendra Singh found Mantu Kumar, Udai Kumar, Pinku Ravidas guilty of murdering the 31-year-old IIT-Kanpur alumni and awarded life term to them. Dubey, a project engineer of the National Highway Authority of India (NHAI) who had exposed several cases of large-scale flouting of rules and corrupt practices in the construction project, was gunned down in the early hours of November 27, 2003 in front of the Circuit House in Gaya when he was going to his residence after alighting from train from Varanasi.

Mantu was convicted under sections for murder(Section 302 IPC), voluntary causing hurt in committing robbery (Section 394 IPC) and the Arms Act for possessing unlicensed weapon. The other two accused were convicted of murder committed in furtherance of common intention (Section 302/34 IPC) and also for voluntary causing hurt in committing robbery.

After the three were convicted on Saturday, Dhananjay Dubey, brother of the victim, said he was "really disappointed" as those convicted were "purely innocent" and claimed that the real culprits were still on the loose. Dubey had even written directly to the then Prime Minister Atal Bihari Vajpayee detailing the financial and contractual irregularities in the construction project.

The murder had sparked protests across the country amidst calls for a legislation to protect whistleblowers who expose corruption. The CBI, which had taken over the investigation of the case from Bihar police on December 14, 2003, had filed a chargesheet in the case on September 3, 2004. During the investigation, CBI arrested four persons, namely Mantu, Udai, Pinku and Sharvan Kumar, all residents of Katari village in Gaya, Bihar, the investigating agency said.

"They had all assembled near Circuit House, Gaya on the fateful intervening night of November 26/27, 2003. Around 3.30 AM on November 27 when Dubey was passing in front of Circuit House, Gaya in a cycle-rickshaw, the accused persons robbed him of his belongings and during the ensuing scuffle, Mantu shot him dead with a .315 country-made weapon," it said in a statement in New Delhi.

The CBI said a briefcase containing documents belonging to Dubey including his Identity Card were recovered from an abandoned well and also the country-made pistol were recovered during investigation. The agency said Sharvan gave full and voluntary disclosure about the incident and was made an approver.

Source : Sunday Times, p1, March 28, 2010

MORE TEETH TO IT:

SOON, SEXUAL HARASSMENT COULD BECOME NON-BAILABLE

The Maharashtra government has proposed to make sexual harassment offences against women a non-bailable offence. An announcement to this effect was made by minister of state for home Ramesh Bagwe in the legislative assembly here on Friday.

The need for a stringent law for offenders in sexual harassment cases was raised by BJP legislator Sudhir Mungantiwar by way of a nonofficial Bill. It is observed that people are not scared of bailable offences as they are confident of getting out on bail. To deal with such a mindset, the government should amend the law and make it a non-bailable offence, he added.

In his reply, Bagwe admitted that there was need for harsh action against those involved in such activities. A letter seeking approval to amend the law has been forwarded to the Union government, he stated. Mungantiwar also drew the attention of the assembly to the increasing obscene advertisements aired on television channels and the print media. People get lured by advertisements which promise friendship through phones or the internet. This results in huge telephone bills which the victims find difficult to pay. Finally to arrange the money, the victim gets involved in criminal activities, Mungantiwar said and demanded a ban on such advertisements.

Bagwe pointed out that laws to prohibit such incidents already exist in the legal system. Many people have been prosecuted in connection with these charges.At present I do not have the figures, but I can table them before the assembly later, he added.

The minister further assured the BJP legislator that the government would positively consider his suggestions. A committee of MLAs would be set up to look into the issues raised during the debate, he stated and at his request, Mungantiwar withdrew the non-official Bill.

Source : Times of India, p19, March 27, 2010

Questions

Section — A Objective Type

1. What is gender equality ?
2. What is work place harassment ?
3. What is harassment of women at work place ?
4. Name the fundamental rights of women as given in Indian Constitution ?
5. What are Human rights ?
6. Expand NHRC.
7. What is whistle blowing ?
8. State any two merits of whistle blowing.
9. State any two demerits of whistle blowing.
10. What you mean by job reservation in private sector ?
11. What is gender discrimination ?
12. What is glass ceiling ?
13. Who are internal whistle blowers ?
14. Who are external whistle blowers ?
15. Expand CEDAW.

Section — B Analytical Type

1. Explain the different forms of gender discrimination.
2. Explain the concept gender equality.
3. Explain the nature of human rights.
4. Explain the different types of harassment of women workforce.
5. Bring out the fundamental rights guaranteed to women under Indian Constitution.
6. What are advantages of whistle blowing ?
7. State the disadvantages of whistle blowing.
8. What are the objectives of NHRC?
9. What are the objectives of UN Protocol on human rights?

Section — C Essay Type

1. Bring out in great detail the concepts — Gender Equality and Gender Discrimination with decided cases.
2. Discuss the different forms of sexual harassment of women at workplace.
3. Describe the fundamental rights guaranteed to women under the Indian Constitution.
4. Explain the functions of NHRC with leading cases.
5. Discuss the salient features of UN Protocol on Human Rights.
6. Is job reservation in private sector feasible — Deliberate.
7. Whistle blowing is both positive and negative. Comment.
8. Bring out the supreme court guidelines on protecting women rights at workplace.

ENVIRONMENT PROTECTION ACT, 1986

Module Objectives

After reading this chapter, you should be able to:

- Know the concepts of environment, environment pollution, environment pollutants, hazardous substance.
- Diagonise the different types of pollution.
- Know the concept of global warming, causes for ozone layer depletion, remedies to reduce ozone layer depletion and powers of the Central Government protocol and promote environment in India.

THE ENVIRONMENT PROTECTION ACT, 1986

The Environment (Protection) Act 1986 is a new piece of legislation enacted by the Government of India after the Bhopal tragedy under article 253 of the constitution. The purpose of the act is to protect and improve the human environment and to prevent hazards to human beings, animals, plants and property. This act enables the central Govt. to co-ordinate the activities of different Central and State Authorities formed under previous laws such as Water (Prevention and Control of Pollution) Act 1974, Air (Prevention and Control of Pollution) Act 1981.

12.1 DEFINITIONS

(1) **Environment (Sect. 2(a)):** It includes water, air and land and the inter relationship which exists between water, air and land and human being, other living creatures, plants, Micro organisms and property.

(2) **Environmental Pollutant (Sect. 2(b)):** It means any solid, liquid or gaseous substance present in such concentration as be injurious to environment. Now noise has also been accepted as an environmental pollutant.

(3) **Environment pollution (Sect. 2(c)):** It means the presence in the environment of any environmental pollutant. It includes all extraneous (foreign) materials that are harmful to human, animal and plant life. The common type of environmental pollution are air pollution, water pollution, land pollution, solid waste pollution, noise pollution, oil pollution, market pollution and thermal pollution.

(4) **Hazardous Substance (Sect. 2(d)):** It means any substance having chemical or physico-chemical properties, that are liable to cause harm to human being, other living creatures and plants or the environment.

(5) **Occupier (Sect. 2(f)):** It means a person who has control over the factory and also includes the person who is in possession of the substance.

12.2 TYPES OF POLLUTION

The major forms of pollution are listed below along with the particular pollutants relevant to each of them:

1. Air Pollution

Air pollution is the introduction of chemicals, particulate matter, or biological materials that cause harm or discomfort to humans or other living organisms, or damages the natural environment, into the atmosphere.

The atmosphere is a complex, dynamic natural gaseous system that is essential to support life on planet Earth. Stratospheric ozone depletion due to air pollution has long been recognized as a threat to human health as well as to the Earth's ecosystems.

An air pollutant is known as a substance in the air that can cause harm to humans and the environment. Pollutants can be in the form of solid particles, liquid droplets, or gases. In addition, they may be natural or man-made.[1]

Pollutants can be classified as either primary or secondary. Usually, primary pollutants are substances directly emitted from a process, such as ash from a volcanic eruption, the carbon monoxide gas from a motor vehicle exhaust or sulfur dioxide released from factories.

Secondary pollutants are not emitted directly. Rather, they form in the air when primary pollutants react or interact. An important example of a secondary pollutant is ground level ozone - one of the many secondary pollutants that make up photochemical smog.

The release of chemicals and particulates into the atmosphere. Common gaseous air pollutants include Carbon monoxide (CO), Sulfur dioxide (SO2), Chlorofluro carbons (CFCs) and Nitrogen oxides (NO) produced by industry and motor vehicles.

Air pollution comes from both natural and man made sources. Though globally manmade pollutants from combustion, construction, mining, agriculture and warfare are increasingly significant in the air pollution equation. Motor vehicle emissions are one of the leading causes of air pollution Principal stationary pollution sources include chemical plants, coal-fired power plants, oil refineries, petrochemical plants, nuclear waste disposal activity, incinerators, large livestock farms (dairy cows, pigs, poultry,etc.), PVC factories, metals production factories, plastics factories, and other heavy industry. Agricultural air pollution comes from contemporary practices which include clear felling and burning of natural vegetation as well as spraying of pesticides and herbicides.

Air pollution is the presence of materials in air in such concentration which are harmful to man and his environment. Various causes of air pollution are shown in Table 12.1:

Table 12.1: Causes of Air Pollution

Category	Examples	Important pollutants
1. Chemical plants	Petroleum refineries, fertilizers, cements, papermills, ceramic clay products, glass manufacture	H_2S, sulphur oxide, fluorides, organic vapours and dust
2. Crop spraying	Pesticides and weedicides	Organophosphates, chlorinated hydrocarbons, lead, arsenic
3. Fuel burning	Domestic burning, thermal power plants	Sulphur and nitrogen oxides
4. Metallurgy plants	Aluminum refineries and steel plant	Metal flumes (Pb and Zn) fluorides and particulates
5. Nuclear device testing	Bomb explosions	Radioactive fall out, Sr-90, Cs-137, C-14 etc.
6. Ore preparations	Crushing, grinding and screening	Uranium and beryllium dust, other particulates
7. Spray painting, ink, solvent cleansing	Printing and chemical separations, furniture, dyeing	Hydrocarbons and other organic vapours
8. Transportation	Cars, trucks, aeroplanes and railways	CO, NO, NO2, Pb, smoke, soot, smoke organic vapours etc.

The major cause of pollution in urban areas are automobiles which inefficiently burn petroleum, release 75% noise, 80% air pollutants. Concentration of industries on area is another major cause, e.g., cotton dust in Ahmedabad, Surat and nearby areas.

Some other examples of using energy and polluting the air are:

- Turning on a light
- Watching TV
- Listening to a stereo
- Washing or drying clothes
- Using a hair dryer
- Playing a video game

2. Water Pollution

By the release of waste products and contaminants into surface runoff into river drainage systems, leaching into groundwater, liquid spills, waste water discharges, eutrophication and littering.

Types of Water Pollution

Of late one of the biggest concern is the problem of water pollution has. Water pollution is caused when pollutants spill into a body of water and cause adverse affects. Basically there are two different types of water pollution as sources.

These sources are listed as

— point sources of pollution and non-point sources of water pollution.

A non-point source of water pollution comes from runoff diverting pollutants directly into a source of water such as pesticides or fertilizers being washed into a storm gutter and then being carried away into nearby streams and rivers. A non-point source of pollution happens when a sewer pipe leaks toxic substances into a river.

There are many types of water pollution. Herbicides, pesticides and industrial compounds release chemical pollutants into the water which are very toxic substances causing pollution. One more type that affects the water systems is the Organic Pollution. Organic pollution is caused by manure or sewage. The main source of organic pollutants is from large feed lots and major farming practices that produce an extremely large amount of wastes.

When organic matter overwhelms a body of water it basically causes the oxygen to deplete which kills fish and plants. Apart from this, high levels of nitrogen and phosphates also cause the decrease in oxygen in the water and create "dead zones" where algae grows in an abundance killing plants and fish.

One other type of water pollution is the Thermal pollution that occurs when water is used as a coolant near a power plant or industrial facility. The water gets heated up and then returned at a higher degree than it was when it was taken out. This in turn causes a decrease in oxygen levels which affects the plants and marine life. Unlike chemical pollution, organic pollution and thermal pollution, one more type of water pollution is the ecological pollution that is caused by nature. Ecological pollution is caused from landslides, dead animals drowning in the water supply, and volcanic eruptions.

The different types of water pollution come from many different sources such as—

- farms that use large amounts of pesticides and fertilizers which cause the increase of nitrates and phosphates in the water.
- Run off from nearby farms also causes water to become cloudy which blocks the sunlight from reaching the plants along the bottom of the water system.
- When the plants do not receive enough sunlight they die which further stresses the water systems by reducing the amount of oxygen in the water.

Some other types of water pollution come from businesses.

3. Soil Contamination/Pollution

This occurs when chemicals are released by spill or underground leakage. Among the most significant soil contaminants are hydrocarbons, heavy metals, herbicides, pesticides and chlorinated hydrocarbons.

Soil pollution is caused by the presence of xenobiotic (man-made) chemicals or other alteration in the natural soil environment. This type of contamination typically arises from the rupture of underground storage tanks, application of pesticides, percolation of contaminated surface water to subsurface strata, oil and fuel dumping, leaching of wastes from landfills or direct discharge of industrial wastes to the soil. The most common chemicals involved are petroleum hydrocarbons, solvents, pesticides, lead and other heavy metals. This occurrence of this phenomenon is correlated with the degree of industrializations and intensities of chemical usage.

The concern over soil contamination stems primarily from health risks, from direct contact with the contaminated soil, vapors from the contaminants, and from secondary contamination of water supplies within and underlying the soil. Mapping of contaminated soil sites and the resulting cleanup are time consuming and expensive tasks, requiring extensive amounts of geology, hydrology, chemistry and computer modeling skills.

Types of Soil Pollution

There are many different types of soil pollution, each stemming from different origins. Each type of soil pollution causes different effects on the ground and can permanently damage the land for future use.

Underground Tanks

- Underground storage tanks can be ruptured from improper safety guards during construction projects or simple wear from time. Many times, these tanks contain fuels or other fluids that damage the soil.

Runoff

- Runoff from farmland and agricultural fields causes soil pollution that can damage animal and plant life. In addition, rainwater can wash the chemicals used by farmers into water sources, which end up in soil far away from the site.

Soil Amendments

- Soil amendments, byproducts from industry, can be used to amplify the nutrients within soil. However, many times, these products stem from industrial waste. Materials such as ash, lime and bio-solids can leave the soil contaminated over the long-term.

Landfills

- Landfills contain products that can leak into the soil. Sulfates, nitrates, heavy metals and other unnatural products pollute the ground.

4. NOISE POLLUTION

Noise pollution (or environmental noise) is displeasing human-, animal- or machine-created sound that disrupts the activity or balance of human or animal life. The word noise comes from the Latin word nausea meaning seasickness.

The source of most outdoor noise worldwide is transportation systems, including motor vehicle noise, aircraft noise and rail noise. Poor urban planning may give rise to noise pollution, since side-by-side industrial and residential buildings can result in noise pollution in the residential area.

Other sources of indoor and outdoor noise pollution are car alarms, emergency service sirens, office equipment, factory machinery, construction work, grounds keeping equipment, barking dogs, appliances, power tools, lighting hum, audio entertainment systems, loudspeakers, and noisy people.

Noise health effects are both health and behavioural in nature. The unwanted sound is called noise. This unwanted sound can damage physiological and psychological health. Noise pollution can cause annoyance and aggression, hypertension, high stress levels, tinnitus, hearing loss, sleep disturbances, and other harmful effects. Furthermore, stress and hypertension are the leading causes to health problems, whereas tinnitus can lead to forgetfulness, severe depression and at times panic attacks.

Chronic exposure to noise may cause noise-induced hearing loss. Older males exposed to significant occupational noise demonstrate significantly reduced hearing sensitivity than their non-exposed peers, though differences in hearing sensitivity decrease with time and the two groups are indistinguishable by age 79. A comparison of Maaban tribesmen, who were insignificantly exposed to transportation or industrial noise, to a typical U.S. population showed that chronic exposure to moderately high levels of environmental noise contributes to hearing loss.

High noise levels can contribute to cardiovascular effects and exposure to moderately high levels during a single eight hour period causes a statistical rise in blood pressure of five to ten points and an increase in stress and vasoconstriction leading to the increased Noise Pollution Effects on Humans Noise pollution effects on human health is a matter of great concern. The reason being the adverse consequences that high noise levels have on human health. Noise pollution can affect us in several ways, some of which are listed below:

Effects of Noise Pollution

Hearing Problems: Exposure to noise can damage one of the most vital organs of the body, the ear. Hearing impairment due to noise pollution can either be temporary or permanent. When the sound level crosses the 70dB mark, it becomes noise for the ear. Noise levels above 80 decibels produce damaging effects to the ear. When ear is exposed to extreme loud noise (above 100 decibels) for a considerable period of time, it can cause irreparable damage and lead to permanent hearing loss.

Cardiovascular Issues: A noisy environment can be a source of heart related problems. Studies have shown that high intensity sound cause a dramatic rise in blood pressure as noise levels constrict the arteries, disrupting the blood flow. The heart rate (the number of heartbeats per minute) also increase. These sudden abnormal changes in the blood increase the likelihood of cardiovascular diseases in the long run. Read more on cardiovascular diseases.

Sleep Disturbances: This is one of the noise pollution effects that can deter your overall well being. Noise can interrupt a good night's sleep, and when this occurs, the person feels extremely annoyed and uncomfortable. People deprived of uninterrupted sleep show a sharp dip in their energy levels which often results into extreme fatigue. This can considerably decrease a person's ability to work efficiently.

Interference in Verbal Communication: A noisy environment that produces more than 50-60 decibels simply does not allow 2 people to communicate properly. Interpreting the speech of a second person becomes quite difficult and may lead to misunderstandings.

Mental Health Problems: Exposure to loud sound can lead to elevated stress levels as well as stimulate violent behaviour. A constant noise in the vicinity can also trigger headaches, make people tense and anxious, and disturb emotional balance, blood pressure noted above as well as to increased incidence of coronary artery disease.

12.3 GLOBAL WARMING

Global warming is when the earth heats up (the temperature rises). It happens when greenhouse gases (carbon dioxide, water vapour, nitrous oxide, and methane) trap heat and light from the sun in the earth's atmosphere, which increases the temperature. This hurts many people, animals, and plants. Many cannot take the change, so they die.

While some would call global warming a theory, others would call it a proven set of facts. Opinions differ vehemently. Let us consider global warming to be both a premise that the environment of the world as we know it is slowly, but very surely increasing in overall air and water temperature, and a promise that if whatever is causing this trend is not interrupted or challenged life on earth will dynamically be affected.

The prevailing counter opinion is that all that is presently perceived to be global warming is simply the result of a normal climactic swing in the direction of increased temperature. Many proponents of this global warming ideology have definitive social and financial interests in these claims.

Global warming and climate change are aspects of our environment that cannot be easily or quickly discounted. Many factions still strongly feel that the changes our Earth is seeing are the result of a natural climatic adjustment. Regardless of one's perspective the effects of global warming are a quantifiable set of environmental results that are in addition to any normal changes in climate. That is why the effects of global warming have catastrophic potential. Global warming may well be the straw that breaks the camel's back. It could turn out to be the difference between a category three hurricane and a category four. Global warming as caused by greenhouse gas emissions can lead us to a definite imbalance of nature.

The premise of global warming as an issue of debate is that industrial growth coupled with non-structured methods we as humans use to sustain ourselves has created a situation where our planet is getting progressively hotter. We have seemingly negatively effected our environment by a cycle of harmful processes that now seem to be feeding upon themselves to exponentially increase the damage to our ecosystem.

Causes of Global Warming

The primary cause of global warming is Carbon Dioxide emissions.

The primary cause of global warming is Carbon Dioxide emissions. CO_2 is being pumped into our atmosphere at an insane pace; 8 billion tons of CO_2 entered the air last year. Of course some of this is due to natural activity such as volcanic eruptions and people breathing. But the Earth is equipped to easily absorb those into the normal regenerative process. No, the beginning of global warming was caused by fossil fuels being burned and emitting plenty of CO_2.

Currently in the world 40% of all CO_2 emissions are caused by power plants. These are burning coal, natural gas and diesel fuel. Some power plants burn garbage. Some burn methane made from garbage. And discounting those super green electrical generating plants designed to issue negligible pollutants, all of our power plants let loose into the atmosphere CO_2.

33% of all the CO_2 sent forth is the product of cars and trucks. Internal combustion engines burning fossil fuels...gasoline and diesel spew forth a retching amount of CO_2.

3.5% of all CO_2 emissions are released from aircraft traveling our friendly skies. Unfortunately, jets and other aircraft deliver their payload of pollutants directly into the troposphere.

Global warming is the increase in the average temperature of Earth's near-surface air and oceans since the mid-20th century and its projected continuation. Global surface temperature increased 0.74 ± 0.18 °C (1.33 ± 0.32 °F) between the start and the end of the 20th century. The Intergovernmental Panel on Climate Change (IPCC) concludes that most of the observed temperature increase since the middle of the 20th century was very likely caused by increasing concentrations of greenhouse gases resulting from human activity such as fossil fuel burning and deforestation. The IPCC also concludes that variations in natural phenomena such as solar radiation and volcanic eruptions had a small cooling effect after 1950. These basic conclusions have been endorsed by more than 40 scientific societies and academies of science, including all of the national academies of science of the major industrialized countries.

Greenhouse Effect

The greenhouse effect is when the temperature rises because the sun's heat and light is trapped in the earth's atmosphere. This is like when heat is trapped in a car. On a very hot day, the car gets hotter when it is out in the parking lot. This is because the heat and light from the sun can get into the car, by going through the windows, but it can't get back out. This is what the greenhouse effect does to the earth. The heat and light can get through the atmosphere, but it can not get out. As a result, the temperature rises.

The greenhouse effect is when the temperature rises because the sun's heat and light is trapped in the earth's atmosphere.

The greenhouse effect is the process by which absorption and emission of infrared radiation by gases in the atmosphere warm a planet's lower atmosphere and surface. It was discovered by Joseph Fourier in 1824 and was first investigated quantitatively by Svante Arrhenius in 1896. Existence of the greenhouse effect as such is not disputed, even by those who do not agree that the recent temperature increase is attributable to human activity. The question is instead how the strength of the greenhouse effect changes when human activity increases the concentrations of greenhouse gases in the atmosphere.

Global Warming and Environment

Global warming is affecting many parts of the world. Global warming makes the sea rise, and when the sea rises, the water covers many low land islands. This is a big problem for many of the plants, animals, and people on islands. The water covers the plants and causes some of them to die. When they die, the animals lose a source of food, along with their habitat. Although animals have a better ability to adapt to what happens than plants do, they may die also. When the plants and animals die, people lose two sources of food, plant food and animal food. They may also lose their homes. As a result, they would also have to leave the area or die. This would be called a break in the food chain, or a chain reaction, one thing happening that leads to another and so on.

The oceans are affected by global warming in other ways, as well. Many things that are happening to the ocean are linked to global warming. One thing that is happening is warm water, caused from global warming, is harming and killing algae in the ocean.

Algae is a producer that you can see floating on the top of the water. (A producer is something that makes food for other animals through photosynthesis, like grass.) This floating green algae is food to many consumers in the ocean. (A consumer is something that eats the producers.) One kind of a consumer is small fish. There are many others like crabs, some whales, and many other animals. Fewer algae is a problem because there is less food for us and many animals in the sea.

Global warming is doing many things to people as well as animals and plants. It is killing algae, but it is also destroying many huge forests. The pollution that causes global warming is linked to acid rain. Acid rain gradually destroys almost everything it touches. Global warming is also causing many more fires that wipe out whole forests. This happens because global warming can make the earth very hot. In forests, some plant and tree leaves can be so dry that they catch on fire.

12.4 DANGEROUS CHEMICALS

Some other chemicals that cause air pollution and are bad for the environment and people are:

Ozone: Ozone is produced when other pollution chemicals combine. It is the basic element of smog. It causes many different kinds of health issues dealing with the lungs. It can damage plants and limit sight. It can also cause a lot of property damage.

Ozone is a colourless gas found in the upper atmosphere of the Earth and formed by the action of ultraviolet radiation on oxygen.

VOCs (volatile organic compounds, smog formers): VOCs are let into the air when fuel is burned. This chemical can cause cancer. It can also harm plants.

NOx (nitrogen dioxide): This chemical forms smog. It is also formed by burning sources of energy, like gas, coal, and oil, and by cars. This chemical causes problems in the respiratory system (including the lungs). It causes acid rain, and it can damage trees. This chemical can eat away buildings and statues.

CO (carbon monoxide): The source of this chemical is burning sources of energy. It causes blood vessel problems and respiratory failures.

PM-10 (particulate matter): The source of this chemical is plowing and burning down fields. It can cause death and lung damage. It can make it hard for people to breathe. The smoke, soot, ash, and dust formed by this chemical can make many cities dirty.

Sulfur Dioxide: This chemical is produced by making paper and metals. This chemical can cause permanent lung damage. It can cause acid rain which kills trees and damages building and statues.

Lead: This chemical is in paint, leaded gasoline, smelters, and in lead storage batteries. It can cause many brain and nerve damages and digestive problems.

Ozone

Ozone is a colourless gas found in the upper atmosphere of the Earth and formed by the action of ultraviolet radiation on oxygen. Ozone forms a layer in the stratosphere, which protects life on Earth from the harmful effects of ultraviolet radiation.

Today, one of the most discussed and serious environmental issues is the ozone layer depletion, the layer of gas that forms a protective covering in the Earth's upper atmosphere. Ozone is formed when oxygen molecules absorb ultraviolet photons and undergo a chemical reaction known as photo dissociation or photolysis, where a single molecule of oxygen breaks down to two oxygen atoms. The free oxygen atom (O), then combines with an oxygen molecule (O2) and forms a molecule of ozone (O3). The ozone molecules, in turn absorb ultraviolet rays between 310 to 200 nm wavelength and thereby prevent these harmful radiations from entering the Earth's atmosphere. In the process, ozone molecules split up into a molecule of oxygen and an oxygen atom. The oxygen atom (O) again combines with the oxygen molecule (O2) to regenerate an ozone (O3) molecule. Thus, the total amount of ozone is maintained by this continuous process of destruction and regeneration.

Ozone layer depletion first captured the attention of the whole world in the later half of 1970 and since then, many discussions and researches have been carried out to find out the possible effects and the causes of ozone depletion.

Ozone layer depletion first captured the attention of the whole world in the later half of 1970 and since then, many discussions and researches have been carried out to find out the possible effects and the causes of ozone depletion. Many studies have also been directed to find out a possible solution.

OZONE LAYER

The ozone layer protects the Earth from the ultraviolet rays sent down by the sun. If the ozone layer is depleted by human action, the effects on the planet could be catastrophic.

The ozone layer protects the Earth from the ultraviolet rays sent down by the sun. If the ozone layer is depleted by human action, the effects on the planet could be catastrophic.

Ozone is present in the stratosphere. The stratosphere reaches 30 miles above the Earth, and at the very top it contains ozone. The suns rays are absorbed by the ozone in the stratosphere and thus do not reach the Earth.

The Ozone Layer Over Time. Image Credit: Institute for Studies in Development, Environment, and Security.

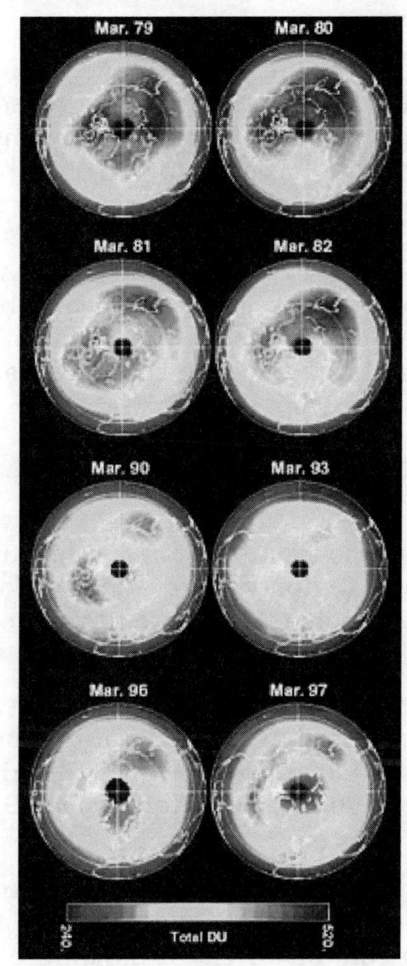

The Ozone Layer Over Time. Image Credit: Institute for Studies in Development, Environment, and Security.

Ozone is a bluish gas that is formed by three atoms of oxygen. The form of oxygen that humans breathe in consists of two oxygen atoms, O_2. When found on the surface of the planet, ozone is considered a dangerous pollutant and is one substance responsible for producing the greenhouse effect.

The highest regions of the stratosphere contain about 90% of all ozone.

In recent years, the ozone layer has been the subject of much discussion. And rightly so, because the ozone layer protects both plant and animal life on the planet.

The fact that the ozone layer was being depleted was discovered in the mid-1980s. The main cause of this is the release of CFCs, chlorofluorocarbons.

Antarctica was an early victim of ozone destruction. A massive hole in the ozone layer right above Antarctica now threatens not only that continent, but many others that could be the victims of Antarctica's melting icecaps. In the future, the ozone problem will have to be solved so that the protective layer can be conserved.

The Ozone Hole

The discovery of the Antarctic "ozone hole" by British Antarctic Survey scientists Farman, Gardiner and Shanklin (announced in a paper in Nature in May 1985) came as a shock to the scientific community, because the observed decline in polar ozone was far larger than anyone had anticipated. Satellite measurements showing massive depletion of ozone around the south pole were becoming available at the same time. However, these were initially rejected as unreasonable by data quality control algorithms (they were filtered out as errors since the values were unexpectedly low); the ozone hole was detected only in satellite data when the raw data was reprocessed following evidence of ozone depletion in *in situ* observations. When the software was rerun without the flags, the ozone hole was seen as far back as 1976.

Causes for Ozone Layer Depletion

The discovery of the Antarctic "ozone hole" by British Antarctic Survey scientists Farman, Gardiner and Shanklin (announced in a paper in Nature in May 1985) came as a shock to the scientific community, because the observed decline in polar ozone was far larger than anyone had anticipated.

Ozone depletion occurs when the natural balance between the production and destruction of stratospheric ozone is tipped in favour of destruction. Although natural phenomena can cause temporary ozone loss, chlorine and bromine released from man-made compounds such as CFCs are now accepted as the main cause of this depletion.

It was first suggested by Drs. M. Molina and S. Rowland in 1974 that a man-made group of compounds known as the chlorofluorocarbons (CFCs) were likely to be the main source of ozone depletion. However, this idea was not taken seriously until the discovery of the ozone hole over Antarctica in 1985 by the British Antarctic Survey.

Chlorofluorocarbons are not "washed" back to Earth by rain or destroyed in reactions with other chemicals. They simply do not break down in the lower atmosphere and they can remain in the atmosphere from 20 to 120 years or more. As a consequence of their relative stability, CFCs are instead transported into the stratosphere where they are eventually broken down by ultraviolet (UV) rays from the Sun, releasing free chlorine. The chlorine becomes actively involved in the process of destruction of ozone. The net result is that two molecules of ozone are replaced by three of molecular oxygen, leaving the chlorine free to repeat the process:

$Cl + O3 \rightarrow ClO + O2$

$ClO + O \rightarrow Cl + O2$

Ozone is converted to oxygen, leaving the chlorine atom free to repeat the process up to 100,000 times, resulting in a reduced level of ozone. Bromine compounds, or halons, can also destroy stratospheric ozone. Compounds containing chlorine and bromine from man-made compounds are known as industrial halocarbons.

Emissions of CFCs have accounted for roughly 80% of total stratospheric ozone depletion. Thankfully, the developed world has phased out the use of CFCs in response to international agreements to protect the ozone layer. However, because CFCs remain in the atmosphere so long, the ozone layer will not fully repair itself until at least the middle of the 21st century. Naturally occurring chlorine has the same effect on the ozone layer, but has a shorter life span in the atmosphere.

The ozone layer acts like a giant sunshade, protecting plants and animals from much of the sun's harmful ultraviolet radiation.

Ozone (O_3) forms a layer in the stratosphere, 15-40 km above earth surface. If the ozone in the atmosphere from ground level to a height of 60 km could be assembled at the earth's surface, it would comprise a layer of gas only about 3 mm thick.

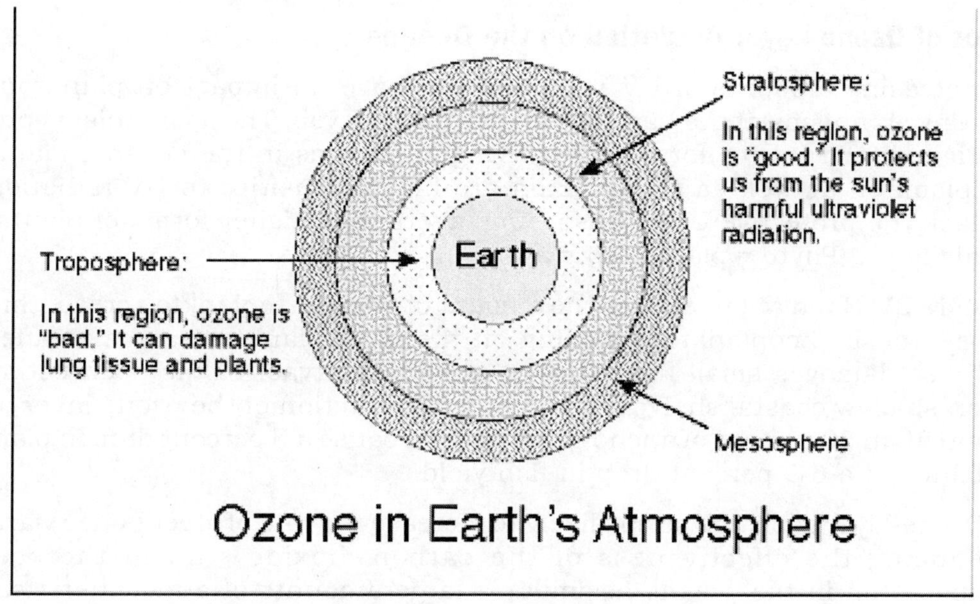

Source: Nasa; Shuttle Solar Backscatter Ultraviolet Instrument

Global stratospheric ozone levels have declined, which means that the ozone layer is changing. Stratospheric ozone has large natural temporal and spatial variations, up to 30 percent variation may be regarded as normal. However, we now have evidence of a significant thinning of the ozone layer during spring and summer. This is observed in both the northern and the southern hemispheres at middle and high latitudes. During the last 10-15 years, the ozone layer above the northern hemisphere has been reduced by 5-6 percent in spring per decade. The latest tests (January-March 1995) have shown very large reductions, with a maximum of more than 30 percent reduction compared to normal.

A depletion of the ozone layer will increase the UV-radiation at ground level. Increasing doses of UV-B may cause skin cancer, eye cataracts, damage to the immune system in animals as well as human beings, and have an adverse impact on plant growth.

The maps show UV intensity at noon calculated from sun angle and satelitte measurements of the ozone layer. The model assumes clear sky conditions at sea level and average sun reflection. With increased altitude and reflection - for instance snow conditions in mountain areas — the UV dose can be considerably higher.

The UV index used in the maps above has been developed by Environment Canada. It runs on a scale from 0 to 10, with 10 being a typical mid-summer, sunny day in the tropics. A relative scale ranging from low to extreme is also applied: In extreme conditions (UV Index higher than 9) light, sensitive and untanned skin may burn in less than 15 minutes.

UV radiation will affect human health through for example sunburn, snow blindness, other eye damage, early ageing of the skin and rising rates of skin cancer. It may also cause suppression of the immune response system. It will likewise affect the productivity of aquatic and terrestrial eco-systems. Single-celled algae, chlorophyll and plant hormones are especially sensitive to UV radiation.

Impact of Ozone Layer Depletion on the Oceans

Increasing amounts of UV radiation will have an impact on plankton and other tiny organisms at the base of the marine food web. These organisms provide the original food source for all other living organisms in the oceans. Plankton-phytoplankton as well as zooplankton are highly sensitive to UV radiation, as they lack the protective UV-B-absorbing layers that higher forms of plants and animals have. (Phyto = plant. Zoo = animal).

More UV-B radiation reduces the amount of food phytoplankton create through photosynthesis. Zooplankton, feeding off the phytoplankton, are also affected. UV-B also damages small fish, shrimp and crab larvae. It has been estimated that on shallow coastal shelves, a 16 percent reduction of the ozone layer would kill more than 50 percent of anchovy larvae, and cause a 5 percent drop in plankton numbers and a 6-9 percent drop in fish yield.

Ozone-layer depletion seems likely to increase the rate of greenhouse warming, by reducing the effectiveness of the carbon dioxide sink in the oceans. Phytoplankton in the oceans assimilates large amounts of atmospheric carbon dioxide. Increased UV radiation will reduce phytoplankton activity significantly. This means that large amounts of carbon dioxide will remain in the atmosphere. A 10 percent decrease in carbon dioxide uptake by the oceans would leave about the same amount of carbon dioxide in the atmosphere as is produced by fossil fuel burning.

On Land Plants

A high increase in UV radiation may disrupt many ecosystems on land. Rice production may be drastically reduced by the effects of UV-B on the nitrogen assimilating activities of micro-organisms. With a diminishing ozone layer, it is likely that the supply of natural nitrogen to ecosystems, such as tropical rice paddies, will be significantly reduced.

Most plants (and trees) grow more slowly and become smaller and more stunted as adult plants when exposed to large amounts of UV-B. Increased UV-B inhibits pollen germination.

air pollution

UV-B stimulates the formation of reactive radicals — molecules that react rapidly with other chemicals, forming new substances. The hydroxyl radicals, for example, stimulate the creation of tropospheric ozone and other harmful pollutants. Smog formation creates other oxidized organic chemicals, such as formaldehydes. These molecules can also produce reactive hydrogen radicals when they absorb UV-B. In urban areas, a 10 percent reduction of the ozone layer is likely to result in a 10-25 percent increase in tropospheric ozone.

More UV-B radiation seems likely to cause global increases in atmospheric hydrogen peroxide. This is the principal chemical that oxidizes sulfur dioxide to form sulfuric acid in cloud water, making it an important part of acid rain formation.

Damage to Materials

UV-radiation causes many materials to degrade more rapidly. Plastic materials used outdoors will have much shorter lifetimes with small increases of UV radiation. PVC sidings, window and door frames, pipes, gutters, etc. used in buildings degrade faster.

Ultraviolet Radiation

Ultraviolet radiation is divided into three types, according to wavelength.

UV-A radiation, emitted at wavelengths of 315-400 nm (1 nanometer is a millionth of a millimeter, or 10 - 9m) is unaffected by ozone reduction, and is not as harmful as UV-B.

UV-B radiation, emitted at 280-315 nm, is affected by decreases in atmospheric ozone. It is UV-B that causes most of the damage to plants and animals.

UV-B damage depends on the amount of atmospheric ozone that can act as a filter, the angle of the sun in the sky, and cloud cover, which shields the surface from some of the ultraviolet radiation. The ozone layer is usually thinnest at the tropics and thickest towards the poles. As stratospheric ozone diminishes, proportionately more of the ultraviolet radiation reaching the Earth's surface will arrive in the shorter UV-B wavelengths.

UV-C radiation, which is lethal, is emitted at wavelengths of 200-280 nm. Fortunately, UV-C is completely absorbed by atmospheric ozone and oxygen. Even with severe ozone reduction, UV-C radiation would still be absorbed by the remaining ozone.

Since the ozone layer absorbs UVB ultraviolet light from the Sun, ozone layer depletion is expected to increase surface UVB levels, which could lead to damage, including increases in skin cancer. This was the reason for the Montreal Protocol. Although decreases in stratospheric ozone are well-tied to CFCs and there are good theoretical reasons to believe that decreases in ozone will lead to increases in surface UVB, there is no direct observational evidence linking ozone depletion to higher incidence of skin cancer in human beings. This is partly due to the fact that UVA, which has also been implicated in some forms of skin cancer, is not absorbed by ozone, and it is nearly impossible to control statistics for lifestyle changes in the populace.

Increased UV

Ozone, while a minority constituent in the Earth's atmosphere, is responsible for most of the absorption of UVB radiation. The amount of UVB radiation that penetrates through the ozone layer decreases exponentially with the slant-path thickness/density of the layer. Correspondingly, a decrease in atmospheric ozone is expected to give rise to significantly increased levels of UVB near the surface.

Increases in surface UVB due to the ozone hole can be partially inferred by radiative transfer model calculations, but cannot be calculated from direct measurements because of the lack of reliable historical (pre-ozone-hole) surface UV data, although more recent surface UV observation measurement programmes exist (e.g. at Lauder, New Zealand).

Because it is this same UV radiation that creates ozone in the ozone layer from O_2 (regular oxygen) in the first place, a reduction in stratospheric ozone would actually tend to increase photochemical production of ozone at lower levels (in the troposphere), although the overall observed trends in total column ozone still show a decrease, largely because ozone produced lower down has a naturally shorter photochemical lifetime, so it is destroyed before the concentrations could reach a level which would compensate for the ozone reduction higher up.

Biological Effects

The main public concern regarding the ozone hole has been the effects of increased surface UV and microwave radiation on human health. So far, ozone depletion in most locations has been typically a few percent and, as noted above, no direct evidence of health damage is available in most latitudes. Were the high levels of depletion seen in the ozone hole ever to be common across the globe, the effects could be substantially more dramatic. As the ozone hole over Antarctica has in some instances grown so large as to reach southern parts of Australia and New Zealand, environmentalists have been concerned that the increase in surface UV could be significant.

Effects on Humans

UVB (the higher energy UV radiation absorbed by ozone) is generally accepted to be a contributory factor to skin cancer. In addition, increased surface UV leads to increased tropospheric ozone, which is a health risk to humans. The increased surface UV also represents an increase in the vitamin D synthetic capacity of the sunlight.

The cancer preventive effects of vitamin D represent a possible beneficial effect of ozone depletion. In terms of health costs, the possible benefits of increased UV irradiance may outweigh the burden.

1. Basal and Squamous Cell Carcinomas — The most common forms of skin cancer in humans, basal and squamous cell carcinomas, have been strongly linked to UVB exposure. The mechanism by which UVB induces these cancers is well understood — absorption of UVB radiation causes the pyrimidine bases in the

DNA molecule to form dimers, resulting in transcription errors when the DNA replicates. These cancers are relatively mild and rarely fatal, although the treatment of squamous cell carcinoma sometimes requires extensive reconstructive surgery. By combining epidemiological data with results of animal studies, scientists have estimated that a one percent decrease in stratospheric ozone would increase the incidence of these cancers by 2%.

2. Malignant Melanoma — Another form of skin cancer, malignant melanoma, is much less common but far more dangerous, being lethal in about 15-20% of the cases diagnosed. The relationship between malignant melanoma and ultraviolet exposure is not yet well understood, but it appears that both UVB and UVA are involved. Experiments on fish suggest that 90 to 95% of malignant melanomas may be due to UVA and visible radiation whereas experiments on opossums suggest a larger role for UVB. Because of this uncertainty, it is difficult to estimate the impact of ozone depletion on melanoma incidence. One study showed that a 10% increase in UVB radiation was associated with a 19% increase in melanomas for men and 16% for women. A study of people in Punta Arenas, at the southern tip of Chile, showed a 56% increase in melanoma and a 46% increase in nonmelanoma skin cancer over a period of seven years, along with decreased ozone and increased UVB levels.

3. Cortical Cataracts — Studies are suggestive of an association between ocular cortical cataracts and UV-B exposure, using crude approximations of exposure and various cataract assessment techniques. A detailed assessment of ocular exposure to UV-B was carried out in a study on Chesapeake Bay Watermen, where increases in average annual ocular exposure were associated with increasing risk of cortical opacity. In this highly exposed group of predominantly white males, the evidence linking cortical opacities to sunlight exposure was the strongest to date. However, subsequent data from a population-based study in Beaver Dam, WI suggested the risk may be confined to men. In the Beaver Dam study, the exposures among women were lower than exposures among men, and no association was seen. Moreover, there were no data linking sunlight exposure to risk of cataract in African Americans, although other eye diseases have different prevalences among the different racial groups, and cortical opacity appears to be higher in African Americans compared with whites.

4. Increased Tropospheric Ozone — Increased surface UV leads to increased tropospheric ozone. Ground-level ozone is generally recognized to be a health risk, as ozone is toxic due to its strong oxidant properties. At this time, ozone at ground level is produced mainly by the action of UV radiation on combustion gases from vehicle exhausts.

Interest in Ozone Layer Depletion

While the effect of the Antarctic ozone hole in decreasing the global ozone is relatively small, estimated at about 4% per decade, the hole has generated a great deal of interest because:

- The decrease in the ozone layer was predicted in the early 1980s to be roughly 7% over a 60 year period.
- The sudden recognition in 1985 that there was a substantial "hole" was widely reported in the press. The especially rapid ozone depletion in Antarctica had previously been dismissed as a measurement error.

- Many were worried that ozone holes might start to appear over other areas of the globe but to date the only other large-scale depletion is a smaller ozone "dimple" observed during the Arctic spring over the North Pole. Ozone at middle latitudes has declined, but by a much smaller extent (about 4-5% decrease).
- If the conditions became more severe (cooler stratospheric temperatures, more stratospheric clouds, more active chlorine), then global ozone may decrease at a much greater pace. Standard global warming theory predicts that the stratosphere will cool.
- When the Antarctic ozone hole breaks up, the ozone-depleted air drifts out into nearby areas. Decreases in the ozone level of up to 10% have been reported in New Zealand in the month following the break-up of the Antarctic ozone hole.
- Remedies to overcome global warming.

Responses to Global Warming

The broad agreement among climate scientists that global temperatures will continue to increase has led some nations, states, corporations and individuals to implement responses. These responses to global warming can be divided into mitigation of the causes and effects of global warming, adaptation to the changing global environment, and geoengineering to reverse global warming.

Mitigation of global warming is accomplished through reductions in the rate of anthropogenic greenhouse gas release.

Mitigation of global warming is accomplished through reductions in the rate of anthropogenic greenhouse gas release. The world's primary international agreement on reducing greenhouse gas emissions, the Kyoto Protocol, now covers more than 160 countries and over 55 percent of global greenhouse gas emissions. As of February 2010, only the United States, historically the world's largest emitter of greenhouse gases, has refused to ratify the treaty. The treaty expires in 2012. International talks began in May 2007 on a future treaty to succeed the current one. The 2009 United Nations Climate Change Conference met in Copenhagen in December 2009 to agree on a framework for climate change mitigation. No binding agreement was made.

Climate change mitigation are measures or actions to decrease the intensity of radiative forcing in order to reduce global warming. Mitigation is distinguished from adaptation, which involves acting to minimize the effects of global warming. Most often, mitigations involve reductions in the concentrations of greenhouse gases, either by reducing their sources or by increasing their sinks.

Means of Mitigation

Scientific consensus on global warming, together with the precautionary principle and the fear of abrupt climate change is leading to increased effort to develop new technologies and sciences and carefully manage others in an attempt to mitigate global warming. Unfortunately most means of mitigation appear effective only for preventing further warming, not at reversing existing warming.

The Stern Review identifies several ways of mitigating climate change. These include reducing demand for emissions-intensive goods and services, increasing efficiency gains, increasing use and development of low-carbon technologies, and reducing non-fossil fuel emissions.

The energy policy of the European Union has set a target of limiting the global temperature rise to 2 °C [3.6 °F] compared to preindustrial levels, of which 0.8 °C has already taken place and another 0.5 °C is already committed. The 2 °C rise is typically associated in climate models with a carbon dioxide concentration of 400-500 ppm by volume; the current level as of January 2007 is 383 ppm by volume, and rising at 2 ppm annually. Hence, to avoid a very likely breach of the 2 °C target, CO_2 levels would have to be stabilised very soon; this is generally regarded as unlikely, based on current programs in place to date. The importance of change is illustrated by the fact that world economic energy efficiency is presently improving at only half the rate of world economic growth.

At the core of most proposals is the reduction of greenhouse gas emissions through reducing energy use and switching to cleaner energy sources. Frequently discussed energy conservation methods include increasing the fuel efficiency of vehicles (often through hybrid, plug-in hybrid, and electric cars and improving conventional automobiles), individual-lifestyle changes and changing business practices.

Newly developed technologies and currently available technologies including renewable energy (such as solar power, tidal and ocean energy, geothermal power, and wind power) and more controversially nuclear power and the use of carbon sinks, carbon credits, and taxation are aimed more precisely at countering continued greenhouse gas emissions.

More radical proposals which may be grouped with mitigation include biosequestration of atmospheric carbon dioxide and geoengineering techniques ranging from carbon sequestration projects such as carbon dioxide air capture, to solar radiation management schemes such as the creation of stratospheric sulfur aerosols. The ever-increasing global population and the planned growth of national GDPs based on current technologies are counter-productive to most of these proposals.

Quota on Fossil Fuel Production

Most mitigation proposals imply — rather than directly state — an eventual reduction in global fossil fuel production. Also proposed are direct quotas on global fossil fuel production.

Pacala and Socolow

Pacala and Socolow of Princeton have proposed a program to reduce CO_2 emissions by 1 billion metric tons per year or 25 billion tons over the 50-year period. The proposed 15 different programs, any seven of which could achieve the goal, are:

1. more efficient vehicles ? increase fuel economy from 30 to 60 mpg (7.8 to 3.9 L/100 km) for 2 billion vehicles,
2. reduce use of vehicles ? improve urban design to reduce miles driven from 10,000 to 5,000 miles (16,000 to 8,000 km) per year for 2 billion vehicles,
3. efficient buildings ? reduce energy consumption by 25%,
4. improve efficiency of coal plants from today's 40% to 60%,

5. replace 1,400 GW (gigawatt) of coal power plants with natural gas,
6. capture and store carbon emitted from 800 GW of new coal plants,
7. capture and reuse hydrogen created by #6 above,
8. capture and store carbon from coal to syn fuels conversion at 30 million barrels per day (4,800,000 m3/d),
9. displace 700 GW of coal power with nuclear,
10. add 2 million 1 MW wind turbines (50 times current capacity),
11. displace 700 GW of coal with 2,000 GW (peak) solar power (700 times current capacity),
12. produce hydrogen fuel from 4 million 1 MW wind turbines,
13. use biomass to make fuel to displace oil (100 times current capacity),
14. stop de-forestation and re-establish 300 million hectares of new tree plantations,
15. conservation tillage ? apply to all crop land (10 times current usage).

Nature.com argued in June 2008 that "If we are to have confidence in our ability to stabilize carbon dioxide levels below 450 p.p.m. emissions must average less than 5 billion metric tons of carbon per year over the century. This means accelerating the deployment of the wedges so they begin to take effect in 2015 and are completely operational in much less time than originally modelled by Socolow and Pacala."

12.5 ENERGY EFFICIENCY AND CONSERVATION

Developing countries use their energy less efficiently than developed countries, getting less GDP for the same amount of energy.

Figure 4. World Marketed Energy Use by Fuel Type, 1980-2030

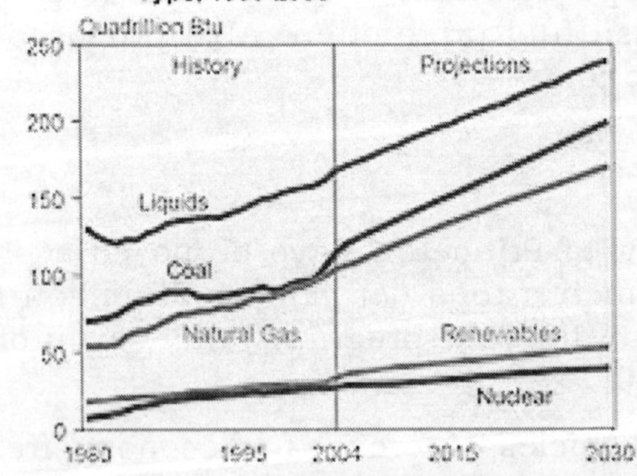

Sources: **History:** Energy Information Administration (EIA), *International Energy Annual 2004* (May-July 2006), web site www.eia.doe.gov/iea. **Projections:** EIA, System for the Analysis of Global Energy Markets (2007).

The Energy Information Administration predicts world energy usage will rise in the next few decades.

Reducing fuel use by improvements in efficiency provides environmental benefits and as well as net cost savings to the energy user. Building insulation, fluorescent lighting, and public transportation are some of the most effective means of conserving energy, and by extension, the environment. However, Jevons paradox poses a challenge to the goal of reducing overall energy use (and thus environmental impact) by energy conservation methods. Improved efficiency lowers cost, which in turn increases demand. To ensure that increases in efficiency actually reduces energy use, a tax must be imposed to remove any cost savings from improved efficiency.

Energy conservation is the practice of increasing the efficiency of use of energy in order to achieve higher useful output for the same energy consumption. This may result in increase of national security, personal security, financial capital, human comfort and environmental value. Individuals and organizations that are direct consumers of energy may want to conserve energy in order to reduce energy costs and promote environmental values. Industrial and commercial users may want to increase efficiency and maximize profit.

On a larger scale, energy conservation is an element of energy policy. The need to increase the available supply of energy (for example, through the creation of new power plants, or by the importation of more energy) is lessened if societal demand for energy can be reduced, or if growth in demand can be slowed. This makes energy conservation an important part of the debate over climate change and the replacement of non-renewable resources with renewable energy. Encouraging energy conservation among consumers is often advocated as a cheaper or more environmentally sensitive alternative to increased energy production.

The Energy Landscape

Residential buildings, commercial buildings, and the transportation of people and freight use the majority of the energy consumed by the United States each year. Specifically, the industrial sector uses 38 percent of total energy, closely followed by the transportation sector at 28 percent, the residential sector at 19 percent, and the commercial sector at 16 percent. On a community level, transportation can account for 40 to 50 percent of total energy use, and residential buildings use another 20 to 30 percent.

In developed nations, the way of life today is completely dependent on abundant supplies of energy. Energy is needed to heat, cool, and light homes, fuel cars, and power offices. Energy is also critical for manufacturing the products used every day, including the cement, concrete and bricks that shape our communities.

While the U.S. represents only five percent of the world's population, it consumes 25 percent of its energy and generates about 25 percent of its total greenhouse gas emissions. U.S. citizens, for example, use more energy per capita for transportation than do citizens of any other industrialized nation—which in part, reflects the greater distances traveled by Americans compared with citizens of other nations.

Urban Planning

Urban planning also has an effect on energy use. Between 1982 and 1997, the amount of land consumed for urban development in the United States increased by 47 percent while the nation's population grew by only 17 percent.[17] Inefficient land use development practices have increased infrastructure costs as well as the amount of energy needed for transportation, community services, and buildings.

At the same time, a growing number of citizens and government officials have begun advocating a smarter approach to land use planning. These smart growth practices include compact community development, multiple transportation choices, mixed land uses, and practices to conserve green space. These programs offer environmental, economic, and quality-of-life benefits; and they also serve to reduce energy usage and greenhouse gas emissions.

Approaches such as New Urbanism and Transit-oriented development seek to reduce distances travelled, especially by private vehicles, encourage public transit and make walking and cycling more attractive options. This is achieved through medium-density, mixed-use planning and the concentration of housing within walking distance of town centers and transport nodes.

Smarter growth land use policies have both a direct and indirect effect on energy consuming behaviour. For example, transportation energy usage, the number one user of petroleum fuels, could be significantly reduced through more compact and mixed use land development patterns, which in turn could be served by a greater variety of non-automotive based transportation choices.

Building Design

New buildings can be constructed using passive solar building design, low-energy building, or zero-energy building techniques, using renewable heat sources. Existing buildings can be made more efficient through the use of insulation, high-efficiency appliances (particularly hot water heaters and furnaces), double- or triple-glazed gas-filled windows, external window shades, and building orientation and siting. Renewable heat sources such as shallow geothermal and passive solar energy reduce the amount of greenhouse gasses emitted. In addition to designing buildings which are more energy efficient to heat, it is possible to design buildings that are more energy efficient to cool by using lighter-coloured, more reflective materials in the development of urban areas (e.g., by painting roofs white) and planting trees. This saves energy because it cools buildings and reduces the urban heat island effect thus reducing the use of air conditioning.

Transport

Modern energy efficient technologies, such as plug-in hybrid electric vehicles, and development of new technologies, such as hydrogen cars, may reduce the consumption of petroleum and emissions of carbon dioxide.

A shift from air transport and truck transport to electric rail transport would reduce emissions significantly.

Increased use of biofuels (such as biodiesel and biobutanol, that can be used in 100% concentration in today's diesel and gasoline engines) could also reduce emissions if produced environmentally efficiently, especially in conjunction with regular hybrids and plug-in hybrids.

For electric vehicles, the reduction of carbon emissions will improve further if the way the required electricity is generated is low-carbon (from renewable energy sources).

Effective urban planning to reduce sprawl would decrease Vehicle Miles Travelled (VMT), lowering emissions from transportation. Increased use of public transport can also reduce greenhouse gas emissions per passenger kilometer.

Alternative Energy Sources

Nuclear power currently produces over 15% of the world's electricity. Due to its low remittance of greenhouse gases (comparable to wind power) and reliability it is seen as a possible alternative to fossil fuels, but is controversial for reasons of capital cost and possible environmental impacts. Also, there are political impacts in some countries.

Life-cycle Greenhouse Gas Emissions Comparisons

Most comparisons of life cycle analysis (LCA) of carbon dioxide emissions show nuclear power as comparable to renewable energy sources.

A life cycle analysis centered around the Swedish Forsmark Nuclear Power Plant estimated carbon dioxide emissions at 3.10 g/kWh and 5.05 g/kWh in 2002 for the Torness Nuclear Power Station. This compares to 11 g/kWh for hydroelectric power, 950 g/kWh for installed coal, 900 g/kWh for oil and 600 g/kWh for natural gas generation in the United States in 1999.

The Vattenfall study found Nuclear, Hydro, and Wind to have far less greenhouse emissions than other sources represented.

The Swedish utility Vattenfall did a study of full life cycle emissions of nuclear, hydro, coal, gas, solar cell, peat and wind which the utility uses to produce electricity. The net result of the study was that nuclear power produced 3.3 grams of carbon dioxide per KW-Hr of produced power. This compares to 400 for natural gas and 700 for coal (according to this study). The study also concluded that nuclear power produced the smallest amount of CO_2 of any of their electricity sources.

Enrichment

The bulk of CO_2 emission from nuclear power plants can be eliminated if nuclear power plants themselves generate the electricity required during the uranium enrichment process (already being done in France and to some extent by the Tennessee Valley Authority's many nuclear units in the U.S.). In addition, gas centrifuge technology has/will greatly reduced the energy required for enrichment, thus reducing the LCA carbon emissions per kilowatt-hour.

Nuclear Fuel Reserves

Current uranium production is expected to be adequate at current consumption rates for about a century (from uranium mining, see also peak uranium).

There are a number of alternative nuclear fission technologies, such as breeder reactors, (see generation IV reactors) which could vastly extend fuel supplies if successfully developed and utilized.

Lower-risk Thorium Cycles have been Demonstrated in the Past

Nuclear fusion is another variant of providing nuclear energy, but it will not provide any immediate mitigation to global warming as the time horizon for its commercial deployment is expected to be after 2050.

Renewable Energy

This three-bladed wind turbine is the most common modern design because it minimizes forces related to fatigue.

One means of reducing carbon emissions is the development of new technologies such as renewable energy such as wind power. Most forms of renewable energy generate no appreciable amounts of greenhouse gases except for biofuels derived from biomass, as well as some biofuels derived from fossil fuel sources.

Helioculture is a newly developed process which is claimed to be able to produce 20,000 gallons of fuel per acre per year, and which removes carbon dioxide from the air as a feedstock for the fuel.

Generally, emissions are a fraction of fossil fuel-based electricity generation. In some cases, notably with hydroelectric dams — once thought to be one of the cleanest forms of energy-there are unexpected results. One study shows that a hydroelectric dam in the Amazon has 3.6 times larger greenhouse effect per kW·h than electricity production from oil, due to large scale emission of methane from decaying organic material.[32] This effect applies in particular to dams created by simply flooding a large area, without first clearing it of vegetation. There are however investigations into underwater turbines that do not require a dam.

Currently governments subsidize fossil fuels by an estimated $235 billion a year. However, in some countries, government action has boosted the development of renewable energy technologies-for example, a program to put solar panels on the roofs of a million homes has made Japan a world leader in that technology, and Denmark's support for wind power ensured its former leadership of that sector. In 2005, Governor Arnold Schwarzenegger promised an initiative to install a million solar roofs in California, which became the California Solar Initiative.

In June 2005, the chief executive of BT allegedly became the first head of a British company to admit that climate change is already affecting his company, and affecting its business, and announced plans to source much of its substantial energy use from renewable sources. He noted that, "Since the beginning of the year, the media has been showing us images of Greenland glaciers crashing into the sea, Mount Kilimanjaro devoid of its ice cap and Scotland reeling from floods and gales. All down to natural weather cycles?

Eliminating Waste Methane

Methane is a significantly more powerful greenhouse gas than carbon dioxide. Burning one molecule of methane generates one molecule of carbon dioxide. Accordingly, burning methane which would otherwise be released into the atmosphere (such as at oil wells, landfills, coal mines, waste treatment plants, etc.) provides a net greenhouse gas emissions benefit. However, reducing the amount of waste methane produced in the first place has an even greater beneficial impact, as might other approaches to productive use of otherwise-wasted methane.

In terms of prevention, vaccines are in the works in Australia to reduce significant global warming contributions from methane released by livestock via flatulence and eructation.

Carbon Intensity of Fossil Fuels

Natural gas (predominantly methane) produces less greenhouse gases per energy unit gained than oil which in turn produces less than coal, principally because coal has a larger ratio of carbon to hydrogen. The combustion of natural gas emits almost 30 percent less carbon dioxide than oil, and just under 45 percent less carbon dioxide than coal. In addition, there are also other environmental benefits.

A study performed by the Environmental Protection Agency (EPA) and the Gas Research Institute (GRI) in 1997 sought to discover whether the reduction in carbon dioxide emissions from increased natural gas (predominantly methane) use would be offset by a possible increased level of methane emissions from sources such as leaks and emissions. The study concluded that the reduction in emissions from increased natural gas use strongly outweighs the detrimental effects of increased methane emissions. Thus the increased use of natural gas in the place of other, dirtier fossil fuels can serve to lessen the emission of greenhouse gases in the United States.

Reforestation and Avoided Deforestation

Almost 20% (8 $GtCO_2$/year) of total greenhouse-gas emissions were from deforestation in 2007. The Stern Review found that, based on the opportunity costs of the landuse that would no longer be available for agriculture if deforestation were avoided, emission savings from avoided deforestation could potentially reduce CO_2 emissions for under \$5/tCO_2, possiblly as little as \$1/tCO_2. Afforestation and reforestation could save at least another 1GtCO2/year, at an estimated cost of \$5/tCO_2 to \$15/tCO_2. The Review determined these figures by assessing 8 countries responsible for 70% of global deforestation emissions.

Pristine temperate forest has been shown to store three times more carbon than IPCC estimates took into account, and 60% more carbon than plantation forest. Preventing these forests from being logged would have significant effects.

Further significant savings from other non-energy-related-emissions could be gained through cuts to agricultural emissions, fugitive emissions, waste emissions, and emissions from various industrial processes.

Carbon Capture and Storage

Carbon capture and storage (CCS) is a plan to mitigate climate change by capturing carbon dioxide (CO_2) from large point sources such as power plants and subsequently storing it away safely instead of releasing it into the atmosphere. Technology for capturing of CO_2 is already commercially available for large CO_2 emitters, such as power plants. Storage of CO_2, on the other hand is a relatively untried concept and as yet (2007) no powerplant operates with a full carbon capture and storage system. When this technique is used with biomass, the technique is known as biomass energy with carbon capture and storage and may be carbon negative.

CCS applied to a modern conventional power plant could reduce CO_2 emissions to the atmosphere by approximately 80-90% compared to a plant without CCS.

Storage of the CO_2 is envisaged either in deep geological formations, deep oceans, or in the form of mineral carbonates. Geological formations are currently considered the most promising, and these are estimated to have a storage capacity of at least 2000 Gt CO_2. IPCC estimates that the economic potential of CCS could be between 10% and 55% of the total carbon mitigation effort until year 2100

In October 2007, the Bureau of Economic Geology at The University of Texas at Austin received a 10-year, $38 million subcontract to conduct the first intensively monitored, long-term project in the United States studying the feasibility of injecting a large volume of CO_2 for underground storage. The project is a research program of the Southeast Regional Carbon Sequestration Partnership (SECARB), funded by the National Energy Technology Laboratory of the U.S. Department of Energy (DOE). The SECARB partnership will demonstrate CO_2 injection rate and storage capacity in the Tuscaloosa-Woodbine geologic system that stretches from Texas to Florida. The region has the potential to store more than 200 billion tons of CO_2 from major point sources in the region, equal to about 33 years of U.S. emissions overall at present rates. Beginning in fall 2007, the project will inject CO_2 at the rate of one million tons per year, for up to 1.5 years, into brine up to 10,000 feet (3,000 m) below the land surface near the Cranfield oil field about 15 miles (24 km) east of Natchez, Mississippi. Experimental equipment will measure the ability of the subsurface to accept and retain CO_2.

Non-CO2 Climate Actors

Action has been suggested on soot, HFCs and other climate drivers, in addition to that proposed for CO_2. Emissions of some of these actors are considered by the Kyoto Protocol.

Geo-engineering

Geoengineering is seen by some as an alternative to mitigation and adaptation, but by others as an entirely separate response to climate change. Carbon sequestration is a form of mitigation, but is not mitigation as defined by climate activists. To them, the term is clearly defined as exclusively associated with reduction of greenhouse gas emissions.

Chapter 28 of the National Academy of Sciences report Policy Implications of Greenhouse Warming: Mitigation, Adaptation, and the Science Base (1992) defined geoengineering as "options that would involve large-scale engineering of our environment in order to combat or counteract the effects of changes in atmospheric chemistry." They evaluated a range of options to try to give preliminary answers to two questions: can these options work and could they be carried out with a reasonable cost. They also sought to encourage discussion of a third question - what adverse side effects might there be. The following types of option were examined: reforestation, increasing ocean absorption of carbon dioxide (carbon sequestration) and screening out some sunlight. NAS also argued "Engineered countermeasures need to be evaluated but should not be implemented without broad understanding of the direct effects and the potential side effects, the ethical issues, and the risks."

Solar Radiation Management

Some scientists have suggested using aerosols and/or sulfate dust to alter the Earth's albedo, or reflectivity, as an emergency measure to increase global dimming and thus stave off the effects of global warming. A 0.5% albedo increase would roughly halve the effect of CO_2 doubling. In 1974, Russian expert Mikhail Budyko suggested that if global warming became a problem, we could cool down the planet by burning sulfur in the stratosphere, which would create a haze. Paul Crutzen suggests that this would cost 25 to 50 billion dollars/year. It would, however, increase the environmental problem of acid rain (although optimized engineering is thought to reduce this to insignificant levels) and drought.

An alternative technique, which may be more benign, is marine cloud brightening. Others have proposed building a literal solar shade in space.

Greenhouse Gas Remediation

Carbon sequestration has been proposed as a method of reducing the amount of radiative forcing. Carbon sequestration is a term that describes processes that remove carbon from the atmosphere. A variety of means of artificially capturing and storing carbon, as well as of enhancing natural sequestration processes, are being explored. The main natural process is photosynthesis by plants and single-celled organisms. Artificial processes vary, and concerns have been expressed about their long-term effects.

Although they require land, natural sinks can be enhanced by reforestation and afforestation carbon offsets, which fix carbon dioxide for as little as $0.11 per metric ton.

Biochar

Charcoal, or biochar, created by pyrolysis of biomass can be buried to create terra preta. The production of biochar may or may not involve energy recovery. The intention is that the carbon in the biomass is removed from the atmosphere for a longer period of time than would otherwise be the case.

Bio-energy with Carbon Capture and Storage, BECCS

During its growth, biomass traps carbon dioxide from the atmosphere through photosynthesis. When the biomass decomposes or is combusted, the carbon is again released as carbon dioxide. This process is part of the global carbon cycle. Through the use of biomass for energy and materials, eg. in biomass fuelled power plants, parts of this cycle is controlled by man. Combining these biomass systems with carbon capture and storage technologies, so called bio-energy with carbon capture and storage, BECCS, is achieved. BECCS systems results in net-negative carbon dioxide emissions, ie. the removal of carbon dioxide from the atmosphere. In comparison with other geoengineering options, BECCS has been suggested as a low-risk, near-term tool to effectively remove carbon from the atmosphere.

Carbon Air Capture

It is notable that the availability of cheap energy and appropriate sites for geological storage of carbon may make carbon dioxide air capture viable commercially. It is, however, generally expected that carbon dioxide air capture may be uneconomic when compared to carbon capture and storage from major sources - in particular, fossil fuel powered power stations, refineries, etc. In such cases, costs of energy produced will grow significantly. However, captured CO_2 can be used to force more crude oil out of oil fields, as Statoil and Shell have made plans to do. CO_2 can also be used in commercial greenhouses, giving an opportunity to kick-start the technology. Some attempts have been made to use algae to capture smokestack emissions, notably the GreenFuel Technologies Corporation, who have now shut down operations. This technology has not reached commercial level yet.

Seeding Oceans with Iron

The so-called Geritol solution to global warming, first proposed by oceanographer John Martin, is a carbon sequestration strategy whimsically named for a tonic advertised to treat the effects of iron-poor blood. It is motivated by evidence that seeding the oceans with iron will increase phytoplankton populations, and thereby draw more carbon dioxide from the atmosphere. A report in Nature, 10 October 1996, by K. H. Coale *et al.*, measured the effects of seeding equatorial Pacific waters with iron, finding that 700 grams of CO_2 were fixed by the resulting phytoplankton bloom per 1 gram of iron seeded. Lenton and Vaughan found this technique to be potentially useful, but limited in its total capacity.

Opponents of this approach argue that fertilizing the ocean is dangerous and lacks any guarantee of efficacy. The original researchers themselves assert that, far from being a panacea for global warming, iron seeding may be entirely ineffective. Among their concerns are that nobody knows where the carbon goes after it is absorbed by phytoplankton. Instead of being drawn down to the ocean floor and acting as a carbon sink, the carbon could be reabsorbed by the water, effectively negating any initial gain. They also express concern that any attempt at geoengineering could result in massive, unpredictable changes to the environment. They point out that, considering the immense damage caused by adding nutrients to lakes and ponds, it would be a logical conclusion that adding nutrients to the ocean would also cause environmental damage. Large-scale growth in phytoplankton could reduce oxygen levels, creating dead zones where the ocean cannot support marine-life. They suggest that there is even the possibility that blooms would release more carbon dioxide equivalent greenhouse gas in the form of methane than it would sequester.

Societal Controls

Another method being examined is to make carbon a new currency by introducing tradeable "Personal Carbon Credits." The idea being it will encourage and motivate individuals to reduce their 'carbon footprint' by the way they live. Each citizen will receive a free annual quota of carbon that they can use to travel, buy food, and go about their business. It has been suggested that by using this concept it could actually solve two problems; pollution and poverty, old age pensioners will actually be better off because they fly less often, so they can cash in their quota at the end of the year to pay heating bills, etc.

12.6 GOVERNMENTAL AND INTERGOVERNMENTAL ACTION

Earth Summit

The Earth Summit is the informal and best-known name for the United Nations Conference on Environment and Development (UNCED).

The Earth Summit, held in Rio de Janeiro from June 3 to June 14, 1992, was unprecedented for a United Nations conference, in terms of both its size and the scope of its concerns. One hundred and seventy two governments participated with 108 at level of heads of State or Government. Some 2,400 representatives of non-governmental organizations (NGOs) attended, with 17,000 people at the parallel NGO Forum.

The issues addressed included:

- systematic scrutiny of patterns of production — particularly the production of toxic components, such as lead in gasoline, or poisonous waste
- alternative sources of energy to replace the use of fossil fuels which are linked to global climate change
- new reliance on public transportation systems in order to reduce vehicle emissions, congestion in cities and the health problems caused by polluted air and smog
- the growing scarcity of water

An important achievement was an agreement on the Climate Change Convention which in turn led to the Kyoto Protocol. Another was agreement to "not carry out any activities on the lands of indigenous peoples that would cause environmental degradation or that would be culturally inappropriate." The conference also reinforced the Convention on Biological Diversity, and made a start towards redefinition of money supply measures that did not inherently encourage destruction of natural eco-regions and so-called uneconomic growth.

The Earth Summit resulted in the following documents:

- Agenda 21
- Convention on Biological Diversity
- Forest Principles
- Framework Convention on Climate Change
- Rio Declaration on Environment and Development

Further development and implementation these issues was undertaken by various entities within the UN:

- United Nations Development Programme
- United Nations Environment Programme
- United Nations Industrial Development Organization
- United Nations Conference on Trade and Development

At its close, Maurice Strong, the Conference Secretary-General, called the Summit a "historic moment for humanity." Although Agenda 21 had been weakened by compromise and negotiation, he said, it was still the most comprehensive and, if implemented, effective programme of action ever sanctioned by the international community.

The Earth Summit influenced all subsequent UN conferences, which have examined the relationship between human rights, population, social development, women and human settlements — and the need for environmentally sustainable development. The World Conference on Human Rights, held in Vienna in 1993, for example, underscored the right of people to a healthy environment and the right to development, controversial demands that had met with resistance from some Member States until Rio.

Critics, however, point out that many of the agreements made in Rio have not been realized regarding such fundamental issues as fighting poverty and cleaning up the environment. Moreover, they say business leaders have used the Rio accords to greenwash their corporate image, giving the impression they have improved their behaviour when in many cases this has not been the case.

Other criticisms were that the format of the Summit inhibited the discussion of sustainable development by putting development and environment functions in separate compartments, and uniting trade and development concerns, rather than trade and environment concerns, as would be required if tax, tariff and trade policy were actually to be changed to accommodate environmental concerns.

Earth Summit 2002

The World Summit on Sustainable Development organised by the United Nations (UN) in Johannesburg was held in August and September of 2002. Also called Earth Summit 2002, it brought together over 100 heads of state and 40,000 delegates to try and set up the goals needed to halt poverty around the world whilst saving the environment at the same time.

Here are a Few Facts on Earth Summit 2002
• It was the largest UN conference to date, with over 100 heads of state and 40,000 delegates attending. • It covered everything from measures to cut poverty, improve sanitation, improve ecosystems, reduce pollution, and improve energy supply for poor people. • It fell exactly 10 years after the Earth Summit in Rio de Janeiro which focused world governments on environmental issues for the first time. • Two weeks of preparatory meetings took place in Bali, Indonesia to reach agreements on the key plans that could be realistically met. • Kofi Annan, the UN Secretary General, put water, energy, health, agriculture and biodiversity at the top of his list of commitments from the summit. • South Africa, the host of Earth Summit 2002, plans to provide clean water to all South Africans by 2008, having already created access for 7 million of the poorest people since 1994. • The European Union (EU), which currently spends 1.4 billion euros (£880 million) on water projects worldwide each year, will focus

particularly on water supply and sanitation in Africa, boosting management of water resources and providing better coordination of water-related development aid.

The summit also aimed to make agreements for the following issues:

- To cut by half by 2015 the proportion of people living on less than $1 a day.
- To cut by half by 2015 the number of people suffering from hunger.
- To cut by half by 2015 the 1.1 billion people without access to safe drinking water.
- To cut by a significant amount the 2.4 billion people who live without inadequate sanitation, and improve sanitation in institutions, such as schools; and promote safe hygiene.
- To launch an action programme to reduce the number of people who lack access to modern energy.
- To improve the living standards for at least 100 million people who live in slums, by 2020.
- To adopt and implement policies and measures that will promote sustainable production and consumption, using the "polluter-pays" principle.
- To increase corporate, environmental and social responsibility and accountability.
- Establish programmes for energy efficiency in poor countries.
- Promote waste prevention and reduction by encouraging production of reusable goods and biodegradable products.
- Implement programmes against deforestation, erosion, land degradation, loss of biodiversity and disruption of water flows.
- Promote the development of sustainable tourism.
- Put particular emphasis on development in Africa.
- Develop programmes to reduce by two-thirds by 2015 the mortality rates for children under the age of five.

Kyoto Protocol

The main current international agreement on combating climate change is the Kyoto Protocol, which came into force on 16 February 2005. The Kyoto Protocol is an amendment to the United Nations Framework Convention on Climate Change (UNFCCC). Countries that have ratified this protocol have committed to reduce their emissions of carbon dioxide and five other greenhouse gases, or engage in emissions trading if they maintain or increase emissions of these gases.

Copenhagen 2009

The first phase of the Kyoto Protocol expires in 2012. The United Nations Climate Change Conference in Copenhagen in December 2009 was the next in an annual series of UN meetings that followed the 1992 Earth Summit in Rio. In

1997 the talks led to the Kyoto Protocol, Copenhagen is the world's chance to agree a successor to Kyoto that will bring about meaningful carbon cuts.

Resolutions in Copenhagen

The world witnessed for almost two weeks how the negotiations went on during the UN global climate conference in the freezing cold Danish capital. The conference, the biggest in the history of mankind for the cause of environment, witnessed the participation of over 130 heads of government and states from around the globe, where every one initially remarked that the summit must not be failed.

But the latest series of negotiation and discussion proved that the division between the developed and developing remained intact. The repeated opposition and adjournment of the meetings delayed the acceptance of the resolutions. The summit, which was supposed to get concluded by Friday night, continued till Saturday evening.

Finally Obama initiated for a breakthrough of the conference, where he convinced BASIC countries, namely, India, China, Brazil and South Africa to give approval for an agreement.

An hour-long meeting if the US President with the Indian Prime Minister, Chinese Premier Wen Jiabao, Brazilian President Lula Da Silva and South African President Jacob Zuma had resulted in a US-BASIC deal, where all parties agreed to take appropriate actions to prevent the global warming exceeding the level of 2 degree Celsius.

Moreover, all the government heads of BASIC and the US had ensued for $30 billion as aid to the poor and developing nations in the next three years. It has also agreed to support the US proposed global fund of $100 billion a year by 2020.

Of course, not every one was happy with the deal. There were opposition from various other developing nations, where they argued that they cannot 'accept a text originally agreed by the United States, China, India, Brazil and South Africa as the blueprint of a wider United Nations plan' to fight climate change.

It was opposed by Cuba, Sudan, Nicaragua, Bolivia, Venezuela, Tuvalu, Costa Rica etc, whereas the host country also showed reservation to the deal. The Danish Prime Minister and also COP15 president Lars Løkke Rasmussen said that he was not in favour of the proposal.

However Japan, Norway, African nations and also the European Union nations came out with support for the proposal.

The British Prime Minister Gordon Brown claimed the deal as a beginning was acceptable to him. He admitted that 'it was not an easy task' and asserted that the Copenhagen climate deal offers hope. German Chanellor Angela Merkel also agreed on the proposal but said she 'expected more.'

The Indian Environment Minister Jairam Ramesh expressed happiness that a good deal for the entire developing world was resolved in the Copenhagen summit.

Someway happy notes were aired by the UN Secretary General Ban Ki-moon also when termed the exercise as an important beginning. He admitted that it was not satisfactory to a number of delegates as the deal 'may not be everything everyone had hoped for'. But he firmly commented that finally 'we have a deal in Copenhagen', which has an immediate operational effect.

Encouraging Use Changes

Carbon Emissions Trading

The European Union Emission Trading Scheme (EU ETS) is the largest multi-national, greenhouse gas emissions trading scheme in the world. It commenced operation on 1 January 2005, and all 25 member states of the European Union participate in the scheme which has created a new market in carbon dioxide allowances estimated at 35 billion Euros (US$43 billion) per year. The Chicago Climate Exchange was the first (voluntary) emissions market, and is soon to be followed by Asia's first market (Asia Carbon Exchange). A total of 107 million metric tonnes of carbon dioxide equivalent have been exchanged through projects in 2004, a 38% increase relative to 2003 (78 Mt CO_2e).

With the creation of a market for trading carbon dioxide emissions within the Kyoto Protocol, it is likely that London financial markets will be the centre for this potentially highly lucrative business; the New York and Chicago stock markets may have a lower trade volume than expected as long as the US maintains its rejection of the Kyoto.

Twenty-three multinational corporations have come together in the G8 Climate Change Roundtable, a business group formed at the January 2005 World Economic Forum. The group includes Ford, Toyota, British Airways and BP. On 9 June 2005 the Group published a statement[64] stating that there was a need to act on climate change and claiming that market-based solutions can help. It called on governments to establish "clear, transparent, and consistent price signals" through "creation of a long-term policy framework" that would include all major producers of greenhouse gases.

The Regional Greenhouse Gas Initiative is a proposed carbon trading scheme being created by nine North-eastern and Mid-Atlantic American states; Connecticut, Delaware, Maine, Massachusetts, New Hampshire, New Jersey, New York, Rhode Island and Vermont. The scheme was due to be developed by April 2005 but has not yet been completed.

Carbon Tax

In 1991, Sweden introduced the world's first carbon tax. The UK has had a Climate Change Levy on fossil-fuel-based electricity generation since 2001. Plans for a carbon tax in New Zealand were abandoned after the 2005 elections.

In May 2008, the Bay Area Air Quality Management District, which covers nine counties in the San Francisco Bay Area, passed a carbon tax of 4.4 cents per ton.

Non-governmental Approaches

Legal Action

In some countries, those affected by climate change may be able to sue major producers, in a parallel to the lawsuits against tobacco companies. Although proving that particular weather events are due specifically to global warming may never be possible, methodologies have been developed to show the increased risk of such events caused by global warming.

For a legal action for negligence (or similar) to succeed, "Plaintiffs ... must show that, more probably than not, their individual injuries were caused by the risk factor in question, as opposed to any other cause. This has sometimes been translated to a requirement of a relative risk of at least two." Another route (though with little legal bite) is the World Heritage Convention, if it can be shown that climate change is affecting World Heritage Sites like Mount Everest.

Legal action has also been taken to try to force the U.S. Environmental Protection Agency to regulate greenhouse gas emissions under the Clean Air Act, and against the Export-Import Bank and OPIC for failing to assess environmental impacts (including global warming impacts) under NEPA.

According to a 2004 study commissioned by Friends of the Earth, ExxonMobil and its predecessors caused 4.7 to 5.3 percent of the world's man-made carbon dioxide emissions between 1882 and 2002. The group suggested that such studies could form the basis for eventual legal action.

Personal Choices

While many of the proposed methods of mitigating global warming require governmental funding, legislation and regulatory action, individuals and businesses can also play a part in the mitigation effort. Environmental groups encourage individual action against global warming, often aimed at the consumer. Common recommendations include lowering home heating and cooling usage, burning less gasoline, supporting renewable energy sources, buying local products to reduce transportation, turning off unused devices, and various others. A geophysicist at Utrecht University has urged similar institutions to hold the vanguard in voluntary mitigation, suggesting the use of communication technologies such as videoconferencing to reduce their dependence on long-haul flights.

Business Opportunities and Risks

In addition to government action and the personal choices individuals can make, the threat posed by global warming provides business opportunities to be exploited and risks to be mitigated.

There has also been business action on climate change.

On 9 May 2005 Jeff Immelt, the chief executive of General Electric (GE), announced plans to reduce GE's global warming related emissions by one percent by 2012. "GE said that given its projected growth, those emissions would have risen by 40 percent without such action."

On 21 June 2005 a group of leading airlines, airports and aerospace manufacturers pledged to work together to reduce the negative environmental impact of the aviation industry, including limiting the impact of air travel on climate change by improving fuel efficiency and reducing carbon dioxide emissions of new aircraft by fifty percent per seat kilometre by 2020 from 2000 levels. The group aims to develop a common reporting system for carbon dioxide emissions per aircraft by the end of 2005, and pressed for the early inclusion of aviation in the European Union's carbon emission trading scheme.

12.7 TERRITORIAL POLICIES OF MITIGATION

United States

Efforts to reduce greenhouse gas emissions by the United States include their energy policies which encourage efficiency through programs like Energy Star, Commercial Building Integration, and the Industrial Technologies Program. On 12 November 1998, Vicc President Al Gore symbolically signed the Kyoto Protocol, but he indicated participation by the developing nations was necessary prior its being submitted for ratification by the United States Senate.

The US and Global Warming Mitigation

In 2007, Transportation Secretary Mary Peters, with White House approval, urged governors and dozens of members of the House of Representatives to block California's first-in-the-nation limits on greenhouse gases from cars and trucks, according to e-mails obtained by Congress. The U.S. Climate Change Science Program is a group of about twenty federal agencies and US Cabinet Departments, all working together to address global warming.

US Attempts to Suppress Science of Global Warming

The U.S. government has pressured American scientists to suppress discussion of global warming, according to the testimony of the Union of Concerned Scientists to the Oversight and Government Reform Committee of the U.S. House of Representatives. "High-quality science" was "struggling to get out," as the Bush administration pressured scientists to tailor their writings on global warming to fit the Bush administration's skepticism, in some cases at the behest of an ex-oil industry lobbyist. "Nearly half of all respondents perceived or personally experienced pressure to eliminate the words 'climate change,' 'global warming' or other similar terms from a variety of communications." Similarly, according to the testimony of senior officers of the Government Accountability Project, the White House attempted to bury the report "National Assessment of the Potential Consequences of Climate Variability and Change," produced by U.S. scientists pursuant to U.S. law. Some U.S. scientists resigned their jobs rather than give in to White House pressure to underreport global warming.

Mitigation in Developing Countries

In order to reconcile economic development with mitigating carbon emissions, developing countries need particular support, both financial and technical. One of the means of achieving this is the Kyoto Protocol's Clean Development Mechanism (CDM). The World Bank's Prototype Carbon Fund is a public private partnership that operates within the CDM.

In July 2005 the U.S., China, India, Australia, as well as Japan and South Korea, agreed to the Asia-Pacific Partnership for Clean Development and Climate. The pact aims to encourage technological development that may mitigate global warming, without coordinated emissions targets. The highest goal of the pact is to find and promote new technology that aid both growth and a cleaner environment simultaneously. An example is the Methane to Markets initiative which reduces methane emissions into the atmosphere by capturing the gas and using it for growth enhancing clean energy generation. Critics have raised concerns that the pact undermines the Kyoto Protocol.

However, none of these initiatives suggest a quantitative cap on the emissions from developing countries. This is considered as a particularly difficult policy proposal as the economic growth of developing countries are proportionally reflected in the growth of greenhouse emissions. Critics of mitigation often argue that, the developing countries' drive to attain a comparable living standard to the developed countries would doom the attempt at mitigation of global warming. Critics also argue that holding down emissions would shift the human cost of global warming from a general one to one that was borne most heavily by the poorest populations on the planet.

In an attempt to provide more opportunities for developing countries to adapt clean technologies, UNEP and WTO urged the international community to reduce trade barriers and to conclude the Doha trade round "which includes opening trade in environmental goods and services."

Population Control

Various organizations promote population control as a means for mitigating global warming. Proposed measures include improving access to family planning and reproductive health care and information, reducing natalistic politics, public education about the consequences of continued population growth, and improving access of women to education and economic opportunities.

Population control efforts are impeded by there being somewhat of a taboo in some countries against considering any such efforts. Also, various religions discourage or prohibit some or all forms of birth control.

Population size has a different per capita effect on global warming in different countries, since the per capita production of anthropogenic greenhouse gases varies greatly by country.

Costs of Mitigation

The Stern Review proposes stabilising the concentration of greenhouse-gas emissions in the atmosphere at a maximum of 550ppm CO_2e by 2050. The Review estimates that this would mean cutting total greenhouse-gas emissions to three quarters of 2007 levels. The Review further estimates that the cost of these cuts would be in the range -1.0 to +3.5% of GDP, with an average estimate of approximately 1%. Stern has since revised his estimate to 2% of GDP. The Review emphasises that these costs are contingent on steady reductions in the cost of low-carbon technologies. Mitigation costs will also vary according to how and when emissions are cut: early, well-planned action will minimise the costs.

One way of estimating the cost of reducing emissions is by considering the likely costs of potential technological and output changes. Policy makers can compare the marginal abatement costs of different methods to assess the cost and amount of possible abatement over time. The marginal abatement costs of the various measures will differ by country, by sector, and over time.

Limitations of Mitigation

Mitigation technologies aimed at reducing emissions, as opposed to enhancing sinks, do not seek to remove greenhouse gases from the atmosphere. As such, their efficacy at reversing global warming is limited.

12.8 POWERS OF THE CENTRAL GOVERNMENT (Sect. 3 to 6)

The central Govt. has the power under the Act to take necessary steps or measures to protect and improve the quality of the environment and prevent and control environmental pollution.

The powers of the central Govt. are briefed here, under headings:

I. Measure to Protect and Improve Environment (Sect. 03)

The Central Govt. has the power in all or any the following:

1. to co-ordinate the actions by the state Govt.
2. to plan and control a nation wide programme for the prevention, control and abatement of environmental pollution.
3. to prescribe standards for the quality of environment.
4. to prescribe different standards for emission (or discharge of environmental pollution) from different sources as to the quality and composition of emission.
5. to restrict areas in which any industries shall not be carried out.
6. to lay down procedure and safe guards for preventing the accidents that may cause environmental pollution.
7. to lay down procedure and safeguards for handling of hazardous substances.
8. to examine the manufacturing processes and materials that may cause environmental pollution.
9. to conduct investigations and research on the environmental pollution problems.
10. to inspect the factories, plants, machinery equipment, materials and manufacturing processes so as to give directions to the officers to take necessary step to prevent and control environmental pollution.
11. to establish or recognise environmental laboratories and institutes.
12. to collect and distribute information on environmental pollution.

For the purpose of performing the above said powers and functions, the central Government may **set up an authority, by an order**, published in the official Gazettee.

II. Appointment of Officers and their Powers Functions (Sect. 4)

The Central Govt. may also appoint officers and give them powers and functions under this act. Such officers shall work under the direction of the Central Govt. and the other authorities set up under the act.

III. Power to give Direction (Sect. 5)

Under the act the Central Govt. may give directions in writing to the officers and authorities on

(1) closing or regulating of any industry operation or process.

(2) stopping or regulating of the supply of electricity and water.

IV. Rules to Regulate Pollution (Sect. 6)

The central Govt. may make rules (through notification in the official Gazettee) on all or any of the matters mentioned in sect. 3. Such rules are:

1. Fixing the standard of quality of air, water and soil.
2. Fixing Maximum limit for notice and other environment pollution.
3. Framing procedure for the handling of hazardous substances and also restriction on handling of such substances in different areas.
4. Prohibiting and restricting the location of industries in different areas.
5. Laying procedures and safeguards for preventing a accidents that may cause environmental pollution.

12.8 PREVENTION, CONTROL AND ABATEMENT (make less) OF ENVIRONMENTAL POLLUTION (Sect.7 – 15)

(1) Preventing Emission in Excess of Standards (Sect. 7)

Any person carrying on any industry or process shall not discharge (emit) any environmental pollution over and above the standard prescribed.

(2) Procedure for Handling Hazardous Substances (Sect. 08)

A person shall handle any hazardous substances only according to the prescribed procedures and after satisfying the safety measure prescribed under the act.

(3) Duties of Persons Creating Environmental Pollution (Sect. 09)

The duties of the persons causing environmental pollution under Act are given below:

(1) He must Mitigate (lessen the seriousness) environmental pollution.

(2) He must inform the prescribed authorities about the (possible) occurence of environmental pollution.

(3) He must help these authorities in preventing or reducing the environmental pollution and

(4) He must bear the expenses incurred on the remedial measures.

(4) Power of Entry and Inspection (sect. 10)

Under the act, the person empowered by the central Govt. can enter into any premises (1) for performing the functions of central Govt. given to him. (2) for examining and testing any equipment, industrial plant, record, register and document and (3) to seize any such equipment if can be used as evidence in the court of law for punishing the person responsible for environmental pollution.

If any person carrying on any industry or process (1) fails to help these authority or (2) intentionally prevents him from doing their functions will be punished under code of criminal procedure of (1973).

(5) Power to make Samples and Procedure (Sect. 11)

The central Govt. or the person empowered by it can take the samples of air, water, soil or other substances for thc purpose of Analysis, from any factory. The sample so taken to be put in a container and shall be marked and sealed and also shall be signed by the person taking the sample and the occupier.

Then the sealed containers with samples shall be sent to the laboratory established or recognised under Sect. 12, for analysis by the person taking the sample.

(6) Establishment of Environmental Laboratories (Sect 12)

Under the Act, the Central Govt. through notification in the official Gazettee, may establish or recognise one or more environmental laboratories and lay down the functions to be performed by them.

(7) Appointment of Govt. Analyst (Sect 13)

The Central Govt. may appoint any qualified persons as govt. Analysts for the purpose of analysis of samples of air, water, soil etc. The appointment may be notified in the official Gazettee.

(8) Report of Analysis (Sect 14)

This Govt. Analyst may prepare a report of the analysis. Such report prepared and duly signed by the Govt. Analyst may be used as evidence in the court of law.

(9) Penalty (Sect 15)

Any person who fails to implement or violates any provisions of this act shall be punished, with imprisonment of upto 5 years or a fine of Rs. 1,00,000 or both. And if the failure continues the defaulter shall have to pay additional fine of upto Rs. 5,000 for every day during which failure continues.

12.9 SOUND POLLUTION

Noise has come to be regarded as a major urban pollutant, capable of causing annoyance and hearing loss, and perhaps even adverse psychological and psychological effect. Exposure to high noise levels pose the greatest harm to human function. The consequences are signified in a higher rate of accidents, general ill-health, occupational diseases and decrease in productivity.

Sound is the form of energy giving the sensation of hearing. It is produced by longitudinal mechanical waves in elastic matter and transmitted by the oscillation of atoms and molecules of matter. Noise is unwanted sound. The human ear is capable of receiving sound waves and transmitting signals to the brain to create the sensation of hearing. **As per the ILO convention No. 148,** "Noise" covers all sounds which can result in hearing impairment or are harmful to health, or otherwise dangerous. In objective terms, noise is random vibrations.

The Frequency of Sound

The frequency of the sound is the rate at which the variation in air pressure takes place. It is expressed as the number of cycles per second and the unit is Hertz (Hz). Human hearing is sensitive to frequency in the range of 16,000 to 20,000 Hz.

A two-fold frequency range corresponds to one octave. It has a centre frequency that is 2 times the lower cut-off frequency, and the upper cut-off frequency, is twice the lower. Following are preferred centre frequencies for noise level measurement 31.5, 63, 125, 250, 500, 1,000, 2000, 4000 and 8,000 H.Z.

Types of Noise

Noise is classified as a *continuous or steady-state and impulse type of noise.*

(a) ***Impulse Noise:*** the noise consists of one or more bursts of sound energy, each of a duration less than about one second. This type of noise is transient, e.g., Gunshot. The impulse must be less than half a second duration and have a magnitude of at least 40 dB within that time.

(b) ***Steady State or Continuous Noise:*** Industrial noise is often produced because of impact between metal parts. If there are many impacts per second as in riveting machine, fluctuations in the noise level are small, and the noise produced is usually treated as normal, broad brand, steady state or continuous type of noise.

NOISE MEASUREMENTS

Noise measurement gives us an objective method of comparing annoying sounds under different conditions. *Sound level meter* is an instrument which indicates sound pressure levels in the audible range. It consists of microphone and electronic circuit, including an attenuator, an amplifier, weighing net works and indication meter. It give the sound pressure level in dB (decibels).

Second type of instrument is *impulse analyser.* Frequency analysers or octave band analysers, are the types most commonly used. They are connected to sound level meters. The frequency range of each band is such that upper hand limit is twice the lower.

Graphic record of sound level may be obtained by connecting a sound level meter to graphic level recorder which plots the sound levels on paper chart.

Noise dosimeters are also available. The personal dosimeter is designed to be attached to the worker for all parts of shift to monitor his exposure directly. The instrument indicates the percent of allowable exposure.

1. Method of Noise Measurement

Sound level meters should be well calibrated before measuring the noise levels. The noise should be measured at the worker's ear level if the objective is to determine whether or not noise are high enough to lead to permanent hearing damage. Further microphone of the sound level meter should be located at least one meter away from hard surface such as walls. Sound level meters are fitted with a *'fast' and 'slow'* response switch. For steady sound the *'fast'* position is used and for fluctuating sound levels the *'slow'* position is used to damp down thc movements of meter needle.

Threshold Limit Values (TLVs)

As regards noise, these TLVs refer to sound pressure levels and duration of exposure that worker may be repeatedly exposed without adverse effect in their ability to hear and understand normal speech.

Threshold Limit Value for Noise

Duration Per day	*Sound level dB (A)*
16	80
8	85
4	90
2	95
1	100
1/2	105
1/4	110
1/8	115

No exposure to continuous or intermittent in excess of 115 dB (A).

It is also recommended that exposure to impulsive or impact noise shall not exceed the limits. No exposure in excess of 140 decibels peak sound pressure level are permitted.

Sound Level	*Impacts Per Day*
140	100
130	1,000
120	10,000

EFFECTS OF NOISE

When dealing with the ill effects of noise, three important factors are considered: its quality, the sensitivity of the individuals, and duration of exposure of noise. The quality of noise is defined as its intensity, component frequencies and vibratory pattern.

Auditory Effects

The chief effect of noise, is that the hearing cells in the inner ear are damaged acutely due to a very severe impact noise of high sensitivity, such as explosion, or due to exposure to high levels over a long period. A sudden rapture of an eardrum on short exposure to high impact noise level, temporary threshold shift and noise induced hearing loss are auditory effects.

Loss of hearing is either temporary or permanent in nature, depending on the length and severity of noise exposure. A temporary hearing loss lasting few seconds to a few days result due to high intensity noise for short duration. However, this is reversible and normal hearing may be restored in a few days. Much more serious regular and prolonged exposure to some kinds of noise of moderate intensity maintained through successive working days over a period of years or single short exposure of very high intensity noise may cause a loss of hearing which is permanent and irreversible. This is called noise hearing loss.

Non-auditory Effects

The other effects of noise on different systems to persons who are in good health are given below.

1. ***Annoyance:*** This make a person or worker tired soon and his quality and efficiency may come down.
2. ***Interference with Communication:*** Any operation that requires oral communication will suffer from a noise environment. Interference with communication can create a misunderstanding in information is to be transmitted from one person to another.
3. ***Difficulty in Hearing Safety Alarms:*** In a noisy environment a person or worker may fail to hear a safety alarm due to the masking effect of noise, this may cause delayed action in case of emergencies.
4. ***Other Effects:***
   (a) Higher incidence of circulatory problems.
   (b) Peripheral blood flow disturbances.
   (c) Interference with performance and irregularities in heart rate.
   (d) Lack of concentration.
   (e) Nausea, headache, insomnia loss of appetite, peptic ulcer, tumour.
   (f) Effect on pregnant mother: (i) Birth defect, (ii) Still birth, (iii) Baby with low weight.
   (g) Noise of high intensity leads to constriction of smaller blood vessels in fingers and eyes.

LEGISLATION ON NOISE

The 42nd Amendment of the Constitution passed in 1976, inserted Articles 48-A and 51-A, to protect and improve the environment. Since, then, it has become a constitutional obligation of the State to improve and protect the environment.

There is no law in India so far which deals exclusively with problems of excessive noise and its control. However, a few States enacted Statutes, e.g., Rajasthan Noises Control Act, 1963, Bihar control of use and play loudspeakers Act 1955, Madhya Pradesh control of Music and Noises Act, 1951. The environmental (Protection) Act, 1986, included noise a physical pollutant and empowered the Central Government to prescribe the maximum allowance limits for different areas.

The International Labour Organisation (ILO) Convention No. 148 concerning the protection of workers against occupational hazards in the working environment due to air pollution, noise and vibration was adapted in 1977. According to Article 4, national laws should prescribe the measures to be taken for prevention and control of and protection against, occupational hazards in the working environment due to noise.

Section 87 of the Factories Act, 1948, following are the permissible noise limits:

Permissible Exposure in Case of Continuous Noise

Total time of exposure Per day, in hours	*Second pressure levels dB (A)*
8	90
6	92
4	95
3	97
2	100
1.5	102
1.0	105
0.75	107
0.50	110
0.25	115

- No exposure to excess of 115 dB (A) is to be permitted.

Permissible Exposure Levels of Impulsive or Impact Noise

Peak Sound pressure Level in dB	*Permitted number of impulsive*
140	100
135	375
130	1,000
125	3,160
120	10,000

- No exposure in excess of 140 dB (A) is to be permitted.

Operation of Super Flights: This constitutes an especially loud and startling impulsive sound produced by the shock wave of a faster than sound air plane (e.g., Concord) flying above a person. In addition to adverse effects on human beings, these shock waves can also causes structural damage to buildings, shatter glass and move light objects. For this reason many countries have not permitted the operation of supersonic flight over their lands.

Questions

Section — A Objective Type

1. Name the Environmental Laws.
2. What are "Externalities" under Environmental Law?
3. Name two renowned environmentalists in India.
4. What is zero-economic growth?
5. Define environment.
6. Define environmental pollutant.
7. Define environmental pollution.
8. What is hazardous substance as per Environmental Protection Act, 1986?
9. Define an Occupier.
10. Define stream as per Water Act, 1974.
11. What is Water Pollution?
12. What is Sound Pollution?
13. Name the different types of Noise.
14. What is Noise Pollution?
15. What is Impulse Noise?
16. What is Steady Noise?
17. Name the instrument for measurement of Noise.
18. What is Threshold Limit Values (TLVs)?
19. What is Auditory Effects? Give examples.
20. What are Non-auditory Effects? Give examples.
21. What is sustained economic development?
22. What is global warming ?
23. State any two causes for global warming.
24. What is green house effect ?
25. What is ozone ?
26. What is Ozone layer ?
27. What is depletion of Ozone Layer ?
28. What is ultravires radiation ?
29. State the two ill effects of Ozone layer depletion.
30. State any two remedies for global warming.
31. What is fossil fuel ?
32. What is deforestation ?
33. What is climate change ?
34. What is carbon trading ?
35. What is carbon credit ?
36. State the two ill effects of global warming on human beings.

Section — B Analytical Type

1. Analyse the liability rules for environmental externalities.
2. Discuss opportunity costs of zero growth.
3. Describe environmental effects of zero economic growth.
4. What are the rules for prevention, control and Abatement of Envrionmental Pollution?
5. Describe the measures to protect and improve environment as per Environment Protection.
6. Explain the powers and functions of Central Pollution Control Board as per the Air Act, 1981.

7. Briefly explain the penalties provision under the Air Act, 1981.
8. Explain the constitution and composition of Central Board under the Water Act, 1974.
9. What are the powers and functions of the Central Board under the Water Act, 1974.
10. Describe the functions of State Board under the Water Act, 1974.
11. Briefly discuss the penalty provisions under the Water Act, 1974.
12. Briefly discuss the Central and State Water Laboratory.
13. Briefly write a note on Legislation pertaining to noise.
14. List the causes for global warming.
15. Differentiate between global warming and global cooling.
16. State the causes for Ozone Layer depletion.
17. Name the five gases which are responsible for global warming.

Section — C Essay Type

1. Discuss the optimal intervention into the environment.
2. Write a note on Environment v/s Economic Growth.
3. What is zero Economic Growth? Analyse the Environmental effects of the same.
4. Explain the powers and Rules of Central Government in respect of prevention and control of Environmental Pollution.
5. Explain the salient features of the Air (Prevention and Control of Pollution) Act, 1981.
6. Explain the salient features of the Water (Prevention and Control of Pollution) Act, 1974.
7. Write a note on Sound and Noise pollution.
8. Write short note on earth summit 1992 and 2002.
9. Discuss fully the kyoto protocol agreement on climate change.
10. Discuss the mechanism for carbon trading.
11. Bring out the salient resolutions of Copenhagen summit.
12. Discuss the causes and remedies of global warming.

INDEX